Family Patterns,
Gender Relations

Edited by
Bonnie Fox

FOURTH
EDITION

OXFORD
UNIVERSITY PRESS

OXFORD
UNIVERSITY PRESS

Oxford University Press is a department of the University of Oxford.
It furthers the University's objective of excellence in research, scholarship,
and education by publishing worldwide. Oxford is a registered trade mark of
Oxford University Press in the UK and in certain other countries.

Published in Canada by
Oxford University Press
8 Sampson Mews, Suite 204,
Don Mills, Ontario M3C 0H5 Canada

www.oupcanada.com

Copyright © Oxford University Press Canada 2014

The moral rights of the author have been asserted

Database right Oxford University Press (maker)

First Edition published in 2014
Second Edition published in 2001
Third Edition published in 2009

Library and Archives Canada Cataloguing in Publication

Family patterns, gender relations / edited by Bonnie Fox.—Fourth edition

Includes bibliographical references and index.
ISBN 978-0-19-544747-7 (pbk.)

1. Families. 2. Sex role. 3. Parenthood. 4. Marriage. I. Fox, Bonnie, 1948-, editor of compilation

HQ734.F2417 2014   306.85   C2013-902375-5

Cover images: Mother and father with child © digitalskillet/iStockphoto,
Mother with newborn © lostinbids/iStockphoto; Mothers with child © Dean Mitchell/iStockphoto;
Father and daughter © Aldo Murillo/iStockphoto; Mother and daughter © knape/iStockphoto;
Men on couch © track5/iStockphoto; Grandmother and child © OJO_Images/iStockphoto

Oxford University Press is committed to our environment.
Wherever possible, our books are printed on paper which comes from
responsible sources.

Printed and bound in the United States of America

1 2 3 4 — 17 16 15 14

Contents

Preface

Sociology offers understanding of our everyday experiences, including our problems, with its focus on the social context that shapes our lives. But this understanding often comes only after students learn to question what they think they already know—especially about social phenomena as familiar as family. Like previous editions, this fourth edition of *Family Patterns, Gender Relations* begins by challenging any assumption that heterosexual nuclear families with conventional gender roles are natural, or somehow shaped by biology. Unlike previous editions, in order to provide the tools necessary to understand families, this book also begins with an introductory chapter that reviews the variety of theoretical approaches that social scientists use to study family and gender. The chapter also proposes a working definition of family and describes more fully the feminist political economy approach that informs my thinking about family and gender, and many of the chapters in this anthology.

To shed some light on why families are organized the way they are today, the chapters in Part Two present rich descriptions of various family patterns. Studying variations in people's living arrangements, their intimate relationships, their methods of acquiring subsistence, and the way they care for children (i.e., different patterns of what we call "family") allows students to begin to understand what social factors affect how families are organized. The chapters in this section describe the organization and characteristic social relations in foraging societies and those common to peasant and artisan households in pre-industrial England and France. These chapters also describe the many factors associated with the development of industrial capitalism that are behind the conventional nuclear-family pattern and modern ideas about gender, sexuality, and motherhood. The section ends with an examination of the gender inequality common to working-class families in which women are home full-time, as they typically were in the 1950s.

The chapters in Part Three are about the social relations involved in making and sustaining families. They explore some of the complexities of intimate relationships, and especially the gender and power dynamics at work in relationships between men and women. They also examine the conventional and unequal patterns that often accompany parenthood for heterosexual couples, as well as the ways different housing arrangements can address the challenges of motherhood, the ways that some men are caring for their children, and the ways lesbian mothers are creating alternative family patterns. This part of the book ends with discussions of the incompatibility of employment and family responsibilities for dual-earner couples in Canada today, as well as the problems inherent in employing women from Third World countries as nannies to address the need for child care when women are employed.

Part Four is about families negotiating changes of various kinds: the challenges of immigrants seeking to establish their families in a new country, the struggles of First Nations people coping with a dire post-colonial legacy, and the difficulties many

Canadians face in feeding and housing themselves in a labour market that produces bad jobs and a country in which the "safety net" has been gutted by years of neoliberal cutbacks. Several chapters look at divorce—not only its causes but also how both children and adults go on to fashion new relationships and families following divorce.

The chapters in Part Five turn to other important matters shaping people's family lives. Chapter 27 reviews the causes of serious violence against women, a problem that is more closely related to family than some might think. The other two chapters discuss the social context of family life—specifically, Canadian family law and social policies affecting men, women, and children as family members. Chapter 29 describes family policies in Quebec and offers a strategy to address the problem of the incompatibility of employment and family responsibilities facing so many Canadian couples today.

Because this book is a collection of articles and book chapters that discuss a variety of topics, it differs from textbooks that offer a summary and synthesis of the field of family sociology. This difference allows instructors and students more space to develop their own understanding of family. To help in that endeavour, each chapter begins with a brief introduction that situates it by describing the large issue, questions, research findings, or debates the writer is addressing. The readings in each chapter were selected because they explore key issues at the heart of family life and relationships today, represent solid scholarship carried out from a variety of theoretical and methodological perspectives, and develop clear arguments that should stimulate reflection and discussion. The vast majority are also about Canada.

Overall, I hope that this book conveys the understanding that men and women make their families in historically specific circumstances, that families can be organized in many different ways, that today's political economy poses problems for many Canadians, and that people are challenging both gender norms and conventional ways of organizing families. At a time when a greedy political economy poses obstacles to people trying to build their lives around caring for their children and each other, knowledge and understanding can be sources of empowerment.

Acknowledgements

Many people helped me in the making of this book. I was especially fortunate to have Kate Bezanson, Kara Somerville, and Melanie Beres offer to write new chapters. Diane-Gabrielle Tremblay also generously updated her previously published piece on Quebec's family policies and Sedef Arat-Koç once again updated her analysis of the situation of nannies in Canada. Judy Beglaubter was especially adept at turning up articles and books as I searched for work that met my long list of criteria for inclusion in the book. Katherine Lyons, Hae Yeon Choo, Mary Jane Mossman, and Glenda Wall also gave useful advice and suggestions along the way. I send thanks to all of these colleagues. Special thanks go to Meg Luxton for ongoing inspiration and generous collaboration. Her insights and her work have been absolutely central to my thinking, teaching, and writing over the years.

The enthusiasm of many of the students in my family and gender courses at the University of Toronto, in 2012 and 2013, has also fuelled my interest in developing teaching materials that use a critical sociological perspective to help make sense of personal life. Thanks go to them and to Melissa Moyser, Judy Beglaubter, and Louise Birdsell Bauer for excellent teaching assistance.

As always, I feel lucky to work with the people at Oxford University Press. A more patient and good-spirited editor than Lisa Peterson would be hard to find. And Wendy Yano did excellent copy editing. I thank them and everyone at Oxford University Press who contributed to the production of this book, including the anonymous reviewers. Finally, my heartfelt thanks to everyone whose friendship I have treasured over the last few years—to Harriet Eisenkraft, Gary Klein, Ester Reiter, Eileen O'Shaughnessy, Art Perlman, Parvin Ghorayshi, Susan Berkowitz, Meg Luxton, Janet Kelenson, Judy Taylor, Peggy McDonough, Diana Worts, Sedef Arat-Koç, and Mustafa Koç. To my mother, Yvonne Bengel, for her optimism in old age and her unflagging love. To my siblings, Mary Conley, Sharon Stein and Tom Bengel, and to the large extended Fox family, for being wonderful family. To my husband, John Fox, for solving all the mysteries my computer continues to pose and giving sage advice on too many matters to list and love I can count on. And to my very creative son, Jesse Fox, who is wise beyond his years and kinder than anyone else I know.

Literary Credits

Mary Louise Adams. "Sexuality and the Postwar Domestic 'Revival'", in *The Trouble with Normal: Postwar Youth and the Making of Heterosexuality* (Toronto: University of Toronto Press, Inc.), 18–38. Copyright © 1997. Reprinted with permission of the publisher.

Sedef Arat-Koç. "The Politics of Family and Immigration in the Subordination of Domestic Workers in Canada", revised version of "In the Privacy of Our Own Home", *Studies in Political Economy* 28 (Spring 1989). Used with permission.

Elizabeth Church. "Kinship and Stepfamilies", in *Voices: Essays on Canadian Familes*, 2nd ed. (Thomson Nelson, 2003), 56–75.

Dawn H. Currie. "'Here Comes the Bride': The Making of a 'Modern Traditional' Wedding in Western Culture", *Journal of Comparative Family Studies* 24, 3 (Autumn 1993): 403–19. Reprinted with permission.

Andrea Doucet. "Fathers and Emotional Responsibility", from *Do Men Mother?: Fathering, Care, and Domestic Responsibility*, (Toronto: University of Toronto Press, Inc.), 109–36. Copyright © 2006. Reprinted with permission of the publisher.

Gillian A. Dunne. "Opting into Motherhood: Lesbians Blurring the Boundaries and Transforming the Meaning of Parenthood and Kinship", *Gender & Society* 14, 1 (Feb.): 11–35. Copyright © 2000 Sociologists for Women in Society. Reprinted by permission of SAGE Publications, Inc.

Felicity Edholm. "The Unnatural Family", in *The Changing Experience of Women*, eds. Elizabeth Whitelegg et al. (Oxford: Blackwell Publishing, 1982). Reprinted with permission of the publisher.

Yen Le Espiritu. "'We Don't Sleep Around Like White Girls Do': Family, Culture, and Gender in Filipina American Lives", *Signs* 26, 2 (Winter, 2001): 415–40, The University of Chicago Press.

Jo-Anne Fiske and Rose Johnny. "The Lake Babine First Nation Family: Yesterday and Today", in *Voices: Essays on Canadian Families*. 2nd ed., ed. Marion Lynn (Scarborough, ON: Nelson Thomson Learning, 2003), 181–98.

Rosemary Gartner, Myrna Dawson, and Maria Crawford. Excerpts from "Woman Killing: Intimate Femicide in Ontario, 1974–1994", in *Resources for Feminist Research* 26, 3, 4 (1998). Reprinted by permission.

Tamara K. Hareven. "Dynamics of Kin in an Industrial Community", in *Families, History, and Social Change* (Boulder, CO: Westview Press), 52–69. Copyright © 2000. Reprinted by permission of Westview Press, a member of Perseus Books Group.

Eleanor B. Leacock, ed. "Women in an Egalitarian Society: The Montagnais-Naskapi of Canada", in *Myths of Male Dominance* (New York: Monthly Review Press, 1981), 33–8, 44–50, 51–4, 57–62. Reprinted by permission of the publisher.

Meg Luxton. "Wives and Husbands", in *More Than a Labour of Love: Three Generations of Women's Work in the Home* (Toronto: Canadian Scholars' Press, Inc./Women's Press, 1980). Reprinted by permission of Canadian Scholars' Press, Inc.

Meg Luxton. "Family Coping Strategies: Balancing Paid Employment and Domestic Labour". Used by permission of Meg Luxton.

Guida Man. "From Hong Kong to Canada: Immigration and the Changing Family Lives of Middle-class Women from Hong Kong", in *Voices: Essays on Canadian Families*, 1st ed., ed. M.M. Lynn (Toronto: Nelson Education Ltd). Copyright © 1996. Reproduced by permission www.cengage.com/permissions.

Maxine L. Margolis. "Putting Mothers on the Pedestal", in *Mothers and Such: View of American Women and Why They Change* (Berkeley: University of California Press, 1984). Reprinted with

Part I

Family in Perspective

Because people hold such firm beliefs about family, it is important to raise and address basic questions at the start of any sociological study of families. For example, what definition of *family* will be broad enough for scholars who aim to understand family patterns in different times and in different cultures? Indeed, are family arrangements different across human societies, or are some basic patterns universal because they are "natural" or given by biology? What are the different theoretical approaches that sociologists use to study families? And what are the major changes and trends in family patterns in Canada today? These are the questions that are addressed in the first two chapters of this book.

Chapter 1

Analyzing the Familiar: Definitions, Approaches, and Issues at the Heart of Studying Families

Bonnie Fox and Meg Luxton

The dominant image of family is one of loving, supportive, and caring relationships. Family is one of the few places where most people can hope to find such relationships, and where many do find them. The conditions in which people build their lives today—especially the decline in good secure jobs, the increase in typical work hours, and the cutbacks to social services—strengthen the appeal of, and even the need for, the support system that marriage and family promise to provide. These same conditions also make it harder for people to build families. Moreover, for some people, family is a place of disappointment and even pain and abuse.

In Canada today, a diversity of family patterns reflects broad changes in the conditions of daily life—changes that present opportunities for some, but constraints and handicaps for others. Fewer people are marrying and divorce rates have been high since the mid-1980s. In the wake of divorce, lone-parent families are an increasing proportion of all families and blended families are sizeable in number. An alternative to marriage—cohabitation—has become increasingly popular. Same-sex couples have also increased in number, some of them married and raising children, more of them not married and without children. Married couples with children living at home are now a minority of all Canadian families. And living alone has become very common. Meanwhile, as more and more young adults

stay home through their twenties, more family households involve multiple generations. As well, both immigrants and lone parents often live with their parents or siblings, in **extended-family** households, at some point in their lives.

This diversity in family patterns presents challenges as well as intriguing questions to those interested in understanding family arrangements, issues, and problems. But the current diversity of family patterns means that deriving even a definition of *family* is not easy. Developing analyses of family-related problems and their sources is even more challenging. In this chapter, we review what is at stake in developing a definition of family, and then offer a definition that accommodates not only family diversity in Canada today but also cross-cultural and historical variations in family patterns (that is, their typical composition, organization, and social relations). Then, we review many of the key theoretical approaches available to those who study family and gender, and highlight their strengths and weaknesses. Finally, we describe key family trends in Canada today and offer some explanation of their sources.

Definitions of Family

When people use the term *family*, they usually assume that what they mean by family is clear. Yet the term has a variety of meanings depending on the context. A university student going home to spend the holidays with her family likely means her parents and siblings. An adult woman who plans to quit her job to have a family is referring to children. A recent immigrant to Canada who says he misses his family may mean his spouse and children who have not yet immigrated, or he may live with his **nuclear family** but still miss his parents, in-laws, and siblings who were part of his daily life before he came to Canada. Someone who explains that her family was killed in the Holocaust probably means an extended kin group. Still someone else who describes a group of friends as "my real family" is identifying people who provide significant emotional and personal support. At the same time, when a play or film is advertised as "family entertainment," the implication is that few people will find it offensive. And when politicians claim to support "family values," they usually mean something quite different from people who support queer families.[1]

The complexities, contradictions, and confusions surrounding the way *family* is used occur in part because families are so familiar and everyday definitions of family taken for granted. Almost everyone is a member of a family and lives for significant periods of time in a family, so they assume that they know very well what *family* means. The nuclear family has been such a widely accepted form for so long in Canada that getting married, having children in the context of marriage, and living as a nuclear family seem natural to many people. Family relationships are often so emotionally significant and so tied to deeply unconscious feelings that most people find it hard to question common assumptions about family. The image of the heterosexual nuclear family based on marriage also dominates popular culture—in spite of significant numbers of common-law

couples and lone parents as well as increasing numbers of same-sex couples.

The ease with which people accept heterosexual marriage norms and nuclear-family forms also comes from the way ideas about marriage and "the family" are central to common-sense ideologies. The belief that biology is a "given," that it determines various social phenomena—such as institutions like family as well as personality and behaviour— is strong in this culture. Thus, the biology of reproduction seems to "naturally" produce the heterosexual nuclear-family pattern, including conventional gender divisions of work and responsibility. Nevertheless, the notion that the nuclear family is a natural unit must be interrogated if for no other reason than that it has important practical consequences.

The belief that biology is socially determining serves the interests of some. Fathers who have never taken care of their children can make custody claims on the strength of their biological relationship. Single mothers may be pressured to name the biological father when registering their child's birth; in some cases, they have been denied access to social assistance if they fail to name the father. For others, the prominence of biology generates important debates about whether sperm donors have the right to privacy or whether their biological offspring have the right to know the identity of the donor. At the same time, new possibilities of assisted reproduction, including sperm donors and surrogate mothers, challenge old conceptions of parenthood. And gay and lesbian couples increasingly are having and raising children. These changing practices, and the debates they evoke, produce new complexities and uncertainties about family forms and definitions.

As understandings about family have become more contentious, the political stakes have risen. Since the 1980s, governments have adopted a neoliberal philosophy that challenges the welfare-state assumption that citizens have the right to services that ensure their social security and well-being. Governments have cut back on the programs that provided a modest safety net for most people. Advocates of **neoliberalism** have mobilized "family values" discourses to promote their central idea that families, and not the state, are responsible for people's welfare. In 1994, for example, the newly elected Conservative Ontario Premier, Mike Harris, justified his government's plans to cut welfare and social services by insisting that people should rely less on government services and more on families, friends, neighbours, and communities (Luxton 2006: 264). The idea that families should and can be self-reliant is problematic, however, especially in a period when governments are reducing supports and protections for their citizens. The competing demands of paid employment and family responsibilities, as many people face longer work weeks, unemployment, and even poverty, make it harder for families to support their members (Bezanson 2006). Right-wing, "pro-family" groups have played on people's anxieties and anger about these social changes and focused those feelings on changing family patterns. They blame many social problems on those who do not conform to heterosexual nuclear-family forms, especially mothers who take on paid employment. Such groups have very effectively invoked "the family" to symbolize a mythical (and apparently lost) past and lobbied for a return to "traditional family values"—a reassertion of the importance of heterosexual nuclear families in which men are the income earners and women are home full-time and thus available to provide unpaid care (Coontz 1992; Gairdner 1992).

Formal Definitions

Family is a legal term involving particular definitions that entail specific rights and obligations for certain people. Biological and adoptive parents are required to provide material support for their children and are normally entitled to custody of, or access to, those children. Other people who may have deep emotional relations with children are not recognized by law. Thus, a woman who may have lived with her divorced partner's children on a daily basis and cared for them for years has no legal claim to them, while the father's parents do—even though they may have seen the children only once a year as they grew up. An estranged father may have greater access to a child's school record and confidential discussions with the teachers about the child's performance at school than someone who has cared for the child every day after school for years. State-regulated institutions such as schools or hospitals use marriage and family relations to determine which people will be informed and consulted about the status of a person in the institutions. Critically ill patients may find that family members with whom they have had little contact are admitted to their rooms and entitled to make significant medical decisions, whereas friends who have provided daily support and who best know their wishes are excluded. Similarly, even when someone designates an heir in a will, the "immediate family" has some legal grounds to challenge that will and claim a right to the inheritance.

At the same time, legal definitions have been challenged and changed as a result. In 2005, same-sex partners won the legal right to marry in Canada—challenging and changing the legal definition of family. Similarly, definitions of family embedded in immigration law have shaped immigration to Canada, but new Canadians have also challenged prevailing definitions of family. Under current legislation, a Canadian citizen or permanent resident may sponsor her or his spouse, common-law or **conjugal** partner, and dependent children to come to Canada as permanent residents. They can also sponsor their parents, grandparents, and certain other specified close kin. But other categories of people are excluded, even if they have the same or more important relationships. Refugees who have raised children who are not legally theirs are refused the right to bring those children with them. People with several spouses are required to identify the "one" recognized in immigration law. At the same time, waves of immigrants have raised new questions about how marriage partners are best chosen and argued that extended kin groups are important networks of emotional and material support that warrant loyalty and legal recognition.

These examples show that the way we conceptualize family matters. Embodying deeply held cultural assumptions, the concept of family informs legislation, social policies, and practices that govern our lives. It also shapes decisions we make as individuals about how to live our lives. And it limits or expands our imagination as we think about the future.

Standard definitions of family, especially those used by governments to determine social policy, typically focus on a number of characteristics that identify a social unit rather than social relationships with social and emotional significance. Statistics Canada currently defines a "census family" as a married couple and the children, if any, of either or both spouses; a couple living common law and the children, if any, of either or both partners; or a lone parent of any marital status with at least one child living in the same dwelling. A couple may be of opposite or same sex. Children may be children by birth or adoption (regardless of their age or marital status) as long as they live in the dwelling and

do not have their spouse or child living there. Grandchildren living with their grandparent(s), but with no parents present, also constitute a census family (Statistics Canada 2006a). An "economic family" refers to a group of two or more persons who live in the same dwelling and are related to each other by kinship, marriage, common law, or adoption. A couple may be of opposite or same sex and foster children are included. A broader concept, "economic family" includes two co-resident census families who are related to one another, co-resident siblings, and nieces or nephews living with aunts or uncles (Statistics Canada 2006b).

These definitions reflect the growing diversity in Canadian family patterns. They recognize lesbian and gay partnerships and marriages. Yet, by restricting *family* to spouses or partners and people related by kinship or adoption, and by insisting on co-residence, these definitions exclude some people who may be considered family members. When definitions of family are not based on activities and functions—much less the social relations responsible for them—biology and legal status are easily accepted as determinants of family. Margrit Eichler (1988) has argued that when definitions based on form rather than social relations or activities and functions are used in policies to establish eligibility for family support, they can threaten the welfare of some individuals and undermine the economic bases of some families. People choosing to live collectively; friends sharing financial resources and providing each other necessary daily support; and people in other types of relationships who share material resources, provide daily support services, and have deep emotional connections are all excluded. When used to set policy on access to loved ones, such definitions can separate needy people from those who give them care and support (e.g., visiting rights in hospitals).[2]

Anthropologists have shown that family and kinship are social creations and not products of biology (Sahlins 1976; Goody 1976; Collier, Rosaldo, and Yanagisako 1982; see Chapter 2). Throughout human history, the composition and organization of domestic groups have varied tremendously. In other words, the group that lives together, co-operates to produce its subsistence, and cares for children has not always consisted of people tied by kinship or marriage. Logically, then, social relationships and functions, and not biological or residential relations, might be the way to identify family.

A Working Definition of Family

On the one hand, a definition of family that focuses on the household—as do Statistics Canada's definitions—makes sense; on the other hand, there are reasons to define family without regard to residence. The relations of greatest emotional intensity in the lives of many people—though associated feelings may vary between deep love and profound pain—often involve the people with whom they live. But co-residence isn't always a measure of the most significant relationships in people's lives. Children whose parents have divorced may have their closest family relationships in two or more households. Conversely, the equation of family with household may be one reason why men who are divorced and no longer living with their children often fail to pay court-ordered child support (Eichler 1997). Because relations of care and support that are central to family may stretch across households, definitions equating family with household can be limited. When anthropologist Carol Stack (1974) studied a poor African American community in the 1970s, where male–female relationships were unstable and a high percentage of babies were born outside marriage, she found that both the labour market for Black men with high-school diplomas and the welfare system undermined male–female relationships. She also found that because households could not sustain themselves amidst poverty and a weak social safety net, women-centred networks of kin and friends who continuously swapped scarce resources were essential to daily survival—and thus provided a powerful adaptation to poverty. In light of this finding, Stack (1974: 31) defined *family* as "the smallest, organized, durable network of kin and non-kin who interact daily, providing domestic needs of children and assuring their survival."

Stack was assuming that what family most fundamentally involves is the maintenance of life on a daily and generational basis. We agree that in conceptualizing and studying family it is more useful to consider the social relationships and processes by which people's ongoing needs are met than to focus on household, kinship, and legal status. As a working definition of family, then, we propose that *family* refers to the social relationships that people create to care for children and other dependents on a daily basis, and also to ensure that the needs of the adults are met. Feminist social scientists refer to the work of caring for children and meeting adult needs as "**social reproduction**" (Gill and Bakker 2003; Bezanson and Luxton 2006). Barbara Laslett and Johanna Brenner (1989: 382–3) have explained what social reproduction means as follows:

> Among other things, social reproduction includes how food, clothing, and shelter are made available for immediate consumption, the ways in which the care and socialization of children are provided, the care of the infirm and elderly, and the social organization of sexuality. Social reproduction

can thus be seen to include various kinds of work—mental, manual, and emotional—aimed at providing the historically and socially, as well as biologically, defined care necessary to maintain existing life and to reproduce the next generation.

By focusing on the social relations and activities that ensure daily life, this definition includes people considered "family" by the law, social conventions, and (in some cases) the people involved. But the main objective of this expansive working definition is to enable researchers and students to identify the groups of people who carry out the activities at the heart of what family involves—although families assume different forms or patterns in different times and cultures.

Focusing on the social relations that provide for the care of loved ones derives from one of many theoretical approaches. And researchers' approaches are important. They shape the assumptions they make, which guide the questions they ask, the information (or data) they collect to address them, and how they interpret what they find. Different approaches offer different ways of conceptualizing family—that is, of defining it and of understanding its relationship to the rest of society, as well as the social significance of biology, and the nature of gender and sexuality.

Different Theoretical Approaches to Studying Family

Structural Functionalism, Its Critics, and Related Approaches

Theoretical approaches reflect the period in which they are developed and the assumptions and concerns of those who develop them. They

are, then, suited to address different questions. In the conservative (Cold War) climate of the post–World War II period, Harvard sociologist Talcott Parsons developed an approach known as **structural functionalism**, which reflected a common belief that steady progress characterized human history, and that current nuclear-family patterns were superior to others (Cheal 1991; Coontz 1992; May 1988). Parsons's focus on structure reflected his concern about the organization of society and institutions like family, which he assumed to be stable. For him, society was like an organism whose institutions and social arrangements functioned to keep the overall structure intact. According to Parsons, anything dysfunctional would be disruptive, so the social order would either reorganize to restore functional relations or sustain social crisis.

In conceptualizing families, Parsons began with the question of the "functional requisites" of societies—that is, what was essential for any society to reproduce itself (Parsons 1951; Parsons et al. 1953). His answer to this question was that the heterosexual breadwinner/homemaker family was best suited to the tasks of having and raising children and ensuring the well-being of adults. Conceptualizing family in terms of the functions it performed for society was central to Parsons's approach: Parsons assumed that what he referred to as "the family" existed because of the functions it performed for the good of society—any society.

A central, functional feature of "the family," according to Parsons, was the division of work between a man and a woman in which the man assumed the "instrumental" role and the woman the "expressive" role (Parsons and Bales 1955; Zelditch 1960). Derived from findings of experimental laboratory research on how small groups accomplish tasks, the assumption in this argument that homemaking and child care did not involve real work reflected 1950s sexism and a market-driven blindness to unpaid work. It also served to reinforce popular beliefs that conventional gender divisions were natural, if not inevitable.

Nearly as soon as Parsonian functionalism became prominent in the 1950s and 1960s, criticism of it developed from a number of different perspectives (Maryanski and Turner 2000). For example, a general criticism was made about the faulty teleological nature of the argument—the notion that social phenomena come into being in order to meet needs (or serve functions), rather than as a result of a particular history. Another criticism was its conservatism, as evident in Parsons's assumption that "what is *must* be because of the vital functions which are being fulfilled" (Morgan 1975: 43). Additionally, some pointed out that the logic of Parsons's argument about the essential nature of conventional nuclear families was circular: Once this form of family is defined as the best unit for childrearing (as he did), its necessity is virtually given. The provocative question whether it *is* best for children to grow up in heterosexual nuclear families is one this argument sidestepped, as it ignored the possibility that intimate relationships organized differently could perform that function equally well, or even better.

What is useful about a functionalist approach is its aim to explain how social arrangements like a particular family pattern *fit* in a particular society. For example, Parsons argued that the heterosexual nuclear-family pattern "fit" an industrial economy, in that its small size (compared to the extended-family pattern he assumed was common to pre-industrial societies) was suited to the geographic mobility necessary in a changing labour market. But Parsons's functionalist approach, and especially its assumption that what is functional (or good) for the social order is good

for the individual, lost much of its popularity in the 1970s (Maryanski and Turner 2000).

Criticism of Parsonian arguments that led to new conceptualizations of family in sociology came from the generation of women who grew up in the 1950s and revived feminism in the following decade. One of the issues that fired the women's liberation movement in the 1960s was young women's recognition of the inequality inherent in their mothers' sole responsibility for housework and child care—unpaid, undervalued work and therefore, for many, unfulfilling as a lifetime occupation (Friedan 1963). Women's consignment to this work meant that, aside from an array of problems associated with being home all day, their needs are secondary to those of the male breadwinner (Gavron 1966; Luxton 1980; Oakley 1974; see Chapter 8). Moreover, far from a functional fit with the capitalist economy, women's responsibility for children and households reduces their ability to compete with men for good jobs. Because workplaces assume an ideal worker who has no family responsibilities that encroach on their devotion to their paid work, mothers especially have experienced reduced access to good jobs and earnings (Acker 1990; Budig and England 2001; Luxton and Corman 2001; Stone 2007; Zhang 2009).

Feminists pointed out that in emphasizing the functional nature of the gender-based division of household labour, as well as conceptualizing household work in terms of "roles," Parsons's work also overlooked the conflicts and inequalities common to heterosexual nuclear families, as well as the possibility of abuse, neglect, and even violence occurring in families. Feminists argued that gender inequality and power imbalances are inherent in a division of work between men and women in which men are the sole income earners

(Thorne 1982; Luxton 1980). Because Parsons's emphasis on functionality overlooked the contradictions, and thus tensions and conflict, in family relations it could not predict, or even make sense of, changes that have occurred in family patterns over time—and that are ongoing. Further, by asserting that the family form predominant among white middle-class Americans was functional and even natural, Parsons paved the way for those who insisted that other family patterns—especially those common in poor African-American communities (Hill 2005; Stack 1974)—were deviant (see Moynihan 1965). Feminists of colour and anti-racist scholars instead showed how racism and poverty ravaged family and gender relations, but also described family patterns that provided support and enabled survival despite the devastating impact of racism (Collins 1990; Jones 1985). In a similar way, gay and lesbian scholars described the loving care people gave partners stricken by AIDS and the families fashioned by people who were socially ostracized and without the conventions provided by **heteronormativity** (Arnup 1997; Stacey 2012; Weston 1991).

The functionalist approach nevertheless retains some influence because it aligns so closely with common-sense views of family. In the 1990s, for example, sociologist David Popenoe (1993: 539) published an article in the leading family sociology journal, lamenting what he identified as unprecedented decline (since the 1960s) of the heterosexual nuclear family, which (in a play on words) he labelled the "nucleus" of society. As evidence of this decline, he cited lower birth rates, which he saw as indicating the lesser value of children; women's labour force involvement, which indicated for him their "rejection" of the role of wife; and lower rates of marriage, which he argued spelled people's "retreat"

from marriage. For Popenoe (1993: 531), these trends meant that Americans had (consciously) rejected the "traditional nuclear family." The cause, he (1993: 538) argued, was that a focus on self-fulfillment, even selfishness, had replaced familism, which for him involves people not only valuing family but also subordinating their personal interests to the perpetuation of family. Popenoe's (1993: 529) main concern—that "families are not as successful at meeting the needs of society as they once were"—assumed that the interests of individuals and those of society were opposed. He also assumed that the intentions and choices of individuals were what had driven the decline of "the family"—an odd approach for a sociologist, given its insensitivity to the ways social context, especially changing opportunities and constraints, shape the choices and decisions individuals make. Failing to contextualize changes such as women's involvement in the labour force, Popenoe resorted to blaming individuals' selfishness for the fact that people now live more of their lives outside of families than they did in the 1950s. In so doing, he provided little understanding of the changes that worried him. But he did succeed in showing the limitations of a Parsonian functionalist approach.

Meanwhile, feminist criticism extended beyond the work of Parsons to critical reviews of the way sociologists usually conceptualized and studied families. They pointed out that family sociologists typically assumed that the nuclear family, in which men are income providers and women full-time homemakers and mothers, was the only normal form of family (Thorne 1982). Aside from denying the rich diversity of family patterns across different races, cultures, and social classes, the "monolithic bias" that characterized family sociology implied that nurturing, caregiving, and mutual support were found exclusively in families and characterized all family relationships (Eichler 1988). Feminists questioned a romanticized view of "the family" as a "haven in a heartless world" (Lasch 1977) and the assumption that all family members, in all families, were equally cared for and supported. Their research showed the inequalities that homemakers experienced, the power inherent in solo breadwinning, that money was unequally available to (and of benefit to) all family members, and that violence was not so rare in families (Komter 1989; Luxton 1980; Pahl 1989; Woolley and Marshall 1994). In short, feminists undermined any monolithic notion of family by revealing the different experiences of different family members and the inequalities inherent in different family positions. Meanwhile, anti-racist scholars documented conditions of inequality and violence facing families in racialized communities—such that the existence of family is itself a triumph (Dill 1988; Collins 1990).

Feminists also challenged the taken-for-granted public–private dichotomy that implied that nuclear families are separated from, and impervious to, the social world outside them. Studies of single-earner working-class couples showed that men's jobs affect household schedules: Tensions and needs produced on the job come home with men and therefore affect the work of their partners (Luxton 1980; Rubin 1976). Research on middle-class and upper-class households revealed the many kinds of work that full-time homemakers did (behind the scenes) that were essential to their husbands' careers (which led sociologists to use the term "two-person career" [Papenek 1978]). The public–private dichotomy also implies that nuclear families are self-sufficient, when instead support from kin and non-kin living outside the household is often essential to the care of family members, especially children, and especially now

that so many mothers are employed (Hansen 2005; Neysmith et al. 2005). Research on poor African-American communities shows that marriage was never the primary basis of parenthood and child rearing in that community, that the extended family was more important than the nuclear family, and that women-centred networks extending across households—and not male–female relationships—were critical for meeting daily subsistence needs in that community, at least until recent decades (Hill 2005; Stack 1974; Sudarkasa 1998). Research also shows the importance of extended-family relations in First Nations communities (Dubinsky 2010).

Despite feminist critique, scholars interested in supporting conventional family patterns have been persistent. In the early 1990s, economist Gary Becker (1991: ix) developed an "economic or rational choice approach to the family," which asserted that the optimal family arrangement is for men to concentrate on earning money and women to do household work. Becker argued that this pattern was the product of individuals acting to maximize their well-being—or couples strategizing to maximize family well-being—something he assumed motivated all the choices people make in life. For Becker, the market valuation of two partners' earning potential shapes how their time is divided between paid work and unpaid household work, and how household work is allocated between two people. The argument is problematic in its assumption that two partners have the same interests, that what is optimal for the household is optimal for each adult in it, and that women and men have equal bargaining power in their negotiations. Assuming that rationality governs the choices that people make in their personal lives is also problematic given the complex influence of personal history, identity, circumstance, cultural ideals, and the dynamics of intimate relationships on our behaviour. Becker's model also ignores social organization, and therefore the way people's social circumstances—their gender, their social class, their race or ethnicity—establish the opportunities and constraints that shape the choices they make.

Over the years, however, some family sociologists have used a variant of **rational-choice theory** known as **exchange theory**. In interpreting interpersonal relationships, exchange theorists assume that people's actions are motivated by cost–benefit calculations. For example, they interpret the kind of support and help that family members give each other—including the help that parents and their adult children often exchange—as motivated by calculations about what people owe each other for past support, or the benefits and obligations they accrue from helping each other. Most sociologists would instead contextualize exchanges among kin, to understand their nature and meaning—and include gender in the analysis, as women are the usual caregivers in this society.

Feminist Approaches

There is no single feminist theory of, or approach to, understanding family. Rather, different approaches address different questions and provide different perspectives on both gender and family. Concern about gender inequality and a desire to eliminate it unites them. Most feminist scholars also assume that no particular kind of family is natural or biologically determined, and instead believe that family patterns are the products of specific social histories and that even the effects of childbearing and rearing on women's lives depend upon social context. Most also recognize that forms of family that are built on a division of work between women and men produce gender inequality, although that inequality varies by class, race, and ethnicity (Luxton 2006).

Feminist **political economy** is an approach that has been especially important in Canada. Political economists assume that in every society there is a relationship between the way people produce their livelihood and wealth—food, shelter, clothing, and other goods—and the way the human population is produced both across generations and daily. This relationship is never simple or direct. Nevertheless, the type of work people do to sustain life—whether that involves foraging, pastoralism, agriculture, industrial or post-industrial **capitalism**—creates conditions for certain patterns of childbearing and rearing, which in turn both require and make possible other types of work, especially for women (Seccombe 1992; 1993).

For example, in foraging societies where small nomadic groups of people live by hunting and gathering the animals and vegetation available around them, women tend to bear fewer children than women in agricultural societies because they have them at later ages, with greater intervals between them (Howell 1979). Because there is no wealth to inherit in foraging societies, there is no social concern about the legitimacy of children, and therefore no control over women's sexuality (Leacock 1981). Instead, all children are welcome as members of the society and the group as a whole tends to accept responsibility for them (Turnbull 1962; Lee 1979). Because children are cared for collectively and because work is under the control of the worker, women in foraging societies are not required to concentrate on child care instead of participating in the other work necessary to sustain community life (Lee 1979; Leacock 1981; see Chapter 3).

In contrast, peasant farmers who individually hold land and must produce their subsistence by working that land tend to have more children with smaller intervals between them. Because family members constitute the main labour force in pre-industrial agricultural economies, women have more children and childbearing is more central to their lives; they therefore do work that is closer to the household and fit child care in amidst their other work (Draper 1975; Harris 1981; Tilly and Scott 1978; see Chapter 4). In societies where some kin groups accumulate wealth, inheritance becomes a major social concern and certain children are designated the legitimate heirs of specific individuals. In many agricultural societies where kin membership in the father's **lineage** both entitles the individual to rights in the land and its produce and legitimates the individual's claim to inheritance rights, children's legitimacy is ensured by powerful social controls over women's sexuality (Lerner 1986).

Aside from the relationship between the organization of production and the organization of reproduction, the requirements of production and the nature of wealth have also been related systematically to the form, composition, and structure of households, as well as to gender relations. Thus, in societies where people had to forage daily to meet subsistence needs, a near-communal organization in which scarce resources were shared, and economic decisions were made collectively, was the wisest survival strategy (Leacock 1981; see Chapter 3). Group membership was fairly fluid and gender relations **egalitarian** (Draper 1975; Leacock 1981; Lee 1979). In contrast, in the feudal and early modern periods, as in earlier Roman and Germanic societies—when agricultural and artisanal production were the bases of the economy—the household was the unit of economic production and household members constituted the labour force. Indeed, the word *economy* comes from the Greek word for "household." Recruitment to, and membership in, the household was dictated primarily by changing household labour requirements. Men who owned land had a basis for power over everyone—men, women, and children—who lived in the household. These were patriarchal societies, but the less property households had, the less unequal were relations between men and women (Blumberg 1978).

Family patterns in Canada and much of the rest of the world today show the influence of the capitalist economy. Historically, a transformation in the nature of family life began when the site where most subsistence goods were produced moved out of households into workplaces devoted exclusively to production. As industrial capitalism developed, the implications of traditional divisions of labour between women and men changed: Women's work was increasingly **privatized** (i.e., done in a private situation and defined as "the family's" responsibility) as men's work was **socialized**, earning wages that symbolized their hard labour. The nature of the household also changed, and the separation of household and workplace meant that coordinating child care and productive work became a problem (Davidoff and Hall 1987; Coontz 1988).

In the nineteenth century, middle-class reaction to the development of an economy that seemed impersonal and even immoral involved defining family as the exclusive site of loving care and women as naturally suited to provide that care (Collier et al. 1992; Cott 1977; Mintz and Kellogg 1988). From early in the nineteenth century, middle-class European, Canadian, and American households increasingly became centres exclusively for raising children, caring for family members' physical and emotional needs, and homemaking (Davidoff and Hall

1987; Mintz and Kellogg 1988; Ryan 1981; see Chapter 6). Meanwhile, working-class families waited a long time before men's (1950s) earnings could support a full-time homemaker (Coontz 1992; Fox 1993). In the nineteenth century, working men in unions reacted to their low wages and employers' strategy to keep them low (by using women as a low-paid competition) by campaigning for a "**family wage**" (M. May 1985). Defined as a wage earned by men and sufficient to support women and child "dependents," the family wage—as ideal and, eventually for some, reality—supported conventional divisions of work based on gender in working-class families.

Socialist feminists have argued that capitalism depends on the daily presence of workers who are able to labour, to produce their earnings, but also to produce profits for their employers. They have argued that the **labour power** or capacity to work, which workers sell to an employer, is reproduced (or maintained) on a daily basis in the home, as homemakers feed and otherwise care for them (Luxton 1980; Luxton and Corman 2001; Fox 1980; Picchio 1992; Seccombe 1993). Thus, nuclear families and the unpaid domestic labour done by homemakers are central to a capitalist economy, as well as to family members' well-being. Moreover, this labour and various other kinds of work common in a capitalist economy produce inequality.

While a political-economic approach is concerned with how economic relations influence family organization and gender relations, and the myriad effects of people's social class on their lives, radical feminists focused exclusively on gender. Asking the important question why household work has been "women's work," they argued that marriage is a kind of labour contract, that spousal relations are similar in nature to class relations as husbands

benefit from (or appropriate) the unpaid labour of their wives (Delphy 1970). This exploitation at the heart of marriage is, according to radical feminists, the product of **patriarchy**, a system based on relations among men that aim to control women, especially their labour (Hartmann 1981). While this explanation rests on an assumption that men and women are essentially different (Fox 1988), this feminist approach has made valuable contributions by highlighting the privileges men have enjoyed because of women's homemaking, but also by bringing the issue of violence against women to the fore and by revealing how pervasive assumptions of heteronormativity have marginalized gays, lesbians, and transgendered people (Ingraham 1999).

Less critical of the way society is organized, liberal feminists have been concerned primarily with issues of equal opportunity and equal treatment for women. One of their chief concerns has been ongoing gender socialization, by parents as well as myriad other people and institutions. A key question they have raised is whether men have come to share the housework and child care as their female partners have earned an increasing portion of the household income. An important indicator of gender inequality in families, this question has generated much research. The main finding is that women continue to bear unequal responsibility for domestic work and that, in dual-earner couples, they work more hours (of paid plus unpaid work) every week than their male partners (Bianchi et al. 2006: 71; Stalker 2006). Couples are especially likely to adopt conventional allocations of work when they have young children (Ornstein and Stalker 2012; Stalker 2006).

The way the work is allocated between two adults is not the only issue that dual-earner couples face, however. Middle-class couples have increasingly shifted housework and child care to the shoulders of other women. A dearth of affordable good daycare spaces has meant that women with well-paying professional and managerial jobs have relied on women migrants to work in their homes as nannies and housekeepers. Feminists whose research is on race and immigration have revealed both the conditions that, in countries like the Philippines, have fostered mass migration to do domestic work and the conditions of the work that make the workers vulnerable to abuse (Arat-Koç 1989; Bakan and Stasiulis 2001; Parrenas 2001; see Chapter 17).

A very different stream of feminist thought involves a conceptual framework for thinking about social phenomena known as **poststructuralism**. Poststructuralists typically argue that theoretical approaches that focus on social structure and material conditions are problematic because they assume that there is a reality that can be discovered, and scholars exploring that presumed reality engage in research without concern about the assumptions embedded in their methods. Instead, poststructuralists assume that their task is not to discover "truth" but rather to reveal the ways in which particular truths are produced, given legitimacy, and thus acquire enormous power over how people live. They focus on popular discourses and their power to shape social reality—for example, to rationalize current social arrangements. At the same time, poststructuralism assumes that any cultural construction of meaning will inevitably contain evidence of the alternative meanings it suppresses or denies. The poststructural project is to examine the silences, absences, and discontinuities in discourse and, in so doing, deconstruct key ideas, knowledge, or ideologies in the culture and the power relations underlying them and supported by

them. Thus, a key value of poststructuralism for studies of family is its critical attention to language, influential discourses, and other cultural influences.

Some poststructuralist scholars have focused on deconstruction rather than constructing understanding. Judith Butler and others have challenged the concepts of sex and gender, and specifically the view that biology produces two sexes and that gender differences are stable characteristics of individuals. Butler (1990) argues that repetitive socially coerced gender performances, which aspire to replicate a normative gender ideal, produce the sexed body and gender identity. For Butler, gender is performance. She argues as well that women's experiences are so diverse that it makes no sense to discuss "women" as a group. In so doing, she ignores the way in which women are treated similarly in this society, and that the idea of gender difference is embedded in the organization of social institutions.

Other poststructuralists have focused their attention on meaning and subjectivity, as these constitute an essential dimension of social reality. They raise important questions such as why individuals come to "choose" to take up particular positions, or roles, in social institutions like family—for example, why so many women choose to become wives and mothers, roles that entail lifelong obligations (and inequalities) (Weedon 1987). In answer to questions like this, poststructuralists turn to the study of popular discourses, and the subject positions these offer people. They assume that subjectivity is neither unified nor fixed, and that it is continually produced as individuals engage with a range of popular discourses (Weedon 1987). For example, Martha McMahon (1995) has argued that in deciding whether or not to allow themselves to get pregnant, women engage with popular discourses about "good" and "bad" womanhood. She argues that a decision to stop using contraception is often a decision not to become a "selfish woman" (i.e., one who never cared for children). Similarly, Glenda Wall's (2004) examination of popular educational material produced by Canadian governments for mothers—literature on "the early years," or what she calls the "new brain science" which holds mothers responsible for their children's cognitive development—has helped explain what compels women with young children to practise very intensive (and demanding) forms of mothering.

Poststructuralists are not alone in highlighting individual agency, or the choices that individuals make. An approach developed by American sociologists known as "doing gender" conceptualizes gender as something that people achieve in the course of interpersonal interaction, when they behave in conformity with expectations about gender. In an article that introduced this approach, Candace West and Don Zimmerman (1987) argued that living in a society in which gender produces "one of the most fundamental divisions" means that people are continually held accountable to expectations of gender-appropriate behaviour, and therefore must do gender (West and Zimmerman 1987: 137). In doing gender, women and men "sustain, reproduce and render legitimate the institutional arrangements that are based on sex category"—such as conventional nuclear families (West and Zimmerman 1987: 146). The doing-gender approach helps explain why women consistently "choose" to do much of the housework, even when employed full-time. Doing housework not only produces family meals and a clean house; it also produces gender, in the form of social approval and a sense of proper gender identity (Berk 1985). Doing "women's work" has no such effect for men.

The many studies that this perspective has generated have provided countless examples of how people do gender in conforming ways. Ironically, then, although this approach seems to highlight individual agency, it has generated virtually no research on people "undoing" gender, or doing gender in a nonconventional way (Deutsch 2007). Because the approach provides no understanding of how material and social conditions influence behaviour, it offers no insight into why and how people could "undo" gender—a critical objective of feminist work (Fox 2009: 30–34).

While the doing-gender approach is concerned with behaviour and how it is interpreted in social interaction, a longstanding sociological approach known as **symbolic interactionism** attends to the interpretations or meaning that people make in social interaction, and the sense of self (or identity) that results. Sense of self emerges, according to this approach, in a reflexive process that involves making meaning of personal experiences in social interactions occurring in particular cultural contexts. For both approaches, the meanings and images at play in interaction are of key concern; interaction is symbolic. But central to a symbolic-interactionist approach is a view of the individual as actively interpreting symbols or images rather than being held accountable by others to social norms (as in doing gender) or simply influenced by the environment (Stryker 2006).

In an interesting example of a symbolic-interactionist approach, Martha McMahon (1995) explored the meaning of motherhood for a sample of Canadian women. She found that for both working- and middle-class women, motherhood involved nothing less than an experience of personal transformation. She argued that a maternal identity provides

women "access to feelings and personal qualities that are characteristically feminine":
When women become mothers, they feel they
become more loving and caring—characteristics associated with femininity in this culture
(McMahon 1995: 145).

It is not uncommon for researchers to
combine several approaches. Using insights
from poststructuralism, the doing-gender
approach, and sociology in general, Marjorie
DeVault (1991), for example, argues that women
construct family when they prepare and serve
family meals—that is, when they plan meals
around every member's likes, dislikes ,and
nutritional needs; coordinate family members'
schedules; prepare the food; and orchestrate
conversation around the dinner table (DeVault
1991: 53). In making family meals, women are
producing a sense of collectivity that is family, and thus are producing family. The reasons why women do this work, according to
DeVault, include the doing of gender, but also
men's greater bargaining power, which often
allows them to avoid doing that work; women's
childhood training by their mothers; and their
own motherhood (which entails responsibility
for children's well-being). DeVault's analysis
includes consideration of both social organization and individual agency.

As these examples illustrate, poststructural and related approaches to the study of
gender provide considerable insight into how
and why individuals, especially women, make
family—often, in conventional ways. Feminist
political economists have worked to understand how families are organized, and their
resulting social relations, as these are related
to the economy and as they are implicated in
class, race, and gender inequalities. And other
feminist approaches have brought to light and
examined a variety of dimensions of gender
inequality in families.

Other Approaches

In what seems to be a reaction to feminism,
changes in gender relations, and increased family diversity, some psychologists have offered
arguments that conventional heterosexual
nuclear families are natural. **Evolutionary
psychology** (formerly sociobiology) arguments
crudely adapt Charles Darwin's model of the
evolution of physiological traits to argue that
some human behaviour—especially behaviour
maximizing the reproduction of individuals'
genes—is natural because it was selected over
the millions of years of human evolution, and
is thus genetically inherited (Fausto-Sterling
1985: 168; Segal 1999). According to these
arguments, differences in women's and men's
behaviour related to sexuality and parenting
are biologically determined.

Instead of offering hypotheses that can be
tested empirically, evolutionary psychologists
offer stories that contain simple explanations
of gender differences evident in daily life. To
support these stories, they select things already
apparent to serve as "evidence." One such argument is that over the course of human evolution, behaviour that maximized "reproductive
success"—sexual aggressiveness by males
and sexual selectivity and good nurturing by
females—was "naturally selected." Thus, over
many generations, these behavioural traits were
increasingly manifest in the genetic offspring of
individuals bearing the traits (see Barash 1979;
Daly and Wilson 2000; Wilson 1975).

Recent stories by evolutionary psychologists are about the different adaptive problems
faced by females over the course of human evolution, as they struggled to survive pregnancy
and care for their offspring, and by males who
were never certain of paternity—and the differences in the nature of their behaviour over
many generations (see Buss 2008). However the

story is told, the argument is that differences between women and men are natural, and somehow wired "in our genes." Additionally, most evolutionary psychologists assert that "marriage is essentially universal" in human history given both men's and women's (and even non-human animals') innate desire to collaborate in producing and protecting their genetic progeny (Daly and Wilson 2000: 94).

Critiques of these arguments, which often come from biologists, highlight myriad problems, the most obvious of which involves their reduction of the complex causes of human behaviour to biology—which never operates outside of an environment (Bleier 1984; Fausto-Sterling 1985, 2000; Fine 2010; Lewontin, Rose, and Kamin 1984). Biologist Anne Fausto-Sterling (1985) points out that empirical evidence and experimental testing, which are fundamental to science, are virtually absent in evolutionary psychology arguments. She also argues that it would not have been adaptive for early humans to act to *maximize* reproductive success, or have as many dependent children as possible.

Evolutionary psychologists seem unacquainted with anthropological evidence that sheds light on early human behaviour. For 99 per cent of human history, humans lived in small groups that acquired their subsistence from foraging (or hunting and gathering): Human evolution occurred in this context (Lee 1979: 1). The anthropological evidence indicates that foragers' main survival strategy involved living in small groups of people—not necessarily kin—who could live together peaceably, and (most important) co-operate and share resources on a daily basis (Blackwood 1984; Draper 1975; Leacock 1981; Lee 1979; Turnbull 1962). Individuals' survival depended on daily reciprocity among group members and not dependence on a

spouse. Moreover, because a foraging group could support only so many dependants, the numbers of children had to be kept low. And women likely got help with child care from other women and men in the group; the responsibility for children was likely shared, not private (Turnbull 1962).

There are alternatives to the assumption that our behaviour is hard-wired in our brains. *Homo sapiens* is the product of a long history in which brain size increased tremendously, making possible language and thus communication, better problem solving, and co-operation with others (Bleier 1984). Tools, knowledge, and ways to solve the problems of daily living could then be taught and thus passed down through the generations. In short, the evolution of culture is likely the big story.

Common to all sociological approaches is the assumption that social factors shape gender and family patterns. In addition to the approaches discussed here, some sociologists would include "life cycle" as an approach. Rather than employing a particular theoretical perspective, however, researchers who do life-cycle analyses typically combine sensitivities derived from one or more approaches—materialist (as is political economy) or cultural. Researchers using a life-cycle approach typically focus on the effects of age, period (i.e., living in a particular time), and cohort (i.e., sharing with a group of similar-age people a common event such as date of birth), whether examining individuals or institutions such as family.

Trends and Ongoing Dilemmas in Family and Personal Life Today

After decades of economic and political restructuring, and cultural changes that began in the 1960s, family patterns and individuals' life cycles are very diverse. The importance of employment in women's lives has challenged the conventional gender-based divisions that organized heterosexual nuclear families for several generations and, as a result, unsettled old patterns. The incompatible demands of employment and family have put direct daily pressures on women, often leaving them to do two "shifts" of work—paid employment and domestic work—every day. Women's employment has also created rising expectations that men assume their share of household work and responsibility (Hochschild 1989; Luxton and Corman 2001; see Chapter 18). But women who can afford it have typically hired other women—often women of colour, with temporary work permits—to care for children or frail seniors and to do housework (Bakan and Stasiulis 2005; see Chapter 17).

The difficulty of finding good jobs and the increase in educational credentials necessary to do so have had clear effects on personal histories and family patterns. Canadian adults are now more likely to cohabit than marry when they begin their first live-in relationship with an intimate partner. Large numbers of Canadians, of all ages, now cohabit. As well, the average age at first marriage is much older than previously, and more people are living their entire lives without ever marrying. Birth rates are low, divorce rates are high, and more people are living alone. Young adults also leave home much later than they did decades ago, or return after leaving. Overall, there is considerable diversity of family patterns in Canada today: common-law couples with and without children; lone parents; lesbian, gay, and trans couples with and without children; blended or reconstituted families with children born to different parents and porous boundaries; "accordion families," stretching and shrinking according to the changing needs of adult

children (Newman 2012); transnational families with close kin ties that extend across countries; extended families with more than two generations living under the same roof; as well as married heterosexual couples with children at home. In fact, in 2006 fewer than 35 per cent (34.6 per cent) of Canadian families consisted of married couples living with children under 24 years of age—the conventional nuclear family, and one many people still imagine when they think of family (Statistics Canada 2007).

Sociologists offer different explanations of this diversity and the flux in individuals' lives that accompanies it. For Anthony Giddens (1992), the historic decline in household-as-productive unit, the erosion of patriarchy, and especially the uncoupling of sex and reproduction have enabled the development of what he calls the "pure relationship"—one based solely on intimacy and satisfying sex. According to Giddens, a long (progressive) history of economic, social, and cultural change has enabled more democratic and fulfilling personal relationships, but also less stable ones and therefore much more flux over the lives of individuals. Agreeing with Giddens about the importance of love as the object and basis of contemporary relationships, Ulrich Beck and Elizabeth Beck-Gernsheim (1995), in *The Normal Chaos of Love*, also argue that such bonds are inherently contradictory: Because intimate relationships derive from a quest for happiness and self-fulfillment, individuals are also often impelled to follow their desires out of one relationship and into another. And because women are no longer economically dependent on men, their lives are more similar to men's in this regard. Beck and Beck-Gernsheim also argue that individuals no longer follow a standard life cycle—in which finishing education is followed by finding a job, leaving home, marrying, and having children—and that individuals' lives are now "planning projects" in which they continually make choices about what they want and decisions about how they will live (Beck-Gernsheim 2002). Individuals are involved in a continually reflexive process of choice making through their lives, according to Beck and Beck-Gernsheim. To explain this trend, they identify not only a culture of individualism but also an economy that produces insecure jobs and thus forces individuals to focus much of their energy and time on securing their livelihood. Insightful in some ways, this argument is also shortsighted. The increasingly long hours that adults spend earning their livelihood are very often made possible because a partner is managing the household, if not also doing the cooking and cleaning. And adults who are scrambling to earn basic subsistence are more likely to succeed if they have a partner involved in the same struggle. Aside from the emotional support that a committed relationship can afford, most adults benefit materially from having a partner who shares the responsibility for earning and the necessary work involved in sustaining a household.

Cultural changes such as increased individualism and heightened pursuit of happiness have no doubt influenced today's family and personal

patterns. But changes in the political economy—in the economy and in state policies—are behind both cultural change and increased diversity in families and personal life cycles.

The most profound of those changes in families, since the post–World War II period, has been women's long-term employment outside the home and the rise of dual-earner families. The majority of adult women are employed, including those with young children (and partners). In 2009, over 77 per cent of women 25 to 54 years of age were employed (Statistics Canada 2012b). That year, almost 74 per cent of women with children under 16 years of age, and living with a partner, were employed (compared with only 38.3 per cent in 1976): Fully 66.5 per cent of mothers with a child under three years old (and a partner), 70.5 per cent of women whose youngest child was three to five years old (and who had a partner), and 79.2 per cent of women whose youngest child was six to fifteen years old (and who had a partner) were employed (Statistics Canada 2012c) (see Table 1.1). Given the dearth of good, affordable child care spaces in Canada (except in Quebec), lone mothers with young children are less likely to be employed: Only

Table 1.1 Employment rate of women with children by family status and age of youngest child, 1976-2009, by percent.

Year	Female lone parents				Women with partners			
	Youngest child less than 3	Youngest child 3 to 5	Youngest child 6 to 15	Youngest child less than 16	Youngest child less than 3	Youngest child 3 to 5	Youngest child 6 to 15	Youngest child less than 16
1976	27.6	45.1	54.0	48.3	27.6	36.0	45.5	38.3
1986	29.8	47.2	60.1	51.7	51.1	55.6	62.2	57.4
1996	32.9	46.2	62.6	53.1	61.0	63.3	71.5	66.6
2006	46.3	66.2	76.6	69.9	66.5	70.1	78.6	73.6
2009	45.9	66.0	75.7	68.9	66.5	70.5	79.2	73.8

Source: Statistics Canada, Labour Force Survey. 2012c. <www.statcan.gc.ca/pub/89-503-x/2010001/article/11387/tbl/tbl004-org.htm>. Downloaded 14/09/2012. Reproduced and distributed on an "as is" basis with the permission of Statistics Canada.

45.9 per cent of lone mothers with a child under three years of age were employed in 2009, while 66.0 per cent with a child three to five years of age and 75.7 per cent with a child eight to fifteen years of age were employed that year (Statistics Canada 2012c). The mass influx of women into the paid labour force over the decades has prevented many families from living in poverty and enabled many others to enjoy a middle-class standard of living, including home ownership. Women's earnings have become more essential because men's real earnings have not risen since the early 1980s, periodic recession has wracked the economy in recent decades, and economic restructuring has worsened the terms of employment— producing more bad jobs (that are part-time, pay low wages, and offer both poor benefits and insecurity) and weakening the power of unions (Cranford et al. 2003; Fudge and Vosko 2001; Fuller 2005). The social consequences of women's employment, in terms of the extent to which gender divisions of work and responsibility in the home will fully erode or even change significantly, remain to be seen. Men do more child care and housework than they did decades ago, but women are still doing considerably more; they are still the ones who bear the bulk of the daily responsibility for children and households, and the ones who alter their employment to accommodate changing family needs (Beaujot and Liu 2005; Ornstein and Stalker 2012; Stalker 2006).

Coinciding with the influx of married women into the labour force decades ago was the advent of very effective contraception. Once sex was decoupled from pregnancy for many women, their experience of sex changed. Sex outside marriage became far more likely and, over time, girls' and women's sexual behaviour became more like boys' and men's (Armstrong et al. 2010). At the same time, employment in good jobs and building a career both have come to require longer years in school, so young adults spend many more years living as singles than they did decades ago, and a "singles" lifestyle has become much more popular.

Related to the extended period of time before young adults end their schooling and get full-time jobs is the dramatic rise in the popularity of cohabitation since the mid-1970s (LeBourdais and Lapierre-Adamcyk 2004: 930). Starting with the cohort of women and men born in the 1970s and entering adulthood in the 1990s, cohabitation has become the more common type of first intimate live-in relationship for Canadians—more common than marriage. It is especially popular in Quebec, where it now has a status that is very similar to marriage: Quebec couples regularly have and raise children in committed common-law relationships (LeBourdais and Lapierre-Adamcyk 2004: 933). It is common in Nunavut, Northwest Territories, and Yukon as well. In the rest of Canada, common-law relationships are not necessarily seen as comparable to marriage; but they are common, especially (but not exclusively) in younger age groups. In 2011, 16.7 per cent of all Canadian families consisted of common-law couples with or without young children, and 16.3 per cent of children under the age of 15 lived with cohabiting parents (Statistics Canada 2012a, 2012e) (see Table 1.2).

The popularity of cohabitation is a significant change in personal and family life, as it is different in nature than marriage. Heterosexual couples who cohabit are more likely to keep their earnings separate and they have somewhat more equal allocations of the housework than do married heterosexual couples (South and Spitze 1994). Common-law relationships are also significantly easier to terminate than

Table 1.2 Distribution (in percentage) of census families by family structure, Canada, 1961 to 2011.

Year	Married couples	Common-law couples[3]	Lone-parent couples
1961	91.6	0.0	8.4
1971	90.6	0.0	9.4
1981	83.1	5.6	11.3
1991	77.3	9.8	13.0
2001	70.5	13.8	15.7
2011	67.0	16.7	16.3

Source: Statistics Canada. 2012e. Censuses of population, 1961 to 2011. <www12.statcan.gc.ca/census-recensement/2011/as-sa/98-312-x/2011003/fig/desc/desc3_1-1-eng.cfm>. Uploaded on 19/09/2012. Reproduced and distributed on an "as is" basis with the permission of Statistics Canada.

marriage and of shorter duration (LeBourdais and Lapierre-Adamcyk 2004, Smock 2000).

People decide to cohabit for a variety of reasons—as in the case of marriage. These reasons vary by gender and class (Sassler and Miller 2011; see Chapter 10). They also range widely between practical financial issues at one extreme, and increased commitment (and a step toward marriage or an alternative to it) at the other extreme (Huang et al. 2011; Sassler and Miller 2011; Syltevik 2010). Young working-class men and women begin cohabiting more quickly than do those who are middle class, and often for practical reasons (Sassler and Miller 2011). Cohabitation, then, is often not the product of choice so much as circumstance (Thomas 2006). Practical reasons (e.g., splitting the cost of rent) may prompt a decision to live together, and some couples then remain in common-law relations because of an ongoing inability to save enough money or secure a stable enough position in the labour force to make the long-term commitment that marriage entails (Sassler and Miller 2011; Smock et al. 2005).

In the case of young middle-class adults, cohabiting also likely appeals because it is more contingent than marriage on both partners' continuing satisfaction with the relationship, and is easier to terminate. Living common-law suits a culture in which love is the primary reason why adults build and stay in relationships. But it also suits a labour market in which two young adults must spend many years acquiring the educational credentials necessary to get a good job and, beyond schooling, build their careers. As well, some people reject the importance of legal marriage and opt for common-law relationships as an alternative.

Some researchers have argued that common-law relationships are more like being single than being married (Smock 2000). The equally significant trend in terms of family, then, is the fact that first marriage now occurs later than it did decades ago, and that higher percentages of adults have never married (and likely never will). The average age at first marriage for Canadian women, in 2004, was 28.5 years and, for men, 30.5 years (Vanier Institute of the Family 2010: 39). These average ages are the highest in the last 180 years in Canada, and fully seven years older than the average for people born in the 1930s and 1940s, who married in the 1950s and 1960s (Gee 1987; Fox with Yiu 2009: 182). Clearly, young adults face a labour market that demands higher educational credentials, and thus a longer time in school, than was the case for earlier genera-tions. But more is involved in the later ages of first marriage.

For Americans at least, getting married is now a decision that people make after having accomplished a minimum of material security, as well as emotional security in a relation-ship. Research on middle- and working-class Americans, as well as that on poor women in the United States, indicates that both men and women feel that they must have achieved some financial security before they marry (Edin and Kefalas 2005; Furstenberg 1996; Smock et al. 2005). This conviction is stronger for young adults who are working class (with high-school education or less) than those who are middle class (with at least some post-secondary edu-cation) (Pew Research Center 2010). Across social classes, however, when Smock et al. (2005: 692) examined the factors that affect cohabitors' decision to marry, they found that financial matters were key—having suf-ficient money to not "be struggling economi-cally," the likelihood that a man especially will be a stable breadwinner, but also being able to afford a "real wedding" and having a few other material accomplishments (like owning a home or being debt-free). Thus, "[p]eople with higher education and better economic prospects are more likely to become married, to stay married, and to have children within marriage" in the United States (Smock et al. 2005: 681). According to the Pew Institute (2010: 1), in the US the "decline in marriage has occurred along class lines."

Andrew Cherlin (2004: 855) argues that because people now see marriage as contin-gent on some financial stability, getting mar-ried now signifies personal achievement. He argues that marriage "has evolved from a marker of conformity to a marker of prestige" (Cherlin 2004: 855). The ongoing popularity of "modern traditional" weddings (Currie 1993) or "white weddings" (Ingraham 1999), featur-ing lavish displays of consumer indulgence and huge price tags, clearly symbolizes the financial achievements of the marrying couple. Weddings also symbolize that two people have successfully built a committed relationship at a time when securing a position in the labour force threatens to leave little time and energy for personal life. Historically late ages at first marriage attest to the difficulties of acquiring financial security in an economy that mostly produces part-time, insecure (service-sector) jobs with low earnings and poor benefits.

Marriage continues to be popular, how-ever, and its popularity is no doubt partly because of its promise of greater financial secu-rity. For both women and men, in same-sex or other-sex relationships, two sources of income mean higher earnings than one. In fact, one of the largest social/financial divides today is that between those adults living in couples and those who live alone (Brannen 1998; McLanahan and Casper 1995). Especially in a neoliberal polit-ical climate in which individuals are increas-ingly responsible for their own support and the social safety net gets weaker and weaker, there are obvious material and financial benefits to having an income-earning partner and being in a relationship in which resources are shared.

Nevertheless, fewer people now are mar-ried than was true decades ago. For example, in 1971, 82 per cent of Canadian women 25 to 29 years of age were married; in 2001, only 37.3 per cent were married. For men 25 to 29, in 1971, 74 per cent were married; in 2001 only 25.6 per cent were married (Beaujot et al. 1995; Fox with Yiu 2009) (see Table 1.3). This decline was not only a result of delaying marriage. For adults 35 to 39 years of age there is a similar trend. In 2001, only 60.7 per cent of women 35 to 39 years of age were married, compared to 1971

Table 1.3 Percent of Women and Men Presently Married, in a Union (Married or Cohabiting), Separated or Never Married—1981 and 2001

	1981				2001			
	Married	Total in union	Separated	Never married	Married	Total in union	Separated	Never married
Women								
15-19	3.6	6.5	0.1	93.4	0.6	3.0	0.2	96.8
20-24	36.5	45.9	2.1	52.0	10.2	25.6	1.3	73.1
25-29	65.9	73.0	3.8	23.2	37.3	57.3	5.1	37.6
30-34	75.5	80.2	9.4	10.5	55.1	71.4	10.4	18.2
35-39	78.1	81.7	11.0	7.3	60.7	74.4	15.2	10.3
40-44	79.2	82.0	11.9	6.1	63.3	74.7	19.2	6.1
45-49	78.8	80.9	13.3	5.8	65.0	74.3	22.5	3.2
50-54	76.4	78.1	15.8	6.0	66.4	73.6	24.6	1.8
Men								
15-19	0.7	1.4	0.1	98.5	0.3	1.0	0.2	99.6
20-24	19.8	26.9	0.9	72.2	4.5	14.2	0.6	85.2
25-29	55.6	63.7	2.6	33.7	25.6	44.7	2.7	52.6
30-34	73.1	79.1	6.0	15.0	47.3	64.7	6.5	28.8
35-39	79.1	83.8	6.8	9.3	56.8	71.6	10.5	17.9
40-44	81.2	84.8	7.4	7.8	62.2	74.5	14.5	11.0
45-49	81.8	84.6	7.9	7.5	66.2	76.5	17.5	6.0
50-54	81.6	83.7	8.4	7.8	70.2	78.8	18.8	2.4

Sources: Beaujot, R., E. Gee, F. Rajulton and Z. Ravanera, 1995: 10, 41; 2001 Census, cat. no. 95F0405XCB2001004 and 95F0407XCB2001004

when fully 89 per cent of women that age were married. The decline in percentage married for men 35 to 39 years old was from 88 per cent to 56.8 per cent (Beaujot 1995; Fox with Yiu 2009). By 2004, only 46 per cent of women and 44 per cent of men in Canada are expected to marry by age 50 (Vanier Institute of the Family 2010: 36). Clearly, marriage is no longer the only way to live as an adult, and not the only way to create a family. It is also the case that more and more adults are living alone: Over the last several decades, even though cohabiting has increased, the percentages of women and men who are not living in any kind of union

(married or common-law) have increased. As Table 1.3 shows, by 2001, only about three of four Canadian men and women between the ages of 40 and 55 were living in a union (that is, either married or cohabiting).

Women are also having children at older ages and having fewer children. More women are remaining childless as well. The average age when women have their first child has increased from 23 years in the 1960s to over 27 in 2002 (Statistics Canada 2006c: 41). Since the mid-1970s, birth rates have declined for teens, even more so for women 20–24, and especially for women 25–29; at the same time, they rose for women over 30 (Statistics Canada 2006c: 41–42). As well, the number of births per woman has declined since the mid-1970s: The total fertility rate decreased from well over 3.5 (children per woman) in the late 1950s to below 2 in the early 1970s, where it has stayed since then (Statistics Canada 2012d). Most of this decline occurred in the 1960s as women flooded into the labour force, effective contraception became widely available, and the pitfalls of full-time home-making became more obvious (in the climate created by the women's liberation movement).

More recent changes have further discouraged women from having many children. Not only has the cost of raising a child increased but also the social definition of "good mothering" has inflated tremendously in the US and Canada in recent years, as young adults face a tighter labour market (Fox 2006, 2009; Hays 1996; Wall 2004). And although women's educational accomplishments have increased and their opportunities in the labour force improved, mothers are in a worse labour-force position than other women. On average, they experience a drop in hourly earnings for every child they have (Budig and England 2001; Zhang 2009). These changes have contributed to the other major change in women's child-bearing: The percentage of women who are childless has increased, starting with the first cohort of baby boomers (Fox with Yiu 2009; Gee 1987). The estimate is that 14 per cent of women born between 1947 and 1949 never had children (Edmonston et al. 2010). Even among "ever-married" women born between 1947 and 1951, over 10 per cent (10.7 per cent) were childless in 1991 (Fox with Yiu 2009). Estimates are not available for later cohorts of Canadian women, but increasing percentages of American women are childless.

There is evidence that more people wish to marry and have children than do either of those things. For example, Barry Edmonston and colleagues (2010) estimate that since 1990 only between 7 and 8 per cent of adult Canadian women have intended to remain childless through life but a higher percentage have done so. A variety of social factors are no doubt behind disjuncture between hope and reality.

In addition to declining rates of marriage, divorce has also been high in Canada for decades, after a major increase in the 1970s and another increase following 1985 legislation that made divorce much easier to obtain. In 2004, Statistics Canada estimated that 37.9 per cent of all marriages occurring that year would end in divorce before their thirtieth anniversary, if the then-current rates persisted (Vanier Institute of the Family 2010: 44). This estimate indicates high rates of divorce, but not nearly as high as in the US. Moreover, divorce rates have been pretty stable since the 1990s.

One consequence of divorce is the increased commonality of lone-parent families, which by 2011 comprised 16.3 per cent of all Canadian families (see Table 1.2). Almost one in five children lived with a lone parent that year (Statistics Canada 2012e). Even higher percentages of children live with one parent over the course of their lives. For example, fully one-third of children born in 1988–9 lived in a one-parent family by age 15 (Vanier Institute of the Family 2006: 62). How many children whose parents have divorced have an ongoing relationship with their non-residential parent is unknown. But not all live only with their mothers; some live with extended-family members.

An important difference between woman-headed, lone-parent families—who constituted over 80 per cent of lone-parent families in 2006—and other types of families (including lone-parent families headed by men) is that they have much lower average incomes: Lone mothers are more likely to be poor and on social assistance. In 2007, 23.6 per cent of female lone-parent families had incomes that fell below the government's "low-income cut-off point" (which indicates poverty) (Vanier Institute of the Family 2010: 104). Until recently, over half of lone-mother families were poor. Relative improvements in their situation are the result of women's higher levels of education (and thus earning power) and women's growing employment and longer hours of work—trends that have likely reached their limit (Vanier Institute of the Family 2010: 104). More stringent eligibility requirements for social assistance in recent decades (e.g., work requirements), coupled with an ongoing dearth of good, affordable child care (in all provinces but Quebec), continue to undermine the livelihood of families in which one adult must do both the earning and caring (Beaujot 2000).

The other family pattern produced by divorce involves blended (or reconstituted) families—involving remarried or cohabiting couples with children from previous relationships. In 2011, 12.6 per cent of Canadian families were "blended" and one of every ten children was living in them (Statistics Canada 2012a). Inherent in these families is the need for ongoing negotiations, at least initially, between adults and stepchildren, among children with different parents, between ex-spouses, and with an array of extended kin and new partners of former spouses (see Chapter 26). These negotiations may be more complicated and ongoing when children move back and forth between two households. And as paid jobs demand more and more of people's time, these negotiations are more burdensome. At the same time, blended families that work well enjoy some positive features relative to other types of families. For example, the fact that many children in them have more than two adults who are attentive to their needs and

committed to their welfare is a benefit for those children—although the children themselves likely need to help negotiate relationships among adults (see Chapter 25) and the adults share parental responsibilities with more than one other person; similarly, having a larger network of extended-family connections can be of benefit to both children and adults.

Another fairly new family pattern developed in response to economic change. Families are now more likely to have their young adult children (in their twenties and even thirties) living with them—those who have never left home or have returned after either finishing university or having a relationship end. Between 1981 and 2001, the percentage of Canadians in their late twenties and early thirties who live with their parents doubled—from 12 to 24 per cent for those 25 to 29 years of age and 5 to 11 per cent for those 30 to 34 (Beaupre et al. 2006: 9). According to some Canadian researchers, "most of this increase took place during the early 1980s and early 1990s, periods in which Canada endured two of the most severe labour recessions since the 1930s" (Beaupre et al. 2006: 9). By 2006, 60.3 per cent of 20- to 24-year-olds were living in the parental home, as were 26 per cent of 25- to 29-year-olds (Vanier Institute of the Family 2010: 73; Statistics Canada 2012e). Since 2001, over 40 per cent of Canadians aged 20 to 29 have been living in their parents' home; in 2011, 42.3 per cent lived there (Statistics Canada 2012e).

Katherine Newman (2012: xix) has called these families "accordion families" because "the contours of the household are stretching . . . [as] there are few other choices, particularly in societies with weak welfare states." Her research indicates that "accordion families are . . . a natural response to economic insecurity"(33). Young adults have found it more and more difficult to leave home because of worse economic opportunities, higher unemployment, and more costly higher education (as well as higher costs of housing in large cities). Newman (2012) sees this as "the private toll of global capitalism." It is much more prevalent in Italy and Japan, where the welfare state is very weak, and not occurring at all in Sweden and Denmark, where the social supports to citizens (even young adults who have never been employed) are generous. While hardly a new phenomenon for working-class families and poor families, middle-class families are now also providing an "important buffer against the ups and downs of the market" (Newman 2012: 135). In so doing, baby-boom parents are parenting for longer than they anticipated. Yet, in providing continuing support to their children, they afford them a much better chance at eventual success in the labour market.

Finally, in recent decades, another important trend in family life has developed: the increase in families built on same-sex relationships. The diversity among them is considerable. But common for all same-sex couples is the absence of a clear blueprint for making family. These couples have had to consciously and reflexively create their own ways of making and sustaining family. Decades ago, most had to build family from friendships, having been rejected by their families of origin; in essence, than, they very consciously "chose" the families they created (Weston 1991). Although queers are now more likely to have ongoing and close relations with their parents and siblings than they were years ago, same-sex families nevertheless often involve a number of novel patterns. For decades, gay men have built relations of caring for lovers and friends dying of AIDS to whom they held

no kin- or marriage-based obligations. Today, gays are forming committed love relationships and marriages that do not necessarily involve monogamy (Stacey 2012). With somewhat different objectives, lesbian couples work to create egalitarian allocations of work and responsibility in their households (Dunne 1996; Bernstein and Reimann 2001). And for same-sex couples parenthood—which is necessarily the result of much planning—also involves important innovations, which include both parents sharing the role of primary caregiver and ongoing relations with sperm or egg donors (Dunne 1996; Nelson 1996; see Chapter 15).

Conclusion

Many questions about family patterns remain. And a more complete understanding of contemporary and historical patterns is necessary before large questions can be adequately addressed. The lessons to be gained from examining social history should contribute to an understanding of the social forces shaping family organization today. Unless these are understood and assessed as structural obstacles to change or forces promoting change, people cannot successfully move on to tackle current problems and explore avenues of change for solving them. With the conceptualization of family that is proposed here (and that emerges from feminist theory), fruitful questions about family should arise, including ones about the nature of current changes in family life and obstacles to a family organization that ensures people's well-being and empowerment. Perhaps, women and men can even begin to find answers to their questions.

● Notes

1. The term *queer* is widely used to refer to all people who identify as lesbian, gay, bisexual, trans, intersexual, or in other ways do not identify as "straight" or heterosexual, or who wish to challenge the privileging of heterosexuality. "Queer families" typically refers to those who do not wish to identify as heterosexual and nuclear and may include a wide range of people who consider themselves families (Bernstein and Reiman 2001).

2. The emphasis in Eichler's criticism is that family membership and treatment as a family member handicaps individuals. Individuals' marital or family status—and not their personal characteristics—establish their eligibility for state benefits: family relationships may disqualify people for benefits (e.g., a handicapped person loses disability

if attached to a spouse with a reasonable income). Eichler's solution is to treat people as individuals in terms of claims on social resources. We agree, but are concerned about the implicit juxtaposition in her argument between individual and collective/community. The social forces that individualize and isolate us are so strong that advocating another such force is unsettling. The problem, as Eichler points out, is that the state is seeking to shift responsibility for people's welfare onto families and simultaneously undermine them. Promotion of universal social services, as well as guaranteed individual access to them and to a decent income, would alleviate the problem.

3. Data on common-law couples are not available prior to the 1981 Census.

● References

Acker, J. 1990. "Hierarchies, Jobs, Bodies: A Theory of Gendered Organizations." *Gender & Society* 4, 2: 139–58.

Arat-Koç, S. 1989. "In the Privacy of Our Own Home: Foreign Domestic Workers as Solution to the Crisis of the Domestic Sphere in Canada." *Studies in Political Economy* 28: 33–58.

Armstrong, E.A., L. Hamilton, and P. England. 2010. "Is Hooking Up Bad for Young Women?" *Contexts* 9, 3: 22–7.

Arnup, K. 1997. "In the Family Way: Lesbian Mothers in Canada," in *Feminism and Families: Critical Policies and Changing Practices*, ed. M. Luxton (Halifax: Fernwood), pp. 80–97.

Bakan, A., and D. Stasiulis. 2001. *Negotiating Citizenship* (Toronto: University of Toronto Press).

Barash, D. 1979. *The Whisperings Within* (New York: Harper and Row).

Beaujot, R. 2000. *Earning & Caring* (Peterborough, ON: Broadview Press).

Beaujot, R., and J. Liu. 2005. "Models of Time Use in Paid and Unpaid Work." *Journal of Family Issues* 26, 7: 924–46.

Beaujot, R., E.M. Gee, F. Rajulton, and Z. Ravanera. 1995. *Family Over the Life Course* (Ottawa: Statistics Canada, cat. no. 91-543).

Beaupre, P., P. Turcotte, and A. Milan. 2006. "When Is Junior Moving Out? Transitions from the Parental Home to Independence." *Canadian Social Trends* 82: 9–16.

Beck, U., and E. Beck-Gernsheim, 1995. *The Normal Chaos of Love* (Cambridge: Polity Press).

Beck-Gernsheim, E. 2002. *Reinventing the Family* (Cambridge: Polity Press).

Becker, G.S. 1991. *A Treatise on the Family* (Cambridge, MA: Harvard University Press).

Bernstein, M., and R. Reimann. 2001. *Queer Families, Queer Politics* (New York: Columbia University Press).

Berk, S.F. 1985. *The Gender Factory* (New York: Plenum).

Bezanson, K. 2006. *Gender, the State, and Social Reproduction* (Toronto: University of Toronto Press).

Bezanson, K., and M. Luxton, eds. 2006. *Social Reproduction* (Montreal & Kingston: McGill–Queen's Press).

Bianchi, S., J. Robinson, and M. Milkie. 2006. *Changing Rhythms of American Family Life* (New York: Russell Sage Foundation).

Blackwood, E.B. 1984. "Sexuality and Gender in Certain Native American Tribes: The Case of Cross-Gender Females." *Signs* 10, 1: 27–42.

Bleier, R. 1984. *Science and Gender: A Critique of Biology and Its Theories on Women* (New York: Pergamon Press).

Blumberg, R.L. 1978. *Stratification* (Dubuque, Iowa: Wm. C. Brown Co.).

Brannen, Julia. 1998. "Employment and Family Work: Equalities and Inequalities," in *Women, Work and the Family in Europe*, eds Eileen Drew, Ruth Emerek, and Evelyn Mahon (New York: Routledge), pp. 76–86.

Budig, M., and P. England. 2001. "The Wage Penalty for Motherhood." *American Sociological Review* 66, 2: 204–25.

Buss, D. 2008. "Psychological Sex Differences through Sexual Selection." *American Psychologist* 50, 30: 164–71.

Butler, J. 1990. *Gender Trouble* (New York: Routledge).

Cheal, D. 1991. *Family and the State of Theory* (Toronto: Oxford University Press).

Cherlin, A.J. 2004. "The Deinstitutionalization of American Marriage." *Journal of Marriage and Family* 66: 848–61.

Collier, J., M.Z. Rosaldo, and S. Yanagisako. 1992. "Is There a Family? New Anthropological Views," in *Rethinking the Family*, ed. B. Throne with M. Yalom (Boston: Northeastern University Press), pp. 25–39.

Collins, P.H. 1990. *Black Feminist Thought* (London: Harper Collins).

Coontz, S. 1988. *The Social Origins of Private Family Life* (London: Verso).

———. 1992. *The Way We Never Were* (New York: Basic Books).

Cott, N. 1977. *The Bonds of Womanhood* (New Haven, CT: Yale University Press).

Cranford, C., L. Vosko, and N. Zukewich. 2003. "The Gender of Precarious Employment in Canada." *Industrial Relations* 58, 3: 454–79.

Currie, D. 1993. "'Here Comes the Bride': The Making of a 'Modern Traditional' Wedding in Western Culture." *Journal of Comparative Family Studies* 24, 3: 403–19.

Daly, M., and M.I. Wilson. 2000. "The Evolutionary Psychology of Marriage and Divorce," in *The Ties That Bind*, ed. L.J. Waite (New York: Aldine de Gruyter), pp. 91–110.

Davidoff, L., and C. Hall. 1987. *Family Fortunes* (London: Hutchinson).

Delphy, C. 1984 [1970]. "The Main Enemy," in *Close to Home*, ed. C. Delphy (Amherst, MA: University of Massachusetts Press), pp. 57–77.

Deutsch, F. 2007. "Undoing Gender." *Gender & Society* 21, 1: 107–27.

DeVault, M. 1991. *Feeding the Family* (Chicago: University of Chicago Press).

Dill, B.T. 1988. "Our Mothers' Grief: Racial-Ethnic Women and the Maintenance of Families." *Journal of Family History* 13, 4: 415–31.

Draper, P. 1975. "!Kung Women: Contrasts in Sexual Egalitarianism in Foraging and Sedentary Contexts," in *Toward an Anthropology of Women*, ed. R.R. Reiter (New York: Monthly Review Press), pp. 77–109.

Dubinsky, K. 2010. *Babies Without Borders* (Toronto: University of Toronto Press).

Dunne, G. 1996. *Lesbian Lifestyles: Women's Work and the Politics of Sexuality* (Toronto University of Toronto Press).

Edin, K., and M. Kefalas. 2005. *Promises I Can Keep* (Berkeley: University of California Press).

Edmonston, B., S.M. Lee, and Z. Wu. 2010. "Fertility Intentions in Canada: Change or No Change?" *Canadian Studies in Population* 37, 3–4: 297–337.

Eichler, M. 1988. *Families in Canada Today,* 2nd edn (Toronto: Gage).

———. 1997. *Family Shifts* (Toronto: Oxford University Press).

Fausto-Sterling, A. 1985. *Myths of Gender* (New York: Basic Books).

———. 2000. *Sexing the Body* (New York: Basic Books).

Fine, C. 2010. *Delusions of Gender: How Our Minds, Society, and Neurosexism Create Difference* (New York: WW Norton & Co.).

Fox, B. 1988. "Conceptualizing 'Patriarchy.'" *Canadian Review of Sociology and Anthropology* 25, 2: 163–83.

———. 1993. "The Rise and Fall of the Breadwinner-Homemaker Family," in *Family Patterns, Gender Relations*, ed. B. Fox (Toronto: Oxford University Press), pp. 147–57.

———. 2006. "Motherhood as a Class Act: The Many Ways in which 'Intensive Mothering' Is Entangled with Social Class," in *Social Reproduction*, eds K. Bezanson and M. Luxton (Montreal & Kingston: McGill–Queen's University Press), pp. 231–62.

———. 2009. *When Couples Become Parents* (Toronto: University of Toronto Press).

Fox, B., ed. 1980. *Hidden in the Household* (Toronto: Women's Press).

Fox, B., with J. Yiu. 2009. "As Times Change: A Review of Trends in Family Life," in *Family Patterns, Gender Relations,* 3rd edn (Don Mills, ON: Oxford University Press), pp. 180–208.

Friedan, B. 1963. *The Feminine Mystique* (New York: Dell Publishing Co.).

Fudge, J., and L. Vosko. 2001. "Gender, Segmentation and the Standard Employment Relationship in Canadian Labour Law and Policy." *Economic and Industrial Democracy* 22: 271–310.

Fuller, S. 2005. "Public Service Employment and Gender Wage Inequalities in British Columbia: Assessing the Effects of a Shrinking Public Sector." *Canadian Journal of Sociology* 30, 4: 405–39.

Furstenberg, F. 2006. "The Future of Marriage." *American Demographics* 18: 34–40.

Gairdner, W. 1992. *The War Against the Family* (Toronto: Stoddart).

Gavron, H. 1966. *The Captive Wife* (Harmondsworth: Routledge & Kegan Paul).

Gee, E. 1987. "Historical Changes in the Family Life Course of Canadian Men and Women," in *Aging in Canada: Social Perspectives*, 2nd edn, ed. V. Marshall (Markham: Fitzhenry and Whiteside), pp. 265–87.

Giddens, A. 1992. *The Transformation of Intimacy* (Cambridge: Polity Press).

Gill, S., and I. Bakker, eds. 2003. *Power, Production, and Social Reproduction* (London: Palgrave Macmillan).

Goody, J. 1976. *Production and Reproduction* (Cambridge: Cambridge University Press).

Hansen, K.V. 2005. *Not-So-Nuclear Families* (New Brunswick, NJ: Rutgers University Press).

Harris, O. 1981. "Households as Natural Units," in *Of Marriage and the Market*, eds K. Young, C. Wolkowitz, and R. McCullough (London: CSE Books), pp. 49–68.

Hartmann, H. 1981. "The Unhappy Marriage of Marxism and Feminism: Towards a More Progressive Union," in *Women and Revolution*, ed. Lydia Sargent (Boston: South End Press), pp. 1–41.

Hays, S. 1996. *The Cultural Contradictions of Motherhood* (New Haven: Yale University Press).

Hill, S.A. 2005. *Black Intimacies* (Walnut Creek, CA: Alta Mira Press).

Hochschild, A.R. 1989. *The Second Shift* (New York: Viking).

Howell, N. 1979. *Demography of the Dobe Kung* (New York: Academic Press).

Huang, P.M., P.J. Smock, W. Manning, and C.A. Bergstrom-Lynch. 2011. "He Says, She Says: Gender and Cohabitation." *Journal of Family Issues* 32, 7: 876–905.

Ingraham, C. 1999. *White Weddings* (New York: Routledge).

Jones, J. 1985. *Labor of Love, Labor of Sorrow* (New York: Basic Books).

Komter, A. 1989. "Hidden Power in Marriage." *Gender & Society* 3, 2: 187–216.

Lasch, C. 1977. *Haven in a Heartless World: The Family Beseiged* (New York: Basic Books).

Laslett, B., and J. Brenner. 1989. "Gender and Social Reproduction: Historical Perspectives." *Annual Review of Sociology* 15: 381–404.

Leacock, E.B. 1981. *Myths of Male Dominance: Collected Articles on Women Cross-Culturally* (New York: Monthly Review Press).

LeBourdais, C., and E. LaPierre-Adamcyk. 2004. "Changes in Conjugal Life in Canada: Is Cohabitation Progressively Replacing Marriage?" *Journal of Marriage and Family* 66: 929–42.

Lee, R.B. 1979. *The !Kung San* (Cambridge, UK: Cambridge University Press).

Lerner, G. 1986. *The Creation of Patriarchy* (New York: Oxford University Press).

Lewontin, R.C., S. Rose, and L.J. Kamin. 1984. *Not in Our Genes* (New York: Pantheon Books).

Luxton, M. 1980. *More Than a Labour of Love* (Toronto: Women's Press).

———. 2006. "Friends, Neighbours, and Community: A Case Study of the Role of Informal Caregiving in Social Reproduction," in *Social Reproduction: Feminist Political Economy Challenges Neo-Liberalism*, eds K. Bezanson and M. Luxton (Montreal & Kingston: McGill–Queen's University Press), pp. 263–95.

Luxton, M., and J. Corman. 2001. *Getting By in Hard Times* (Toronto: University of Toronto Press).

McLanahan, S., and L. Casper. 1995. "Growing Diversity and Inequality in the American Family," in *State of the Union*, ed. R. Farley (New York: Russell Sage Foundation).

McMahon, M. 1995. *Engendering Motherhood* (New York: The Guilford Press).

Maryanski, A., and J.H. Turner. 2000. "Functionalism and Structuralism," in *Encyclopedia of Sociology,* 2nd edn, Vol. 2, eds E.F. Borgatta and R.J.V. Montgomery (New York: Macmillan Reference USA), pp. 1029–37.

May, E. 1988. *Homeward Bound* (New York: Basic).

May, M. 1985. "Bread Before Roses: American Working Men, Labor Unions and the Family Wage," in *Women, Work, and Protest*, ed. R. Milkman (Boston: Routledge & Kegan Paul), pp. 1–21.

Mintz, S., and S. Kellogg. 1988. *Domestic Revolutions* (New York: The Free Press).

Morgan, D. 1975. *The Family and Social Theory* (London: Routledge & Kegan Paul).

Moynihan, D.P. 1965. "The Negro Family: The Case for National Action" (Washington, DC: Government Printing Office).

Nelson, F. 1996. *Lesbian Motherhood* (Toronto: Toronto University Press).

Newman, K.S. 2012. *The Accordion Family* (Boston: Beacon Press).

Neysmith, S., K. Bezanson, and A. O'Connell. 2005. *Telling Tales* (Halifax: Fernwood).

Oakley, A. 1974. *Woman's Work* (New York: Pantheon Books).

Ornstein, M. and G. Stalker. 2012. "Canadian Families' Strategies for Employment and Care for Preschool Children." *Journal of Family Issues* (online) May 22, DOI 10.1177/0192513X12442824.

Pahl, J. 1989. *Money and Marriage* (London: Macmillan).

Papenek, H. 1978. Men, Women and Work: Reflections on the Two-Person Career. *American Journal of Sociology* 78, 4: 852–71.

Parrenas, R.S. 2001. *Servants of Globalization* (Stanford: Stanford University Press).

Parsons, T. 1951. *The Social System* (New York: The Free Press).

Parsons, T., and R.F. Bales. 1955. *Family, Socialization and Interaction Process* (New York: Free Press).

Parsons, T., R.F. Bales, and E. Shils. 1953. *Working Papers in the Theory of Action* (New York: Free Press).

Pew Research Center. 2010. "The Decline of Marriage and Rise of New Families." Pew Research Center: A Social & Demographic Trends Report. Accessed April 25, 2013 http://www.pewsocialtrends.org/files/2010/11/pew-social-trends-2010-families.pdf.

Picchio, A. 1992. *Social Reproduction* (Cambridge: Cambridge University Press).

Popenoe, D. 1993. "American Family Decline, 1960–1990: A Review and Appraisal." *Journal of Marriage and Family* 55, 3: 527–42.

Rubin, L.B. 1976. *Worlds of Pain* (New York: Basic Books).

Ryan, M. 1981. *Cradle of the Middle Class* (Cambridge: University of Cambridge Press).

Sahlins, M. 1976. *The Use and Abuse of Biology* (Ann Arbor: The University of Michigan Press).

Sassler, S., and A. Miller. 2011. "Class Differences in Cohabitation Processes." *Family Relations* 60: 163–77.

Seccombe, W. 1974. "The Housewife and Her Labor Under Capitalism." *New Left Review* 83 (Jan.–Feb.): 3–24.

——. 1992. *A Millennium of Family Change* (London: Verso).

——. 1993. *Weathering the Storm*. (London: Verso).

Segal, L. 1999. *Why Feminism?* (New York: Columbia University Press).

Smock, P.J. 2000. "Cohabitation in the U.S.: An Appraisal of Research Themes, Findings, and Implications." *Annual Review of Sociology* 26: 1–20.

Smock, P.J., W. Manning, and M. Porter. 2005. "'Everything's There Except Money': How Money Shapes Decisions to Marry Among Cohabitors." *Journal of Marriage and Family* 67: 680–96.

South, S., and G. Spitze. 1994. "Housework in Marital and Nonmarital Households." *American Sociological Review* 59, 3: 327–47.

Stacey, J. 2012. *Unhitched* (New York: New York University Press).

Stack, C. 1974. *All Our Kin* (New York: Harper & Row).

Stalker, G. 2006. "Gender Convergence and Life Course: Differentiation in Canadian Use of Time." *Leisure & Society* 29, 1: 159–190.

Statistics Canada. 2006a. http://www.statcan.ca/english/concepts/definitions/cen-family.htm.

——. 2006b. http://www.statcan.ca/english/concepts/definitions/eco-family.htm.

——. 2006c. *Women in Canada,* 5th edn (Ottawa: Minister of Industry).

——. 2007. Catalogue no. 97-553-XIE. Figures 1 and 13.

——. 2012a. *The Daily*. 2011 Census of Population. www.statcan.gc.ca/daily-quotidien/120919/dq120919a-eng.htm. Accessed 19/09/2012.

——. 2012b. www.statcan.gc.ca/pub/89-503-x/2010001/article/11387/tbl/tbl1004-eng.htm. Accessed 14/09/2012.

——. 2012c. www.statcan.gc.ca/pub/89-503-x/2010001/article/11387/tbl/tbl1006-eng.htm. Accessed 14/09/2012.

——. 2012d. www.statcan.gc.ca/pub/89-503-x/2010001/article/11546/c-g/c-g004-eng.htm. Accessed 15/10/2012.

——. 2012e. www12.statcan.gc.ca/census-recensement/2011/as-sa/98-312-x/2011003/fig/desc/desc3_1-1-eng.cfm. Accessed 25/04/2013.

Stone, P. 2007. *Opting Out?* (Berkeley: University of California Press).

Stryker, S. 2006. "Symbolic Interaction Theory," in *Encyclopedia of Sociology*, 2nd edn, eds E. Borgatta and R. Montgomery (New York: Macmillan Reference USA), pp. 3095–102.

Sudarkasa, N. 1998. "Interpreting the African Heritage in Afro-American Family Organization," in *Families in the U.S.: Kinship and Domestic Politics*, eds Haren V. Hansen and Anita Ilta Garey (Philadelphia: Temple University Press), pp. 91–130.

Syltevik, L.J. 2010. "Sense and Sensibility: Cohabitation in 'Cohabitation Land.'" *The Sociological Review* 58, 3: 444–462.

Thomas, C.A. 2006. "The Roles of Registered Partnerships and Conjugality in Canadian Family Law." *Canadian Journal of Family Law* 22, 2: 223–57.

Thorne, B. 1982. "Feminist Rethinking of the Family: An Overview," in *Rethinking the Family*, ed. B. Thorne with M. Yalom (New York: Longman), pp. 1–24.

Tilly, L., and J. Scott. 1981. *Women, Work and Family* (New York: Holt, Rinehart and Winston).

Turnbull, C.M. 1962. *The Forest People* (Garden City, NY: Doubleday).

Vanier Institute of the Family. 2010. *Families Count* (Ottawa: Author).

Wall, G. 2004. "Is Your Child's Brain Potential Maximized? Mothering in the Age of New Brain Research." *Atlantis* 28, 2: 41–50.

Weedon, C. 1987. *Feminist Practice & Poststructuralist Theory* (Oxford: Basil Blackwell).

West, C., and D. Zimmerman. 1987. "Doing Gender." *Gender & Society* 1, 2: 125–51.

Weston, K. 1991. *Families We Choose* (New York: Columbia University Press).

Wilson, E.O. 1975. *Sociobiology: The New Synthesis* (Cambridge, MA: Harvard University Press)

Woolley, F., and J. Marshall. 1994. "Measuring Inequality Within the Household." *Review of Income and Wealth* 40: 415–31.

Zelditch, M. 1960. "Role Differentiation in the Nuclear Family," in *Modern Introduction to the Family*, eds Norm Bell and Ezra Vogel (New York: Free Press), pp. 329–38.

Zhang, X., 2009 (March). "Earnings of Women With and Without Children." *Perspectives on Labour and Income*. Statistics Canada.

Zheng, W., C.L. Costigan, R. Hou, R. Kampen, C.M. Schimmele, and M. Eichler. 1988. *Families in Canada Today* (Toronto: Gage).

Chapter 2

Perhaps the most important assumption about "the family" in popular culture is that the heterosexual nuclear pattern is somehow natural. This family form seems to follow naturally from the biology of reproduction and therefore seems to be universal. This chapter challenges assumptions that family patterns are "given" by biology and thus are natural and universal. Written decades ago by an anthropologist, it examines basic aspects of family life—like the relationship between mother and child—and shows tremendous diversity across human societies. Felicity Edholm's discussion challenges us to question what we take for granted. In showing that family is socially constructed—as an idea and as a set of social relations—she also raises questions about the factors and forces that are significant influences on families in any society.

The Unnatural Family

Felicity Edholm

. . . It was, and still is, widely argued that some form of the family, and, in some cases, of the nuclear family, was universal and was found in all societies. Only recently has this accepted wisdom been challenged and it has still not been dislodged. One major reason for its resilience in anthropology, apart from the crucial political, economic, and ideological significance of the family in the nineteenth- and twentieth-century Western world, is that groups very similar to those which we identify as the family do exist in the majority of societies known to anthropologists. Furthermore, anthropologists have tended to assume that an adequate explanatory definition of any given social or cultural trait can be extended to similar traits in other cultures. But as one anthropologist has commented: "because the family seems to be the predominant unit we must not be bemused into thinking that it is the 'natural' or 'basic' one" (Fox 1967: 38). . . .

It is usually assumed that the family, a co-residential unit containing parents and their own children, is the natural primary unit within which domestic and sexual relations and socialization will take place; that relationships between members of a family are unique and specific, and are recognizably different from relationships with individuals outside the family; that there is, at least for the early years of life, an inevitably deep and necessary dependence between a mother and her children, and that there is some sense of obligation and interdependence between those who are members of the family, particularly between parents and children; that incest taboos operate within the family unit; and that property, status, and positions pass within the family. It is also usually assumed that there is considerable interdependence, both social and sexual, between men and women and that this is revealed within the family/the household.

The most critical areas of kinship to examine in order to have some understanding of the family are those which offer the greatest challenge to preconceptions and which have significant effect on the construction of kinship relations insofar as they affect the assumptions we have outlined above. Five areas will be explored: conception, **incest**, parent/child relations and adoption, marriage, households and residence.

Conception

The question of who our kin, our relations, are is answered in numerous ways, even for the primary parent–child relation. Notions of blood ties, of biological connection, which to us seem relatively unequivocal, are highly variable. Some societies of which we have anthropological record recognize only the role of the father or of the mother in conception and procreation. The other sex is given some significance but is not seen, for example, as providing blood . . . as having any biological connection. Only one parent is a "relation," the other parent is not. In the Trobriand Islands, for example, it is believed that intercourse is not the cause of conception; semen is not seen as essential for conception (Malinowski 1922). Conception results from the entry of a spirit child into the womb; the male role is to "open the passage" to the womb, through intercourse, and it is the repeated intercourse of the same partner which "moulds" the child. A child's blood comes from its mother's side and from her siblings, her mother and mother's brother, not from the father. A child will not be related by blood to its father, but will look like its father since he has through intercourse created its form. Fathers continue after birth to have a very close and intimate relationship with their children and it is this contact which also is seen as creating the likeness, as moulding the child in his/her father's image.

Other societies recognize the crucial importance of semen in the formation of a child, but believe that it is essential for conception that either the semen of more than one man is involved—or that fertility is only possible given a mixture of different semen; thus a newly married woman in Marind-Anim society (in New Guinea) is gang-raped at marriage and on subsequent ritual occasions (Van Baal 1966). Semen is understood as being necessary for growth throughout childhood and adolescence and elaborate male homosexual activities ensure that adolescent boys are in receipt of semen.

The Lakker of Burma on the other hand consider that the mother is only a container in which the child grows; she has no blood connection with her children, and children of the same mother and different fathers are not considered to be related to each other (Keesing 1976). These cases are extreme but have important implications in that they indicate that relations which seem to us to be self-evidently biological are not universally seen as such. "Natural," "biological" relations are not inevitably those which organize human relations at a very fundamental level since what is understood as "biological" is socially defined and therefore is expressed in different ways.

Incest

Incest is another area of human relations which is widely discussed in terms of some kind of innate, instinctive abhorrence for sexual relations with "close kin" and is often attributed to a subconscious realization of the genetic danger of inbreeding. (It is not uniformly accepted that inbreeding is inevitably disadvantageous.)

Incest taboos, defined as prohibitions on sexual relations between individuals socially classified as kin, as relations, are nearly universal. But the prohibition does not inevitably apply to the individuals whom we would identify as primary kin. The most dramatic exceptions to incest are found in certain royal dynasties (Egypt, Hawaii) where inbreeding (brother–sister) was enforced in order to keep the purity of the royal line, as well as in

Ptolemaic and Roman Egypt where apparently father–daughter and brother–sister sexual relations were relatively common. In most other known societies, sexual relations between those socially recognized as "biologically" related are taboo. The Trobrianders, for example, do not consider the children of one father and different mothers to be related and sexual relations between those children are thus entirely legitimate, whereas sexual relations with women who have the same mother, or whose mothers are siblings, are taboo. The Lakker of Burma do not consider that the children of the same mother have any kinship links. "Incest" does not apply to these non-kin and sexual relations are permitted. In other societies in which, for example, the category of mother or sister is extended to include all males or females of the same generation who are descended through one parent from a common grandfather, or great-grandfather, it is frequently this whole group which is sexually unavailable. It is the social definitions of significant kinship relations that are important in defining incest rather than any concept of natural, biological imperatives militating against sexual intercourse within a "natural family unit."

Parent/Child Relations: Adoption

It is nearly universally accepted in all anthropological texts on the family, however prepared they are to accept the fact that the nuclear family is not ubiquitous, that the "mother–child tie is inevitable and given," that the "irreducible and elementary social grouping is surely the mother and her children." This is seen as determined by the imperatives of infantile dependence and the need for breast milk and is also related to other psychological needs on the part both of the mother and

of the child. It is in this context instructive to consider the implications of the widespread practice of adoption. In many societies, children do not live with their "real" parents, but often stay with their mothers until some time after they have been weaned, when, as they say in N. Ghana, they have "gained sense" (at about six). However, throughout Melanesia and Polynesia, children are adopted just after weaning or, in some instances, well before— a phenomenon which is considered as absolutely acceptable. In some instances babies are adopted and breastfed by their adopted mother. Margaret Mead (1935: 193) describes such a situation among the Mundugumor in New Guinea: "even women who have never borne children are able in a few weeks, by placing the child constantly at the breast and by drinking plenty of coconut milk, to produce enough, or nearly enough, milk to rear the child, which is suckled by other women in the first few weeks after adoption."

In Tahiti, young women often have one or two children before they are considered, or consider themselves to be, ready for an approved and stable relationship. It is considered perfectly acceptable for the children of this young woman to be given to her parents or other close kin for adoption while she is freed to continue what is seen as the "business of adolescence." The girl can decide what her relationship to the children will be, but there is no sense in which she is forced into "motherhood" because of having had a baby; "motherhood" in such a situation can be seen as a status reached by women at a particular stage of development, as involving a psychological and social readiness, not something inevitably attached to the physical bearing of children.

In nearly all the societies in which adoption of this kind is common (and where anthropologists have discussed it at length) it is clear that the adopted child will still maintain contact with its "natural" parents and will know what their relationship to each other is. A Tahitian man (himself adopted) was asked about children's relations to their parents: "if you are not adopted you are grateful to your biological mother because she gave birth to you. On the other hand, when you are taken in your infancy by somebody it isn't worthwhile to think any more about your mother. The woman who took you in is just the same as your biological mother. Your gratitude is because you were an infant and you were taken" (in Levy 1970: 81). One of the interesting aspects of this definition of the relationship between parents and children is the sense in which it is seen as so critically dependent on gratitude—from child to parent—since it is recognized that adults choose to bring up the child and do not have a necessary sense of responsibility or instinctive love for it. The implications of such attitudes for all social relations are clearly considerable.

Again, in most of these societies it is agreed that the adopted child is more the foster father's than the true father's. Margaret Mead (1935), writing on the Manus of New Guinea, described the very considerable personality similarities she saw between fathers and their adopted children. The relationship between fathers and children is extremely close; fathers feed and spend a lot of time with their children. The "likeness," of which the Trobriand Islanders speak, between father and children, is also, in many other Melanesian and Polynesian societies, seen as due to the close personal contact between them. The father–child relationship is seen as a crucial and, above all, as a social relationship, one which is created by social contact, not one which exists because of a "blood relationship." In Tahiti, it is considered an ultimate shame for adopted children to leave the house of their adopted parents since the relationship between those who have lived together and have grown "familiar" ("matau") with each other (the essential ingredient for all good relations) is seen as inevitably far closer than that between biological, "natural" parents.

It is instructive in this context to consider the United Nations' study on the *Adoption of Children in Western Nations* in which it is argued that in the West, society attributes "a sacred character . . . to family bonds" (Levy 1970). The extent to which this attribution is ideological is even more evident once we have understood the extraordinary narrowness of our definitions of familiar, "natural" relations.

Marriage

It has been claimed that some form of marriage is found in all human societies. The definitions of marriage, however, again give some indication of the kind of complexity that is involved in the attempt to provide universals. One famous definition by Goodenough (1970: 12–13) defines marriage in these terms:

> Marriage is a transaction and resulting contract in which a person (male or female, corporate or individual, in person or by proxy) establishes a continuing claim to the right of sexual access to a woman—this right having priority over rights of sexual access others currently have, or may subsequently acquire, in relation to her (except in a similar transaction) until the contract resulting from the transaction is terminated, and in which the woman involved is eligible to bear children.

Other definitions stress, above all, the significance of marriage in determining parentage—in allocating children to different groups. The definitions have to be understood in relation to the kinds of social arrangements which are entirely inconsistent with our notions of marriage.

The Nayar of northern India provide one of the most problematic cases of "marriage" (Schneider and Gough 1972). The basic social group among the Nayar is the Taravad, a unit composed of men and women descended through the female line from a common ancestress. Thus it is brothers and sisters, mothers and children who cohabit. A child becomes a member of the mother's Taravad, not the father's. A Nayar girl was involved, before she reached puberty, in a formal ritual with a man from an equivalent caste to her own, and then was able to take as many lovers as she wished; the "husband"—the man who had been involved in the ritual—only had a very minimal ritual attachment to his "wife," although he too could be one of her lovers. (Not all lovers came from the same caste.) Husbands and fathers, in such a context, are entirely peripheral to the domestic life of their wives and children—and never cohabit.

Among the Nuer of the Nile Basin, one of the most common forms of marriage is what has been called "ghost" marriage (the anthropologist Evans-Pritchard who worked among the Nuer estimates that nearly 50 per cent of all marriages correspond to this form). Ghost marriage refers to the situation in which a man dies unmarried or with no children of his own. If this happens, a close kinsman (related to him through his father's line) will marry a wife "to his name" and children born of this union will be seen as the dead man's children. A man who has been involved in marrying this way and bearing children for another man will, when he dies and if he has not contracted a second marriage in his own name—only possible if his wife dies—have to become in his turn a proxy father

and a subsequent ghost marriage will be contracted. If a married man dies his widow then should ideally be married by a brother or close male kin of the dead man and, again, children born of this union will be considered to be those of the dead man, not of the living husband.

The Nuer also have another contractual form of "marriage" in which an old and important, usually barren, woman may marry a younger woman. Nuer marriages are contracted through the "husband" giving the bride price (cattle) to the wife's group. The children born to this younger woman will then, for particular purposes such as inheritance, be considered as the children of the old woman; their "father." Marriages of this kind indicate the importance among the Nuer both of becoming a parent, or rather a male parent, in order to become an ancestor—for only "fathers" with offspring are remembered and have status as ancestors—and also of the inheritance of property. Nuer marriages also demonstrate that the marriage indicates a contract between a group of related "men," who are seen in some sense as equivalents, and a woman married to one of them.

These two widely differing examples illustrate one of the other critical elements in the relations defined by marriage: the difference between the "legally" recognized father or mother and the person who was involved in conception, or birth. In both the cases cited above, the person we would see as the father, he who had impregnated the woman, is not given any social recognition at all; it is the person, not necessarily male, who is given the social position of father who is recognized through the ritual of "marriage." The two males are distinguished in the anthropological literature thus: the biological father is the *genitor*, the biological mother the *genetrix*, the "socially" recognized father the *pater*, the socially recognized mother the *mater*. In cases of **polyandry**, where a woman is "married" to more than one man, as is the case among the Toda, one of the men will perform a ritual which makes him the *pater*, and the child and subsequent children will belong to this group. In some of the societies (very few) in which polyandry exists, it is a group of brothers who share a wife. In some cases a group of sisters will be "married" to a group of brothers and in such situations the children belong to the family group. Individual paternity is thus socially less important than membership of a family unit.

Paternity is of crucial importance in societies in which status, positions, and property are transmitted through the male line. The notion of the group, related through the male line, can in some societies have such force that sexual relations between a woman and any male from the same group as that into which she was born (and such a group can include a considerable number of individuals, all the descendants of a common great-grandfather, for example) are regarded as incestuous. We can see with the example of the Nayar (although the Nayar do constitute an exceptional case) that paternity has far less social significance if all important social attributes are gained through inheritance down the female line. (It is important to recognize that such a system of inheritance does not imply that men are marginalized . . . but that it is brothers rather than husbands who are the significant social males.)

Even in situations in which the attribution of paternity is so important we cannot simply assume that the concepts of legitimacy and illegitimacy are clear-cut. In many societies of this kind there are all kinds of arrangements for the allocation of children—which are not wholly dependent on the concepts of the determining factor of parenthood.

Household and Residence

Our conception of what constitutes the family is dependent not only on what we have called kinship ties but equally in terms of residence, domestic units, or households. Given the range of kinship relations that we have briefly explored, it is inevitable that a wide range of different residential patterns exist. Moreover, households will not only be composed of individuals whose relations to each other are based on different criteria but the size and composition over time of such households will vary, as will their relation to production, to other units, and to social positions.

There are three basic forms of residence as isolated by anthropologists: **vivilocal**, where a married couple and their children live with the kin of the husband; **matrilocal**, where the couple live with the kin of the wife; and **neolocal**, where the couple live independently of either group of kin. This scheme is however further complicated by the fact that in many societies in which descent is traced through the female line (**matrilineal** societies), the children might initially live with the mother and father with the father's kin, and then later move to live with their mother's kin; in other words, with their mother's brothers, those from whom they will inherit property, status, or position. Often in such societies (such as the Trobriand Islanders) daughters never live with their mother's kin—they stay with their fathers until they marry and then move to their husband's kin. The complication of residence patterns is considerable—one of the factors which these different patterns demonstrate is that households as units of parents and their children are not a necessary or permanent social arrangement. The extent to which individuals are identified with any one household, both as children and as adults, varies considerably. In most matrilineal societies men will circulate and often a man will split his available time and space between kin and conjugal roles. In some societies of this kind, men will live alternately in two places, or will frequently visit two different units, or move at different stages from one to another. In the case of the polyandrous Toda, a woman married to different men will circulate between their different households (Rivers 1906). Children similarly will shift residence in many societies—in many instances, because of the "institution" of fostering whereby, from the age of about five, children are sent to be brought up by non-parental kin. Claims to have a foster child are formally expressed as the rights held by a man in his sister's children—and by a woman in her brother's daughter—but it is much more extensive than this, and there are many instances of children living with their grandparents (Goody 1969: 192). Households then can often be extremely fluid units, with shifting membership.

In most of the known societies of the world, monogamy is the exception rather than the rule. Some anthropologists claim that over 90 per cent of the world's cultures involve plural polygamous marriages. We have already referred to polyandry, one woman with several husbands, but by far the most common form of **polygamy** is **polygyny**—one man with several wives.

In some polygynous societies, almost invariably those in which descent is traced through the male line, households consist of a series of relatively self-contained living quarters in which a man and his wives, each with her own children, live, one wife in a relatively autonomous domestic unit. In others, domestic arrangements are dominated by a group of brothers with their wives and their offspring.

The domestic existence of each smaller unit within such a group is determined by the existence of the larger group and is ultimately dependent on the authority of those males who are in control of the unit as a whole.

In such situations it is again difficult to arrive at a useful definition of such a unit if we are concerned to consider households purely as kinship entities. Is such a mother and children unit an entity or is it a sub-household within a much larger household?

The Tiv of Nigeria provide an example of this latter form of "household." Tiv kinship groups live in compounds, a circular arrangement of huts and granaries, in the centre of which is an open space—"the centre of Tiv family life." The compound head is the senior, eldest man. He settles disputes, supervises the productive activities of the group, and controls magic. His several wives live in separate units in the compound which is also inhabited by his junior children, unmarried daughters, and married sons and their families. In addition, there may be a younger brother and his family, and/or outsiders.

As is argued by the anthropologists involved, while in a sense each wife who has a separate hut and her children constitute a separate domestic unit, the larger compound group—a **patrilineal** extended family augmented by outsiders—is the central domestic unit of everyday Tiv life and of collective economic enterprise (Bohannon and Bohannon 1968).

It is only when we consider the household in terms of this latter—its productive capacities—that we can make sense of this kind of domestic unit usually found in agricultural communities. Households and domestic units are not only an arrangement of people related to each other through parent–child ties, but in societies such as the Tiv, they form units of production and have to be analyzed and understood as such.

Kinship ties have thus been seen by some anthropologists as constituting the relation of production. The Tiv compound, for example, is essentially a means of reuniting and controlling necessary labour, both productive and reproductive. Clearly, households in many societies have to be analyzed as units of production and consumption, and as providers of labour. The form of the household must therefore be analyzed in terms of the economic structure of the society as a whole and cannot simply be seen as a unit containing the "family," essentially defining sets of affective relations. Precisely because the Western ideal of the nuclear family is so ideologically and spatially separated from wage labour, the recognition of the profound economic significance of household formation in other societies has posed considerable problems for anthropologists. It has been even more difficult for Western sociologists to re-examine the economic role of the family within their own society in the light of the understanding gained through anthropological analysis.

Polygynous households of the kind described above are common in Africa, south of the Sahara, and however different their form, they are usually crucial productive units. In New Guinea, very different domestic arrangements exist and these cannot be analyzed in terms of the same economic determinants. In Marind-Anim and many other New Guinea societies, domestic organization constructs very considerable separation between men and women. Special men's houses provide the focal point for all male life (often including sleeping and eating) and there are often stringent taboos on women having access to such houses and, in general, on contact between males and females.

Conclusion

The family, particularly the nuclear family, can be seen, through comparative analysis, as just one very specific means of organizing the relations between parents and children, males and females. It is not, as has so often been claimed, some kind of "natural" instinctive and "sacred" unit. Even the bond between mothers and their own children, which is seen in almost mystic terms as the fundamental biologically determined relationship, can be seen as far less important than we are generally led to believe. Universal definitions of human relations must be constantly questioned and the whole notion of the "natural" must, in terms of human relations, be challenged, and the "unnatural"—in these terms the social construction of relationships—must be fully recognized.

● References

Bohannon, P., and L. Bohannon. 1968. *Tiv Economy* (Northwestern University Press).

Carroll, V. 1970. *Adoption in Eastern Oceania* (The University of Hawaii Press).

Evans-Pritchard, E.E. 1951. *Kinship and Marriage among the Nuer* (Oxford: Clarendon Press).

Fox, R. 1967. *Kinship and Marriage* (Harmondsworth, UK: Pelican).

Goodenough, W.H. 1970. *Description and Comparison in Cultural Anthropology* (Chicago: Aldine Publishing).

Goody, J.R. 1969. *Comparative Studies in Kinship* (London: Routledge & Kegan Paul).

Keesing, R.M. 1976. *Cultural Anthropology, a Contemporary Perspective* (New York: Holt, Rinehart and Winston).

Levy, R.I. 1970. "Tahitian Adoption as a Psychological Message," in *Adoption in Eastern Oceania*, ed. V. Carroll (The University of Hawaii Press).

Malinowski, B. 1922. *Argonauts of the Western Society* (London: Routledge & Kegan Paul).

Mead, M. 1935. *Sex and Temperament in Three Primitive Societies* (New York: William Morrow & Co.).

Rivers, W.H.R. 1906. *The Todas* (New York: Macmillan).

Schneider, D., and E.K. Gough. 1972. *Matrilineal Kinship* (Berkeley: University of California Press).

Van Baal, J. 1966. *Dema: Description and Analysis of Marind-Anim Culture (South New Guinea)* (The Hague: Martinus Nijhoff).

Part II

Family Diversity Over Time

Across different cultures, human societies have featured diverse family patterns. Family arrangements have also changed significantly throughout history. The following chapters provide an indication of how differently human societies have organized the work of social reproduction. Because the chapters describe people living in very different circumstances, they also provide an opportunity to address the question why family patterns are so different. To understand family patterns, it is important to get a sense of the dynamic relationship between the way people typically acquire their livelihood, on the one hand, and the way the social relations involved in sexuality, childbearing, child care, and consumption are organized, on the other hand.

When we compare gender and family patterns in societies based on foraging, agriculture, and industrial capitalism, we see some significant contrasts. From these, we can begin to see how different ways of acquiring a livelihood involve different gender relations and family arrangements. For example, in foraging (or hunting and gathering) societies, survival depends upon co-operation and dependence on a group larger than the nuclear family. Married couples and their children do not live in private households, gender relations are egalitarian, and children are cared for and indulged by all adults. For peasants, in contrast, who grow crops on land (owned by the man) to produce their daily subsistence, the male household head exerts authority over his wife and children—the latter valued mostly for their labour and kept home or sent away (to live and work in other households) depending upon economic considerations.

Many of today's family and gender patterns emerged with the development of industrial capitalism. They did so in part from the new organization of production. They also resulted from the ways people responded to their situation, as they struggled to feed their families and build meaningful lives.

Chapter 3

What follows are selections from the writings of the late anthropologist Eleanor B. Leacock. These provide rich descriptions of gender and family relations among the Montagnais-Naskapi, an Aboriginal people who survived by hunting and gathering. Leacock's research involved close examination of the "Jesuit Relations" (diaries kept by the Jesuits working in the seventeenth century in what is now Quebec, and Newfoundland and Labrador); it also included her own fieldwork in Labrador during the 1950s and 1960s. The parts of her essays presented here (written decades ago) provide us not only with descriptions of family and gender relations in a foraging society but also a sketch of her argument about how the ways that foragers acquired their livelihood shaped both their family organization and the gender relations typical in their society. Leacock also provides vivid descriptions of how family and gender changed as these people abandoned hunting for trapping and trading

with Europeans (and as the Jesuits, working on behalf of France as well as their church, devoted themselves to undermining Native traditions).

Leacock describes a society in which people lived in small groups and acquired their subsistence by co-operating with each other daily. At the heart of that co-operation was a division of labour based on gender that did not entail systemic gender inequality. The **autonomy** that women had in this society, Leacock argues, was related to the dependence that all people had on the group: because people depended on each other daily—because co-operation and generosity were central to daily subsistence—people accorded each other considerable freedom. This autonomy, and the absence of private property, formed the basis of the gender egalitarianism common in foraging societies. Elsewhere, Leacock defined **egalitarian** relations as those in which no group of people are in a position that would allow them to impose their will on others.

Women in an Egalitarian Society: The Montagnais-Naskapi of Canada

Eleanor B. Leacock

In the past, the Montagnais-Naskapi of the eastern Labrador Peninsula lived by hunting moose, caribou, beaver, bear, hare, porcupine, and other small game; by fishing, and by catching water fowl. The Indians hunted with bows and arrows, spears, and a variety of traps. Meat that was not eaten was smoke-dried for storage. In the summer they gathered nuts, berries, and roots.

The Montagnais-Naskapi lived in tents constructed of 20 to 30 poles, converging at the top and covered with large rolls of birchbark and animal hides. A tent might be shared by about 18 people. They wore breechcloths, leggings and moccasins, and robes with detachable sleeves, made from leather by the women. In the winter, travel was by foot on snowshoes and long narrow sledges, which were dragged along forest trails by a cord strung across the chest. Canoes made of birchbark were used in the summer.

Until very recently, the Montagnais-Naskapi still lived for the most part in tents, wore moccasins, and often the women retained their traditional hairstyle with the hair wound on two little wooden knobs over the ears. They manufactured their own canoes, snowshoes, fish spears, sleds, and toboggans using the "crooked knife"—a sharpened steel file, curved upwards at the end and hafted in a piece of wood. They seldom settled in one place for more than a few weeks; entire families moved hundreds of miles or more in the course of a year.

The Indians spoke their own language, told their own stories, and taught their children to read and write in the phonetic script they developed long ago when European books and letters gave them the idea. Thus, many anthropologists considered the Indians' use of some modern technology, and their adoption of some Western social and religious practices, to be the sum total of the changes that have taken place in their lifestyle.

However, a close study of the observations made centuries ago by traders and missionaries shows what profound changes have taken place in the way the Montagnais-Naskapi live. Le Jeune, a Jesuit missionary, lived with a Montagnais band in the winter of 1633–4 and his accounts give a picture of their life in the days when they depended on hunting not only for food but for everything from clothes to snowshoe webbing. Three or four families, usually related, lived together in a single, large tent; men, women, and children travelled together, each working and contributing to the group to the extent he or she was able.

Le Jeune relates that three tent groups joined forces and decided to winter together on the south shore of the St Lawrence River some miles below Quebec. Leaving their canoes at the coast, they went inland and travelled about, shifting their camp 23 times in the period from 12 November to 22 April. The winter was a hard one, since the lack of snow made it impossible to trace moose successfully. One of the three tent groups left the other two so that they might spread out over a wider area.

Eventually a heavy snowfall alleviated the situation, and large game was killed in sufficient numbers so that some of the meat could be dried and stored. In the spring, the tent group Le Jeune was with split up temporarily, some members keeping to the highlands to hunt moose, the others following the stream beds where beaver were to be found. Gradually the entire party collected again at the coast where the canoes had been cached.

Within the group, the social ethic called for generosity, co-operation, and patience, and Le Jeune commented on the good humour, the lack of jealousy, and the willingness to help that characterized daily life. Those who did not contribute their share were not respected, and it was a real insult to call a person stingy.

The Montagnais had no leaders; the "chiefs" Le Jeune referred to were apparently men of influence and rhetorical ability. Everyone was impressed with the skill of the speaker who put forth the Montagnais view of French-Indian relations when he greeted Champlain in 1632. Such men were spokesmen, who acted as intermediaries with the French or with other Indian groups, but they held no formal power, a situation the Jesuits tried to change by introducing formal elections. . . .

Important matters were resolved through considered discussion. Le Jeune was impressed by the patience with which people listened as others spoke, rather than all talking at once. At that time leadership in specific situations fell to the individual who was most knowledgeable.

For instance, during Le Jeune's stay when food was scarce and the Indians had to move in search of it, he wrote: "When our people saw that there was no longer any game within three or four leagues of us, a Savage, who was best acquainted with the way to the place where we were going, cried out in a loud voice, one fine day outside the cabin: 'Listen men, I am going to mark the way for breaking camp tomorrow at daybreak.'"

The principle of autonomy extended to relations between men and women. Though some observers saw women as drudges, Le Jeune saw women as holding "great power" and having "in nearly every instance . . . the choice of plans, of undertakings, of journeys, of winterings." Indeed, independence of women was considered a problem to the Jesuits, who lectured the men about "allowing" their wives sexual and other freedom and sought to introduce European principles of obedience.

Compare this lifestyle with that of an Indian man living to the northeast of Quebec a few decades ago, who depended upon the produce of his trapline for most of his livelihood. He worked within a definite territory which was probably passed down to him by his father, father-in-law, or another older relative. During the trapping season he left his family at a permanent camp, or perhaps even at the fur trading post, and he travelled back and forth along his line of some 300 to 400 steel traps, preferably in the company of a partner or grown son, but at times alone. Only in the summer did he join his fellow band members at the trading post, and only in this season would all the trappers live together with their families for a reasonably long period of time.

The change in this Indian's life had come about because he was no longer primarily a hunter. He was first and foremost a trapper, dependent upon the goods his furs procured for him at the local trading post. True, his ancestors always hunted and traded furs. Avenues of exchange and communication in Aboriginal America had apparently been kept open from time immemorial. However, this trade was primarily for luxury items and for social purposes. It was not of great economic importance; the economy of the Indians was still based almost entirely on hunting for immediate use.

Then Europe, breaking the bonds of the small, self-contained **feudal** communities of the Middle Ages, slowly began to develop into a commercial and urban civilization. Explorers covered the earth; trade with American Indians, and the fur trade in particular, was of no small importance. Even before the end of the sixteenth century, British and French companies were competing among themselves for a monopoly of the St Lawrence trade.

To the Indians, the trade opened up a source of new and more effective tools and weapons, of cloth which did not have to be tanned and worked, and of foods which could be more readily transported and stored. However, it demanded an unending flow of furs, and trapping fur-bearing animals began to displace the hunting of large game in the Indian economy. Within a few generations the Indians near the earliest trade centres around Quebec had become dependent upon trade goods as the mainstay of their existence. When the fur-bearing animals in their immediate area became scarce, they became the middlemen between the Europeans and the Indians who lived farther to the north and west.

On the face of it, there seems little reason why it should make much difference when men turned to trapping rather than hunting as a major pursuit. But through the fur trade it came to supersede and replace all other basic economic activities. And tending a trapline was a more individual type of activity than hunting. When men became trappers, the sexual definition of functions and spheres of interest became sharper, for the wife and children began to be set apart as the family who were provided for, as compared to the men who were the providers. At the same time, there was a breaking up of the "family bands" (the two or three tent groups that usually stayed together) into smaller units approaching the "nuclear" family.

A connected change that took place in Montagnais-Naskapi life was an increasingly clear-cut differentiation between the spheres of men's work and women's work. In the past, both sexes were almost continuously engaged in satisfying the immediate needs of the extended family group. There was a rough and ready division of labour, based on expediency, with the men doing most of the large game hunting and the women preparing the food, making the clothes and tents, and tending the small children. When necessary, the women helped with the hunting, and if a woman was busy elsewhere, a man would readily look after the children. *The Mistassini Diaries*, written a century ago by Hudson's Bay Company members, mention Indian women in western Labrador who were the heads of families and even handled their own traps.

The lack of a marked division of labour prevailed until recently in the camp of the Northwest River Indians. A man and his wife would come together from the woods, each carrying a log. A father and daughter might saw wood together. A man might hold a fussing child while the mother calmly did something else, feeling no compulsion to take over. A whole family would go off in a canoe to pull in the fishnets. Two young women would pick up some guns and go off to hunt rabbits. It is only when one comes to the technical processes that one noticed a division of skills that

seems to be rigid: the men were the woodworkers, making the canoes and snowshoes, and the women handled the skins, scraping, tanning, working, and sewing them.

Another change that can be observed among the Montagnais-Naskapi is a shift toward smaller family units. Only on rare occasions did two or three Indian families of eastern Labrador still share a tent. One result of the breaking up of large "extended" families into smaller units, based on a married couple and their children, was that the circle of people upon whom the children depend began to shrink. Le Jeune reveals the feelings of a seventeenth-century Indian father, who chided the French, saying, "Thou hast no sense. You French people love only your own children; but we love all the children of our tribe." In 1950, however, there was a growing emphasis among the Indians on having one's "own" son who will help one on the trapline.

On the other hand, it must be said that the general loving attitude toward all children still prevailed. Time and again one noticed an adult's casual and spontaneous concern for the needs of whatever child happened to be around. Nor could one pick out an orphan or "adopted" child by the way he or she was treated. Such children were in no way set apart from the life of the group but were gratefully taken in and cherished by another family.

These are only a few of the developments that have been taking place in Montagnais-Naskapi life. Any number of others could be studied—changing forms of property and attitudes toward possessions, courtship practices, recreation and amusement, methods of child rearing, and so on. However, the same fundamental point would be made by examination of any important area of living: that the Montagnais-Naskapi Indians are not a people who simply accepted some European traits and rejected others but a people who actively adjusted their whole way of life to meet the demands of a new occupational calling.

By 1950, most Montagnais-Naskapi had moved into relatively large centres of permanent settlement. Three important towns were Schefferville, near a large interior iron mine; Seven Islands, a railhead on the St Lawrence River; and Happy Valley, near the Goose Bay Air Base on the eastern coast. While most Indians who lived in these towns were wage labourers at the enterprises near their homes, work was often seasonal, and some still derived a major part of their income from winter trapping. Many young Indians were moving to cities for work and schooling and some were joining local and national Indian groups that concern themselves with the problems and futures of Native Canadians. As part of this future many young Indians found that they wanted to retain some of the Indian tradition of a close group life, in tune with the waters and forests, the animals and bird life, the natural surroundings of their ancestors.

What was the status of the Montagnais-Naskapi women in the early seventeenth century when the French were establishing a foothold in the upper St Lawrence valley? As is often the case, a look through accounts written at the time yields contrasting judgments. One may read that "women have great power . . . A man may promise you something and if he does not keep his promise, he thinks he is sufficiently excused when he tells you that his wife did not wish him to do it" (Thwaites 1906, 5: 179). Or one may read that women were virtual slaves:

The women . . . besides the onerous role of bearing and rearing the children, also transport the game from the place where it has fallen; they are the hewers of wood and drawers of water; they make and repair the household utensils; they prepare the food; they skin the game and prepare the hides like fullers; they sew garments; they catch fish and gather shellfish for food; often they even hunt; they make the canoes, that is, skiffs of marvelous rapidity, out of bark; they set up the tents wherever and whenever they stop for the night—in short, the men concern themselves with nothing but the more laborious hunting and the waging of war . . . Their wives are regarded and treated as slaves. (2: 77)

Fortunately, the ethnohistorical record for the Montagnais-Naskapi is full enough so that contradictions between two statements such as these can be resolved. The view that the hard work of Native American women made them slaves was commonly expressed by European observers who did not know personally the people about whom they were writing. The statement about female authority, however, was written by a man who knew the Montagnais-Naskapi well and recognized that women controlled their own work and made decisions accordingly. Paul Le Jeune, superior of the Jesuit mission at Quebec, had spent a winter in a Montagnais lodge in order to learn the language and understand the culture of the people he was supposed to convert and "civilize." He commented on the ease of relations between husbands and wives in Montagnais society, and explained that it followed from "the order which they maintain in their occupations," whereby "the women know what they are to do, and the men also; and one never meddles with the work of the other" (5: 133). "Men leave the arrangement of the household to the women, without interfering with them; they cut and decide and give away as they please without making the husband angry. I have never seen my host ask a giddy young woman that he had with him what became of the provisions, although they were disappearing very fast" (6: 233).

Le Jeune sought to change this state of affairs, and he reported to his superiors in Paris on this progress in "civilizing" the Montagnais-Naskapi through what became a fourfold program. First, he saw permanent settlement and the institution of formally recognized chiefly authority as basic. Second, Le Jeune stressed the necessity of introducing the principle of punishment into Montagnais social relations. Third, central to Le Jeune's program was education of Montagnais-Naskapi children. . . .

Montagnais-Naskapi culture posed a stumbling block for the Jesuits in that the Montagnais did not practise corporal punishment of children. Le Jeune complained, "The Savages prevent their instruction; they will not tolerate the chastisement of their children, whatever they may do, they permit only a simple reprimand" (5: 197). Le Jeune's solution was to propose removing the children from their communities for schooling: "The reason why I would not like to take the children of one locality in that locality itself, but rather in some other place, is because these Barbarians cannot bear to have their children punished, even scolded, not being able to refuse anything to a crying child. They carry this to such an extent that upon the slightest pretext they would take them away from us, before they were educated" (6: 153–5).

Fourth, essential to Le Jeune's entire program was the introduction of European family structure with male authority, female fidelity, and the elimination of the right to divorce. Lecturing a man on the subject, Le Jeune said the man "was the master and that in France women do not rule their husbands" (5: 179). The independence of Montagnais women posed continual problems for the Jesuits. Le Jeune decided that

it is absolutely necessary to teach the girls as well as the boys, and that we shall do nothing or very little, unless some good household has the care of this sex; for the boys that we shall have reared in the knowledge of God, when they marry Savage girls or women accustomed to wandering in the woods will, as their husbands, be compelled to follow them and thus fall back into barbarism or to leave them, another evil full of danger. (5: 145)

Le Jeune's account of his problems, successes, and failures in introducing hierarchical principles into the ordering of interpersonal relations among the Montagnais-Naskapi affords a clear record of the personal autonomy that was central to the structure and ethics of their society—an autonomy that applied as fully to women as to men.

Montagnais-Naskapi Economy and Decision-making

The Montagnais-Naskapi lived by hunting and trapping wild game—caribou, moose, beaver, bear, hare, porcupine, and water fowl, by fishing, and by gathering wild berries and other vegetable foods. Like foraging peoples everywhere, they followed a regular pattern of seasonal movement according to the provenience of the foods on which they depended. The Montagnais with whom Le Jeune worked summered on the shores of the St Lawrence River, where groups of several hundred people gathered to fish, socialize, and make and repair canoes, snowshoes, and other equipment. In the fall, groups of some 35 to 75 people separated out to ascend one or another of the rivers that emptied into the St Lawrence. During the winter hunting season, these bands might split up into smaller groups in order to spread out over a wide area in search of game. However, they kept in touch with each other so that if some were short of food, they could turn to others for help.

The smallest working unit was the group that lived together in a large cone-shaped lodge—some 10 to 20 people, or, in Western terms, several nuclear families. In early times, as later, residential choices were probably flexible, and people moved about in accord both with personal likes and dislikes and with the need for keeping a reasonable balance in the working group between women and men and young and old. Upon marriage, however, a man ideally moved into his wife's lodge (Thwaites 1906, 31: 169). Accordingly, mentions of a Montagnais man's family might include the man's wife's sister, or a son-in-law, or a father-in-law (6: 125; 9: 33; 14: 143–5). Yet three brothers and their wives shared the lodge in which Le Jeune lived. Le Jeune is silent about the relationships among the wives who, judging from hunting-group compositions in recent times, could easily have been sisters or parallel cousins.[1] In any case, Le Jeune's diary shows that the arrangement was not permanent.

Ethnographic evidence as well as the *Jesuit Relations* indicates that decisions about movements were made by the adult members of whatever group was involved. There is no question about women's importance in making such decisions. In fact, one recorder stated that "the choice of plans, of undertakings, of journeys, of winterings, lies in nearly every instance in the hands of the housewife" (68: 93). Individuals might be chosen as spokespersons to mediate with the French, but such "chiefs" held no formal authority within the group. Le Jeune noted that "the Savages cannot endure in the least those who seem desirous of assuming superiority over the others; they place all virtue in a certain gentleness or apathy" (16: 165).

They imagine that they ought by right of birth, to enjoy the liberty of wild ass colts, rendering no homage to anyone whomsoever, except when they like. They have reproached me a hundred times because we fear our Captains, while they laugh at and make sport of theirs. All the authority of their Chief is in his tongue's end; for he is powerful insofar as he is eloquent; and, even if he kills himself talking and haranguing, he will not be obeyed unless he pleases the Savages. (6: 243)

Le Jeune was honest enough to state what he saw as the positive side of Montagnais egalitarianism:

As they have neither political organization, nor office, nor dignities, nor any authority, for they only obey their Chief through goodwill toward him, therefore they never kill each other to acquire these honours. Also, as they are contented with mere living, not one of them gives himself to the Devil to acquire wealth. (6: 231)

In his final judgment, however, Le Jeune remained bound by his culture and his missionizing commitment: "I would not dare assert that I have seen one act of real moral virtue in a Savage. They have nothing but their own pleasure and satisfaction in view" (6: 239–41).

The Jesuit Program for Changing Montagnais Marriage

As indicated above, Le Jeune's original assumption—that he could win the Montagnais to Christianity through converting the men—changed when he learned how far Montagnais family structure was from that of the French. He realized that he would have to give special attention to women as well as men if he was to eliminate the Montagnais' unquestioned acceptance of divorce at the desire of either partner, of polygyny, and of sexual freedom after marriage.

"The young people do not think that they can persevere in the state of matrimony with a bad wife or a bad husband," Le Jeune wrote. "They wish to be free and to be able to divorce the consort if they do not love each other" (16: 41). And several years later, "The inconstancy of marriages and the facility with which they divorce each other are a great obstacle to the Faith of Jesus Christ. We do not dare baptize the young people because experience teaches us that the custom of abandoning a disagreeable wife or husband has a strong hold on them" (22: 229).

Polygamy was another right that women as well as men took for granted: "Since I have been preaching among them that a man should not have more than one wife, I have not been well received by the women; for, since they are more numerous than the men, if a man can only marry one of them, the others will have to suffer. Therefore, this doctrine is not according to their liking" (12: 165). And as for the full acceptance of sexual freedom for both women and men, no citation can be more telling of the gulf between French and Montagnais society than Le Jeune's rendition of a Montagnais rebuff:

> I told him that it was not honourable for a woman to love anyone else except her husband, and that this evil being among them, he himself was not sure that his son, who was there present, was his son. He replied, "Thou hast no sense. You French people love only your own children; but we love all the children of our tribe." I

began to laugh, seeing that he philosophized in horse and mule fashion. (6: 255)

Converts to Christianity wrestled with the dilemmas posed by the French faith. A recently married young man wished to be faithful to his wife but felt himself "inclined toward infidelity." Deeply disturbed by his criminal wish, he entreated to be imprisoned or publicly flogged. When his request was refused, "He slips into a room near the Chapel and, with a rope that he finds, he beats himself so hard all over the body that the noise reaches the ears of the Father, who runs in and forbids so severe a penance" (22: 67).

In 1640, eight years after Le Jeune's arrival in New France and the setting up of a Jesuit mission, the governor called together a group of influential Montagnais men, and "having recommended to the Christians constance in their marriages—he gave them to understand that it would be well if they should elect some chiefs to govern them" (18: 99). Accordingly, the Montagnais sought advice from the Jesuits, who supervised the election of three captains. The men then "resolved to call together the women to urge them to be instructed and to receive holy Baptism." The women were used to holding councils of their own to deal with matters of concern to them and reported surprise at being lectured to by the men:

> Yesterday the men summoned us to a council, but the first time that women have ever entered one; but they treated us so rudely that we were greatly astonished. "It is you women," they said to us, "who keep the Demons among us; you do not urge to be baptized . . . when you pass before the cross you never salute it, you wish to be independent. Now know that you will obey your husbands and you young people

know that you will obey your parents, and our captains, and if any fail to do so, we will give them nothing to eat." (18: 107)

Women's responses ranged from zealous compliance to rebelliousness. . . . [Some] women continued to have lovers, to solicit married men to take a second wife, and to defy or leave their husbands. One convert complained, "My wife is always angry; I fear that the Demons she keeps in my cabin are perverting the good that I received in holy Baptism." . . .

Another particularly revealing incident offers an important comment on Montagnais ethics, and indicates the growing distance between the missionized Montagnais, with their acceptance of corporal punishment, and the unconverted. A Jesuit called some "chief men" together and, after commending them on putting a stop to "the disorderly conduct that occasionally occurred among them," expressed astonishment at their permitting a young baptized woman to live apart from her husband. The captain responsible for her replied that "he had tried all sorts of means to make her return to her duty and that his trouble had been in vain; that he would, nevertheless, make another effort." The Jesuit father counselled him to consult his people and decide upon what was to be done for such disobedience: "They all decided upon harsh measures. 'Good advice,' they said, 'has not brought her to her sense; a prison will do so.' Two captains were ordered to take her to Kebec and . . . have her put in a dungeon." The woman fled, but they caught her and tried to take her by canoe to Quebec. At this

> some Pagan young men, observing this violence, of which the Savages have a horror, and which is more remote from their customs than heaven is from Earth,

made use of threats, declaring that they would kill anyone who laid a hand on the woman. But the Captain and his people, who were Christians, boldly replied that there was nothing that they would not do or endure in order to secure obedience to God. Such resolution silenced the infidels.

To avoid being imprisoned, the woman "humbly begged to be taken back to Saint Joseph, promising thenceforward she would be more obedient." Le Jeune stated,

> Such acts of justice cause no surprise in France, because it is usual there to proceed in that manner. But, among these peoples . . . where everyone considers himself from birth, as free as the wild animals that roam in their great forest . . . it is a marvel, or rather a miracle, to see a peremptory command obeyed, or any act of severity or justice performed. . . .

Long-range Impact of the Jesuit Program

. . . Perhaps no incident in the *Relations* more poignantly reveals the cultural distance to be spanned by Montagnais converts than that in which a French drummer boy hit a Montagnais with his drumstick, drawing blood.

> The Montagnais onlookers took offence, saying, "Behold, one of thy people has wounded one of ours, thou knowest our custom well; give us presents for this wound." The French interpreter countered, "Thou knowest our custom; when any of our number does wrong, we punish him. This child has wounded one of your people; he shall be whipped at once in

[their] presence." When the Montagnais saw the French were in earnest about whipping the boy, they began to pray for his pardon, alleging he was only a child, that he had no mind, that he did not know what he was doing; but as our people were nevertheless going to punish him, one of the Savages stripped himself entirely, threw his blanket over the child and cried out to him who was going to do the whipping: "Strike me if thou wilt, but thou shalt not strike him." And thus the little one escaped. (5: 219)

This incident took place in 1633. How was it possible that scarcely 10 years later, adults could be beating, withholding food from, and even, if the report is accurate, doing such things as throwing hot ashes on children and youths? Above, I have referred to the punitiveness toward the self and others that accompanied the often tormented attempt on the part of converts to reject a familiar set of values and replace it with another. This psychological response is familiar. To say this, however, merely presses the next question: Why did some Montagnais feel so strongly impelled to make this attempt? The answer is that the Jesuits and their teachings arrived in New France a full century after the economic basis for unquestioned co-operation, reciprocity, and respect for individual autonomy began to be undercut by the trading of furs for European goods. On the basis of new economic ties, some Montagnais-Naskapi were interested in attaching themselves to the mission station and the new European settlement, thereby availing themselves of the resources these offered. By the same token, some were prepared to accept the beliefs and ritual practices of the newcomers, and to adopt—or attempt to adopt—new standards of conduct.

Elsewhere, I have documented the process whereby the stockpiling of furs for future return, to be acquired when the trading ships arrived, contradicted the principles of total sharing based on subsistence hunting, fishing, and gathering (Leacock 1954). The process has subsequently been well described for the Canadian sub-Arctic generally, and it has been pointed out that parallel processes are involved when a horticultural people become involved in exchange relations with a market economy (Murphy and Steward 1955).

At the same time that the fur trade was undercutting the foundation for Montagnais-Naskapi values and interpersonal ethics, the terrible scourge of epidemic disease, the escalation (or introduction) of warfare, and the delusion of relief from anxiety offered by alcohol were also undermining Montagnais-Naskapi self-assurance. Alfred Goldsworthy Bailey (1969) has described the effects of these developments in a review of the conflict between European and eastern Algonkian cultures during the sixteenth and seventeenth centuries. Fear of disease, particularly smallpox which raged in the decade after the priests' arrival, was only equalled by fear of the Iroquois. The prolonged and intricate torture of Iroquois prisoners, into which women entered with even more zeal than men, was a grim expression of profound fearfulness and anger. Alcohol, which temporarily elated the spirits, led to fights around the European settlement; in 1664 there is a reference to a case of rape committed under its influence (48: 227).

This is not to say, however, that Montagnais-Naskapi society as a whole was thoroughly disrupted. The violence that occurred around the European settlement contrasts not only with the friendliness, gaiety, and lack of quarrelling that Le Jeune described during the winter he spent in the interior in 1633–4 but also with the general co-operativeness and goodwill—albeit laced with raucous banter and teasing—that characterized Montagnais-Naskapi life in later centuries in the rest of the Labrador Peninsula. Quebec was, after all, a gateway to the North American interior, and fur trading posts and mission stations pushed ever westward. The non-racist policy of building a French colony in part with re-socialized Indians was abandoned and replaced by a hardening colour line. In time, all Montagnais-Naskapi became Catholic, but without the closer supervision of the Jesuits, they retained established religious practices and added Catholic sacraments and prayer. During the summer of 1951, the "shaking-tent rite," in which a religious practitioner converses with the gods, both gaining useful information and entertaining the audience in the process, was still being practised in eastern Labrador.

The pace of change in most of the Labrador Peninsula was slow, as Indians living far from centres of early settlement and trade gradually became drawn into a fur-trapping economy. In the summer of 1950, I was able to document the final stages of transition in southeastern Labrador, at a time when the next major change was about to transform life for French and English fishermen and fur trappers as well as Montagnais-Naskapi hunter trappers; a railroad was being built into a huge iron mine deep in the north central part of the peninsula. When I was there, conditions in the north woods were still such that the traditional Montagnais-Naskapi ethic of cooperativeness, tolerance, and non-punitiveness remained strong.

What about the relations between women and men? . . . Burgesse (1944) has written that

labour is fairly equitably divided between the sexes under the economic system of the Montagnais. Each sex has its own particular duties but, within certain limits, the divisions between the types of work performed are not rigid. A man would not consider it beneath his dignity to assist his wife in what are ordinarily considered duties peculiar to the woman. Also, women are often enough to be seen performing tasks which are usually done by men. On being questioned in regard to this aspect of their economics, the Montagnais invariably reply that, since marriage is a union of co-equal partners for mutual benefit, it is the duty of the husband to assist his wife in the performance of her labours. Similarly, it is the duty of the wife to aid the husband. . . .

The Montagnais woman is far from being a drudge. Instead she is a respected member of the tribe whose worth is well appreciated and whose advice and counsel is listened to and, more often than not, accepted and acted upon by her husband. (4–7) . . .

Women retained control over the products of their labour. These were not alienated, and women's production of clothing, shelter, and canoe covering gave them concomitant practical power and influence, despite formal statements of male dominance that might be elicited by outsiders. In northern Labrador in the late nineteenth century, dependence on trading furs for food, clothing, and equipment was only beginning. Band cohesion was still strong, based on the sharing of meat, fish, and other necessities, and on the reciprocal exchange of goods and services between women and men.

By the middle of this [twentieth] century, the economic balance had tipped in favour of the ultimate dependence upon the fur trade (and, in many cases, wage labour) throughout the entire Labrador Peninsula.

The Montagnais-Naskapi lived in nuclear-family units largely supported by the husband and father's wages or take from the trapline. Nonetheless, the resources of the land were still directly used, were still available to anyone, were acquired co-operatively insofar as it was most practical, and were shared. Furthermore, partly through their own desire and partly in accord with the racist structure of Western society, the Montagnais-Naskapi maintained their status as a semi-autonomous people and were not separated into an elite minority versus a majority of marginal workers. Thus, a strong respect for individual autonomy and an extreme sensitivity to the feelings of others when decisions were to be made went with a continuing emphasis on generosity and co-operativeness, which applied to relations between as well as within the sexes.

In my own experience living in a Montagnais-Naskapi camp, I noted a quality of respectfulness between women and men that fits Burgesse's characterization. I also observed such behaviour as an ease of men with children, who would take over responsibility even for infants when it was called for, with a spontaneity and casual competence that in our culture would be described as "maternal." Nonetheless, men were "superior" in ways commonly alluded to in anthropological literature. The few shamans who still practised their art (or admitting practising it to an outsider) were men; band chiefs were men; and patrilocality was both an ideal and statistically more common among newlyweds than matrilocality. In short, Montagnais-Naskapi practice at this time fitted what is considered in the anthropological literature to be usual for people who live (or have recently lived) by direct acquisition and use of wild products; strongly egalitarian, but with an edge in favour of male authority and influence.

Seventeenth-century accounts, however, referred to female shamans who might become powerful (Thwaites 1906, 6: 61; 14: 183). So-called outside chiefs, formally elected according to government protocol to mediate with white society, had no more influence within the group than their individual attributes would call for; and matrilocality had only recently given way to patrilocal, post-marital residence. As markedly different as Montagnais-Naskapi culture continued to be from Western culture, the ethnohistorical record makes clear that it had been constantly restructuring itself to fit new situations and that the status of women, although still relatively high, has clearly changed.

● Note

1. Parallel cousins are the children of two sisters or two brothers (and their spouses). Children of a brother and a sister (and their spouses) are called "cross-cousins." As is common in many kin-based societies, the Montagnais-Naskapi terms for parallel cousins were the same as for siblings, while the terms for cross-cousins, who were desirable marriage partners, connoted something like "sweetheart" (Strong 1929).

● References

Bailey, A.G. 1969. *The Conflict of European and Eastern Algonkian Cultures, 1504–1700* (Toronto: University of Toronto Press).

Burgesse, J.A. 1944. "The Woman and the Child among the Lac-St-Jean Montagnais," *Primitive Man* 17.

Leacock, E. 1954. "The Montagnais 'Hunting Territory' and the Fur Trade," *American Anthropologist* 78.

Murphy, R.F., and J.H. Steward. 1955. "Tappers and Trappers: Parallel Processes in Acculturation," *Economic Development and Cultural Change* 4.

Strong, W.D. 1929. "Cross-cousin Marriage and the Culture of the Northeastern Algonkians," *American Anthropologist* 31.

Thwaites, R.G., ed. 1906. *The Jesuit Relations and Allied Documents*, 71 vols (Cleveland: Burrows Brothers).

Chapter 4

What follows is a selection from Louise Tilly and Joan Scott's book *Women, Work and Family*, which examines women's work on farms and in urban shops in England and France between 1700 and 1950. The selection contains a fine description of the dynamics of pre-industrial households in the eighteenth century. At the time, land was being purchased in large amounts by commercial capitalists (for the production of wool), and many peasants thus lost the land that allowed them to produce their daily subsistence; in turn, they were forced into waged work. Tilly and Scott, however, mostly describe the life of peasant farmers and urban craftspeople as it was in a pre-industrial economy in which households were both units of production and units of consumption. This "household economy" involved a continual need to balance the supply of labour against the requirements of consumption. The heads of households did so by increasing or decreasing the number of people living in their household. The enduring and essential core of these households was, however, the married couple because the work carried out by both husbands and wives was essential to the support of their households.

We learn from Tilly and Scott's summary of their research that the work of producing subsistence so dominated daily life in pre-industrial English and French households that the nature of family life, and likely even the quality of personal relationships, was largely dictated by economic considerations and pressures. Household residents came and went as labour requirements changed, marriages were delayed as couples waited to acquire the property necessary to support a new household, and the interests of households generally took precedence over the interests of the individuals in them. High death rates also shaped the lives of children and adults—in dramatic ways.

Tilly and Scott's detailed description of the position of women—both single and married—gives us a pretty clear picture of one side of the division of labour based on gender in these peasant and artisan households. Because women did essential work, Tilly and Scott suggest (as some other historians have argued) that there was a "rough equality" between husbands and wives. In contrast, other historians point to the gross inequality in the legal status of married women and men, including the legal approval of husbands' use of corporal punishment against "disobedient" wives, and cultural definitions of husbands as household authorities. They argue that gender relations were patriarchal—that is, that men with property exerted authority and control over all the members of their households.

The Family Economy in Pre-industrial England and France

Louise A. Tilly and Joan W. Scott

Economy and Demography

In the cities and the countryside of eighteenth-century England and France economic life was organized on a small scale. The visual image one gets from reports of the period is of small farms dotting the countryside and of small shops lining the crowded narrow streets of cities. . . . The centre of life for rural people, whatever the size of their holding, was a farm. The centre of the farm was the household in which they lived and around which work was organized.

For those engaged in rural and urban manufacturing the household was both a shop and a home. . . . In the craft shop and on the land most productive activity was based in a household, and those labouring often included family members. This form of organization is often referred to as the household or domestic mode of production. It had important consequences for family organization. The labour needs of the household defined the work roles of men, women, and children. Their work, in turn, fed the family. The interdependence of work and residence, of household labour needs, subsistence requirements, and family relationships constituted the "**family economy.**"

The specific form of the family economy differed for craftsmen and peasants. And in the city and the country there were important differences between the prosperous and the poor, between those families with property and those who were propertyless. Nonetheless, in all cases production and family life were inseparably intertwined. And the household was the centre around which resources, labour, and consumption were balanced.

Rural Economies

Most people lived in rural areas and worked in agriculture during the eighteenth century. Estimates based on scattered local studies show that in 1750 agriculture employed about 65 per cent of all English people and about 75 per cent of the French population (Cipolla 1976: 74). The forms of agricultural organization differed in France and England.

In France, the most typical rural household in the eighteenth century was the peasant household. In the course of the century the pressures of increased population and of high rents and taxes drove many families off the land or left them severely impoverished. . . . Some families barely subsisted on their land, others not only produced for themselves but marketed a crop of grapes, grains, olives, and the like. Some families manufactured cloth or clothing to supplement their earnings. Others hired themselves out as part-time labourers as well as tilled their own soil. Whatever the expedients they adopted to make ends meet, these rural people remained peasants, and the family's life ultimately was organized around the property, no matter how small the holding (Baehrel 1961; Goubert 1965b: 148; Hufton 1974; 1975).

The composition of the peasant household could vary considerably over the years. At any time those living and working together constituted a "family" whether or not they were related by blood. "The peasant concept of the family includes a number of people constantly eating at one table or having eaten from one pot . . . peasants in France included in the concept of the family the groups of persons locked up for the night behind one lock" (Thorner, Kerblay, and Smith 1966; Flandrin 1976: 103).

Although the terms *family* and *household* were often used interchangeably, and although servants took their meals with family members, the number of non-kin in the household of a propertied peasant depended on the composition of his own family. The propertied peasant had to balance labour and consumption. His resource—land—was fixed. The amount of work to be done and thus the number of labourers needed changed in the course of the family's life cycle. A young couple could adequately provide for its own needs, with the assistance perhaps of some day labourers at planting and harvest times. As children were born, they also had to be fed, and the availability of the mother to work away from the hearth decreased. The consumption needs of the family exceeded its labour power, and so at this point outside labour was recruited. Young men and women were added to the household as servants. They usually worked in exchange for room and board, rarely for cash wages. They were available for work because their own families either could not support them or did not need their labour. (One study suggested that 30 per cent of all rural workers in England at the end of the seventeenth century were servants, and that 60 per cent of all those 15 to 24 years old in rural England were servants.) As the peasant's own children grew up, the need for outside help diminished. When several children lived in the household, there might be more labour available than the size of the landholding warranted. At this point, farmers might rent or buy additional land. More typically, in the land-poor regions of western Europe, children would leave home to seek employment. They usually worked in other households as servants (Macfarlane 1970: 209; Berkner 1972; Kussmaul-Cooper 1975b).

In England some people still supported themselves on small farms during the eighteenth century, but they were a decreasing group. The growth of agricultural capitalism, particularly in the form of sheep-herding to produce wool for sale, led to the **enclosure** of large areas of land and the gradual, and violently resisted, dispossession of small farmers. Despite their protests and resistance, English farmers lost the struggle to retain their land and their right to farm it (see Thompson 1975 and Hay et al. 1975 for details). By 1750 land ownership was concentrated "in the hands of a limited class of very large landlords, at the expense both of the lesser gentry and the peasants . . ." (Hobsbawm 1968: 15). . . .

The dispossessed became agricultural labourers working for wages on the large farms, or they turned to **cottage industry**. Those involved in cottage industry worked at home on account for a merchant entrepreneur. In England the typical form of cottage or domestic industry was wool and, later, cotton weaving. In both England and France, merchants brought raw materials to rural cottages and then picked up the woven cloth which they had finished in towns or large villages. By having cloth woven in the countryside, the merchants managed to escape the control of the guilds, organizations of urban craftsmen, which closely supervised production in the cities. Although cottage weavers, like agricultural labourers, worked for wages, they worked in their own households, controlling the pace and organization of production. The family was the unit of production and of consumption, the household was the locus of work and residence. The family economy thus existed in the cottages of domestic weavers (and hosiers and nail or chain-metal workers) as it did in the households of propertied peasants.

Agricultural labourers, on the other hand, left home to earn wages elsewhere. "Thus an amazing number of people have been reduced from a comfortable state of partial independence to the precarious condition of hireling" (Davies 1965: 41). Family members often worked together. And the aim of everyone's work was to secure enough to support the family, both by bringing home some cash and by labouring in exchange for food. Among these families, family membership meant shared consumption, but not shared production. In this case the family economy became a "family wage economy." The unit's need for wages, rather than for labourers, defined the work of family members.

Work in Urban Society

Cities in both England and France had similar economic and occupational structures in the early modern period. They were essentially centres of consumer production and of commerce. The dominant form of activity differed from city to city. Yet city life differed markedly from life in the country. Gathered within city walls was a diverse population linked by an exchange of goods, services, and cash.

The varieties of urban life can be illustrated by examining several cities. For the early modern period, we will describe York, England, and Amiens, France. Both these cities were typically "pre-industrial" in economy and social structure. York was a Cathedral town, engaged in commerce, while the principal business of Amiens was small-scale, largely artisanal textile manufacture. . . .

The specific jobs available to men and women differed according to the economic structure of each city. In York most manufacture involved luxury products: bell casting, glass painting, and pewter and clock making

were among those listed. . . . Although the fortunes of the city (once the "second capital" of English society) seemed to be declining by the end of the eighteenth century, it remained a centre of handicrafts and trade. . . .

In the provincial capital of Amiens most people were engaged in the woollen trades. Various tax lists enable us to determine the occupations of others in the city, although these lists give out a partial description, since only the wealthier people in the city were taxed. Most artisans and shopkeepers on the lists were in textiles, food, and the building trades. A list from 1722 indicates a number of servants, too (Deyon 1967: 546).

Despite differences in specific trades in each city, the forms of organization were similar. Economic units were small, often overlapping with households. The scale of production was also small, for the quality and quantity of activity in commerce and manufacture were controlled by guild or other forms of regulation and by the availability of only limited amounts of capital. Life was more specialized in urban than in rural society. Food and clothing production, for example, was carried on in separate settings from the households of most urban residents. Rather than make most of what it needed, the urban family bought what it needed in the market or in shops. Shoemakers, for example, made shoes for sale, but they purchased their other clothing and food. Because of this division of labour, urban families were involved in many more consumer activities than their rural counterparts, and cash was regularly used as a means of exchange.

Manufacture and trade, however, were geared primarily to the demand of the local population. Hence the production of food and clothing and the construction of housing were the largest urban manufacturing sectors. Together they employed, according to one estimate, from 55 to 65 per cent of a city's working population (Cipolla 1976: 75).

In Amiens, as in York, guilds regulated the training and activities of skilled craftsmen. The number of workers in a trade was limited and, except in a few cases such as millinery and shawl making, the masters and **apprentices** were male. Craftsmen often worked at home or in small shops assisted by family members, apprentices and **journeymen**, and servants. Indeed, the dynamic of the self-employed artisan's household was much like that of the peasant's, for labour supply and consumption needs had to be balanced. An artisan had to produce and sell enough goods so that he could feed his family. Competition from others in the trade was controlled by guilds, which limited the numbers of those who became masters. Yet labour demands were variable within a trade; some work was seasonal, there were periods of great activity, other periods of slump. An artisan's family members often served as extra hands, as unpaid assistants in time of high demand. In addition, if family members alone could not furnish the necessary labour, an artisan hired assistants, who lived in the household as long as their labour was needed. On the other hand, if he could not use the labour of his family members at his trade, a craftsman often sent them off to find work elsewhere. His children joined another household as apprentices or domestic servants.

Although craftsmen produced most goods in workshops in their homes and used their families as labour units, the economy of the city provided many opportunities for work away from home. Men and women earned wages as servants or as street merchants, or as assistants to artisans or construction workers. The wage workers included journeymen who had no chance to advance to mastership, masters who had lost their small capital in bad times and now worked for others, daughters and sons of craftsmen whose shops could not absorb their labour, migrants to the city, unskilled workers, and widows with no capital but with a family to support.

Servants formed a substantial portion of urban populations in the seventeenth and eighteenth centuries. Their precise numbers are often difficult to determine since they were not always listed separately in tax and demographic records. Nonetheless, from those records which clearly identified servants, it has been estimated that perhaps 16 per cent of those between the ages of 15 and 65 in European cities in this period were servants. Hufton suggests that in eighteenth-century French cities, servants could represent as much as 13 per cent of the working population. In Aix in 1695, some 27 per cent of the working population were servants. The term *servant* designated a broad category of employment (Hufton 1974: 4). Any household dependant, whether performing domestic or manufacturing tasks, was a servant. There were servants in the households of the rich and in the households of craftsmen and petty artisans. They were young men or women who joined a family economy as an additional member. Indeed the language used to describe servants denoted their dependent and age status. "Servant" was synonymous with "lad" or "maid"—a young, unmarried, and therefore dependent person.

Wage labourers, on the other hand, lived in households of their own, bound together, like the families of agricultural labourers, by the need to earn money which would pay for their subsistence. Their presence in cities is attested to by the rolls of charitable organizations, which gave them bread when they could not earn enough, and by the complaints of guilds against their activity. Petty artisans, unskilled and casual labourers, carters, and street hawkers were commonly listed. In Paris in 1767, when an Order-in-Council enjoined the registration of non-guild members selling food, clothing, or lodging to the public, the list included "retailers and repairers of old clothes and hats, of rags and of old ironware, buckles and hardware . . . sellers of medicines for eyes, corns, and assorted afflictions. . . ." In the families of wage labourers, all members old enough to seek employment did so.

The work of each person brought little remuneration; the combined earnings of family members were often barely enough for the support of the group. In these families, individuals sold their labour power in order to support the family unit; they were "in fact if not in principle . . . proletarian[s]" (Landes 1969: 44). Theirs was a "family wage economy."

Production and Consumption

In both England and France, in city and country, people worked in small settings, which often overlapped with households. Productivity was low, the differentiation of tasks was limited. And many workers were needed. The demand for labour extended to women as well as men, to everyone but the youngest children and the infirm. Jobs were differentiated by age and by sex, as well as by training and skill. But among the popular classes, some kind of work was expected of all able-bodied family members.

The work of individuals was defined by their family positions. An observer of twentieth-century French peasants described their household economy in terms which also portray peasant and artisan families in the seventeenth and eighteenth centuries: "The family and the enterprise coincide: the head of the family is at the same time the head of the enterprise. Indeed, he is the one because he is the other . . . he lives his professional and his family life as an indivisible entity. The members of his family are also his fellow workers" (Mendras 1970: 76). But whether or not they actually worked together, family members worked in the economic interest of the family. In peasant and artisan households, and in proletarian families, the household allocated the labour of family members. In all cases, decisions were made in the interest of the group, not the individual. This is reflected in wills and marriage contracts which spelled out the obligation of siblings or elderly parents who were housed and fed on the family property, now owned by the oldest son. They must work "to the best of their ability" for "the prosperity of the family" and "for the interest of the designated heir" (Bernard 1975: 30). Among property-owning families the land or the shop defined the tasks of family members and whether or not their labour was needed. People who controlled their means of production adjusted household composition to production needs. For the propertyless, the need for wages—the subsistence of the family itself—sent men, women, and children out to work. These people adjusted household composition to consumption needs. The bonds holding the proletarian family together, bonds of expediency and necessity, were often less permanent than the property interest (or the inheritable skill) which united peasants and craftsmen. The composition of propertied and propertyless households also differed. Nevertheless, the line between the propertied and the propertyless was blurred on the question of commitment to work in the family interest.

One of the goals of work was to provide for the needs of family members. Both property-owning and proletarian households were consumption units, though all rural households were far more self-sufficient than urban households. Rural families usually produced their own food, clothing, and tools, while urban families bought them at the market. These differences affect the work roles of family members. Women in urban families, for example, spent more time marketing and less time in home manufacture. And there were fewer domestic chores for children to assist with in the city. In the urban family, work was oriented more to the production of specific goods for sale, or it involved the sale of one's labour. For the peasant family, there were a multiplicity of tasks involved in working the land and running the household. The manner of satisfying consumption needs thus varied and so affected the kinds of work family members did.

When the number of household members exceeded the resources available to feed them, and when those resources could not be obtained, the family often adjusted its size. Non-kin left to work elsewhere when children were old enough to work. Then children migrated. Inheritance systems led non-heirs to move away in search of jobs, limited positions as artisans forced children out of the family craft shop, while the need for wages led the children of the propertyless many miles from home. People migrated from farm to farm, farm to village, village to town, and country to city in this period. Although much migration was local and rural in this period, some migrants moved to cities, and most of these tended to be young and single when they migrated. . . . Village compatriots tended to live near one another. Young men and boys often migrated to be apprenticed to a craftsman who himself came from their village. Young women and girls followed their brothers to Amiens and became domestic servants (Deyon 1967: 7–10).

Migration increased in times of economic crisis, when food was scarce and when, even with everyone working, families could not feed all their members. The precariousness of life in rural and urban areas in the seventeenth and eighteenth centuries has been documented dramatically in studies such as those by Pierre Goubert and Olwen Hufton. These studies have shown that large numbers of ordinary people barely survived on the fruits of their labour. At the end of a lifetime of work, an artisan or peasant might have nothing more than a few tools or the small piece of land with which he began. Simply feeding one's family in these circumstances was a constant preoccupation. An increase in the price of bread, the basic staple in the diet of the popular classes, could easily make a family's earnings inadequate for its survival. . . .

Even if the price of bread remained stable, other factors might unbalance a family's budget. Agricultural or trade depressions could severely strain a family's resources. At these times there were bread riots as people collectively sought food for their families. If matters did not improve, individual families might send children off to seek their fortunes away from home, as servants, apprentices, or vagrants. Sometimes the father of the family left home in search of work. He thereby relieved the household of the need to feed him, since he could contribute nothing to its support. He also left the family to an uncertain, but probably poverty-stricken, future.

If the adult members of the family could continue working, then young children were sent away to restore the balance between consumption and work. When families were desperate, parents might expose or abandon a last-born child. Older children, still too young to work productively, were sent off also, to whatever their fate might hold. Fictional characters such as Hansel and Gretel and Hop-O'-My-Thumb, children deliberately lost by parents who could not feed them, had real counterparts. Deyon's study of seventeenth-century Amiens indicates that during food shortages in 1693–4 and 1709–10 the number of abandoned children rose. These were not only infants but children as old as seven (Deyon 1967: 357). Another recent study of the records of charity in eighteenth-century Aix-en-Provence reveals that children were regularly enrolled at an orphanage because their families could not feed them. Only a third of these were actually orphans. Once a child entered the orphanage, he or she was likely to be joined by a sibling. In other cases, a child would return home and be replaced in the orphanage by a sibling. Families used the orphanage as a temporary measure, enrolling a child and then withdrawing him or her as economic circumstances allowed. Hence one girl entered the Aix orphanage in 1746, "rejoined her family briefly in 1747, then returned . . . later left again, and . . . re-entered . . . in 1755" (Fairchilds 1976: 10).

The location and organization of work differed among the households of rural and urban people and among the propertied and the propertyless. So did the levels of consumption vary and the manners of satisfying family needs. Yet in all cases the family was both a labour unit and a consumption unit, adjusting its size and assigning work to its members to meet its needs in both spheres.

Demography: Marriage

The demographic patterns of early modern England and France reflected the need to balance people and resources. Death frequently influenced these patterns. Perhaps the most sensitive indicator of the relationship between resources and population was the age at which couples married. The precise age at marriage varied from city to country and from region to region depending on inheritance laws and on specific conditions. Yet among the popular classes the crucial differences were between the propertied and the propertyless.

Marriage was, among other things, an economic arrangement, the establishment of a family economy. It required that couples have some means of supporting themselves and, eventually, their children. For peasant children this meant the availability of land; for artisans, the mastery of a skill and the acquisition of tools and perhaps a workshop. Wives must have a **dowry** or a means of contributing to the household. Among families with property these resources most often were passed on from generation to generation.

In England, inheritance by the oldest son prevailed. In France this custom of **primogeniture** was not universal. In some areas of France, particularly in the west, an heir and his wife lived with his parents, in a **stem family** arrangement. In northern France, on the other hand, a young man had to postpone marriage until a house was vacant. This meant until the death of one or both parents. Land was passed to one child—usually, though not necessarily, the oldest son. He paid his siblings a cash settlement which represented their share of the family land. A brother could use his money to buy some land of his own or to set himself up in a trade. A sister used her money as a dowry. Often the heir had to mortgage the property to pay off his sisters and brothers. Sometimes, too, the money was not available. Then the heir's siblings might remain on the family farm as unmarried labourers in their brother's household, working in exchange for room and board. "A peasant reckons this way; my farm can feed no more than one, at most two, sons; the others may have to remain unmarried or seek their fortune elsewhere" (Braun 1966: 46; see also Flandrin 1976: 180–1).

Among artisans, trade regulations prevented early marriage. Apprentices and journeymen were not allowed to marry until they had completed their training. In some cases, the duration of apprenticeship was as much a function of the artisans' desire to control workers' access to their trade as it was of the difficulty of the skills taught. Apprentices' and journeymen's associations reinforced the control by expelling from their ranks anyone who married. A young man was ready to marry only when he had an established niche in the system of production.

The need for a dowry meant that young women, too, often had to wait for the death of their parents to receive a settlement. In the weaving centre of Manchester, for example, in the period 1654–7, more than half of the girls marrying for the first time had recently lost their fathers. Other girls, those who worked to accumulate savings for a dowry, had to spend many years gathering a small sum (Armengaud 1975: 145).

The result of these requirements was a relatively late age at marriage in both England and France; women were generally 24 or 25 years old, men 27. The late age at marriage of women meant that couples had fewer children than they would have had if the woman had been 19 or 20 at marriage. If she married at 25, the woman was actively engaged in childbearing for only a portion of her fertile years. (There was little sexual intercourse outside of marriage, and very low rates of illegitimacy. During the eighteenth century in France, the illegitimacy rate increased from 1.2 to 2.7 per cent of all births.) Thus relatively late marriage functioned as a kind of birth control, in the sense that it limited the size of the completed family (Goubert 1965a; Henry 1965).

Among the propertyless, there were no resources to inherit. When a young man and woman were able to earn wages, they could marry. Not only must an individual be able to work, however, but work which paid wages must be available. (Servants, for example, could not marry since a requirement of their jobs was that they live in the household they served, that they remain unmarried, and that they receive much of their payment in room and board, not cash.) One study has shown that in Shepshed, England, during the seventeenth century, the coming of domestic industry provided jobs and cash wages and led to a lowered age of marriage (Levine 1976; see also Braun 1966). In other areas, the growth of commercial agriculture, and the consequent demand for agricultural labourers, may have had the same effect.

Among the poorest, marriage sometimes did not take place at all. The absence of property and the lack of any expectation that it would be acquired, made legalization of sexual relationships unnecessary. From the seventeenth century comes this comment on the urban poor: "They almost never know the sanctity of marriage and live together in shameful fashion" (Fairchilds 1976: 33). These people, however, were exceptions. In general, those without property did marry. They married younger than their peasant and artisan counterparts and, as a result, their wives bore more children over the course of the marriage. But most expected to be able to live on the fruits of their labour. A couple marrying in Amiens in 1780 acknowledged their poverty, but wrote a contract anyway, agreeing that if they did manage to make some money, the future bride would have "by preciput 150 livres of the estate and the survivor would have the bed and bedclothes, . . . his or her clothes, arms, rings, and jewels" (Deyon 1967: 254).

Some people never married, of course. In general, permanent celibacy was more common in cities than in the country. There were examples of unmarried brothers or sisters remaining sometimes on farms with a married sibling. More commonly, however, these individuals migrated to a city in search of work. The occupational structure of particular cities often determined the marital fate of many of its migrants. In Lyons, for example, the women who came to work in the silk industry greatly outnumbered the men. As a result, during the eighteenth century, some 40 per cent of adult women were still single at age 50 in that city. (In towns where men outnumbered women, more women were married.) In Amiens, with its mixed occupational structure, 20 per cent of the women over 40 in one wealthy parish were single at death. The rate was 13 per cent in two poorer parishes. Domestic servants in the wealthy parish account for the difference.

Birth and Fertility

Once a couple married, at whatever age, they began to have children. About half of all first babies were born less than a year after their parents' marriage. Studies of French villages indicated that subsequent children were then born about 25 to 30 months apart. This interval was apparently the result of two factors, postpartum abstinence from intercourse, and nursing, which postpones the onset of ovulation. Among working-class families in cities, birth intervals were shorter because mothers sent their children to **wet nurses** rather than nursing them themselves and because infant mortality was high. In both cases, women became fertile sooner than they would have if they had nursed an infant. In Amiens, for example, in a parish of small shopkeepers, artisans, and workers, children were born about two years apart. In Lyons, where work in the silk industry demanded a great deal

of a mother's time and where children were regularly sent to wet nurses, birth intervals were even shorter: births occurred there at the rate of one per year (Wrigley 1969: 124; Armengaud 1975: 52; Flandrin 1976: 197).

There is some evidence to indicate that couples sometimes practised deliberate birth control. One study, of the English village of Colyton in Devon in the seventeenth century, seems to show that couples were deliberately limiting the size of their families. Its author, E.A. Wrigley, suggests that a longer than usual interval between the next-to-last and the last birth is an indicator of attempted fertility control. This first attempt of couples to avoid conception failed, of course, but the longer birth interval is evidence of their effort. Such control as there was was probably achieved by means of *coitus interruptus*, or withdrawal, the most widely known and widely practised technique (Wrigley 1966: 123). Most other studies, however, using the same kinds of data and the same method of family reconstitution, do not point to deliberate family limitation before the late eighteenth century. Yet complete families were not large: four or five children at most, more often only two or three who lived to adulthood. Why?

First, standards of nutrition and health were very low. Analyses of the diet of the popular classes in this period show consistent evidence of malnutrition, a factor which inhibited conception and which promoted miscarriage. Poor nutrition of a mother increased the likelihood that her infant would be stillborn or weak. And it affected the supply of milk she had to nurse it. In addition, poor nutrition made many women infertile before 40 or 45— the usual age of menopause (Meuvret 1965; Le Roy Ladurie 1969).

Second, mortality rates were very high. If infants did not die at birth because of unsanitary or crude childbirth procedures, they died within the first year of life. Young children, too, died in large numbers. Finally, many marriages were shortened by the death of one of the spouses. Childbirth resulted in a high incidence of maternal death. In one fishing village in France, one-third of all marriages were broken by death within 15 years. Men's opportunities for remarriage were usually greater than those of women. As a result, women did not engage in intercourse during all of their fertile years and hence did not bear children. Given the odds that death would strike a young child or a spouse, there was little need to employ birth control (Armengaud 1975: 53). Death was the natural regulator of family size in early modern England and France.

Death and Mortality

Premature death was a frequent experience of family life in this period. Death rates nearly matched birth rates, producing a very slow growth of population. The crude birth rate was about 35 per thousand; the death rate 30 per thousand. Moreover, until around 1730, there were years with dramatically high death rates, reaching 150, 300, and even 500 per thousand in some localities. These deaths were the result of widespread crop failures and consequent starvation, or of epidemics of diseases like the plague. The last plague epidemic struck in southern France in 1720–2 (Cipolla 1964: 77; Clarkson 1971: 28–9), but new diseases caused killing epidemics well into the twentieth century. Demographers usually place the end of extreme and widespread mortality due to disease and starvation in the early eighteenth century.

Yet even in relatively stable times, death rates were very high by modern standards—a rate of 30 per thousand is more than triple the present-day rate in western Europe. Studies of French villages show that about one-quarter of all infants born alive died during their first year of life, another quarter died before they reached the age of 20. Urban death rates were even higher. In Amiens, for example, during the seventeenth century, 60 to 70 per cent of all burials were of persons under 25. Although rates varied from parish to parish and among villages, the overall situation was similar in England and France. Goubert aptly summarized the mortality experience of pre-industrial families: "It took two births to produce one adult" (Goubert 1965a: 468).

The life expectancy at birth for people in this period was 30 years. Of course, that figure included infant and child mortality. If a person lived to age 25, the likelihood was much greater than at birth that she or he would live to 50 or 60. Yet, although systematic evidence is hard to accumulate, it is clear that adult mortality was also quite high. The figures on orphans and widows are revealing in this connection. Laslett's analysis of the English village of Clayworth found that during the period 1676–88, "32 per cent of all resident children [under 14] had lost one or both of their parents." A study of all children in households in 19 English communities from 1599 to 1811 indicates that some 20 per cent were orphans. For France, Jean Fourastié has drawn a hypothetical portrait of family life for a man at the end of the seventeenth century. In that situation marriage would be broken by the death of a spouse after an average of 20 years. The average age of a child orphaned in this way would be 14 years (Fourastié 1959: 427; Laslett 1974; Armengaud 1975: 74–7).

Many children were left orphans when their mothers died in childbirth. Ignorance of the need for sanitary conditions, the crude attempts of midwives to force a baby from the womb, and the general poor health of pregnant women made for high rates of maternal mortality. Age-specific mortality tables drawn for small seventeenth- and eighteenth-century villages show women dying in larger numbers than men between ages 24 and 40—the child-bearing years.

The death of a parent left not only orphans but widows or widowers. The existence of these people is attested to by notices of second marriage, particularly of men, and by charity rolls and tax lists, on which widows' names predominated. Fourastié's calculations show that of 1,000 men married at age 27 and surviving to age 50, nearly half would have lost their wives. Many of these men would have remarried and would have also lost a second wife. (The calculations for women would be similar except that fewer widows remarried.) Overall, in eighteenth-century France "at least 30 per cent of all marriages were second weddings for one of the partners." Most parishes had many widows in them. In Châteaudun, at least half of the seamstresses and spinners listed on tax rolls in 1696 were widows. In eighteenth-century Bayeux, over 46 per cent of all textile workers in the linen and woollen trades were widows (Fourastié 1959: 425; see also Couturier 1969: 64; Lebrun 1971: 190; Hufton 1974: 116; Baulant 1976: 105). The poor widow, struggling to support her children, was a familiar figure in the towns and villages of the period.

Early modern populations could do little medically to control mortality. Nutrition was poor, little was known about hygiene, and medical science had not developed. In 1778, a French demographer noted that "it is still a problem whether medicine kills or saves more men" (Armengaud 1975: 70; see also Dupaquier 1976). The result was that every person who survived to adulthood experienced the loss of close relatives: a father, mother, sisters, and brothers. Few children knew their grandparents, few grandparents lived to see the birth of a first grandchild. Orphanhood, widowhood, and the loss of children were common experiences. In calculations about family size, about fertility and household labour supply, the expectation of death played an important part.

These, then, were the economic and demographic characteristics of England and France during the seventeenth and eighteenth centuries. Agriculture was more important than manufacturing, and most people lived in rural areas. In France, small-scale property holding and artisanal manufacture were typical. In England, by 1750, there had been consolidation of agricultural holdings and a consequent increase in the size of farms, on the one hand, and in the proportion of people without property, on the other hand. Work in both countries was relatively undifferentiated and productivity was low. On the demographic side, fertility and mortality were both high, so population growth was very slow. A relatively high age of marriage and a degree of non-marriage served to reduce fertility. From the perspective of the household, most aspects of life were affected by the need to maintain scarce resources and consumers in a delicate balance. Family life and economic organization were inseparably entwined. Premature death was a familiar experience in each household. Within this context were shaped the position and activities of women.

Single Women in the Family Economy

Most single women belonged to households, either as daughters or servants. Most were young, but whatever their age, single women were regarded as dependants of the household in which they lived and worked. Under the domestic mode of production most work was organized around a household, the basic unit of which was a married couple. Girls either worked at home or for another family. If they were to escape this state of dependency, they had to marry, for single adult women were effectively children. The language of the day equated a girl with a maid, a maid with a servant. Age, marital status, and occupation were inseparably intertwined.

Single women were often effectively servants for their families, if not in the households of strangers. Those employed in other areas, textiles for example, usually lived with a family or with other women like themselves. Even in religious orders, single women joined a family of celibate sisters. Prostitutes usually lived in groups. Economically it was extremely difficult to be single and independent. In the best of jobs female wages were low, one-third to one-half of what men's were (Hauser 1927; Hufton 1975). The only way for a woman to achieve a measure of economic security, as well as adult status, was to marry. If she did not marry, her position was anomalous. If she became a nun, of course, she gained protection and recognition, although her role and autonomy were limited. An unmarried woman outside a convent was vulnerable to material hardship and sexual exploitation.

Although aggregate figures are not available for this period, local studies indicate that in rural areas marriage took place at a relatively late age and nearly all women did marry. In urban areas, rates of celibacy among women could be higher because of differences in sex ratios and as a result of the concentration of specialized occupations for single women (Hollingsworth 1969: 160–8). Most of these occupations, like domestic service or religious orders, involved a family-like dependency.

Single Women's Work

All women began their working lives as daughters, serving the family economy of which they were a part. The specific jobs they did were a consequence of their family's place in the productive process, of the nature of the enterprise in which it was engaged.

A daughter began assisting at home as soon as she was able to work. Indeed, at an early age, her role was no different from that of male children, and many accounts make no distinction when describing children's work. Girls and boys were given small tasks to do as early as four or five years of age. In rural areas they cared for farm animals and helped at harvesting and gleaning. In cottages where families engaged in rural industry, young children washed and sorted wool or learned to spin. . . . As they grew older, girls usually assisted their mothers, boys their fathers. In agricultural areas, daughters helped with dairying, cared for poultry, prepared food, and made cloth and clothing. During planting and harvesting they joined family members and hired hands in the fields. . . .

In cities also, daughters worked for their families. The craftsman's household was also his workshop and his family members were among his assistants, whether he wove silk or wool, sewed shoes or coats, made knives, or baked bread. . . . If the father worked elsewhere, daughters assisted their mothers as market women, laundresses, or seamstresses. . . . When she worked at home a daughter served a kind of apprenticeship to her mother, learning the domestic, agricultural, or technical skills she would need as an adult.

Not all girls remained working at home until marriage, however. The labour needs of her family defined the type of work a daughter might do at home, but also whether or not she would remain there. Family labour was differentiated by age and sex. So, if a family had no need for a daughter's labour, she would be sent to a job somewhere else. Peasants with two or three working children and more than one daughter would send younger daughters away to earn their keep. Weavers, who needed several spinners to supply thread for their looms, jealously guarded their daughters at home, while bakers or shoemakers whose sons, male apprentices, and wives were an ample labour force, regularly sent their daughters away. Families thus adjusted their labour supply by sending off daughters not suited for certain work and taking on male apprentices in their stead.

The ability of a family to feed its children was another influence on where a daughter worked. For subsistence farmers with small holdings, the cost of maintaining a daughter might be greater than the value of her labour. It would be cheaper to hire and feed a few local labourers during the harvest season than to provide for one's own child all year long. Moreover, in time of economic crises, the numbers of "surplus children," those who could not be supported, would grow, and daughters and sons would be sent off to seek jobs as servants or apprentices.

Death was yet another factor which sent daughters to work away from home. The death of a parent often left the widow or widower less means to support the children. In the French town of Châteaudun during the sixteenth to eighteenth centuries, for example, daughters of wine growers remained at home until marriage. They participated in all aspects of domestic and household work and were given ample dowries when they married. The death of a father, however, immediately changed the pattern. At that point, the mother took up a trade and sold the family holding or passed it to one of her sons. Daughters who were

too young to marry or "who could not marry immediately became chambermaids in town or farm servants in the country." The luckiest of these found places at the homes of other wine growers (Couturier 1969: 181).

The remarriage of a widowed parent could also result in the dislocation of the children of the first marriage, either because the stepparent resented feeding and caring for children who were not his or her own or because conflicts and jealousies became unbearable. Folk tales such as Cinderella and Snow White capture an aspect of these relationships. . . .

Even if both parents were alive, however, the economic resources of the family might be insufficient for the establishment of more than one child with the means to live independently as a married adult. Daughters needed a dowry, and families customarily provided them with it. In rural areas, depending on laws of inheritance, a girl was given either a sum of money or movable property, usually household and farm furnishings. Again depending on local practices, she might receive a full settlement at her marriage or be promised a payment after the death of her parents. In cities, craftsmen gave their daughters household furnishings, cash, skills, or tools. In country and city, the size of the family contribution to a dowry or settlement was very small among the lower classes. Often, the family's contribution had to be supplemented. An artisan's daughter had an advantage over her rural counterpart in this situation, for the skills she had were highly valued. Unlike the heavy manual labour of a farm, trade skills guaranteed a lifetime of relatively high wage-earning possibilities or of assistance to one's husband at his trade. These were acceptable as substitutes for the dowry required of rural girls. But, in either case, if a dowry was needed for a woman's contribution to a marriage and the family (or some other source) could not provide it, a girl had to earn it herself (Clark [1919] 1968: 194; Hufton 1975: 9).

When for one or a combination of reasons daughters left home to work, they usually entered another household. In the country, domestic service was the typical occupation of a young girl. Of course, in areas of rural textile manufacture, particularly in England, in the early eighteenth century, spinners were in great demand. It took the work of four spinners to supply thread enough for one weaver. . . . Spinsters lived either at home or in the weaver's household. But even in areas where spinning and lacemaking jobs were available, girls sometimes went into service at age 12 or 13, after having done textile work as a child. Cities offered other opportunities and urban-born girls took advantage of them. Such girls might be apprenticed to a crafts or tradeswoman. Others might work for wages in a local enterprise, usually related to textile or garment manufacture. . . . But in cities, as in the country, the main occupation for young girls was domestic service. In Ealing in 1599, for example, almost "three-quarters of the female children [between ages fifteen and nineteen] seem to have been living away from their parents," most often as servants (Macfarlane 1970: 209; Perrot 1975: 425).

In a period when most productive activity was organized within or around a household, service was the major occupation for young, single women. Service involved a variety of chores, not only the ones the twentieth century associates with domestic work. A servant was a household dependant who worked in return for board and wages. The low cost of her labour, the availability of young, single women to work, the need in producing households for an extra hand, made the employment of a servant a fairly common practice. Service was the customary means by which households

exchanged labour supply and balanced their own labour and consumption needs.

In upper-class families a girl "in service" was a maid of one kind or another, a laundress, charwoman, serving maid, or nursemaid. In household productive units she was an extra hand, available to do whatever work was required. She might be a dairymaid or harvester on a farm; in textile towns she was "a resident industrial employee." In Lyons, for example, a *servante* did domestic chores and helped prepare the silk to be woven. As with a daughter, the nature of the family enterprise defined her work, except that a servant girl usually did the dirtiest and most onerous of the chores that needed to be done (Le Roy Ladurie 1969: 477; Hufton 1975: 3). In return for her work she was fed, housed, and clothed and paid a wage at the end of her term, which usually lasted a year. This meant that a servant had little or no money to spend on herself during the year and was entirely dependent on her employers. . . .

When daughters left home to work they did not always sever family ties. Their parents often helped them find jobs, and provided homes for them between terms of service. One study suggests that female farm servants in England returned to their families far more frequently than did males (Kussmaul-Cooper 1975a: 6). Moreover, kin networks were a common means used by those seeking jobs. In the country, peasants and agricultural labourers sought work for their daughters at neighbouring farms or in a nearby village or large town. . . .

A girl's ability to maintain contact with [her] family depended on how far she had journeyed from home. . . . In general, . . . the continuing demand for cheap female labour in towns and on farms made it possible for most girls to remain within a short distance of home, sustained by occasional visits, by parcels of food, and by the expectation of returning there to marry.

The death of a girl's parents, of course, modified this pattern. Orphans were on their own, lacking family connections to help them find work or to sponsor their migrations. Without resources, with no one to turn to for help, orphans had to settle for whatever work they could find, throwing themselves on the mercy of an employer, a charitable organization, or the state. They were more vulnerable, more open to exploitation, more likely to end up in trouble as criminals, prostitutes, and mothers of illegitimate children. . . .

The work of a young single woman was circumscribed by a limited range of occupational opportunities. The type and location of her work was defined by her family's needs. A daughter worked, as everyone did in lower-class families in this period, to help support the unit of which she was a part. In addition, her work prepared her for marriage, by giving her training and skills and sometimes also by enabling her to accumulate the capital she needed for a dowry.

Courtship and Marriage

A girl was ready for marriage when she had accumulated some capital or received it from her family, when she was ready to help establish a productive unit, a household. The amount was not necessarily very large. In France, some cash, a bed, sheets, and some pots were frequently all a girl brought to her new household. . . . Often a girl's small earnings supplemented the family contribution.

Unless she migrated far away, or unless she was an orphan, a girl's marriage usually involved her family in a variety of ways. First, her family's economic situation limited her choice of a husband to someone of roughly comparable means. The size of the dowry the family promised or provided was a reflection of its property holdings or trade prosperity. An artisan's craft position was itself an important consideration, for access to a tightly controlled craft might be gained for a son-in-law. Among property-owning peasants, parents often vetoed suitors whose family holdings did not measure up to their own. Marriage was a chance to extend or renew family capital. . . .

Second, the parental community of residence and work was most often the one within which a girl found a husband. In rural areas, young women met young men in the village, at local social gatherings, or in the household of an employer. In France, the veillée offered young people a means of meeting one another, under the watchful eye of parents and neighbours and in activities which were usually segregated by sex. The *veillée* was the rural custom of gathering in the largest, warmest barn on cold winter evenings. . . .

In the city, a girl might marry an apprentice or journeyman in her father's shop, or the son of another craftsman. Networks of labour and trade were important sources of marriage partners. In Amiens, such "corporative endogamy" was the rule. Young men in the same trades married one another's sisters with great frequency; apprentices married their master's daughters or widows (Deyon 1967: 340). But apprentices or journeymen might also choose a servant girl in the household. The small capital she had saved from her service brought to the couple the possibility of buying a loom and setting up a shop of their own (Hufton 1975: 7–9). Since social, occupational, and family life were so closely intertwined, one's associate at work often became a marriage partner.

Among the propertyless, of course, marriage crossed occupational lines, but geographic **endogamy** was the norm. Artisans and peasants as well as the unskilled and prop-ertyless tended to marry others from the same parish or a neighbouring one. . . .

Social and geographic endogamy had important implications for marriage and for premarital sexual behaviour. It meant that family and communal ties, as well as the rela-tionship between the two individuals, bound a couple together and governed their behaviour. In many areas, engaged couples began sleep-ing or living together before marriage. Local custom varied, of course. In areas of France and England, studies have documented the practice. In addition, the fact that rates of pre-nuptial conception tended to be higher in cities than in rural areas suggests that such cohabi-tation was more common in cities. Premarital sexual activity was tolerated because marriage was expected to and usually did take place. Hence, although some brides were pregnant at the altar, bastards were relatively few. Using marriage and birth registers from 77 parishes in rural England, from 1540 to 1835, P.E.H. Hair found that between one-third and one-sixth of all brides were pregnant at their weddings (Hair 1966; Hollingsworth 1969: 194). Indeed, pregnancy often seems to have precipitated a couple's marriage. In small vil-lage communities, or among groups of urban craftsmen, families could put a great deal of pressure on a young man who had begun to regret his choice of a mate and was hesitating about marriage. Such social pressure tended to ensure that marriage usually followed engage-ment, especially if pregnancy intervened.

The women who bore illegitimate children were often those with no ties to their families of origin. Several English studies have indi-cated that most illegitimate births came from the poorest and most vulnerable women in the community. . . .These were people whose sexual behaviour was not that different from their more prosperous counterparts. The difference was that "the relatively more secure position [of the better-off] meant that their behaviour was more certain of ultimate legitimation" (Levine and Wrightson 1980). In other words, prosperous parents were in a better position to enforce the promise of marriage which had compromised their daughters. On the other hand, girls with no parents or those who were a long distance from home were most vulner-able. Servant girls in cities were often open to exploitation by their employers or by young men they met. Indeed, rates of illegitimacy and of child abandonment were highest among domestic servants. These women could not appeal to parental, religious, or community authority to help them make a seducer keep his promise.

Young women were protected not only by their parents but by community institutions as well. In many rural areas, the rituals of court-ship and marriage involved vigilant groups of young people who regulated the morals and sexual activity of the village. Adolescent boys particularly policed the behaviour of courting couples, sometimes even influencing a man's choice of a mate. A wide discrepancy in the ages of the couple, for example, or promiscuity or adultery, could attract the ridicule of local youths. They would engage in elaborate rituals, following the couple, mocking them, singing profane songs under the woman's window. A bad-smelling bush planted before a girl's door indicated her low moral standing. A group of young men might fight or fine strangers court-ing local girls (Davis 1971; Gillis 1974: 20). Unwed mothers as well as married men who seduced single girls would be "**charivaried**" or, in England, hear the sound of "rough music" at their door. . . . In the village community these proceedings had the effect of legal sanctions. The charivari set and enforced standards of acceptable sexual conduct. Natalie Davis has pointed out that they also regulate the activities of the youths themselves, preventing too-early marriage and premarital promiscuity.

Organizations of craftsmen, too, watched over the activities of journeymen and apprentices. The rules of journeymen's organizations included the requirement that members not marry until they had completed their training and were in a position to help support a family. Guilds also had rules which prohibited young men from seducing girls and which enforced their regulations with fines and expulsion (Cadet 1870: 118, citing S. Daubie). Of course, those outside the guild structure were not subject to such rules. In general, the movement of people into, out of, and within cities made the regulation of sexual and social behaviour more difficult, especially among the unskilled. Hence rates of illegitimacy were higher in cities, and concubinage was a more common practice.

A woman's courtship and her marriage involved her family in a number of important ways. A young man usually asked a young woman's family for her hand. Then the families of the engaged couple assembled to draw up a contract which specified the economic terms of the marriage. The wedding was celebrated by family and community members. In the country, whole villages turned out to eat, drink, and dance in celebration of the consecration of a union; in cities all the craftsmen of a particular trade (many of whom were also related) attended the festivities. Among the propertyless and the unskilled the wedding might be less elaborate, but dancing was free and people could clap and sing if there was no money to hire music. These rituals and festivities marked the couple's entry into adulthood, the creation of a new family, the beginning of an independent existence. Among property holders marriage might ally two families and joint property holdings. In the lower ranks of society marriage was simply the establishment of a new family economy, the unit of reproduction and of work without which "one cannot live" (Armengaud 1975: 144; Stone 1975: 48–9).

The characteristics of marriage among the popular classes clearly were different from those in the upper classes. Among wealthy families there was strict parental control over marriage. Parents sought to preserve their status and wealth by allying their children with a limited group of similarly wealthy families. Children's marriages extended networks of power and influence. The lineage must be protected, the patrimony enlarged and transmitted from one generation to the next. In these cases property was the basis for status and political power, hence family control over children's marriages was vital for the preservation of the elite position of aristocrats or local notables. There was, for example, a close association between the transmission of wealth and political power in Vraiville, a French village studied by Martine Segalen. There all the mayors for ten generations were descendants of, or married to, one of the thirteen most eminent families (Segalen 1972: 104). The families carefully chose spouses for their children from among a very small group of large property holders.

Among the popular classes parental consent and family contracts did not mean the same thing. Within the social and economic limits already described, individual choice of a spouse was permitted. Parental consent functioned as a verification of the couple's resources. Parents wanted to be sure a child would find his or her new family situation roughly equal to that of the family or origin. Moreover, the contract involved not the acquisition of resources for the patrimony but the surrendering of resources by families to the new family. Families, rather than the individuals to be married, drew up the contracts because they were the units of social identification and of membership for all individuals. The children were leaving one family to establish another and they were transferring their resources, their means of support, from one household to another. Relatively few persons, men or women, went through an intermediate stage of independence—economic or social—as they passed from their family of origin to their family of procreation. Individuality in the modern sense was socially and legally limited.

The age of marriage was constrained by the fact that family and social resources were limited. Like their husbands, wives were expected to bring a contribution to the marriage, in the form of capital, household furnishings, or marketable skills. Marriage itself signified the beginning of a new enterprise, of an economic partnership of husband and wife. It was "the founding of a family" (Armengaud 1975: 144). And it was the emergence of this new family, the recreation of a social and economic unit, the beginning of a new enterprise that families and communities celebrated at a wedding. . . .

Married Women in the Family Economy

The married couple was the "simple community of work, the elementary unit" in the preindustrial household (Gouesse 1972: 1146–7). The contribution of each spouse was vital for the creation and survival of the family. From its outset, marriage was an economic partnership. Each partner brought to the union either material resources, or the ability to help support each other. Peasant sons brought land, craftsmen brought their tools and skill. Daughters brought a dowry and sometimes a marketable skill as well. The dowry of a peasant or artisan daughter was usually a contribution

to the establishment of the couple's household. These might include "a bit of cash, furniture, linen, tools. Sometimes a loom, one or two skeins of wool, several pounds of wool and silk, a boat, a thousand eels for a fish merchant, sometimes a house or part of a house in the city, a meadow and some plots of land in the country" (Deyon 1967: 341). . . .

Among the propertyless there was only the promise of work and wages. In Amiens in 1687, François Pariès, a mason, and Marie Hugues declared in their contract that they had no material possessions and that "they are mutually satisfied with their well-being and with one another" (Deyon 1967: 254). The point was that the wife as well as the husband made an economic contribution (or a promise of one) which helped set up the new household. In addition, however, it represented a commitment to help support the new family. The resources brought to the marriage were only a beginning. The continuing labour of each partner was required to maintain the couple and, later, its children. In the course of a lifetime, the work of husband and wife was the major source of the family's support. Families were productive and reproductive units, centres of economic activity, and creators of new life. Married women contributed to all aspects of family life and thus fulfilled several roles within their households. They engaged in production for exchange and production for household consumption, both of which contributed to the family's economic well-being. And they performed the reproductive role of bearing and raising children.

Married Women's Work

A married woman's work depended on the family's economic position, on whether it was involved in agriculture or manufacturing, whether it owned property or was property-less. But whether labour or cash were needed, married women were expected to contribute it. The fact that a woman bore children influenced the kind of work she did, but it did not confine her to a single set of tasks, nor exclude her from participation in productive activity. The organization of production in this period demanded that women be contributing members of the family economy. It also permitted women to control the time and pace of their work, and to integrate their various domestic activities.

Within the pre-industrial household, whether on the farm or in the craft shop, among property holders and wage earners, there was a division of labour by age and by sex. The levels of skill expected of children advanced with age, with young children performing the simplest and crudest chores. Certain kinds of heavy work were reserved for men, but women also did many heavy tasks which today are considered too arduous for females. Hauling and carrying were often women's tasks. Rural and urban wives sometimes had occupations of their own, or they shared their husbands' occupations performing specified tasks within the productive process. Indeed, the jobs women did reflected the fact that they performed several functions for the family. The normative family division of labour tended to give men jobs away from the household or jobs which required long and uninterrupted commitments of time or extensive travel, while women's work was performed more often at home and permitted flexible time arrangements.

Rural Women

On farms, men worked in the fields, while women ran the household, made the family's clothes, raised and cared for cows, pigs, and poultry, tended a garden, and marketed surplus milk, vegetables, chickens, and eggs.

A French peasant saying went: "No wife, no cow, hence no milk, no cheese, neither hens, nor chicks, nor eggs . . ." (Armengaud 1975: 75). The sale of these items often brought in the only cash a family received. Women's participation in local markets reflected their several family roles. They earned money as an outgrowth of activities concerned with family subsistence; and they might use the money to purchase food and supplies for their families. Their domestic and market activities overlapped, and both served important economic functions for the family. Moderately prosperous farm families owed their success to a variety of resources, not the least of which was the wife's activity. . . .

Wives of propertyless labourers also contributed to the family economy. They themselves became hired hands, "working in the fields and doing all kinds of hard jobs." Others became domestic textile workers. Still others alternated these activities. When Vauban, justifying his fiscal recommendations under Louis XIV, described the family of an agricultural labourer, he emphasized the importance of the wife's ability to earn money: "by the work of her distaff, by sewing, knitting some stockings, or by a bit of lacemaking, according to the region" (Morineau 1972: 236; see also Flandrin 1976: 113). Without this and her cultivation of a garden and some animals, "it would be difficult to subsist." Home work most commonly involved spinning or sewing. Lacemaking, straw plaiting, glove making, knitting, and needlework were the major areas of domestic manufacture. Pinchbeck estimates that lacemaking alone employed as many as 100,000 women and children in seventeenth-century England. About a million women and children worked in the clothing trades as a whole in England in that period (Pinchbeck [1930] 1969: 203; Clark [1919] 1968: 97). And in France, as rural industry took hold in some areas, the numbers of women employed in spinning rose. Women earned low wages spinning, perhaps five sous a day in Picardy at the end of the seventeenth century (Guilbert 1966: 30–1). Male weavers earned double that amount. Yet the individual wage a married woman could earn was less important than was her contribution to a joint effort. Spinning and weaving together were the complementary bases of the family economy.

When no home work was available, a wife marketed her household activities, shopping for others at the market, hawking some wares: extra pieces of linen she had woven or lengths of thread she had spun and not used. Rural women also became wet nurses, nursing and raising the children of middle-class women and of urban artisans who could afford to pay them. . . . Maurice Garden suggests that close to a third of all babies born in Lyons (some 2,000 of 5,000 to 6,000) were carted off to the countryside. Until the late eighteenth century these included the children of the upper classes as well as of artisan and shopkeeping families (Garden 1970: 324). Most often, however, the more prosperous families hired wet nurses who lived in the household. The wet nurse "business" was most developed, it appears, in large pre-industrial urban centres where married women played an active role in artisan and commercial enterprise. . . .

Married women, then, would often alternate different kinds of work, putting together a series of jobs in order to increase their earnings or to earn enough to help their families survive. Indeed the absence of employment for the wives of wage earners was often given as the reason for a family's destitution.

Although women tended to work at or near home, they did not do so exclusively. On farms, the rhythm of the seasons with their periods of intensive labour brought women into the fields to sow and harvest, as well as to glean. . . . In areas where small property holders worked as agricultural labourers or as tradesmen, women tended the family plot and men worked away from home "except for about a week in hay harvest, and for a few days at other times, when the gathering of manure or some work which the women cannot perform" required the men's assistance (Pinchbeck [1930] 1969: 20). In the vineyards of the Marne "the wife [was] really the working partner of her husband: she share[d] all of his burdens," cultivating the grapes (Flandrin 1976: 113).

On the other hand, there was household work which included the entire family. In villages in France, for example, the kneading and preparation of bread (which was baked in a communal oven) "mobilized the energies of everyone in the house every other week in the summer and once a month in winter" (Bernard 1975: 30). And the winter slaughter of a pig took all family members and sometimes some additional help. When the farm or the household needed labour, it incorporated all hands, regardless of sex, in periods of intense activity. At other times, though work roles were different, they were complementary. The family economy depended upon the labour of both husband and wife.

Urban Women

Wives of skilled craftsmen who worked at home usually assisted their husbands, sharing the same room, if not the same bench or table. The wife sometimes prepared or finished materials on which the husband worked. Thus wives spun for their weaver husbands, polished metal for cutlers, sewed buttonholes for tailors, and waxed shoes for shoemakers. Sometimes a wife's work was identical to her husband's. . . . If the wife was not her husband's constant companion at the loom, however, or if spinning was her customary job, she still must be able to take his place when he had other tasks, when he was ill, or when he died. . . . The fact that all family members worked together and benefited jointly from the enterprise meant that some jobs were learned by both sexes and could be interchangeable. It meant, too, . . . that the family's joint economic activity was the first priority for everyone.

If the products made at home were sold there, then a craftsman's wife was usually also a shopkeeper. She handled transactions, kept accounts, and helped supervise the workers in the shop. Many of these women hired servants to free them from "the routine of domestic drudgery." When work pressed, as it did in the Lyonnais silk trade (where the typical female occupation was silk spinning or assistance with weaving), mothers sent their infants off to nurses rather than break the rhythm of work in the shop (Clark [1919] 1968: 156; see also Hufton 1975: 12).

Yet, if a wife was her husband's indispensable partner in many a trade, and even if her skill equalled his, she remained his assistant while he lived. Married women were granted full membership in certain guilds only after their husbands had died and then so long as they did not remarry. Occupational designations in all but the food and clothing trades usually were male. Women were referred to as the wives of the craftsmen, even when they were widows and practising in the trade on their own. . . .

Some women did have crafts or trades of their own in the cities of England and France in 1700. Most of these were associated with the production and distribution of food and clothing. The all-female *corporations* in seventeenth-century France include seamstresses, dressmakers, combers of hemp and flax, embroiderers, and hosiers. In addition, there were fan and wig makers, milliners, and cloak makers (Guilbert 1966: 21–2). Lists from English cities are similar.

In many of these trades women regularly took on apprentices. In millinery, for example, an apprenticeship lasted from five to seven years and required a substantial fee. The women ran their enterprises independently of their husbands, whose work often took them away from home. . . .

Women were represented, too, in the retail trades, assisting their husbands and running their own businesses as well. In England, brewing once was a female monopoly. It was so no longer by the eighteenth century, but women still practised the trade. Women were also bakers, grocers, innkeepers, and butchers . . . .

By far the most numerous group of married women working independently were the wives of unskilled labourers and journeymen. They were women in precarious economic situations, since their husbands never earned enough money to cover the household needs. These women had no skills, nor did they have capital for goods or a shop. No family productive enterprise claimed their time. So they became petty traders, and itinerant peddlers selling such things as bits of cloth or "perishable articles of food from door to door" accompanied by their children (Clark [1919] 1968: 150, 290; Hufton 1974). The street was their shop; their homes were their workplaces; and their work required no investment in tools or equipment. . . .

The time required of women differed greatly in different situations. During harvesting and planting, wives worked day and night in the fields. Wives of urban butchers and bakers spent many hours in the family shop. Lyons' silk spinners paid others to nurse their babies. Women doing casual labour had to spend long hours earning a few pence or sous. Yet the work of most married women permitted a certain flexibility, some control over the time and pace of work. Some studies estimated that in the course of a year, a woman probably spent fewer days at cash-earning activities than did her husband. While a man worked about 250 days a year, a woman worked about 125 to 180 days. The studies, based on contemporaries' analyses of family budgets of French weavers in 1700 and agricultural labourers in 1750, assumed that a married woman worked less "because of the supplementary demands of her sex: house-keeping, childbirth, etc." (Morineau 1972: 210, 221). In the fields, women could stop work to nurse a baby or feed a young child. In craft and retail shops, they could allocate some time for domestic responsibilities. In addition, they could include young children in certain aspects of their work, teaching them to wind thread or clean wool. Those who walked the street selling their wares were invariably accompanied by their children. Yet rather than "working less," as contemporaries described it, it seems more accurate to say that demands on women's time were more complex. In this period, the type of work women did meant that even if home and workplace were not the same, a woman could balance her productive and domestic activities.

Widows

We have described so far a "normal" situation, in which both husband and wife were alive. Yet mortality statistics indicate that quite frequently death changed this picture. The death of a husband disrupted the family division of labour and left the wife solely responsible for maintaining the family. Sometimes, of course, there were children to assist her, to run the farm, or earn some wages. But often they were too young or too inexperienced to contribute much.

In the best of circumstances, a widow gained the right to practise her husband's craft. She became legal representative of the family,

and her mastery and autonomy were publicly recognized. . . .

Widowhood, however, was usually a difficult situation. Deprived of a husband's assistance, many women could not continue a family enterprise and instead sought new kinds of work . . . . In cities, women who did the most onerous jobs were often widows whose need led them to take any work they could find. Many of these women were unable to support themselves despite their work, for wages were so low. The jobs available to these women—as seamstresses, or unskilled work-ers—were notoriously poorly paid. Hence it was impossible for women and their families to live on earnings alone. So they often sent their children off to charitable institutions, or to fend for themselves. Widows and orphans made up the bulk of names on charity lists in the seventeenth and eighteenth centuries. . . .

Remarriage was clearly the happiest solution for a widow, since an economic partnership was the best means of survival. Widows and widowers did remarry if they could. One study of the Parisian region found that in the sixteenth, seventeenth, and eighteenth centuries men remarried within a few months or even weeks of their wives' deaths (Baulant 1976: 104). Among the lower classes, the rates of remarriage were much higher than among the upper classes, who were protected from penury by the money or property specifically designated for widowhood in marriage contracts. Prosperous widows were sometimes prevented from remarrying by children who did not want their inheritance threatened. If she could find a husband, a second marriage for a widow of the popular classes meant a restoration of the household division of labour. If she had a craft shop or some land, a widow might attract a younger man eager to become a master craftsman or a farmer. (As the husband of a master's widow a man was legally entitled to take over the mastership.) But if she had no claim to property or if she had to relinquish those claims because of the difficulty of maintaining the enterprise alone, she would marry a man whose economic situation was considerably worse than her first husband's. In these instances, farm wives, for example, would become agricultural field labourers or, perhaps, spinners (Couturier 1969: 139).

In most cases, however, widows failed to find new spouses and they had to manage on their own. Widowers more often chose younger, single women as their second wives. A widow's advanced age or the fact that she had children lessened her chances of finding a husband. (Sometimes the price of remarriage was the abandonment of her children, since a prospective husband might be unwilling or unable to contribute to their support. But even this alternative might be preferable to the precarious existence of a widow on her own who might have to abandon her children anyway.) The charity rolls and hospital records of the seventeenth and eighteenth centuries starkly illustrate the plight of a widow with young children or of an elderly widow, desperately struggling and usually failing to earn her own bread. "Small wonder," comments Hufton (1974: 117), "the widow and her brood were common beggars. What other resource had they?"

Although there were fewer of them (they either remarried or simply abandoned their children), widowers too were on the charity lists. Like the widows, these men had great difficulty supporting themselves and their dependent children. Such men and women were eloquent testimony to the fact that the line between survival and starvation, between poverty and destitution, was an extremely thin one. They clearly demonstrate as well that two partners were vital to family survival.

The family division of labour reflected an economy based on the contributions of husband and wife. The loss of one partner usually meant the destruction of the family economy. Although the jobs they performed may have differed, the work of husband and wife were equally necessary to the household. It was this partnership of labour that struck one observer in eighteenth-century France:

> In the lowest ranks [of society], in the country and in the cities, men and women together cultivate the earth, raise animals, manufacture cloth and clothing. Together they use their strength and their talents to nourish and serve children, old people, the infirm, the lazy and the weak. . . . No distinction is made between them about who is the boss; both are . . . (Hufton 1974: 38)

It is not entirely clear that a partnership of labour meant there existed a "rough equality" between husband and wife in all areas of family life (this is the position of Power 1975: 34). It is clear, however, that the survival of the family depended on the work of both partners. . . . Tasks performed were complementary. The differentiation of work roles was based in part on the fact that women also had to bear children and manage the household, activities which were necessary, too, to the family economy. The family economy reproduced itself as the basic economic unit of production. Children were important as well for the sustenance of aged and dependent parents.

Married Women's Domestic Activity

The wife's major domestic responsibility was the provision of food for the family. The work of all family members contributed directly or indirectly to subsistence, but wives had a particular responsibility for procuring and preparing food. In the peasant family, "the duties of the mother of the family were overwhelming; they were summed up in one work: food" (Le Roy Ladurie 1969: 481). In the unskilled labourer's home, too, the wife raised chickens, a cow, a pig, or a goat. Her garden supplemented the miserable wages she earned sewing and those her husband made in the fields. Urban wives frequented markets, where they haggled and bargained over the prices of food and other goods. Some also kept small gardens and few animals at home. Whether she grew food or purchased it—whether, in other words, she was a producer or consumer—the wife's role in providing food served her family. A wife's ability to garden and tend animals, or to bargain and to judge the quality of items for sale, could mean the difference between eating decently and not eating at all. In more desperate circumstances, women earned the family's food by begging for it or by organizing their children to appeal for charity. They supervised the "economy of make-shift," improvising ways of earning money or finding food, and going without food in order to feed their children. One curé in Tours compared such women to "the pious pelican of the *Adoro Te*, who gave her blood to feed her young." Hufton's careful study of the poor in eighteenth-century France has led her to conclude that "the importance of the mother within the family economy was immense; her death or incapacity could cause a family to cross the narrow but extremely meaningful barrier between poverty and destitution" (Hufton 1971: 92).

Food was the most important item in the budgets of most families. Few families had any surplus funds to save or to spend on anything other than basic necessities. A French artisan's family, for example, whose members earned 43 sols a day, spent in 1701 approximately 36 sols on food: bread, herring, cheese, and cider.

Poorer families ate less varied fare. Rural and urban wage earners in eighteenth-century France could spend more than half of their income on bread alone (Lefebvre 1962: 218; Morineau 1972: 210; Hufton 1974: 46–8).

The fact that she managed the provision of food gave the wife a certain power within the family. She decided how to spend money, how to allocate most of the family's few resources. She was the acknowledged manager of much of the monetary exchange of the family and her authority in this sphere was unquestioned. Legally, women were subordinate to their husbands. And some were clearly subject to physical mistreatment as well. Recent studies of criminality, violence, and divorce among the lower classes during the seventeenth and eighteenth centuries indicate that wife beating occurred and that women were at a disadvantage in seeking redress in court.

The law tolerated male adultery and punished it in females; and it also tolerated violence by men against their wives (Abbiateci et al. 1971; Castan 1974; Phillips 1976). The studies, of course, focus on examples of family breakdown and disharmony which reached the criminal courts. They do not, therefore, adequately describe the day-to-day dealings of husband and wife, nor do they detail *distribution* of power within the household. Yet it is precisely the distribution that is important. Men had the physical and legal power, but women managed the poor family's financial resources. Within the households of the popular classes there seem to have been not just one but several sources of power. Men did not monopolize all of them. Wives' power in the household stemmed from the fact that they managed household expenditures for food. Among families which spent most of their money on food this meant that the wife decided how to spend most of the family's money.

. . .

Childbirth and Nurture

The role of food provider was an important aspect of a married woman's productive economic activity and it was also tied to her reproductive role. For it was she who bore and nurtured children, she who clothed and cared for them. Children were the inevitable consequence of marriage; child-bearing was an exclusively female activity. Married women expected to spend much of their married lives pregnant or caring for young children. High infant mortality rates and ensuing high fertility meant that at least two-thirds of a wife's married years involved reproductive activity. For women the risks and pain of childbirth, the need to spend some time nursing an infant, the supervision and feeding of children were all part of the definition of marriage.

. . .

Well into the nineteenth century babies were delivered by untrained women. As Hufton (1974: 14) has put it, "The actual birth of the child was surrounded by a 'complicity' of females." Childbirth created a bond among women. They not only shared the experience but also assisted and nursed one another as best they could.

Yet after the birth of a baby, in the list of household priorities the care of children ranked quite low. Work and the provision of food for the family had first claim on a married woman's time. In the craft shop or on the farm, skilled or unskilled, most labour was time intensive. Men and women spent the day at work, and what little leisure they had was often work related. Hence in the rural *veillée* people would gather in barns on winter evenings to keep warm, to talk, but also to repair farm tools, to sew, to sort and clean fruit and vegetables. In cities when women were not formally employed or when their paid work

was through, they put in long hours spinning, buying and preparing food, or doing laundry. Household tasks were tedious and no labour-saving technology lightened the chores of a working woman. She simply did not have time to spare to devote specifically to children. The demands of the family enterprise or the need to earn wages for the unskilled could not be postponed or put aside to care for children, who, in their earliest years, represented only a drain on family resources. Busy mothers in French cities sent their babies out to be nursed by wet nurses if they could afford it. . . . Death rates among children put out to nurse were almost twice as high as among infants nursed by their own mothers. Even infants who remained at home, however, did not receive a great deal of care. The need for special attention for young children simply was not recognized. . . .

The needs of family economy and not children's individual needs or the needs of "childhood" determined whether or not children remained at home from infancy onward. If they were not put out to a wet nurse, children might be sent into service or apprenticeship at age seven or eight. They were expected to work hard and were sometimes subjected to harsh treatment by their masters and mistresses. (Court records are full of accounts of young servants and apprentices fleeing from cruel employers.) On the other hand, if the family needed their labour, children worked at home.

Children were a family resource only if their labour could be used. In propertied families, of course, one child was also important as an heir. As soon as they were able, young children began to assist their parents in the work of the household. In time of scarcity, those not working might be abandoned or sent away, for they were of limited usefulness to the household as it attempted to balance labour and food.

As family labourers, children were accorded no special treatment. They simply worked as members of the family "team." Their interest and their needs were not differentiated from the family interest. The mother's services to the family were therefore services to them as well. Although she spent time as a child-bearer, a mother allocated little time to activities specifically connected with child rearing . . .

Production was most often located in the household, and individuals for the most part controlled the time and pacing of their work. Production for the market was often an outgrowth of production for household consumption. Although household chores were time-consuming, they did not demand a broad range of skill or expertise. Childbirth

interrupted a woman's routine and claimed some of her time, but after a few days, a woman was usually back to work, taking time out only to nurse the infant. Views of children and standards of child care were such that children were either sent away at a young age or were incorporated into adult routines and adult work. Hence it was possible for a married woman to earn wages or to produce for the market, to manage her household, and to bear children. Each activity influenced the others, but no single activity defined her place nor claimed all of her time. In the course of her lifetime, indeed in the course of a year or a day, a married woman balanced several types of activity and performed them all. She was the cornerstone of the family economy.

● References

Abbiateci, A., et al. 1971. *Crimes et criminalité en France, XVIIe–XVIIIe siècles* (Paris: Colin).

Allison, K.J., and P.M. Tillot. 1961. "York in the Eighteenth Century," in *A History of Yorkshire*, ed. P.M. Tillot (London: The Institute of Historical Research).

Armengaud, A. 1975. *La famille et l'enfant en France et en Angleterre du XVIe au XVIIIe siècles: Aspects démographiques* (Paris: Société d'édition d'enseignement supérieur).

Baehrel, R. 1961. *Une Croissance: La Basse Provence rurale (fin du XVIe siècle–1789)* (Paris: SEVPEN), 109–20.

Baulant, M. 1976. "The Scattered Family: Another Aspect of Seventeenth-century Demography," in *Family and Society*, eds R. Forster and O. Ranum (Baltimore: Johns Hopkins).

Berkner, L. 1972. "The Stem Family and the Development Cycle of the Peasant Household: An Eighteenth Century Austrian Example," *American Historical Review 77* (Apr.): 398–418.

Bernard, R.-J. 1975. "Peasant Diet in Eighteenth-century Gevaudan," in *Diet from Pre-industrial to Modern Times*, eds Forster and Forster (New York: Harper & Row).

Braun, R. 1966. "The Impact of Cottage Industry on an Agricultural Population," in *The Rise of Capitalism*, ed. D. Landes (New York: Macmillan).

Cadet, E. 1870. *Le Mariage en France* (Paris: Guillamin).

Castan, Y. 1974. *Honnêteté et relations sociales en Languedoc (1715–1780)* (Paris: Plon).

Cipolla, C. 1964. *The Economic History of World Population*, rev. edn (Baltimore: Penguin).

———. 1976. *Before the Industrial Revolution: European Society in the Eighteenth Century* (New York: Norton).

Clark, A. [1919] 1968. *The Working Life of Women in the Seventeenth Century* (London: G. Routledge & Sons; reissued by Frank Cass).

Clarkson, L.A. 1971. *The Pre-industrial Economy of England, 1500–1750* (London: Batsford).

Couturier, M. 1969. *Recherches sur les structures sociales de Châteaudun, 1525–1789* (Paris: SEVPEN).

Davies, D. 1965. "The Case of Labourers in Husbandry, 1795," in *Society and Politics in England, 1780–1960*, ed. J.F.C. Harrison (New York: Harper & Row).

Davis, N. 1971. "The Reasons of Misrule: Youth Groups and Charivaris in Sixteenth-century France," *Past and Present 50*: 42–75.

Deyon, P. 1967. *Amiens, Capitale provinciale: Etude sur la société urbaine au 17e siècle* (Paris, The Hague: Mouton).

Dupaquier, J. 1976. "Les Caractères originaux de l'histoire démographique française au XVIIIe siècle," *Revue d'histoire moderne et contemporaine 23* (Apr.–June).

Fairchilds, C. 1976. *Poverty and Charity in Aix-en-Province, 1650–1789* (Baltimore: Johns Hopkins University Press).

Flandrin, J.-L. 1976. *Familles: Parenté, maison, sexualité dans l'ancienne société* (Paris: Hachette).

Fourastié, J. 1959. "De la vie traditionnelle à la vie 'tertiare,'" *Population 14*.

Garden, M. 1970. *Lyon et les lyonnais au XVIIIe siècle* (Paris: Les Belle-Lettres).

Gillis, J.R. 1974. *Youth and History* (New York: Academic Press).

Goubert, P. 1965a. "Recent Theories and Research on French Population between 1500 and 1700," in *Population in History: Essays in Historical Demography*, eds D.V. Glass and D.E.C. Eversley (Chicago: Aldine).

———. 1965b. "The French Peasantry of the Seventeenth Century: A Regional Example," in *Crisis in Europe, 1540–1660: Essays from Past and Present*, ed. T. Aston (London: Routledge & Kegan Paul) and *Beauvais et le Beauvaisis*.

Gouesse, J.-M. 1972. "Parenté, famille et mariage en Normandie aux XVIIe et XVIIIe siècles," Annales: *Economies, Sociétés, Civilisations 27*.

Guilbert, M. 1966. *Les Fonctions des femmes dans l'industrie* (Paris, The Hague: Mouton).

Hair, P.E.H. 1966. "Bridal Pregnancy in Rural England in Earlier Centuries," *Population Studies* 20 (Nov.): 233–43.

Hauser, H. 1927. *Ouvriers du temps passé* (Paris: Alcan).

Hay, D., et al. 1975. *Albion's Fatal Tree* (New York: Pantheon).

Henry, L. 1965. "The Population of France in the Eighteenth Century," in *Population in History: Essays in Historical Demography*, eds D.V. Glass and D.E.C. Eversley (Chicago: Aldine).

Hobsbawm, E.J. 1968. *Industry and Empire: An Economic History of Britain since 1750* (London: Weidenfeld and Nicolson).

Hollingsworth, T.H. 1969. *Historical Demography* (London: The Sources of History Limited in Association with Hodder and Stoughton Ltd.).

Hufton, O. 1974. *The Poor of Eighteenth Century France, 1750–1789* (Oxford: Clarendon Press).

———. 1975. "Women and the Family Economy in Eighteenth Century France," *French Historical Studies* 9 (Spring): 1–22.

Kussmaul-Cooper, A. 1975a. "The Mobility of English Farm Servants in the Seventeenth and Eighteenth Centuries," unpublished paper, University of Toronto (cited with permission).

———. 1975b. "Servants and Laborers in English Agriculture," unpublished paper, University of Toronto (cited with permission).

Laslett, P. 1974. "Parental Deprivation in the Past: A Note on the History of Orphans in England," *Local Population Studies* 13 (Autumn): 11–18.

Lebrun, F. 1971. *Les Hommes et la mort en Anjou aux 17e et 18e siècles* (Paris, The Hague: Mouton).

Lefebvre, G. 1962. *Etudes Orléannaises*, Vol. I (Paris: CNRS).

Le Roy Ladurie, E. 1969. "L'Amenorrhée de famine (XVIIIe–XXe siècles)," *Annals: ESC* 24e Année (Nov.–Dec.): 1589–601.

Levine, D. 1976. "The Demographic Implications of Rural Industrialization: A Family Reconstitution Study of Shepshed, Leicestershire, 1600–1851," *Social History* (May): 177–96.

Macfarlane, A. 1970. *The Family Life of Ralph Josselin* (Cambridge: Cambridge University Press).

Mendras, H. 1970. *The Vanishing Peasant: Innovation and Change in French Agriculture*, trans. J. Lerner (Cambridge, MA: MIT Press).

Meuvret, J. 1965. "Demographic Crisis in France from the Sixteenth to the Eighteenth Century," in *Population in History: Essays in Historical Demography*, eds D.V. Glass and D.E.C. Eversley (Chicago: Aldine).

Morineau, M. 1972. "Budgets populaires en France au XVIIIe siècle," *Revue d'histoire économique et sociale 50*.

Perrot, J.-C. 1975. *Genèse d'une ville moderne: Caen au XVIIIe siècle* (Paris, The Hague: Mouton).

Phillips, R. 1976. "Women and Family Breakdown in Eighteenth Century France: Rouen 1780–1800," *Social History* 2 (May): 197–218.

Pinchbeck, I. [1930] 1969. *Women Workers and the Industrial Revolution, 1750–1850* (London: G. Routledge; reissued by Kelley).

Power, E. 1975. *Medieval Women* (Cambridge: Cambridge University Press).

Segalen, M. 1972. *Nuptialité et alliance: Le Choix du conjoint dans une commune de l'Eure* (Paris: G.P. Maisonneuve Larose).

Thompson, E.P. 1975. *Whigs and Hunters* (London: Allen Lane).

Thorner, D., B. Kerblay, and R.E.F. Smith, eds. 1966. *A.V. Chayanov on the Theory of Peasant Economy* (Homewood, IL: Richard D. Irwin).

Wrigley, E.A. 1966. "Family Limitation in Pre-industrial England," *Economic History Review*, 2nd series, 19 (Apr.): 89–109.

———. 1969. *Population and History* (London: Cambridge University Press).

Chapter 5

There are longstanding debates among sociologists about the impact of the development of industrial capitalism on working-class families in the nineteenth century. Influential early arguments held that the process whereby families lost their ability to support themselves—most commonly, when peasants and family farmers lost their land—produced a breakdown of family. The erosion of a "household economy" meant the breakup of families as working groups. Economic partnerships of husbands and wives, and supervision of children's work by parents, gave way to the abuses and exploitation characteristic of early factories. The daily stress and struggle associated with poverty and economic insecurity put additional strains on spousal relationships at a time when husbands and wives were negotiating their new circumstances.

Family and industrial work were not entirely at odds for the working class in the nineteenth century, however. Family was not just altered in the profound changes associated with **proletarianization** and industrialization; as well, much about family shaped the industrialization of work. Sonya Rose's research (reported in *Limited Livelihoods*) shows that the gendered relations of authority and divisions of work characteristic of patriarchal household production served as the model that factory owners adopted as they organized their workplaces: men supervised women and children, skilled work (and the training for it) was reserved for men and boys, and men earned higher wages than women.

Additionally, even as old patterns were unsettled, family relations were mobilized by working-class people to help them survive in their new situation. Because working-class men were unable to earn wages sufficient to support a family, the earnings of sons and daughters, and the shopping, cooking, budgeting, and other domestic skills of housewives, were critical to the livelihood of families. Moreover, kinship networks were important during the nineteenth century, as extended-family members played a vital role in people's migration to factory towns and their survival strategies once there. At the same time, the authority of male household heads was undermined in an economy where men were both "wage slaves" and inadequate providers, and their children earned money essential to the household.

In response to their situation, working-class men campaigned for a "family wage" which would enable them to support their wives and children (whom they defined as "dependent"); in short, they strategized to uphold their position as head of their household. In a context of rapid economic restructuring, skilled male workers also struggled to protect their better-paid jobs. In response to factory owners' use of low-paid women workers to undermine the position that skilled workmen held, those men regularly took action to exclude women from skilled and high-paying jobs. Thus, new notions of gender and family developed as working-class men responded to their changing position in the marketplace.

Sociologist Tamara Hareven did extensive research on French Canadians who migrated to Manchester, New Hampshire, between 1880 and 1930, to work for wages in a large textile mill located there. She found that kin served as an "informal recruitment and hiring agency" that helped people migrate, find housing and jobs, and learn the skills essential to success in the mill. In fact, relatives often worked side by side in the mill—assisting each other in their work—and lived near each other in the town. The following selection, which relies heavily on her book *Amoskeag*, describes the ongoing kinship support that occurred among relatives, as well as the sacrifices that individuals made for the sake of their parents, children, and siblings.

Dynamics of Kin in an Industrial Community

Tamara K. Hareven

Kin Assistance in Critical Life Situations

The interdependence of kin in the factory was part of a larger role that kin fulfilled as the very source of security and assistance in all aspects of life. Within the family, relatives provided major support over the entire life course, both on a routine basis and in times of stress. Kin assistance was essential both in coping with the insecurities dictated by the industrial system, such as unemployment and strikes, and in coping with personal and family crises, especially death.

The basic axis of kin assistance, both in families living in nuclear households and in extended ones, was that of siblings with each other and parents with their children. Most mutual assistance among kin was carried out between brothers and sisters and between adult children and aging parents, even after they had left their common household. Older brothers and sisters were expected to care for their younger siblings as a matter of course, even to act as surrogate parents in the event of the death of a parent. Given the wide age spread of children within the family, it was not unusual for the oldest child to be about the age at which he or she could have been a parent of the youngest child.

Grandmothers and aging aunts cared for grandchildren and for nieces and nephews, without necessarily living in the same household. They also cooked meals, cleaned house, and mended clothes when a mother was working. Older female relatives assisted young women in childbirth and took care of the other children in the family while the mother was recovering. Relatives cared for each other during illness (at a time when people rarely stayed in hospitals). Relatives reared orphans, along with their own children, and also took in invalids and retarded family members. Male relatives helped each other in the repair and maintenance of their apartments or homes; when they owned farmland outside the city, they co-operated in planting and harvesting. They shared tools and implements, traded services and transportation.

As siblings left home and established their own households, modes of assistance in the nuclear family were broadened to include extended kin. In addition to this basic interaction of the core siblings and parents, nuclear families were enmeshed in larger kinship networks that often spanned two or three generations and were expanded through marriage. The distance of the relationship affected, of course, the intensity of the interactions. Instead of close involvement with child rearing, health care, and the collective work and maintenance of the household, assistance was of a more casual nature. The level of obligation varied depending on how closely kin were related. In times of crisis or in the absence of other sources of support, however, more distant kin often took on major responsibilities as well.

Even though nuclear families resided in separate households, they extended their reach beyond the household by sharing and exchanging resources and labour with their kin. Autonomous nuclear households drew their strength and support from extended kin. Living in proximity to one's kin was essential for survival, particularly in periods when transportation was difficult or when a shortage in housing occurred. Despite the predominance of the nuclear household, relatives opened up their homes to each other during periods of transition or need. Some newlywed couples initially lived either with their parents, usually the wife's parents, or with an older brother and sister. Couples often shared housing temporarily with relatives after their arrival in Manchester or during periods of scarcity. Generally, however, they adhered to the custom of separate residence of the nuclear family from extended kin. They lived near each other, often in the same building, separate but available in time of need.

The social space of the Simoneau family in Manchester illustrates the conscious effort of kin to reside near each other and the flexibility kin exercised in extending to each other temporary help with housing. When the oldest son first arrived to settle in Manchester in 1908, he lived in a boarding house. When his widowed father and younger siblings joined him two years later, the family lived in a tenement close to the mills. Shortly thereafter, they moved to the West Side of Manchester to be near other relatives. His father married a woman from his hometown who lived nearby in Manchester. She brought her niece, who had been living with her, into the household. The niece later married the oldest Simoneau son.[1]

As each of the Simoneau sons and daughters married, they set up separate residences within several blocks of their father's house. When only two unmarried teenage children remained, the father moved to the nearby village of Goffstown. Because commuting to work in the mill was difficult for the young daughter still living at home, she moved in with her married sister in Manchester. The father lived in Goffstown until his death, at which point the youngest son moved to Boston. The other siblings continued to live in proximity to each other. Two brothers and their wives shared housing temporarily, first during the 1922 strike, when a brother lost his home because of unemployment, and again after the shutdown of the Amoskeag, when another brother sold his home and moved to Nashua to seek work. Upon his return, he and his family moved in with the oldest brother for a limited period while looking for their own place to live.

The experience of people who had no relatives to assist them demonstrates the bitter price paid for isolation from kin. Lottie Sargent's father, for example, had no relatives in the city. After his wife died in childbirth, he took Lottie as a baby to bars and clubs, where the "ladies of the night" kept an eye on her. Eventually, he placed her in the orphanage until he remarried; then he took her into his newly established household. Another example of the consequences of isolation from kin is provided by Cora Pellerin, who had no relatives in Manchester to take care of her two daughters. When both she and her husband were working in the mill, she had a housekeeper. But during her husband's prolonged illness, she had to place the children in the Villa Augustina, a Catholic boarding school. To both Cora and her daughters, it was a heart-rending experience:

I had never been to a school with the nuns. It was hard for me to put them in there. It is a big, big building, and it seemed that it was just like a jail. That's the way I felt inside. I used to go and see them every Wednesday night, and they'd come home every Saturday. They'd have supper with me and leave every Sunday afternoon at four o'clock. If they didn't come, it was because they'd been bad and were being punished. I used to cry on my way home. I wiped my eyes before seeing my husband because if he'd notice it, he'd take the girls out. (*Amoskeag*: 211)

Even though a systematic measure for the consistency of kin assistance is not available, it is clear from the interviews that assistance from distantly related kin was frequent. The people interviewed were conscious of kinship ties that often included extended kin to whom one might be related through in-laws or cousins. Thus, in addition to the actual communication with kin, the mental kinship map, which was often reinforced by an elaborate genealogy, encompassed distantly related kin as well.

The fluidity and informality in the functions and roles of kin in Manchester was characteristic of the overall kinship structure in American society. Normatively defined in American culture, rather than legislated, the obligations among extended kin have always been flexible and voluntary (Parsons 1943: 22–8). The boundaries for extended kin were loosely defined, centering on the nuclear family as a focus. Goode characterizes kin in contemporary American society as "ascriptive friends." Kin are involved in mutual reciprocity as friends, but "they may not intrude merely because they are relatives" (Goode 1963: 76):

There is no great extension of the kin network. . . . Thus the couple cannot count on a large number of kinfolk for help. Just as these kin cannot call upon the couple for services. . . . Neither couple nor kinfolk have many *rights* with respect to the other, and so the reciprocal *obligations* are few. . . . the couple has few moral controls over their extended kin, and these have few controls over the couple. (italics in original; Goode 1963: 8)

As opposed to more generationally defined kinship systems in traditional agrarian societies, where the place of each member was more clearly determined within the kinship system and where obligations among kin were more rigidly legislated and defined, the extended kinship system in Manchester (and in the United States generally) was loosely defined. Kin relations and obligations revolved around individuals or the nuclear family.

In Quebec, children's opportunities and obligations were ranked in relation to inheritance practices,[2] whereas French Canadians in Manchester adopted a more flexible and voluntary system. However, they followed several basic implicit rules governing kin assistance, which also specified that nuclear-family members (and later parents and their adult children) were first in priority for assistance. Customarily, couples also drew a line between in-laws and their family of orientation. The closest kin connections followed a mother–daughter dyad—adult women were usually engaged in closer exchanges with their own mothers than with their mothers-in-law and drew explicit boundaries with their husbands' families.

This sequence of priorities usually led to a multi-layered pattern of kin interaction over the life course. As younger children grew up, older siblings helped them find jobs. They aided younger sisters, especially in preparing for marriage and in setting up households. In addition, they cared for aging parents and often continued to assist their siblings later in life. Older children thus were sometimes caught in a squeeze between helping younger siblings and caring for aging parents simultaneously. Marie Anne Senechal, for example, had no sooner finished rearing her younger siblings than she encountered the responsibility of caring for her aging father and continuing to aid her siblings in their adult years.

Within each family or kin group, one member, usually a woman, emerged as the "**kin keeper.**" Larger networks had several kin keepers, but within a nuclear family, the task usually fell upon one member. Most commonly, the oldest daughter or one of the older daughters was cast in the role of kin keeper when a crisis arose, such as the death of the mother. Ora Pelletier viewed herself as a kin keeper (even though she was not the oldest daughter):

> But if they need me, if they have any trouble or you know they're in trouble or they're worried about something or if they need a recipe or something they always call me like if I was the mother . . . No matter what happens you know they will call me and ask me. Ask me for advice, or, "Do you remember how Mom used to do this or that?" (interview with Ora Pelletier)

Kin keepers usually retained their role throughout their lives. Although needs and responsibilities changed, their centrality to the kin group as helpers, arbiters, and pacifiers continued over life and became even more pivotal with age. Kin keepers were at times designated by parents in advance or were thrust into that position by circumstances and by their skills and personalities. Given the wide age spread

of children within the family, designating the oldest or middle children as kin keepers was an important strategy for large families.

Some kin keepers remained single because the responsibility of care extended and escalated as they grew older. They commanded greater authority among their siblings, nieces, and nephews and were in the centre of family communication. Kin keepers kept track of different family members who immigrated or who married and left town; they scheduled family reunions and celebrations of birthdays and anniversaries. When adult siblings were in conflict with each other, kin keepers tried to resolve the feud by acting as intermediaries.

Kin keeping thus carried with it prestige and respect, in addition to the many tasks and services. For a woman, in particular, this position also bestowed a power and influence she rarely held within her nuclear family, where the father was the source of authority and the final arbiter. But kin keeping was also confining and bestowed many obligations on the person so designated.

Marie Anne Senechal explained how she became a kin keeper. The oldest daughter, she was left at age 20 with 11 children, including two infants, when her mother died. She opposed her father's plan to place the non-working children in an orphanage, and along with her work in the mill, she took charge of them. Committed to rearing her siblings, Marie Anne allowed her sister, two years her junior, to get married, knowing that this decision sealed her own fate—the entire care of the home would be on her shoulders forever. "It's my fault that my sister got married. I should have told her not to. She was 18, and she was the one who was taking care of the house. She asked for my advice, and I said, 'Well, an old maid doesn't have a very good name.' . . . I pushed my sister to get married." But the sister's departure was not free of guilt. "When she left with him [her husband], all of us were at the window; all the little kids. She never forgot our faces in the window. As long as she lived, she always said, 'Marie Anne, why did I get married and leave you all by yourself?'"(*Amoskeag*: 280–1).

Florida Anger, the oldest daughter, helped with the rearing of her younger siblings even though both parents were alive. She and her sisters and brothers worked together in the mill, and her parents assigned her the task of making sure her siblings actually went to work and stayed with their jobs. She also helped at home with child rearing and housework. After they married, her younger sisters turned to her for assistance, especially during the illness and death of a child of one of her sisters. Throughout their adult lives, her brothers and sisters sought her help. She mediated the quarrels over the use of their father's insurance money and his car after his death and subsequently tried to reconcile her feuding siblings when petty conflicts arose.

How were the multiple patterns of kin assistance that extended over the entire life course and flowed back and forth across a wide geographic region enforced? Why did kin assist each other over long time periods? What prepared them to pay the high personal cost of self-sacrifice that often led to the postponement or denial of marriage for women?

The most eloquent explanation advanced for kin assistance has been the theory of exchange relations, which Michael Anderson employs in his study of nineteenth-century textile workers in Lancashire (1971). His emphasis on instrumental relationships is particularly relevant to this study. Using economic exchange theory, Anderson argues that the basis for kin assistance was exchange in services and in supports during critical life situations. The motives that led kin to help each other, he argues, were "calculative": parents aided their children with the expectation of receiving assistance in old age; and more distant kin helped each other in the hope of receiving returns when they were in need. These calculative relationships were reinforced by strong societal norms dictating mutual obligations among relatives. Anderson thus sees kin assistance as a series of exchanges revolving around self-interest and reinforced by social norms.[3] Although the time period is different, the Manchester workers share several characteristics with Lancashire's labourers. In both communities, kin provided the almost exclusive source of assistance for a low-resource population with a high proportion of migrants. However, the interviews of former Manchester workers, which provide crucial information on their own perceptions of instrumental relationships, make it clear that certain aspects of kin assistance cannot be entirely explained by economic exchange theory.

In the context of Manchester, instrumental relationships fell into two categories: short-term routine exchanges in services and assistance in critical life situations and long-term investments in exchanges along the life course. In addition to those forms of assistance previously discussed, kin provided money on a short-term basis and traded skills, goods, and services. For example, mill workers supplied their relatives with cheap cloth and received farm products in exchange. Plumbers and masons traded services with each other, and storekeepers exchanged merchandise for medical or legal assistance from relatives.

Long-term investments were more demanding and less certain in their future returns, and the most pervasive exchange along the life course was that between parents and children—old-age support in return for child rearing. Under conditions of frequent migration, exchanges across the life course also occurred among aunts and uncles and their nieces and nephews, with the former frequently acting as surrogate parents for their newly arrived young relatives in Manchester. Such exchanges were horizontal as well as vertical. Horizontally, aunts and uncles were fulfilling obligations to or reciprocating the favours of brothers or sisters by taking care of their children; vertically, they were entering into exchange relationships with their nieces and nephews, who might assist them later in life. Godparents also represented long-term exchanges. Because godparents assumed obligations of future assistance to their godchildren, the people selecting them preferred relatives or non-relatives with resources.

Although the benefits of short-term exchanges are easily understandable, it is difficult to accept calculative motives as the exclusive base of long-term kin assistance, especially when the rewards were not easily visible. For example, those women who substantially delayed or even sacrificed an opportunity for marriage to fulfill their obligation to care for younger siblings or aging parents did so for no apparent reward. Men and women supported members of their nuclear families even when a more distant relative might have been a better long-term contributor to an exchange bargain. These forms of kin behaviour exceed benefits that could be measured by economic exchange.

Young family members who subordinated their own careers to family needs did so out of a sense of responsibility, affection, and familial obligation rather than with the expectation of eventual gain. Within this context, kin assistance was not strictly calculative. Rather, it expressed an overall principle of reciprocity over the life course. Reciprocity, as Julian Pitt-Rivers (1973) defines it,

is undifferentiated in that it requires that a member of the group shall sacrifice himself for another, that kinsmen shall respect preferential rules of conduct toward one another regardless of their individual interests. Such reciprocity as there is comes from the fact that other kinsmen do likewise. Parents are expected to sacrifice themselves for their children but they also expect that their children will do the same for theirs. The reciprocity alternates down the chain of generations, assuming that the grand parental generation will be repaid in the persons of the grandchildren. (101)

The sense of duty to family was a manifestation of family culture—a set of values that entailed not only a commitment to the well-being and self-reliance or survival of the family but one that took priority over individual needs and personal happiness. The preservation of family autonomy was valued as a more important goal than individual fulfillment. Family autonomy, essential for self-respect and good standing in the neighbourhood and the community, was one of the most deeply ingrained values: it dictated that assistance be sought among kin. Few of the people interviewed turned for help to the church, ethnic mutual-aid associations, public welfare, or charity. (It must be remembered that given the stigma attached to receiving charity, many may not have admitted they were aided in this manner.) The first significant acceptance of public welfare occurred in the 1930s when workers turned to the Federal Emergency Relief Administration and the Works Progress Administration after enduring weeks of unemployment and the subsequent shutdown of the mills.

In a regime of insecurity, where kin assistance was the only continuing source of support, family culture by necessity dictated that family considerations, needs, and ties guide or control most individual decisions. Collective family needs were not always congruent with individual preferences. Migrating to Manchester, locating jobs and housing, and conversely leaving the mills and returning to Canada were all embedded in family strategies rather than in individual preferences.

At times, such family decisions ignored individual feelings to a degree that would seem callous from the vantage point of our times; Mary Dancause, for example, was at age four sent back by her parents to live with relatives in Quebec when she had an eye disease. When she reached age 12, her parents uprooted her from a loving environment in Quebec to bring her back to Manchester to take care of younger siblings. She recalled her bitterness and loneliness: "I was so lonesome, I cried so much, you won't believe it. My mother would be working in the kitchen and I would be talking to myself: 'I want to go back, I want to go back'" (interview with Mary Dancause).

Her older brother, who had also been left behind but who was not summoned back, decided to strike out on his own for Manchester. When he knocked on his parents' door, his father did not recognize him. "There was a knock at the back door. 'We don't want anything,' Father said, and he banged the door. So my brother went around to the front. He rang the bell, and my father said, 'It's you again.' Brother said, 'Wait a minute, can I talk to you?' He told him, 'I'm your son'" (*Amoskeag*: 51).

Both career choices and economic decisions were made within the family matrix. Families might be described as being composed of units that were switched around as the need arose. Each unit was relied upon and used when appropriate. Following such strategies, families timed the movement of members in response to both individual schedules and external conditions. Family strategies revolved around a variety of decisions: when to migrate, when to return, when those who were left behind should rejoin the family in Manchester, who should be sent to explore other working opportunities, who should be encouraged to marry, and who should be pressured to stay at home.

The subordination of individual needs to family decisions did not always take place without conflict. Many interviewees who had made personal sacrifices expressed long-repressed anger and pain during the interview. Anna Fregau Douville, for example, as the last child of working age who could support her parents, left school and started working at age 14 and postponed her own marriage. When Anna finally announced she was going to get married, her sisters pressured her to cancel her engagement, claiming that her fiancé was a drunkard. Actually, "they were scheming to get me to support my folks until they died. . . . But my mother told me, 'Anna, don't wait too long. What if I die or your father dies? Then you'd insist on staying with me, and you'll lose your boyfriend.'" She got married and lived two houses away from her parents. Although Anna was determined to live her life independently of her family, she was never quite free of guilt. Having grown up in a large family where she experienced first-hand the pressures imposed by kin, Anna subsequently set strict boundaries with her husband's family immediately following her marriage: she refused to pay her mother-in-law's debts and made it clear to her husband and her in-laws that they could not rely on her to compensate for their extravagances:

> I put my foot down the first year that I got married. . . . When his parents used to come and visit me and ask to borrow money . . . I said, "Listen, I don't go down

to your house to bother you. I'm happy with my husband and get the hell out. Don't ever come here and try to borrow anything from him or from me." . . . My husband agreed with me. He said, "I'm glad that you can open up with them. I couldn't talk that way to my own family." (*Amoskeag*: 291)

Interestingly, despite her resentment of extended family obligations and her own bitterness toward her siblings, Anna Douville kept the most complete family albums and follows the traditional Quebec custom of maintaining a family genealogy. Her personal resentment of the intrusions of kin into her own privacy was divorced from her ideological commitment to keeping a complete family record for posterity.

Anna's refusal to provide assistance to her husband's family represented a common pattern among women who had been deeply enmeshed in responsibilities with their own kin. Once they married, they refused involvement with their husbands' relatives to avoid taking on new obligations, having just emerged from their own families' burdens. Cora Pellerin, for example, postponed her marriage until the death of her fiancé's ailing mother rather than join his household and take on the responsibility of caring for her. When she married, Cora closed her home to her husband's older sister. She allowed her housekeeper to give her husband's sister an occasional meal, but she did not admit her as a regular member of the household even though her sister-in-law could have acted as a babysitter and a housekeeper. Eventually, her sister-in-law moved to a convent (interview with Cora Pellerin).

Marie Anne Senechal, who spent most of her life rearing her own siblings and finally married when she was in her sixties, drew a firm line with her husband's sister. Even though she allowed her own siblings to live in her house, she would not tolerate her sister-in-law. Marie Anne drove her out of the house, finally, after provoking a quarrel. Ora Pelletier, whose six older sisters worked in the mills, was ostracized by her siblings ever since she cashed in their father's insurance policy after his death and used the money for her own needs. She felt entitled to the money because she was the last remaining daughter at home and had taken care of her father until his death. Alice Olivier still resented being sent to work in the mill at age 14 while her two brothers were sent to the seminary at Trois-Rivières in Canada. At age 60, she returned to high school to fulfill her old dream of an education. The interview took place just at the point when she was about to graduate from high school. After all these years she finally confronted her mother, asking her why she had sent her to work instead of letting her stay in school (*Amoskeag*: 268–9).

And Marie Anne Senechal, who defended her lifelong sacrifices for her family without any aura of martyrdom, finally wiped away a tear at the end of the interview and said: "I thought I'd never marry. I was 67 years old when I got married. . . . It was too much of a wait, when I think of it now, because I would have been happier if I'd got married. . . . I knew I wasn't living my own life, but I couldn't make up my mind" . . . (*Amoskeag*: 281–2).

Migration and the Continuity of the Kinship System

Although historians and sociologists have long recognized the importance of kin in communities of destination in facilitating migration and settlement, less attention has been paid to the role of relatives remaining in the communities of origin. Kin who remained in Quebec fulfilled a crucial function in providing backup assistance and security for the migrating family. Availability of continued support in the community of origin was therefore an essential consideration in the decision to migrate.

The networks of relatives, besides serving as important backups, also enabled workers to experiment with different employment opportunities, to send their sons to scout for better jobs, and to marry off their daughters. "Long-distance" kin, like those nearby, were sources of security and assurance in times of crisis and often served as a refuge. Some people who worked until their later years of life retired to their villages of origin. Some unmarried pregnant women, for whom life in Manchester was unbearable because of shame and social pressure, went to live in convents in Quebec until their children were born and then either remained there or returned to work in Manchester. Some parents left young children with relatives in Quebec until they found jobs and housing in Manchester. Others sent sick children back to Quebec to recuperate with relatives . . .

In Manchester, as in mid-nineteenth-century and twentieth-century East London or Preston, kinship networks were embedded in the city's neighbourhoods. But the social space of French-Canadian kin extended from Quebec to Manchester and spread over New England's industrial map. French-Canadian kinship behaviour in Manchester thus demonstrates the importance of intensive kin networks in one's immediate neighbourhood and workplace, as well as persistence of distant kinship ties laced through a larger geographic region.[4] Geographic distance did not disrupt basic modes of kin co-operation but led, rather, to a revision of priorities and forms of assistance. Under certain conditions, migration

strengthened kinship ties and led to new kin functions, which evolved as changing conditions dictated. . . .

Continuities and Discontinuities in the Functions of Kin

To understand fully the role of kin in twentieth-century Manchester, one must place it in historical perspective. Ideally, the kinship patterns of French Canadians in Manchester should be compared to those of their communities of origin in rural Quebec. Unfortunately, only two studies of kinship in Quebec are available for comparison: an ethnographic study of the village of St Denis by Horace Miner (1939) and a more recent study of urban kinship ties in Montreal by Philippe Garigue (1967).[5]

Were the kinship patterns characteristic of St Denis transported to Manchester? In the absence of a full-fledged comparison of family structure, demographic behaviour, women's labour-force participation, and family economy for Manchester and the Quebec parishes of origin, it would be impossible to answer this question conclusively. This discussion is limited, therefore, to a comparison with the kinship patterns found in Quebec by Miner and Garigue, respectively. In rural St Denis, kin were at the base of the organizational structure. They controlled the channels of land transmission and all major aspects of assistance and discipline. Symbols of kin permeated religious life, and reverence for ancestors constituted an important component of socialization. Even marriage partners were chosen within the kinship network. Kin directed and dominated most important career decisions. In outlining the stages of the family cycle in rural Quebec, Miner stressed the farmer's perception of the interrelatedness of generations: "Life is like a turning wheel. The old turn over the work to the young and die, and these in turn get old and then turn the work to their children. Yes, life is like a wheel turning" (Miner 1939: 85). Particularly important for comparative purposes is Miner's emphasis on the interchangeability of sons for inheritance rather than on primogeniture. The father decided which son would inherit the farm and launched the other sons into the outside world by providing them with assistance to migrate to the towns to find jobs or by helping with their education. After the father's death, the other brothers customarily left the household, because it was considered a disgrace to live in a brother's home. Also important, for comparative purposes, was the prevalence of mutual assistance and shared effort, especially among brothers who farmed in the same village or in nearby villages.

Migration to Manchester shifted the economic base of the family from landholding to industrial work. It therefore disrupted the basic territorial continuity and the interlocking of generations within the family cycle. The move to an industrial economy obviously exposed the French-Canadian immigrants to different occupational careers and economic organization. Accordingly, it necessitated a reorganization of family roles and a redefinition of kinship rules. The stem family structure found by Miner in St Denis was not present in Manchester. As indicated earlier, sons and daughters in Manchester tended to set up their own households after marriage even though they did not move far away from their parents. At most, some spent the first two years of marriage in their parents' household. Once removed from the land, fathers in Manchester lost the bargaining power and control they had held by virtue of their land ownership. Thus, the move to industrial cities

may have weakened the patriarchal authority of traditional rural families.

However, despite this major change, migration to Manchester did not result in a breakdown of kinship ties. Traditional family structures were not disrupted through the migration of sons and daughters. Migration was an essential component of the family cycle in Quebec. Non-inheriting sons left home to work in cities, often in textile towns such as Trois-Rivières. Daughters usually entered domestic service or textile work. Migration to Manchester was, therefore, part of the larger historic pattern of rural–urban migration of Quebec sons and daughters at specific stages of the family cycle.

The factory system in some ways reinforced family ties. Industrial work allowed adult sons and daughters to remain in the parental household until marriage and to establish their own households nearby after marriage. In this respect, life in an industrial town (provided the entire nuclear family had migrated) offered greater opportunities for cohesion and contact among relatives throughout their lives. The dispersal of children by inheritance practices did not affect families in Manchester. As long as employment in the mills was available, children and parents continued to work in the same place, thus allowing continued interaction with parents as well as siblings.

Life in the industrial town added new functions to an already long repertory of kin interaction. The legacy of rural Quebec to industrial Manchester—the principle and practice of kin solidarity—was extremely significant in the adaptation of rural workers to industrial conditions. Once villagers left the land, their kin ceased to be the exclusive organizational base of social life and lost many of their sanctions. However, a corporate view of family life and an orientation to a collective family economy was maintained in Manchester, at least in the first generation. The principle of resource exchanges across the life course took new forms, such as the provision of housing, child care, the teaching of skills, and brokerage within the factory.

A comparison of the organization and behaviour of kin in Manchester with that of kin in urban Quebec communities is also illuminating. Garigue (1956) found large kinship networks in Montreal, which were vitally linked with relatives in their rural community of origin, as well as in a number of other French-Canadian communities. These networks did not contain scattered nuclear families but instead exhibited concentrations in each location of kin clusters that, as part of a larger network, maintained contact with each other in several different communities. Individuals and nuclear families generally migrated to join a specific cluster. Migrants often moved to a certain urban community because other relatives lived there. The pattern outlined by Garigue places kinship ties in Manchester into a larger world of French-Canadian networks, a cell in a larger series of clusters—many located in Quebec.

This examination of the kinship patterns in Manchester and its comparison with Quebec raises crucial historical questions: What changes in kinship patterns resulted from migration and settlement in new communities? What behaviours were transferred with modifications and which remained intact? Answers hinge on an overall understanding of the transmission of pre-migration organizations and traditions to new settings. A systematic distinction between complete transfers of traditional patterns or their modification and new adaptation will considerably advance our understanding of the role of kin in adaptation to modern, industrial life.

The French-Canadian case in Manchester suggests that what has been considered a survival of pre-modern patterns may also represent modern responses to new industrial conditions. French-Canadian immigrants initially transported kinship ties and traditional practices of kin assistance to Manchester. They subsequently adapted their kin organization to the industrial system by developing new modes of interaction and new functions.

Although the basic kinship ties had been imported from rural Quebec, their functions, responsive to the demands of industrial production, were different from those customarily performed by kin in rural society. Functioning in an industrial environment required a familiarity with bureaucratic structures and organizations, adherence to modern work schedules, planning in relation to the rhythms of industrial employment, specialization in tasks, and technological skills. The roles assumed by kin—hiring young relatives and manipulating the pace of production—required a mastery of "modern" processes, a high level of expertise, and sophistication. The role of kin in these areas, as well as in the more personal areas, such as housing, required a comprehension of the complexity and diversity inherent in an urban industrial system. The selective use of kinship ties by the workers of Manchester represented, therefore, both earlier practices and their modification.

The selectivity used by immigrants in adapting their traditional ties and resources to industrial conditions is most significant in this process. **Modernization theory** has frequently viewed integration with kin as an obstacle to geographic mobility and adaptation to modern ways (Moore 1965; Inkeles and Smith 1974). The Manchester case suggests, rather, that kin not only facilitated migration to industrial communities but also served as agents of adaptation and modernization by providing role models and by offering direct assistance. Under the insecurities of the factory system, the selective use of kinship was part of survival strategies and under certain circumstances also facilitated mobility.

● Notes

1. These patterns of residence were reconstructed from city directories and addresses listed in the Amoskeag Company's employee files.
2. For definitions and descriptions of traditional kinship systems, see Fox (1967), Arensberg and Kimball (1968), Fortes (1969), and Lèvi-Strauss (1969). For a historical analysis of legal changes governing American family and kinship organization, see Farber (1973).
3. For a theoretical discussion of the instrumentality of kin in modern society, see also Bennett and Despres (1960).
4. Compare also with Litwak's assertion that geographic propinquity is not an essential condition for the maintenance of extended kinship ties (1960).
5. Recently, the extent to which St Denis is representative of most rural Quebec communities has been questioned. No comparable studies for other Quebec communities are available, however.

● References

Anderson, M.S. 1971. *Family Structure in Nineteenth century Lancashire* (Cambridge, UK: Cambridge University Press).

Arensberg, C.M., and S.T. Kimball. 1968. *Family and Community in Ireland*, 2nd edn (Cambridge, MA: Harvard University Press).

Bennett, J.W., and L.A. Despres. 1960. "Kinship and Instrumental Activities," *American Anthropologist* 62: 254–67.

Farber, B. 1973. *Family and Kinship in Modern Society* (Glenview, IL: Scott Foresman & Co).

Fortes, M. 1969. *Kinship and the Social Order* (Chicago: Aldine Publishing Co).

Fox, R. 1967. *Kinship and Marriage: An Anthropological Perspective* (London: Penguin).

Garigue, P. 1956. "French-Canadian Kinship and Urban Life," *American Anthropologist* 58: 1090–1101.

——. 1967. *La vie familiale des Canadiens Français* (Montréal: Les Presses de l'Université de Montréal).

Goode, W. 1963. *World Revolution and Family Patterns* (New York: Free Press).

Hareven, T.K. and R. Langenbach. 1978. *Amoskeag: Life and Work in an American Factory City.* (New York: Pantheon Books)

Inkeles, A., and D. Smith. 1974. *Becoming Modern: Individual Change in Six Developing Countries* (Cambridge, MA: Harvard University Press).

Lèvi-Strauss, C. 1969. *The Elementary Structures of Kinship* (Boston: Beacon Press).

Litwak, E. 1960. "Geographical Mobility and Extended Family Cohesion," *American Sociological Review* 25: 385–94.

Miner, H.M. 1939. *St Denis: A French-Canadian Parish* (Chicago: University of Chicago Press).

Moore, W.E. 1965. *Industrialization and Labor: Social Aspects of Economic Development* (Ithaca, NY: Cornell University Press).

Parsons, T. 1943. "The Kinship System of the Contemporary United States," *American Anthropologist* 45: 22–38.

Pitt-Rivers, J. 1973. "The Kith and the Kin," in *The Character of Kinship*, ed. J. Goody (Cambridge, UK: Cambridge University Press).

Chapter 6

In addition to a working class, a middle class composed of businessmen, professional men, and their families developed during the rise of industrial capitalism. For the most successful people in this class—especially the capitalists able to build factories—work oriented to the market was moving outside the household, and thus the nature of the household was changing. In response, a gender ideology known as "separate spheres" developed, which provided an explanation of the dramatically changed social landscape. The developing separation between public and private sectors was seen as mirroring differences between men and women, which were increasingly understood to be natural. Women were defined as naturally nurturing, and even virtuous, while men were seen as naturally suited to a competitive economy. The emerging middle class also embraced domesticity as a badge of identity—one symbolizing morality. Loving, caring, unselfish, and virtuous behaviour came to be seen as residing in family and the home. The home, in essence, became a "haven in a heartless world" (in the words of the late Christopher Lasch)—a contrast to the economy, which was popularly seen as exploitative and immoral.

Today, the feature of family life that is perhaps most difficult to problematize is the mother–child relationship. Our practices of assuming that biological mothers bear full responsibility for their children, that they should provide most (or all) of their children's care (especially in their infancy), and that motherhood should assume priority in their life until their children are grown are hard to question. Yet this is an unusual pattern, historically and across different cultures—even

today. Moreover, there is no evidence that this is the best way to meet the needs of children.

This chapter traces the historical development of the ideas that define motherhood as we know it. American anthropologist Maxine Margolis (writing in the 1980s) situates the rise of new ideas about childhood and motherhood in the changes occurring in households—and thus family life—in the nineteenth century, as an economy based on household production gave way to industrial capitalism. Margolis provides a clear description of the structural, or social-organizational, changes that promoted these new ideas, especially what she calls "the invention of motherhood." Assumed in her discussion is the importance of urbanization to the germination and popularization of these ideas. The conditions of family farming militated against any changes to the view of children as valuable solely for their usefulness as labourers. Thus, the transformation in popular thinking about childhood and motherhood that Margolis describes for the United States likely occurred later in Canada, as the shift to urban living was slower here. But these ideas were common here too—at least in English-speaking Canada—by the end of the nineteenth century (see Neil Sutherland's *Children in English-Canadian Society*).

Margolis also provides some evidence about the people who created and promoted the new ideology of motherhood. These were women as well as men, and what united them were concerns based on social class and race. In both countries, in the later part of the nineteenth century, the same interests produced moral-reform movements with the objective of protecting and perpetuating nation states they saw as white, middle class, and Protestant (see

Mariana Valverde's *The Age of Light, Soap and Water: Moral Reforms in English Canada, 1885–1925*). Motherhood, then as now, was a public concern for political, as well as other, reasons.

Social historians know less about what social relations and daily life were like for middle-class North Americans than they do about cultural ideals and popular ideas. Canadian historian Francoise Noel (in *Family Life and Sociability in Upper and Lower Canada, 1780–1870*) has, however, searched through diaries and personal correspondence for evidence about the personal lives of propertied middle- and upper-class families in Upper and Lower Canada between 1780 and 1870. She describes marriages based on love and companionship, as well as property sufficient to support an independent household. The love and affection she finds between spouses, and the concern about children's development and grief over their death, indicate strong similarities with couples today. But the incredible sociability of these nuclear families stands in contrast with the ideals of privacy and independence that became so central to family life in the twentieth century. According to Noel, nineteenth-century couples met and even honeymooned in the company of family, especially parents. Members of extended families stayed with each other for long visits, and neighbours and friends were in and out of each other's homes frequently. Noel argues that mutual assistance—among neighbours especially—was very important to family life in Canada at that time.

Putting Mothers on the Pedestal

Maxine L. Margolis

Motherhood as we know it today is a surprisingly new institution. In most of human history and in most parts of the world even today, adult, able-bodied women had been, and still are, too valuable in the productive capacity to be spared for the exclusive care of children.

Jessie Bernard
The Future of Motherhood, 1974

Debates about the conflict between motherhood and work have lessened in intensity over the last decade as millions of middle-class wives and mothers have taken jobs and as employment for these women has become the norm rather than the exception. But these developments have not met with unanimous approval. Just think of the demand by groups like the Moral Majority for a return to "traditional family values," code words for the presence of a full-time housewife–mother in the home. Nevertheless, biting denunciations of working mothers—so common during much of this century—are much less frequent today. Most women are pleased to be living in an era in which they are free to take a job or even pursue a career and in which their economic contribution to their families is recognized. They probably feel less uneasy about working because it is no longer an article of faith that their employment is harmful to their children. But what is often overlooked is that this is not the first time in American history when work and motherhood were thought compatible and when women's productive activities were seen as essential to their families' well-being.

Ideas about the "correct" maternal role have often changed over the last 250 years in the United States. Not until the nineteenth century, for example, did a child's development and well-being come to be viewed as the major, if not the sole, responsibility of his or her mother, who was then urged to devote herself full-time to her parental duties. In contrast, during the eighteenth century child rearing was neither a discrete nor an exclusively female task. There was little emphasis on motherhood *per se* and both parents were simply advised to "raise up" their children together.

These and other changes in ideas about motherhood are not isolated cultural artifacts resulting from random ideological fashions. I will argue that these value changes were and are moulded by changes in the nature of the family and the American economy. I intend to review the process whereby motherhood as a full-time career for middle-class women first arose as women's role in the domestic economy diminished, "work" was removed from the household, the family became more isolated from the larger community, the need for education and skilled children increased, and the birth rate declined. As a result of these developments, with minor variations, the exclusivity of the mother–child dyad and the incessant duties of motherhood emerged beginning in the 1830s as givens in American child-rearing manuals and other prescriptive writings aimed at the middle class.

One of the principal factors that have influenced the middle-class mother's role and the ideology surrounding it is the decline of domestic production. During the **colonial** period when women were responsible for the manufacture and use of a wide variety of household products essential to daily living, women could not devote themselves full-time to motherhood. But in the early nineteenth century, as manufacturing left the home for the factory, middle-class women found themselves "freed up" to spend more time on child care. And before long they were told that such full-time care was essential.

The daily presence or absence of men in the home also shaped the American definition of motherhood. During colonial times when men, women, and children all worked together in or near the household, there were no firm distinctions in parental responsibilities. It was the duty of both parents to rear their children, and fathers were thought to be especially important to a proper religious education. But when a man's work began to take him away from the home for most of the day—an arrangement that began with the onset of industrialization nearly 200 years ago—child-rearing responsibilities fell heavily on the mother. And, once again, middle-class mothers were told that this was in the nature of things.

Household size and its contacts with the outside world have also influenced the mother role. Prior to the nineteenth century, when most households were larger than the nuclear family, when they consisted of more people than just a married couple and their children, the presence of other adults who could take a hand in child care diluted maternal responsibility. Because the household was the site of both life and work, because there was a constant coming and going of people, the mother–child tie was but one of many relationships. As the country industrialized in the nineteenth century, however, the home and the place of work became separate. Women then remained as the only adults in the household and the mother–child relationship was thrown into sharp relief. Mothers took on all the burdens of child care, and their performance of these tasks became a major concern. Why? Because the middle-class mother was advised that she and she alone had the weighty mission of transforming her children into the model citizens of the day.

Fertility rates also influence the mother role, but not always in the way one might expect. It seems logical that the more children a woman has the more she will be defined by her maternal role, for the care and feeding of a large brood demand so much time. But this was not always the case. The emphasis on motherhood in the nineteenth century *increased* as fertility among the middle class *decreased*. One explanation of this anomaly lies in what has been called the "procreative imperative" (Bernard 1974: 7; Harris 1981: 84). This refers to the promotion of cheap population growth by powerful elements in society which benefit from the rearing of "high quality" children. As industrialization continued, the need for skilled labour correspondingly increased. Thus, the reification of maternity during the nineteenth century reflects a dual attempt to stem the falling birth rate in the middle class and increase the quality of children through long-term mother care. The emphasis on maternity was also a way of solving what became known as "the woman question." Once a woman's productive skills were no longer needed, what was to occupy her time? The answer was summarized in a single word: *motherhood.*

This preoccupation with motherhood and the corollary assumption that an exclusive mother–child relationship is both natural and inevitable is by no means universal. Ethno-graphic evidence clearly points out the variability of child care arrangements and the ideologies that justify them. One study of 186 societies from around the world, for example, found that in less than half—46 per cent—mothers were the primary or exclusive caretakers of infants. In another 40 per cent of the societies in the sample, primary care of infants was the responsibility of others, usually siblings. An even more striking finding is that in less than 20 per cent of the societies

are mothers the primary or exclusive caretakers *after* infancy. The authors of this study conclude: "According to our ratings, in the majority of these societies mothers are not the principal caretakers or companions of young children" (Weisner and Gallimore 1977: 170; for information on cross-cultural differences in child-rearing values see Lamber, Hamers, and Frasure-Smith 1979).

How are we to explain this conclusion which contradicts the deeply held modern American belief in the central role of the mother in child care? A number of factors are involved in the explanation, but one clue is that the living arrangement we take so much for granted—the married woman's residence in a nuclear-family household made up exclusively of parents and children—is extremely rare cross-culturally. Such households are found in only 6.1 per cent of the societies listed in the massive Human Relations Area Files, the largest systematic compilation of cross-cultural data in the world (Weisner and Gallimore 1977: 173). So in the majority of societies other kin present in the household relieve the mother of some of the burden of child care.

Another factor that influences the degree of maternal responsibility is the nature and location of women's productive activities. In societies with economies based on hunting and gathering or agriculture, young children typically are taken care of by an older sibling or by their mother or other female relative while these women are gathering or gardening. But in industrial societies where the workplace and the household are separate, production and child care are incompatible. It is in these same societies—ones in which women's activities typically are limited to the domestic sphere—that we find the duties of parenting weighing most heavily on the mother (Brown 1970: 1073–8; Klevana 1980).

A study of mothers in six cultures points up the relative rarity of Western industrial child care patterns. In the American community represented in the study, 92 per cent of the mothers said that they usually or always took care of their babies and children by themselves. The other five societies displayed considerably less maternal responsibility for child care. In the words of the authors: "The mothers of the US sample have a significantly heavier burden (or joy) of baby care than the mothers in any other society." They explain: "Living in nuclear families isolated from their relatives and with all their older children in school most of the day the [American] mother spends more time in charge of both babies and older children than any other group" (Minturn and Lambert 1964: 95–7, 100–1, 112–13).[1]

These studies suggest that the preoccupation of American experts with the mother–child relationship almost certainly is a result of social and economic developments in the United States and Western industrialized societies in general, societies that are characterized more than most others by exclusive mother–child care arrangements. What we have come to think of as inevitable and biologically necessary is in great measure a consequence of our society's particular social and economic system. We are certainly not unique in believing that our brand of mother–child relationship is natural and normal. People in every culture firmly believe that their child-rearing practices stem from nature itself (Berger and Luckmann 1966: 135).[2]

Raise up Your Children Together: The Colonial Period to 1785

A distinct maternal role would have been incompatible with the realities of life during colonial times. The mother–child relationship was enmeshed in the myriad daily tasks women performed for their families' survival. They kept house, tended gardens, raised poultry and cattle, churned milk into butter and cream, butchered livestock, tanned skins, pickled and preserved food, made candles, buttons, soap, beer, and cider, gathered and processed medicinal herbs, and spun and wove wool and cotton for family clothes. The wives of farmers, merchants, and artisans were kept busy with these duties and the wives of merchants and artisans often helped in their husbands' businesses as well. Child rearing therefore largely centred on teaching children the skills needed to keep the domestic economy going. Child rearing was not a *separate* task; it was something that simply took place within the daily round of activities. It is little wonder that in 1790 a New England mother could write that her two children "had grown out of the way" and are "very little troble [sic]" when the younger of the two was still nursing (quoted in Cott 1977: 58; quoted in Bloch 1978b: 242).

The agrarian economy of the seventeenth and eighteenth centuries presented no clearcut separation between the home and the world of work; the boundary between the pre-industrial family and society was permeable. Male and female spheres were contiguous and often overlapped, and the demands of the domestic economy ensured that neither sex was excluded from productive labour. Fathers, moreover, took an active role in child rearing because they worked near the household. Craftsmen and tradesmen usually had their shops at home and farmers spent the long winter months there. The prescriptive literature of the day rarely or imprecisely distinguished between "female" or domestic themes and the "masculine" world of work. The few colonial domestic guides addressed both men and women under the assumption that they worked together in the household (Sklar [1841] 1977; Ariès 1965).

Scholars now agree that the colonial family was not an extended one as was once thought; the best estimates are that at least 80 per cent were nuclear (but not nuclear in the same way as the small isolated nuclear family of the industrial era). The colonial family was nuclear in the formal sense in that parents and children were at its core, but mothers and fathers usually were not the only adults living in the household. Some families took in maiden aunts, or perhaps an aged parent, others had apprentices or journeymen, while domestic servants were common in the households of the prosperous. Moreover, because the typical colonial couple had six to eight offspring, children ranging from infancy to adolescence were commonly found in the same household. Finally, the practice of "putting out" children and taking others in ensured that at least some children were not brought up exclusively by their parents. What is central to the discussion here is that during the colonial period children's relationships were not nearly as mother-centred as they later came to be in the smaller industrial variant of the nuclear family. Given the composition of the colonial American household, children must have received support from and been disciplined by a number of adults—their parents, apprentices or servants, older siblings, and perhaps other relatives as well (Demos 1970; Greven 1973; Bloch 1978b; Degler 1980: 5).

Children themselves were hardly recognized as a separate human category in the American colonies of the seventeenth and eighteenth centuries. "There was little sense that children might somehow be a special group with their own needs and interests and capacities," writes one historian. Virtually all of the child-rearing advice of the day emphasized that children were "meer Loans from God, which He may call for when He pleases." Parents were told to bring up their children as good Christians and discipline was emphasized, but no mention was made of developing the child's personality, intelligence, or individuality. Quite to the contrary, most sermons dwelt on the importance of breaking the child's "will" (Wadsworth [1712] 1972; Mather [1741] 1978; Demos 1970: 57–8).

Some children were "put out" to work as early as six or seven years of age, and those who remained with their parents were expected to help with household chores. Girls as young as six could spin flax and boys helped in farming tasks or fetched wood. Childhood was at best a span of years lasting considerably less than a decade. Even had a family wanted a prolonged, leisurely childhood for its offspring, this was a luxury few could afford (Calhoun [1917] 1960; Demos 1970: 141).

Since infant mortality rates were high, parents expected to lose some of their children. Infant mortality in the seventeenth century, for example, ranged from 10 to 30 per cent in different parts of the colonies; this high rate was acknowledged in the sermons of the day. . . .

Although not a great deal is known about seventeenth- and eighteenth-century advice on child rearing and parental roles—the few manuals of the period were of English origin—we can glean some indication of parental duties in the American colonies from the sermons of the day. In a 1712 sermon entitled "The Well-ordered Family, or, Relative Duties," Benjamin Wadsworth, pastor of the Church of Christ in Boston, distinguished mothers' responsibilities from fathers' when he urged the former to "suckle their children." But then he went on to say: "Having given these hints about Mothers, I may say of Parents (Comprehending both Father and Mother) they should provide for the outward supply and comfort of their Children.

They should nourish and bring them up." In the lengthy discussion of religious instruction and the teaching of good manners and discipline that followed, all of Wadsworth's injunctions were addressed to "Parents." . . .

Colonial clergymen were generally consistent in their sermons treating parental roles. Fathers were to supervise the secular and religious education of their children, teaching them to fear and respect God, but mothers also were advised of their responsibilities in this training. Both parents were admonished to set good examples for their children, and both were held responsible for their children's general well-being. Except for the greater authority bestowed on the father as head of the family, the prescribed roles for parents made no important distinctions on the basis of sex. Similarly, even in funeral sermons for women, there was little mention of motherhood as opposed to the more generalized concept of parenthood. In the few sermons specifically addressed to mothers, the duties laid out were the same as those addressed to both parents, and "none of these were distinctly maternal obligations" (Frost 1973; Masson 1976; Bloch 1978a: 106; Ulrich 1979).[3]

To be sure, women were thought to have special ties to their children during infancy, and infants were described as "hers" by both men and women. The realities of reproduction were certainly recognized, and here we find special advice to mothers. A number of clergy inveighed against the practice of wet nursing, which in fact was quite rare in the American colonies. In describing the duties of a righteous woman, Cotton Mather admonished: "Her care for the Bodies of her Children shows itself in the nursing of them herself. . . . She is not a Dame that shall scorn to nourish in the world, the Children whom she has already nourished in her Womb." Wet nursing was condemned

because it was thought contrary to God's will and dangerous to the physical health of the child, not because it was believed to interfere with the development of a bond between mother and child. Some ministers actually warned women against "excessive fondness" for their children (Mather [1741] 1978: 105; Bloch 1978a: 105; Norton 1980: 90, 94).

Once children reached the age of one or two, when their survival was more certain, all directives regarding child rearing were addressed to *both* parents. Fathers were expected to take a larger role once children reached an educable age. This was particularly true among the Puritans, who believed that the "masculine" qualities of religious understanding and self-discipline were essential in child rearing. One of the few distinctions made in the sermons of the day was in vocational training; this was the responsibility of the parent of the same sex as the child, although sometimes responsibility was removed from the family entirely. Children, particularly boys, often were sent out at age nine or 10 to apprentice in other households, while children from other families were taken in to serve as apprentices (Ryan 1975: 60; Bloch 1978a: 107; 1978b: 242; Kessler-Harris 1981: 29).

A cult of motherhood did not exist because it would have been incongruous in this setting. Women were far too busy to devote long hours to purely maternal duties, and fathers, older siblings, and other adults were also on hand to see to children's needs and discipline. Moreover, because of high mortality rates, a woman was not likely to become obsessive about her children, some of whom would not survive to adulthood. It is not surprising that, as one scholar had remarked of the colonial period, ". . . motherhood was singularly unidealized, usually disregarded as a subject, and even at times actually denigrated." Although women bore and cared for very young children, this role received less emphasis in the prescriptive literature than nearly any other aspect of women's lives. Motherhood, when it was discussed at all, was merged with the parental, domestic, and religious obligations of both sexes (Bloch 1978a: 101, 103–4).

The Transition: 1785–1820

The cult of motherhood is usually associated with the middle and late nineteenth century, but we can see its roots in the prescriptive literature of the very late eighteenth century and the first decades of the nineteenth century. During these years the earliest hints of a special and distinct maternal role began appearing in sermons, domestic guides, medical volumes, and childrearing manuals; for the first time writers began stressing the critical importance of maternal care in early childhood.

It is significant that these years also witnessed the beginnings of the industrial revolution. Markets slowly expanded, agriculture efficiency increased, transportation costs decreased—all developments that led to greater specialization in the economic division of labour. What is centrally important to my argument is that home industry, which typified the colonial period, began to wane. Gradually home manufacture for family use was replaced by standardized factory production for the wider market. The first industry that moved from the home to the factory was textile manufacture, one of women's traditional household tasks. As early as 1807 there were a dozen large textile mills in New England, and by 1810 farm families could buy cloth in village shops and from itinerant peddlers (Smith 1796: 58; Brownlee 1974: 77; Ryan 1975: 91; Cott 1977: 24).

The replacement of homespun by manufactured goods was nonetheless a gradual process.

In 1810, Secretary of Treasury Albert Gallatin estimated that "about two-thirds of the clothing, including . . . house and table linen used by the inhabitants of the United States, who do not reside in cities, is the product of family manufactures." In terms of monetary value this was about ten times the amount produced outside the home. Class membership and place of residence were primary factors in the reduction of home manufacture; more prosperous families, urban dwellers, and those living in the older settled areas of the east led the way in the substitution of store-bought goods for homemade ones (quoted in Degler 1980: 361).

While women's role in the domestic economy gradually diminished, important changes also were taking place in the family. By the late eighteenth century the domestic sphere had begun to contract; there were fewer servants than there had been earlier, the practice of taking in apprentices and journeymen had all but ceased, and with the expansion of economic opportunities fathers were spending less time at home. The physical separation of the home and the place of work already was under way for artisans, merchants, and professionals. But while fewer adults remained in the household, children were now living in it until they reached adolescence. With the demise of the **"putting out" system**, middle-class children were no longer apprenticed to other families and by 1820 they generally lived at home until about the age of 15. The nuclear family itself became smaller as the birth rate declined, particularly in the more densely populated eastern regions of the country. A study of Gloucester, Massachusetts, found that women who married before 1740 had an average of 6.7 children, while those who married after that date averaged 4.6 children. Similarly, by the late eighteenth century in Andover, Massachusetts, women typically had five or six children when their grandmothers had averaged seven or eight (Greven 1970; Bloch 1978a: 114; 1978b: 251; Degler 1980).

Not only was the middle-class household smaller in size but with the onset of industrialization it was no longer a wholly self-contained unit whose members were bound by common tasks. For the first time the place, scope, and pace of men's and women's work began to differ sharply. As a distinct division of labour gradually arose between the home and the world of work, the household's contacts with the outside decreased. By the first decades of the nineteenth century the term *home* had come to be synonymous with *place of retirement or retreat* (Cott 1977).

Ideologies about the nature of children also began to change. By 1800 the Calvinist belief in infant damnation had begun to give way to the Lockean doctrine of the **tabula rasa**, which stressed the lack of innate evil (or good), and the importance of experience in moulding the child. In 1796 one physician wrote, "that any children are born with vicious inclinations, I would not willingly believe." Children, at least middle-class children, began to be seen as individuals. They were no longer viewed as "miniature adults" whose natural inclinations toward evil had to be broken: childhood was becoming a distinct period in the life cycle. The dictum that children were to be treated as individuals with special needs and potentials requiring special nurturing placed a new and heavy responsibility on parents; failure in child rearing could no longer "be blamed on native corruption," explains one historian (Smith 1796: 108; Frost 1973: 87; Slater 1977).

These altered views of children coincided with the decline of the birth rate in the late eighteenth and early nineteenth centuries. The decline in New England, for example, was greatest between 1810 and 1830, and, according to one scholar, during these years "the new sensibility toward children first became highly visible" (Slater 1977: 73). But the lower birth rate, implying fewer children per family and perhaps more attention paid to each child, only partially explains the fundamental change in thinking about children. Both the gradual redefinition of women's role and the redefinition of childhood were linked to larger societal changes affecting middle-class life.

The prescriptive literature on child care in these years was in many ways transitional between the stark dicta of the colonial clergy and the effusive writings of the later nineteenth-century advice givers. Prior to about 1830 such literature did not enjoy mass circulation but appeared in periodical articles, printed sermons, and occasional treatises. All of it came under the rubric "domestic education" and was written by ministers, physicians, and parents for a white, middle- and upper-middle-class audience. Most pertinent here was the transitional image of the role of middle-class mother. Motherhood in fact was being revamped. Duties that had once belonged to both mothers and fathers or to fathers alone were now becoming the near exclusive province of mothers. One historian of the period notes that "now fathers began to recede into the background in writings about the domestic education of children." Treatises on the treatment of childhood diseases, diet, hygiene, and exercise for young children now addressed mothers alone. Some of the medical texts also offered advice on the psychological management of young children, stressing for the first time the importance of the mother's influence during the impressionable years (Slater 1977; Bloch 1978a: 112–13).

Arguments against **wet nursing** also took on a new cast. Whereas earlier commentators condemned the practice for its ill effects on a child's health, writers now added that wet nursing tainted the child's character. One of the earliest references to a special relationship between mother and child appears in this context. A 1798 tract printed in England (but read in America) urged women to nurse their children so as to avoid "the destruction, or at least the diminution of the sympathy between mother and child." Nursing was no longer simply a woman's religious duty but the key to her future happiness as well. "Those children who are neglected by their mothers during their infant years," wrote Dr Hugh Smith in 1796, "forget all duty and affection toward them, when such mothers are in the decline of life." The same author exalted in the joys of breastfeeding: "Tell me you who know the rapturous delight, how complete is the bliss of enfolding in your longing arms the dear, dear fruits of all your pains!" (Smith 1796: 54, 57; quoted in Frost 1973: 72).

Another early guide is Dr William Buchan's *Advice to Mothers*, published in Boston in 1809. The growing importance of the maternal role is obvious here. "The more I reflect on the situation of a mother, the more I am struck by the extent of her powers," wrote Dr Buchan. Clearly not all mothers are equal: "By a mother I do not mean the woman who merely brings a child into the world, but her who faithfully discharges the duties of a parent—whose chief concern is the well-being of her infant." But mothers walked a narrow line between neglect and overindulgence. "The obvious paths of nature are alike forsaken by the woman who gives up the care of her infant to a hireling . . . who neglects her duties as a mother; and by her who carries these duties to excess; who makes an idol of her child" (Buchan [1809] 1972: 3, 77). This is the first mention of a theme that was to be heard over and over again in the prescriptive writings of the nineteenth and much of the twentieth centuries. Mothers must be ever on

guard to do their job properly—always lurking in the background of the advice books were the pitiful figures of mothers who had failed, mothers who had not taken their duties seriously, or mothers who had performed them with excessive zeal. . . .

Emphasis on the mother role was not limited to advice manuals. Between 1800 and 1820 a new theme appeared in many New England sermons: mothers are more important than fathers in shaping "the tastes, sentiments, and habits of children." One New Hampshire minister proclaimed in 1806: "Weighty beyond expression is the charge devolved to the female parent. It is not within the province of human wisdom to calculate all the happy consequences resulting from the persevering assiduity of mothers." While sermons of the day did not deny all paternal responsibility, they made clear that raising children was a specialized domestic activity that was largely the province of mothers. As one scholar of the period notes, this "emphasis departed from (and undermined) the patriarchal family ideal in which the mother, while entrusted with the physical care of her children, let their religious, moral, and intellectual guidance to her husband" (quoted in Cott 1977: 86; quoted in Bloch 1978a: 112).

Although little is known about the actual childrearing practices in the early nineteenth century, it is clear that the aim of the advice manuals and the sermons dealing with the topic was to increase the amount of time and attention mothers devoted to infants and small children. For the first time in American history the care of young children was viewed as a full-time task, as a distinct profession requiring special knowledge. What had once been done according to tradition now demanded proper study. Even arguments favouring women's education now came to be couched in terms of the woman's role as mother; women were to be educated because the formation of the future citizens of the republic lay in their hands (Sicherman 1975: 496). It is ironic, indeed, but by no means coincidental, that as their sphere narrowed and became more isolated, middle-class women were told that their sphere's importance to the future of the new nation was boundless.

Historian Ruth H. Bloch notes that economic factors exercised a "push–pull" effect on child-rearing responsibilities. As the domestic production of middle-class mothers began to wane and their domestic work lost its commercial value, fathers began to spend more and more time working outside the home, as did other adults who had once resided in the household (Bloch 1978b: 250). Women, left alone at home with their children, who were now living there until adolescence, began to assume almost complete responsibility for child care. The prescriptive literature, with its newly expanded definition of motherhood, was thus a response to these structural changes in society. In essence, as the female role in domestic production declined, the middle-class woman was told to focus on reproduction.

Motherhood, A Fearful Responsibility: 1820–70

The concept of the mother role which prevailed from the late eighteenth century to about 1820 was, in the words of one historian, "a rare and subdued hint of the extravagant celebration of motherhood to come" (Abbott 1833: 162; Calhoun [1918] 1960: 52; Ryan 1975: 126). Beginning in the 1820s and gaining momentum in the 1830s and 1840s, a flood of manuals and periodical articles gave advice on the maternal role, exulted in the joys of motherhood, and told women that good mothering was not only the key to their own and their children's happiness but crucial to the nation's destiny as well.

This period between 1820 and 1860 was one of rapid industrialization; industrial production in fact doubled every decade. . . . The most salient change occurring during these years was the eventual demise of the self-sufficient household. The growth of industry, technological advances, improvements in transportation, and the increasing specialization of agriculture made more goods available, and the household became more and more reliant on the market to meet its needs. In simple terms, the period between 1820 and 1860 witnessed the substitution of store-bought goods for home-manufactured goods, and this development had a profound impact on women's work. Even as early as the 1820s women's domestic production had diminished in scope and variety to the extent that they were left with only a residue of their former household duties. In New England by 1830 home spinning and weaving were largely replaced by manufactured textiles, and by mid-century women's productive skills had become even more superfluous; butter, candles, soap, medicine, buttons, and cloth were widely available in stores. By 1860 women's contribution to household production continued to a significant extent only in remote frontier regions. The noted feminist and abolitionist Sarah Grimké remarked on the decline of home manufacture in 1838: "When all manufactures were domestic, then the domestic function might well consume all the time of a very able-bodied woman. But nowadays . . . when so much of woman's work is done by the butcher and the baker, by the tailor and the cook, and the gas maker . . . you see how much of woman's time is left for other functions" (Cott 1977; Ehrenreich and English 1978; quoted in Degler 1980).

The removal of production from the home to the factory led to the breakdown of the once close relationship between the household and the business of society. For the first time "life," that is, the home, was divided from "work." Not only had the two spheres become separate, they were now seen as incompatible; the home was a retreat from the competitive world of commerce and industry, a place of warmth and respite where moral values prevailed. The business of the world no longer took place at home.

These economic and social developments were of course not unique to the United States. A similar series of events occurred in England in the seventeenth century. There, in the words of one scholar of the period, "the old familial economic partnership of husband and wife was being undermined. The wife was being driven from her productive role. The concept of the husband supporting his family was replacing mutuality in earning power . . . [the wife's] place might still be in the home, but her husband was no longer an integral part of it" (Thompson 1974: 75).

The American household continued to shrink throughout the nineteenth century. By 1850 the ancillary household members had moved out—an unmarried sister might be teaching school in town and greater numbers of domestic servants were leaving the middle-class household to take factory jobs. . . . Part of this decrease, however, resulted from a falling birth rate.

Ideas about the nature of children continued to evolve. The neutral *tabula rasa* of the first decades of the nineteenth century was supplanted by the idea of the "sweet angels of the Romantic era." After 1830 children were routinely depicted as beings of great purity and innocence. They were naturally close to God and their virtuous proclivities had only to be gently moulded to ensure eternal salvation.

Closely allied with this idealized image of the young was the conviction that *mothers and mothers alone* had the power to transform malleable infants into moral, productive adults. For this reason many warned against the dangers of hiring nurses, for even the best nurse was never an adequate substitute for the mother herself. Only a mother's care and influence, not that of fathers, older siblings, relatives, or servants, could fulfill the special physical and spiritual needs of the growing child. Motherhood had not only become a career-like responsibility but the responsibility had grown longer and longer in duration. By the mid-nineteenth century middle-class children remained at home until well into adolescence, and throughout the century there was a tendency to prolong dependence. Children left home at a later and later age (Slater 1977; Wishy 1968: 40; Degler 1980: 69).

Some scholars claim that the nineteenth century's concern with the child as an individual and with proper child-rearing methods was the result of a decline in infant mortality. Parents, they argue, became more certain that their children would grow to adulthood and so were willing to invest more time and energy in them. Historian Carl Degler faults this thesis, citing data that suggests that infant mortality did not decline. In fact, infant mortality might even have been higher than the official statistics indicate with the likelihood of a high mortality rate among unreported births. One could argue on this basis that at least part of the growing concern for the child was because infant mortality rates did remain so high. Catherine Beecher and other manual writers contended that proper child care would help to prevent the deaths of infants and young children (Beecher [1841] 1977; Degler 1980: 72–3).

Population growth from reproduction did in fact decline steadily as the birth rate fell throughout the nineteenth century. By 1850 the average white woman was bearing only half as many children as her grandmother had. Even more striking is the 50 per cent decline in the completed fertility rate for the century as a whole; it fell from 7.04 children per white woman in 1800 to 3.56 in 1900. The question, of course, is why did women bear fewer children? In the words of anthropologist Marvin Harris, in an industrializing, urbanizing society children "tend to cost more and to be economically less valuable to their parents than children on farms" (Degler 1980: 181; Kessler-Harris 1981: 34; Harris 1981: 81).

Children in agrarian societies cost relatively little to raise and they help out by doing a variety of tasks even when they are young. But in cities the expense of rearing children increases as does their period of dependency; most or all of the items a child needs must be purchased, and schooling is required before the child can become economically independent. In essence, urban children contribute less and cost more. Therefore, as the nineteenth century progressed, the shift in the costs and benefits of having children particularly affected the middle class, whose children required longer and longer periods of socialization before they could make it on their own outside the home. The rearing of "quality" children, children who enjoyed a long period of dependency while they were schooled to take their "rightful" position in society, was an ever more costly process. Is it any wonder then that the average middle-class family had fewer and fewer children as the century progressed?

The immense outpouring of advice manuals and other prescriptive writings after 1830 cannot be adequately explained by continued high levels of infant mortality or even by the fact that women were having fewer children and simply had the time to make a greater investment in each one. Another factor in the advice-giving boom was the nation's slowly growing need for children who would be reared to become professionals or to take the business and management positions being created by the industrializing process. What better and cheaper way to accomplish this than by urging middle-class women to devote many years and large quantities of their (unpaid) time and energy to nurturing the future captains of business and industry?

Another key to understanding the paeans to motherhood is the falling fertility rate of the middle class. But the relationship is by no means a simple one. It seems logical that if women had been taking these paeans seriously they would have had more rather than fewer children, and it is of course naïve to assume that fertility decisions are made on the basis of advice books. I believe the line between the two is as follows: as fertility declined among the white middle class, there was growing alarm in certain quarters. Where were the future leaders in business and industry to come from? Who was going to manage the nation's burgeoning industries? At a time when the fertility of the non-white and the foreign-born was higher than that of native-born whites, the country's elite feared that the "backbone" of the nation was being diluted by "lesser types." The glorification of maternity which was directed at potential mothers of the "backbone," was an attempt, albeit an unsuccessful one, to encourage their reproductive activity.[4]

Scholars are not certain just how people in the nineteenth century controlled their fertility, but there is evidence that American women began practising abortion more frequently after 1840. One historian estimates one abortion for every 25 or 30 live births during the first decades of the century, a proportion that rose to about one in every five or six live births during the 1850s and 1860s. Most contemporary physicians agreed that the primary motive for abortion was control of family size, and they cited as evidence the fact that by far the largest group practising abortion was married women. It is significant that prior to the nineteenth century there were no laws prohibiting abortion during the first few months of pregnancy. The procedure was not illegal until "quickening," that is, until the first movements of the fetus are felt at about four months. The first laws banning abortion were passed between 1821 and 1841; during those two decades 10 states and one territory specifically outlawed its practice. By the time of the Civil War nearly every state had laws prohibiting abortion at all stages of fetal development (Gordon 1977: 52, 57n; Mohr 1978: 50, 20).

I do not think that mere coincidence accounts for concern about the falling birth rate, laws banning abortion, and the publication of numerous child care manuals and articles lauding the maternal role, all appearing at roughly the same time. The outpourings of the advice givers reflected the wider anxiety about middle-class women's declining fertility and sought to counteract it by dwelling on the joys of motherhood for their white, middle-class audience.

The contraction of women's productive activities in the now smaller and more isolated nuclear household provided the necessary setting for this expanding emphasis on the mother role. There was now a sizeable, literate audience of homebound women who could be advised of the importance of motherhood and given suggestions of time-consuming methods for its proper discharge. In short, as the domestic sphere contracted and middle-class women found their lives increasingly centred around their husbands and children, they were advised of the gravity of their redefined role.

What higher calling was there than shaping the future leaders of the nation?

Maternal Ideals

A number of recurrent themes in nineteenth-century child-rearing manuals and periodical articles were only weakly developed or were entirely absent from the prescriptive writings of an earlier era. Foremost among these are that child care is the exclusive province of women, that motherhood is their *primary* function, and that mothers, and mothers alone, are responsible for their children's character development and future success or failure. By the 1830s motherhood had been transformed into a mission so that "the entire burden of the child's well-being in this life and the next" was in its mother's hands (*The Ladies' Museum* 1825; Sunley 1963: 152). These themes, moreover, were not limited to child-rearing manuals. Popular novels, poems, and biographies of famous men all stressed the important role of the mother in shaping her child's fate. Middle-class women were told that they had it in their power to produce joy or misery, depending on how they performed their parental duties. These sentiments were echoed in a burgeoning literature on "female character" which claimed that women were innately nurturant, domestic, and selfless, all qualities that made them "naturals" at child rearing.

One of the most striking features of the child-rearing advice of the mid-nineteenth century is the disappearance of references to fathers. While some earlier tracts were addressed exclusively to mothers, most were written for "parents," and there was even an occasional "advice to fathers" manual. This shift from *parental* to *maternal* responsibility is evident in Philip Greven's collection of sermons, treatises, and other sources of advice on child rearing dating from 1628 to 1861 (Greven 1973). The first eight excerpts, originally published between 1629 and 1814, are all addressed to "parents." It is not until John Abbott's 1833 essay "On the Mother's Role in Education" that the maternal role is highlighted and mothers are given the primary responsibility for child care.

Mothers were offered abundant advice on the feeding, dressing, washing, and general management of infants and young children. They were told how to deal with teething, toilet training, masturbation, and childhood diseases. But the mother's physical care of her children was a minor task compared to her job of socializing them. Women were advised that their every thought and gesture, no matter how seemingly inconsequential, carried a message to the child. Women were to be ever on their guard lest they impede their offspring's moral development.

Many writers stressed the sentimental benefits of an activity that received no material rewards. "How entire and perfect is the dominion over the unformed character of your infant. Write what you will, upon the printless tablet, with your wand of love," wrote Mrs Sigourney in *Letters to Mothers* (1838).

Women's education is justified, some advice givers claimed, because of women's influence on the next generation. *Maternal* education, however, was what they really sought. In an 1845 tome, for example, Edward Mansfield cited three reasons for educating women: "that they should as *mothers*, be the fit teachers of infant men. That they should be the fit teachers of American men. That they should be the fit teachers of Christian men" (Mansfield 1845: 105; emphasis in original).

Motherhood, as depicted in the prescriptive writings of the mid-nineteenth century, was a full-time occupation demanding time-consuming unpaid labour. "It truly requires all the affection of even a fond mother to administer dutifully to the numerous wants of a young child," wrote William Dewees. Mrs Sigourney agreed. She saw a mother as "a sentinel who should never sleep at her post," recommending that women get household help to perform manual tasks so that the mother "may be able to become the constant directress of her children." There is no question that mothering was work; infants should be fed on demand, and toilet training and "moral education" should begin at a few months of age. Cleanliness was stressed and clothes were to be washed often and changed as soon as they got dirty. Furthermore, the good mother would keep careful records of her children's behaviour and development. The Reverend Abbott told mothers to "study their duty," while Mrs Sigourney urged women to "study night and day the science that promotes the welfare of our infant" (Abbott 1833: 169; Sigourney 1838: 28, 82, 87; Dewees 1847: 64–5).

Mothers, according to the advice givers, were perfectly suited to care for their children; no one else could do the job as well or, one might add, as cheaply. As far as the mother's duties permitted, she was to "take the entire care of her own child," advised the popular domestic writer, Lydia Maria Child. During the first "sacred" year, concurred Mrs Sigourney, "trust not your treasure too much to the charge of hirelings. Have it under your superintendence night and day. The duty of your office admits of no substitute." But what of other family members? Are they of no help? Yes: "brothers and sisters, the father, all perform their part, but the mother does the most," opined the author of a *Parents Magazine* article, who went on to issue a stern warning. Children whose mothers did not "take the entire care of them" faced real danger; a mother "cannot be long relieved without hazard or exchanged without loss"

(Child [1831] 1972: 4; Sigourney 1838: 16, 32, 87; *Parents Magazine* 1841: 156).

A corollary of the focus on mothers was the disappearance of fathers from the child-rearing manuals of the nineteenth century. Advice books assumed that children spent most of their time with their mothers, not their fathers, even though by law and custom final authority was patriarchal. Paternal responsibilities were rarely spelled out. For example, in answering the question "Is there nothing for fathers to do?" Reverend Abbott responded that there are many paternal duties "which will require time and care." But the only duties he actually stipulated for fathers were "to lead their families to God" and to teach their children to "honour" their mother. Although some advice givers saw fathers as the primary disciplinarians in the family, others urged mothers to punish their children's misbehaviour before fathers returned home in the evening. Even daily prayers, once led by the father as head of the household, had now become the province of the mother (Abbott 1833: 155–6).

The occasional references to fathers in the prescriptive writings of the day either remarked on their sovereignty in the home or noted their real responsibilities outside of it. A father's duties, advised the *Ladies' Companion*, are "the acquisitions of wealth, the advancement of his children in worldly honour—these are his self-imposed tasks."

By the mid-nineteenth century a gooey sentimentality had come to distinguish motherhood from fatherhood. A sample from a "ladies' magazine" of the day reveals the tone: "Is there a feeling that activates the human heart so powerful as that of maternal affection? Who but women can feel the tender sensation so strong? The father, indeed, may press his lovely infant to his manly heart, but does it thrill with those feelings which irresistibly overcome the mother?" (*Ladies' Literary Cabinet* 1822: 5).

These patterns of ideological change are also apparent in an analysis of sixteenth- to nineteenth-century child-rearing responsibilities in England. English manuals of the sixteenth and seventeenth centuries told parents to "co-rear" their children: eighteenth-century manuals depicted mothers as the primary child rearers but expressed some anxiety about this; by the nineteenth century mothers were the primary rearers "without anxiety" (Stewart, Winter, and Jones 1975: 701).

In America by mid-century good mothering was not only essential to the well-being and future of the child but the lack of such exclusive care was considered a threat to the very moral fibre of the nation. "The destiny of a nation is shaped by its character," Reverend Beckwith proclaimed, "and that character . . . will ever be found to be molded chiefly by maternal hands." "When our land is filled with pious and patriotic mothers, then will it be filled with virtuous and patriotic men," agreed Reverend Abbott. But it is clear that women's contribution to the young republic was to be indirect. In the words of Daniel Webster: "It is by promulgation of sound morals in the community, and more especially by the training and instruction of the young that woman performs her part toward the preservation of a free government . . ." (Abbott 1833: 153; Beckwith 1850: 4; quoted in Kuhn 1947: 34).[5] As part of the effort to convince middle-class women of their crucial role in the nation's destiny—a role wholly dependent on the diligent performance of their maternal duties—moral educators frequently cited the mothers of famous men.

Many advice writers dwelt long and graphically on the general evils that sprang from poor mothering. An 1841 issue of *Parents Magazine* contained a case study of a convict, whose life of crime was analyzed in the following terms: "His mother, although hopefully pious, never prayed with him in private. . . . There was no maternal association in the place of their residence." Then a warning was issued: "Reader, are you a parent? . . . *Train up a child in the way he should go.*" Even such cataclysms as the French Revolution, with its "atheism, licentiousness, and intemperance," could be avoided by "seizing upon the infant mind and training it up under moral and religious influence," suggested another author in the same magazine. Mrs Elizabeth Hall, writing in *The Mother's Assistant,* made the point succinctly: "Perhaps there is no proposition that is so hackneyed, and at the same time so little understood, as that women are the prime cause of all the good and evil in human actions. . . . Yes, mothers, in a certain sense the destiny of a redeemed world is put into your hands" (Hall 1849: 25; quoted in Kuhn 1947: 67; emphasis in original). Mothers were given a strong message. They were the potential source of *both* evil and good in the world, so that they had best be mindful of the proper performance of their maternal duties.

Many authors pointed out that while women should not go out into the world, the mother role, because of its far-reaching influence, still gave women a lofty position in society. "Though she may not teach from the portico nor thunder from the forum . . . she may form and send forth the sages that shall govern and renovate the world," wrote Catherine Beecher, the popular domestic educator. "The patriotism of women," Mrs Sigourney agreed, "is not to thunder in senates"—it is to be expressed in the "office of maternal teacher." A writer in *Ladies' Magazine* noted that a mother's influence is "unseen, unfelt," but through it "she is forming the future patriot, statesman, or enemy of his country; more than this she is sowing the seeds of virtue or vice which will fit him for Heaven or for eternal misery" (Beecher 1829: 54; Sigourney 1838: 13, 16; *Ladies' Magazine* 1840: 246).

The rewards of motherhood were extravagantly described by the advice givers. To wit: "My friends," wrote Mrs Sigourney, "if in becoming a mother, you have reached the climax of your happiness, you have also taken a higher place on the scale of being." Since children have the power to change their mothers for the better and bring them joy, no matter how difficult the tasks of motherhood, a mother "would willingly have endured a thousandfold for such a payment." Children also could provide their mothers with eternal salvation. "Does not the little cherub in his way guide you to heaven, marking the pathway by the flowers he scatters as he goes?" queried Mrs Child. There was no doubt that children were the keys to feminine fulfillment. The love of children, proclaimed an editorial in *Godey's Lady's Book,* "is as necessary to a woman's perfect development, as the sunshine and the rain are to the health and beauty of the flowers." Not only was a woman's entire happiness dependent on her civilizing task, her very identity was derived from it. "A woman is nobody. A wife is everything . . . and a mother is, next to God, all powerful," trumpeted a writer in a Philadelphia newspaper at mid-century (quoted in Calhoun [1918] 1960: 84–5; Child [1831] 1972: 9; Sigourney 1838: 2, 24; *Godey's Lady's Book* 1860: 272).

This preoccupation with motherhood is baffling unless firmly set within its larger social and economic context. The demise of the self-contained household economy, the isolation of a much reduced living unit, the segregation of the home from the workplace, and the resultant segregation of daily life into male and female spheres were all elements in the stage setting in which this ideology emerged. These factors, rather than any strong domestic propensity in women, explain the overweening emphasis on the mother role. On this point I take issue with the historian Carl Degler, who writes that since only women bore and could feed children in the early years, it is not surprising that "the ideology of domesticity stressed that women's destiny was motherhood." But hadn't women always borne and nursed children? Why does this ideology appear in full strength only after 1820? In the words of another historian, Mary Ryan, why for the first time was "childhood socialization, and not merely the physical care of infants . . . subsumed under the category of motherhood"? Why, asks another student of the subject, if there had always been mothers, had motherhood just been invented? The answer lies in the structural changes occurring in nineteenth-century society, changes that led to the increased seclusion of women and children in the home, the decreasing burden of household manufacture, the need for "high quality" children, and the growing concern with the declining birth rate of the white middle class. These changes more than adequately explain why motherhood, as never before, "stood out as a discrete task" (Ryan 1975: 84; Cott 1977: 84; Degler 1980; Dally 1982: 17).

● Notes

1. This study does not measure the actual amount of time mothers spent with their infants, only whether mothers had primary or exclusive care of them.
2. This is what has been called "the most important confidence trick that society plays on the individual—to make appear as necessary what is in fact a bundle of contingencies."
3. I am indebted to Bloch's two articles for the sources contained in this and the next section of the chapter. They are the most thorough research on the prescriptive literature of the colonial period and early nineteenth century that I have found.
4. Although the fear of "race suicide" is usually associated with the very late nineteenth and early twentieth centuries and with the figure of Theodore Roosevelt, there were in fact references to it prior to the Civil War. See L. Gordon, *Woman's Body, Woman's Right* (New York, 1977), Ch. 7, and A.W. Calhoun, *A Social History of the American Family: Since the Civil War* (New York, [1919] 1960), Ch. 11.
5. Somewhat later the British sociologist Herbert Spencer, who was widely read in the United States, propounded a similar idea when he wrote that "Children . . . had to be long nurtured by female parents" for "social progress" to take place (quoted in L. Duffin, "Prisoners of Progress: Women and Evolution," in *The Nineteenth Century Woman*, eds S. Delmot and L. Duffin [New York, 1978], 78).

● References

Abbott, Rev. J.S.C. 1833. *The Mother at Home* (New York: American Tract Society).

Ariès, P. 1965. *Centuries of Childhood* (New York: Vintage).

Beckwith, G.C. 1850. "The Fate of Nations Dependent on Mothers," *The Mother's Assistant* 15: 4.

Beecher, C. 1829. *Suggestions Respecting Improvements in Education* (New York: Hartford, Packard, and Butler).

——. [1841] 1977. *A Treatise on Domestic Economy* (New York: Schocken).

Berger, P.L., and T. Luckmann. 1966. *The Social Construction of Reality* (New York: Doubleday).

Bernard, J. 1974. *The Future of Motherhood* (New York: Penguin).

Bloch, R.H. 1978a. "American Feminine Ideals in Transition: The Rise of the Moral Mother, 1785–1815," *Feminist Studies* 4: 106.

——. 1978b. "Untangling the Roots of Modern Sex Roles: A Survey of Four Centuries of Change," *Signs* 4: 242.

Brown, J.K. 1970. "A Note on the Division of Labor by Sex," *American Anthropologist* 72: 1073–8.

Brownlee, W.E. 1974. *Dynamics of Ascent: A History of the American Economy* (New York: Alfred A. Knopf).

Buchan, W. [1809] 1972. *Advice to Mothers*, reprinted in *The American Physician and Child Rearing: Two Guides 1809–1894* (New York: Arno Press).

Calhoun, A.W. [1917] 1960. *A Social History of the American Family: The Colonial Period* (New York: Barnes and Noble).

———. [1918] 1960. *A Social History of the American Family: From Independence through the Civil War* (New York: Barnes and Noble).

Child, L.M. [1831] 1972. *The Mother's Book* (New York: Arno Press).

Cott, N.F. 1977. *The Bonds of Womanhood: "Woman's Sphere" in New England, 1780–1835* (New Haven: Yale University Press).

Dally, A. 1982. *Inventing Motherhood* (London: Burnett Books Ltd.).

Degler, C.N. 1980. *At Odds: Women and the Family in America from the Revolution to the Present* (New York: Oxford University Press).

Demos, J. 1970. *A Little Commonwealth: Family Life in Plymouth Colony* (New York: Oxford University Press).

Dewees, W. 1847. *A Treatise on the Physical and Medical Treatment of Children*, 10th edn (Philadelphia: Blanchard and Lea).

Ehrenreich, B., and D. English. 1978. *For Her Own Good: 150 Years of the Experts' Advice to Women* (New York: Anchor).

Frost, J.W. 1973. *The Quaker Family in Colonial America: A Portrait of the Society of Friends* (New York: St Martin's Press).

Gordon, L. 1977. *Woman's Body, Woman's Right* (New York: Penguin).

Greven, Jr, P.J. 1970. *Four Generations: Population, Land, and Family in Colonial Andover, Massachusetts* (Ithaca, NY: Cornell University Press).

———. 1973. *Child Rearing Concepts, 1628–1861* (Itasca, IL: Peacock).

Hall, E.S. 1849. "A Mother's Influence," *The Mother's Assistant* 1: 25.

Harris, M. 1981. *America Now: The Anthropology of a Changing Culture* (New York: Simon and Schuster).

Kessler-Harris, A. 1981. *Women Have Always Worked* (Westbury, NY: The Feminist Press).

Klevana, W.M. 1980. "Does Labor Time Increase with Industrialization? A Survey of Time Allocation Studies," *Current Anthropology* 21: 279–98.

Kuhn, A.L. 1947. *The Mother's Role in Childhood Education: New England Concepts 1830–1860* (New Haven: Yale University Press).

Ladies' Literary Cabinet. 1822. 5 (Jan.): 5. *Ladies' Magazine*. 1840. "Influence of Women—Past and Present," 13: 246.

The Ladies' Museum. 1825. "Maternity" 1 (Sept.): 31.

Lamber, W.E., J.F. Hamers, and N. Frasure-Smith. 1979. *Child Rearing Values: A Cross-national Study* (New York).

Mansfield, E. 1845. *The Legal Rights, Liabilities, and Duties of Women* (Salem, MA: John P. Jewett).

Masson, M.W. 1976. "The Typology of the Female as a Model for the Regenerate: Puritan Teaching, 1690–1730," *Signs* 2: 304–15.

Mather, C. [1741] 1978. *Ornaments of the Daughters of Zion*, 3rd edn (Delmar, NY: Scholars Facsimiles and Reprints).

Minturn, L., and W.W. Lambert. 1964. *Mothers of Six Cultures* (New York: John Wiley).

Mohr, J.C. 1978. *Abortion in America: The Origins and Evolution of National Policy 1800–1900* (New York: Oxford University Press).

Norton, M.B. 1980. *Liberty's Daughters: The Revolutionary Experience of American Women* (Boston: Houghton Mifflin).

Parents Magazine. 1841. "The Responsibility of Mothers," 1 (Mar.): 156.

Ryan, M.P. 1975. *Womanhood in America: From Colonial Times to the Present* (New York: New Viewpoints).

Sicherman, B. 1975. "American History," *Signs* 1: 461–85.

Sigourney. 1838. *Letters to Mothers* (Hartford: Hudson and Skinner).

Sklar, K.K. [1841] 1977. "Introduction," in C.E. Beecher, *A Treatise on Domestic Economy* (New York: Schocken).

Slater, P.G. 1977. *Children in the New England Mind* (Hamden, CN: Archon).

Smith, H. 1796. *Letters to Married Women on Nursing and the Management of Children*, 2nd edn (Philadelphia: Mathew Carey).

Stewart, A.J., D.G. Winter, and A.D. Jones. 1975. "Coding Categories for the Study of Child Rearing from Historical Sources," *Journal of Interdisciplinary History* 5: 701.

Sunley, R. 1963. "Early Nineteenth Century American Literature on Child Rearing," in *Childhood in Contemporary Cultures*, eds M. Mead and M. Wolfenstein (Chicago: University of Chicago Press).

Thompson, R. 1974. *Women in Stuart England and America* (Boston: Routledge & Kegan Paul).

Ulrich, L.T. 1979. "Virtuous Women Found: New England Ministerial Literature, 1668–1735," in *A Heritage of Her Own*, eds N.F. Cott and E.H. Pleck (New York: Touchstone).

Wadsworth, B. [1712] 1972. "The Well-ordered Family, or, Relative Duties," in *The Colonial American Family: Collected Essays* (New York: Arno).

Weisner, T., and R. Gallimore. 1977. "My Brother's Keeper: Child and Sibling Caretaking," *Current Anthropology* 18.

Wishy, B. 1968. *The Child and the Republic: The Dawn of Modern American Child Nurture* (Philadelphia: University of Philadelphia Press).

Chapter 7

Some important social trends in personal life that developed in the nineteenth century continued in the early decades of the twentieth century (e.g., the decline in birth rates and the organized campaigns for women's rights). The belief that marriage should be founded on love was growing in popularity before the twentieth century as well. But early in that century the imagery associated with marriage became even more positive. Amidst growing concern about "the family," given the decline in birth rates among middle-class Americans and rising rates of separation and divorce, writers and researchers in the United States began to define the sexual pleasure of both husbands and wives as essential to the health of any marriage. As Hollywood simultaneously glorified romantic relationships between men and women, marriage came to represent the promise of emotional and sexual happiness, as well as steadfast love.

Also new in the early twentieth century was the notion that heterosexuality signified one's personal identity. This idea took on special significance for men. As fears that newly common white-collar jobs threatened the masculinity of the men doing them, active heterosexuality came to signify a man's masculinity.

The 1950s was another decade in which people's sexual behaviour was interpreted as evidence of their identity and moral character. But the 1950s was unique as a decade in the history of family life, for the most part. In it, long-term trends like the fall in birth rates were reversed; age at marriage also fell and nearly every adult married. Canadians and Americans embraced family life and domestic roles—expecting to find happiness in them—in a way they never had before.

In her book *The Trouble with Normal*, Mary Louise Adams explores the ways heterosexuality was constructed and promoted as the natural and only "normal" form of sexual expression in the post–World War II period in Canada. Adams examines popular post-war discourses that aimed to define what constituted normal sexual expression, and thus (indirectly) normal sexual identity. Her work is informed by the work of Michel Foucault, who argued that public discourses about sexuality are an important means by which powerful groups exert power over individuals. They do so, according to Foucault, when they so firmly establish what is "normal" that people take measures to regulate their behaviour in order to conform. While Adams's book is mostly about sexuality, this chapter highlights the tremendous symbolic importance that the heterosexual nuclear family assumed during the Cold War of the 1950s. The rhetoric about family that Adams describes was not confined to the 1950s, however. Students born much later than that period will recognize some of the same ideas coming from the mouths of politicians and other public figures today.

Sexuality and the Post-war Domestic "Revival"

Mary Louise Adams

In present-day popular culture, the post-war period is routinely depicted by a predictable mix of Ozzie and Harriet, suburban bungalows, and rock 'n' roll teen culture. On the one hand, the period has come to represent a lost era of family values for which many now yearn; on the other hand, it is seen as a time of unceasing conformity, repression, and blandness, broken only by the tyrannies of McCarthyist anti-Communism. In Canada, any of a number of recent studies—Doug Owram's *Born at the Right Time*, Franca Iacovetta's *Such Hardworking People*, and Reg Whitaker and Gary Marcuse's *Cold War Canada*, among others—is capable of shattering these simplistic views.[1] While the post-war period was a time when social conformity was valued by many and when popular culture frequently traded in images of smiling suburban housewives, it was also a period that saw tremendous changes on the social landscape—such as a steady increase in the numbers of working women and huge increases in the numbers of immigrants coming to Canada from southern and eastern European countries.

Canadian sociologists and historians have dealt constructively with this contradictory image, avoiding the false polarization that has characterized some post-war scholarship in the United States: Was the period a time of repression or a time of social change? In her recent anthology *Not June Cleaver*, American historian Joanne Meyerowitz takes other feminist historians to task for focusing too much attention on the conservatism of the post-war years and not enough on women's resistance. Her argument seems to be directed primarily at Elaine Tyler May's book, *Homeward Bound*, which discusses the links between United States foreign policy during the Cold War and prevailing ideologies of gender and domesticity. While recognizing the era's conservatism, Meyerowitz claims that the emphasis on the constraints women encountered in the period "tends to downplay women's agency and to portray women primarily as victims. It obscures

the complexity of post-war culture and the significant social and economic changes of the post-war era . . . the sustained focus on the white middle-class domestic ideal . . . sometimes renders other ideals and other women invisible."[2] But surely it is not a matter of either/or, or that researchers need to give priority to one of these projects over the other. The point of studying dominant cultural discourses—mainstream ideals—as May has done, is that we all have to negotiate them, whether we subscribe to them, are marginalized by them, or actively resist them. There can be no understanding of agency—the resistance Meyerowitz wants to reclaim—without an understanding of the context within which it occurs.

Domesticity and Security in Post-war Canada

While the term *post-war* is a convenient way of marking a time period, it cannot be emphasized enough that it refers to the specific social configurations that arose as six years of war came to an end. So, for instance, when we talk about post-war prosperity we need to remember that this prosperity arose in the wake of tremendous loss and disruption.

In 1945, the Canadian domestic economy underwent substantial change as both public and private sectors shifted production and services away from military requirements. While peace was obviously welcomed, many Canadians feared the type of economic downturn that had followed the First World War: Would the economy collapse with the end of military production? Such post-war concerns about economic security were complicated by the emotional and social upheavals that resulted from attempts to reintegrate into civilian life the million men and women who had been in the armed forces. More than 40,000

Canadians had been killed during the war, and thousands more had been injured either physically or mentally.[3] It is not surprising, then, that homecomings did not always provide a happy ending to long and difficult separations.

As victory celebrations subsided, Canadians struggled with the changes the war had brought to the home front. War work had introduced thousands of women and teenagers to relatively lucrative industrial jobs. Many children and teenagers had been free of adult supervision, with fathers in the military and mothers doing war work. Workers of all ages who had migrated to cities in search of wartime jobs experienced for the first time the freedom of living in communities away from their relatives. Further demographic changes occurred as tens of thousands of immigrants and refugees arrived from Europe, many from countries and ethnic/religious backgrounds not widely represented (or forcefully kept out) in previous waves of immigration: Jews, Czechs, Poles, Hungarians, Ukrainians, Russians, Yugoslavians, Italians. The degree to which these and other social changes would, or could, be integrated into the fabric of post-war life was open to considerable debate—as, for instance, in the widespread discussions about the place and acceptability of married women workers in the peacetime labour market, or those about the desirability of having Jews and southern and eastern Europeans enter the country.[4]

According to historian Doug Owram, the physical and emotional disruptions caused by the war, and the significant social changes it motivated, oriented Canadians toward home, family, and stability to a degree unparalleled in other historical periods in this country. Owram suggests that giving precedence to home and family was a primary value of the post-war era and is central to any understanding of the economy, gender relations, politics,

or other aspects of those years.[5] As represented by married, middle-class, heterosexual couples and their legitimate offspring, the ideal family was at once seen as a source of affectional relationships, the basis of a consumer economy, a defence against Communism, and a salient metaphor for various forms of social organization, from the nation to the high-school class. In the 1940s and 1950s, writes Joy Parr, "Domestic metaphors . . . proclaimed the promise of peace."[6]

During the Depression of the 1930s, fears about security and the future were easily attributed to material deprivation and the social disruptions that followed from it. But after the Second World War, discourses about an uncertain future existed in spite of considerably improved material circumstances across North America. While 25 per cent of the Canadian population continued to live in poverty into the 1960s, this figure was down substantially from the 50 per cent that had been the average during the interwar years.[7] During the post-war period, the United States and Canada had the highest and second-highest standards of living in the world. Total industrial output rose by 50 per cent in the 1950s. Canadian manufacturing wages doubled between 1945 and 1956 while prices rose only slightly. Unemployment remained between 2.8 and 5.9 per cent, depending on the region, until the mid-1950s.[8] In contrast, the 1933 national unemployment rate had been 20 per cent.[9] Between 1948 and 1961, a decades-old housing crisis began to reverse as building boomed and home ownership jumped from just over 30 per cent to 60 per cent. Clearly, many Canadians were better off than they had been. Still, speech-makers and journalists referred to a collective distrust of the future.

In a 1952 editorial, *Chatelaine* editor Lotta Dempsey tried to put this unease into words.

Writing of a cross-Canada train trip, she noted prosperous-looking people at "every station" and found herself remarking on the difference a single decade could make:

> I listen to conversations of well-fed, well-dressed people enjoying the ease and luxury of modern trains and planes. They seem to have everything . . . everything except some indefinable inner security . . . and faith. Some sense of certain strength to hold and maintain this largesse.
>
> Perhaps we know that the borders of our peaceful land grow thinner as the turmoil of the outside world increases.[10]

After 15 years of domestic uncertainty, Canadians were confronted with the Cold War and they were nervous about "the outside world," the unknown, the other. In the face of such a nebulous threat, there seemed little that an individual could do, and Dempsey counselled her readers to have faith in God.

In the 1950s, Christianity remained a profoundly important discourse in both popular and official media. Certainly, Christian values underlay recurring arguments that placed the heterosexual nuclear family at the centre of a secure future for both individuals and the nation.[11] In 1946, for instance, a Toronto mayor promoted good citizenship by declaring "Christian Family Week." An ad in the *Toronto Daily Star* read: "If our country is to fulfill its destiny, family life, founded on Christian ideals and principles, must be preserved."[12]

Domesticity as Cold War Strategy

In magazines, school board curricula, and instructional films, an idealized image of the nuclear family was promoted as the first line of defence against the perceived insecurity of the Cold War years.[13] Family life would shield Canada from the threat of "outside turmoil." As both Canadian and American historians have shown, in this age of prosperity both international and domestic affairs were suffused by familial discourse and, thus, contributed to the need North Americans expressed for control on a personal level. As American historian Elaine May puts it, the post-war family was located firmly "within the larger political culture, not outside it,"[14] although contemporary representations of the family usually portrayed the opposite.

Cold War rhetoric and the activities that followed from it were not the same in Canada as they were in the States, as Reg Whitaker and Gary Marcuse have shown.[15] Nevertheless, few Canadians could have escaped the American Cold War hype that infused the popular culture of the era—from the predominantly US films and television shows that came across the border to the US magazines that, by 1954, occupied 80 per cent of Canadian newsstand space.[16] At the very least, Canadians and Americans shared both a fear of and a fascination with the bomb. In 1946, the Toronto Board of Education proclaimed the theme of Education Week to be "Education for the Atomic Age,"[17] marking the bomb and nuclear energy as the harbingers of a new era. Four years later, a *Chatelaine* editorial identified the bomb as the "biggest thing in our new half-century." Noting the fear that the bomb inspired in many people, the editorial carefully refrained from mentioning the potential of such an invention to cause mind-boggling harm, referring instead to that fear as "man's [sic] reaction to his own creative powers." *Chatelaine* readers were encouraged to focus on the good that could come of this creativity, to "help abolish those Atom Bomb blues!"[18] *Chatelaine* was nothing if not optimistic; hence the claim that atomic energy might one day provide for "a fantastic new way of life," one with "luxury and security for all."[19] Ironically, a feature on the same page acknowledged that most nuclear research at the time was going into "making bigger and better bombs," not domestic innovations.[20] And while the feature writer didn't mention it, her readers knew what stood in the way of the hoped-for luxury and security, knew why military rather than other forms of research were necessary: Western democracies were on the alert against the threat of Communism.

In Canada, the East–West conflict that eventually came to be known as the Cold War started in 1945 when Igor Gouzenko, a cipher clerk in the Soviet embassy in Ottawa, defected and claimed that the Soviets had been running a spy ring in Canada.[21] Investigations into his allegations focused national attention on the need for internal defences against Communism. According to Len Scher, in his book on the Canadian Cold War, an unsuccessful search for spy rings gave way to efforts to track "domestic dissidents."[22] Between October 1950 and June 1951, the Royal Canadian Mounted Police (RCMP) dealt with 54,000 requests to screen both civil servants and private-sector workers.[23] Those who were most likely to be put under surveillance included labour organizers, members of Communist and socialist organizations, peace activists, and homosexuals. Deviance from any number of mainstream norms, writes Philip Girard, "represented an independence of mind that could no longer be tolerated" during the Cold War. In such a climate, "the unknown"— homosexuals, for instance—"represented a triune denial of God, family, and (implicitly or potentially) country at a time when departing

from any one of these norms was immediately suspect."[24] Deviance also precluded the homogenization that was seen to be central to Canada's strength as a nation. The conformity that is so often identified as a primary aspect of post-war social life wasn't simply a characteristic of increased consumerism and/or the centralization of popular culture and entertainment industries. It was also produced by an approach to citizenship that demanded a willingness to participate in social consensus, to adopt a shared set of behavioural standards and mores.

Democracy and Moral Standards

In 1946, an interdepartmental Security Panel (National Defence, External Affairs, and the RCMP) was established to check on federal civil servants who had been identified by the RCMP as security risks. As Larry Hannant writes, this was not the first time the RCMP had initiated security screening; however, it was the first time the effort had received formal government approval.[25] In the first three months of the panel's operation, the RCMP offered panel officials 5,466 names. Checks on these individuals resulted in 213 "adverse reports," although only 27 of the people in question were determined to be bona fide security risks—possible spies. The remainder had been included on the original list because of "moral" failings or "character" weaknesses, a category that included homosexuals, and parents of illegitimate children, among others.[26] To security officials, these character weaknesses suggested an inability to do the right thing, a tendency to compromise, an impairment of moral fibre. These were the characteristics of someone who might be influenced by Communists or, worse, who might be a Communist. Normal sexual and moral development signalled maturity and an ability to assume responsibility. By contrast, those who transgressed sexual and moral norms were assumed to be immature, trapped in adolescence. How could they be counted on to safeguard their country?

Despite the overenthusiasm of RCMP security checks, writer John Sawatsky claims that Canadian officials abhorred the McCarthyism that swept through the American military and the government bureaucracy.[27] In Canada, the search for the red menace was conducted more quietly, was more "gentlemanly," says Erich Koch, who worked with the CBC International Service in Montreal after the war.[28] There were no televised proceedings, and there was little publicity. People were either fired quickly or were never hired in the first place. Communist sympathies were the original source of concern, but this quickly translated into a fear of anyone who could potentially be blackmailed by a Communist spy: alcoholics, gamblers, and people who visited prostitutes or who had affairs. Also on this list were homosexuals, and though they were no more blackmailable than any of the others, the RCMP formed a special unit, A-3, to root out homosexuals from the civil service. Eventually, writes Sawatsky, the Mounties had files on 3,000 people, including members not only of the civil service but of the general public as well.[29]

In 1952, Canada's immigration law was quietly changed to keep homosexuals out of the country.[30] In the late 1950s and early 1960s, attempts to construct homosexuals as security risks led the RCMP and the Security Panel to recruit psychologists and psychiatrists to assist in the ousting of "perverts" from the civil service. The experts' co-operation culminated in a research project to develop what they called the Fruit Machine, an instrument that would confirm an individual's homosexuality by measuring his reaction to homoerotic imagery. (Men were the primary target of the purge. Lesbians, according to Sawatsky, refused to disclose the names of friends and colleagues, thus limiting the investigations of their networks by the mostly male Mounties.) The effort was, not surprisingly, unsuccessful, and stands as a stunning example of the use of science to support moral regulatory practices.[31]

That homosexuals were identified as particularly dangerous by the guardians of national security suggests the importance of normative sexuality in the social and political landscape of post-war Canada. Certainly the vilification of sexual deviants did much to shore up the primary position of the heterosexual nuclear family as the only legitimate site of sexual expression. But the links made between sexuality and national security also suggest the way that sexuality worked as a site for the displacement of general social and political anxieties. In official discourses, homosexuality was constructed not simply as the tragic fate of particular individuals but as a force so menacing it carried the potential to undermine the strength of the nation. In the face of the Cold War, Communists and spies and those with mysterious and questionable sex habits or morals were almost equal threats to the security of the Dominion.

In this context, having a family became an important marker of social belonging, of conformity to prevailing standards. It was a sign of maturity and adulthood, of one's ability to take on responsibility. The social positions of mother/wife and father/husband defined individuals as contributors to their community and their country. As a psychiatrist argued in *Chatelaine*, the formation of families and the raising of children was, at root, a patriotic obligation. In becoming parents, men and women were "giving to the best of their ability."[32] Thus, the nuclear family came to operate as a symbol of safety—not just on the individual level but on the national level as well.

Discourses about shared values, common goals, and mutual goodwill among Canada's citizens helped to construct an image of the Dominion itself as a family, as Annalee Gölz has argued.[33] In this frame, Communists and sex deviates were disruptions to the larger domestic order. By protecting the borders against perverts, the state was protecting the "home," safeguarding those under its charge. After the war, with the expansion of the welfare state, the government was increasingly positioned as concerned parent of its citizens. Attempts to purge the country of "perverts" and "Commies" suggest that the state, as "head of the family," was attending to more than the material well-being of Canadians. Policies and practices that targeted deviants were an effort to protect and foster moral standards, a primary task of any "concerned parent."

The Family

In a Canadian Youth Commission pamphlet called "Speak Your Peace," the family was identified as "the chief support of the new world."[34] Certainly, as the crucible of consumption, the middle-class family was the chief support of the post-war economy. Essential to the nurturing of workers and the buying of goods, the nuclear family was also understood to be the primary site of moral education and the training ground for the democracy that, in part, was thought to define the age.[35] Hence the anxiety created when various expert voices claimed that "the family" was threatened in the post-war world. If the family failed, would democracy—and, by implication, Canada—fail too? The fact that families were being formed by more people more often than at any other time in this century did little to counter a pervasive sense that "the family" as a social institution was under threat.

As evidence of the family's decline, social critics were most likely to cite figures about divorce rates. At the end of the Second World War, the divorce rate in Canada tripled, "from 56.2 divorces per 100,000 married persons 15 years of age and over in 1941 to 131.9 in 1946." After 1946, the rate fell off, but then it "rose steadily from 1951 to 1968 (88.9 to 124.3)."[36] Most of the early rise was attributable to hastily considered wartime weddings, although increasing opportunities for women to achieve some measure of economic independence may also have been an important factor. The divorce rate served to bolster a protectionist stance toward the family and to justify its ideological fortification by way of, for instance, television programs, school health curricula, and moral panics over sex crime. The state of the family was a central—if not the central—concern of post-war life.

For the most part, the image of "the family" that was used to represent the ideal was drawn from urban, white, Anglo-Saxon, middle-class and upper-middle-class communities. The authors of the massive *Crestwood Heights*, a 1956 study of Toronto's "internal suburb" of Forest Hill, offered the following description:

> In infinite variety, yet with an eternal sameness, [such a community] flashes on the movie screen, in one of those neat comedies about the upper-middle-class family which Hollywood delights to repeat again and again as nurture for the American Dream. It fills the pages of glossy magazines devoted to the current best in architecture, house decoration, food, dress, and social behaviour. The innumerable service occupations bred of an urban culture will

think anxiously about people in such a community in terms of what "they" will buy or use this year. Any authority in the field of art, literature, or science, probably at some time has had, or will have, its name on a lecture itinerary. A teacher will consider it a privilege to serve in its schools. For those thousands of North Americans who struggle to translate the promise of America into a concrete reality for themselves, and even more important, for their children, it is in some sense a Mecca.[37]

The authors of *Crestwood Heights* argued that upper-middle-class families were a marker of "what life is *coming* to be more and more like in North America—at least in the middle classes." In this sense, they wrote, a community like Crestwood Heights "is normative, or 'typical,' not in the sense of the average of an aggregate of such communities but in the sense of representing the norm to which middle-class community life tends now to move."[38] While I agree with their point, that society tends "to move" in such a direction, it bears remembering that it does not necessarily arrive. The experience of the "ideal family"—breadwinner father, stay-at-home mother, and well-adjusted children—was not available to everyone.

If divorce was considered to be the main threat to this idealized image of the nuclear family, working mothers and immigrant families were also serious—and related—challenges to its claim on the Canadian imagination. As many historians have noted, the numbers of married women in the workforce increased rapidly in the post-war period. In the early 1940s, one in 20 women worked outside the home; in 1951 that figure had risen to one in 10, only to rise again, to one in five, by 1961. As Joan Sangster writes, concerns about increases in the numbers of married women working for

pay masked class and race biases; the labour participation rates of recent immigrants, women in some ethnic and racial communities, and women who were poor had not changed.[39]

Between 1946 and 1954, Canada admitted almost a million immigrants.[40] That not all of the new arrivals organized their families in accordance with Canadian middle-class norms led to concerns that "New Canadians" would disrupt post-war efforts to shore up the family as an institution. Settlement services and advocacy groups encouraged immigrants to abandon their own family structures in favour of those thought to be essential to the moral strength of the nation: single-family households presided over by breadwinner fathers and stay-at-home mothers. Franca Iacovetta says that the Cold War gave social workers an opportunity to frame such assimilationist rhetoric as a matter of national urgency "by equating the predominance of respectable, middle-class family values with the superiority of Western democracies such as Canada."[41] That Canadian family norms were neither desirable for many immigrants, who had their own ways of doing things, nor attainable for those facing the hardship of arrival in a new country, did not deter Canadian experts from labelling immigrant families as "deviant" and a threat to both "Canadianization" and the institution of the family itself.[42]

An emphasis on the family was not a new phenomenon in Canada. However, this emphasis took a new shape in the post-war period. Whereas the primary focus of many earlier family discourses had been on women, motherhood, and the development of proper femininity,[43] post-war discourses about the family tended to show (and construct) most concern for the development of properly adjusted—normal—children. Certainly these strands of concern are closely tied together, but what is important here is the way their relationship was characterized. In post-war discourses the construction of appropriate forms of femininity—and masculinity—were seen as the means to the nobler goal of child rearing. In *Crestwood Heights*, the production of the future Crestwood adult was the focus of the community's institutions.[44]

According to the *Crestwood* authors, the upper-middle-class families they studied were relatively isolated social units with limited connection to a wider network of kin. In contrast to "the usual Victorian family," or, presumably, working-class or immigrant families, Crestwood families were units of consumption, rather than production. And, importantly, they allowed "more individuality and freedom" to their members than had earlier forms.[45] These modern families, though not as religious as their predecessors, drew heavily on Judaeo-Christian ethics, "democratic practice," and the advice of "child-rearing experts." Deviation from prevailing norms could result in a family's being defined by such experts as malfunctioning and likely to produce "disturbed" children.[46]

Present-day writers have also noted this tendency of post-war, middle-class families to be relatively self-contained.[47] While 1990s conservatives nostalgically recall the post-war family as a link to earlier times, and as exemplifying enduring "traditional" values, Elaine May claims that "the legendary family of the 1950s . . . represented something new. It was not, as common wisdom tells us, the last gasp of traditional family life with roots deep in the past. Rather, it was the first wholehearted effort to create a home that would fulfill virtually all its members' personal needs through an energized and expressive personal life."[48]

The extent to which the ideal family had come to be constructed in popular discourse as a set of relationships, a source of affectional

and material needs, is evident in a 1950s educational film for adolescents called *A Date with Your Family*. In the film, a teenaged boy and girl arrive home from school full of excitement because they have "an important date . . . dinner with the family," which to them "is a special occasion." Sister changes her clothes to "something more festive" because "the women in this family seem to feel that they owe it to the men of the family to look relaxed, rested, and attractive at dinnertime." Brother studies while sister sets the table. Then he gets Junior ready for dinner. Sister makes a centrepiece of flowers for the dining table. Father comes through the door, and the boys greet him enthusiastically, before Mother calls them all to the dining room where "they converse pleasantly" over their meal. Brother compliments Mother "and maybe sis" on the food because "it makes them want to continue pleasing you." The whole event is a "time of pleasure, charm, relaxation . . . ."[49] For the non-cinematic families who failed to meet this ideal of civility and gratification, it was, nevertheless, a modern standard by which they would be measured, one that took material comforts for granted. It assumed a strict sexual division of labour and a public life in which troubles were manageable enough to be either left at the door or assuaged by family harmony. Certainly this picture of the "united, happy family"[50] was distinct from earlier versions in which affectional needs came second to economic ones and expectations for emotional fulfillment were considerably lower.

In part, idealized images of the post-war family were a consequence of the economic changes and prosperity that favoured consumerism over mutual dependence, suburban bungalows over farms and crowded downtown apartments. But the constitution of the notion of nuclear-family-as-island was also related to post-war desires for individual satisfaction and needs for social stability. Middle-class families were frequently portrayed as offering refuge from the turmoil of the outside world. That they could actually engender isolation and alienation, as we now know from numerous articles in *Chatelaine* and from books like Betty Friedan's *The Feminine Mystique*, was not widely discussed.[51] Nor was the fact that many Canadians, by choice or circumstance, lived in families that bore little resemblance to the middle-class nuclear ideal.

In 1956, *Maclean's* published a special report on "the family" by Eric Hutton. Noting "the comeback of the Canadian family," Hutton characterized it as a resilient but basically unchanging entity, although he also told his readers "the family way of life has changed out of recognition in half a century."[52] It had taken on a particularly modern guise as Canadian young people married at younger ages, gave birth to more children, and, like the parents in *A Date with Your Family*, had more expectations of the whole package than had the generations before them. As Doug Owram writes, "the young adults of the 1940s were the most domestically oriented generation of the twentieth century."[53]

In 1941, the average age of first marriage for women was 25.4 years of age. By 1961 that figure had dropped to 22 years of age. Between 1937 and 1954, the marriage rate for women between the ages of 15 and 19 doubled from 30 per 1,000 to 62 per 1,000.[54] Once married, these women had more children, more quickly, than their mothers did. Between 1937 and 1947, the number of births per 1,000 of the population rose from 20.1 to 28.9, and it continued to rise until 1956. Much of this increase was accounted for by mothers under 25 years of age and by families with three or more children. In 1956, almost 50 per cent of live births

in Canada were third or later children.[55]

Maclean's accounted for the popularity of babies and families in a number of ways: large families, Hutton said, provided security in an insecure world; the baby bonus (established in 1945) and an overall prosperity made them easier to afford; maternal and child health had improved; television encouraged families to spend their leisure time together at home; Princess Elizabeth and Princess Grace of Monaco had made maternity fashionable; and parents—even fathers—had come to realize that children could be fun. According to the provost of Trinity College at the University of Toronto, "the family is returning to favour because so many men are making the discovery that it's the pleasantest company they're ever likely to have in a world that is full of competition and unpleasant episodes."[56] That fathers were under heavy pressure from psychological experts to participate to a greater extent in the life of their children, especially to prevent the abnormal sexual and emotional development of their sons, is not discussed in Hutton's article. Without adequate fathering, some experts said, a boy might become delinquent, turn into a homosexual, or suffer "untold mental distress."[57]

What is also not mentioned in Hutton's article about the comeback of the family is that there was tremendous pressure applied to anyone who failed to follow the trend, as evidenced by the RCMP crackdown on homosexuals. But that episode was only the most obvious aspect of a more widespread trend. In an American survey conducted after the war, only 9 per cent of those questioned believed that single people could be happy.[58] Toronto gynaecologist and author Marion Hilliard (who was herself not married) counterposed single women and married women in ways that made them seem almost like different species. Single women, she said, could only be "out of place at a gathering of married couples." And single women and married women could "only, unwittingly, hurt one another."[59] Even young divorcees and widows, Hilliard wrote pityingly, "fit in nowhere."[60] Single men, in the 1950s, risked being seen as homosexuals, a group whose social currency was non-existent. From her reading of post-war American sociology, Barbara Ehrenreich says that experts claimed a number of reasons why men might not marry: "Some were simply misfortunes, such as 'poor health or deviant physical characteristics,' 'unattractiveness,' and extreme geographical isolation. But high on the list for men were homosexuality, emotional fixation on parent(s), and unwillingness to assume responsibility."[61]

But simply getting married was not enough to satisfy post-war social expectations. Married couples without children were also subject to disapproval and admonishments for not doing their duty to their country.[62] A *Chatelaine* article featured an infertile couple who received constant ribbing from their friends: "How come you two are leading such selfish lives?"; "Aren't you going to prove yourself a man? What are we supposed to think, eh?"[63] Another *Chatelaine* story, a first-person account by a woman who chose not to have children, was roundly denounced in the letters column of two subsequent issues.[64] A reader from Ontario wrote: "That writer who is 'not going to have any' [children] has aroused my indignation to such a point that I must answer, in the face of such malformed humanity . . . I am mother of nine . . . Such a woman is denying herself the greatest of all love and satisfaction, that of mothering a child, and giving life the purpose of your being, the purpose of your Creator, great and true." After a number of similar comments, *Chatelaine* editors intervened on the letters page to set things right: "One moment please! The editors are happy to announce, for all such

readers' peace of mind, that the anonymous writer in question has just telephoned to say 'Hurray,' she is going to have one!"[65]

While this particular exchange can be read as little more than a rally of individual opinions, the importance of post-war professionals in constructing this kind of discussion cannot be overstated. In magazines, on the radio, and in newspapers, experts were increasingly evident as mediators of everyday life and as primary participants in the construction of boundaries between normality and deviance. For instance, the *Chatelaine* letters about the woman's decision not to have a baby appeared exactly one year after the magazine published an article by a psychiatrist criticizing those who chose not to have children, suggesting that they were immature and unpatriotic.[66] The point is not that the letter writers were directly influenced by the earlier article; rather, their comments were part of a larger discourse that was, in part, constructed via expert commentary.

While the middle class often consulted experts voluntarily, or sought out their ideas in print, working-class and immigrant families were likely to encounter these professionals in any number of institutional settings—such as schools, the courts, or social service offices.[67] But even as the general category of "the expert" was gaining prominence, some experts were more revered than others. Psychologists and psychiatrists had a particular appeal in a social system that was based more and more on individualism. Part of the appeal of the mental health professionals stemmed from the influence they had wielded during the war. Their contribution to the screening and rehabilitation of the troops had increased public awareness of their work,[68] and widely circulating discourses about the importance of mental hygiene validated their concerns. But sociologists and medical doctors were also routinely called upon to diagnose social trends, to make pronouncements on behaviours or identities, and to lend legitimacy to certain positions.

It was the increasing influence of psychiatry in post-war North America that constituted babies as evidence of their parents' "normal," gendered, sexual, and emotional development—of their having achieved maturity. Babies were a public sign of married sexuality and, in theory, of marital harmony. Babies could also be seen to signal acceptance of community norms and to confirm that men and women were performing their respective normative gender roles (whether, in fact, they were or not) and assuming the responsibility that came with them.

Those seen to be outside the family, from runaway youths to homosexuals, were anomalies. Hard to classify, they were often the objects of scorn or pity. Discourses about life in the middle-class nuclear family made available a variety of subject positions (albeit gendered and restrictive ones)—parent, sexual being, responsible citizen, consumer—that either were not available or were available in limited ways to adults who were single. Families, narrowly defined—monogamous, heterosexual marriages and the children produced within them—provided an important way of making sense of one's position in the post-war social structure.

Marriage: Site of Legitimate Sex

One of the primary defining factors of the post-war nuclear family was an emphasis on the sexual compatibility between husband and wife and the importance of sex in a conjugal union. According to Steven Seidman, the eroticization of romantic relationships was a trend that had been building throughout the twentieth century.[69] Certainly, reproduction continued to be a primary goal of marital sexual activity, but sex had come to be understood as entailing more than this. In the post-war period, sex was meant to be a source of pleasure and emotional fulfillment for both men and women.[70] In this framework, women's sexuality was, in theory if not in practice, as important as men's.[71] Sex was also perceived to be a "natural" part of a healthy life, even if it wasn't engaged in for the sole purpose of producing babies.

Isolated within their families, away from kin or other members of the community, the ideal post-war couple were meant to draw their support primarily from each other. In some popular constructions of marriage, even close friends were to be shunned in order to protect the sanctity and privacy of the heterosexual bond. One article in *Chatelaine* goes so far as to suggest that "The [wife's] girlfriend is a danger signal, a clear alarm that the marriage is sick and in need of loving attention. . . ."[72] In the same article, a psychiatrist argues that the "primary rule of married life" was "that nothing of intimate consequence be discussed with friends." Marriage was drawn as the most important, indeed as the only important, relationship between adults. Husbands and wives were to gain their "basic sense of belonging, of well-being, of fulfillment" from each other. Sex was the glue that would hold them together. As Steven Seidman argues, sex was the sphere upon which rested the success of the marital bond.[73]

While the role of sex within marriage may have been clear, the role of men and women in that same relationship was seen to be in an incredible state of flux. Once glued together by their sexual attraction, it was not always clear how men and women were to perform their non-sexual conjugal duties. The presence of married women in the labour force—rates rose from 12.7 per cent of all women in paid employment in

1941, to 30 per cent in 1951, to 49.8 per cent in 1961[74]—suggested to some people that the difference between gender roles was diminishing. While this could have been looked upon as a positive gain for women, it was interpreted by many as a demasculinization of men. It was also seen to spell trouble for heterosexual relationships, based as they were on an assumption of essential difference between men and women. In 1954, *Chatelaine* printed this advice to young brides from a Protestant minister:

> Wives you can unman your husband by taking his place. If you are going to go to work, you should work only for a few years ... While working you should still live on your husband's income ... Within one or two years, depending upon your ages, you should quit work and let him support you and live on what he can make ...
>
> The wife should also take pride in being good at her wifely job. In our day it is sometimes difficult for women to adjust themselves to this fact ...
>
> ... Make the man act his part. Do not start to be the man yourself.[75]

Women's advances in the workplace, slim as they were, and new forms of corporate organization contributed to what some contemporary writers have called a post-war crisis of middle-class masculinity.[76] Corporate culture demanded a personality concerned with the thoughts of others, tuned to the needs of others. It was the antithesis of the "rugged individualism" that grounded the versions of white, middle-class masculinity available in popular culture. In his study of conformity in (male) middle-class America, sociologist David Riesman, author of *The Lonely Crowd*, called this the "other-directed" personality.[77] Its characteristics, he said, were more closely matched to a traditional

feminine identity than to a traditional masculine one. In robbing men of their "individuality," "other-direction" feminized men.

On top of this, changes in the structure of the economy and the increasing importance of consumption as a family-based activity shifted men's place of importance in the household. As Barbara Ehrenreich points out in her study of (male and female) middle-class America, men might have earned the money, but women were the ones who spent the bulk of it. Consumption was women's work. Men's paid employment certainly made it possible, but it did not necessarily give men control over it: "In the temple of consumption which was the suburban home, women were priestesses and men mere altar boys."[78]

These transformations in the organization of gender contributed to a stressful negotiation of the relationship between husband and wife. Both women and men were under a tremendous strain to build what *Chatelaine* called "modern marriages": "a new kind of joint-ownership marriage ... which may beat any earlier model back to Adam and Eve." As one psychologist put it, "We are moving from dictatorship to equality in marriage, from the day when the husband's word was law to a time when the wife shares equally in the family decisions. And the working wife is probably doing more for the partnership idea than anything else."[79] Indeed, it was middle-class assumptions about the lack of equality in the marriages of some working-class immigrants that led social workers to label those marriages deviant and in need of "Canadianizing."[80] The popular assumption was that gender roles in marriage were relaxing, but not too far. Expectations remained that women would be responsible for domestic life and men for "breadwinning." In a 1955 investigation of marriage, *Chatelaine* encouraged women to give more rather than less to their homes and families: "And the siren–wife–mother who realizes the once simple business of being a married woman has become a complex and full-time career in itself is at least halfway to licking these [aforementioned] problems"[81]—problems like confusion over roles, loneliness, and boredom.

As Wini Breines writes, despite discourses about "modern marriages" and the "age of equality," men and women continued to experience gender as a deep-rooted site of social difference. While there were more options for white, Anglo-Saxon, middle-class women than there had been in previous decades, few women were encouraged to pursue them. Middle-class women's social worth continued to be measured by their success in raising children and providing a comfortable home for their husbands. Marriage continued to be an inevitability rather than a choice. At the same time, middle-class men were being told to participate more in the affectional life of the family while having to give themselves over to a corporate culture that was constructed on the assumption of their freedom from domestic responsibilities. For both men and women, frustration seemed an inevitable consequence of a relationship that was supposed to reflect "new" forms of gender organization without giving up the old ones. That this package of contradictions was supposed both to inspire and to sustain sexual attraction and pleasure was just one more strain on a relationship that, nevertheless, maintained remarkable levels of popularity right up until the late 1950s.

The Kinsey Reports and the Sexual Climate

Although marriage remained the only legitimate site of sexual activity between adults throughout the late 1940s and the 1950s, post-war sexual discourses did preserve some of the liberalization that had been fostered by the war.[82] Popular culture, especially, became increasingly sexualized by way of sexy movie stars, the so-called "sex appeal" of advertisements, and sexually explicit books and magazines. Divorce rates increased.[83] Some Protestant churches supported the need for sex education and were even prepared to accept its limited introduction into the schools.[84] And, though the birth control movement was hardly at its peak in the 1950s, interest in the pill, which would be released in 1961, was high.[85] Lesbians and gay men in urban centres gained access to limited but important public spaces.[86] Single mothers in Ontario were eligible for the first time to receive mother's allowance. While these and other changes were significant, they existed alongside a more familiar reticence about matters pertaining to sexuality. Thus, even the mention of sex in the public realm continued to elicit reactions of strong disapproval from some people. *Chatelaine* readers, for instance, regularly chastised the editors for succumbing to so-called prurient interests. Questionable material included an article about menstruation for teenage girls, cover illustrations that showed too much leg, and self-help-type features that focused on psychiatric explanations (perceived to be inherently sexual explanations) for emotional and relationship problems.[87]

Nothing crystallizes the various strains of post-war sexual discourse like public response to the Kinsey reports, *Sexual Behavior in the Human Male* (SBHM 1948) and *Sexual Behavior in the Human Female* (SBHF 1953). When the first volume appeared, in an 800-page, hardcover edition, published by a little-known scientific publishing house, it sold a total of 200,000 copies in its first six months. Even the publishers were unaware of the impact the book would have and originally planned to print only 10,000 copies, "one of the more spectacular publishing mistakes of the decade," says Kinsey's associate Wardell Pomeroy.[88] Within a month, Kinsey had received more than 1,000 letters, only six of which, Pomeroy claims, were negative.[89] When the female volume was about to come out in 1953, more than 150 magazines and major newspapers wanted pre-release access to the text. That same year, *Time* declared the sex researcher their man of the year, and Kinsey was, by all accounts, a household name.

In general, reaction to the two books was mixed, and perhaps therefore suggestive of the various ways that sex was understood to fit into North American culture. According to Pomeroy, reaction to the male volume was largely favourable, with most of the criticism it received focusing on the method of the study. In contrast, reaction to the female volume was significantly more negative and tended to focus on the morality of the findings and on the moral basis of the project itself. Clearly, it was one thing to talk about men's sexual activity and quite another to talk of women's. The uproar over the second book eventually led to the termination of funding (from the Rockefeller Foundation) for Kinsey's research.[90] Still, there were many who appreciated the work that Kinsey had done and the impact it could make, even if they weren't particularly thrilled with what the doctor had found. At the very least, reviewers were impressed by the sheer size of Kinsey's sample. The male volume was based on interviews with 5,300 men, the female volume on interviews with 5,940 women. Both samples were diversified in terms of class background, age, region, and religion, but they dealt almost exclusively with white people, a fact not noted in any of the Canadian commentaries. Reviews in liberal Canadian magazines like *Saturday Night, Canadian Forum,* and *Canadian Welfare* were largely positive and took seriously the implications of the research for sexual standards.[91] Even

Chatelaine sent a reporter to Indiana to interview Kinsey at work.[92] In her article, *Chatelaine* writer Lotta Dempsey took pride in being the first Canadian woman to be part of the sex doctor's sample—as a rule, Kinsey only granted press interviews to those who would agree to be interviewed for his study.

Canadian reviewers made little of the fact that Kinsey's material was American. B.K. Sandwell, in a piece for *Saturday Night,* criticized Kinsey's first volume for succumbing to the familiar American habit of not openly identifying itself as American. But Sandwell also concluded that the difference between Canadian and American males was so slight that the absence of Canadians from the study was of little importance.[93] That Kinsey had identified numerous social factors as having an influence on sexual behaviour (education, religion, class, region) was certainly an opportunity for Canadian critics to speculate on the possible sexual implications of Canadianness. But it was an opportunity that seems not to have been taken up.

Before Kinsey, public discussions of sex had taken place in the context of related issues such as birth control, divorce, sexual crime, and venereal disease. While marriage manuals with explicit descriptions of sexual activities had been published throughout the first half of the century, these were not the subject of mainstream, everyday discussion. Certainly, such material was unlikely to find its way into newspapers and magazines. One of Kinsey's main achievements, then, was packaging information about sex in a fashion that could be widely disseminated. In his books, sex was reduced to a series of clean statistics. Kinsey's emphasis on his own scientific background and on the scientific integrity of his study made sex more acceptable as a topic of conversation. In a period when North Americans were enamoured of scientists and experts of all kinds, and were concerned about wartime changes in sexual mores, Kinsey's timing was perfect.

In publishing his findings, Kinsey not only brought sex into public discussion, he brought a lot of different kinds of sex into public discussion: homosexual acts, premarital sex, oral sex, anal sex, and masturbation. In his description of sexual behaviour, heterosexual intercourse was just one of many possible activities in which North Americans engaged to satisfy what Kinsey understood to be a natural need for orgasm. It was this challenge to normative standards of sexual behaviour—to the definition of normal sexuality—that most concerned Kinsey's critics and supporters alike. As Janice Irvine has written, homosexuals and others who wanted to liberalize moral standards used the reports' statistics about sexual diversity to back demands for social tolerance for sexual minorities. On the other hand, "vigilantes" against such changes used the same figures to show the extent of a moral breakdown, "to fuel the post-war backlash" against relaxing sexual mores.[94]

A reviewer in *Canadian Forum* wrote that "what this [diversity of sexual behaviours] does to our concepts of 'normal,' 'excessive,' and the like needs no emphasis . . . ."[95] An editor at *Saturday Night* wrote that there was no problem in the statistics themselves (remarkable as they were); rather, the danger lay in the conclusions people might draw from them. Some people might decide, he said, that "anything that is done by seven-tenths of the population cannot possibly be wrong—a conclusion which reduces morality to a sort of popular plebiscite."[96] In another *Saturday Night* article, Perry Hughes questioned even the ethics of applying statistics to sex. Sex, he wrote, is a "subject that cannot be divorced from its moral and spiritual associations, and which therefore is not a proper subject for statistics at all . . . the

obligation to behave oneself in a certain manner is not affected by the question whether 90 per cent, or 50 per cent, or only 20 per cent of one's fellow citizens behave in that manner."[97] Not everyone was as willing as Kinsey was to base moral norms on statistical ones.

In the years following the Second World War, the heterosexual nuclear family was valued as the "traditional" foundation of the Canadian social structure. The family was reified as a primary stabilizing influence on both individuals and the nation as a whole. Metaphorically and practically, it was assumed to be the basis of the social consensus that was a central part of Cold War discourse and practice. Mainstream discourses suggested that dissent and difference could weaken the face of democracy in the ideological fight against Communism. Canadians were called upon to show an impressive social cohesiveness as evidence of their dedication to the superiority of the Western way of life. A commitment to the family was central to the social homogeneity necessitated by this display.

Inherent in the post-war definition of "the family" was its basis in a sexually charged heterosexual marriage. Elaine May argues that marriage operated to "contain" sexuality, to protect against the social disorder that was thought to be the inevitable result of sex out-of-control.[98] Certainly, this type of anxiety was evident in the vilification of homosexuals practised by agencies of the Dominion government. As a form of social organization and the only site of legitimate sexual behaviour, the family was integral to the definition of deviance. Those who found themselves on the outside of the family existed beyond the bounds of social legitimacy, and so were denied claim to one of the defining features of normality. It was a lesson that adults would emphasize over and over again in their dealings with post-war youth.

● Notes

1. Owram, *Born at the Right Time*; Iacovetta, *Such Hardworking People*; Whitaker and Marcuse, *Cold War Canada*.
2. Meyerowitz, "Introduction," in *Not June Cleaver*, 4; May, *Homeward Bound*.
3. Finkel, Conrad, and Strong-Boag, *History of the Canadian Peoples*, 384.
4. For a discussion of women war workers, see Pierson, "They're Still Women after All"; and Joan Sangster, "Doing Two Jobs." For a discussion of Canadians' reluctance to accept non-northern European immigrants and refugees, see Iacovetta, *Such Hardworking People*.
5. Owram, *Born at the Right Time*.
6. Parr, ed., "Introduction," *A Diversity of Women*, 5.
7. Finkel, Conrad, and Strong-Boag, *History of the Canadian Peoples*, 429–30.
8. Francis, Jones, and Smith, *Destinies: Canadian History since Confederation*, 338–9, 353.
9. Finkel, Conrad, and Strong-Boag, *History of the Canadian Peoples*, 331.
10. Dempsey, *Chatelaine* editorial, 1.
11. See, for example: Canadian Youth Commission, *Youth, Marriage and the Family*; Franks, "A Note to Brides," 29ff; *Marriage Today*, a film produced by McGraw-Hill Book Company, 1950.
12. Advertisement for Christian Family Week, *Toronto Daily Star*, 2 May 1947.
13. The idea that strong families are the root of social stability has been a recurring theme in the face of capitalism's rise and evolution. For a discussion of this, see Ursel, *Private Lives, Public Policy*; Dehli, "Women and Class."
14. May, *Homeward Bound*, 10.
15. Whitaker and Marcuse, *Cold War Canada*.
16. Finkel, Conrad, and Strong-Boag, *History of the Canadian Peoples*, 426–7.
17. Advertisement for Education Week, *Telegram*, 11 Apr. 1946.
18. Sanders, "What's the Biggest Thing in Our New Half Century?," 6.
19. Ibid., 53.
20. Adele White, "Let's Abolish Those Atom Bomb Blues," 6–7ff.
21. Whitaker and Marcuse, *Cold War Canada*, Chs 2–4.
22. Scher, *The Un-Canadians*, 8.

23. Ibid., 9.
24. Girard, "From Subversion to Liberation," 3.
25. Hannant, *The Infernal Machine*, 144. For discussion of the Security Panel, also see Whitaker and Marcuse, *Cold War Canada*, Ch. 7.
26. Girard, "From Subversion to Liberation," 4. Also see Kinsman, "'Character Weaknesses' and 'Fruit Machines.'"
27. Sawatsky, *Men in the Shadows*, 116.
28. Cited in Scher, *The Un-Canadians*, 81.
29. Sawatsky, *Men in the Shadows*, 126.
30. See Girard, "From Subversion to Liberation."
31. Kinsman, "'Character Weaknesses' and 'Fruit Machines'"; Robinson and Kimmel, "The Queer Career of Homosexual Security Vetting in Cold War Canada."
32. Franks, "A Note to Brides," 29.
33. Gölz, "Family Matters."
34. The quotation is from a pamphlet produced by the Canadian Youth Commission, "Speak Your Peace: Suggestions for Discussion by Youth," Bulletin No. 2—*Youth and Family Life*, NAC, MG 28 I 11, Vol. 64 (Ontario Committee).
35. For an example of discussions about the family as a site of democracy, see the National Film Board films *Family Circles*, produced in 1949, and *Making a Decision in the Family* (1957); Osborne, "Democracy Begins in the Home." For discussions about the family as the primary site of moral education, see newspaper debates about the introduction of sex education into school classrooms: "Board of Education Considers Courses in Sex Education"; "No Need for Haste."
36. Alison Prentice et al., *Canadian Women: A History*, 323.
37. Seeley, Sim, and Loosley, *Crestwood Heights*, 3.
38. Ibid., 20 (emphasis in original).
39. Joan Sangster, "Doing Two Jobs," 99–100.
40. Li, *The Making of Post-war Canada*, 97.
41. Iacovetta, "Remaking Their Lives," 143.
42. Iacovetta, "Making 'New Canadians.'"
43. See, for example, Arnup, *Education for Motherhood*; Comacchio, *Nations Are Built of Babies*.
44. Seeley, Sim, and Loosley, *Crestwood Heights*, 4. See also, Owram, *Born at the Right Time*.
45. Seeley, Sim, and Loosley, *Crestwood Heights*, 161.

46. Ibid., 165.
47. See, for example, Owram, *Born at the Right Time*; or May, *Homeward Bound*.
48. May, *Homeward Bound,* 11.
49. *A Date with Your Family,* a Simmel-Meservey Release, produced by Edward C. Simmel and written by Arthur V. Jones (no date, appears to be mid-1950s).
50. Gölz talks about how discursive constructions of the "happy united family" were "interlinked with an idealized notion of the 'Canadian family' as both the social foundation and the metaphorical microcosm of Canadian nationhood." See her "Family Matters," 49.
51. Starting in the late 1940s, Chatelaine published numerous articles about women's fate in the suburban middle-class family. Features and editorials mentioned the "something missing" in women's lives, a sense of unease and dissatisfaction. See, for instance, "Unhappy Wives," 2. For discussion of Chatelaine as a source of material that challenged prevailing ideologies, see Korinek, "Roughing It in Suburbia"; also, Friedan, *The Feminine Mystique*.
52. Hutton, "The Future of the Family: A Maclean's Report," 74.
53. Owram, *Born at the Right Time,* 12.
54. Alison Prentice et al., *Canadian Women,* 311.
55. Ibid.
56. Cited by Hutton, "The Future of the Family," 76.
57. Nash, "It's Time Father Got Back in the Family," 28.
58. Cited in May, *Homeward Bound,* 80.
59. Hilliard, *A Woman Doctor Looks at Love and Life,* 94.
60. Ibid., 99.
61. Ehrenreich, *The Hearts of Men,* 20.
62. Franks, "A Note to Brides," 29ff.
63. Morris, "Give the Childless Couple a Break," 11ff.
64. Anonymous, "I'm Not Having Any," 14.
65. *Chatelaine* (June 1947): 6.
66. The article was "A Note to Brides" by Ruth MacLachlan Franks, MD (see above, nn11, 62).
67. Iacovetta, "Making 'New Canadians.'"
68. Seeley, Sim, and Loosley, *Crestwood Heights,* 426.
69. Seidman, *Romantic Longings,* 118.
70. Marion Hilliard's book and her regular columns in *Chatelaine* frequently espoused the importance of sexual happiness in marriage.
71. For discussions of North American women's sexual dissatisfactions during the 1950s, see Breines, *Young, White, and Miserable*; and Harvey, *The Fifties: A Women's Oral History.*
72. Morris, "Don't Let Your Girl Friends Ruin Your Marriage," 26.
73. Seidman, *Romantic Longings,* 94.
74. Strong-Boag, "Home Dreams," 479.
75. Lautenslager, "A Minister's Frank Talk to Brides and Grooms," 98–9.
76. See, especially, Ehrenreich, *The Hearts of Men.*
77. Riesman, *The Lonely Crowd.*
78. Ehrenreich, *Fear of Falling,* 34.
79. Anglin, "Who Has Won the War between the Sexes?," 12.
80. Iacovetta, "Making 'New Canadians,'" 276.
81. Ibid., 70.
82. Costello, *Love, Sex and War,* 9.
83. In the year after the war, the divorce rate tripled as hastily constructed wartime marriages withered under more prolonged consideration. But between 1947 and 1951 rates were relatively stable. Between 1951 and 1968, the divorce rate rose steadily from 88.9 to 124.3 divorces per 100,000 married persons (Alison Prentice et al., *Canadian Women: A History,* 323).
84. "Church Group Would Study Sex Education."
85. For a discussion of the Canadian birth control movement, see McLaren and McLaren, *The Bedroom and the State.* On excitement about the pill, see Anglin, "The Pill That Could Shake the World," 16–17. Letters for and against Anglin's article appear in *Chatelaine* (Dec. 1953), 3.
86. See Kinsman, *The Regulation of Desire,* and the National Film Board film *Forbidden Love,* directed by Aerlyn Weissman and Lynne Fernie, 1992.
87. The menstruation article, "High School Huddle," was written by Adele White, 26–7. It was followed by both positive and negative letters. The letter complaining about "the ungainly display of limbs" appeared in *Chatelaine* (Nov. 1952): 2. And the complaint about psychiatry, from a reader wondering why "every issue has to have an article about sex," appeared in *Chatelaine* (Oct. 1949): 14.
88. Pomeroy, *Dr Kinsey and the Institute for Sex Research,* 265.
89. Ibid., 273.
90. Ibid., 360, 363.
91. Ketchum, "Turning New Leaves," 44–5; Sandwell, "Statistical Method Applied to Sex Shows New and Surprising Results," 12; Seeley and Griffin, "The

Kinsey Report," 40–2; Rumming, "Dr Kinsey and the Human Female," 7–8; Kidd, *Review of Sexual Behavior in the Human Male*, 45–6. For a less positive critique, see Hughes, "Kinsey Again: Leers or Cheers?," 10ff. For a bona fide anti-Kinsey rant, see the review by "E.J.M.," 50ff.

92. Dempsey, "Dr Kinsey Talks about Women to Lotta Dempsey," 10–11.

93. Sandwell, "Statistical Method Applied to Sex," 12.
94. Irvine, *Disorders of Desire*, 54.
95. Ketchum, "Turning New Leaves," 45.
96. Sandwell, "Statistical Method Applied to Sex."
97. Hughes, "Kinsey Again: Leers or Cheers?," 10.
98. May, *Homeward Bound*, Ch. 4.

● References

Anglin, Gerald. 1953. "The Pill That Could Shake the World," *Chatelaine* (Oct.): 16–17, 99–103.

———. 1955. "Who Has Won the War between the Sexes?," *Chatelaine* (June): 11–13, 66–70.

Anonymous. 1947. "I'm Not Having Any," *Chatelaine* (Apr.): 14, 64, 78.

Arnup, Katherine. 1994. *Education for Motherhood* (Toronto: University of Toronto Press).

Breines, Wini. 1992. *Young, White, and Miserable: Growing Up Female in the Fifties* (Boston: Beacon).

Canadian Youth Commission. 1948. *Youth, Marriage and the Family* (Toronto: Ryerson).

Comacchio, Cynthia R. 1993. *Nations Are Built of Babies* (Montreal and Kingston: McGill-Queen's University Press).

Corrigan, Philip, and Derek Sayer. 1985. *The Great Arch: English State Formation as Cultural Revolution* (Oxford: Blackwell).

Costello, John. 1985. *Love, Sex and War: Changing Values, 1939–1945* (London: Collins).

Dehli, Kari. 1988. "Women and Class: The Social Organization of Mothers' Relations to Schools in Toronto, 1915–1940," PhD diss., University of Toronto, Ontario Institute for Studies in Education.

Dempsey, Lotta. 1949. "Dr Kinsey Talks about Women to Lotta Dempsey," *Chatelaine* (Aug.): 10–11, 59–60.

———. 1952. Editorial. *Chatelaine* (Aug.): 1.

Ehrenreich, Barbara. 1983. *The Hearts of Men: American Dreams and the Flight from Commitment* (New York: Anchor/Doubleday).

———. 1989. *Fear of Falling: The Inner Life of the Middle Class* (New York: HarperCollins).

"E.J.M." 1948. "Review of *Sexual Behavior in the Human Male*," *Canadian Doctor* (July): 50–6.

Finkel, Alvin, and Margaret Conrad, with Veronica Strong-Boag. 1993. *History of the Canadian Peoples, 1867–Present*, Vol. II (Toronto: Copp Clark Pitman).

Foucault, Michel. 1979. *Discipline and Punish: The Birth of the Prison* (New York: Vintage).

———. 1981. *The History of Sexuality*, Vol. I, trans. Robert Hurley (New York: Pelican).

Francis, R. Douglas, Richard Jones, and Donald B. Smith. 1992. *Destinies: Canadian History since Confederation*, 2nd edn (Toronto: Holt, Rinehart and Winston).

Franks, Ruth MacLachlan. 1946. "A Note to Brides: Don't Delay Parenthood," *Chatelaine* (May): 29, 44, 100.

Friedan, Betty. 1963. *The Feminine Mystique* (New York: Dell).

Girard, Philip. 1987. "From Subversion to Liberation: Homosexuals and the Immigration Act 1952–1977," *Canadian Journal of Law and Society* 2: 1–27.

Gölz, Annalee. 1993. "Family Matters: The Canadian Family and the State in the Post-war Period," *Left History* 1, 2 (Fall): 9–49.

Hacking, Ian. 1993. "Normal," a discussion paper prepared for the "Modes of Thought" Workshop (Sept.), Toronto.

Hannant, Larry. 1995. *The Infernal Machine* (Toronto: University of Toronto Press).

Harvey, Brett. 1993. *The Fifties: A Women's Oral History* (New York: HarperCollins).

Henriques, Julian, et al. 1984. *Changing the Subject: Psychology, Social Regulation and Subjectivity* (London: Methuen).

Hilliard, Marion. 1956. *A Woman Doctor Looks at Love and Life* (New York: Doubleday).

Hughes, Perry. 1950. "Kinsey Again: Leers or Cheers?," *Saturday Night* (20 June): 10, 15.

Hutton, Eric. 1956. "The Future of the Family: A *Maclean's* Report," *Maclean's* (26 May): 12–15, 74–9.

Iacovetta, Franca. 1992. "Making 'New Canadians': Social Workers, Women and the Reshaping of Immigrant Families," in *Gender Conflicts*, eds Iacovetta and Valverde, 261–303.

———. 1992. *Such Hardworking People: Italian Immigrants in Postwar Toronto* (Montreal and Kingston: McGill-Queen's University Press).

———. 1995. "Remaking Their Lives: Women Immigrants, Survivors and Refugees," in *A Diversity of Women*, ed. Parr, 136–67.

——— and Mariana Valverde, eds. 1992. *Gender Conflicts: New Essays in Women's History* (Toronto: University of Toronto Press).

Irvine, Janice. 1990. *Disorders of Desire* (Philadelphia: Temple University Press).

Johnson, Richard. 1983. "What Is Cultural Studies Anyway?," *Anglistica* 26, 1, 2: 1–81.

Ketchum, J.D. 1948. "Turning New Leaves," *Canadian Forum* (May): 44–5.

Kidd, J.R. 1949. "Review of *Sexual Behavior in the Human Male*," *Food for Thought* (Feb.): 45–6.

Kinsman, Gary. 1995. "'Character Weaknesses' and 'Fruit Machines': Towards an Analysis of the Antihomosexual Security Campaign in the Canadian Civil Service," *Labour/Le Travail* 35 (Spring): 133–61.

———. 1996. *The Regulation of Desire*, rev. edn (Montreal: Black Rose).

Korinek, Valerie. 1996. "Roughing It in Suburbia: Reading *Chatelaine* Magazine, 1950–1969," PhD diss., University of Toronto.

Lautenslager, E.S. 1954. "A Minister's Frank Talk to Brides and Grooms," *Chatelaine* (May): 18–19, 96, 98–100.

Li, Peter S. 1996. *The Making of Post-war Canada* (Toronto: Oxford University Press).

McLaren, Angus, and Arlene Tigar McLaren. 1986. *The Bedroom and the State* (Toronto: McClelland and Stewart).

May, Elaine Tyler. 1988. *Homeward Bound: American Families in the Cold War Era* (New York: Basic Books).

Meyerowitz, Joanne. 1994. *Not June Cleaver: Women and Gender in Postwar America, 1945–1960* (Philadelphia: Temple University Press).

Morris, Eileen. 1954. "Don't Let Your Girl Friends Ruin Your Marriage," *Chatelaine* (Oct.): 26, 50–1, 55, 58–9.

———. 1955. "Give the Childless Couple a Break," *Chatelaine* (May): 11, 76, 78, 80–1.

Nash, John. 1956. "It's Time Father Got Back in the Family," *Maclean's* (12 May): 28–9, 82–5.

Owram, Doug. 1996. *Born at the Right Time: A History of the Baby Boom Generation* (Toronto: University of Toronto Press).

Parr, Joy, ed. 1995. *A Diversity of Women: Ontario, 1945–1980* (Toronto: University of Toronto Press).

Pierson, Ruth Roach. 1986. *"They're Still Women after All": The Second World War and Canadian Womanhood* (Toronto: McClelland and Stewart).

Pomeroy, Wardell B. 1972. *Dr Kinsey and the Institute for Sex Research* (New York: Harper & Row).

Prentice, Alison, et al. 1988. *Canadian Women: A History* (Toronto: Harcourt, Brace Jovanovich).

Prentice, Susan. 1993. "Militant Mothers in Domestic Times: Toronto's Postwar Childcare Struggles," PhD diss., York University.

Riesman, David. 1950. *The Lonely Crowd* (New Haven: Yale University Press).

Robinson, Daniel J., and David Kimmel. 1994. "The Queer Career of Homosexual Security Vetting in Cold War Canada," *Canadian Historical Review* 75, 3 (Sept.): 319–45.

Rumming, Eleanor. 1953. "Dr Kinsey and the Human Female," *Saturday Night* (15 Aug.): 7–8.

Sanders, Byrne Hope. 1950. "What's the Biggest Thing in Our New Half Century?," editorial *Chatelaine* (Jan.): 6.

Sandwell, B.K. 1948. "Statistical Method Applied to Sex Shows New and Surprising Results," *Saturday Night* (21 Feb.): 12.

Sangster, Joan. "Doing Two Jobs: The Wage-earning Mother, 1945–1970," in *A Diversity of Women*, ed. Parr, 98–134.

Sawatsky, John. 1980. *Men in the Shadows: The RCMP Security Service* (Toronto: Doubleday).

Scher, Len. 1992. *The Un-Canadians* (Toronto: Lester).

Seeley, John R., and J.D.M. Griffin. 1948. "The Kinsey Report," *Canadian Welfare* (15 Oct.): 40–2.

———, R. Alexander Sim, and Elizabeth W. Loosley. 1956. *Crestwood Heights: A Study of the Culture of Suburban Life* (Toronto: University of Toronto Press).

Seidman, Steven. 1991. *Romantic Longings: Love in America, 1830–1980* (New York: Routledge).

Strong-Boag, Veronica. 1991. "Home Dreams: Women and the Suburban Experiment in Canada, 1945–1960," *Canadian Historical Review* 72, 4: 471–504.

Ursel, Jane. 1992. *Private Lives, Public Policy: 100 Years of State Intervention in the Family* (Toronto: Women's Press).

Urwin, Cathy. 1985. "Constructing Motherhood: The Persuasion of Normal Development," in *Language, Gender and Childhood*, eds Steedman, Urwin, and Walkerdine, 164–202.

Whitaker, Reg, and Gary Marcuse. 1994. *Cold War Canada: The Making of a National Insecurity State, 1945–1957* (Toronto: University of Toronto Press).

White, Adele. 1947. "High School Huddle," *Chatelaine* (Sept.): 26–7, 48.

———. 1950. "Let's Abolish Those Atom Bomb Blues," *Chatelaine* (Jan.): 6–7, 53.

Chapter 8

In 1976–77, Meg Luxton interviewed and observed full-time homemakers in working-class families in Flin Flon, Manitoba, a mining town. She chose Flin Flon because the oldest generation of women living there had raised their families in the most primitive of housing conditions—without running water, electricity, or household appliances. Interviewing three generations of Flin Flon women meant that Luxton was able to learn about how their housework and child care changed as their households modernized. Moreover, because Flin Flon was populated mostly with breadwinner/homemaker families it afforded Luxton the opportunity of better understanding the family pattern common in the 1950s.

More Than a Labour of Love, the book in which Luxton reported her findings, examines how a capitalist economy and working-class jobs affect family life—especially the relationships between women and their husbands and women and their children. Luxton explores the gender relations typical of working-class families in which women were full-time homemakers and men were sole breadwinners, and neither the influx of married women into the labour force nor the women's liberation movement had yet occurred. In so doing, she describes the power and privilege that a single male breadwinner was likely to have in his family decades ago.

Wives and Husbands

Meg Luxton

> I [woman] take thee [man]
> To my wedded husband
> To have and to hold
> From this day forward
> For better for worse
> For richer for poorer
> In sickness and in health
> To love, cherish, and to obey
> Till death do us part
> > Solemnization of Matrimony

In her marriage vows, a woman promises "to love, cherish, and to obey" her husband. While couples appear to marry on the basis of free choice and love, their dependence on the wage imposes structural imperatives which undermine their freedom and love. The daily requirements of household survival mean that both adults must subject themselves and each other to dictates which, for the most part, are beyond their control and which are not particularly in their interests.

Consequently, marriage is indeed "for better for worse." While some aspects of marriage are good and women often mention the pleasure and happiness they derive from their marriages, the underlying imperatives create all sorts of tensions which diminish the marital relationship, binding people to each other not by choice based on love but by dependency and a lack of alternatives.[1]

Wage Labour and Domestic Labour

For many working-class women, supporting themselves independently by wage labour is not an inevitable or even a realistic alternative. The sex segregation of the labour market restricts women to the lowest paid, least secure, and most monotonous jobs. Women's wages are so low that it is virtually impossible, especially if they have children, for women to survive.[2] Often in periods of high unemployment or in small towns like Flin Flon, there are simply not enough jobs available for those women who want to work. For these women marriage becomes a primary option—it appears to be the only viable life strategy available to them.

In this way there is a basic economic compulsion to marriage and women's low wages help to keep the nuclear family together. Though women marry on the basis of free choice, they have very few real alternatives because of how those alternatives are structured. By associating themselves with men who are earning relatively higher wages, women probably have a higher standard of living than they might have if they depended on their own wage labour.

This economic dependency permeates and threatens female/male relationships. For family households to survive, the husband must sell his labour power in exchange for wages to an employer on an ongoing, regular basis. Once the men enter the bosses' employ, they are no longer free but come under the direct control of their employer.

The employer's primary objective is to extract from his employees as much of their ability to work as possible, to maximize the product of their labour by the end of the shift. Once workers are employees, they become part of capitalist production and how they work depends on how the capitalist organizes production—his control over his labour force, his capacity to coordinate and rationalize the various operations of his enterprise—in other words, his capacity to harness labour in the production process and to utilize his workers' labour power to the hilt.

Marx described this type of labour, showing vividly its implications for the (male) worker's state of being:

> Labour is external to the worker—that is, it is not part of his nature—and the worker does not affirm himself in his work but denies himself, feels miserable and unhappy, develops no free physical and mental energy but mortifies his flesh and ruins his mind. The worker therefore feels at ease only outside work, and during work he is outside himself. . . . The external nature of work for the worker appears in the fact that it is not his own but another person's, that in work he does not belong to himself but to someone else. (Easton and Guddat 1967: 292)

From the perspective of the worker, the labour process is not for the satisfaction of needs. Rather it demands the denial of needs. Time spent at work is segregated from "real life"; it is time spent for, controlled by, and at the service of another. The man returning after a day of work comes home tired. His capacity to labour has been consumed, so he is spent and depleted. He considers his time off work to be his own, to do with as he pleases. He demands the right to spend his time away from wage work in voluntary activities.

But the experiences of wage work are not so easily shaken. His experiences at work usually leave him tired, frustrated, and irritable. The worker bears the social residue of this alienating labour process and of the oppressive social relations of capitalist production. He needs to find ways of releasing those feelings of tension, of assuaging the dissatisfaction. He wants his leisure time to be free of conflict and to be refreshing, restful, and personally satisfying. He needs the opportunity and the means to re-energize—to reproduce his labour power—before he goes back to work the next day.

A miner who had worked for the Company for 41 years explained how he experienced this process:

> I work hard, see. And it's not great work. And when I gets home I'm tired and fed up and I want to just rest till I feel better. I come home feeling sort of worn down and I need to loosen up and feel human again. At work there is always someone standing over me telling me I have to do this or that. Well, I don't want any more of that at home. I want to do what I want for a change. I want a chance to live when I'm off work.
> (Generation II, b. 1920)[3]

Despite the social relations of production, or perhaps because of them, a man is usually proud of his skill, strength, and intelligence in performing his job. This pride focuses on the wages he receives; a good wage is an expression of his ability as a worker.

For the man the importance of the wage is represented by his home, for it is his wage that buys the house he lives in and provides for his needs and those of his wife and children. A male worker measures his worth by his ability to provide for his family. He is proud to be able to support a wife who can devote all her time and energy to maintaining their household. His self-esteem is derived from his ability to provide and maintain his side of the sexual division of labour. This helps motivate him to continue working. And for his labour he expects that the home will be his castle. For the man there is a distinct separation between his workplace and his home, between work time and leisure time. He usually assumes that his wage labour fulfills his obligations within the division of labour of the family household. When a man comes home he is finished work:

> He is at home when he is not working and when he is working he is not at home. His work, therefore, is not voluntary, but coerced, forced labour. It is not the satisfaction of a need but only a means to satisfy other needs. Its alien character is obvious from the fact that as soon as no physical or other pressure exists, labour is avoided like the plague. (Easton and Guddat 1967: 292)

No such separation exists for the woman. Her workplace is her home, and for her, work time and leisure time are indistinguishable. She discharges her obligations within the division of labour by doing all those things that are necessary to ensure that the adult members of the household are available for work every day—able and relatively willing to work. In this way she ensures, as far as possible, the regular continuance of the wage on which she depends in order to meet her own physical and social needs. Because the labour power of her husband is exchanged for a wage, while hers is not, the needs of the husband and the requirements of his wage labour always take precedence over other household considerations. Part of the woman's work includes caring for her husband, creating a well-ordered and restorative home for him to come back to. In the process her work becomes less visible and its importance is less acknowledged. The wife is subordinated to the husband.

The sexual division of labour, although inherently hierarchical, makes the participants mutually dependent. While the dependency of women is greater economically and socially, men are dependent on their wives not only for the physical aspect of domestic labour but also for important psycho-emotional support. Within the household division of labour, it falls to the woman to provide for the immediate needs of the wage worker. All aspects of women's work, from its schedules and rhythms to the most subtle personal interactions, are touched and coloured by the type of wage work the men are doing, by the particular ways in which their labour power is consumed by capital.

If the man is engaged in shift work, the household then operates around two, or sometimes three, often contradictory schedules. It is the woman's task to service each routine and to prevent each of them from coming into conflict. This process is well illustrated by one housewife's day. The woman gets up at 7 a.m., feeds the baby, then gets the three older children up, fed, and off to school by 8:45 a.m. Meanwhile, her husband who is on the graveyard shift (midnight to 8 a.m.) comes in from work and wants a meal, so once the children are fed she prepares his dinner. Then he goes to bed and sleeps until about 6 p.m. During the day she must care for the toddler, do her housework, feed and visit with the older children who come home for lunch from noon to 1:30 p.m. and return again at 4 p.m. All of this occurs while "daddy is sleeping" and the noise level must be controlled to prevent him from being disturbed. At 5 p.m. she makes supper for the children and at 6 p.m. she makes breakfast for him. By 8:30 p.m., when the children are in bed, he is rested and ready to socialize while she is tired and ready to sleep. Another woman in a similar position described it this way:

> It totally disrupts my life, his shift work. I have to keep the kids quiet—I'm forever telling them to shut up—and I can't do my work, because the noise wakes him. It makes my life very difficult.
> (Generation II, b. 1941)

The impact of shift work on family life is subtle and difficult to pin down. Workers on weekly rotating shifts cannot sleep properly and their eating patterns are disrupted. The result is general irritability, headaches, constipation, and a host of other physical ailments. The social and psychic effects are more elusive.[4] Flin Flon women generally maintained that the graveyard shift was the hardest for them. Some of them did not like being alone with small children at night. Others said they never had time with their husbands, who went to bed as the women were getting up:

> Those changing shifts are awful. It's a constant reminder that his work comes first, over any other needs his family might have. We can never get ourselves organized into any regular pattern because our lives are always being turned upside down.
> (Generation III, b. 1947)

The requirements of the husband's wage work affect the women's work in a variety of other ways. Women usually have to pack a lunch for their husbands. They may have to wash and repair work clothes. Most significantly, they have to organize their time around their husband's time. All of the women interviewed said that they got up before their husbands in the morning because it was their responsibility to wake them and get their breakfast ready in time for them to leave for work.

A song from a play about mining towns illustrates how women have to organize their time around the Company's schedules:

> "Who says we don't work to the whistle?
> With us it just don't show.
> We got to have dinner on the table before that whistle blow."
> (Winnipeg Women's Liberation 1978)

Or, as a Flin Flon housewife described it:

Lots of people say what a housewife does isn't work. Well, it is work, and it's just like men's work only it isn't paid and it isn't supervised. But I have things I have to do at certain times. The main difference is, my work is regulated by his work. And whatever I have to do is somehow always overshadowed by the requirements of his work.
(Generation II, b. 1934)

Beyond doing these immediate tasks, the housewife must enter into a far more complex and profound relationship with her husband, for she must also ensure his general psycho-emotional well-being.

The types of demands placed on domestic labour in trying to meet the husband's needs are partly a function of the specific way in which the husband's labour power has been consumed by capital. For example, levels of mental or physical fatigue vary according to the job as do the types of stress, kinds of injuries, size of appetite, and so on. What restoring his ability to work actually involves depends to a large extent on the personality and personal preferences of the individuals in the marriage. These various constraints and possibilities account for some of the differences between households.

In many cases the men develop their own ways of dealing with their work-related tensions. Their wives simply have to recognize their patterns and allow them to do what they want. Some men want to be left alone for a while when they get home. Others insist on going to the pub for a few drinks before coming home. Three of the women interviewed said their husbands insisted that supper be on the table when they walked in the door. These men refused to talk to anyone until they had eaten.[5] In some households the wife and children had to be home waiting for him when he arrived home from work:

Bill likes to play with the kids when he comes in, so I always make sure we're home and the kids are washed and changed.
(Generation III, b. 1955)

In others the children had to be neither seen nor heard when their fathers first returned from work:

When Mike comes in he likes a quiet time with a beer and no kids, so I have to make sure the kids keep quiet and don't bug him in any way.
(Generation III, b. 1950)

Men who do heavy physical labour such as shovelling muck (broken rock) or very noisy work, such as drilling, may need a quiet time alone to relax when they first get off work. Those working under the direct supervision of a boss may choose to release the tensions generated by drinking, playing with their children, or yelling at their families. Some men like to spend their free time at home watching television. Others like to go visiting or have friends over. Some prefer to go off with their male friends to the bush for hunting or fishing or to the pub for drinking. Others like to be very active in voluntary organizations, municipal politics, union politics, or other activities that take them out of the home and away from their families. Whatever their choice, the women's task is to facilitate.

This is a subtle process. Though the tendency for women is to do things "his way" women are not powerless within marriage. They do have a certain amount of leeway and considerable influence, and they regularly exercise discretion about how much they let their husbands' needs structure their lives. When the man is not present, the housewife can do things "her way." She can sometimes expand and alter his tastes. Depending on the quality of their relationship, she can even get him to do things her way.

If the relationship is poor, the wife may do all she can to make her husband's life miserable by regularly asserting her own will in deliberate opposition to his. When there is no conflict between them, she may do things his way because she loves him and wants to make him happy. Finally, many women will say that they do things their husband's way because they believe that is the way a household should function. In fact, the events they describe suggest that what is often designated "his way" is often really "their way."

On some level all of the woman's work takes into account her husband's preferences. This was reflected repeatedly in the decisions Flin Flon women made about what to buy, what to cook, what to wear. When asked why they prepared the foods they did, most women replied that they made what their husbands liked. Often women mentioned that they liked certain foods or were interested in trying a different type of cooking but they refrained because their husbands' tastes had priority. They also bought clothes with their husbands' tastes in mind. A friend and I were shopping for shoes. She tried on a pair that she liked very much. After much indecision she rejected them because "Henry just wouldn't like them." In another instance a woman spent several hours preparing her dress and getting ready for a formal party. When her husband came in he took one look at her and commented that he had never liked that dress. She immediately went to change her clothes.

An older woman recalled moving into a new house from a two-room cabin in 1940. The new house was completely modern, and they had enough money to furnish it as they liked:

> We settled in slowly. We did one room at a time. We would sit down and discuss the room and what we wanted to do with it. We would talk it out together, then I would go and buy the things we needed and set it up. I always did it the way he wanted. After all, it was his money what bought it and he should have his house as he likes.
>
> (Generation II, b. 1915)

This woman described a co-operative process of decision-making and then, without mentioning any conflict or deferral, she said it was his way. How much this suggests that her preferences are guided by him and how much it reflects her notion of how things should be is impossible to determine.

Love and Affection

All of these types of interactions have an impact on the social relations of marriage. One of the striking features of marital relations in Flin Flon over the last three generations is that, as soon as limitations imposed by their working conditions were modified, Flin Flon residents altered their marital arrangements. Love, affection, and caring have changed considerably over the last 50 years. Largely because of their respective work patterns, women and men in the early period had little time to spend socializing together. Sometimes men had to work away from home for months at a time. Even when they lived at home, they often worked for 12 and 14 hours each day six days a week. The woman's housework required long, uninterrupted days.

Older women described their expectations of marriage as "making a family." For them the sexual division of labour was explicitly embodied in their interpersonal relations as well. A couple co-operated to form a household and to have children. They recognized very distinct women's and men's spheres in their leisure activities. As working time decreased for both women and men, the quality of their relationships changed. The shortened workweek and the improvements in housework meant that men could be at home more often and that women had more opportunities to take a few hours "off."[6]

Younger women described their marriages as "partnerships." While they adhered to the traditional division of labour based on work, they seemed to share more activities with their husbands and they expected to be "friends" with them. Over the last 50 years wives and husbands have increasingly spent more time together. Couples seem to expect more demonstrated affection, intimacy, friendship from each other. A young woman described how her marriage differed from her mother's:

> They didn't seem to expect much of each other. They lived together and I know they cared, but they each went their own ways. I don't think that's right. I want to have more closeness with my husband. I think husbands and wives should be each other's best friends.
>
> (Generation III, b. 1952)

Comparing observations of an older woman recalling her past and a young woman describing her present confirms this changed perspective:

> When we was married [1926] and moved here we knew we each had our own harness to pull. Jake worked for the railway and later for the Company and he worked long hours for most of the week. I recollect

he worked 12 to 14 hours each day Monday to Saturday and on Sunday he slept or went out for a drink with his mates. He brought home the wages; that were his job. Me, I looked after the house and took care of the kids and made sure his clothes were clean and his meals were on the table. That were my job.

> (Generation I, b. 1895)

> Jim's my best friend in the world. I don't like to do anything unless he can too. Well he works for the Company, eh, and I take care of the house and the kids but all the time he's home we do things together.
>
> (Generation III, b. 1949)

Besides changing work patterns, other social forces, such as the increasing isolation of the family, have affected marital relationships. In the early period in Flin Flon social life involved regular collective activities. Large groups of people held dances, floating card games, berry-picking outings, and socials organized by groups of individuals who came together for a specific event. Women were central to organizing these get-togethers.

Over the years there has been a shift from community-based entertainment to smaller family events. The number of communal activities has decreased and are organized either by businesses or formal organizations. Women are still active, but the scope of their decision-making and authority has been reduced. Where women once organized for both the community and their families, they now organize primarily for their families.

This shift has reduced women's social horizons and increased their orientation toward the family. An older woman described her experience:

When we first came here the town was small and there weren't no Trout Festival Association or Rotary or whatnot to organize things. So we did it. Oh I remember lovely times, big dances and lots of fun. The men were all working odd hours so we women would do it and everybody would go. . . . Now it seems everything is done for us. There's this or that event, all organized in advance for you, and families go to them or not. It's not the same somehow.

(Generation I, b. 1901)

As she suggests, this change is partly as a result of the municipal infrastructure. However, other factors have also contributed to the changing social patterns.

Before people in Flin Flon owned cars, groups of people sometimes got rides in horse-drawn wagons into the bush to collect berries or to go hunting, picnicking, or exploring:

Before we had the car we often used to go in groups for a wagon ride somewhere. Now we just all go off separately in our own cars.

(Generation II, b. 1923)

Another source of major social change was the development of television:

Before the TV come we used to have a regular, floating card game with the people on the street. We'd go from house to house playing cards and having a whale of a time.

(Generation I, b. 1898)

Used to be, we'd go visiting. Folks would go out for a walk and drop in and chat, have a beer. Nowadays we just all stay home and watch telly.

(Generation II, b. 1931)

The result of these changes is that families have become more dependent on their own leisure activities. When female and male spheres were quite separate, women were less concerned with entertaining their husbands and more involved with the community at large. Their increased isolation within the family, coupled with the modern expectation of friendship and companionship, has meant that wives and husbands are more dependent on each other and therefore more vulnerable to personal whim:

I don't like to go out visiting without Mike. It just doesn't seem right. We like to do things together. But he hasn't been feeling like going out since he started working the night shift, so I haven't been going out either. I miss it.

(Generation III, b. 1951)

Sexuality

I don't know what sex is all about. Sometimes I wish you could just do it because it feels good. But of course you can't. You're not supposed to do it till you're married. You might get pregnant. He wants it and you don't. There's all these different things happening all at once. And you don't know what's right or wrong or why it's all happening. Oh sex! Who would have thought anything so simple could be so complex?

(Generation III, b. 1950)

The "long arm of the job" stretches from the workplace into the bedroom and exerts its grip on the most intimate part of marriage. Sexuality is so complex that it operates on many levels and has different meanings in different situations. In some ways it is an expression of human need, of pleasure, and of the social togetherness of lovers. In other ways it is an oppressive and repressive relationship which grinds the tenderness and love out of people, leaving behind the frustration, bitterness, and violence. From the perspective of domestic labour, there is an aspect of sexuality that is work. On one level marriage can be understood as an exchange between wife and husband—her domestic work, including sexual access, for his economic support.[7]

This underlying exchange becomes apparent in the prelude to marriage, the period in which women are recruited for domestic labour. The process of dating—of selecting a mate for marriage—is, of course, not experienced as an exchange by the people participating in it. The economic necessity for women and the sexual motivation for men are hidden under massive layers of ideology, propaganda, and confusion. People date and marry for many reasons, often because "that is the way things work." They are usually so caught up in the process that they do not have time to reflect on it. Although very few Flin Flon women and men had analyzed the forces that underpin their lives, they did experience the power of those forces. In dating practices, for example, women generally dated men their own age or older. Men rarely dated older women. While a couple may have agreed to share the costs on a date, men were generally expected to pay. Most significantly, women were not supposed to initiate a relationship. They had to wait until a suitable man approached them.

This means that the balance of forces in any female/male relationship is likely to be unequal. Men tend to have the advantage of being older, having economic power and social authority. Women rarely have access to as much money and they cannot act forthrightly.

They are forced to manipulate and insinuate—to set things up so that men will ask them out and, ultimately, ask them to marry.

This inequality permeates sexual activities. Whatever their real feelings (and often they do not know what their real feelings are), both women and men get involved in the process of serious dating where women trade sexual "favours" for a "good time" and economic rewards. On some level the participants are aware of this underlying exchange.

The women know that if they hold out too long, they risk losing the man to someone who is less resistant. Three young women were evaluating their relationships with their current, steady boyfriends. All three men were working. One woman, age 16, had been out with her 17-year-old boyfriend six times. She commented:

> Tomorrow will be our seventh date. Last time he really wanted me to neck with him but I wouldn't. I only let him kiss me goodnight when he took me home. I don't think I can get away with that again this date. I'm going to have to let him go further or he'll never take me out again.

Her boyfriend had been working for the Company for two years. He owned a car and had sizeable savings. He had also stated publicly that when he married, as a wedding present he would give his wife the down payment for the house of her choice. Because of his resources he was considered a "good catch."

Her 15-year-old friend replied:

> Yeh, John [age 16] and me were necking last weekend and we got real close. He wants to go all the way but I said no way. Not till I get married. But he laughed and said I'd be an old maid if I never made out

till then. I'm afraid that if I give in, I'll get pregnant, but if I don't, then I'll lose him.

The third woman, 16 years old, agreed:

Yeh! Boys always expect you to go all the way. And if you won't, then they go find someone else who will. Andy [her 18-year-old boyfriend of six months] said that it wasn't worth his while taking me out all the time, spending his money on me, if I didn't come across.

The men had a similar understanding. One 17-year-old man returned from a date in a foul mood. He complained bitterly that he had had a "lousy time" because:

Jesus, I took her out for supper and we went to a show, and when I took her home she would do nothing but peck my face and say, "Thank you for the nice time." I spent all that money on her, and was real nice to her too and that's all the thanks I get.

Men try to cajole and coerce women "to go all the way." Women resist, give in a bit, resist some more. Everyone knows the risks involved and when a woman finally "gives in" and "allows" the man to go all the way, two related but opposed social expectations come into play. The first is the assumption that pregnancy is the woman's responsibility. If she does not take precautions to prevent conception, she must face the consequences alone. The second is that men do have responsibilities. If a couple have sexual relations and the woman gets pregnant, then they will probably marry.

Once a woman is pregnant, the man is not bound by the same constraints in the situation. Unlike the woman, he can decide or choose whether or not to accept some of the responsibility for her pregnancy. If he does not accept it, then she has been "knocked up" and as a single woman she is subject to material and social hardships. If the man does accept some responsibility, they get married. For the woman this is clearly the preferred choice. It indicates to her as well as to others that he thinks enough of her to want to marry. It makes her a "good woman." However, her dependency on him establishes yet another tension in their relationship.

Many Flin Flon women expressed feelings of gratitude because their husbands had married them. Some spoke of feeling indebted to men who offered to marry them:

Bob is my honey. When I told him I was pregnant he didn't give me no hassle. He just said right off, "Why then we'll get us married and I'll be a daddy." He was so good to me.

(Generation III, b. 1955)

I owe him so much. You know, I got that way and I wasn't going to tell him, only my sister said she would if I didn't. At first he was mad. But he agreed we'd get married.

(Generation III, b. 1956)

Many women expressed anxiety that their husbands had married them only because they were pregnant. These women talked about how they and their children were burdens that the man had "nobly" taken on. One woman, married for over 30 years and the mother of five children, described her fears:

I think maybe he hates me deep down. We had to get married and then I had four more after that one. So he didn't want to marry me. I don't think he ever loved me. But he stuck with us. It was a sort of noble gesture on his part back then. I don't think he knew what it would mean.

(Generation II, b. 1924)

After the first child is born couples are confronted with a series of problems and decisions that focus on sex, children, and domestic work. Here, more than anywhere else perhaps, the different interests of women and men are illuminated. For men the issue seems relatively straightforward. They have an acknowledged and socially recognized desire for sexual intercourse. They tend to assume both that birth control is the responsibility of the woman and that having children is part of marriage. They also generally favour having several children.

For women the question is far more complex. While a few women have come to terms with their sexuality and have apparently satisfying and active sex lives, most young women find sexuality problematic. They say that they rarely enjoy sex except as an indication that their husbands still love them. They are ignorant about their own sexual needs and are terrified of getting pregnant. A standard complaint raised by women of all ages was that their husbands wanted sex "too often":

> He's forever wanting it. Never a weekend goes by but he isn't after me to sleep with him. I don't understand why men want it so often.
>
> (Generation II, b. 1929)

This discrepancy between the experiences of women and men is reflected in interactions between friends or cohorts of the same sex. Men at work joke about making it or "scoring" with their wives on a regular basis. Older men comment regularly on younger men's work patterns by assuring them that the reputed laziness of the younger men occurs because they have such

active sex lives. Older men caution younger men to wait until they have been married for 10 years; then they will not have sex so often and will be able to get a good day's work done.

Women regularly console each other for having "over-sexed" husbands who constantly make demands on them. Older women reassure younger women that after they have been married for 10 years or so their husbands will not want sex so much. It will then happen only a couple of times a year and the younger women will not have to worry any more. A young woman who had been married for three years commented:

> My husband wants sex too much. I think he is oversexed. If he had his way, we'd make out every day!
>
> (Generation III, b. 1950)

Her older neighbour reassured her:

> My man used to be that way too, but he got over it. Just wait a few more years and yours will slow down too. It's hard on you now, but it gets better.
>
> (Generation II, b. 1925)

While the primary reason women give for avoiding sex is the fear of pregnancy, the contradictions they experience are compounded by the fact that their work is continuous and tiring. When a man gets home from work he expects to relax. For a woman home is work and she can rarely relax. Relaxing and concentrating on sex may be almost impossible for the woman if she is listening for the children, or has just finished cleaning up and is trying to organize herself for the next day:

> Then he wants to make out, but I just can't. My head is racing, thinking of all the stuff

to be done tomorrow morning, and I'm tired and just want to collapse asleep. And part of me is always listening for the baby.

(Generation III, b. 1954)

In general, their tension about pregnancy and the nature of their work combine to make women reluctant sexually. Just as patterns of love, affection, and caring have changed over the last 50 years, so too have patterns of sexuality. In her analysis of "the marriage bed," Lillian Rubin (1976: 44) found that in the last 50 years American sexual practices have changed tremendously. "The revolution in American sexual behaviour is profound." She also found that while working-class couples were having sex more frequently and with greater variation, it was at the man's initiative. The women felt great ambivalence and insecurity about sex.

In Flin Flon it also appears that women of the third generation experienced greater confusion, bewilderment, and pressure about sexuality than their mothers and grandmothers did before them. One explanation is that as sexuality is increasingly identified with leisure activities, popularity, and personal expression, it acquires increased significance for both women and men. Another explanation emerges from an analysis developed by Michael Schneider (1975) regarding the dynamic between wage work and male sexuality. Schneider notes the oppressive characteristics of wage work, where the work processes and the machines take over the worker. The body of the worker moves in response to predetermined patterns. His mind has to obey the logic of work processes determined by someone else. Fundamentally, he is denied his humanity.

One area that capitalism does not directly control at work is his sexuality. Because this is one area left to the man, it becomes an important one for him to develop and express. Schneider also notes that as labour has been steadily degraded by capitalism, sex has become increasingly important as a focus of survival for the individual. In sex, male workers have increasingly sought solace and release and an assertion of power, which means there is now more sexual pressure on women.

Older Flin Flon women described sex as a duty a woman is obliged to provide for her man. Because they believed that male sexual needs are direct and urgent, they said it was the responsibility of women to meet them. They rarely referred to any sexual drive on the part of women:

> A woman doesn't need that like a man. Men need it regular or they go a bit nutty. So women have to give it to them. You just leave it up to them; just let them do what they want.
>
> (Generation I, b. 1894)

These women received no direct sexual education. Instead they received extremely contradictory messages. Sex was "not nice" and something to be avoided. Sex was a duty that a woman performed willingly and passively for her husband. They learned to repress and deny their sexual feelings while submitting to men. Older Flin Flon women said that their usual sexual experience was limited to the missionary position, which maximizes the passivity of women. Younger women described a considerably wider range of sexual activities. The sexual revolution of the 1960s expanded knowledge about sexual physiology and sexual practices. As various studies have shown, more people are practising more variations in their sexual behaviour now than in the 1940s.[8]

Rubin found that men were interested in changing their sexual behaviour and pushed women to experiment. She also found that women viewed men's attitudes, including their concern for female orgasm and gratification, as a mixed blessing. She concluded:

> As long as women's sexuality is subjected to capricious demands and treated as if regulated by an "on–off" switch, expected to surge forth vigorously at the flick of the "on" switch or to subside at the flick of the "off," most women will continue to seek the safest path and remain quietly some place between "on" and "off." (Rubin 1976: 92)

"Quietly somewhere between on and off" is an apt description of the way most younger Flin Flon women talked about their sexuality:

> Sometimes I get real excited and I really want it but what we do doesn't really do it to me so then I feel frustrated and irritable. So it's better if I never get turned on.
> (Generation III, b. 1952)

> I usually don't get turned on very much but sometimes he's just so nice and he loves me so much that I feel sort of like it.
> (Generation III, b. 1951)

> Mostly I don't think about sex, but if I get too turned off then it's awful when he wants it, so I can't shut myself off completely.
> (Generation III, b. 1954)

The passive lover is a natural extension of the "good girl." Women who for years learned to deny their sexual needs cannot suddenly reverse those years and "turn on." But for younger men sexuality is an important part of the way they have learned to express their feelings. As one man explained:

> I love her and I want her to know how deeply I feel and I can't understand why she won't let me show her [by having sex].
> (Generation III, b. 1945)

His bewilderment was genuine; so was his affection. Rubin (1976: 47) describes the uncertainty that women and men experience when they confront each other's sexual expectations:

> The cry for understanding from both men and women is real. Each wishes to make the other understand, yet, given the widely different socialization practices around male and female sexuality, the wish is fantasy. As a result, he asks; she gives. And neither is satisfied.

For women the recent sexual patterns that men have introduced are bound up in contradictions. Men want women to be more active, to participate more energetically in sex, to initiate it more often. They want greater variety, particularly oral sex. They also want to feel that women are enjoying sex. But women and men have not generally learned how to share mutual pleasure. Instead men tend to exert even more pressure on women and then appropriate women's pleasure for themselves.

So women become more active, take the initiative, and either have orgasms or fake them, still mostly to satisfy the men:

> He keeps telling me he wishes I'd start things off sometimes. But when I do he's always busy or too tired or I'm interrupting him. I think he wants me to start things when he wants them to start.
> (Generation III, b. 1945)

For some women, sex is still a duty, but a duty that now includes being active:

He wants me to be real turned on and excited. He sort of likes it when I pant and moan and wiggle around.

(Generation III, b. 1941)

Some women do what their husbands want out of resignation or fear:

I don't care any more. I just let him do what he wants, and if he wants me to do something I do it. So what?

(Generation III, b. 1946)

When he wants it he has to get it or he gets mad and beats me up, so I always do as he wants.

(Generation III, b. 1957)

Just as women are afraid when dating that if they hold back they may lose the men, some wives are afraid that if they do not participate in sex, they will lose their husbands to other women, to the pub, or to male friends:

I do whatever he wants. Otherwise I figure he'll run off with other women—ladies of the night types.

(Generation III, b. 1945)

I try to act real interested and sexy just as he's leaving for work so he'll be interested and come straight home after work.

(Generation II, b. 1935)

I always seduce him just before we go to a party. That way I figure he won't be interested in other women. He'll be too pooped.

(Generation III, b. 1946)

For some women sexual co-operation is a way of inducing or rewarding good behaviour.

Some even recognize the sexual–economic exchange that underlies marriage:

If I want something, I just get all sexy and loving, and after I tell him what I want.

(Generation III, b. 1956)

If he does something really nice, like help me with the dishes or take me out somewhere to something special, then I always try to make love to him so he'll know I liked what he did.

(Generation II, b. 1933)

When I want something for the house, like a new washing machine or something, then I just make love like crazy for a while and then stop. Then I tell him what I want and say that if he wants more loving he has to buy it.

(Generation III, b. 1949)

For many other women, however, sex is a way of expressing their feelings of affection and caring. For them "making love" is literally that. Sex both expresses and reinforces the love they feel for their husbands:

I love that guy. So I try to show him.

(Generation III, b. 1947)

He's a sweetie. I love him so I make love with him lots.

(Generation III, b. 1948)

He's a wonderful man. I love him. It's the best way I can let him know.

(Generation III, b. 1953)

Love and affection can hold women back sexually. Some women decide that there is no percentage in "turning on." To turn on is to assert one's own needs. Sex traditionally revolves around the man's advances, his schedules, his rhythms, his climax—his needs. For a woman to be turned on seems to contest this one-sidedness. Women often subordinate their needs and wants to ensure family harmony. Sublimating their sexuality to their husbands' may be an expression of this pattern, an attempt on the part of the wife to express her love for her husband.

> Sometimes I'd like to say stop when he is pounding away at me. Then I'd tell him to slow down, to touch me the way I dream about. And I imagine us making love beautifully. And I like it and I love him. But if I did, I know he'd feel hurt. It's important to him that he thinks I like the way he makes love. If I started suggesting things he'd feel bad. So I don't.
>
> (Generation III, b. 1948)

The sublimation of sexuality in the interests of marital harmony may be one reason sexual activity apparently decreases as the marriage ages. Sixty of the women interviewed reported that as their marriages progressed, their level of sexual activity decreased. It may be that, faced with their inability to resolve all the contradictions that surround sexuality, many couples give up. They minimize their sexual activities rather than continue to confront the tensions:

> When we were first married, sex was really difficult. I never liked it and he knew that and it made him feel bad. Gradually it just didn't seem worth it to go on. So we don't do it much any more.
>
> (Generation II, b. 1931)

Family Violence Is a Hateful Thing

Men and women come to marriage from very different positions and their experiences of work and marriage create different understandings. At best these contrary positions are barriers which must be struggled against. For most couples they become sources of tension and all too frequently the tension leads to hostility and conflict.

At work men are powerless, so in their leisure time they want to have a feeling that they control their own lives. Because they are responsible for the household's subsistence, men often feel that they have the right to control the arrangements of the household and the people who live there. As the wage *earner*, the man is the wage *owner*. He is the property owner in the family; his power is rooted in real property relations. This property prerogative is the basis of the unequal relations of the family. Structured into household relations therefore is a "petty tyranny" which allows the man to dominate his wife and children. Such male domination derives partly from the fact that domestic labour is predicated on wage labour and therefore caters to the needs of the wage worker. It is reinforced partly by societal norms of male dominance and superiority. Male chauvinism easily flourishes in such a setting. Some men exercise their "petty tyranny" by demanding that their wives be at home when they get off work. The reason men give for making this demand is partly a reflection of their desire to assert their authority:

> She's my wife and she should be there when I get off.
>
> (Generation II, b. 1919)

> You [to wife] be home when I get off. That's where you belong.
>
> (Generation III, b. 1946)

Knowing that they can demand that their wives be at home waiting for them is a mechanism for releasing some of the feelings of powerlessness the wage work engenders:

It makes me feel good to know she is at home waiting for me, like there's a place where I'm a man. I think about that when I'm at work.

(Generation III, b. 1953)

One result of the economic relationship between women and their husbands is to bind the men to their jobs. While divorce from the means of production structurally compels men to do wage work, once a man has a dependent wife and children he incurs responsibilities and debts, which means that he cannot afford to stop working. While a single man can choose to quit a particular job when it becomes too unpleasant, a married man cannot. Objectively the woman becomes a force in keeping the man tied to his job. From her position of economic dependency, a wife adds more pressure to the structural compulsion to work.

Historically the Company has hired married men precisely because they create a more stable workforce. Sometimes women themselves recognize this aspect of their relationship:

I know he hates his job. It's a terrible job. But he can't quit 'cause of me and the kids. We need his wages.

(Generation III, b. 1953)

Subjectively, women act as pressure to keep their husbands not only at work but working regularly and responsibly. Many men deal with their dislike of work by quitting periodically, or less drastically, by going late, taking time off, or slacking on the job. Such behaviour is directly threatening to the household standard of living as it affects the amount of money the men bring home. It is in the women's interests to try to prevent the men from taking time off. When a man considers doing so, his wife may point out that they are in debt and need his money. Thus some men see their wives as constantly nagging, forcing them to work when they hate it. This induces tensions between the needs of women as domestic workers and the response of the men to wage work, tensions which are often expressed as hostilities between the sexes. A woman whose husband regularly skipped shifts expressed her sense of frustration and anger at men:

Men. They're just no good. They are lazy and irresponsible and selfish. Look at Jim, he just skipped another shift and how are we going to make do?

(Generation II, b. 1929)

On the other hand, the responsibility of being breadwinners generates in men all sorts of pressure and fear, which in turn are often projected onto women (Guettel 1974: 14). This hostility is reinforced by women's work as tension managers for their husbands.

When men express their work-related tensions, anxieties, and hostilities at work, it is economically threatening to the employer. When their protest is collectively expressed, for example in a general strike, the results are politically threatening to the capitalist state. Therefore, both employers and the state employ sophisticated means to minimize this potential. The threat of firing is the most significant means of repressing outbursts in the workplace. Labour legislation, especially laws against wildcat strikes, and the armed force of the police protect the interests of the state.

On the other hand, family violence is not directed against either employers or the state.

While in recent years, primarily because of pressures from the women's liberation movement, family violence has gradually come to be considered socially deviant, it is still not recognized as a major social problem. Very little is done by either employers or the state to prevent family violence.

If no mechanisms are available by which workers can channel their work-related tensions into forms of struggle at the workplace, they carry those tensions and angers home with them. Part of reproducing the worker's labour power must therefore include ways of displacing those work-related fears and hostilities:

> When he comes home from work, I really think it's up to me to help him relax and feel good. If he's grumpy and tired, I cheer him up.
> (Generation II, b. 1926)

This part of women's work in reproducing labour power is the most hidden and profound. It is also of vital importance for her work and her life. While part of this tension management is done for the sake of the man, another part is for herself and the children. Women do not want to live with fights and the threat of violence every day. They defuse tension, refrain from a certain argument, or protect their husbands from things that will upset them in order to maintain peace:

> I remember how I always used to try and meet him at the door with a cup of tea. He liked his tea. If I made him feel better after work, then our home was a happy one.
> (Generation I, b. 1900)

In some instances, women are the recipients of overt anger and rage. Some examples will illustrate what this means in practice. A 32-year-old man had worked for the Company for 16 years. His current supervisor did not like him and they had regular clashes at work. He came home almost every night tense and irritable. His wife described what happened at night:

> We go to sleep and then sometimes in the middle of the night I wake up because he is groaning and punching me and crying out angry stuff at his boss. Sometimes he punches me real hard and once he broke my nose. Course he didn't mean to and it wasn't me he was mad at. It was his boss, but still. So I get out of bed and go make tea and wake him up and talk to him, then he settles down and we go back to sleep. It happens maybe two or three times a week.
> (Generation III, b. 1949)

The wife received the brunt of the rage and violence that her husband bottled up and repressed at work. She considered it her duty to get up and make him tea and comfort him, even though she had an infant to feed at 6 a.m. She was constantly tired and sometimes dozed off in the middle of a conversation. She apologized for doing so by explaining:

> See Joe has a hard time at work so I have to get up with him in the night, so I don't get too much sleep these days.

In another case, a 28-year-old man had worked for the Company for 12 years. He too had a supervisor with whom he fought regularly. His solution to his work-related tensions was to get drunk or stoned on marijuana every night after work. His wife was concerned for his health and worried that he drank or smoked "all that hard-earned cash." When he was "ripped" he tended to think that she was the hated boss and he lashed out at her:

Once he came at me with the kitchen knife saying I was [the boss] and he wasn't going to take no more shit from me. Another time he took a swipe at me and broke my glasses. Usually though he just yells at me that I can take my fucking job and shove it or something like that. I just keep out of reach till he calms down.

(Generation III, b. 1951)

Growing out of the various power struggles that occur between men and their work and between wives and husbands is sex-based hostility where male contempt for women is expressed through physical violence.

Wife beating is one of the hidden crimes in this society. In recent years the women's liberation movement has pointed out how widespread it is. The few studies that have been done show unequivocally that wife beating is a phenomenon that occurs with equal frequency among families of all classes (Eekelaar and Katz 1975; Borland 1976; D'Oyley 1978; Martin 1978; Renvoize 1978; MacLeod 1980). It is part of the larger problem of generalized violence against women and must be understood in that context. For working-class families, it is compounded by the pressures and dependency generated by the proletarian condition:

My husband beats me, usually on payday. He gets mad and hates me. His violence is a really hateful thing.

(Generation II, b. 1935)

Why do women put up with such treatment? They do so partly because there are no resources to give them the support necessary to deal with the abuse. Flin Flon has no hostels for women; the police will not interfere in what they term "domestic squabbles"; and economically the women have no resources to

leave. Equally important is the fact that most women feel it is their responsibility to "stick it out" because marriage is "till death do us part" and tension managing is part of their work. Of the hundred women interviewed, only three were divorced. Most women, when male violence erupts, "just keep out of reach" until it subsides.

One woman who was beaten regularly by her husband was recovering after a particularly bad attack in which her arm was broken. What she said explains in part why so many women accept the abuse they receive from their husbands:

He puts up with shit every day at work and he only works because he has me and the kids to support. Weren't for us he'd be off trapping on his own, with no boss breathing down his neck. He hates his job. He's got all that mad locked up inside with nowhere for it to go. So sometimes he takes it out on me and the kids. Well I sort of don't blame him I guess.

(Generation II, b. 1935)

Thus a terrible but logical and extreme extension of their roles as tension managers is for women, as the victims, to blame themselves and to feel guilty for having induced male hostility and aggression.

Meeting Women's Needs

Domestic violence is the most extreme form of women's oppression within the family. However, in a myriad of other less obvious ways the subordinate character of domestic labour denies women their full humanity.

Domestic labour is responsible for reproducing the labour power of all the adults of the household. In other words, the woman is responsible for reproducing not only her husband's capacity to work each day but her own as well. In some ways, domestic labour is similar to wage work. It is frequently physically and mentally exhausting and monotonous. While it is not alienated in the sense that wage labour is alienated, it is the epitome of self-sacrificing labour. Because it is unpaid, women can justify it as reasonable and honourable work only by considering it a "labour of love." This definition reinforces its self-sacrificing quality and encourages women themselves to underplay the extent to which it is much more than a labour of love. In daily life this means that women's needs are not always met.

When household resources are scarce, it is the women who cut back their consumption first. There is a working-class tradition of women eating less than their husbands and children, denying themselves sustenance they badly need so that other household members can have more.[9]

In many Flin Flon households, on the day before payday there was very little food in the house. A number of women regularly did not eat that day because there was only enough for one or two people.

> He's got to eat or he can't do his work and the baby needs food to grow, but it won't hurt me to skip a meal for once.
> (Generation III, b. 1958)

Women's sleeping time is also vulnerable to demands from other household members. In some households where men worked the night shift, their wives got up at 3 a.m. either to greet them coming off shift or to send them off to work. When those women had school-aged children, they also had to get up at 7:30 a.m. so their sleep was disrupted and inadequate. When other household members were sick or frightened or simply unable to sleep at night, the women got up with them to comfort, feed, and care for them. A number of women talked about how tired they felt all the time. They attributed this "housewife's fatigue" to regularly interrupted sleep.

Even when women were ill, they had to carry on with their work. Those women who were actively engaged in domestic labour reported that their husbands were sick enough to stay in bed an average of four days each year. Their husbands went to bed when they got sick, and the women took care of them in addition to doing their regular work. The women themselves were sick enough to warrant staying in bed an average of eight days each year. However, they unanimously agreed that, no matter how sick they were, they could not take time off to go to bed. They continued with their regular work despite their illness. In every case, women took time off work only when they were hospitalized—for a major illness or having a baby. Women said they enjoyed their stays in hospital when their babies were born. They relished the rest and being catered to.

The 22 women who were retired said that a similar pattern continued even when the couple was older and nearing retirement. In older people, illness was compounded by the fact that many of the men had work-related injuries or illnesses, which meant they required constant nursing. Even though the women were also often ill or crippled by age-related diseases, such as arthritis and rheumatism, they still continued to nurse the men. A number of women said that dealing with an ill spouse finally forced them to retire:

> I kept on managing my house for 20 years after my husband retired. He had bad lungs [from working underground] and at last he took to bed and needed regular

nursing. Well I kept at it for about a year, but I wasn't strong enough so I finally had to give it up.

(Generation I, b. 1888)

Reproducing labour power also involved ensuring that workers have a chance to recuperate, relax, and engage in leisure activities that are not related to their regular work. For domestic workers, especially with young children, meeting this need is almost impossible. There is no time when the woman is totally free from work-related responsibilities. Even when she is relaxing, she is on call. Women recognize that their situation differs from their husbands':

I guess I have to take care of all of them and then I have to take care of myself too.
(Generation III, b. 1955)

How come there's no one to take care of me?
(Generation II, b. 1934)

When they are tired, or can't find something or they want something, I do it for them. When I want something I get it for myself.
(Generation III, b. 1945)

When women described their activities during a typical day, they frequently mentioned periods when they took time "off" to visit with friends, watch TV, or just sit down for a cup of tea and a cigarette. However, even during these breaks, those with young children must be alert to their activities. And all too often, women described their breaks as time not only to relax but also to "do a bit of mending or sewing."

The responsibility of constantly caring for the needs of others means that it is often difficult for women to determine what their own needs are:

When I wake up early I like to lie in bed and have a think about my life. It's the only time I have to myself and what I need, you know, to get me through my day. Like I know what he needs—his lunch box and a hot supper—and what they need—clean clothes and their lunch. And they all need love I guess. But what do I need?
(Generation II, b. 1936)

Sometimes the work women do becomes so merged with their identity that they have trouble distinguishing them. They confuse their own needs with those of their families. This confusion is reflected in the way women sometimes describe family needs. A woman buying a jacket for her six-year-old child remarked: "I need this jacket. It's getting cold these days."

The lack of clarity that women have about their own needs as domestic workers begins with marriage when most couples set up households and the women establish the social relations of their work based on inexperience and lack of knowledge. The first few years of household formation are critical, for it is during this period that patterns of work, personal interactions, and the particular expression of the division of labour within the household are established. Once established they are extremely difficult to change.

A woman with three children under 10 years of age observed that when her first baby was born she was so interested and excited by the new baby that she wanted to take care of it herself. She never asked her husband to help out with child care. When the second and third children were born, the novelty had worn off, her energy was dissipated, and she wanted him to become involved:

But he just wouldn't. He said he'd never changed a nappy and he wasn't about to start. In fact, he used to point out regularly that I had insisted on doing it alone with the first one and why had I suddenly changed my tune now?

(Generation III, b. 1948)

Because of their initial experience and lack of knowledge, women frequently flounder around for several years trying to understand what is happening to them and trying to get some control over the situation.

At the same time, they are caught up in the demands of young children, keeping a house, and relating to their husbands. Many of them end up in the same situation as the Red Queen in Lewis Carroll's *Through the Looking Glass*, having to run as fast as they can simply to stay in one place.[10] An older woman recalled her feelings of bewilderment and confusion during this early period of her marriage:

I never quite got on top of things. I kept thinking that if I could just get a week of peace I could think things through and then I'd be okay. But everything was always rushing here and there and I didn't ever catch up. Now I sort of have a routine and a pattern of work. But I never chose it. It just happened by default.

(Generation I, b. 1907)

Most women are not deliberate martyrs; they make a concerted effort to ensure that their own needs for relaxation and support are met at some level. They develop strategies, such as organizing their workplace and the social relations of their work in the most convenient and convivial ways possible. This means that women are interested in adopting any new developments in household technology, in the organization of their work or in new products and materials.

Another strategy involves organizing their work so that they can assert themselves as they choose when their husbands are not around. Most women organize this part of their time around their own interests:

When he's not here I do things how I want. I scrub my floors or do my wash or go visit or play with the kids—whatever I want to do and how I want to do it. When he gets off, I have to make sure I'm on time for work, I have to be home waiting for him and I do what he wants while he's there. That way he feels good, we have a good time together and I get my own time too.

(Generation III, b. 1947)

As a third strategy women establish and maintain networks of co-workers, friends, and neighbours to provide a milieu in which they can pool their knowledge about their work and share information, goods, and services. All of the women interviewed described these networks as vitally important to them. On an average, women spent three to four hours each day visiting, either in person or on the phone, with friends and neighbours. During these visits women combine a number of activities. They enjoy each other's company while exchanging information about their work and their lives. Simultaneously they care for their children and continue doing some aspect of their housework, such as ironing or cooking:

I try to visit with my friends as often as possible. It helps me get through my day. We sit and chat about this and that. We watch the kids. I help do the laundry or whatever.

(Generation III, b. 1949)

They also rely a great deal on assistance and support from female relatives. Of the 20 women interviewed who had mothers living in Flin Flon, 19 said that they saw their mothers at least twice a week. Of the 88 active domestic workers interviewed, 72 said they relied on a close female relative, mother, mother-in-law, daughter, or sister to help out in crisis situations. Women in 63 households said they visited with a close female relative at least once each week and that those women provided assistance, information, and affection:

> My sister and my husband's mother are just always there when I need them. If I want to pop out to the store, one of them will mind the baby. If I'm feeling low, I go for a visit.
>
> (Generation III, b. 1951)

Through their women friends and relatives, housewives can improve the social relations of their work and meet some of their own needs for work-related tension managing. Even women who considered their husbands to be their best friends asserted that women friends were special and important:

> Well, my husband, he's my husband and I love him, and he knows me better than anyone and he's my best friend. But Sarah is something else. I see her every day and we chat and when I'm down she cheers me up and when I'm in a muddle she sorts me out and when things aren't good with my husband, she hugs me.
>
> (Generation III, b. 1948)

Frequently, several women got together to do some part of their work collectively. Two or three women went shopping in one car, and as they shopped they pooled ideas about good deals and menu suggestions. They looked out for each other's children and borrowed money

from each other. On occasion, several women assembled in one house to spend the day cooking. They usually did this when the food such as pierogies, cabbage rolls, or preserves required lots of chopping or a long cooking time and constant watching. The women prepared a large quantity of food to be shared among all of them. I participated in two collective cooking activities. One day three of us worked from 9 a.m. to 5:30 p.m. and made 435 pierogies. On another day, four of us worked from 10:30 a.m. to 4:30 p.m. and made 193 cabbage rolls. Working together turned an onerous job into an interesting social occasion.

Most of the women interviewed said that periodically when their children were young they arranged with another woman to exchange childcare services. Two women with children of similar ages took turns looking after each other's children for a number of hours each week. This gave each of the mothers some time "off" to spend as they wished.

Because individual women work most of the time in the isolation of their own home, these relations with other women combine both the need for co-workers with whom to share information and advice and the need for friends with common interests. It is these relationships that provide much of the tension managing that domestic workers need. Women pointed out that their husbands rarely did domestic work and consistently undervalued both its difficulty and its worth. Other women, who from their own experience understood the requirements and rigours of the work, were more helpful in providing support, reassurance, and comfort for work-related problems:

> Sometimes I feel so tired and out of sorts with my family. I can't really talk to David about it. He tries but he really doesn't

understand, and anyway sometimes he's part of the problem, if you know what I mean. My mother or my sister or my neighbour next door, I just go and have a good cry with them and then I feel better.
(Generation III, b. 1942)

Women's efforts to improve the conditions of their work, and their families' lives, and all the contradictions inherent in that, have an impact beyond their immediate household and friendship networks.

The tension between women's short- and long-term interests as domestic labourers and as members of their class was illustrated during the period of contract negotiations between the union and the Company in 1976. A number of women noted that the negotiations directly affected them and their ability to do their work. One woman pointed out the contradictions between the immediate objective conditions of her work, the long-term interests of that work, and her subjective understanding of her class interests. Her immediate interests were the regularity of the wage, ensuring that money kept coming into the household purse. Her long-term interests as a domestic labourer were concerned with the magnitude of the wage and its increase. As a member of her class she had to grapple with the short-term/long-term trade-offs that are always part of class struggle:

I don't want a strike because I can't live on strike pay. I just can't feed my kids on strike pay. But I think we should strike because that company makes so much money off those men and it thinks it can get away with murder. We need to stand up to the Company and show them that they can't go on trashing us workers any more.
(Generation II, b. 1926)

There is a long tradition of miners' wives acting militantly in support of the miners in class-struggle situations.[11] In both strikes in Flin Flon, in 1934 and 1971, the wives of strikers played an important role in the union struggles. They organized strike support committees, went on the picket lines, and regularly indicated both their support for the men and their own interests in winning the strike.

A woman who was active in the 1971 strike described her experiences and noted the connections between her work in the home and her husband's wage work:

The men were on strike and their families were hurting. A bunch of us women were talking. Some of them wanted to end the strike—they were scared and just wanted life to be normal again. But others understood better that it was our strike too. We needed more money and better conditions for our men, [and this] meant better conditions at home. Miserable angry workers make rotten husbands. . . . So we went on the picket line and did what we could.
(Generation II, b. 1929)

By seizing the initiative, women begin to gain some control over their working conditions and their lives. This gives them strength to struggle against the inequalities of their marriages. It undermines their subordination and helps to make better, rather than worse, the position of wife in industrial-capitalist society.

● Notes

1. The most important lack of alternatives is the fact that heterosexual, monogamous marriage is generally considered to be the only normal life choice for everyone. People who choose to be single, to have children alone, to have no children, to live with several people, lesbians, homosexuals, and bisexuals, even couples who live together without marrying—all are subjected to some degree of social sanction and disapproval. As long as this is so people cannot "choose" freely to marry.

2. The situation of women wage earners with respect to the sex-segregated job market and the unequal pay differentials between women and men was well documented in 1970 by the *Report of the Royal Commission on the Status of Women in Canada* (Ottawa: Information Canada, 1970). More up-to-date figures from the Department of Labour, Women's Bureau, are summarized by Pat Armstrong and Hugh Armstrong in *The Double Ghetto* (Toronto: McClelland & Stewart, 1978). These more recent figures confirm that the pay differential between women and men is, if anything, increasing.

3. Luxton interviewed 60 women who had set up their households between the 1920s and 1970s: five did so in the 1920s, 15 in the 1930s, and 10 from each of the later decades. (She interviewed other women as well, but this was her initial sample.) She divided these 60 women into three "generations" (which she signified with I, II, and III). The first generation established their households in the most primitive of conditions, and the last had houses that were equipped with modern services and technology. Whenever she quotes them, Luxton indicates the birth date (b.) of each woman.

4. For a study of the impact of shift work on the social relations of the family, see P.E. Mott, *Shift Work: The Social, Psychological, and Physical Consequences* (Ann Arbor: University of Michigan Press, 1965), 18.

5. This is a typical pattern for working-class families. Denis et al. cite the example of the man who threw

his supper into the fire even though he admitted that it was particularly good food. His wife had gone out and arranged for another woman to prepare his meals for him. They quoted him when he explained that he threw out the dinner because it was his wife's job to prepare his meal and she could not allocate her work to someone else. N. Denis, F. Henriques, and C. Slaughter, *Coal Is Our Life: An Analysis of a Yorkshire Mining Community* (London: Tavistock Publications, 1969), 182.

6. Michael Young and Peter Willmott in *The Symmetrical Family: A Study of Work and Leisure in the London Region* (London: Routledge & Kegan Paul, 1973) suggest that the shorter workweek for wage workers and the improved situation for domestic workers created by household technology have resulted in a new type of family relations where the sexual division of labour is breaking down. They note that men have begun to spend a bit more time around the house helping out with domestic work and that women are increasingly taking on wage work. They hypothesize from these observations that a basic equality is evolving within the family. They are able to make such a statement only because they have never stopped to investigate what actually does constitute domestic labour. While it is true that men are helping out more around the house, they are still "helping out." The internal household labour is still the primary responsibility of women.

7. While marriage laws vary, one universal feature is the recognition that legal marriage must be "consummated"; that is, sexual intercourse must take place. If it does not, the marriage may be annulled, which essentially means that the marriage never occurred.

8. A summary of the major studies on North American sexuality since Kinsey, see Ruth Brecker and E. Brecker, *An Analysis of Human Sexual Response* (New York: Signet, 1966); M. Hunt, *Sexual Behavior in the 1970s* (Chicago: Playboy

Press, 1974); Shere Hite, *The Hite Report* (New York: Dell Books, 1976).

9.   For a good discussion on how and why women subordinate their needs to those of their husbands, see Laura Oren, "The Welfare of Women in Labouring Families: England 1860–1950," in M. Hartman and L.W. Banner, eds, *Clio's Consciousness Raised: New Perspectives on the History of Women* (New York: Harper and Row, 1974); M.L. McDougall, "Working Class Women During the Industrial Revolution, 1780–1860" (Houghton Mifflin, 1977); Jane Humphries, "The Working Class Family, Women's Liberation, and Class Struggle: The Case of Nineteenth-century British History," *The Review of Radical Political Economics: Women, Class, and the Family* 9, 3 (Fall 1977).

10. In Lewis Carroll's *Through the Looking Glass* (London: Penguin Books, 1971), Alice meets the Red Queen and they begin to run just as fast as they can because they want to stay in the same place. Alice suggests that this is unusual but the Queen assures her: "Now here you see, it takes all the running you can do to keep in the same place. If you want to get somewhere else, you must run at least twice as fast as that." A number of women who had read this story saw a similar pattern in their own lives.

11. For information on the role of women in miners' strikes in North America, see M.E. Parton, ed., *The Autobiography of Mother Jones* (Chicago: Charles H. Kerr, 1974); and Kathy Kahn, *Hillbilly Women* (New York: Avon Books, 1973). The important part that women play in primary resource strike situations was graphically portrayed by Barbara Kopple in her film *Harlan County, USA* (1975). For a sketchy outline of the role of women in the Flin Flon strikes, see Valerie Hedman, Loretta Yauck, and Joyce Henderson, *Flin Flon* (Flin Flon, MB: Flin Flon Historical Society, 1974). *The Wives Tale/L'histoire des femmes* is a film about the 1978 strike against Inco in Sudbury, Ontario.

● References

Borland, M., ed. 1976. *Violence in the Family* (Manchester: Manchester University Press).

Denis, N., F. Henriques, and C. Slaughter. 1969. *Coal Is Our Life: An Analysis of a Yorkshire Mining Community* (London: Tavistock Publications).

D'Oyley, V., ed. 1978. *Domestic Violence* (Toronto: Ontario Institute for Studies in Education).

Easton, L.D., and K.H. Guddat, eds and trans. 1967. *Writings of the Young Marx on Philosophy and Society* (New York: Doubleday).

Eekelaar, J.M., and S.N. Katz. 1975. *Family Violence* (Toronto: Butterworths).

Guettel, C. 1974. *Marxism and Feminism* (Toronto: The Women's Press).

MacLeod, L. 1980. *Wife Battering in Canada: The Vicious Circle* (Ottawa: Canadian Advisory Council on the Status of Women).

Martin, J.P., ed. 1978. *Violence and the Family* (New York: John Wiley).

Renvoize, J., ed. 1978. *Wed of Violence* (London: Routledge & Kegan Paul).

Rubin, L. 1976. "The Marriage Bed," *Psychology Today* (Aug.): 44.

Schneider, M. 1975. *Neurosis and Civilization* (New York: The Seabury Press).

Winnipeg Women's Liberation. 1978. *Newsletter* (Feb.).

Part III

Families Today: The Social Relations That Make Families

In a culture dominated by the marketplace, people are confronted with seemingly endless choices about how to live. But influencing the choices that men and women make about their lives are a number of social factors and forces pushing them to make families.

Normative heterosexuality promotes marriage and family. The subtle and unsubtle repression of "inappropriate" sexual and gender expression in children and young people—especially boys—and the eroticization of relationships between girls and boys, and women and men, produce adults who are likely to be drawn to relationships with the other sex. Meanwhile, as an ever-present backdrop, the marketplace and especially the music, advertising, and film industries rely on glorified images of heterosexual romantic love to sell their products. Moreover, there is a strong belief in Canadian culture that only people related by blood or marriage can be truly committed to each other: Family continues to be seen as the exclusive site of love and caring relationships. And there is more at work than belief, ideals, and ideology. In the absence of many other sources of community and solidarity, families seem to be the only real foundation of close and caring relationships for many of us.

Ongoing gender differences also pull men and women together to form families. A variety of social processes, including social pressures, produce girls who have learned how to care for others and do the emotion work central to intimacy, and boys who typically have not. Continuing differences in women's and men's opportunities and results in the labour force also promote interdependence between men and women. Although fewer and fewer men earn enough singlehandedly to support a family, many single women are still unlikely to earn enough to support themselves and children. Moreover, motherhood in countries like Canada, where little social support is given to parents, reinforces women's sense of dependence on a partner. And many men are dependent on women to sustain their relationships with children, as is evident in the frequency with which men's relationships with their children weaken or die in the wake of divorce.

Interestingly, the social forces that have recruited most people to form heterosexual nuclear families have weakened in recent decades. The ideologies of romantic love and even motherhood—as women's primary career, which relegates all else to the background—now compete against some other ideas, albeit only vaguely developed ones. And the majority of women do not depend financially on men, as they did decades ago. Substantial numbers of women as well as men are dedicating themselves to their careers or jobs and avoiding long-term relationships, and choosing to have children on their own. As well, heterosexuality is no longer the only socially accepted form of sexual expression or foundation of committed relationships: Same-sex couples are creating families and raising children.

Families have also changed. In heterosexual nuclear families, the increased likelihood that both adults are employed unsettles conventional arrangements based on gender. Women's employment also exposes a contradiction built into nuclear-family living—that it takes more than two adults to care for children. Without good, affordable daycare, upper- and middle-class couples typically rely on a paid employee, a nanny who is usually a woman of colour; other couples frequently depend on babysitters. In the former families, then, household work is divided along the lines of race and class as well as gender. There are problems inherent in that arrangement.

The following chapters examine how women and men negotiate sexuality; the decisions to date, live together, and marry; the planning of their wedding; parenthood; and doing household work. In spite of change in the direction of gender equality over several decades, the research presented here indicates that women and men continue to wield different degrees of bargaining power when negotiating sex and building intimate heterosexual relationships. Gender differences are strongest when heterosexual couples become parents, and especially when their children are young. At the same time, men are increasingly involved in the care of their children. Moreover, growing numbers of same-sex partners are forging new, more egalitarian family arrangements than those characteristic of heterosexual couples.

Section 1

Negotiating Adult Intimacy

Chapter 9

In her description of the family survival strategies of nineteenth-century Quebeckers working in New England textile mills, Tamara Hareven elaborates on the "kin work" typically done by an elder daughter in every family. These women cared for their parents in their old age but also, over the years, nurtured relationships among grown siblings and maintained ties with far-flung relatives. With a similar focus on the work central to families, Meg Luxton describes the wide-ranging work that 1970s working-class wives did in order to ensure their husbands' daily return to jobs they hated, to earn the money essential to their families' livelihood. Having sex was, according to Luxton, an essential part of this social-reproductive work done by homemakers.

In this chapter, Yen Le Espiritu describes the kin work expected of women in Filipino families that have migrated to the United States, work that is central to family and community identity in a racist country. She also describes the symbolic nature of womanhood and women's sexuality in this racialized migrant community. In so doing, Espiritu provides an explanation of these parents' attitudes toward their daughters' sexuality.

"We Don't Sleep Around Like White Girls Do": Family, Culture, and Gender in Filipina American Lives

Yen Le Espiritu

I want my daughters to be Filipino especially on sex. I always emphasize to them that they should not participate in sex if they are not married. We are also Catholic. We are raised so that we don't engage in going out with men while we are not married. And I don't like it to happen to my daughters as if they have no values. I don't like them to grow up that way, like the American girls.
— Filipina immigrant mother

I found that a lot of the Asian American friends of mine, we don't date like white girls date. We don't sleep around like white girls do. Everyone is really mellow at dating because your parents were constraining and restrictive.
— Second-generation Filipina daughter

Focusing on the relationship between Filipino immigrant parents and their daughters, this article argues that gender is a key to immigrant identity and a vehicle for racialized immigrants to assert cultural superiority over the dominant group. In immigrant communities, culture takes on a special significance: not only does it form a lifeline to the home country and a basis for group identity in a new country, it is also a base from which immigrants stake their political and sociocultural claims on their new country (Eastmond 1993, 40). For Filipino immigrants, who come from a homeland that was once a US colony, cultural reconstruction has been especially critical in the assertion of their presence in the United States—a way to counter the cultural Americanization of the Philippines, to resist the assimilative and alienating demands of US society, and to reaffirm to themselves their self-worth in the face of colonial, racial, class, and gendered subordination. Before World War II, Filipinos were barred from becoming US citizens, owning property, and marrying whites. They also encountered discriminatory housing policies, unfair labour practices, violent physical encounters, and racist as well as anti-immigrant discourse.[1] While blatant legal discrimination against Filipino Americans is largely a matter of the past, Filipinos continue to encounter many barriers that prevent full participation in the economic, social, and political institutions of the United States (Azores-Gunter 1986–87; Cabezas, Shinagawa, and Kawaguchi 1986–87; Okamura and Agbayani 1997). Moreover, the economic mobility and cultural assimilation that enables white ethnics to become "unhyphenated whites" is seldom extended to Filipino Americans (Espiritu 1994). Like other Asians, the Filipino is "always seen as an immigrant, as the 'foreigner-within' even when born in the United States" (Lowe 1996, 5). Finally, although Filipinos have been in the United States since the middle of the 1700s and Americans have been in the Philippines since at least the late 1800s, US Filipinos—as racialized nationals, immigrants, and citizens—are "still practically an invisible and silent minority" (San Juan 1991, 117). Drawing from my research on Filipino American families in San Diego, California, I explore in this article the ways racialized immigrants claim through gender the power denied them by racism.

My epigraphs, quotations of a Filipina immigrant mother and a second-generation Filipina daughter, suggest that the virtuous Filipina daughter is partially constructed on the conceptualization of white women as sexually immoral. This juxtaposition underscores the fact that femininity is a relational category, one that is co-constructed with other racial and cultural categories. These narratives also reveal that women's sexuality and their enforced "morality" are fundamental to the structuring of social inequalities. Historically, the sexuality of racialized women has been systematically demonized and disparaged by dominant or oppressor groups to justify and bolster nationalist movements, colonialism, and/or racism. But as these narratives indicate, racialized groups also criticize the morality of white women as a strategy of resistance—a means of asserting a morally superior public face to the dominant society.

By exploring how Filipino immigrants characterize white families and white women, I hope to contribute to a neglected area of research: how the "margins" imagine and construct the "mainstream" in order to assert superiority over it. But this strategy is not without costs. The elevation of Filipina chastity (particularly that of young women) has the effect of reinforcing masculinist and patriarchal power in the name of a greater ideal of national/ethnic self-respect. Because the control of women is one of the principal means of asserting moral superiority, young women in immigrant families face numerous restrictions on their autonomy, mobility, and personal decision making. Although this article addresses the experiences and attitudes of both parents and children, here I am more concerned with understanding the actions of immigrant parents than with the reactions of their second-generation daughters.

Studying Filipinos in San Diego

San Diego, California has long been a favoured area of settlement for Filipinos and is today the third-largest US destination for Filipino immigrants (Rumbaut 1991, 220).[2] As the site of the largest US naval base and the Navy's primary West Coast training facility, San Diego has been a primary area of settlement for Filipino navy personnel and their families since the early 1900s. As in other Filipino communities along the Pacific Coast, the San Diego community grew dramatically in the 25 years following passage of the 1965 Immigration Act. New immigration contributed greatly to the tripling of San Diego county's Filipino American population from 1970 to 1980 and its doubling from 1980 to 1990. In 1990, nearly 96,000 Filipinos resided in the county. Although they made up only 4 per cent of the county's general population, they constituted close to 50 per cent of the Asian American population (Espiritu 1995). Many post-1965 Filipino immigrants have come to San Diego as professionals—most conspicuously as health care workers. A 1992 analysis of the socio-economic characteristics of recent Filipino immigrants in San Diego indicated that they were predominantly middle-class, college-educated, and English-speaking professionals who were more likely to own than rent their homes (Rumbaut 1994). At the same time, about two-thirds of the Filipinos surveyed indicated that they had experienced racial and ethnic discrimination (Espiritu and Wolf, forthcoming).

The information on which this article is based comes mostly from in-depth interviews that I conducted with almost 100 Filipinos in San Diego.[3] Using the "snowball" sampling technique, I started by interviewing Filipino Americans whom I knew and then asking them to refer me to others who might be willing to be interviewed. In other words, I chose participants not randomly but rather through a network of Filipino American contacts whom the first group of respondents trusted. To capture the diversity within the Filipino American community, I sought and selected respondents of different backgrounds and with diverse viewpoints. The sample is about equally divided between first-generation immigrants (those who came to the United States as adults) and Filipinas/os who were born and/or raised in the United States. It is more difficult to pinpoint the class status of the people I interviewed. To be sure, they included poor working-class immigrants who barely eked out a living, as well as educated professionals who thrived in middle- and upper-class suburban neighbourhoods. However, the class status of most was much more ambiguous. I met Filipinos/as who toiled as assembly workers but who, through the pooling of income and finances, owned homes in middle-class communities. I also discovered that class status was transnational, determined as much by one's economic position in the Philippines as by that in the United States. For example, I encountered individuals who struggled economically in the United States but owned sizable properties in the Philippines. And I interviewed immigrants who continued to view themselves as "upper class" even while living in dire conditions in the United States. These examples suggest that the upper/middle/working-class typology, while useful, does not capture the complexity of immigrant lives. Reflecting the prominence of the US Navy in San Diego, more than half of my respondents were affiliated with or had relatives affiliated with the US Navy.

My tape-recorded interviews, conducted in English, ranged from three to ten hours each and took place in offices, coffee shops, and homes. My questions were open-ended and covered three general areas: family and immigration history, ethnic identity and practices, and community development among San Diego's Filipinos. The interviewing process varied widely: some respondents needed to be prompted with specific questions, while others spoke at great length on their own. Some chose to cover the span of their lives; others focused on specific events that were particularly important to them. The initial impetus for this article on the relationship between immigrant parents and their daughters came from my observation that the dynamics of gender emerged more clearly in the interviews with women than in those with men. Because gender has been a marked category for women, the mothers and daughters I interviewed rarely told their life stories without reference to the dynamics of gender (see Personal Narratives Group 1989, 4–5). Even without prompting, young Filipinas almost always recounted stories of restrictive gender roles and gender expectations, particularly of parental control over their whereabouts and sexuality.

I believe that my own personal and social characteristics influenced the actual process of data collection, the quality of the materials that I gathered, and my analysis of them. As a Vietnam-born woman who immigrated to the United States at the age of 12, I came to the research project not as an "objective" outsider but as a fellow Asian immigrant who shared some of the life experiences of my respondents. During the fieldwork process, I did not remain detached but actively shared with my informants my own experiences of being an Asian immigrant woman: of being perceived as an outsider in US society, of speaking English as a second language, of being a woman of colour in a racialized patriarchal society, and of negotiating intergenerational tensions within my own family. I do not claim that these shared struggles grant me "insider status" into the Filipino American community; the differences

in our histories, cultures, languages, and, at times, class backgrounds, remain important. But I do claim that these shared experiences enable me to bring to the work a comparative perspective that is implicit, intuitive, and informed by my own identities and positionalities—and with it a commitment to approach these subjects with both sensitivity and rigour. In a cogent call for scholars of colour to expand on the premise of studying "our own" by studying other "others," Ruby Tapia argues that such implicitly comparative projects are important because they permit us to "highlight the different and *differentiating* functional forces of racialization" (1997, 2). It is with this deep interest in discovering—and forging—commonalities out of our specific and disparate experiences that I began this study on Filipino Americans in San Diego.

"American" and Whiteness: "To Me, American Means White"

In US racial discourse and practices, unless otherwise specified, "Americans" means "whites" (Lipsitz 1998, 1). In the case of Asian Americans, US exclusion acts, naturalization laws, and national culture have simultaneously marked Asians as the inassimilable aliens and whites as the quintessential Americans (Lowe 1996). Excluded from the collective memory of who constitutes a "real" American, Asians in the United States, even as citizens, remain "foreigners-within"—"non-Americans." In a study of third- and later-generation Chinese and Japanese Americans, Mia Tuan (1998) concludes that, despite being long-time Americans, Asians—as racialized ethnics—are often assumed to be foreign unless proven otherwise. In the case of Filipinos who emigrated from a former US colony, their formation as racialized minorities does not begin in the United States but rather in a "homeland" already affected by US economic, social, and cultural influences (Lowe 1996, 8).

Cognizant of this racialized history, my Filipino respondents seldom identify themselves as American. As will be evident in the discussion below, they equate "American" with "white" and often use these two terms interchangeably. For example, a Filipina who is married to a white American refers to her husband as "American" but to her African American and Filipino American brothers-in-law as "black" and "Filipino," respectively. Others speak about "American ways," "American culture," or "American lifestyle" when they really mean white American ways, culture, and lifestyle. A Filipino man who has lived in the United States for 30 years explains why he still does not identify himself as American: "I don't see myself just as an American because I cannot hide the fact that my skin is brown. To me, American means white." A second-generation Filipina recounted the following story when asked whether she defined herself as American:

> I went to an all-white school. I knew I was different. I wasn't American. See, you are not taught that you're American because you are not white. When I was in the tenth grade, our English teacher asked us what our nationality was, and she goes how many of you are Mexican, how many of you are Filipino, and how many of you are Samoan and things like that. And when she asked how many of you are American, just the white people raised their hands.

Other Asian Americans also conflate *American* and *white*. In an **ethnographic** study of Asian American high-school students,

Stacey Lee reports that Korean immigrant parents often instructed their children to socialize only with Koreans and "Americans." When asked to define the term *American,* the Korean students responded in unison with "White! Korean parents like white" (Lee 1996, 24). Tuan (1998) found the same practice among later-generation Chinese and Japanese Americans: the majority use the term *American* to refer to whites.

Constructing the Dominant Group: The Moral Flaws of White Americans

Given the centrality of moral themes in popular discussions on racial differences, Michele Lamont (1997) has suggested that morality is a crucial site to study the cultural mechanisms of reproduction of racial inequality. While much has been written on how whites have represented the (im)morality of people of colour (Collins 1991; Marchetti 1993; Hamamoto 1994), there has been less critical attention to how people of colour have represented whites.[4] Shifting attention from the otherness of the subordinate group (as dictated by the "mainstream") to the otherness of the dominant group (as constructed by the "margins"), this section focuses on the alternative frames of meaning that racially subordinate groups mobilize to (re)define their status in relation to the dominant group. I argue that female morality—defined as women's dedication to their families and sexual restraint—is one of the few sites where economically and politically dominated groups can construct the dominant group as other and themselves as superior. Because womanhood is idealized as the repository of tradition, the norms that regulate women's behaviours become a means of determining and defining group status and boundaries. As a consequence, the burdens and complexities of cultural representation fall most heavily on immigrant women and their daughters. Below, I show that Filipino immigrants claim moral distinctiveness for their community by re-presenting "Americans" as morally flawed, themselves as family-oriented model minorities, and their wives and daughters as paragons of morality.

Family-oriented Model Minorities: "White Women Will Leave You"

In his work on Italian immigrant parents and children in the 1930s, Robert Anthony Orsi (1985) reports that the parents invented a virtuous Italy (based on memories of their childhood) that they then used to castigate the morality of the United States and their US-born or -raised children. In a similar way, many of my respondents constructed their "ethnic" culture as principled and "American" culture as deviant. Most often, this morality narrative revolves around family life and family relations. When asked what set Filipinos apart from other Americans, my respondents—of all ages and class backgrounds—repeatedly contrasted close-knit Filipino families to what they perceived to be the more impersonal quality of US family relations.[5] In the following narratives, "Americans" are characterized as lacking in strong family ties and collective identity, less willing to do the work of family and cultural maintenance, and less willing to abide by patriarchal norms in husband/wife relations:

American society lacks caring. The American way of life is more individual rather than collective. The American way is to say I want to have my own way.

(Filipina immigrant, 54 years old)

Our [Filipino] culture is different. We are more close-knit. We tend to help one another. Americans, ya know, they are all right, but they don't help each other that much. As a matter of fact, if the parents are old, they take them to a convalescent home and let them rot there. We would never do that in our culture. We would nurse them; we would help them until the very end. (Filipino immigrant, 60 years old)

Our [Filipino] culture is very communal. You know that your family will always be there, that you don't have to work when you turn 18, you don't have to pay rent when you are 18, which is the American way of thinking. You also know that if things don't work out in the outside world, you can always come home and mommy and daddy will always take you and your children in. (Second-generation Filipina, 33 years old)

Asian parents take care of their children. Americans have a different attitude. They leave their children to their own resources. They get baby sitters to take care of their children or leave them in day care. That's why when they get old, their children don't even care about them. (Filipina immigrant, 46 years old)

Implicit in negative depictions of US families as uncaring, selfish, and distant is the allegation that white women are not as dedicated to their families as Filipina women are to theirs. Several Filipino men who married white women recalled being warned by their parents and relatives that "white women will leave you." As one man related, "My mother said to me, 'Well, you know, don't marry a white person because they would take everything that you own and leave you.'" For some Filipino men, perceived differences in attitudes about women's roles between Filipina and non-Filipina women influenced their marital choice. A Filipino American navy man explained why he went back to the Philippines to look for a wife:

> My goal was to marry a Filipina. I requested to be stationed in the Philippines to get married to a Filipina. I'd seen the women here and basically they are spoiled. They have a tendency of not going along together with their husband. They behave differently. They chase the male, instead of the male, the normal way of the traditional way is for the male to go after the female. They have sex without marrying. They want to do their own things. So my idea was to go back home and marry somebody who has never been here. I tell my son the same thing: if he does what I did and finds himself a good lady there, he will be in good hands.

Another man who had dated mostly white women in high school recounted that when it came time for him to marry, he "looked for the kind of women" he met while stationed in the Philippines: "I hate to sound chauvinistic about marriages, but Filipinas have a way of making you feel like you are a king. They also have that tenderness, that elegance. And we share the same values about family, education, religion, and raising children."

The claims of family closeness are not unique to Filipino immigrants. For example, when asked what makes their group distinctive, Italian Americans (di Leonardo 1984), Vietnamese Americans (Kibria 1993), South Asian Americans (Hickey 1996), and African Americans (Lamont 1997) all point proudly to the close-knit character of their family life. Although it is difficult to know whether these claims are actual perceptions or favoured self-legitimating answers, it is nevertheless important to note the gender implications of these claims. That is, while both men and women identify the family system as a tremendous source of cultural pride, it is women—through their unpaid housework and kin work—who shoulder the primary responsibility for maintaining family closeness. As the organizers of family rituals, transmitters of homeland folklores, and socializers of young children, women have been crucial for the maintenance of family ties and cultural traditions. In a study of kinship, class, and gender among California Italian Americans, di Leonardo argues that women's kin work, "the work of knitting households together into 'close, extended families,'" maintains the family networks that give ethnicity meaning (1984, 229).

Because the moral status of the community rests on women's labour, women, as wives and daughters, are expected to dedicate themselves to the family. Writing on the constructed image of ethnic family and gender, di Leonardo argues that "a large part of stressing ethnic identity amounts to burdening women with increased responsibilities for preparing special foods, planning rituals, and enforcing 'ethnic' socialization of children" (1984, 222). A 23-year-old Filipina spoke about the reproductive work that her mother performed and expected her to learn:

> In my family, I was the only girl, so my mom expected a lot from me. She wanted me to help her to take care of the household. I felt like there was a lot of pressure on me. It's very important to my mom to

have the house in order: to wash the dishes, to keep the kitchen in order, vacuuming, and dusting and things like that. She wants me to be a perfect housewife. It's difficult. I have been married now for about four months and my mother asks me even now and then what have I cooked for my husband. My mom is also very strict about families getting together on holidays, and I would always help her to organize that. Each holiday, I would try to decorate the house for her, to make it more special.

The burden of unpaid reproductive and kin work is particularly stressful for women who work outside the home. In the following narrative, a Filipina wife and mother described the pulls of family and work that she experienced when she went back to school to pursue a doctoral degree in nursing:

The Filipinos, we are very collective, very connected. Going through the doctoral program, sometimes I think it is better just to forget about my relatives and just concentrate on school. All that connectedness, it steals parts of myself because all of my energies are devoted to my family. And that is the reason why I think Americans are successful. The majority of the American people they can do what they want. They don't feel guilty because they only have a few people to relate to. For us Filipinos, it's like roots under the tree, you have all these connections. The Americans are more like the trunk. I am still trying to go up to the trunk of the tree but it is too hard. I want to be more independent, more like the Americans. I want to be good to my family but what about me? And all the things that I am doing. It's hard. It's always a struggle.

It is important to note that this Filipina interprets her exclusion and added responsibilities as only racial when they are also gendered. For example, when she says, "the American people they can do what they want," she ignores the differences in the lives of white men and white women—the fact that most white women experience similar competing pulls of family, education, and work.

Racialized Sexuality and (Im)morality: "In America, . . . Sex Is Nothing"

Sexuality, as a core aspect of social identity, is fundamental to the structuring of gender inequality (Millett 1970). Sexuality is also a salient marker of otherness and has figured prominently in racist and imperialist ideologies (Gilman 1985; Stoler 1991). Historically, the sexuality of subordinate groups—particularly that of racialized women—has been systematically stereotyped by the dominant groups.[6] At stake in these stereotypes is the construction of women of colour as morally lacking in the areas of sexual restraint and traditional morality. Asian women—both in Asia and in the United States—have been racialized as sexually immoral, and the "Orient—and its women—has long served as a site of European male-power fantasies, replete with lurid images of sexual licence, gynecological aberrations, and general perversion" (Gilman 1985, 89). In colonial Asia in the nineteenth and early twentieth centuries, for example, female sexuality was a site for colonial rulers to assert their moral superiority and thus their supposed natural and legitimate right to rule. The colonial rhetoric of moral superiority was based on the construction of colonized Asian women as subjects of sexual desire and fulfillment and European colonial women as the paragons of virtue and the bearers of a redefined colonial morality (Stoler 1991). The discourse of morality has also been used to mark the "unassimilability" of Asians in the United States. At the turn of the twentieth century, the public perception of Chinese women as disease-ridden, drug-addicted prostitutes served to underline the depravity of "Orientals" and played a decisive role in the eventual passage of exclusion laws against all Asians (Mazumdar 1989, 3–4). The stereotypical view that all Asian women were prostitutes, first formed in the 1850s, persisted. Contemporary American popular culture continues to endow Asian women with an excess of "womanhood," sexualizing them but also impugning their sexuality (Espiritu 1997, 93).

Filipinas—both in the Philippines and in the United States—have been marked as desirable but dangerous "prostitutes" and/or submissive "mail-order brides" (Halualani 1995; Egan 1996). These stereotypes emerged out of the colonial process, especially the extensive US military presence in the Philippines. Until the early 1990s, the Philippines, at times unwillingly, housed some of the United States's largest overseas air force and naval bases (Espiritu 1995, 14). Many Filipino nationalists have charged that "the prostitution problem" in the Philippines stemmed from US and Philippine government policies that promoted a sex industry—brothels, bars, and massage parlors—for servicemen stationed or on leave in the Philippines. During the Vietnam War, the Philippines was known as the "rest and recreation" centre of Asia, hosting approximately ten thousand US servicemen daily (Coronel and Rosca 1993; Warren 1993). In this context, *all* Filipinas were racialized as sexual commodities, usable and expendable. A US-born Filipina recounted the sexual harassment she faced while visiting Subic Bay Naval Station in Olongapo City:

One day I went to the base dispensary. . . . I was dressed nicely, and as I walked by the fire station, I heard catcalls and snide remarks being made by some of the firemen. . . . I was fuming inside. The next thing I heard was, "How much do you charge?" I kept on walking. "Hey, are you deaf or something? How much do you charge? You have a good body." That was an incident that I will never forget. (Quoted in Espiritu 1995, 77)

The sexualized racialization of Filipina women is also captured in Marianne Vilanueva's short story "Opportunity" (1991). As the protagonist, a "mail-order bride" from the Philippines, enters a hotel lobby to meet her American fiancé, the bellboys snicker and whisper *puta* (whore): a reminder that US economic and cultural colonization in the Philippines always forms a backdrop to any relations between Filipinos and Americans (Wong 1993, 53).

Cognizant of the pervasive hypersexualization of Filipina women, my respondents, especially women who grew up near military bases, were quick to denounce prostitution, to condemn sex labourers, and to declare (unasked) that they themselves did not frequent "that part of town." As one Filipina immigrant said,

Growing up [in the Philippines], I could never date an American because my dad's concept of a friendship with an American is with a GI. The only reason why my dad wouldn't let us date an American is that people will think that the only way you met was because of the base. I have never seen the inside of any of the bases because we were just forbidden to go there.

Many of my respondents also distanced themselves culturally from the Filipinas who serviced US soldiers by branding them "more Americanized" and "more Westernized." In other words, these women were sexually promiscuous because they had assumed the sexual mores of white women. This characterization allows my respondents to symbolically disown the Filipina "bad girl" and, in so doing, to uphold the narrative of Filipina sexual virtuosity and white female sexual promiscuity. In the following narrative, a mother who came to the United States in her thirties contrasted the controlled sexuality of women in the Philippines with the perceived promiscuity of white women in the United States:

> In the Philippines, we always have chaperons when we go out. When we go to dances, we have our uncle, our grandfather, and auntie all behind us to make sure that we behave in the dance hall. Nobody goes necking outside. You don't even let a man put his hand on your shoulders. When you were brought up in a conservative country, it is hard to come here and see that it is all freedom of speech and freedom of action. Sex was never mentioned in our generation. I was 30 already when I learned about sex. But to the young generation in America, sex is nothing.

Similarly, another immigrant woman criticized the way young American women are raised: "Americans are so liberated. They allow their children, their girls, to go out even when they are still so young." In contrast, she stated that, in "the Filipino way, it is very important, the value of the woman, that she is a virgin when she gets married."

The ideal "Filipina," then, is partially constructed on the community's conceptualization of white women. She is everything that they are not: she is sexually modest and dedicated to her family; they are sexually promiscuous and uncaring. Within the context of the dominant culture's pervasive hypersexualization of Filipinas, the construction of the "ideal" Filipina—as family-oriented and chaste—can be read as an effort to reclaim the morality of the community. This effort erases the Filipina "bad girl," ignores competing sexual practices in the Filipino communities, and uncritically embraces the myth of "Oriental femininity." Cast as the embodiment of perfect womanhood and exotic femininity, Filipinas (and other Asian women) in recent years have been idealized in US popular culture as more truly "feminine" (i.e., devoted, dependent, domestic) and therefore more desirable than their more modern, emancipated sisters (Espiritu 1997, 113). Capitalizing on this image of the "superfemme," mail-order bride agencies market Filipina women as "'exotic, subservient wife imports' for sale and as alternatives for men sick of independent 'liberal' Western women" (Halualani 1995, 49; see also Ordonez 1997, 122).

Embodying the moral integrity of the idealized ethnic community, immigrant women, particularly young daughters, are expected to comply with male-defined criteria of what constitute "ideal" feminine virtues. While the sexual behaviour of adult women is confined to a monogamous, heterosexual context, that of young women is denied completely (see Dasgupta and DasGupta 1996, 229–31). In the next section, I detail the ways Filipino immigrant parents, under the rubric of "cultural preservation," police their daughters' behaviours in order to safeguard their sexual innocence and virginity. These attempts at policing generate hierarchies and tensions within immigrant families—between parents and children and between brothers and sisters.

The Construction(s) of the "Ideal" Filipina: "Boys Are Boys and Girls Are Different"

As the designated "keepers of the culture" (Billson 1995), immigrant women and their behaviour come under intensive scrutiny both from men and women of their own groups and from US-born Americans (Gabbacia 1994, xi). In a study of the Italian Harlem community from 1880 to 1950, Orsi reports that "all the community's fears for the reputation and integrity of the domus came to focus on the behaviour of young women" (1985, 135). Because women's moral and sexual loyalties were deemed central to the maintenance of group status, changes in female behaviour, especially that of growing daughters, were interpreted as signs of moral decay and ethnic suicide and were carefully monitored and sanctioned (Gabbacia 1994, 113).

Although details vary, young women of various groups and across space and time—for example, second-generation Chinese women in San Francisco in the 1920s (Yung 1995), US-born Italian women in East Harlem in the 1930s (Orsi 1985), young Mexican women in the Southwest during the interwar years (Ruiz 1992), and daughters of Caribbean and Asian Indian immigrants on the East Coast in the 1990s (Dasgupta and DasGupta 1996; Waters 1996)—have identified strict parental control on their activities and movements as the primary source of intergenerational conflict. Recent studies of immigrant families also identify gender as a significant determinant of parent–child conflict, with daughters more likely than sons to be involved in such conflicts and instances of parental derogation (Rumbaut and Ima 1988; Woldemikael 1989; Matute-Bianchi 1991; Gibson 1995).

Although immigrant families have always been preoccupied with passing on their native culture, language, and traditions to both male and female children, it is daughters who have the primary burden of protecting and preserving the family. Because sons do not have to conform to the image of an "ideal" ethnic subject as daughters do, they often receive special day-to-day privileges denied to daughters (Haddad and Smith 1996, 22–24; Waters 1996, 75–76). This is not to say that immigrant parents do not place undue expectations on their sons; rather, these expectations do not pivot around the sons' sexuality or dating choices.[7] In contrast, parental control over the movement and action of daughters begins the moment they are perceived as young adults and sexually vulnerable. It regularly consists of monitoring their whereabouts and forbidding dating (Wolf 1997). For example, the immigrant parents I interviewed seldom allowed their daughters to date, to stay out late, to spend the night at a friend's house, or to take an out-of-town trip.

Many of the second-generation women I spoke to complained bitterly about these parental restrictions. They particularly resented what they saw as gender inequity in their families: the fact that their parents placed far more restrictions on their activities and movements than on their brothers'. Some decried the fact that even their younger brothers had more freedom than they did. "It was really hard growing up because my parents would let my younger brothers do what they wanted but I didn't get to do what I wanted even though I was the oldest. I had a curfew and my brothers didn't. I had to ask if I could go places and they didn't. My parents never even asked my brothers when they were coming home." As indicated in the following excerpt, many Filipino males are cognizant of this double standard in their families:

My sister would always say to me, "It's not fair, just because you are a guy, you can go wherever you want." I think my parents do treat me and my sister differently. Like in high school, maybe 10:30 at night, which is pretty late on a school night, and I say I have to go pick up some notes at my friend's house, my parents wouldn't say anything. But if my sister were to do that, there would be no way. Even now when my sister is in college already, if she wants to leave at midnight to go to a friend's house, they would tell her that she shouldn't do it.

When questioned about this double standard, parents generally responded by explaining that "girls are different":

I have that Filipino mentality that boys are boys and girls are different. Girls are supposed to be protected, to be clean. In the early years, my daughters have to have chaperons and curfews. And they know that they have to be virgins until they get married. The girls always say that is not fair. What is the difference between their brothers and them? And my answer always is, "In the Philippines, you know, we don't do that. The girls stay home. The boys go out." It was the way that I was raised. I still want to have part of that culture instilled in my children. And I want them to have that to pass on to their children.

Even among self-described Western-educated and "tolerant" parents, many continue to ascribe to "the Filipino way" when it comes to raising daughters. As one college-educated father explains,

Because of my Western education, I don't raise my children the way my parents raised me. I tended to be a little more tolerant. But at times, especially in certain issues like dating, I find myself more towards the Filipino way in the sense that I have only one daughter so I tended to be a little bit stricter. So the double standard kind of operates: it's all right for the boys to explore the field but I tended to be overly protective of my daughter. My wife feels the same way because the boys will not lose anything, but the daughter will lose something, her virginity, and it can be also a question of losing face, that kind of thing.

Although many parents discourage or forbid dating for daughters, they still fully expect these young women to fulfill their traditional roles as women: to marry and have children. A young Filipina recounted the mixed messages she received from her parents:

This is the way it is supposed to work: Okay, you go to school. You go to college. You graduate. You find a job. *Then* you find your husband, and you have children. That's the whole time line. *But* my question is, if you are not allowed to date, how are you supposed to find your husband? They say "no" to the whole dating scene because that is secondary to your education, secondary to your family. They do push marriage, but at a later date. So basically my parents are telling me that I should get married and I should have children but that I should not date.

In a study of second-generation Filipino Americans in northern California, Diane Wolf (1997) reports the same pattern of parental pressures: Parents expect daughters to remain virgins until marriage, to have a career, *and* to combine their work lives with marriage and children.

The restrictions on girls' movement sometimes spill over to the realm of academics. Dasgupta and DasGupta (1996, 230) recount that in the Indian American community, while young men were expected to attend faraway competitive colleges, many of their female peers were encouraged by their parents to go to the local colleges so that they could live at or close to home. Similarly, Wolf (1997, 467) reports that some Filipino parents pursued contradictory tactics with their children, particularly their daughters, by pushing them to achieve academic excellence in high school but then "pulling the emergency brake" when they contemplated college by expecting them to stay at home, even if it meant going to a less competitive college, or not going at all. In the following account, a young Filipina relates that her parents' desire to "protect" her surpassed their concerns for her academic preparation:

> My brother [was] given a lot more opportunity educationally. He was given the opportunity to go to Miller High School that has a renowned college preparatory program but [for] which you have to be bussed out of our area.[8] I've come from a college prep program in junior high and I was asked to apply for the program at Miller. But my parents said "No, absolutely not." This was even during the time, too, when Southside [the neighbourhood high school] had one of the lowest test scores in the state of California. So it was like, "You know, mom, I'll get a better chance at Miller." "No, no, you're going to Southside. There is no ifs, ands, or buts. Miller is too far. What if something happens to you?" But two years later, when my brother got ready to go on to high school, he was allowed to go to Miller. My sister and I were like, "Obviously, whose education do you value more? If you're telling us that education is important, why do we see a double standard?"

The above narratives suggest that the process of parenting is gendered in that immigrant parents tend to restrict the autonomy, mobility, and personal decision making of their daughters more than that of their sons. I argue that these parental restrictions are attempts to construct a model of Filipina womanhood that is chaste, modest, nurturing, and family-oriented. Women are seen as responsible for holding the cultural line, maintaining racial boundaries, and marking cultural difference. This is not to say that parent–daughter conflicts exist in all Filipino immigrant families. Certainly, Filipino parents do not respond in a uniform way to the challenges of being racial-ethnic minorities, and I met parents who have had to change some of their ideas and practices in response to their inability to control their children's movements and choices:

> I have three girls and one boy. I used to think that I wouldn't allow my daughters to go dating and things like that, but there is no way I could do that. I can't stop it. It's the way of life here in America. Sometimes you kind of question yourself, if you are doing what is right. It is hard to accept but you got to accept it. That's the way they are here. (Professional Filipino immigrant father)

> My children are born and raised here, so they do pretty much what they want. They think they know everything. I can only do so much as a parent. . . . When I try to teach my kids things, they tell me that I sound like an old record. They even talk back to me sometimes. . . . The first time my daughter brought her boyfriend to the house, she was

18 years old. I almost passed away, knocked out. Lord, tell me what to do? (Working-class Filipino immigrant mother)

These narratives call attention to the shifts in the generational power caused by the migration process and to the possible gap between what parents say they want for their children and their ability to control the young. However, the interview data do suggest that intergenerational conflicts are socially recognized occurrences in Filipino communities. Even when respondents themselves had not experienced intergenerational tensions, they could always recall a cousin, a girlfriend, or a friend's daughter who had.

Sanctions and Reactions: "That Is Not What a Decent Filipino Girl Should Do"

I do not wish to suggest that immigrant communities are the only ones in which parents regulate their daughters' mobility and sexuality. Feminist scholars have long documented the construction, containment, and exploitation of women's sexuality in various societies (Maglin and Perry 1996). We also know that the cultural anxiety over unbounded female sexuality is most apparent with regard to adolescent girls (Tolman and Higgins 1996, 206). The difference is in the ways immigrant and non-immigrant families sanction girls' sexuality. To control sexually assertive girls non-immigrant parents rely on the gender-based good girl/bad girl dichotomy in which "good girls" are passive, threatened sexual objects while "bad girls" are active, desiring sexual agents (Tolman and Higgins 1996). As Dasgupta and DasGupta write, "the two most pervasive images of women across cultures are the goddess and whore, the good and bad women" (1996, 236). This good girl/bad girl cultural story conflates femininity with sexuality, increases women's vulnerability to sexual coercion, and justifies women's containment in the domestic sphere.

Immigrant families, though, have an additional strategy: they can discipline their daughters as racial/national subjects as well as gendered ones. That is, as self-appointed guardians of "authentic" cultural memory, immigrant parents can attempt to regulate their daughters' independent choices by linking them to cultural ignorance or betrayal. As both parents and children recounted, young women who disobeyed parental strictures were often branded "non-ethnic," "untraditional," "radical," "selfish," and "not caring about the family." Female sexual choices were also linked to moral degeneracy, defined in relation to a narrative of a hegemonic white norm. Parents were quick to warn their daughters about "bad" Filipinas who had become pregnant outside marriage.[9] As in the case of "bar girls" in the Philippines, Filipina Americans who veered from acceptable behaviours were deemed "Americanized"—as women who have adopted the sexual mores and practices of white women. As one Filipino immigrant father described "Americanized" Filipinas: "They are spoiled because they have seen the American way. They go out at night. Late at night. They go out on dates. Smoking. They have sex without marrying."

From the perspective of the second-generation daughters, these charges are stinging. The young women I interviewed were visibly pained—with many breaking down and crying—when they recounted their parents' charges. This deep pain, stemming in part from their desire to be validated as Filipina, existed even among the more "rebellious" daughters. One 24-year-old daughter explained:

My mom is very traditional. She wants to follow the Filipino customs, just really adhere to them, like what is proper for a girl, what she can and can't do, and what other people are going to think of her if she doesn't follow that way. When I pushed these restrictions, when I rebelled and stayed out later than allowed, my mom would always say, "That is not what a decent Filipino girl should do. You should come home at a decent hour. What are people going to think of you?" And that would get me really upset, you know, because I think that my character is very much the way it should be for a Filipina. I wear my hair long, I wear decent makeup. I dress properly, conservative. I am family oriented. It hurts me that she doesn't see that I am decent, that I am proper and that I am not going to bring shame to the family or anything like that.

This narrative suggests that even when parents are unable to control the behaviours of their children, their (dis)approval remains powerful in shaping the emotional lives of their daughters (see Wolf 1997). Although better-off parents can and do exert greater controls over their children's behaviours than do poorer parents (Wolf 1992; Kibria 1993), I would argue that all immigrant parents—regardless of class background—possess this emotional hold on their children. Therein lies the source of their power: As immigrant parents, they have the authority to determine if their daughters are "authentic" members of their racial-ethnic community. Largely unacquainted with the "home" country, US-born children depend on their parents' tutelage to craft and affirm their ethnic self and thus are particularly vulnerable to charges of cultural ignorance and/or betrayal (Espiritu 1994).

Despite these emotional pains, many young Filipinas I interviewed contest and negotiate parental restrictions in their daily lives. Faced with parental restrictions on their mobility, young Filipinas struggle to gain some control over their own social lives, particularly over dating. In many cases, daughters simply misinform their parents of their whereabouts or date without their parents' knowledge. They also rebel by vowing to create more egalitarian relationships with their own husbands and children. A 30-year-old Filipina who is married to a white American explained why she chose to marry outside her culture:

> In high school, I dated mostly Mexican and Filipino. It never occurred to me to date a white or black guy. I was not attracted to them. But as I kept growing up and my father and I were having all these conflicts, I knew that if I married a Mexican or a Filipino, [he] would be exactly like my father. And so I tried to date anyone that would not remind me of my dad. A lot of my Filipina friends that I grew up with had similar experiences. So I knew that it wasn't only me. I was determined to marry a white person because he would treat me as an individual.[10]

Another Filipina who was labelled "radical" by her parents indicated that she would be more open-minded in raising her own children: "I see myself as very traditional in upbringing but I don't see myself as constricting on my children one day and I wouldn't put the gender roles on them. I wouldn't lock them into any particular way of behaving." It is important to note that even as these Filipinas desired new gender norms and practices for their own families, the majority hoped that their children would remain connected to Filipino culture.

My respondents also reported more serious reactions to parental restrictions, recalling incidents of someone they knew who had run away, joined a gang, or attempted suicide. A Filipina high-school counsellor relates that most of the Filipinas she worked with "are really scared because a lot of them know friends that are pregnant and they all pretty much know girls who have attempted suicide." A 1995 random survey of San Diego public high schools conducted by the Federal Centers for Disease Control and Prevention (CDC) found that, in comparison with other ethnic groups, female Filipino students had the highest rates of seriously considering suicide (45.6 per cent) as well as the highest rates of actually attempting suicide (23 per cent) in the year preceding the survey. In comparison, 33.4 per cent of Latinas, 26.2 per cent of white women, and 25.3 per cent of black women surveyed said they had suicidal thoughts (Lau 1995).

Conclusion

Mainstream American society defines white middle-class culture as the norm and whiteness as the unmarked marker of others' difference (Frankenberg 1993). In this article, I have shown that many Filipino immigrants use the largely gendered discourse of morality as one strategy to decentre whiteness and to locate themselves above the dominant group, demonizing it in the process. Like other immigrant groups, Filipinos praise the United States as a land of significant economic opportunity but simultaneously denounce it as a country inhabited by corrupted and individualistic people of questionable morals. In particular, they criticize American family life, American individualism, and American women (see Gabbacia 1994, 113). Enforced by distorting powers of memory and nostalgia, this rhetoric of moral superiority often leads to patriarchal calls for a cultural "authenticity" that locates family honour and national integrity in the group's female members. Because the policing of women's bodies is one of the main means of asserting moral superiority, young women face numerous restrictions on their autonomy, mobility, and personal decision making. This practice of cultural (re)construction reveals how deeply the conduct of private life can be tied to larger social structures.

The construction of white Americans as the "other" and American culture as deviant serves a dual purpose: It allows immigrant communities both to reinforce patriarchy through the sanctioning of women's (mis)behaviour and to present an unblemished, if not morally superior, public face to the dominant society. Strong in family values, heterosexual morality, and a hierarchical family structure, this public face erases the Filipina "bad girl" and ignores competing (im)moral practices in the Filipino communities. Through the oppression of Filipina women and the denunciation of white women's morality, the immigrant community attempts to exert its moral superiority over the dominant Western culture and to reaffirm to itself its self-worth in the face of economic, social, political, and legal subordination. In other words, the immigrant community uses restrictions on women's lives as one form of resistance to racism. This form of cultural resistance, however, severely restricts the lives of women, particularly those of the second generation, and it casts the family as a potential site of intense conflict and oppressive demands in immigrant lives.

● Notes

1. Cordova 1983; Sharma 1984; Scharlin and Villanueva 1992; Jung 1999.
2. Filipino settlement in San Diego dates back to 1903, when a group of young Filipino *pensionados* enrolled at the State Normal School (now San Diego State University).
3. My understanding of Filipino American lives is also based on the many conversations I have had with my Filipino American students at the University of California, San Diego, and with Filipino American friends in the San Diego area and elsewhere.
4. A few studies have documented the ways racialized communities have represented white Americans. For example, in his anthropological work on Chicano joking, José Limón (1982) reports that young Mexican Americans elevate themselves over whites through the telling of "Stupid-American" jokes in which an Anglo American is consistently duped by a Mexican character. In her interviews with African American working-class men, Michele Lamont (1997) finds that these men tend to perceive Euro Americans as immoral, sneaky, and not to be trusted. Although these studies provide an interesting and compelling window into racialized communities' views of white Americans, they do not analyze how the rhetoric of moral superiority often depends on gender categories.
5. Indeed, people around the world often believe that Americans have no real family ties. For example, on a visit to my family in Vietnam, my cousin asked me earnestly if it was true that American children put their elderly parents in nursing homes instead of caring for them at home. She was horrified at this practice and proclaimed that, because they care for their elders, Vietnamese families are morally superior to American families.
6. Writing on the objectification of black women, Patricia Hill Collins (1991) argues that popular representations of black females—mammy, welfare queen, and Jezebel—all pivot around their sexuality, either desexualizing or hypersexualizing them. Along the same line, Native American women have been portrayed as sexually excessive (Green 1975), Chicana women as "exotic and erotic" (Mirande 1980), and Puerto Rican and Cuban women as "tropical bombshells, . . . sexy, sexed and interested" (Tafolla 1985, 39).
7. The relationship between immigrant parents and their sons deserves an article of its own. According to Gabbacia, "Immigrant parents fought with sons, too, but over different issues: parents' complaints about rebellious sons focused more on criminal activity than on male sexuality or independent courtship" (1994, 70). Moreover, because of their mobility, young men have more means to escape—at least temporarily—the pressures of the family than young women. In his study of Italian American families, Orsi reports that young men rebelled by sleeping in cars or joining the army, but young women did not have such opportunities (1985, 143).
8. The names of the two high schools in this excerpt are fictitious.
9. According to a 1992 health assessment report of Filipinos in San Francisco, Filipino teens have the highest pregnancy rates among all Asian groups and, in 1991, the highest rate of increase in the number of births as compared with all other racial or ethnic groups (Tiongson 1997, 257).
10. The few available studies on Filipino American intermarriage indicate a high rate relative to other Asian groups. In 1980, Filipino men in California recorded the highest intermarriage rate among all Asian groups, and Filipina women had the second-highest rate, after Japanese American women (Agbayani-Siewert and Revilla 1995, 156).

● References

Agbayani-Siewert, Pauline, and Linda Revilla. 1995. "Filipino Americans?" In *Asian Americans: Contemporary Trends and Issues*, ed. Pyong Gap Min, 134–68. Thousand Oaks, Calif.: Sage.

Azores-Gunter, Tania Fortunata M. 1986–87. "Educational Attainment and Upward Mobility: Prospects for Filipino Americans." *Amerasia Journal* 13(1): 39–52.

Billson, Janet Mancini. 1995. *Keepers of the Culture: The Power of Tradition in Women's Lives*. New York: Lexington.

Cabezas, Amado, Larry H. Shinagawa, and Gary Kawaguchi. 1986–87. "New Inquiries into the Socioeconomic Status of Pilipino Americans in California?" *Amerasia Journal* 13(1): 1–21.

Collins, Patricia Hill. 1991. *Black Feminist Thought: Knowledge, Consciousness, and the Politics of Empowerment*. New York: Routledge.

Cordova, Fred. 1983. *Filipinos: Forgotten Asian Americans, a Pictorial Essay, 1763–1963*. Dubuque, Iowa: Kendall/Hunt.

Coronel, Sheila, and Ninotchka Rosca. 1993. "For the Boys: Filipinas Expose Years of Sexual Slavery by the U.S. and Japan." *Ms.*, November/December, 10–15.

Dasgupta, Shamita Das, and Savantani DasGupta. 1996. "Public Face, Private Space: Asian Indian Women and Sexuality." In *"Bad Girls/Good Girls": Women, Sex, and Power in the Nineties*, eds Nan Bauer Maglin and Donna Perry, 226–43. New Brunswick, N.J.: Rutgers University Press.

di Leonardo, Micaela. 1984. *The Varieties of Ethnic Experience: Kinship, Class, and Gender among California Italian-Americans*. Ithaca, N.Y.: Cornell University Press.

Eastmond, Marita. 1993. "Reconstructing Life: Chilean Refugee Women and the Dilemmas of Exile" In *Migrant Women: Crossing Boundaries and Changing Identities*, ed. Gina Buijs, 35–53. Oxford: Berg.

Egan, Timothy. 1996. "Mail-Order Marriage, Immigrant Dreams and Death." *New York Times*, May 26, 12.

Espiritu, Yen Le. 1994. "The Intersection of Race, Ethnicity, and Class: The Multiple Identities of Second Generation Filipinos." *Identities* 1(2–3): 249–73.

———. 1995. *Filipino American Lives*. Philadelphia: Temple University Press.

———. 1997. *Asian American Women and Men: Labor, Laws, and Love*. Thousand Oaks, Calif.: Sage.

Espiritu, Yen Le, and Diane L. Wolf. Forthcoming. "The Paradox of Assimilation: Children of Filipino Immigrants in San Diego." In *Ethnicities: Children of Immigrants in America,* eds Ruben Rumbaut and Alejandro Portes. Berkeley: University of California Press; New York: Russell Sage Foundation.

Frankenberg, Ruth. 1993. *White Women, Race Matters: The Social Construction of Whiteness*. Minneapolis: University of Minnesota Press.

Gabbacia, Donna. 1994. *From the Other Side: Women, Gender, and Immigrant Life in the US, 1820–1990*. Bloomington: Indiana University Press.

Gibson, Margaret A. 1995. "Additive Acculturation as a Strategy for School Improvement." In *California's Immigrant Children: Theory, Research, and Implications for Educational Policy*, eds Ruben Rumbaut and Wayne A. Cornelius, 77–105. La Jolla: Center for U.S.-Mexican Studies, University of California, San Diego.

Gilman, Sander L. 1985. *Difference and Pathology: Stereotypes of Sexuality, Race, and Madness*. Ithaca, N.Y.: Cornell University Press.

Green, Rayna. 1975. "The Pocahontas Perplex: The Image of Indian Women in American Culture?" *Massachusetts Review* 16(4): 698–714.

Haddad, Yvonne Y., and Jane I. Smith. 1996. "Islamic Values among American Muslims." In *Family and Gender among American Muslims: Issues Facing Middle Eastern Immigrants and Their Descendants*, eds Barbara C. Aswad and Barbara Bilge, 19–40. Philadelphia: Temple University Press.

Halualani, Rona Tamiko. 1995. "The Intersecting Hegemonic Discourses of an Asian Mail-Order Bride Catalog: Pilipina 'Oriental Butterfly' Dolls for Sale." *Women's Studies in Communication* 18(1):45–64.

Hamamoto, Darrell Y. 1994. *Monitored Peril: Asian Americans and the Politics of Representation*. Minneapolis: University of Minnesota Press.

Hickey, M. Gail. 1996. "'Go to College, Get a Job, and Don't Leave the House without Your Brother': Oral Histories with Immigrant Women and Their Daughters." *Oral History Review* 23(2): 63–92.

Jung, Moon-Kie. 1999. "No Whites: No Asians: Race, Marxism and Hawaii's Pre-emergent Working Class." *Social Science History* 23(3): 357–93.

Kibria, Nazli. 1993. *Family Tightrope: The Changing Lives of Vietnamese Immigrant Community*. Princeton, N.J.: Princeton University Press.

Lamont, Michele. 1997. "Colliding Moralities between Black and White Workers." In *From Sociology to Cultural Studies: New Perspectives*, ed. Elisabeth Long, 263–85. New York: Blackwell.

Lau, Angela. 1995. "Filipino Girls Think Suicide at Number One Rate." *San Diego Union-Tribune*, February 11, A-1.

Lee, Stacey J. 1996. *Unraveling the "Model Minority" Stereotype: Listening to Asian American Youth*. New York: Teachers College Press.

Limón, José E. 1982. "History, Chicano Joking, and the Varieties of Higher Education: Tradition and Performance as Critical Symbolic Action." *Journal of the Folklore Institute* 19(2/3): 141–66.

Lipsitz, George. 1998. *The Possessive Investment in Whiteness: How White People Profit from Identity Politics*. Philadelphia: Temple University Press.

Lowe, Lisa. 1996. *Immigrant Acts: On Asian American Cultural Politics*. Durham, N.C.: Duke University Press.

Maglin, Nan Bauer, and Donna Perry. 1996. "Introduction." In *"Bad Girls/Good Girls": Women, Sex, and Power in the*

Nineties, eds Nan Bauer Maglin and Donna Perry, xiii–xxvi. New Brunswick, N.J.: Rutgers University Press.

Marchetti, Gina. 1993. *Romance and the "Yellow Peril": Race, Sex, and Discursive Strategies in Hollywood Fiction*. Berkeley: University of California Press.

Matute-Bianchi, Maria Eugenia. 1991. "Situational Ethnicity and Patterns of School Performance among Immigrant and Nonimmigrant Mexican-Descent Students." In *Minority Status and Schooling: A Comparative Study of Immigrant and Involuntary Minorities*, eds Margaret A. Gibson and John U. Ogbu, 205–47. New York: Garland.

Mazumdar, Suchetta. 1989. "General Introduction: A Woman-Centered Perspective on Asian American History." In *Making Waves: An Anthology by and about Asian American Women*, ed. Asian Women United of California, 1–22. Boston: Beacon.

Millett, Kate. 1970. *Sexual Politics*. Garden City, N.Y.: Doubleday.

Mirande, Alfredo. 1980. "The Chinano Family: A Reanalysis of Conflicting Views." In *Rethinking Marriage, Child Rearing, and Family Organization*, eds Arlene S. Skolnick and Jerome H. Skolnick, 479–93. Berkeley: University of California Press.

Okamura, Jonathan, and Amefil Agbayani. 1997. "*Pamantasan:* Filipino American Higher Education." In *Filipino Americans: Transformation and Identity*, ed. Maria P. Root, 183–97. Thousand Oaks, Calif.: Sage.

Ordonez, Raquel Z. 1997. "Mail-Order Brides: An Emerging Community." In *Filipino Americans: Transformation and Identity*, ed. Maria P. Root, 121–42. Thousand Oaks, Calif.: Sage.

Orsi, Robert Anthony. 1985. *The Madonna of 115th Street: Faith and Community in Italian Harlem, 1880–1950*. New Haven, Conn.: Yale University Press.

Personal Narratives Group. 1989. "Origins." In *Interpreting Women's Lives: Feminist Theory and Personal Narratives*, ed. Personal Narratives Group, 3–15. Bloomington: Indiana University Press.

Ruiz, Vicki L. 1992. "The Flapper and the Chaperone: Historical Memory among Mexican-American Women." In *Seeking Common Ground: Multidisciplinary Studies*, ed. Donna Gabbacia. Westport, Conn.: Greenwood.

Rumbaut, Ruben. 1991. "Passages to America: Perspectives on the New Immigration." In *America at Century's End*, ed. Alan Wolfe, 208–44. Berkeley: University of California Press.

———. 1994. "The Crucible Within: Ethnic Identity, Self-Esteem, and Segmented Assimilation among Children of Immigrants." *International Migration Review* 28(4): 748–94.

Rumbaut, Ruben, and Kenji Ima. 1988. *The Adaptation of Southeast Asian Refugee Youth: A Comparative Study*. Washington, D.C.: US Office of Refugee Resettlement.

San Juan, E., Jr. 1991. "Mapping the Boundaries: The Filipino Writer in the U.S." *Journal of Ethnic Studies* 19(1): 117–31.

Scharlin, Craig, and Lilia V. Villanueva. 1992. *Philip Vera Cruz: A Personal History of Filipino Immigrants and the Farmworkers Movement*. Los Angeles: University of California, Los Angeles Labor Center, Institute of Labor Relations, and Asian American Studies Center.

Sharma, Miriam. 1984. "Labor Migration and Class Formation among the Filipinos in Hawaii, 1906–46." In *Labor Immigration under Capitalism: Asian Workers in the United States Before World War II*, eds Lucie Cheng and Edna Bonacich, 579–611. Berkeley: University of California Press.

Stoler, Ann Laura. 1991. "Carnal Knowledge and Imperial Power: Gender, Race, and Morality in Colonial Asia." In *Gender at the Crossroads of Knowledge: Feminist Anthropology in the Postmodern Era*, ed. Micaela di Leonardo, 51–104. Berkeley: University of California Press.

Tafolla, Carmen. 1985. *To Split a Human: Mitos, Machosy la Mujer Chicana*. San Antonio, Tex.: Mexican American Cultural Center.

Tapia, Ruby. 1997. "Studying Other 'Others.'" Paper presented at the Association of Pacific Americans in Higher Education, San Diego, Calif., May 24.

Tiongson, Antonio T, Jr. 1997. "Throwing the Baby out with the Bath Water." In *Filipino Americans: Transformation and Identity*, ed. Maria P. Root, 257–71. Thousand Oaks, Calif.: Sage.

Tolman, Deborah L., and Tracy E. Higgins. 1996. "How Being a Good Girl Can Be Bad for Girls." In *"Bad Girls/Good Girls": Women, Sex, and Power in the Nineties*, eds Nan Bauer Maglin and Donna Perry, 205–25. New Brunswick, N.J.: Rutgers University Press.

Tuan, Mia. 1998. *Forever Foreigners or Honorary Whites? The Asian Ethnic Experience Today*. New Brunswick, N.J.: Rutgers University Press.

Villanueva, M. 1991. *Ginseng and Other Tales from Manila*. Corvallis, Oreg.: Calyx.

Warren, Jenifer. 1993. "Suit Asks Navy to Aid Children Left in Philippines." *Los Angeles Times*, March 5, A3.

Waters, Mary C. 1996. "The Intersection of Gender, Race, and Ethnicity in Identity Development of Caribbean American Teens." In *Urban Girls: Resisting Stereotypes, Creating Identities*, eds Bonnie J. Ross Leadbeater and Niobe Way, 65–81. New York: New York University Press.

Woldemikael, T.M. 1989. *Becoming Black American: Haitians and American Institutions in Evanston, Illinois*. New York: AMS Press.

Wolf, Diane L. 1992. *Factory Daughters: Gender, Household Dynamics, and Rural Industrialization in Java.* Berkeley: University of California Press.

———. 1997. "Family Secrets: Transnational Struggles among Children of Filipino Immigrants." *Sociological Perspectives* 40(3): 457–82.

Wong, Sau-ling. 1993. *Reading Asian American Literature: From Necessity to Extravagance.* Princeton, N.J.: Princeton University Press.

Yung, Judy. 1995. *Unbound Feet: A Social History of Chinese Women in San Francisco.* Berkeley: University of California Press.

Chapter 10

In Canadian culture, we tend to assume that whom we date, when we date, whether and when we move in with a boy/girlfriend, and whether we get married are all personal choices. Of course, we know that our circumstances affect these choices. For example, increasingly, people marry only when they have finished school, started a job, and saved a bit of money; so how much financial help parents can provide, how tight the labour market is, and the cost of housing all influence decisions about cohabiting and marrying. What we are likely less conscious of is the influence that gender might have in shaping these important events in people's personal lives. In this chapter, Sharon Sassler and Amanda Miller examine whether and how gender affects couples' decisions about dating, cohabiting, and marrying.

Waiting to Be Asked: Gender, Power, and Relationship Progression Among Cohabiting Couples

Sharon Sassler and Amanda Miller

Cohabitation has become a normative part of the courtship process among American adults. Recent estimates indicate that more than two-thirds of American women lived with a partner by their mid-twenties, and the majority of individuals who married lived with their spouses before the wedding day (Chandra, Martinez, Mosher, Abma & Jones, 2005; Kennedy & Bumpass, 2008). Social scientists have long suggested that men and women are looking for alternatives to the traditional family (Bernard, 1981; Goldscheider & Waite, 1991; Stacey, 1990). Cohabitation is often portrayed as such an arrangement, because it provides the benefits of intimacy and shared economies of scale with fewer expectations for specialization in traditional gender roles (Blumstein & Schwartz, 1983; Clarkberg, Stolzenberg & Waite, 1995). Although numerous studies have explored the factors facilitating or impeding marriage among cohabitors (Gibson-Davis, Edin & McLanahan, 2005; Sassler & McNally, 2003; Smock, Manning & Porter, 2005), these studies have not addressed how gender norms shape power relations within couples and the impact that power relations have on relationship progression.

Building on prior research on romantic relationships and on feminist critiques of how marital power has been studied, we examine how couples discuss their decisions to become a couple, move in together, and raise and negotiate plans for the future. Because the literature on marital power has suggested that gender display is an essential factor undergirding how men and women interact (Potuchek, 1997; Tichenor, 2005; Zvonkovic, Greaves, Schmiege & Hall, 1996), this study is based on the interactionist approach known as "doing gender" (West & Zimmerman, 1987). Our qualitative analysis explores how romantic partners negotiate the process of relationship progression, focusing on several relationship stages where cohabiting couples do (and undo) gender (Deutsch, 2007; West & Zimmerman, 1987). Our findings reveal how interpersonal interactions reflect the social processes that underlie adherence to, as well as resistance against, conventional gender relations and how challenges to the power dynamics and inequities between men and women are managed.

The Manifestation of Power in Romantic Relationships

Family scholars have long been interested in the relationship between power and decision making. A recurrent theme in this research is the extent of asymmetry between partners. Early studies conceptualized power as the ability to get one's way, even in the face of a partner's opposition, and tended to focus on outcomes, such as which partner made the final decisions over major purchases (houses, cars, vacations). They generally found that men had more power in intimate relationships, which was often attributed to their greater economic contributions (Blood & Wolfe, 1960; Gray-Little & Burks, 1983; Szinovacz, 1987).

Gender scholars are increasingly challenging the notion that the basis of power is predominantly material. The majority of women are now employed in the paid labour force, and about one-third earn as much or more than their partners (Winkler, McBride & Andrews, 2005). Yet while women's greater labour force participation has increased their power in certain domains—employed women do less housework, get more child care assistance from partners, and have greater control over money than do their non-working counterparts—women's employment has not equalized their balance of power relative to men (Bianchi, Milkie, Sayer & Robinson, 2000; Pyke, 1994; Sayer, 2005). The increase in cohabitation has also been suggested as a challenge to conventional gender relations, in part because of presumed differences in exchanges between married and cohabiting men and women (Waite & Gallagher, 2000). Cohabitors have weaker expectations for specialization in traditional gender roles (Clarkberg et al., 1995; Sassler & Goldscheider, 2004) and partners generally maintain control over their own resources (Heimdal & Houseknecht, 2003; Vogler, 2005; Winkler, 1997). Furthermore, a subset of cohabitors eschews marriage and its inherent gender inequities (Elizabeth, 2000). Yet research continues to find that cohabiting women remain disadvantaged relative to men, performing a disproportionate share of domestic labour (Ciabattari, 2004; Hohmann-Marriot, 2006). In addition, their economic resources are not significant predictors of equality in spending or in marital transitions (de Ruijter, Treas & Cohen, 2005; Sassler & McNally, 2003; Vogler, 2005).

Feminist scholars have long noted the need to better account for persistent gender inequality in studies of power and decision making. The gender perspective highlights how gender differences in decision-making power result from social norms regarding appropriate behaviours, interactions that reinforce gendered performances, and social institutions that limit possibilities for challenging such behaviour (Ferree, 1990; Martin, 2004; Risman, 2004; West & Zimmerman, 1987). Existing social structures perpetuate beliefs that men's authority is more "legitimate" than women's (Carli, 1999). The consequences—gendered power differences—are seen in both public and domestic realms. To date, however, scholars have not extended studies of gender differences in power to the ways that intimate unions evolve and progress, although the family is a primary location of gender inequality (Tichenor, 1999, 2005; Zvonkovic et al., 1996).

Reviewing the research on marital power, Gray-Little and Burks (1983, p. 522) asserted that "much that goes on between spouses is not reflected in the final outcome of the decision-making process." To better understand how power is exerted by each partner requires the investigation of interactions and a focus on influence strategies, negotiation, and conflict management (Knudson-Martin & Mahoney, 1998; Pyke, 1994; Zvonkovic et al., 1996). A growing body of research explores how partners negotiate decision making, when power is exerted, and situations where conventional gender patterns are challenged or affirmed (e.g., Tichenor, 1999, 2005; Zvonkovic et al., 1996). Komter (1989) argued that existing studies based on conventional resource theory masked how *manifest power* operated to advantage men. In her study of marital decision making, it was usually women who desired change, but men who controlled the outcome. But power is not always evident (McDonald, 1980). Disagreement may not emerge as a result of adherence to dominant values—what Komter termed *hidden power*. In such situations, conflict does not occur because subordinate groups adhere to hegemonic notions of what is natural and appropriate. Women's reliance on men to initiate all stages of romantic relationships because that is "tradition," even if that means deferring or foregoing desired goals, is one example of how hidden power may operate (see also Humble, Zvonkovic & Walker, 2008; Knudson-Martin & Mahoney, 1998).[1] *Covert power* can also operate to suppress negotiation and maintain the status quo—for example, when one partner determines that the timing is not right to address relationship advancement, or a partner no longer raises issues because of fear of destabilizing the relationship or resignation resulting from previous failed attempts (Komter, 1989; Pyke, 1994; Tichenor, 1999, 2005).[2]

Little attention has been paid to how covert power and hidden power operate to establish and perpetuate gender inequality in premarital

romantic relationships. What research exists on this topic suggests that romantic involvement remains an arena where established gender norms are highly entrenched. Notwithstanding young adults' expressions of egalitarianism, male and female students generally expected first dates to proceed in gender-typical ways, with men responsible for initiating and paying (Laner & Ventrone, 1998; Rose & Frieze, 1989; Ross & Davis, 1996). Male partners in dating relationships also reported more decision-making power than female partners (Felmlee, 1994; Peplau, 1979). Women's attempts to influence outcomes are more often indirect, consistent with gender norms (Knudson-Martin & Mahoney, 1998; Komter, 1989; Zvonkovic et al., 1996). For example, one study that asked women to simulate date initiation found that nearly a third of the women (31 per cent) instead showed responsiveness to encourage the man to ask them out (Gilbert, Walker, McKinney & Snell, 1999). Even when relationships do not begin with the traditional "date," men retain greater control over whether a romance ensues or remains a brief physical encounter (England & Thomas, 2006).

Research on cohabitors' relationship progression is sparse. Sassler (2004) examined how young adults entered cohabiting unions, although her study focused on relationship tempo and reasons given for moving in together. Most quantitative research on cohabitors explores the structural factors shaping the decision to move in, marry, or break up rather than how such transitions are negotiated (Manning & Smock, 2002; Sassler & Goldscheider, 2004; Sassler & McNally, 2003; Smock & Manning, 1997). Although several qualitative studies have considered what cohabitation and marriage mean to individual cohabitors and the role economic resources play in conditioning their views of the appropriate time to wed (Gibson-Davis et al., 2005; Reed, 2006; Sassler & Cunningham, 2008; Smock et al., 2005), they do not reveal how couples negotiate discrepant desires.

Cohabiting couples may attempt to challenge conventional gender norms for relationship progression. Nonetheless, cohabitors are still socialized into a culture that assigns greater power and authority to men, so it is not surprising that gender ideology continues to condition the relationship progression of cohabitors; for example, couples engaging in complementary roles are more likely to marry than are their less traditional counterparts (Sanchez, Manning & Smock, 1998). Since cohabitation prior to marriage is now normative, it is important to better understand how and when power relationships that disadvantage women are challenged or affirmed. This study examines how cohabiting couples discuss the progression of their relationships, using inductive, qualitative methods to consider how couples make decisions at several stages. We focus on outcomes, who initiates and controls them, and how such decisions are negotiated, forwarded, or negated. Our study asks whether underlying ideas about gender-appropriate behaviours shape how relationships progress and continue to perpetuate women's subordinate status even in less formal unions.

Method

This study is based on semistructured face-to-face interviews with 30 cohabiting couples (60 individuals). We focused on the working class, where intense change regarding women's and men's opportunities is taking place (Cherlin, 2009; Ellwood & Jencks, 2004). Working-class men's employment prospects and wages have declined with the loss of manufacturing jobs,

resulting in a diminishing gap between the earnings of working-class men and women (Levy, 1998; Rubin, 1994). Furthermore, within the past decade the increase in cohabitation has been greatest among those with a high-school diploma or those who have some postsecondary education but no college degree (Chandra et al., 2005). Finally, the working class has traditionally expressed conservative views regarding gender roles (Komarovsky, 1987; Rubin, 1976, 1994). Our theoretical focus on the working class therefore underscores how gender is negotiated in a population where men's dominant role as provider is threatened.

Recruitment took place in a large metropolitan area (Columbus, Ohio) at a junior college. Community college students come from families with limited economic resources and have relatively low rates of attaining a four-year degree (Goldrick-Rab, 2006). Signs inviting participation were posted on public message boards on the campus. We were also contacted by non-students who saw the postings or were told of our study by acquaintances.[3] The data were collected from July 2004 to April 2005. Respondents were selected if they reported being heterosexual, were aged 18 to 35 years, were currently cohabiting, and shared a residence with their partner for at least three months.

Our study sample was not in the bottom quarter of the income distribution (US Census Bureau, 2000) but nevertheless differed in important ways from those whose characteristics would place them among the solidly middle class (Rubin, 1976). Couples were screened primarily on education and income. When both partners had less than a bachelor's degree, couples were eligible for the study provided they earned more than $18,000 a year. We used occupation as a determinant of class status when a couple's earned income was above the second quartile for Ohio (the highest earners in the sample, e.g., are skilled labourers and a postal worker) and when one partner in a couple had a bachelor's degree but the other did not (two men and two women in the sample). None of the respondents with bachelor's degrees were working at jobs requiring a college education, and their responsibilities did not differ from other sample members without college degrees.[4]

Respondents were interviewed simultaneously in separate rooms to ensure confidentiality and to allow each partner to discuss sensitive issues (Hertz, 1995). Interviews were conducted by both authors and a graduate student who had been involved in the project from its inception. Interviews lasted 1 to 2½ hours. All interviews were digitally recorded and transcribed verbatim. Transcripts were coded line by line by both authors. Emergent codes identified through repeated reading of transcripts were discussed until agreement was reached. Individual partners' stories were read in conjunction with those of their counterparts to reconstruct a couple-level experience of each aspect of relationship progression. Couples' narratives often differed. In these instances, we followed Hertz's recommendations and did not attempt to find one objective "truth," but instead created "a space for both partners to tell different accounts" (Hertz, 1995, p. 434). Names of all respondents have been altered to protect confidentiality.

Couples were asked how their relationship progressed from first meeting until the present and about plans with their current partner. Interviewers probed to ascertain timing of events, which partner initiated a step, when plans were discussed, and thoughts regarding the relationship tempo. We focused on three stages of the relationship, although some couples engaged in two steps at the same time: becoming romantically involved, moving in

together, and discussing the future (particularly engagement and/or marriage). Following the grounded theory approach, *open coding* was used initially to generate topical themes (e.g., male initiation, female initiation, negotiation) for each stage (Strauss & Corbin, 1998). The second stage of analysis involved *axial coding,* or looking at the variability and linkages within topics (i.e., female initiation of cohabitation and discussions of the future). The third level of analysis, *selective coding,* integrates and refines categories to identify a "story line" (Strauss & Corbin, 1998) regarding how gender is done (and challenged) in cohabiting couples.

Descriptive information for the 30 couples is presented in Table 10.1. The mean level of education for participants was some college; in 20 couples both partners had completed some postsecondary education. The average yearly income for men was $22,044, somewhat higher than the women's average of $17,427. The median combined household income of $35,350 was lower than the Ohio median earnings of $45,805 for 2004–5 (Fronczek, 2005). A disproportionate number of couples were interracial, and nearly 40 per cent lived with children, consistent with other studies of cohabiting couples (e.g., Blackwell & Lichter, 2000; Sassler & McNally, 2003).

Findings

We focused on three stages of couples' relationship: (a) how they became romantically involved, (b) decisions to move in together, and (c) discussions of the future (particularly proposals and marriage). For each stage, we assess which partner was given (or took) credit for the outcome of interest, as well as whether and how the process was negotiated. Our findings on romantic relationship initiation are consistent with prior studies (e.g., Laner & Ventrone, 1998; Rose & Frieze, 1989; Ross & Davis, 1996); discussion of that stage is therefore condensed.

Becoming a Couple

Determining how couples became romantically involved is challenging given today's looser relationship patterns. The cohabiting couples in our sample often relied on normative gender scripts. Men were more likely to initiate relationships, and to do so using direct approaches, whereas women demonstrated their receptiveness. Although only 11 couples in our sample describe a formal "date" as the beginning point of their relationship, 10 of these couples attributed the initiation of the relationship to the man. Another 6 couples met on the Internet. No clear patterns regarding gender and initiation emerge from this group. The remaining 13 couples met through friends, common interests, or work, and many describe "hanging out" with their partners in groups before their relationships became romantic.

Although more indefinite relationship progression patterns could challenge normative gender prescriptions, our findings suggest more consistency than contestation with traditional gendered scripts. Seven couples described knowing they were in a romantic relationship because of a sign—a first kiss (or more), leaving flowers in a locker, or the presentation of chocolates. In six of these seven couples, men were the instigators of these direct but non-verbal signifiers. Other men expressed their interest in a romantic relationship. Stacy recalled that Andre, while giving her a ride home from a social gathering, told her, "I have a crush on you," after which their relationship rapidly developed. Women, in contrast, were far more likely to rely on indirect strategies to transition friendship into romance or to clarify whether the couple was involved.

Explaining why a particular date was their "official" anniversary, Aliyah said, "I asked him one day, like 'Well, what do you consider me as?' and he was, like, 'Well, you're my girlfriend.'" The men in these couples have more power to determine whether hanging out evolves into a romantic relationship, consistent with research on hook-ups (England & Thomas, 2006). That may be because non-normative gender behaviours are apt to be met with resistance. Several respondents revealed that women who pursued the first date or first sexual encounters with partners were, in the words of one rueful woman, "shot down." At least in the initial stages, men have greater power to formalize the establishment of relationships, a sign of manifest power (Komter, 1989). That women in our sample are much less likely to initiate these relationships also provides some evidence of men's hidden power.

Moving in Together

The process whereby couples determined to move in together provides a unique opportunity to examine how decisions are made regarding shared living, as well as how differences are negotiated. Women were far more likely to suggest the couple move in together than they were to ask men out on a date; in fact, they are as likely as the men to suggest cohabiting. Yet deeper probing reveals the ways that structural gender inequities continue to shape relationship strategies and, subsequently, reflect power.

The majority of couples share similar stories about how they came to live together. Nine couples concurred that the male partner was the one to initially raise the idea that they should share a home, with an additional two men suggesting it in response to their partner's indirect pleas for a place to live. Three

Table 10.1   Demographic Characteristics of Cohabiting Couples

Variables	Measures	Means
Age	Mean age: Men	26.4
	Mean age: Women	24.4
Couple-level income[a]	Mean combined income	$38,971
	Median combined income	
Couple-Level Measures		*N*
Relative age	Man >4 years older	4
	Woman >4 years older	2
	Both within 4 years	24
Educational attainment	Both high school or less	1
	1 ≤ high school, 1 some college	5
	Both some college or associate degree	20
	1 high school, 1 BA	1
	1 some college, 1 BA	3
Relative schooling	Man has more education	7
	Woman has more education	7
	Equal levels of schooling	16
Race	Both White	13
	Both Hispanic	1
	Both Black	4
	Mixed race	12
Relative earnings[a]	Man earns 60% or more	13
	Woman earns 60% or more	6
	Each partner earns within 40% to 60%	11
Marital Status	Both never married	24
	One never married, one previously married	6
Parental status	Both no children	16
	Both share children[b]	5
	Man has children (not woman)	6
	Woman has children (not man)	2
	Each has child from prior relationship	1
Duration of cohabitation[c]	3-6 months	8
	7-11 months	2
	12-23 months	5
	24-35 months	7
	3 years or more	8
N		30 couples (60 individuals)

a. Determined by summing each partner's reported individual income. In one instance, where the male partner did not report his income, we relied on his partner's report of both their incomes.

b. In two instances, the couples share a child and the male partner also has a child from a prior relationship.

c. Five couples have broken up and gotten back together; their living together duration is from the initial cohabitation to the interview date.

of the four long-distance Internet couples reported that the man instigated discussion of living together, with housing needs mentioned as a primary reason for doing so. Bill and Maria resided in different states and met on the Internet. Asked how they decided to move in together, Maria said, "I think it was him bringing it up and saying, 'You know, why don't you just move in?'" The greater convenience of shared living was most often mentioned as a reason that men proposed living together. Vic, who met Carly in his neighbourhood bar, recalled how he raised the subject. "I think it was in mid-April, I said, 'You know, you're here all the time. . . . Why aren't your clothes here? Why aren't you here, you know, sort of, officially?'" Eugene suggested cohabiting when his partner experienced housing problems, recalling,

> [Susan] explained to me her situation when she was about to get kicked out of her house and she had like a week to get out or pay the rent. So she said "I really need a place to stay." And I wasn't gonna say, you know, well, you can go live elsewhere.

Another third of the couples in our sample agreed that the female partner initially raised the idea of living together; in one additional couple, the woman suggested that her partner move in with her in response to his housing needs. Examining how the subject of living together was broached reveals how normative gender roles are challenged, as well as maintained. Only four women in this group used a direct approach to suggesting cohabitation. Brian mentioned how they gradually began spending every night together, then divulged that Shelly had initiated the talk of their living together. Shelly's discussion revealed what preceded that request:

I'd say he "officially" moved in like maybe in March, because like when he was staying there that whole time, like he finally started staying there like seven days a week. And I wasn't making him pay the bills and he wasn't offering, and I was [thinking] like, "This is so messed up, like how are you not even offering?" Like it started really to get me, like I was [thinking] "Ask him to pay, to see if he wants to. Is he gonna move out?" But one day I was just like "We got to talk. You've got to start paying 50 per cent because I can't do this." So that was when the living together became, like, official.

Her response reveals the considerable anxiety she felt in being frank. In fact, women's direct attempts were sometimes checked, as Keisha reveals. "I was the one that came up with the suggestion," she said laughingly. "He was kind of leery about it, too, when I first came with the suggestion." Asked what happened next, she replied:

> So, yeah, so after I pushed that conversation with him about that, he thought about it for a while. First kept on telling me he didn't know. He had to think about it. So, suddenly, out of the blue, like maybe a couple months later . . . he said, "You know, I put some thought into what you was talking about." And he said "Yeah, that does sound like a plan."

Although several male-initiated couples also deferred moving in, they all indicated that the reason for delay was to save enough money for a deposit or to search for an apartment. Even when women are willing to initiate relationship progression, doing so is perceived as risky and outcomes uncertain. Furthermore, men's ability to defer the decision highlights their control over decision making, or the use of manifest power to determine when changes are agreed on.

Another four women used indirect approaches to raise the topic of living together. These respondents faced little resistance from their partners. Two women suggested that they become roommates. Tyrone recalled, "She was like, 'We move in together, we could split the rent, we could be roommates,' and she stressed the point of roommates," after which he laughed. Another man whose partner broached the topic of living together said that he found her qualms about assertiveness endearing. Jake said, "She did one of those, like, 'I'm going to ask you a question and I don't want you to freak out about it, 'cause it's like one of those things where I am being too forward.'" Although these women demonstrated hesitation about initiating the discussion to live together for fear of overturning normative gender expectations (being "too forward"), their partners enjoyed being asked and were receptive. This suggests an area where social interactions can minimize gender divergence. The final two women raised the need to live together in response to pregnancies; both their partners agreed that moving in together was "a given," consistent with other qualitative studies on relationship progression (Reed, 2006).

Of the remaining eight couples, three reported that decisions to live together were jointly made. Another five disagreed about who had initially raised the subject or how living together actually transpired. In two couples, for example, the female partner interpreted words in ways the man had not intended. Crystal credited Ron with suggesting she move in, adding, "He just asked me to bring some things over and to start keeping things there so I didn't have to go home." Ron asserted that his offer to make life more convenient for her was not an invitation to move in. Neither of these men, however, contested shared living so much that partners felt uncomfortable enough to move out. There was no consistent pattern in the remaining three couples who did not concur on how their living decision transpired.

Reasons respondents gave for why they moved in suggest that for many women, structural factors, such as gender disparities in wages, the shortage of affordable housing, and an absence of reliable transportation, often conditioned their initiating discussing of living together (whether directly or indirectly). Housing issues were mentioned most frequently by couples where the woman had instigated the discussion of shared living, whereas male-initiated cohabitors cited convenience as their primary reason. Gender disparities in earnings might account for women's greater challenges affording housing; alternatively, while many of the respondents said they could move back in with their family, women in particular were unwilling to do that. The way decisions to move in together were discussed, and whose residence couples moved into, revealed other manifestation of power. Several men did not act on the initial suggestion to live together. Eric, who said he initially laughed when Dawn raised the idea, later suggested she move in with him. Negotiation about where to move was most evident for three involved non-custodial fathers, two of whom insisted their partner move for them. Laura mentioned that "she made a compromise" and moved to Columbus, because Simon wanted to be able to see his young son as much as possible. Gender disparities also emerged in where couples first lived. Half of the 30 couples moved into the man's home. Only seven couples made their home in the woman's apartment; this was more likely to happen when the woman raised the idea, or had more earnings or education. The remaining eight couples relocated to a new apartment.

Discussions of the Future

Cohabitors are a diverse group, and a considerable number have no interest in marrying (Elizabeth, 2000). Nonetheless, there are strong normative expectations that cohabiting young adults are contemplating marriage. Not all couples have discussed future plans with partners, in response to past experiences, adherences to gendered scripts, or because relationships are too new; others have curtailed such conversations. But most of the respondents in our sample report periodic or ongoing discussions of marriage, sometimes in response to seeing something on television or following an invitation to a wedding. How these talks progress, the roles men and women play in forwarding or impeding such talks, and the decisions couples ultimately make suggest that while normative gender roles continue to have considerable weight, women in cohabiting couples are challenging conventional female roles.

Earlier research suggests that many cohabitors do not raise serious discussions of future plans until well after they have moved in together (Sassler, 2004), often because the transition to shared living has occurred rapidly. Three couples in our sample agree that they have never discussed marriage. Asked whether she and her partner Eugene had talked about marriage, Susan replied, "Not really. We still don't really, I mean, 'cause it's the future. You don't know really much about it, it can change." Though she did think that they would probably get married, the way Susan describes her understanding—as "kind of like this unspoken thing that we're gonna stay together"—typifies many cohabiting relationships. Two of these couples have been dating and cohabiting for under a year.

Yet other respondents who have been involved for similar lengths of time have raised the issue of marriage, especially when they are opposed to marriage. Four couples in our sample have verbally agreed that they never want to formalize their unions through marriage. "I think we discussed marriage like probably the first date we had or something," Mitch explained, "just because I wanted to get it out in the open that I didn't want to get married ever. Not unless, like, for insurance or tax purposes." The four women in these couples are equally dismissive of marriage. Several reported vigilance in ensuring their partners understood that they were not interested in bearing children. Stacy recollected a discussion she had with her partner Andre when they first got involved:

> But I told him the first day, the first day, before we even had sex I told him, "Look. If you want to date me, that's cool. I want to date you, too. . . . But I'm not having your puppies and I'm not getting married, so if you're looking for marriage or puppies you better look to somebody else. It's not me. I'm not that girl."

In another three couples, only one partner was marriage averse; two previously married women had no interest in marrying again, and the man in the third couple claimed he would never be responsible enough for marriage (and his partner agreed). By rejecting the possibility of marriage, they control the matrimonial future of their partners as long as they remain coupled.

Marriage either is or has been a topic of discussion for the remaining 20 couples, in varying forms. Several women revealed they had been reluctant to discuss desires for marriage and children on first moving in together. Brandi explained, "It was just kind of like an off-subject, you just don't ask, you know?" Asked why, she responded, "I didn't want to put pressure on him to think that just because we live together that this is like forever." Dawn's restraint was driven by previous experience, saying, "I tried not to talk about marriage because I talked about it with my last boyfriend, and it just really didn't make things very good." Both were reluctant to destabilize their relationships by suggesting to their partners that they were too desirous of marriage. An additional five respondents indicated that they had curtailed marriage talk in response to their current partners' reactions. The three women provided similar stories, of how marriage talk discomfited their partners—a reaction that a male partner verified. Shane revealed that Sandra no longer talked much about their future:

> And eventually she realized that I was so undecided and, like, not ready that she just kind of backed off without saying anything like that. She just kind of stopped pressing the issue. So I'm pretty sure it's something she still thinks about and it's probably still on her mind. But she hasn't been bugging me about it.

Women's fear that talk of marriage will be unwelcome demonstrates how covert power advantages men. But power to curb marriage talk was also wielded by two women. Maria explained, "About a year ago he stopped demanding that we had to be married, because I told him that if we had to be married, then I was going to break up with him, because I couldn't promise that." Both women had been previously married, had children, and were tenuous about their desires to remarry. Both were also the primary providers in their relationships, suggesting that their resources may have been one source of their power.

More than one-third of the couples in our sample ($n = 12$) are actively negotiating the relationship, its progression and desired outcomes. Many of the women in these couples attempted to challenge normative gender constructions involving male initiation of relationship advancement. At least one partner in 10 couples indicated that the woman has stated a desire to get engaged or married. Women often revealed that they hinted or joked about getting engaged but few admitted to raising the issue directly. Stories of the woman's desires to expedite a proposal were also mentioned by the men. Anthony conveyed how his partner, Diana, tipped her hand, saying, "We were at the mall the other day, and she was like, 'Oohh, look at these rings,' and she keeps saying stuff like, you know, 'My birthday's coming up pretty soon. I'd like some jewelry.'" Although women may attempt to promote their desires, those in this sample faced considerable opposition to realizing their goals. Aliyah mentioned that she brings up marriage once or twice a month, but admitted, "I usually have to force him into talking about it. He doesn't like talking about it, but once I get him into it, he will talk about it."

In discussing reasons for deferring marriage, both men and women note that they wanted to be earning more, to have decreased their debt, completed school, or saved money for a house or a wedding before getting engaged, consistent with prior research (Gibson-Davis et al., 2005; Smock et al., 2005). The cost of engagement rings also featured in these talks; men sometimes said they had to save up for a ring, whereas women mentioned the pressure their partners felt to buy a "nice enough" ring. But another reason also emerged—ambivalence about marriage. This sentiment was expressed mainly by men, several of whom stated that marriage was not on their minds. Notwithstanding Diana's hints, Anthony was content with the status quo. "Everything's working out right now the way it is and we just want it to be that way for now, you know?" he said. Asked about a possible time-table, he replied, "Maybe eventually down the road." Terrell responded to Aliyah's feints by stating, "I ain't ready, I don't want to talk about it." Six women expressed some dissatisfaction with this situation. Dawn, for example, said, "I just feel like he wants to, he wants control of the situation. He wants to do it when he's ready for it." And although admitting that finishing school before getting married was the right thing to do, she also felt that prospect was quite far away. "I don't know, the way he's going, he might be another two years," she said, mentioning that he was already in his sixth year of school. Only one man reported pushing for marriage more than did his partner.

The men in our sample appeared far more confident in their partners' desires to marry them than the women did with respect to their mates. In fact, men often asserted that their partners were anxious to get engaged. Stan reported, "Oh, she's waiting for, itching for that," whereas Bill declared, "She seems to be okay with waiting until I graduate. I mean, she would like to get married now. If I walked up to her and said, 'Let's get married tomorrow,' she'd get married." The consistency of such statements reflects men's conviction that they control the pace of the relationship progression. Women often verified men's assertions. Keisha noted that Stan tells her to be patient, whereas Dawn replied, "I'm just waiting for my boyfriend to ask me."

Furthermore, exploration revealed that men's dominant position rests largely in the enactment of becoming engaged. Among nearly all the couples where marriage was a possibility (and even among some of those rejecting marriage), the man is expected to be the one to "pop the question." Most of these couples adhere to conventional views, referencing "tradition" as a justification. Ron said, "I mean, that's just a guy thing," and added, "It's how it should be," a sentiment his partner Crystal seconded. Because neither of these partners believes that women should propose, the power to advance the relationship rests in the hands of the men.

Both partners do not always agree that proposing is the male prerogative. Two men who had been discussing engagement with their partner said they would welcome being proposed to, as proposing was often viewed as a burden; one other man, who had not discussed marriage with his partner, also expressed the belief that having his partner ask him to marry her would be, in his words, "cool." Simon thought being proposed to would be "awesome," further clarifying, "I do think more women should propose. I think that is a turn on. It would be a turn on for me." However, these men's partners were not eager to take on that role. Simon's partner, Laura, affirmed that she would never think of proposing to Simon. Asked why, she stated, "'cause that's the man's job. The man is supposed to do it." Asked what the woman's job was, she replied, "To say yes. To wear the ring." Several of the women indicated that for them to propose smacked of desperation. Brandi said, "I think it would just be kind of strange, and I don't know how he'd react to that." Dawn jokingly asked, "What girl really wants to be the one that has to propose?" then said in a pathetic voice, "Will you take me as your wife?" before laughing. But Dawn's partner, Eric, mentioned that in the past she had joked about proposing; asked his response, he said, "I'm like, 'Well, if you do, I'm going to say no!'" In view of Eric's reply, Dawn's best option appears to be to wait until he is ready.

The two women who felt that either partner could propose, or who had tried to do so, were met with resistance. Asked how they would feel if their partner proposed, men frequently said they would be shocked or surprised, or worse, that they would laugh. "It would be hilarious," Spencer commented. Terrell's response revealed how firmly entrenched men's prerogatives are. Faced with a hypothetical proposal from Aliyah, Terrel said, "I would laugh and then I would be like, "Come on, girl, get off your knees. Stop playing around." Then I would eventually go do it for real—the real way, how it's supposed to be done." Even if women desire to take control of their relationship's progression, they need the consent of their partners. Men's demonstration of manifest power suggests that for most of these couples a woman's proposal would be disappointing or (as in the case of Dawn) refused. Yet two couples did mention that the woman had proposed; in neither instance are both partners satisfied with the outcome, and both couples indicate that the man would be "redoing" the proposal in the near future. In one case the female partner had tried to set up a scenario where he would ask her, but slipped and "accidentally" asked him instead. The other man was discomfited by his partner's proposing. Though he called Maria his fiancée, Bill did not wear the engagement ring she gave him, saying, "I don't know of guys having engagement rings or anything."

Yet individuals' attempts to convince partners to take a step are not all futile. Several respondents mentioned that over time their partners have influenced them to do something they had not previously considered—demonstrating convincing power. This occurred with two men, who persuaded partners to get engaged (although one woman says she subsequently broke it off). Harry was eventually able to sway Marta into talking about marriage and at his interview revealed that he was currently planning his proposal. Men also reported doing (or planning) something they believed their female partner wanted more than they did. For some men, it was proposing, or giving their partner a ring; for other men, the ultimate sacrifice was in deciding to get married.[5] Ray said that he had proposed to Julie, stating,

> I think at the time it was mostly for her, because it was something that she really wanted and I didn't want to lose her. So I was willing to do it just so that, you know, I wouldn't lose her.

Jerry, who reported being "kind of against" marriage, said "I still, even though I am going to propose to her, it's more for her gratification. I mean, I don't think it's necessary to get married." And finally, Simon, who preferred that Laura propose, said that he would end up doing it, as it was what she wanted. These supposed sacrifices were generally for hypothetical actions that had yet to take place.[6] That these respondents took account of their partner's desires rather than their own suggests that control can be negotiated, at least when partners seek to keep each other happy.

Discussion and Conclusions

This study examined whether cohabiting couples attempted to "undo gender" by challenging normative expectations that male partners assume primary responsibility for relationship progression. We analyzed how relationships progressed for a sample of 30 working-class cohabiting couples (60 respondents). Our findings suggest that cohabitation serves as an arena where normative gender roles are sometimes undone, at least when it comes to establishing cohabiting unions. Nonetheless, couples reinforce normative gender enactments at numerous relationship points, including initiating relationships and transforming them into more formal arrangements, such as engagement. Individuals' strategies to attain their desired ends highlight the persistence of men's dominant position, through the operation of manifest, covert, and hidden power.

Women did not leave all relationship decisions in the hands of their male partners. They frequently raised the topic of moving in together, and many also advocated strongly for formalizing their relationships via engagement. Cohabitation is an "incomplete institution" (Cherlin, 2004), with few clear guidelines regarding whether and how it should progress. Our findings suggest that cohabitation is a welcome alternative for couples who do not desire children or marriage. However, we do not find such relationships are any more likely to be female driven. That women remained more likely to use indirect approaches, and expressed concerns about their assertiveness when they did suggest living together, reveals the challenges experienced by those tentatively trying on new roles. In addition, although the women were as likely as the men to suggest living together, the primary reason given by women who initiated shared living was related to housing needs. Low wages available for women, particularly those with less than a college degree, rather than resource power therefore seem to condition women's relationship strategies. Women also demonstrate agency in discussing marriage, although we found that when marital goals are not shared women are generally less able than men to obtain their desired outcome. Even though a few women were able to get a less sanguine partner to at least contemplate engagement, far more couples revealed that when they held discrepant views regarding the desirability of marriage, women's desires had less weight. Women's power may be limited to

their ability to end an already formed union (cf., England & Kilbourne, 1990).

Men's responses to women's attempts to "undo gender" highlight the importance of couple-level analysis for studies of relationship power. Although some men tacitly welcomed female partner's assertiveness, describing it as endearing or sexy, male partners were not always accepting of women's attempts to play a more assertive role in the progression of intimate relationships. Several of the men whose female partner raised the possibility of living together put off decisions, and relatively few welcomed the idea of women proposing. The male prerogative of proposing, though sometimes seen as a burden because of expectations that it be unique and memorable, endows men with considerable outcome power. In fact, quite a few of the men in our sample reveled in their ability to control the timing and pace of relationship progression; 7 of the 12 men who have discussed their relationship's future believe that their partners are eager to get engaged. Men's ability to play the dominant role in romantic relationships by controlling the proposal leaves women who desire to marry, in the words of both the male and female respondents, "waiting to be asked." Nonetheless, in most instances the female partners are complicit in this enactment of male control. As with other traditional norms that disadvantage women, the right of the male proposal is also interpreted as an expression of love and caring (Ferree, 1990). Thus, women are not just failing to ask their partners to marry them because they fear disapproval or are unwilling to flout normative gender roles but because they want to be asked.

Consistent with other studies on the division of domestic labour and spending (Miller & Sassler, 2010; Tichenor, 1999, 2005; Zvonkovic et al., 1996), our findings provide greater support for the gender perspective than for relative resource theory. Women who have more education than their partners or who earn equivalent amounts or more do not have greater say in advancing their relationships in the direction and at the pace they desire. Most women, regardless of their earnings, were not the ones who instigated the formation of the couple as a romantic unit. There is also no consistent relationship between women's relative earnings and initiating the discussion of living together, no doubt because housing needs featured so prominently among the women who did raise the topic. Most conclusively, regardless of the resources they commanded, women did not have—and did not claim—the right to propose. And although couples do mention the need to be more financially established as a reason to defer marriage (Gibson-Davis et al., 2005; Reed, 2006; Smock et al., 2005), our findings suggest the importance of assessing whether marital delay also reflects power imbalances between men and women, especially when men are less desirous of marriage than their partners.

Our sample consists of intact, cohabiting couples who had not (yet) married or broken up. This study is therefore limited in that it likely underrepresents those couples least satisfied with their relationship progression, as both partners would not have agreed to participate. Relying on retrospective interviews might also result in fewer mentions of failed negotiations. Nonetheless, we did get reports from both partners regarding their thoughts about their relationship, how it progressed, and their desired outcomes. There is also the possibility that cohabiting couples characterized by unconventional (female initiated) relationship progression were more likely to have broken up (Felmlee, 1994), or wed. As with most qualitative studies, our sample is not representative

of the population of all cohabitors. Cohabitors may engage in different relationship strategies in other regions where housing costs are higher. Finally, the working class may pursue different relationship strategies than do their more advantaged counterparts, given greater challenges to men's abilities to assume the provider role. Results emerging from other studies of working and lower-middle-class cohabitors regarding men's role in relationship progression (e.g., Sassler & Cunningham, 2008; Smock et al., 2005), however, provide some confirmatory support for our findings.

In conclusion, cohabitation appears to be an arena where normative gender roles can be contested. Women often instigate relationship progression, by suggesting couples move into shared living arrangements or raising talk of marriage. Nonetheless, men continue to play dominant roles in both initiating whether couples become romantically involved and in formalizing these unions via proposing, largely because of hegemonic norms regarding male prerogatives. Although both women and men contest how gender is performed, the way these cohabiting couples enact what it means to be male and female are more likely to privilege cohabiting men in the arena of relationship progression. Couples' initial behaviours lay the groundwork for future expectations and behaviours (e.g., Humble et al., 2008; Laner & Ventrone, 1998). In fact, such power differentials also emerge in other areas (Ciabattari, 2004), suggesting that should these couples wed, similar patterns would emerge in their marriages. In our sample, cohabitation mainly served to reinforce rather than challenge extant gender norms. In other words, adherence to conventional practices even among those residing in informal unions perpetuated women's secondary position in intimate relationships.

● Acknowledgments

The authors are grateful for the helpful comments of Liana Sayer, Daniel Lichter, and Betty Menaghan. The authors thank Sarah Favinger for her assistance in data collection. The authors would like to acknowledge The Ohio State University for providing funding for stages of the project via a University Seed Grant awarded to the first author.

● Authors' Note

A previous version of this article was presented at the 2006 Annual Meeting of the American Sociological Association.

● Notes

1. Zvonkovic, Greaves, Schmiege, and Hall (1996) also identified ways that men's *hidden power* operated to reduce active contention. They provide several examples of how wives naturalize accepting men's right to ultimately make family decisions when the couple was not in consensus.

   "We usually talk and come to full agreement, or I give in and do what he wants on . . . [a] majority of things," one woman stated, explaining "I love him, and minor disagreements are a part of life" (Zvonkovic et al., 1996, p. 98).

2. Several examples of *covert power* emerge in Tichenor's (2005) study of how couples negotiate men's dominant role among couples where the man earns substantially less than his wife; the author discusses the power asymmetry that advantages men but not women, and women's perceptions that such imbalances were dangerous or threatening to couple stability and harmony.

3. Two couples who contacted us were referred by others that had been interviewed; we limited our acceptance of these referrals to one per couple, in order to ensure that the sample is not composed of couples who are all interrelated (Berg, 1988). A third couple was referred by an acquaintance of one of the researchers.

4. For example, one of the women with a college degree reported working at a job that was identical to that mentioned by several of her less educated counterparts, telemarketing; another man with a college degree in theater reported working at a job with computers that was similar to one held by another man who had a few classes from a technical school.

5. We distinguish between proposing and marriage based on respondents' actions. For example, Ray and Julie had been engaged for about five years at the time of their interview and had not yet picked a wedding date. Among other couples, discussions of wedding plans seemed to precipitate an acceptance that marriage was in the cards, perhaps because talks about when and where to marry were more concrete.

6. Only one of the men who had been ambivalent about engagement had actually proposed, though Jerry revealed that he had already purchased the ring and planned and paid for the vacation where he intended to ask his partner Natalie to marry him.

● References

Berg, S. (1988). Snowball sampling. In S. Kotz & N.L. Johnson (eds), *Encyclopedia of statistical sciences* (Vol. 8, pp. 528–32). New York, NY: Wiley.

Bernard, J. (1981). The good provider role: Its rise and fall. *American Psychologist, 36*, 1–12.

Bianchi, S., Milkie, M., Sayer, L., & Robinson, J. (2000). Is anyone doing the housework? Trends in the gender division of household labor. *Social Forces, 79*, 191–228.

Blackwell, D.L., & Lichter, D.T. (2000). Mate selection among married and cohabiting couples. *Journal of Family Issues, 21*, 275–302.

Blood, R., & Wolfe, D. (1960). *Husbands and wives.* Glencoe, IL: Free Press.

Blumstein, P., & Schwartz, P. (1983). *American couples.* New York, NY: William Morrow.

Carli, L. (1999). Gender, interpersonal power, and social influence. *Journal of Social Issues, 55*, 81–99.

Chandra, A., Martinez, G.M., Mosher, W.D., Abma, J.C., & Jones, J. (2005). Fertility, family planning, and reproductive health of U.S. women: Data from the 2002 National Survey of Family Growth. *Vital Health Statistics, 23*, 1–160.

Cherlin, A.J. (2004). The deinstitutionalization of American marriage. *Journal of Marriage and Family, 66*, 848–61.

———. (2009). *The marriage go round: The state of marriage and family in America today.* New York, NY: Knopf.

Ciabattari, T. (2004). Cohabitation and housework: The effects on marital intentions. *Journal of Marriage and Family, 66*, 118–25.

Clarkberg, M., Stolzenberg, R., & Waite, L. (1995). Attitudes, values, and entrance into cohabitational versus marital unions. *Social Forces, 74*, 609–26.

de Ruijter, E., Treas, J.K., & Cohen, P.N. (2005). Outsourcing the gender factory: Living arrangements and service expenditures on female and male tasks. *Social Forces, 84*, 305–22.

Deutsch, F.M. (2007). Undoing gender. *Gender & Society, 21*, 106–27.

Elizabeth, V. (2000). Cohabitation, marriage, and the unruly consequence of difference. *Gender & Society, 14*, 87–110.

Ellwood, D.T., & Jencks, C. (2004). The uneven spread of single parent families: What do we know? In K. Neckerman (ed.), *Social inequality* (pp. 3–77). New York, NY: Russell Sage Foundation.

England, P., & Kilbourne, B. S. (1990). Markets, marriages, and other mates: The problem of power. In R. Friedland & A.F. Robertson (eds), *Beyond the marketplace: Rethinking economy and society* (pp. 163–88). New York, NY: Basic Books.

England, P., & Thomas, R.J. (2006). The decline of the date and the rise of the college hook-up. In A. Skolnick & J. Skolnick (eds), *Families in transition* (14th edn, pp. 151–62). Boston, MA: Allyn & Bacon.

Felmlee, D.H. (1994). Who's on top? Power in romantic relationships. *Sex Roles, 31*, 275–95.

Ferree, M.M. (1990). Beyond separate spheres: Feminism and family research. *Journal of Marriage and the Family, 52*, 866–84.

Fronczek, P. (2005). *Income, earnings, and poverty from the 2004 American Community Survey.* Retrieved from www.census.gov/prod/2005pubs/acs-01.pdf.

Gibson-Davis, C., Edin, K., & McLanahan, S. (2005). High hopes but even higher expectations: The retreat from marriage among low-income couples. *Journal of Marriage and Family, 67*, 1301–13.

Gilbert, L.A., Walker, S.J., McKinney, S., & Snell, J.L. (1999). Challenging discourse themes reproducing gender in heterosexual dating: An analog study. *Sex Roles, 41*, 753–75.

Goldrick-Rab, S. (2006). Following their every move: An investigation of social-class differences in college pathways. *Sociology of Education, 79*, 61–79.

Goldscheider, F., & Waite, L. (1991). *New families, no families? The transformation of the American home.* Berkley: University of California Press.

Gray-Little, B., & Burks, N. (1983). Power and satisfaction in marriage: A review and critique. *Psychological Bulletin, 93*, 513–38.

Heimdal, K., & Houseknecht, S. (2003). Cohabiting and married couples' income organization: Approaches in Sweden and the United States. *Journal of Marriage and Family, 65*, 525–38.

Hertz, R. (1995). Separate but simultaneous interviewing of husbands and wives: Making sense of their stories. *Qualitative Inquiry, 1*, 429–51.

Hohmann-Marriott, B. (2006). Shared beliefs and the union stability of married and cohabiting couples. *Journal of Marriage and Family, 68*, 1015–28.

Humble, A., Zvonkovic, A., & Walker, A. (2008). "The Royal We": Gender ideology, display, and assessment in wedding work. *Journal of Family Issues, 29*, 3–25.

Kennedy, S., & Bumpass, L.L. (2008). Cohabitation and children's living arrangements: New estimates from the United States. *Demographic Research, 19*, 1663–92.

Knudson-Martin, C., & Mahoney, A.R. (1998). Language and processes in the construction of equality in new marriages. *Family Relations, 47*, 81–91.

Komarovsky, M. (1987). *Blue-collar marriage.* New Haven, CT: Yale University Press.

Komter, A. (1989). Hidden power in marriage. *Gender & Society, 3*, 187–216.

Laner, M., & Ventrone, N. (1998). Egalitarian daters/traditionalist dates. *Journal of Family Issues, 19*, 468–77.

Levy, F. (1998). *The new dollars and dreams.* New York, NY: Russell Sage Foundation.

McDonald, G.W. (1980). Family power: The assessment of a decade of theory and research, 1970–1979. *Journal of Marriage and the Family, 42*, 841–54.

Manning, W., & Smock, P. (2002). First comes cohabitation and then comes marriage? A research note. *Journal of Family Issues, 23,* 1065–88.

Martin, P.Y. (2004). Gender as a social institution. *Social Forces, 82,* 1249–73.

Miller, A., and Sassler, S. (2010). Stability and Change in the Division of Labor Among Cohabiting Couples. *Sociological Forum, 25*(4):677–701.

Peplau, L.A. (1979). Power in dating relationships. In J. Freeman (ed.), *Women: A feminist perspective* (pp. 121–37). Palo Alto, CA: Mayfield.

Potuchek, J. (1997). *Who supports the family? Gender and breadwinning in dual-earner marriage.* Stanford, CA: Stanford University Press.

Pyke, K.D. (1994). Women's employment as a gift or burden? Marital power across marriage, divorce, and remarriage. *Gender & Society, 8,* 73–91.

Reed, J.M. (2006). Not crossing the "extra line": How cohabitors with children view their unions. *Journal of Marriage and Family, 68,* 1117–31.

Risman, B. (2004). Gender as a social structure: Theory wrestling with action. *Gender & Society, 18,* 429–50.

Rose, S., & Frieze, I.H. (1989). Young single's scripts for a first date. *Gender & Society, 3,* 258–68.

Ross, L., & Davis, A.C. (1996). Black-white college student attitudes and expectations in paying for dates. *Sex Roles, 35,* 43–56.

Rubin, L. (1976). *Worlds of pain: Life in the working class family.* New York, NY: Basic Books.

———. (1994). *Families on the fault line: America's working class speaks about the family, the economy, race, and ethnicity.* New York, NY: HarperCollins.

Sanchez, L., Manning, W., & Smock, P. (1998). Sex-specialized or collaborative mate selection? Union transitions among cohabitors. *Social Science Research, 27,* 280–304.

Sassler, S. (2004). The process of entering into cohabiting unions. *Journal of Marriage and Family, 66,* 491–506.

Sassler, S., & Cunningham, A. (2008). How cohabitors view childbearing. *Sociological Perspectives, 51,* 3–28.

Sassler, S., & Goldscheider, F. (2004). Revisiting Jane Austen's theory of marriage timing: Changes in union formation among American men in late 20th century. *Journal of Family Issues, 25,* 139–66.

Sassler, S., & McNally, J. (2003). Cohabiting couples' economic circumstances and union transitions: A re-examination using multiple imputation techniques. *Social Science Research, 32,* 553–78.

Sayer, L.C. (2005). Gender, time, and inequality: Trends in women's and men's paid work, unpaid work, and free time. *Social Forces, 84,* 285–303.

Smock, P., & Manning, W. (1997). Cohabiting partners' economic circumstances and marriage. *Demography, 34,* 331–41.

Smock, P., Manning, W., & Porter, M. (2005). Everything's there except money: How money shapes decisions to marry among cohabitors. *Journal of Marriage and Family, 67,* 680–96.

Stacey, J. (1990). *Brave new families: Stories of domestic upheaval in late twentieth century America.* New York, NY: Basic Books.

Strauss, A., & Corbin, J. (1998). Basics of qualitative research: Techniques and procedures for developing grounded theory. Thousand Oaks, CA: Sage.

Szinovacz, M.E. (1987). Family power. In M.B. Sussman & S.K. Steinmetz (eds), *Handbook of marriage and the family* (pp. 651–93). New York, NY: Plenum Press.

Tichenor, V. (1999). Status and income as gendered resources: The case of marital power. *Journal of Marriage and the Family, 61,* 638–51.

———. (2005). Maintaining men's dominance: Negotiating identity and power when she earns more. *Sex Roles, 53,* 191–205.

US Census Bureau. (2000). *Census 2000 Summary File 1 (SF 1) and Summary File 3 (SF 3), Ohio.* Retrieved from http://factfinder.census.gov.

Vogler, C. (2005). Cohabiting couples: Rethinking money in the household at the beginning of the 21st century. *Sociological Review, 53,* 1–29.

Waite, L.J., & Gallagher, M. (2000). *The case for marriage.* New York, NY: Doubleday.

West, C., & Zimmerman, D. (1987). Doing gender. *Gender & Society, 2,* 125–51.

Winkler, A.E. (1997). Economic decision-making by cohabitors: Findings regarding income pooling. *Applied Economics, 29,* 1079–90.

Winkler, A.E., McBride, T.D., & Andrews, C. (2005). Wives who outearn their husbands: A transitory or persistent phenomenon for couples? *Demography, 42,* 523–35.

Zvonkovic, A., Greaves, K., Schmiege, C., & Hall, L. (1996). The marital construction of gender through work and family decisions: A qualitative analysis. *Journal of Marriage and the Family, 58,* 91–100.

Chapter 11

Getting married represents a very meaningful passage for many couples. Thus, weddings hold powerful significance for those couples who decide to marry. Students of sociology might try to uncover the meaning of these ceremonies for the people who engage in them. One way of doing so is to examine the rituals and symbols in the ceremonies—the father "giving away" the bride, the ring exchange, the bride's white gown. We might also ask people who follow such "traditions" in their ceremonies why they do so.

Sociologist Dawn Currie takes a different approach. She examines not only what their marriages meant to the women and men she interviewed but also how they planned their wedding ceremonies. Currie's interviews were done in the 1990s, yet this article retains its relevance: expensive "traditional" weddings continue to be popular. The interviews occurred years after legal definitions of marriage in Canada changed to reflect ideals of greater gender equality in marriage. In the late 1970s and early 1980s, English-speaking provinces across the country changed their family laws in a way that omitted old assumptions about women's and men's different rights and responsibilities in marriage. But what Currie finds in this small study raises questions about the extent to which gender relations have changed.

"Here Comes the Bride": The Making of a "Modern Traditional" Wedding in Western Culture

Dawn H. Currie

Changes in marriage and family dynamics during the past 25 years have given rise to new questions for sociologists of the family. Following legislative changes in the 1960s, the divorce rate in Canada has increased steadily, so that up to one-third of marriages today are likely to end in divorce.[1] As indicators of marital instability rose in most Western industrialized societies, commentators declared a "crisis in the family" (see Gittins 1985). However, against trends of family breakdown the vast majority of Canadians continue to marry, and also to remarry after divorce. On this basis some writers claim that marriage and the family are "alive and well," or even "getting better." . . . On the other hand, feminists draw attention to the frequency of violence against wives by husbands and the unequal division of domestic labour which characterizes most heterosexual households. For these writers, the modern nuclear family is interpreted as a central factor in women's continued oppression in the West, and thus as being in need of further dismantling (see Burt, Code, and Dorney 1988; Boulton 1983; Thorne 1982; Barrett and McIntosh 1982). Given the public documentation of trends which underlie this latter claim, and a rising consciousness about gender parity among Canadians, feminists are beginning to ask why the traditional nuclear family persists.

The answer to this question is complex, and thus is the matter of ongoing academic debate. Here, one enduring aspect of traditional family life is explored: the everyday activity of "getting married." While the past few decades have seen growth in alternatives to marriage (Wilson 1990), Canadians continue to perceive legal marriage as an indicator of greater commitment, even when they are already living in common-law unions. Baker (1990: 48) notes that the wedding ceremony itself is frequently seen as a "rite of passage" to adult status. Many families save for years and spend considerable sums on wedding clothing and receptions, even though the event itself is short-lived. For those marrying, church weddings remain important. Although they declined from 91 per cent of marriages in 1972 to 70 per cent in 1982, this figure has levelled off (Nett 1988: 211).[2] At the same time, Nett (1988: 211) notes that conventional wedding ceremonies and receptions are filled with customs which are unambiguously patriarchal and that much of the symbolism in church weddings is sexist. The bride is the object of attention, the exchange occurs between the [bride's father] and the man to be her husband, the ring is a remnant of bride price, the white gown symbolizes virginity, and the throwing of rice fertility. She interprets the persistence of these customs as a reminder that emotions, and not fact-based knowledge, surround the activity of the wedding. This emphasis upon the emotional aspects of weddings is characteristic of the work appearing in most textbooks on the sociology of the family, and it is quite likely that this view of wedding customs as "irrational" accounts for the lack of research interest in weddings.

While sociologists generally refer to these unions as "conventional weddings," during my research I came to call these occurrences "modern traditional" weddings, a term which captures the notion of paradox. Participants in my study acknowledged that marriage as a union "for life" is a now outdated view, and few brides promised to "love, honour, and obey" their spouses. Despite slight modifications of wedding vows, however, participants consciously followed "tradition," and in so doing acted out rituals with not entirely progressive meanings. My primary interests therefore were to explore why traditional weddings remain popular and to examine the role which the wedding itself plays in the reproduction of gendered family relations.

The Study

This paper is based on interviews with a small non-random sample of 13 brides and three grooms.[3] Criteria for participation in the study were simply that respondents were either planning a wedding or had been recently married with a conventional wedding. Brides and grooms participating in the weddings included in this study ranged from 21 to 44 years of age. The occupational and economic status of the brides varied, and included "pink collar" work in sales and clerical positions as well as professional and managerial employment. All women interviewed intended to continue working after marriage, and many planned to combine marriage, employment, and motherhood. The majority of couples had been living together prior to their wedding, and a small number of prospective grooms had been previously married. Interviews, which were unstructured and open-ended, focused on the meaning of weddings to respondents and documented the activities involved in making weddings happen.

With one exception, the weddings in this study occurred in a church.[4] Receptions which followed included anywhere from 25 to over 300 participants, although most involved at least 100 guests. Brides wore white, full-length gowns, and for many respondents the choice of the bridal gown was among the most important decisions. Despite that fact that all weddings were planned as religious ceremonies, however, religious beliefs emerged as important to only three couples. More typically, respondents spoke of the symbolic importance of "following tradition":

> We did want to have a church wedding. . . . Neither of us have any feelings, I guess, against the Church or for the Church. I was brought up more-or-less Lutheran. I'm not really a strong frequenter, but still I did want to get married in a church. (Elizabeth, 27-year-old sales representative)

> For some reason I didn't think it would be a proper wedding if I didn't have the traditional. (Margie, 23-year-old employee of Parks and Recreation)

> I think it's a reflection of the tradition that I like. . . . When I hear the word "tradition," . . . I think along the lines of something solid, something quality. Something's traditional, or has been a tradition because it has stood the test of time, and that's the whole idea about marriage. (Brian, 28-year-old jewelry designer)

While the notion of following tradition may seem deceptively simple, what this entails proved to be much more extensive than what I had anticipated. More surprisingly, perhaps, in most cases wedding preparations entailed more work (and expense) than even respondents themselves had anticipated or actually desired. This could result in a sense of wedding plans being out of the control of respondents, or of the wedding excluding them:

> If I'd had my way, it would have just been really small and simple, and that was what

we initially intended. . . . I just felt caught up in this big thing that I didn't have any control over, and people just kept pressing me to do this or that. . . . I was under a lot of stress. (Helen, 21-year-old student)

> We never initially intended to have a big deal. I think, maybe I wanted to wear a nice dress or something, but I didn't have this idea—and neither did Bill—of a great big wedding. It just kind of happened. . . . We kind of conceded to the fact that this was more for other people than for us, which is really ironic. (Michelle, 22-year-old student)

As researcher, therefore, I could not assume that as social agents, respondents were either fully aware, or in control, of events which made their wedding. However, this did not mean that respondents were simply acting on their emotions: indeed, weddings required many months of research and rational planning on the part of participants. Thus I was curious as to how weddings came to take on "a life of their own."

The Symbolism of Getting Married: Wedding as Commitment

As sociologists have noted elsewhere, although social actors generally view themselves as behaving in a rational manner, they can seldom tell researchers why they engage in specific behaviours. This proved to be true in the case of getting married. Jane and Brian, for example, had lived together off-and-on for over six years. In thinking about why they decided to marry, Jane, a 26-year-old nurse, reflected that:

> I don't know—I feel quite married right now, but there's something that's not there.

It's not a negative thing, and it's not "Oh god, I have to have this thing," but it's not there and I have no idea what it is. I've looked elsewhere for it. I think the actual "I do" is the end of something and the beginning of something [else], although it really is the same thing. . . . I guess it really boils down to [the fact that] it seems like the right thing to do for all sorts of reasons.

While the bride in this case obviously couldn't really say what marriage meant to her, her husband-to-be articulated the associations which many of the other respondents made between marriage and a commitment which would lend their relationship a new sense of stability. In response to the same question, Brian maintained that the wedding signified:

We're going to stick together through thick and thin. We commit ourselves to each other before God. It's holy. It has an aura about it. We're saying that we're going to be together till the day we die.

Overall, this sense of commitment and stability was the most common theme concerning the meaning of the marriage to respondents. Patty, a 22-year-old clerk at Eaton's who had been engaged for nine months prior to the wedding, maintained that:

I think there is still a sense of confidence and—what's the word? Confidence, I guess, that you are together and even though it is a piece of paper, in a sense, in a more important sense there is that bond. . . . I don't know. I think just the fact that you've made the decision and made it clear that commitment is significant.

Similarly:

I think it's the "for better or for worse" thing. . . . If things get really bad and you're living together, you think, "OK, I'll split." But if you're married, and you know that you are both really committed, then it means that you can work through that thing together. I could see in Dick that he had that kind of intent, just from our conversations and stuff. We both had this similar idea about marriage. (Helen)

Just living together just seems—there's no commitment then to stick around, to really work at it. I guess this silly piece of paper and this ceremony just enforced that we are committed to each other to spend a life together and we were really going to make a good stab at it, if that makes any sense. (Faye, 23-year-old nurse)

Since commitment can be signalled in any number of ways, it is interesting to ask how the wedding ceremony, in particular, communicates this meaning to participants. Here the attendance of the wedding by extended family members is important. Like many other celebrations, a wedding may be the time during which family membership and ties are affirmed and renewed:

I think I'll feel a little more part of the family. I'll be the "son-in-law"—there's a title right there, not just a boyfriend, not quite a son. (Brian)

I see it as a celebration of friends and family. In other words, a celebration of people who are important for us from our past and our present, who are suggesting something nice for our future by being there. (Larry, 30-year-old computer operator)

For many respondents, including extended family members meant that planning the wedding was driven by the need to include appropriate relatives:

> I talked to my parents and my mom went through her address book which she's had since she probably got married and found all the relatives that had to be invited. . . . So we just went to our parents and our parents told us who we were supposed to invite from our families and then we added to that. (Rachael, 23-year-old university graduate)

The pressure to include relatives often determined the planning of the wedding:

> It was kind of important for me to have people there like my mother and my father, and my brother and close family. The same with Jim. Anything above and beyond that was, well initially we had this idea that we were just going to have this very small wedding. We were to invite our parents and our siblings, and it turned into more than that . . . there were aunts and uncles, and relatives who were close enough to come, so [trails off]. (Helen)

> We didn't want a large wedding in the first place. I had originally said it would be nice with about 75 people, but with all my relatives and Rob's relatives and friends we couldn't pick out—it was just impossible to cut it back that much. (Elizabeth)

Patty had 450 people on their guest list:

> The guest list, I think, is probably always hard. When I look over the list, when it came almost time for the wedding I kept thinking, "Well, why did we invite them

and not these people?" I'm sure if I did it differently there'd be a lot of people that I probably wouldn't put on the list that I did. . . . I felt that there were people we could leave off, yet I wondered why we invited these people.

Christine managed to keep their guest list down to 130 people, although they were "having a tough time of it":

> Well, we talked about it. And we figured we didn't really want more than 100 people because it was fairly expensive. Then, my parents—they said that—well, the caterer's giving us a little bit of a deal. My dad's a fisherman and he's giving them some fish. So we're getting a good deal there. . . . But we really felt a little uncomfortable. We don't want to have that many people because it does get expensive.

Initially, it appeared that this need to include more participants than intended accounted for the amount of planning and preparations. Joan, a 30-year-old dental assistant who emphasized the religious importance of her marriage over all other aspects, remarked:

> There's so much preparation that you're excited about it, but you want it to be over, too . . . It's just—the caterers, the church, the florist, the photographer, and—you don't just visit these people once, it's a couple of times. Check the flowers, see whether they're okay, and talk to the photographer and go over details, you know. It's just like—it was a lot of work.

"Going All the Way": The Work of Getting Married

On the surface, it might appear that the work

and expense of weddings were simply a function of the size of events. During interviews, however, it became evident that this was not the case. For the large part, both the amount of planning and expense were the results of paying attention to details which, although often seen as "not really necessary," were important to respondents. A case in point is Patty and Eric, who had a relatively small wedding with 100 guests. Although Patty had just relocated to Vancouver from Toronto, and as a consequence had also been recently unemployed, her wedding cost $8,500 ("not counting the wedding bands"). In explaining their expenditures, she noted that they "did a few things that you wouldn't have to do":

> A lot of little things. Like we rented a limousine for four hours which is fairly expensive, and rented a car for our parents to drive in. They could of used their own, but we wanted them to have a nicer sleek white [car]. And we put the fathers in tuxedos, the ushers in tuxedos—we paid for all of that. The ring bearer, we paid for his tuxedo. The two flower girls, we bought their dresses and accessories. We had real flowers, too.

Respondents referred to this as "going all the way":

> I figure that if we're going to do the ceremony in a traditional way, that we might as well do it all the way. I just feel like why do part of it? Might as well just do it all. (Michelle)

Going all the way meant taking care of the minutest details. In the final analysis, it was the drive to have things "picture perfect" that determined the amount of work and expense:

The issue for us was what looked good in the church. I wanted a kind of rosy colour, but Sharla said "It'll look awful in the church, because the church is orange." . . . So we even went so far as to get swatches of different colours and take them to the church. We hadn't chosen this exact colour, but knew that maybe this was what would look the best [shows interviewer wedding photos]. (Patty)

> You're so vulnerable because you want to look your best. It's important that you look nice. And they [salespeople] say, "Well, it really would make your dress just look that much better if you have the right bra under it." . . . And nylons. I did notice at all the bridal shops you'll get—of course, your dress—but they've got necklaces and some even sell, not so much makeup, just things that would really add to it all. (Faye)

Getting things perfect required careful planning:

> We also had to make an appointment to see the photographer within two weeks, just to get our last minute checklist. . . . That kind of thing. Buy a guest list and pen, organize my girlfriends—I didn't want them wondering what to do so I typed out lists for all of them. Phoned the organ music at the church, call Purdy's to confirm the chocolates were ready and available for picking up, and I bought yards and yards of fabric, of ribbon, because I was going to tie little royal blue bows around each box of chocolates. I purchased candles for the wedding. I purchased car decorations—I bought tons of these little plastic pompom kits two weeks before—not even thinking it was going to take me about three hours a

box, and I had eight boxes. I was working full-time right up to the end. (Faye)

Looking back, it seemed to respondents that "one thing just led to the next":

> You know about the basic steps. You have to have a place to get married, and you have to have a place to have the reception. You need a cake, you need a dress, you need flowers, and then, of course—oh yes, there's the car, and then there's decorations for the car, and then there's choosing the wine, and the menu, and then there's this and that.... One thing just leads to the next. (Joan and Brian)

> I did feel that there was a lot of unnecessary pressure to have the wedding this way or you have to have this. ... One example I'll give you was shoes for my bridesmaids. I was originally going to have them wear white shoes so they could wear them again, you know, practical pumps. But then after awhile I said "No. These dresses would really look much nicer if they had dyed satin shoes." And so, even while they were being dyed I thought "Oh, this is a waste. This is so unnecessary, both for the girls and overall." (Patty)

> I had an image in my mind, like a pretty wedding, so I wanted to have a nice dress. Then it seemed to me that there was a lot of things that went along with having a nice dress. ... If you're spending a lot of money on your dress then you've got to invite people to come and see it. So, we started getting relatives coming. Then you've got to have some place for them to go after the wedding, for food and stuff like that. As it turned out, we had a

reception, which we weren't planning on. (Helen)

Joan and Brian found planning so complex that they used a professional wedding consultant:

> I just got so fed up and I said "I don't want to do this any more." So I phoned a wedding consultant, and she said "Well, what are you having problems with?" ... The woman who helped us was most helpful, very helpful, asking "Have you done this yet?"

Unlike Joan and Brian, however, most respondents could not afford to hire a consultant, who usually charges an hourly fee. Heather and Larry, who had been living together for two years before deciding to get married, initially expected to have about 80 guests. As plans progressed, however, their guest list grew to 160. In order to keep the costs down, they decided to have the wedding in the small town where the bride's parents live rather than in Vancouver, the groom's home. They had been planning their wedding for the past year, and Larry estimated that for the last six months they were "putting in at least two hours a day." Larry explained how he kept track of planning:

> We have our schedule already organized for the week before and up to the date. We have all our costs put on a spreadsheet so we can see various things. We have a database for the invitations and the reply cards, and the gifts. It's the only way of keeping track of so many people and so many little things.

Heather put her commuting time to good use:

> I spend a lot of time on the SkyTrain making notes. My big fear is "What am I

forgetting?" So I read the magazines and if I see something I make a note. So I've got an hour to get to work and I just make notes. But the problem is I get home and I'm so tired.

Although Larry's active involvement in planning was not typical of all interviews, Heather's reliance on bridal magazines to be sure that she was "doing the right thing" was shared by other brides. Even though wedding traditions appealed to respondents because they symbolize generational ties, respondents in this study did not rely on the knowledge of mothers or other relatives who had been married. In fact, it was typical for respondents to minimize the role of their mothers, either avoiding them altogether or including them in a token way:

> I'd organized it so well in the first place, as I say, right down to the flowers and my flower arrangements so I would say things—because of course I didn't want her [mother] to feel excluded at all—I would ask her advice about something, or a suggestion, or whatever, but it was just to make her feel that she was involved in it. (Sara, 34-year-old secretary)

> She [mother] was just there for practical advice and helping, and things like that—I actually did it more so that she feels involved. (Rachael)

Almost without exception, respondents used books and magazines to find out how to plan their wedding:

> I got library books out. I did that because I wanted to make sure I covered all the details. I knew the basics for planning a

wedding, I think, but I didn't want to miss anything out. That's where a book came in handy, because then I had everything there. I knew I wasn't missing anything. I had a little list of things to do. (Margie)

> I bought a book—a bride magazine. It had what to do the first six months, what you should do three months before the wedding, one month before. So that's what I did. . . . I just checked it off every time I accomplished or got something done. It really worked good because otherwise, without that list I'd be a mess [Joan shows an appointment calendar—one month showed 11 of 27 days on which there were notations for wedding chores—next two months were busier].

> I was so excited when I first found a wedding planner! . . . This actually has been an extension of my body for the whole engagement, this dear old red book [points to her wedding planner]. . . . I had pages marked. At four months, things I needed to do, at two months, and one week. *Modern Bride* made it all so neat and uncomplicated. You could just make a phone call and check it off. (Faye)

The problem is, however, that bridal magazines and planners did not always simply make the wedding plans easier. In many cases, women wanted their weddings to match what they saw in bridal magazines. The most typical example was in choosing a wedding gown:

> I bought *Modern Bride* and got an idea for what kind of dress I wanted. . . . I wanted to spend a week just looking for a wedding dress. I was up early every day on my own

and must have hit 90 per cent of the wedding dress stores in Vancouver and the lower mainland. . . . I went to that many stores because I'd feel better if I could say I'd been really thorough. It was important to me that I didn't buy something that I liked and then was wondering "Oh, did I miss a dress that was even nicer somewhere else?" But at the same time, I kept saying "I'll know when I find it" and "It is just taking me that many places to find it." (Faye)

I was looking through a magazine—a small BC magazine—and there was a dress designer that had some really wild dresses. I saw one which really struck me, so I played with her design and changed a few things, and did this and that. . . . I showed her [dressmaker] my idea, and she wasn't really sure about it at first, . . . but it's turned out much better than I even expected. (Jane)

However helpful bridal planners were, they also added to the sense of what needed to be done:

I bought these two bridal magazines. That's when I really started to realize how much work it was going to be. Those books are full of "this month you have to do this," and "this month you have to do that," and "make sure you've gone here." (Rachael)

In this way, although respondents bought wedding planners to be reassured that plans would proceed smoothly, these planners could precipitate worry about things going right:

I had eight months to plan. I sort of laid out what I had to do each month, I was pretty organized. About two weeks before the wedding I panicked, I just felt "all this

stuff to do." Two weeks before, I panicked. So I just rushed for those two weeks and got everything done. (Elizabeth)

As well, following wedding planners and bridal magazines could add to the expense:

What we did say was "Let's spend as little as possible for the wedding, but don't—uhm, don't not buy something because we don't feel that we have the money." I mean, if it's important, go for it, just maybe try to get it on sale or the cheapest one of them. (Faye, whose wedding cost $15,000)

During interviews, respondents often spontaneously suggested that they had spent far more than they thought was reasonable, or even stated that weddings themselves were a "waste of money":

I think it's a waste of money, and I don't think that's what a wedding—forget the marriage part—is about. I don't think it's about mortgaging your house. (Rachael)

It's a trap. They just want you to spend money. I wanted to make it simple and low cost—like my shoes were $29. I really cut corners. My dress was half-price, even though it was still expensive. (Joan)

That was the dress [shows wedding photos], and it just happened to be on sale, too. It was regularly $880 and I got it for $580, so I was really happy with it. I mean, I wasn't trying on dresses, as much as I would have loved them, that were over $800 or $900. That to me, I mean that's ludicrous. I mean, $580 is ludicrous actually, but I could justify that, [pause] still. (Faye)

One result was that many couples began their newlywed life in debt:

> We haven't paid them all yet. . . . [we made] a lot of down payments. (Patty)

> There'll be—what we did was we just "balanced" it—tried to put as much as possible on credit cards. That way we deferred it for another month until we did have some more money in the bank account. (Elizabeth)

However, debt was not the only strain which wedding preparations could place on the new couple. While purchasing products may appear to decrease the amount of work associated with weddings compared to the past when gowns were hand-sewn and receptions prepared by the bride's family rather than catered, shopping itself is work. Bridal magazines emphasize the importance for the prospective couple to be well informed about competing products. For example:

> Now that you and your fiancé will be shopping for wedding bands, it's to your advantage to walk into the store as educated consumers. With so many beautiful rings to choose from, you'll want to know what distinguishes one from the other. (*Modern Bride*, Apr./May: 194)

As with any major purchase, consumers are advised to "do their homework." For those trying to minimize expenditures, this meant shopping around for bargains:

> I think the trick is to make the effort and take the time to really shop around and ask a lot of questions. You know this is your day and you want it exactly how you

want it. Don't compromise because what you want is out there and you can find it, and you can get it at a reasonable price. You just have to be willing to do some footwork. (Jane, targeted $4,000 but thought that $5,000 would be more realistic)

> I looked for the cheapest things. I really wanted to keep it inexpensive. . . . I checked around all the local places and checked out prices. I mean, I must have gone to about four different places checking invitations, and I must have gone to about four different photographers to check out prices. (Margie)

Probably aware of the frustration which shopping might entail, magazines reassured readers that it will be worth the extra work:

> Be patient, shop wisely and most of all, have faith. In the end you'll find the perfect gown. After all, didn't you find the perfect guy? (*Today's Bride*, Summer 1989: 14)

Ironically, avoiding these pressures by making rather than buying things had the effect of increasing the amount of work:

> A lot of the rest of the stuff we're doing ourselves—that's why we spend so much time doing it [preparing]. . . . It just makes you a bit tired. Some days you'd rather just go home and go to sleep, but you know you have to go and do this. (Heather)

In this way, debt is not the only strain placed upon the newlywed couple. Reflected above but also in most of the interviews, consumption is primarily "women's work." Like many brides, Sara assumed most of the responsibility for the actual work of the wedding:

Because I was doing so much of the wedding it annoyed me to be organizing right down to the minute—who was saying what, what speeches were going to be made, who I wanted to have a speech made to. That annoyed me because I felt that it was the groom's thing, but he said "No. No, I want you to do it." . . . Obviously, all this is not going to be a man's job, I guess.

Although Sara initially saw this division of labour as a source of conflict, she came to accept the wedding as her work:

At first I thought, "Why am I doing it?" I thought he was being, uhm—lazy was actually how I first termed it, lazy. And then, knowing him, you know, his integrity and how he is a super-organized man himself, I thought "No, no, no. This is great. In fact, if anything it was a compliment to me." But at the beginning, you won't see it at all, because I certainly couldn't see it [that way].

As did most brides and grooms:

He affirmed or vetoed decisions! No, I shouldn't say it like that. He wasn't involved a lot in the planning. I planned most of it because I had the time. I checked things out with him and we talked about certain things, like the wedding vows, for instance, things like that. . . . He's the type that gets distracted very easily and if he has too many things on his mind, he gets distressed. (Patty)

Larry referred to a lot of the work as "girls' stuff," especially taking care of details:

I think she spends more hours a day

thinking about the conscious little details which I would miss, than I do.

Brian quite agreed with Joan's comment that "He really is quite useless":

For some reason my mind goes blank. She asks how things should happen on the day of the wedding—"We need cars. Who's going to ride with whom to the wedding?" I couldn't figure it out to save my life. And I don't know why. I have a feeling that it's not in men's genes.

Interestingly, Joan commented that "he just has better and more pressing things to think about." Overall, for most couples the groom's role involved the final say or right to veto:[5]

I was always running ideas past him. He had a lot of input. It's just when it came to actually doing the stuff, he wasn't around. But one time he came over and we picked out the invitations together. (Margie)

He's just playing right along with it. I'd just as soon take responsibility, one way or the other, you know. I'm willing to do it, not because I think I have to, but because it feels better if I just take care of the whole thing. You know, then it's no hassle. But things we want, we decide together. (Michelle)

What we had not agreed upon, for one reason or another, we would discuss. . . . If I went over the limit on something he would certainly pull me up on it and say "Listen, that's not the way to do it." . . . So, he let me go on my own merry way, but when he knew something was "out" he would stop me and say "Now look, I don't want to do that," "I absolutely refuse," or whatever. (Sara)

Reflected poignantly in these quotes, the notion of a "modern traditional" wedding is more than a literary oxymoron: it expresses quite well the contradictory outcome of establishing "modern" relationships in the name of "tradition."

The Quest for Meaning: Re-writing Tradition

As a ritual symbol, the wedding signifies commitment and shared love. Indeed, we have seen that this meaning is stated by respondents as the "reason" to be married rather than to cohabit. However, focusing on weddings as rituals obscures the way in which gender relations are reproduced through this everyday search for stability and personal fulfillment. It is not simply that wedding ceremonies are couched in patriarchal symbolism, as Nett notes: indeed, here we have seen that changing the language and content of wedding vows to convey an egalitarian commitment stands in direct contrast to the way in which the women assumed responsibility for the work of weddings as symbolic of this commitment. For the large part, men participated primarily in decision-making, where they often "had the final say." Thus, although respondents did not vow to "obey" their husbands, the brides-to-be very often avoided conflict by deferring to their partner's wishes. As an extreme example, Rachael radically broke with tradition in choosing her wedding gown—one decision which has been historically the bride's to make:

Then the dress I had in mind, exactly what I wanted and what I found in a magazine,—he hated it. He hated it. He thought

it looked stupid. . . . I couldn't buy it if he didn't like it. I couldn't make the decision myself. I figured if he thinks I'm going to look terrible in it, there's not much use in wearing it, right? (Rachael)

In this research it became important to explain how the actions of respondents came to unintentionally contradict their stated expectations for egalitarian marital relations.

As we have seen, wedding planners and bridal magazines were a major contributing factor to the amount of work involved and to the subsequent feeling that respondents were "out of control" of the events which unfolded. In the final analysis, the commercialized nature of wedding planning accounted for much of the financial stress, as well as the ambivalence, which respondents expressed. Virtually every couple interviewed after their wedding had spent more than anticipated, and respondents were frequently quite critical about their unanticipated level of conspicuous consumption. To point out ways in which wedding planning is about consumption is not to argue simply that respondents were "dupes" of capitalism, however. Here, commodification is interesting as a process through which "modern traditional" weddings appeal to consumers and become primarily women's work. Weddings are a good example of the increasing commodification of ritual elements of social life in Western cultures. Despite widespread economic recession, weddings are "big business": in 1988, the year in which this project was initiated, weddings were a $3.8 billion industry in Canada (*Wedding Bells*, Spring/ Summer 1989: 76).

Specialized books and magazines are the major vehicle of wedding commodification.[6] While it would be overly simplistic to attribute wedding plans entirely to the bridal magazines mentioned by respondents, it is clear that they contributed to women's dilemmas. For this reason, wedding magazines became the subject of further ongoing textual analysis. Of relevance here are the "wedding planners" which respondents universally referred to. In total, 28 such planners appeared in seven magazines purchased during the time that interviews were conducted. Given that bridal magazines are published seasonally and that there is a small, identifiable selection, it is safe to speculate that these lists are the ones referred to by respondents. At any rate, analysis reveals a great deal of similarity and repetition from magazine to magazine, with identical photo-spreads appearing in more than one issue, for example.

As reported by the brides in this study, wedding tasks on each checklist began anywhere from one year to a minimum of six months before the wedding. Reflecting the almost military precision implied in wedding planning, "Wedding Countdown" (*Wedding Bells*, Spring/Summer 1989) identified 54 tasks, while a "Wedding Day Schedule" presented in *Today's Bride* (Winter 1988: 120) listed the same number of items, reminding readers that:

> Your wedding can run smoothly if you take the time to make up your itinerary beforehand. Plan your day from start to finish. Write everything down in proper sequence and, if possible, appoint a close friend to make sure you get to the church on time without forgetting anything.

Separate checklists are usually provided for the groom and the bride. *Today's Bride* (Summer 1989) itemizes 20 tasks for the groom, followed by a list of nine expenditures for which he is responsible. The same magazine carries a companion list of 42 tasks for the bride, which include choosing the groom's attire; ordering,

addressing, and mailing all invitations; and visiting the cosmetician for skin-care and makeup tips. Only a few tasks are included on both lists. Feature articles further added to this bare minimum: *Bride's* (Feb./Mar. 1989), for example, suggests that learning how to dance will add to the success of the wedding day, while *Wedding Bells* (Spring/Summer 1989: 292) features a "Bridal Beauty Countdown" which advises brides to "start early (six months prior) to face your big day beautifully." In this way, the use of bridal magazines is likely to increase the amount of work and planning by drawing attention to extra, additional things that help to make a "perfect" wedding.

Although the necessary tasks in making a wedding prove to be relatively easy to identify in bridal magazines, the reader is likely to be overwhelmed by choices of how to accomplish these tasks: content analysis revealed that 91 per cent of feature articles about the wedding day presented differing options on how to do things. While tasks itemized on the bride's inventory may include, for example, a notation to pick up flowers, order invitations, or remember to have a final dress fitting, each item presupposes a complex series of decisions concerning a seemingly endless array of choices. In part, these choices are guided by etiquette or tradition, which are regularly discussed in magazines. However, articles which discussed wedding etiquette or tradition account for only 3.5 per cent and 2.9 per cent, respectively, of subjects covered in feature articles. In contrast, 33.8 per cent of feature materials concerned how to coordinate wedding details or choose between competing wedding options according to latest trends and fashions. In fact, the emphasis on being "up-to-date" overrides what tradition and etiquette have dictated in the past. An editorial in *Today's Bride* (Winter 1988: 6) declares that "brides should feel free to do away with any tradition or all of them." Within the discourses of bridal magazines, "tradition" refers to a carefully coordinated wedding "theme" rather than an actual wedding practice, reflected in the comment that "fortunately, tradition is honoured when most brides indulge in the luxury of a lavish white ensemble!" (*Bridal Guide*, 1989: 26). While this appeal to tradition imparts historical credentials to white weddings, it is interesting to note that not so long ago *Vogue*—a leading commentator on Western fashion—admonished brides that "there must be no exaggerated décolletage, for Vogue considers the wedding in its traditional light as a religious ceremony" (from the 1920s, quoted in Probert 1984: 16). Here modesty is a remnant of the time when bridal etiquette concerned one's proper sense of social status:

> Extravagance in any of the appointments of the wedding is in extremely bad taste. It is sometimes well to remember the delightful logic of the old lady who said that she did not dress better than she could afford to at home because everybody knew her there . . . and she did not dress better than she could afford when she went to the city because nobody knew her . . . magnificent ornamentation is out of place in a simple chapel or church, and in every place profusion beyond one's means is not only ill-bred but foolish. (Eichler 1921: 49–50)

Lansdell (1983: 81) notes that the element of "fancy dress" began to appear in wedding fashion in the late 1960s, with a noticeable appeal to "tradition" emerging only in the mid-1970s. Thus bridal magazines do not act to simply preserve, or even to restore, old customs, but rather to re-write tradition:

> Whether you are being married for the second, third, or fourth time, your wedding day is still a "first," the beginning of a new partnership, the sharing of joy that this commitment represents. . . . The *old myth* that only a first-time bride may wear white has been replaced with the understanding that white symbolizes the wedding itself rather than the purity of the bride. . . . All of these decisions are strictly personal ones. (Piccione 1982: 130, 134; emphasis mine)

In this way, while white weddings appealed to respondents because they signify tradition, brides are being advised that a traditional wedding is a matter of personal preference, tempered by what experts suggest is in "good taste." Judy Siblin-Rakoff, quoted in *Wedding Bells* as author of a well-known bridal planning book, encourages couples to update wedding customs according to their personalities and taste:

> Despite the allure and integrity of many wedding traditions, today's couples feel that it is important to personalize the event. Bridal consultants point out a host of small details that, when considered together, show how the ceremony, and especially the reception, are changing with the times. . . . "Today's young couples are bright, they have their own careers, they're independent. Their wedding should be their own." (*Wedding Bells*, Spring/Summer 1989: 68)

Similarly, *Today's Bride* exhorts readers that:

> Today's bride is looking for something more than just the essentials. She's looking for something new and interesting, something out of the ordinary, something

exciting. She demands creativity. (*Today's Bride*, Winter 1988: 78)

During interviews, items which respondents referred to as giving their wedding a "personal touch" ironically recurred in other weddings: although commodification promises "consumer magic," it is a contradictory process in that it must appeal to what consumers have in common while addressing their search for individuality (see Fiske 1989a). In this way, because commodification and mass consumption act to standardize products, a personalized wedding can only be achieved through giving attention to a myriad of individual details. In the final analysis, this "attention to details" is what created the work of wedding planning. Perhaps ironically, the stress led some respondents to maintain that:

> At that time I remember feeling "I'll just be glad when it's all over." ... I did want it how I had it, but I was just feeling tired. I was tired. I was tired of thinking of it. (Faye)

As the "big day" drew closer, Helen maintained:

> I never really wanted to call off the marriage, the idea of marriage. The wedding, I really wanted to call [it] off.

Conclusion

As a small exploratory study, generalizations about how, or why, traditional weddings remain popular in Canada cannot be made. However, this in-depth investigation illustrates how traditional weddings reproduced relations of the patriarchal nuclear family for the couples in this study, despite claims by respondents to be establishing "modern" partnerships. This paradox becomes apparent by exploring weddings as activities rather than as simply symbolic ritual. As rituals, weddings symbolize family ties: legally, the wedding acknowledges the couple as husband and wife and, publicly, it links the new couple to an extended network of kin relations. Hidden by this emphasis on the purely symbolic aspect of weddings, however, is the reproduction of unequal marital relations and women's wedding work which these relations reflect. Because respondents expected—or even claimed—to have egalitarian domestic relations, it is perhaps ironic that the couple's first public act already begins to establish a traditional, unequal pattern of domestic labour. It also makes the persistence of traditional white weddings appear to be all the more perplexing. What does this study tell us, then, about the current popularity of the "modern traditional" wedding?

Although it is tempting to simply dismiss the behaviours described in this study as "irrational," such an approach would not help us understand the everyday activities through which dominant social relationships are reconstituted. Here, it is perhaps more fruitful to view traditional weddings as a rational pursuit of a pleasurable occasion to celebrate personal and familial relations.[7] The affirmation of kinship relations was a source of emotional fulfillment for both the women and men in this study. As "the bride's day," weddings remain one of the few public occasions where women's roles in the family are celebrated. This public recognition appealed to many respondents:

> I understand now why people say: "It's the bride's day." It doesn't matter what anybody does, nothing really takes away from your being the centre of attention. (Sara)

> I get to get up in the morning, have a bubble bath, go and get my hair and makeup done, wear something that I would never ever on

any other occasion wear. Just [pause] be absolutely pampered. This sounds really selfish, self-centred as well. But, to be the centre of attention for a while—and also be a reason why all these people we care about are all getting together—it feels good to be a catalyst for something like that to happen. (Jane)

This pleasure does not simply reflect 'false consciousness' on the part of women involved:

Well, I'm a bit of a feminist and I see myself as having more important or more valid things to be thinking about, to concern myself with than what I'm going to look like on my wedding day. It just seems very trivial and insignificant to me, but [pause]. When the day comes, when you do have to think about it, it becomes, then [pause] you know, I loved doing it. (Patty)

As reflected above, despite the stresses associated with extensive planning and preparations, weddings provided respondents with one day of "self-indulgence." It remains to be seen whether the pattern of unequal domestic labour which emerged during wedding preparations is a better predictor of future relations than the premarital expectations of brides. However, the immediate appeal of weddings is in fact due to their transient nature: as a one-day event, the indulgence of a wedding does not require feminists, working wives, or other "non-traditional" participants to compromise the ideals of their everyday, "ordinary" lives. Thus Brian described their wedding day as a "rented fantasy," while Jane maintained:

One day in fairyland. It's going to be fun, no matter why or how! . . . It's a very "me" day. We want this, and we want that, and

it's going to last for the whole day. We're going to get everything out of it.

As a one-day event, they saw their wedding as being distinct from their relationship or marriage:

You really do feel quite special, and that's nice. It is totally separate from actually getting married. There's the getting married and then there's the day of getting married, and all the stuff that goes with it—and I find that sort of thing is very separate. (Jane)

It is this separation which gave rise to their desire for a public celebration:

There's just something about a wedding that stirs your soul. So if all these people we know can come to our wedding, somehow we can let them know that this is the best thing, and let them know that this is the right thing to do. (Brian)

As it did for other couples:

The celebration is the public thing, but the commitment and even the whole building up to the wedding itself is a very private thing. . . . The whole idea of all the little things [wedding details] is because they're part of us making this making what happened in private between the two of us public. (Rachael)

As we have seen, this appeal of "self expression" is kindled by a mass wedding culture that is perpetuated by bridal magazines. Here discourses address the reader's desire to feel connected to the tradition of weddings, albeit encouraging identifiably non-traditional practices. Thus the discourses of bridal magazines do not simply transmit wedding traditions, but in so doing actively re-write what is meant by "tradition." Writers of both bridal books and bridal magazines refer to "tradition—with a new twist. From the proposal to the honeymoon pictures, their way is the Right Way."[8] As we have seen, tradition is thus transformed into a wedding theme rather than being presented as a wedding practice, facilitating the sense that meanings associated with weddings are separate from those which respondents assigned to their marital relations. Perhaps ironically, therefore, however "modern" the material, symbolic elements of their wedding, market processes led respondents to re-enact "traditional" patterns of marital relations.

● Notes

1. The incidence of divorce varies by region. Estimates range from fewer than one-quarter in the Atlantic provinces to almost one-third in British Columbia (*Canadian Social Trends*, No. 13, Summer 1989: 27).

2. As Nett (1988: 211) notes, since remarriages are more likely to involve a civil ceremony or home wedding, this initial decrease probably reflects increases in remarriages. By 1985, more than 20 per cent of marriages of both men and women were second or later marriages (*Canadian Social Trends*, Spring 1987: 3).

3. This study is a pilot study, and generalizations are not intended. Nevertheless, observations and analyses here have interesting implications for understanding aspects of our everyday life.

4. The exception is a Jewish couple, who held a religious ceremony and reception out-of-doors.

5. Here it may be important to note that it is not simply that the husbands-to-be assumed the traditional "burden" of paying for their new wives'

consumption. In most cases the new couple shared the cost of the wedding, and families of both the bride and groom usually helped to cover some of the expenditure.

6. How to plan a wedding is discussed in both wedding guidebooks, available at most bookstores and at the local library, and bridal magazines. The tasks outlined in these guidebooks closely follow those presented in magazines. The most striking difference between guidebooks and magazines is the dominance of photographic layouts in the latter, provided in feature articles but more importantly in advertisements. Undoubtedly, this glossy format accounted for the appeal of magazines over guidebooks.

7. By describing these activities as pleasurable, I do not intend to imply that they are therefore desirable, beneficial, or that they are somehow acts of "resistance," in the way that cultural studies often implies. (See Fiske 1989b, for example.)

8. Comment by editor-in-chief of *Bride's*, Apr./May 1989: 22; emphasis in original.

● References

Baker, Maureen, ed. 1990. "Mate Selection and Marital Dynamics," in *Families: Changing Trends in Canada* (Toronto: McGraw-Hill Ryerson).

Barrett, Michele, and Mary McIntosh. 1982. *The Anti-social Family* (London: Verso).

Boulton, Mary Georgina. 1983. *On Being a Mother* (London: Tavistock).

Burt, Sandra, Lorraine Code, and Lindsay Dorney, eds. 1988. *Changing Patterns: Women in Canada* (Toronto: McClelland and Stewart).

Eichler, Lillian. 1921. *Book of Etiquette*, Vol. I (Oyster Bay, NY: Nelson Doubleday).

Fiske, John. 1989a. *Understanding Popular Culture* (Boston: Unwin Hyman).

———. 1989b. *Reading the Popular* (Boston: Unwin Hyman).

Gittins, Diana. 1985. *The Family in Question: Changing Households and Familiar Ideologies* (London: Macmillan).

Lansdell, Avril. 1983. *Wedding Fashions, 1860–1980* (London: Shire Publications).

Nett, Emily M. 1988. *Canadian Families: Past and Present* (Toronto: Butterworths).

Piccione, Nancy. 1982. *Your Wedding: A Complete Guide to Planning and Enjoying It* (Englewood Cliffs, NJ: Prentice Hall).

Probert, Christina. 1984. *Brides in Vogue since 1910* (London: Thames & Hudson).

Thorne, Barrie, with Marilyn Yalom, eds. 1982. *Rethinking the Family: Some Feminist Questions* (New York: Longman).

Wilson, Susannah J. 1990. "Alternatives to Traditional Marriage," in *Families: Changing Trends in Canada*, ed. Maureen Baker (Toronto: McGraw-Hill Ryerson).

Chapter 12

Sociologist Julia Ericksen's book, *Kiss and Tell*, tells the history of research on people's sexual practices and experiences. She argues that the assumptions that researchers have brought to their work have shaped ideas about sexuality, especially about what is "normal," and women's and men's responsibilities in intimate relationships. The ideas that sex is the glue that holds a marriage together and that women's natural sex drive is oriented to giving pleasure to a man were developed and popularized by sex researchers in the early twentieth century, according to Ericksen. Today, popular women's magazines echo these themes, as they offer tips on sex techniques to their readers.

Nevertheless, with the advent of effective contraception and the "sexual revolution" that followed in the 1960s, important barriers to women's enjoyment of sex eroded. Women's experiences of sex have no doubt become more like men's as a result. But there are many questions that researchers have yet to examine. How do ongoing gender inequalities play out in sexual relations between women and men? If women are the ones who continue to do more of the "emotion work" in heterosexual relationships, how does that affect their sexual experiences? What is the impact of the expectation of monogamy on long-term relationships?

In this chapter, Melanie Beres offers us a glimpse into the sexual experiences of men and women in couples. After interviewing women and men living in New Zealand about sex in their relationships, she teases out some themes in what they said in order to address basic questions about the role of pleasure, desire, and sex acts themselves in people's intimate relationships.

Desire, Pleasure, and Sex in Young Adults' Heterosexual Relationships

Melanie Ann Beres

Michel Foucault argues that sexuality has three main elements that are useful for understanding sexual behaviour: acts, desire, and pleasure. In order to understand sexuality, it is important to develop an understanding of these three components. Foucault contends that at different times and in different social and historical contexts, emphasis is placed, to a greater or lesser extent, on one or two of these elements. To illustrate this point, Foucault provides the following examples:

- the ancient Greek "formula" where emphasis was placed on "acts," rather than pleasure or desire
- the Chinese "formula" in which acts are put aside and pleasure comes first, followed by desire, and "you have to restrain acts in order to get maximum duration and intensity of pleasure"
- the Christian "formula," where emphasis is placed on the control and limit of "desire," where acts become neutral and are used

for procreation and to honour Christian duty, and "pleasure" is wholly excluded (Foucault, 1997; Rainbow, 1997)

Of most relevance to this chapter is Foucault's take on the modern "formula." He argues that "desire" takes precedence, acts are not very important, and no one knows what pleasure is.

Foucault's articulation of the "modern" formula seems rather bleak, particularly if he is right that no one seems to know what pleasure is. Recently I was teaching a senior undergraduate class on sexuality. I asked the students to complete these two phrases: "Sex should be . . . " and "Good sex is . . . ." The majority of responses fell into two major themes, pleasurable and consensual. Words like "fulfilling," "enjoyable," "feel good," "mutual," "negotiated," and "pleasurable" dominated discussion. Perhaps ideas about sex have shifted since Foucault described the modern formula.

The purpose of this chapter is to explore how young heterosexual adults in relationships construct sex and sexuality. I do this by exploring how talk related to desire, pleasure, and acts surfaced in interviews I conducted with heterosexual couples in New Zealand. These couples were recruited for the interviews mostly through informational posters across campus, but also through (snowball sampling based on) contacts in the personal networks of two research assistants. I interviewed 36 individuals altogether, some in couples and some separately. They were the members of 20 couples, but in four cases only the female partner participated in an interview. All of these men and women were between the ages of 18 and 30. Individuals came from a variety of ethnic backgrounds and had been in their relationships for between four months and seven years at the time of the interview.

The analysis that follows builds on feminist discourse analysis of heterosex. Wendy Hollway was a pioneer of this approach when, in 1984, she described three discourses of heterosexuality. First, what she called the "male sexual drive" discourse suggests that men's desire and need for sexual activity is innate—that men have a biologically insatiable urge to have sex and are forever in search of sex. In this discourse, women are positioned as sexual objects. Second, the "have/hold" discourse highlights women's sexuality as defined by the Madonna/whore binary. In this discourse, because the focus for women is on "keeping her man," men are positioned as the objects. Third, the "permissive" discourse challenges monogamy and opposes the have/hold discourse while acting as an "offspring" of the male sexual drive discourse. In the permissive discourse, sex is viewed as natural for both women and men. Thus, women are given "permission" to participate in sexual activity outside of committed relationships, although in a way that supports the male sexual drive discourse.

Hollway builds on a Foucauldian understanding of discourse and power to understand heterosexuality. According to Foucault (1972), a discourse is a set of statements that reveal particular assumptions about the social world. In this case, I am interested in the underlying assumptions of heterosexuality. It is important to note that discourses, in this sense, are not representations about what actually happens during sex, or how people actually feel during sex. Rather, an analysis of the discourses of heterosex helps uncover particular assumptions and understandings about sex that shape and mould our sexual lives. Of particular interest is how these discourses shape the sexual lives of men and women differently. Discourse represents implicit ideas that shape what is considered "normal" or "sexual." These discourses open up spaces for particular actions and relationships. Thus, through this analysis we examine particular underlying assumptions about heterosex and the possibilities for action encouraged in those discourses, as well as the possibilities of subversion. If my students foreshadowed my analysis, then I would expect to see pleasure as central to their constructions. But where does that leave desire and acts?

Sexual Acts

In contrast to the first articulations of my students and Foucault's assertion of the "modern" sexual formula, sexual acts were given primacy in the stories of the people I interviewed. The most common construction of acts relayed by participants was one consistent with the coital imperative (M. Jackson, 1984). The term "coital imperative" was coined in relation to the way that scientific texts implied that intercourse was a natural and inevitable end to sexual activity. The term has since been taken up in a wide range of contexts to outline the way that sex is constructed as coitus, or that "real sex" has not occurred in the absence of penile–vaginal intercourse, and that sex always includes intercourse.

> Margaret: We French kiss if we're going to have sex and we don't if we're not going to have sex. It's just the way. We've never French kissed and then not had sex. Never.

> Stacy: I think with anyone that I've ever had sex with like once I've started to have sex . . . then if I do anything intimate with them, then I have sex with them, like if I kiss someone then it'll lead to sex.

Within participants' stories there was an almost unshakeable assumption that sexual activity would always lead to coitus, particularly once the sexual relationship was established, as described by Stacy. When asked

to define what participants meant by sex in these cases, the answer was that they meant intercourse. Some recognized that there are multiple forms of sex, including oral sex, for example. Yet, sex was not "complete" until intercourse occurred, (presumably) ending with a male orgasm.

> Christine: It pretty much generally always leads to sex, he has um he, it's quite rare for him to orgasm with just oral or hand and touching so pretty much it always leads to sex, yes.

Christine's statement was not unique. Sexual intercourse was central to all discussions of sex. There are a few times when this coital imperative is interrupted, typically when there is some external reason for not engaging in intercourse.

> Mark: No, there've never been any times where we do sexual activity and not have sex, unless of course . . . I don't know, like if she was having her period or something we wouldn't have sex. I don't know, like maybe she'd just give me a blow job or something. Um well there've been times we would've done it [but] I was really drunk couldn't keep it up . . . other than that we always every time if it gets that far we'd be going to have sex.

Mark presents a couple of scenarios where intercourse does not happen. On the surface it may appear that this type of description could subvert the coital imperative, but in the end the primacy of intercourse remains. Mark begins his statement suggesting that sex always happens, and then qualifies this by suggesting appropriate times when exceptions to this rule occur. Exceptions are generally granted when there is some biological reason why intercourse cannot take place; either she is having her period or he cannot have an erection because he is too drunk. By presenting exclusively biological reasons for not engaging in intercourse, Mark reinforces the coital imperative by implying that sex would have taken place without these constraints.

In addition, both Christine's (above) and Mark's descriptions reinforce the male sex drive discourse, which positions men's sexuality as central to heterosex (Hollway, 1984). Within this discourse, men are understood to have an insatiable desire for sex with women. It is expected that men constantly pursue sex. Implied in this discourse are the assumptions that to be fully satiated a man must have an orgasm and that intercourse is the most direct and reliable way to achieve an orgasm. Mark reinforces the primacy of male sexual pleasure and orgasm when he suggests that he would just receive oral sex if his female partner was having her period. Similarly, Christine places strong emphasis on the requirement for sex to include a male orgasm when she mentions that the reason sex includes intercourse is because her partner rarely orgasms with other forms of stimulation. There is no similar trade-off when he is not able to get an erection, nor is there a discussion of ensuring her sexual pleasure while she is having her period.

Search for Variety

In addition to the coital imperative, many participants discussed the importance of bringing variety into their sexual lives.

> Christine: I prefer variety, that's kind of my number one thing! I like variety, I hate routine, which sometimes you seem to get into because you know what each other likes so you kind of do the same thing.

> Julia: I think now we are probably more boring, we just do the same thing most of the time. Um there was a time when I said that I kind of wanted to try a vibrator and I kind of joked about it and alluded to it for ages but would never have had the balls to go and buy one. I got home one day and he'd bought one and he was so proud of himself (laughs).

Christine in particular talked a lot about introducing variety into her sex life. For her and her partner this included having sex with other people in "threesomes" or "foursomes" and using sex toys. Other couples talked about the inclusion of vibrators and sex toys or experimenting with different positions. Conversely, sex without such additions was described as "boring" by Julia and others. Articulations of sex acts focused on variety to achieve pleasure are consistent with popular culture messages about sex and relationships. If we are to believe the covers of many magazines, such as *Cosmopolitan,* the pathway to great sex and great sexual pleasure is variety. Articles on sex inevitably discuss the latest sexual positions and techniques guaranteed to drive lovers wild and rekindle a dwindling sexual relationship.

While the coital imperative shapes the form of sex that participants discussed, this does not automatically imply that sexual acts are given primacy in the constructions of heterosexuality. In order to understand how acts are positioned as primary, we need to take a closer look at pleasure and desire.

Pleasure

Discussions of pleasure in the interviews were fleeting and centred on orgasms. The primary way that pleasure was constructed by couples was through discussion of orgasms. In the first section, I spoke about the importance of the male orgasm for defining "sex." The intense focus on the male orgasm means that men's pleasure can be taken for granted (assuming that pleasure is defined through the orgasm). Thus, when discussing pleasure, the concern revolved around whether or not women were experiencing orgasm.

> Colin: I'd always sort of felt kind of bad that I was getting off but Isabelle wasn't you know; she seemed . . . she's enjoying herself from sex. She's always said "yes" she "loves sex" and that's great and all, but for me when you have an orgasm you get that release. After, I don't know how long it was, we brought the vibrator onto the scene whereby after we have sex Isabelle would use the vibrator and I'd use my fingers inside her and help. The fingers didn't start straight away, that was . . . we found out she liked that. Each time then I'd come from sex and then she would come and now that's the routine or sometimes she'll use the vibrator and we'll come from sex that way while we are having sex at the same time. Um, so now it's like we both get off which makes me feel a lot better about sex cuz I felt bad that she wasn't getting off from it . . . She wasn't actually getting an orgasm out of it. And partly you missing out and now that you've had the whole vibrator thing you wouldn't go back.

While most participants did not discuss pleasure directly, a few did mention orgasms and the role they play in their sexual relationships. Of particular concern were women's orgasms, and ensuring they were happening. Men's orgasms were largely assumed to happen. There was also a conflation of pleasure and orgasm.

As we can see from Colin above, while his partner said that she was getting pleasure from sex without having an orgasm, he believed it was important for her to orgasm and took the initiative to introduce a vibrator into their sex play to help her achieve an orgasm.

This quotation is reminiscent of what Braun et al. (2003) refer to as the discourse of reciprocity. In this discourse, emphasis is placed on ensuring that both women and men experience sexual pleasure, usually equated with orgasm. In Colin's account, it is possible to see how he is positioning himself and his partner within this discourse of reciprocity. He had anxiety about whether he was a "good lover" until he could ensure that his partner experienced orgasm with every sexual experience. While genuinely concerned about his partner's pleasure, he does not believe that she can truly experience pleasure without orgasm. This is reminiscent of what Potts (2000) refers to as the "orgasm imperative." It is not only important, then, for sex to consist of intercourse, but this intercourse must also be accompanied by an orgasm.

It is not just men who discussed the importance of women's orgasms. Women too talked about men giving them orgasms and used this as an indication of the skill of their lover.

> Christine: I'm very satisfied sexually with him. He's definitely given me more orgasms than any other man has [laugh] but the one the one problem is that it can be a little routine. But it's hard not to be when you have to have it in bed with your father sitting in the next room.

Similar to Colin, Christine discusses the importance of the female orgasm, her own. She measures her partner's skill as a lover by noting that he has given her more orgasms than any of her previous lovers. Both Colin and Christine also discuss the woman's orgasm as something that is given by the man. This is consistent with the discourse of reciprocity (Braun et al., 2003), which presents the occurrence of mutual orgasms as an exchange of "gifts" between lovers. Braun et al. suggest there is a complex relationship between the discourse of reciprocity and heterosexuality. This discourse presents the liberating potential in women's sexual experiences (by producing an expectation of women's sexual pleasure). At the same time, it "brings with it the potential to reinscribe aspects of heterosex" (p. 255) consistent with the male sex drive discourse. Thus, while the quotations above provide space for a positive articulation of women's pleasure, they simultaneously reinforce women's sexuality as passive and men's sexuality as active. Women passively receive orgasms from their partners, while men's orgasms were not discussed in this way. Instead, they were taken for granted and assumed to just "happen." Women's orgasms were something that women did not have control of during sex with a partner, but rather something that the skilled male partner gifted to the female partner. This construction reinforces the idea of the active male body acting on the passive female body (Braun et al., 2003; S. Jackson & Scott, 2002).

While discussion of pleasure in the interviews was often veiled and relegated to discussion of the orgasm, it is important to note here that some men and women talked about pleasure. A couple of women were quite direct about being active in pursuing their own pleasure.

> Beth: I really feel that sex is, if you are not making babies, it's supposed to be about fun because we want to have fun and to feel good so I'm just trying to make it always more interesting! For example, to play music and do some silly dance or to dress myself in kinky way like in nurse dirty nurse or something like that.

We can see concern about pleasure in Beth's comment that sex should be about fun, and how she tried various strategies to achieve this goal. As well, Colin explicitly discussed how his partner Isabelle used her vibrator to orgasm if she did not orgasm during sex with him. Other women also discussed the use of vibrators to reach orgasm during or after sex. Their use of the vibrator suggests two things. First, it is not only male sexual partners who are responsible or credited with providing pleasure, despite Christine's statement about how her partner's success as a lover is measured by the number of orgasms he has "given" her. Second, the orgasm is deemed a requirement for a successful ending to a sexual event.

In the context of these interviews, men's pleasure was given primacy, although it was also taken for granted. It was assumed that men would always orgasm with intercourse. Women's pleasure, assumed to be synonymous with their orgasm, was considered more elusive. Men had to exert effort to ensure that women received pleasure. While some women took a more active approach to ensure that they too achieved the pleasure they desired, they still talked about the man gifting them pleasure most of the time. Christine took ownership of her own pleasure when she used a vibrator after intercourse; but this created tension between her and Richard, as Richard took it as a sign that she did not otherwise enjoy sex or that he was not a good lover.

Desire

A discourse about desire is missing in the stories told about women's sexuality. The construction of women's desire contrasted sharply with the construction of men's sexual desire, as perpetual. Both of these constructions are consistent with the male sexual drive discourse in which women are placed in the position of responding to men's sexual desires (Tolman, 2002) and consequently their desires are rendered silent.

> Tracy: I don't know if there's ever been a time that he's not interested. I guess you just like sense his response. Yeah like he just responds in the way I would expect him to.

This quotation from Tracy is in response to a question about times when one partner is interested in sex and the other is not. This type of response from the women in the study was fairly common. For these couples, the question about times when she wanted to have sex and he did not took them by surprise. One woman, who expressed a lot of interest in sex, said that she was waiting for her partner to "man up" and begin initiating sex more frequently. This again reinforces the idea that men should have an ever-present desire for sex.

Concurrent with the assumption of men's perpetual desire is a distinct absence of talk about sexual desire per se. When asking participants about how sex is initiated (by either partner) they often discussed practical reasons for initiating sex that were not about desire for their partner or desire for sex.

> Stacy: I felt like James was a safe person to do that with cause I, um, I just trusted him, he's a very um . . . he's got strong values. Like he smelled really good but it wasn't really a physical thing, it was just that I felt safe with him.

> Tyson: As a general rule we have sex three to four times a week, so that works out to

every second day, but it's pretty rare for us to have sex two days in a row. So you can sort of use that as a guideline. If we go to bed, if we had sex the night before, I don't make any arrangements or I don't bring anything in particular, or I'll be sitting in bed reading my book when she comes out of the shower, or whatever—instead of paying attention to her or things like that. Whereas on the other nights I won't have my book out.

An expression of sexual desire is absent in both of these stories. Combining these quotations highlights two different ways of thinking about sexual desire. First, we can think of desire in terms of whom we desire and to whom we are attracted. A thorough reading of popular cultural materials indicates that we are supposed to believe that upon meeting a new love interest there will be passion, connection, and chemistry.

Accounts of sexual desire in my interviews presented far more sobering accounts of partner selection. While many people talked about finding their partner cute or attractive, Stacy (above) emphasizes that her selection of James as her partner is based on safety. At this point in the interview, she discussed how she had just recently broken up with a boyfriend. She decided that she should have sex with someone to help her get over the break up and James was someone she knew well, trusted, and with whom she felt "safe." It is of course possible that Stacy was feeling desire as well as safe. We see a hint of this when she says that he also smelled good, but this is rendered less significant than her feelings of safety. The story that she told was not one of sexual desire, at least not the kind imbued with passion. Similarly, other women told stories about feeling at ease with their partner.

The second quotation illustrates another way of conceptualizing desire, that is, as a desire for sex at a particular time and place. Tyson is discussing the way that he and his partner time their sexual experiences together. Like many other stories told by participants, the sexual lives of participants were driven by practical issues and the desire to ensure they were experiencing and creating a "regular" and "adequate" sex life. In a similar vein, other participants talked about " . . . Making the effort that I should . . . especially if we haven't had sex for a few days then I think maybe I should keep him happy" (Carla) or, "We've only done it once this week and it's like, 'Oh like really? Oh no' and then it's just forthright, 'We've gotta do it now!' and it's like, 'Okay sweet!'" (Fred).

What these accounts have in common is the way that they structure the sex lives of the participants around what is considered "normal" in terms of frequency of sex. Active sexual desire is absent in these stories. This is not to say that these couples do not desire sex, or that they do not desire their partners. What it does suggest, however, is that a primacy is given to ensuring that couples are presenting themselves as being adequately interested in sex, or "normal" sexually. This ends up reinforcing the primacy of sexual acts. The creation of the "normal" interest in sex is seen perhaps most clearly in the words of Carla:

Carla: Yeah that happens quite regularly. I think both of us probably proposition the other person knowing that the other person is saying "no." Like I'm usually the first person into bed and often he'll come in later and it'll be midnight or something and I have to get up in six hours. And him sort of propositioning me knowing pretty well that he's probably going to get shut down, but if he would have tried a couple of hours earlier I probably would have been keen. I don't know, I like having sex in the morning but he often sleeps in. Sometimes I sort of proposition him when I know my chance is probably not too good as well so it happens. Partially that I think, but also sometimes that there is often this expectation that people are supposed to have sex like you know 10 times a week or whatever. So you know, you kind of put it out there, then you sort of look like you are keen but if it gets shut down well then you know at least it looks like you are wanting to have sex 10 times. So I think maybe sometimes that's why we sort of proposition each other, so it looks like we are not the ones who, you know, we are sort of like putting that each of us do want to have sex sort of thing.

Here, Carla is very clear about why she and her partner regularly proposition one another, and that is to keep up appearances that they are both desiring subjects: that they both desire sex with one another on a regular basis. This quotation speaks to the strength of the coital imperative. The imperative is not just about what happens when sex is initiated such that intercourse takes place with every sexual encounter. Here, the coital imperative also takes the form of regulating how often couples engage in sex or contribute to the feeling that they *should* be engaging in intercourse on a regular basis.

While Stacy is less explicit about the reason behind the need for each of them to initiate sex, the sentiment is similar to Carla's account. Sex is something that requires effort to ensure that they maintain an "adequate" sex life.

Articulations of desire such as those above are reminiscent of Fine's discussion of the "missing discourse of desire" (Fine, 1988). Fine originally coined the term "missing discourse of desire" to describe the absence of talk of female sexual desire in sex education. More recently, Fine's concept of a missing discourse of desire has been used widely to describe the absence of discussion of sexual desire broadly, particularly the absence of discussion of female sexual desire.

An overwhelming number of stories by the people I interviewed evidenced the missing discourse of desire. Yet there were a couple of women who spoke explicitly about desiring sex. Christine articulated explicit desire, as did Carla. Olivia (below) articulates quite clearly that she enjoys and desires sex.

> Olivia: I don't know, I'm strange I think cuz I love sex! I can never get enough of sex!

In some ways, these women challenge the male sex drive discourse by recognizing and articulating their own desires for sex. Olivia's comment is part of a discussion of how she had not experienced much foreplay with previous partners. In past relationships, she laid passively, just accepting her male partner's advances. In the interview, her partner Colin referred to her as being like a starfish at the beginning of the relationship. So, despite articulating a high level of sexual desire, Olivia did not take steps to satiate that desire. Rather, she acquiesced to a version of sex consistent with the male sexual drive discourse and became the passive partner. This behaviour contrasted with Christine's description, where she discussed, in detail, seeking out sex to satiate her own desires.

The missing discourse of desire was evident particularly when participants discussed women's sexuality. Yet when women did occasionally speak of their own desires, their narratives emphasised the expectation on them to want to engage in sex on a regular basis. This is most evident, once again, when we look at the description of the sexual acts and the "drive" to ensure they are participating in enough sex.

Of all the interviews I conducted, none portrayed as explicit an idea of sexual desire than those by the couple I interviewed who decided to abstain from sex until marriage. This couple was very strict about which behaviours they would or would not engage in. They limited their sexual activity to small amounts of open-mouthed kissing. What I found so intriguing about their account of sex in their relationship was the strong role of desire, and both the man and the woman expressed that desire when I interviewed each separately. Desire was central to their understanding of their sexuality, in a way that was absent in the stories of all other couples in the study. Their desire was the reason they limited their sexual interactions. They did not want to get swept up in their desire and "move too quickly" or end up doing things they may not be ready for.

> Luke: . . . I don't know, there just seems to be a whole lot more emotion and passion involved and so it kind of went down a track of, um, I guess what you call making out. You start getting your sex drive going and it's much harder to stop it and I was saying, well this is leading me down a path which I'm losing more and more control.

Within the context of the other interviews where desire was all but absent, the account given by Luke and Tracy stands out because of the role desire plays in their discussion of sex. Desire is central to their understanding of sex.

As someone engaged with feminist theorizing, there are two things that really stand out for me. First, I can be critical of the nature of their account of sex as it is positioned with a biological imperative. Consistent with the coital imperative, the limitations they placed on their sexuality were at least in part because of the belief that they would be so overcome by desire and passion that they would be unable to stop the sexual activity, and would inevitably end up having intercourse. Second, though, it is encouraging and hopeful to see a space where female (and male) sexual desire is expected and celebrated. Desire was present and expected in this relationship. Thinking about the relationship between desire, pleasure, and acts in this context, Tracy and Luke's interview suggests that restricting the sex acts that people engage in may enable and enhance sexual desire.

While this was the only couple where desire permeated the story of the sexual part of their relationship, other participants expressed an emotive version of desire in certain contexts. Another couple began their relationship when one of them was living overseas; their abstinence was imposed by physical separation rather than voluntary. Yet the articulation of desire within the initial part of their relationship resembled the story of Luke and Tracy. Other couples who did not experience a period of imposed abstinence occasionally mentioned this type of desire. This desire was limited to the early stages of their relationship when they were getting to know each other and their descriptions of the first time they engaged in sexual activity with each other.

> Fred: I don't know—maybe the firey-ness within each other is sort of not like the sexual firey-ness, but we don't sort of . . . we seem to work more in unison a bit more.

One question that emerges from these quotations emphasizing desire: what happens to desire once the sexual relationship becomes established? Is desire given primacy until then? For some couples, it would appear that talk of desire is rendered almost absent once a sexual routine is established. It is not clear, however, what might happen in the case of Luke and Tracy when and if they begin a more sexual relationship. Does their story represent a different conceptualization of desire and sex more broadly? Or, are they merely at a different point in their relationship trajectory?

Overall, desire was constructed as simultaneously perpetual and absent. Desire was perpetual in that it was expected that both members of the couple should be interested in sex on a regular basis. This took the form of ensuring that sex was happening on a regular basis rather than anyone talking about the desire to have sex or desiring their partner. The perpetual quality of desire was more prominent for men, where some men and women stated that men "always want sex." While it was not expected that women would be quite so consumed with desire, there was the expectation they would be interested in sex on a regular basis. Desire was also, however, literally absent in that it was rarely spoken about. Desire was not mentioned in regard to when couples chose to have sex. Instead, decisions about when and how often to have sex were based on notions about how frequently couples "should" be having sex or how long it had been since they had had sex together. In this way, desire for both women and men is perpetual and absent.

The Trifecta of Sex

I now return to the original question set out in this chapter. Understandings of desire are shaped by assumptions of men's perpetual sexual desire and an absence of discussion of women's desire. Pleasure is analogous to orgasm and constructed as a necessary component of a "successful" sexual event. When discussing acts, intercourse is positioned as the essential "main event" with importance placed on the variety of sexual positions and sexual acts. Thus, in contrast to Foucault's "modern" formula, I would argue that acts are privileged within this understanding of heterosex, particularly the act of coitus. Participant couples placed importance on having enough "sex" and having intercourse. This came out in discussions of sexual acts as well as in discussions of desire. In many instances, a description of desire was replaced with a discussion of how often couples should have sex. This reinforces the idea that people should be engaging in a certain amount of sex; it is just not clear how much is enough. As such, desire gets relegated to the backseat where it is either implied as perpetual or just absent from discussion.

In a contemporary account of sex in New Zealand, I would argue that acts are privileged. To be a successful sexual actor, it is important that we engage in certain activities. The pathway to increased sexual pleasure and better quality sex is through a broadening array of "acts." This construction that emerged from my participants is consistent with the explosion of advice columns in women's and men's magazines, with headlines celebrating an increasing array of sexual positions and activities to pleasure and tantalize our partners. So, while acts are privileged, they are privileged in this quest for pleasure. Yet pleasure itself is rather narrowly defined, whilst desire remains strangely absent.

● References

Braun, V., Gavey, N., & McPhillips, K. (2003). The "Fair Deal"? Unpacking Accounts of Reciprocity in Heterosex. *Sexualities, 6*(2), 237–61.

Fine, M. (1988). Sexuality, Schooling, and Adolescent Females: The Missing Discourse of Desire. *Harvard Educational Review, 58*(1), 29–54.

Foucault, M. (1972). *Archaeology of Knowlege*. London: Routledge.

———. (1997). On the Genealogy of Ethics: An Overview of Work in Progress. In P. Rabinow (Ed.), *Michel Foucault: Ethics, The Essential Works* (Vol. 1, pp. 253–80). London: Penguin Books.

Hollway, W. (1984). Women's Power in Heterosexual Sex. *Women's Studies International Forum, 7*(1), 63–68.

Jackson, M. (1984). Sex Research and the Construction of Sexuality: A Tool of Male Supremacy? *Women's Studies International Forum, 7*(1), 43–51. DOI: 10.1016/0277-5395(84)90083-9

Jackson, S., & Scott, S. (2002). Embodying Orgasm. *Women & Therapy, 24*(1–2), 99–110. DOI: 10.1300/J015v24n01_13

Potts, A. (2000). Coming, Coming, Gone: A Feminist Deconstruction of Heterosexual Orgasm. *Sexualities, 3*(1), 55–76. DOI: 10.1177/136346000003001003

Rabinow, P. (1997). *Michel Foucault: Ethics, Essential Words of Foucault 1954–1984.* (Vol. 1). London: Penguin Books.

Tolman, D.L. (2002). *Dilemmas of Desire: Teenage Girls Talk about Sexuality.* Cambridge, MA: Harvard University Press.

Section 2

Parenthood

Chapter 13

While cohabiting couples and single women are increasingly having children, many couples marry because they want to be parents. Yet men and women rarely have a sense of how their lives will change with parenthood. And their lives are very likely to change significantly. Heterosexual couples typically become more conventional when they become parents. Because of a strong belief that babies do best with full-time mothers, women with infants typically stay home for as long as they can—often a year, because of the maternity and parental leave now available to many Canadian women. Moreover, when men make higher earnings than women, it seems to make "economic sense" for the woman to be home. As well, the added pressure that parenthood puts on couples' time makes the "path of least resistance" appear to be a division of the work and responsibility between a woman and her partner. When women stay home, however, they often assume responsibility for both the baby and the bulk of the housework. This conventional pattern entails not only gender inequality but also a decline in couples' satisfaction with their marriage.

In this chapter, Bonnie Fox describes some findings from her study involving interviews with women and men who were making the transition to parenthood—findings described more fully in her book *When Couples Become Parents*. She describes some of the subtle dynamics that developed in their relationships over the first year of their baby's life. These relational dynamics provide some insight about why allocations of work and responsibility usually become more conventional in heterosexual couples when they become parents.

When the Baby Comes Home: The Dynamics of Gender in the Making of Family

Bonnie Fox

Couples have babies for all sorts of reasons.[1] For many women and men, the attraction of parenthood is the promise of a special relationship with a precious child and a life that includes nurturing. Having a child is a project that couples ideally take on together, as an extension of their love for each other. And they anticipate that when they become parents they will become a family: couples expect to enrich their lives, hope to deepen their relationship, and imagine living in a more family-centred way than is likely without children.

Indeed, people's lives change when they become parents, and couples often feel more like a family when they become parents. But they typically experience something else with parenthood that they might not have fully anticipated: heterosexual couples usually become more conventional when they become parents, as they typically handle the weight of their new responsibility by dividing the work between partners. As a result, it seems that, for heterosexual couples, divisions of work and responsibility based on gender, and related gender inequalities, are inherent in the making of family—unless women and men resist that development.[2] A key reason why heterosexual couples' lives often become more gender-divided when they become parents is that it takes work to make "family," and women often do more of that work than men.

Many researchers have reported that heterosexual couples typically experience a strengthening of gendered divisions of work and responsibility when they become parents (Cowan and Cowan 1992; Feeney et al. 2001; Fox 2001, 2009; Lewis 1986; MacDermid et al. 1990; Rexroat and Shehan 1987; Sanchez and Thomson 1997; Walzer 1996, 1998). Women tend to take on the bulk of the caring for and thinking about their babies, and a greater proportion of the housework than before they were mothers, while men tend to concentrate more on financial providing while also becoming their babies' playmates and their wives' helpers. Some research indicates that this gendered division of work and responsibility in early parenthood establishes the template for a more lasting division of household work based on gender in families formed by heterosexual couples (MacDermid et al. 1990; Perkins and DeMeis 1996; Rexroat and Shehan 1987). These gendered divisions are central to the gender inequality that is characteristic of many Canadian and American families (Bianchi et al. 2006; DeVault 1991; Hartmann 1981; Hochschild 1989; Luxton 1980; see Chapter 8; A. McMahon 1999). Other researchers have found, however, that inequalities in workload are greatest when couples have young children, and that they decrease as the children age (Ornstein and Stalker 2012).

Of course, not all women have children in the context of a lasting couple relationship: marriage has become far from universal, increasingly predicated on educational, occupational, and financial accomplishment and thus optional (Furstenberg 1996). Lone

motherhood is on the increase, though it has been common for poor African Americans and, to a lesser extent, African Canadians for some time (Calliste 2001; Hill 2005). But images of parenthood in this culture assume the heterosexual couple and nuclear families (Richardson 1993; Wall and Arnold 2007). Indeed, the "experts" on infant care prescribe a kind of child-centred care that requires "intensive mothering" by a full-time mother (at least when children are babies) (Hays 1996). Such mothering assumes a breadwinning partner, as well as middle-class circumstances (Blum 1999; Bobel 2002; Fox 2006).

Gendered divisions of work are not the only products of parenthood that entail gender inequalities. The message that women should devote themselves to intensive mothering defines motherhood in terms of self-sacrifice. In accord with a neoliberal political climate, and policies that move responsibility for care from state-funded agencies and institutions to individuals, mothers' responsibility for their infants has increased in scope over the years (Brodie 1996; Hays 1996). Coupled with messages about the need to "bond" with their babies, and to breastfeed them, are those on the importance of the "early years" to children's cognitive development (Wall 2001, 2004). These increases in mothers' responsibilities no doubt raise the anxiety associated with mothering a helpless infant. Some evidence shows that for white middle-class women at least, the prescriptions in authoritative discourses on mothering are a persistent point of reference and regulation of behaviour (Miller 2007). Moreover, Martha McMahon (1995) has argued that the emotional intensity with which women experience motherhood produces a personal transformation such that women identify more with femininity (that is, more with caring, nurturance, etc.).

But popular expectations of parenthood have been changing. Partners today often embark on their journey into parenthood with intentions of greater sharing than was common in the past: men often intend to be involved in the care of their babies, and women often insist on that involvement (Backett 1987; Coltrane 1996). Women also have more bargaining power and sense of entitlement in their relationships now that they are earning sizeable proportions of household income. Yet, a number of social changes have made parental ties more voluntary for men (Gerson 1997). As a result, the changes that occur in couples' relationships when they become parents are varied and unpredictable.

This chapter discusses two interpersonal dynamics entailing gender inequality that developed in the couple relationships of some first-time parents who were interviewed several times over their first year of parenthood. These dynamics involve women protecting their partners and catering to them in the first few months following the birth of their babies (Fox 2001; Kelleher and Fox 2002). Examining these dynamics reveals something about the subtleties of gender in families and how the project of making family can promote interpersonal dynamics that involve gender inequality. It also indicates how couples' social context and their material and social resources—which are shaped by their social class and their race—affect the ways they handle the challenges of caring for an infant.

A Study of First-time Parents

This discussion is based on a study of the social relations of parenthood, which involved in-depth interviews with couples who were making the transition to parenthood. The women and men who participated in this study volunteered following brief presentations during their prenatal classes on childbirth—including both hospital classes and Lamaze classes (with sizeable fees) and classes sponsored by the Public Health Department (free of charge). The classes were located in diverse neighbourhoods, with populations that substantially varied in terms of social class, race, and ethnicity. I interviewed 10 women and their male partners between 1992 and 1994, in a pilot project; and Diana Worts, Sherry Bartram, and I interviewed 30 more heterosexual couples between 1995 and 1998, in a larger project involving a very similar set of questions. We interviewed these women and men separately, late in the pregnancy and then at two months and one year after the birth of their babies. Shortly after the births—all in a hospital—we interviewed the women alone; six months after the births, we interviewed the women and men together. The interviews were recorded and lasted between one and two-and-a-half hours. The interview guide consisted of a set of semi-structured questions that directed the inquiry but allowed participants considerable scope for response. And we encouraged people to talk about any relevant matters not raised by our questions. Of course, interviews are a poor substitute for 24/7 observation. Interviewing the women five times and the men four times, however, promoted the development of trust and familiarity between them and us. It also meant that we had repeated opportunities to witness daily activities and interactions, as the interviews nearly always took place in people's homes.

Analysis of the interview material involved making summaries of key themes in the experiences of each woman, man, and couple, and of the changes in their lives over the course of the year. To derive tentative answers to my questions, examine hypotheses, and derive general arguments, I developed inductive and deductive codes of interview transcripts, categorized the people and their behaviour, and made systematic comparisons across couples to uncover relationships and patterns. I read all interviews several times, over several years, in a process that moved back and forth between the interview material and tentative findings.

The couples in the study are likely not representative of the population of first-time parents in Toronto in the 1990s, even though the problems and patterns they developed with parenthood seemed typical. The fact that they volunteered for the study while participating in childbirth classes meant, however, that the traits distinguishing them from any other cross-section of parents served the study well. They likely undertook parenthood with more than the usual thoughtfulness and commitment to being "good parents." That distinction no doubt contributed to the diversity of gender arrangements these couples created as they became parents. Thus, several couples shared the baby care and housework; that is, they avoided the conventional patterns that usually develop—an unusual outcome, and one unlikely to appear in a small sample representative of the general population. In turn, the diversity in the patterns that developed for these couples made it easier to identify the factors that influenced, or even caused, those patterns.

The 40 couples were similar in some ways and different in others. All except five couples were married when the study began. Two more were married and a third couple was planning their wedding before the study ended; only two couples intended to remain common-law. The sample was also mostly white and middle-class. Only two couples were immigrants from non-English speaking countries, and only one of them (an East Indian couple) was a visible minority. Four people (two women,

two men) were black Canadians—all of them married to white Canadians. While fairly similar ethnically and racially, these couples differed significantly with respect to education, occupation, and income.[3] Considering both the women's and the men's educational attainment, jobs, income, and whether or not they owned a home, nine couples were working-class and 31 couples were middle-class (and two of these upper-middle-class). Most of the working-class participants had high-school educations, while most of the middle-class people had college or university degrees, and many had post-graduate degrees. Most of the working-class couples had low incomes: six had household incomes below $40 000. Only two middle-class couples had incomes this low; 20 had incomes over $60 000 and 10 had incomes over $100,000. And the differences in occupational status between the two groups were significant.

Most of these couples were dual earners. When the study began, all except four of the men were employed full-time, though three of them were self-employed and working at home. The other four men had part-time jobs. As well, 36 of the 40 women were employed, most of them full-time. After their babies were born, all except two of the women (both working-class) stayed home for at least six months.[4] Twenty-five women returned to paid work before the end of the year, usually at the end of maternity leaves that lasted about six months. Fifteen women were home for the entire year, although five of them spent some time away from baby care (writing, taking classes, or doing some paid work). Three of the men—only one of whom had been working full-time—stayed home full-time with their babies when their partners returned to work.

In spite of the fact that these were mostly white middle-class couples, the patterns they developed were diverse. Circumstances and ideologies of motherhood and gender pushed many couples along "paths of least resistance" involving gendered divisions. But other couples resisted those forces and developed more shared arrangements.

After briefly exploring why the couples in the study wanted to be parents and how the women and men initially reacted to parenthood, this chapter describes two dynamics that developed in their relationships as they coped with the demands of parenthood. One of those dynamics involved the women protecting their partners—who were usually more focused on breadwinning than ever before—from much of the demand and disruption that living with an infant can entail. The other dynamic had to do with the women's strategies for pulling their men into involvement in the care of their baby. Both dynamics involved the women catering to their male partners, and they provide some insight into the nature of the gender inequalities that often develop when heterosexual couples become parents.

Becoming Parents

While these couples became parents for a variety of reasons, and out of a variety of circumstances, parenthood for them was usually intimately connected with their relationship and the desire to become "a family" (or more of a family). As is common, pregnancy was not the result of a rational decision-making process by these women (Currie 1988; M. McMahon 1995). In fact, when we first interviewed them (late in the women's pregnancy), both women and men struggled to tell us why they wanted to be parents. They usually settled on talking about parenthood as a normal part of adulthood, the next stage in life, and the "natural" product of a loving relationship.

For many of the women and men, the answer to our question why they were having a child was simply that "it was time" (see also Ranson 1998). Of course, there were eight couples for whom the pregnancy was *untimely*—unexpected and indeed a shock.

Although the couples typically saw parenthood as a normal life-cycle stage, they also usually saw it as intimately entangled in their relationship. Many people referred to parenthood as a normal extension of their loving relationship. Caitlin[5] said just that: "I think it's the natural culmination of two people who love one another." Helen also described her pregnancy as an extension of her relationship with her partner: "it's an extension of my love for [Gary] and wanting to have a child we created together." Gary felt the same way: he said that parenthood had "something to do with us as a couple." Parenthood was seen as a joint enterprise, firmly situated in these couples' relationships, and often so intimately bound together with the relationship that it could not be imagined independently of it. The women especially saw it that way. While many women said that they had "always" wanted to have a child, they also made clear that doing so required a stable relationship. As Jane said, "it wasn't as though I'd have had one if I weren't in this situation with [Tom]."

Highlighting the entanglement of parenthood and marriage was the fact that pregnancy closely followed marriage for a large number of the women in the study, many of whom had been living with their partners in common-law relationships for several years (see also Beaujot 2000). Nineteen of the 35 women who were married (54 per cent of them) were pregnant within two years of marrying (and at least one other woman had a miscarriage within two years of marriage); another six women (25 altogether, or 71 per cent of the 35) were pregnant within three years of marriage; and another five women (30 altogether, or 86 per cent of the 35) were pregnant within four years of marriage. Vic summed up the connection that many made between marriage and parenthood when he commented, "marriage is something that you do if you want to have a family." Of the five unmarried couples in the study, two had unplanned pregnancies and, as mentioned above, three married or made wedding plans near the time their babies were born.

Even though parenthood was not the product of a reasoned decision, these women and men were clear about what parenthood meant. At one time or another, all of the women and nearly all of the men indicated that parenthood primarily meant assuming responsibility. For example, when she was pregnant, Jane commented, "I see myself as a mother, as taking responsibility." After two months of motherhood, Esther described what being a mother meant to her as follows: "It's a huge responsibility; it's being responsible for unconditional love." Similarly, Andrea explained that for her motherhood meant "an overwhelming sense of responsibility." Keith, like many of the men, had the same definition of parenthood: "I think fatherhood is really responsibility. You're responsible to yourself to bring a person into this world, you're responsible to the other person you're bringing this child into the world with, and you're responsible to the child." And Adam said, "responsibility is the main issue . . . I mean, it's the ultimate step into adulthood, in some ways."

For these couples, parenthood not only meant assuming responsibility; it also involved an expectation of greater personal fulfillment. Participating in the development of a precious child and having a relationship with that child were central to this vision of fulfillment. But so was an image of family. In fact, our everyday language commonly equates having a baby with "having a family." So, like others, Jane explained that "[Tom] wants to have a family. I want to have a family" when she talked about why she decided to get pregnant. Some people talked about their desire to have a "family lifestyle" as a reason for wanting to become parents. Many other couples indicated anticipating a more family-oriented life, focused on their relationship with each other and with their child and the simple pleasures of being together. Robin, for example, expressed this goal in terms of her hope that parenthood would help her avoid becoming "a workaholic" and live a more "reasonable" life. Caitlin explained why she and her husband wanted to be parents by saying, "both of us believe that family life is a good life." And Robert's explanation of Emma's and his decision to have a child was that "it's family. It's the next progression in life. It feels like creating a family, which is very important." Overall, then, parenthood was premised on the couple relationship and it held the promise of family.

When the Baby Comes Home

These women and men typically expected that when their babies came home the women would take on the infant care but that the men would be involved in their care as well. Many of the women were quite adamant, while pregnant, about how important it was to them that their partners be involved in the care of the baby. Moreover, in their responses on a short questionnaire, many of the women and men indicated that they did not think that women were better able than men to care for babies.[6]

Nevertheless, most of these women and men thought that mothers should be the primary people to care for their babies. Social-organizational factors also promoted women's primary, full-time caregiving and men's prioritization of breadwinning. In a majority of the couples, the men made more money than the women did. As well, a majority of the women were entitled to paid maternity leaves of about six months, while whatever paternity leaves the men could get involved days or weeks—and most men felt they would be wise to take vacation time instead, to avoid jeopardizing their positions at work. Accordingly, a slight majority of the women were home on maternity leave for approximately six months, and 15 women were home full-time all year. Only two of the women returned to their paid work before six months: limited finances pushed them to return to work before their babies were three months old. In contrast, a (slight) majority of the men stayed home for only a week, or less, after the birth of their babies. Nearly all of the other men were home for two weeks only, although a few were home for three weeks and a couple of men worked at home.[7]

More subtle divisions between women's and men's roles and responsibilities unfolded very soon after their babies were born. The shape the women were in following birth varied significantly, but only a few of them felt able to resume normal activities right away. Nevertheless, the women felt compelled to learn to care for their babies without delay, in part because they were breastfeeding[8] but also because they were the ones who would be home caring for their infants. In contrast, many of the men seemed to feel they had a choice about learning to care for their babies. And once the women acquired some skills the men often were quick to perceive the differences in skills, and to decide that their wives were "naturals" at mothering.

Jill, for example, went through a very long labour and delivery, during which her husband, Adam, was at a loss to help her—while her birth coach provided considerable support and assistance. The birth left her absolutely exhausted and in need of recovery. Nevertheless, Jill felt that she needed to learn to care for her baby: Adam—though thrilled to be a father—was not stepping forward to do the learning. Two months later, when Jill was discussing the limited amount of baby care that Adam did, she commented, "women aren't born knowing how to look after babies. It's a learning experience for both of us [women and men]." In a similar comment that denied any "natural" maternal instinct, Joanne noted that active mothering "is one of those things where until you're sort of forced to do it you don't jump right into it." The men's reluctance to take the lead in learning to care for their babies, coupled with the fact that the women knew they would have to manage infant care virtually alone once the men returned to work, pushed the women to quickly learn how to care for their babies.

Nevertheless, some of these new fathers had partners who simply could not or would not—because of their physical condition—take on the baby care by themselves immediately after giving birth. In these cases, the men learned with their wives how to soothe their babies, change their diapers, and even bathe them. One man in the study—Sam, who was the only man who stayed home nearly full-time all year—learned these things before his partner, Rosa, and he remained the parent most able to intuit what his baby needed over the course of the year. The dominant pattern for these couples, however, was that the women quickly became the more skilled parents while the men developed varying degrees of comfort doing infant care. This pattern developed in spite of the fact that it would be months before the women felt even somewhat confident about how they were caring for their babies.

In the weeks and months following the birth of their babies, the women's reactions to the infants, and their feelings about full-time motherhood, were extremely varied. Many of the women were clearly spellbound by their babies, and in love with them from the beginning. When her baby was two months old, Esther noted, "I didn't really expect to sort of fall in love with her as much, as completely, as I have." In contrast, other women clearly did not "bond" with their babies for quite some time.[9] They were overwhelmed by the weight of their new responsibility, and struggling with both sleep deprivation and anxiety about whether they were providing adequate care for their baby. A few women were clearly depressed. Following a drug-free labour and delivery, Lara's first reaction to her baby was, "I don't know quite what to do with it!" Lara described her first two months of motherhood—in which her husband (who was beginning a professional career) was away for about 12 hours every day—as a "vast pit of exhaustion." She explained that, "my body was just totally off kilter for quite a while. I was zonked, and I think mentally unstable for a bit because of the sleep issue and the exhaustion." Six months after her baby was born, Lara was very distressed about the fact that she was still not "bonded" with her baby.

The men also had a range of reactions to their babies and to fatherhood. A few men commented about how unequipped and inadequate they felt when faced with their tiny infants (see also Kelleher 2003; Lupton and Barclay 1997). Greg, for example, talked about how a baby seemed "so fragile it could break in two." Some men mentioned how rough and large their hands suddenly seemed when they were with their babies. More generally, in the weeks that followed there was a range in the men's reactions to being fathers. Some men were clearly enthralled by their babies, and talked about how they "love[d] being a father." Caleb's comment about fatherhood was, "I think it's great. It just feels good." In contrast, some men continued to feel very marginal. Lance commented, at two months postpartum, "I don't feel very fatherly."

The degree to which the men became involved in the care of their infants in the early period after the birth varied tremendously. The men's varying involvement was related to differences in their partners' needs (given their physical condition), the women's expectations of the men, the degree to which the men wanted to be involved in baby care or wanted to help their partners, whether or not the men had a history of sharing the housework, and the amount of time they were home. Some of the men devoted their time at home to doing as much baby care as they could, as well as doing housework. Sam's case was unusual: he learned to comfort and care for his baby before his partner did because he defined fatherhood as the priority in his life once his baby was born and because Rosa felt unable to function for some time after giving birth. Some other men learned to care for their babies alongside their partners, did a fair amount of infant care in the period when they were home full-time, and took the babies for much of the time in the evenings, after they returned to work. Some men provided good "help" to their wives, taking their turn giving care through the first few months of parenthood. But fully half of the men in the study gave their partners only limited help: they could and would do some of the tasks involved in infant care but not others, and they "helped" only when asked. A few of the men were very marginal to their babies' lives, and mostly restricted their involvement to holding them and playing with them for a brief period every day, as well as keeping their wives company while the women cared for the baby. While many factors affected the men's involvement in the care of their babies, chief among them was the nature of a couple's relationship, as well as the circumstances of their lives.[10] A pattern that developed for a number of the couples highlights some of these causal factors.

Caring for the Baby, Protecting Dad[11]

Whatever the men's early reactions were to fatherhood, a common reaction the women had to motherhood was a sense of heightened dependence on their partners (Fox 2001, 2009). What they expected of the men varied, from just "being there" physically and emotionally, to recognizing how hard the women were working to provide good care for the baby, to being fully involved in the baby's care whenever they were home. Only a few women gave no indication that they felt more dependent on their partner. Nearly all of the women commented on this sense of dependence by noting that they could "never" make it as a single mother. Jeanne, for example, mentioned what many women clearly felt, that "strong support from her partner is like the number one need [of a mother]." At the same time, the women's full absorption in infant care diminished their ability to give their partners the attention and care they usually gave them (A. McMahon 1999).

The stresses characterizing the weeks and months following birth were an obvious reason why the women were so sure they were dependent on their partners. Most of the women felt overwhelmed by the new demands on them, and the weight of their new responsibility (Rosenberg 1987). Susan described how stunned she was by . . .

how completely and utterly all-consuming and overwhelming the whole thing

is . . . It is the most overwhelming thing. I can see why people go back to work because it's easier, because you can have your coffee when you want to, and go to the bathroom when you want to. I'm not putting down work at all. But as far as having control goes, you do have control at work and you just don't here, until you know what you're doing, which you don't until after the fact, I think.

Having to learn to care for their babies under the pressure of their unpredictable demands, and amidst anxiety about whether they were adequately caring for them, the women were left feeling both overwhelmed and stretched to their physical and emotional limits. Only a few women—those with tremendous amounts of support from their partners and other close family—did not feel overwhelmed by their new responsibility.

Many of the women had a surprising reaction to their sense of increased dependence on their partners: they acted to protect the men from the very demands that the women themselves were finding so stressful (Kelleher and Fox 2002). A majority of the women in the study—though not all of them—worried about and acted to protect their partners in the weeks and even months following the birth of their babies. When they were recovering from childbirth, they worried about how tired the men looked, and even how hard the birth experience had been for them. In spite of sleep deprivation and physical exhaustion, these women protected their husbands' sleep. After being home all day and getting no "break" from their responsibilities, they urged the men to play with the baby instead of cleaning the dirty dishes. They cleaned the dishes while the men played with the baby. In short, many of the women in the study often sacrificed their own needs—especially their need for rest—to safe-guard the men's well-being.

There were several reasons why these women acted to protect their partners in the early months of parenthood. One of them is ideological. It has to do with an equation of individual "choice" with individual responsibility that is common to this culture (M. McMahon 1995; Wall 2001). For most of the women in the study, choosing to have a baby meant accepting full responsibility for that baby. Helen, for example, answered a question about who held the daily responsibility for her two-month-old son by saying that she "definitely" was the one responsible for the baby. When asked how that responsibility felt she said,

> Most of the time it feels, it's wonderful, and it's, you know, I, I think like "this is my child" and, you know, I brought him into the world and he's my responsibility. But other times, some days you just feel sort of overwhelmed, like, who decided to have this baby, you know? Ha ha.

In a later interview, Helen again explained, "I *chose* to have this baby . . . It's my responsibility . . . This is my job now." Helen was not the only woman who equated "choice" with responsibility. The understanding that "it takes an entire village to raise a child" may be folk wisdom in societies where kinship plays a strong role in social organization, but not in ours, where nuclear families are assumed to be the best arrangement for raising children, and a woman home alone all day well-positioned to provide good infant care.

Of course, the equation of "choice" with responsibility rests on the assumption that biological mothers are responsible for their children (Eyer 1996). This assumption is ironic given that women are rarely aware of

the implications of the decision to become a mother. Once their baby is born, women commonly feel remarkably unprepared for motherhood (Miller 2007). In this study, the middle-class women especially felt that they were ready to be parents: they had a good relationship with their spouse, both they and their partners had good incomes and some security in the labour force, they usually owned a home, and they had taken a prenatal class and read about childbirth, if not parenting.[12] Yet, as is common, they typically felt incredibly unprepared once their babies were born.

But these women were right about responsibility: there are remarkably few social supports for new parents; the responsibility for a child rests solely with parents, and especially mothers. One of the chief consequences of the dearth of social support—the fact that the responsibility for young children is a private one—is women's heightened sense of dependence on their partners. The women in the study who most obviously protected their partners were women who were completely financially dependent on them—and the working-class women were more likely to be so dependent. Beth, for example, had only a high-school degree and some experience working part-time as a sales clerk. She came from a dysfunctional family and expressed gratitude about "finding" her husband, Albert, who had a full-time, though low-paid, job. Unable to cook when she got married, Beth was taught by her husband, just before their baby was born. Even though she had no help caring for her baby during the day, she worked hard over the year to cook dinner every evening, and generally "made sacrifices to make sure he's happy, as much as I can." One of the other working-class women in the study, Nancy, was in a position like Beth's, having only minimal job credentials and thus clearly financially dependent on her partner who was a skilled tradesman. Additionally, Nancy was grateful that Simon had agreed to her wishes to have a baby. Even in the early months after the birth of her baby, Nancy got up at dawn every day to prepare breakfast for Simon, who worked very long hours; and before the baby was six months old, she started putting him to bed at 9 p.m. every evening so that she could spend the evenings with Simon (as he insisted).

The working-class women seemed not only more dependent on their partners but also more conscious of and concerned about the men's position as financial providers—and the need to protect that position. Fatherhood intensifies the pressures on men to succeed as breadwinners, and many men in the study reacted to their partners' pregnancy by increasing their hours at work and becoming more determined to improve their position there (Fox 2001). For some of the working-class men—five of the nine men—the increased responsibility as breadwinner meant approximately 60 hours of work every week. In response, their wives felt they could not ask much of the men. Sophia, whose husband worked long hours, often on the night shift, commented, "I can't very well expect him to do work around here when he's working 60-hour weeks."

Middle-class women who were financially dependent on their partners also acted to protect their male partners. Ruth, who had just graduated from university and was only beginning to plan her career, was a full-time homemaker when she got pregnant. She was clear about her calculations behind protecting her husband's sleep:

I can't have him not sleeping when he has to go to work. That's number one. Even though I think he could do with a little less sleep . . . I'd much rather—it's sort of a

strategy I have—I'd much rather have him be stable and healthy so he can help me when I really need it . . . Before I wake him up, I weigh the pros and cons. It's funny how strategic I have to be.

Ruth continued, "so on the weekend, he'd better help—a lot!"

A third reason why many women protected their partners' sleep and a few other privileges was that they saw the men as their primary support and help with infant care. Ruth consciously calculated whether she needed Dave more as breadwinner or as her backup caregiver and chief helper, and when one need outweighed the other. She saw her husband as a breadwinner from Monday morning until he came home on Friday. Other women seemed to be doing the same, and some of them were as clear about it as Ruth. But still other women simply felt that it "made no sense" to have two tired parents rather than one. They wanted the certainty that when they could no longer handle the baby in the middle of the night they could call on someone who could. What is interesting about this reasoning by the women is that they were conceding that the men were only marginal caregivers, that they were *helpers* (Kelleher and Fox 2002; Wall and Arnold 2007). These women accepted the men's limited caregiving.

Another assumption at play in this dynamic involved women feeling that the work they did all day was less valuable than the work the men did, and therefore that the men's needs took precedence over their own. In part, that feeling was because the women were doing *unpaid* work. But it also had to do with their economic dependence on their partners—albeit, often temporary dependence. Sally, for example, said she went through two weeks of worrying about money when her baby was about two months old. Jake, her husband, had a full-time job, but she had earned about as much as he did before getting pregnant. Now that she was home, Sally said, "I just feel like I am not contributing. I feel that a lot." Similarly, Jane, who quit a good job to stay home for a year, talked about going through "a period where it hit me that [baby] and I are more or less dependent on him [her husband] . . . I spent a lot of time thinking . . . It occurred to me and it was frightening when it occurred to me because I've never been dependent, you know, as an adult." Sally's husband, Jake, wanted to do more baby care than Sally allowed him. Jane's husband, Tom, said that he would do whatever Jane asked him to do, but interestingly she rarely asked him to do much baby care. For many of these women, who were used to supporting themselves—and deriving a sense of their own worth, or at least contribution, from money-making—their sudden financial dependence weakened their sense of their own entitlement in their relationships.

Needless to say, these women's feelings also reflected a cultural devaluation of the work that mothers do: somehow the men's need to be wide-eyed in the morning was more important than their own. Indeed, many of the women seemed to feel that they owed something to their partners for "putting up with" the fact that the women had drastically reduced time and energy for giving the men the kind of attention and care that was usual in their relationships. Because the women's care giving was redirected from the men to the babies, the women seemed to feel indebted to their spouses.

A final, less apparent, cause seemed to be behind the tendency for many women to protect their male partners from the disruption and stress of living with a newborn. Many of these women seemed to be protecting their partners not only because they were breadwinners but also because the men—as husbands

and fathers—were central to their developing families. This concern was evidenced by the efforts many of the women made to build their partners' relationships with their babies. Most of the women were more concerned that their babies have a good relationship with their fathers—that the men and babies "bond"—than that the men help them with baby care. To nurture the father–child relationship, these women regularly encouraged the men to play with their baby rather than do housework. They also were strategic about how they involved the men in baby-care tasks. As well, some of the women made an effort to create the kind of home environment that the men were happy to come home to.

Jane, for example, told me when her baby was two months old that

> my priorities are totally different, you know, totally different. [Baby] and [Tom] are the first priorities, and then everything after that fits in whenever. Maybe because of me identifying with [baby's] needs, I'm more conscious of [Tom's] needs.

Having spent little time at home before she got pregnant, Jane was not only making her apartment more home-like, she was also cultivating Tom's bond with his baby. To that end, she urged Tom to play with the baby whenever he asked how he might help. She did the housework while he was with the baby, and in fact ended up doing all of the housework over the year she was home (even though Tom had done some of it before the baby was born).

Other women also promoted the relationship between father and baby by taking on extra work themselves. Some women strategized about when to give the baby to their husbands—and chose times when the infant was clean, fed, and not crying or upset. Apparently, they aimed to ensure a good experience for the men. One of the women was explicit about protecting her partner this way. Carla explained, "I don't want to put him through that [dealing with a fussy baby]. It's not fair. It makes him feel like he's not a competent father." Other women set aside an activity or time for their spouses to be with the baby. Some had their partners feed the baby, with a bottle of 'expressed' breast milk; some had them bathe the baby. In short, some of the women worked to create the men's relationships with their babies, and their involvement in their care, and did so by protecting them from the more stressful and difficult aspects of infant care. They were working to ensure the development of the men's relationships with their babies, and thus their fledgling families.

The men's reactions to the women's attempts to protect them from the stresses of life with a newborn varied. Most of the men who benefitted from this ongoing care by their wives seemed to be oblivious to it. Apparently, they were used to their wives giving them a certain amount of care and privileging their needs. In fact, some of the men told us that because they were the ones who were "working" it was only fair that their partners did the housework and infant care. Justin, for example, commented that, "If I could stop working I'd do all the housework . . . If she wanted to go out working all day long, I'd take it over." Yet, there was also a hint in Justin's comments that he did not feel completely entitled to the privilege he was given at home; he also said, "I like living in a clean place, and she does it well and, you know, she does it. So I get very selfish." A few men, however, were uncomfortable with the women's sacrifices. Gary, for example, commented on Helen's efforts to spare him as follows: "I just thought she worked too hard to insulate me from the problems." And Carla's husband felt that he was marginalized

as a parent. Both of these men wanted to, and expected to, be involved in the care of their babies. As well, there were quite a few men who had no expectation that the women should work any longer over the course of the day than they did, or that they should relax while their wives were busy.

In contrast, a few men whose partners were protective—and some whose partners were not—clearly felt that they needed more of their wives' attention, company, and care than they were getting. These men had a hard time dealing with the women's absorption with the baby, the dramatic changes in daily life, and the women's inability to spend relaxed time with them. They wanted more protection against the disruption to their lives. Joe, for example, struggled with the loss of his wife's attention and time, even though he was thrilled with his baby. At one point, he commented that with fatherhood men "sort of get displaced" when couples become parents.

The men's different reactions to the demands on them and to the redirection of the women's emotional energy are not easily explained. But the men who were both involved in the care of their babies and successful as providers seemed to be much better able to make the adjustment to life with an infant. The men who seemed in need of their wives' ongoing attention were typically marginal to the babies' care and, in most cases, stressed by their financial responsibilities—and not successful providers. Nicholas Townsend (2002) has argued that successful breadwinning is central to men's sense of masculine identity. He also argues that marriage, fatherhood, and employment are a "package deal," and that successful breadwinning is often considered by men to be central to fulfilling the responsibilities of fatherhood (Townsend 2002; Coltrane 1996). The men in the study who did not feel good about themselves—and they were typically unsuccessful as breadwinners—struggled the hardest to adjust to fatherhood and the loss of their partners' attention.

While women's protection of the men was the most common pattern in the postpartum period, some (13) women in the study gave no indication that they were protecting their partners in any way. Indeed, some of these women insisted that their partners pay attention to their own needs as well as to the babies' needs. Susan, for example, was determined that her husband, Charles, be as involved with the baby as she was during his two (vacation) weeks at home. She felt that he had broken a virtual "marriage vow" to do some of the cooking, and she was determined that something similar did not happen with respect to parenthood. Charles did all of the housework (including the cooking) and much of the infant care in the weeks following the birth, when he was home. All but two of the women who did not try somehow to protect their partners were employed when they got pregnant, with jobs and earnings comparable to or better than their partners' (and one of the two women who were exceptions to this rule was working on a doctoral degree). What nearly all of these women had in common was an absence of financial dependence on their male partners. They also typically had advanced educational credentials, an orientation influenced (to varying degrees) by feminism, and often a partner who shared the household work before the couple became parents.

Making Dads

Protecting their partners became an increasingly contradictory strategy for the women as the year wore on because those men who remained marginal to the care of their babies were less committed to their families. Thus, the women's concerns about their developing families and desires that the men be actively involved in the care of their babies moved those who had protected their partners to adopt a new strategy. When the men were not very involved in the care of their infants, the women took action to construct the men's active caregiving (see also Coltrane 1996: 60; Gerson 1993). Helen—whose partner, Gary, commented that she had protected him—noted that, "it takes work to bring the man into the picture and into the, you know, care. Through the care of the baby you can do that, and through, like I say, giving him more responsibility." For Helen, Gary's care of the baby was not her main concern; there was a larger "picture"—their evolving family.

Like Helen, many of the women took action to create the men's involvement with their babies. In the process, they usually created more work for themselves. Often women set aside a baby-care task for the men to carry out (as mentioned above). A few of the women "expressed" milk into a bottle, and had the men feed the baby once a day; more women drew the men into a daily feeding after they moved their babies onto formula. It was also common for women to save their baby's bath for Dad. Marie noted, "I usually try to keep certain things for [Bill], like bathing the baby . . . I figure those are his special moments." Interestingly, this typically meant that the women prepared everything before they turned the job over to their partner—pouring the bath water and ensuring its temperature was right; and lining up the soap, towel, washcloth, baby seat, and clean clothes (Kelleher and Fox 2002). Even less ambitiously, some of the women stuck to the strategy of encouraging the men to play with the baby. In more extreme cases, the women tended to hand over the baby only when the baby was fed, clean, and contented. But invariably, having the man play with the baby meant that the women were doing housework while the men were so engaged. All of these strategies involved the women doing more work.

Less obviously, women worked to create a comfortable home and pleasant "family" experiences. Many women cooked dinner every night, and many did housework during the day so that evenings were free for spending time as a threesome, or during the week so that weekends were free for family activities. Some women did this because they felt that it was part of "the bargain" when they were home and the men were making the money, but others did so even though they felt it was not quite fair, and in spite of growing resentment about the allocation of the work. Susan, for example, talked about making especially appealing dinners, and even eating by candlelight after the early months of parenthood because, "I'm trying to make it a little bit nicer." Having good food and a pleasant dinner was important to her: "We both eat a lot and we didn't want to skip dinner or order pizza—seems so transient and temporary. Awful. You can't have a sense of home." Susan also did housework during the week so that she, Charles, and their baby could spend weekends together. And when asked at six months postpartum what had changed in her life, Susan said,

> I think the most significant thing, and as far as our lives go, what's changed? I think we're probably, we're more of a, we've realized that we're more of a family unit, I think. And it's kind of, we're all willingly one big happy family—more so than just, "oh gosh, there's the baby."

And after a year of motherhood, Susan commented,

> I love the little threesome, the little home scene. I love weekends. They drive me nuts. On Sunday night I'm furious half the time because the joint's a wreck and we didn't get anything done. But we manage to go out for walks together and we play together. And that's so fantastic.

Clearly, making home life pleasant suited Susan's needs, but it also pulled her husband into the project of making family as well: while he had abrogated his "vow" to cook meals before their baby was born, he cooked when Susan was unable to and was very involved in baby care when he was home from work, for the entire year.[13] Nevertheless, Susan struggled with resentment about doing all of the housework.

A majority of the women in the study did more housework than they had before becoming mothers. While few of them explained their increased domesticity with direct claims about making family, many more talked about making the time their partners were home pleasant. Still other women noted that they regularly complimented, indeed praised, their partners' parenting skills—and often in spite of seeing problems with what the men were doing. Sophia said she often had to "bite her tongue" when she watched her husband with their baby, but she nevertheless noted, "I tell [Max] all the time how wonderful he is with her [the baby], and how lucky she is to have a dad like him." Ensuring that the men were developing solid relationships with their babies seemed to be a priority for these women.

Providing a contrast with the women who did extra work to pull their partners into active parenting were the women who took an entirely different strategy: they made sure that they left the men alone with their babies for regular periods of time (after the first several months). Unlike the other women, this strategy did not involve any catering to the men, and instead evidenced the women's sense that they were entitled to some time to themselves. After about four months of motherhood, Emma, for example, made arrangements to go out with friends one night every week, in order to give her husband time with their baby—and while the baby was awake. Some other women did the same, though less regularly, but usually at least partly to put their partners in the position of having to care for the baby. Claire returned to her paid job before her baby was two months old, partly out of financial need, partly "to get out of the house," but also partly to push Jaime (who worked only part-time) to do more infant care while she was gone. The women who adopted this strategy, and gave no indication of catering to their partners to pull them into involvement with the baby, were women with as much bargaining power as the men they lived with—bargaining power that accrued because they earned as much money as the men, and had jobs of equal status to the men's jobs.

In general, the women in the study were more concerned that their partners form a relationship with their babies than that they do significant amounts of infant care. The middle-class women were more determined that the men be involved in infant care. But both middle- and working-class women took measures to draw the men into active parenting involvement of whatever kind. The type of strategy they used, and thus the extent to which it involved catering to the men, was largely a product of the women's relative bargaining power in the relationship: women who were financially dependent on their partners were more likely to cater to the men in some way in their effort to draw them into active involvement. Many women also seemed to be concerned about sustaining their own relationships with their partners, through a period

when they could give the men little attention and when couples' sexual relationships were changed and sometimes non-existent.

Wrapping Up

Motherhood is a source of profound meaning and pleasure in the lives of many women. It is also an experience that positions women differently in this society, making them subject to all of the handicaps associated with being women (Crittenden 2001). It is significant that parenthood enforces and even produces divisions of work and responsibility in the lives of heterosexual couples. There is a longstanding conviction among those who study gender that the fact that women do more child care and housework than men provides one of the main bases of gender inequality in this society, at least in the white population. The low status of this unpaid work, the social isolation it often entails, the service nature of the work, the monetary cost it entails, and the longer hours of work it has meant are all identified as central to that inequality (Budig and England 2001; Hartmann 1981; Luxton 1980; Waldfogel 1997). This chapter examined two relational dynamics that developed for many of the couples in a study of couples becoming parents. These dynamics, and women's sense of increased dependence on their partners that motivated them, shed some light on the causes of the conventional arrangements and increased gender inequality in families that often accompany the transition to parenthood.

Many of the new mothers in this study catered to their partners for the short-term goal of protecting the men from the disruption of life with an infant and the long-term goal of creating "family." These women protected their partners in the early weeks and months after their babies were born, out of a strong sense of dependence on the men as breadwinners and as central to the development of their babies' families. Even when women changed their approach in later months, and worked to pull the men into active involvement in infant care, that effort often involved extra work for the women, which again entailed some catering to the men (see also Fox 2001).

Before these dynamics were established, the initial gender divisions that developed for most of these couples—whereby the women became the main caregivers—were the product of both gender ideologies and social circumstances, especially the fact that the women

knew they would be home caring for their infants, and not women's natural ability for mothering or even the bond they established with their baby. Yet, there were differences among the women in the study, and among the men. Some men did not need to be pulled into baby care or protected from the demands of an infant; some men were quite involved with the baby, and committed to their families from the beginning. This variation among couples and the importance of circumstances—and not "nature"—in establishing the patterns common among these couples make clear the possibility for egalitarian parenting.

● Notes

1. I thank the 40 couples who generously allowed me to interview them at a time in their lives when they were incredibly busy. I am also grateful to Diana Worts and Christa Kelleher for their invaluable insights over the course of this project; to Judith Taylor, Josee Johnston, Anna Korteweg, Cynthia Cranford, Barrie Thorne, Ester Reiter, Meg Luxton, Kate Bezanson, and other colleagues for comments on various pieces of my forthcoming book; and to Bonnie Erickson for the title of this chapter. Also, thanks go to Sherry Bartram and Diana Worts for excellent research assistance, and to Sheila Martineau, Evangeline Davis, Elizabeth Walker, Rebecca Fulton, Ann Bernardo, Sharon Saunders, David Guetter, and Jennifer Bates for careful transcribing. The research on which this chapter is based was made possible by a grant from the Social Sciences and Humanities Research Council, # 410-94-0453.

2. This is not so for lesbian couples. Research on lesbian couples shows that when they make the transition to parenthood they typically do not divide their work and responsibilities between the two adults, in the way that is common to heterosexual couples (Dunne 2000; Nelson 1996).

3. Also, the people participating in the study varied widely in age. Age proved not to be an important predictor of experience, but the "age" of the marriage did have an impact on a number of things.

4. In the 1990s, women living in Ontario who had

been employed full-time for at least six months were eligible for 17 weeks of maternity leave, 15 of which were paid; they could also take 10 weeks of paid parental leave. They applied for money through Unemployment Insurance, and could receive up to 60 per cent of their usual wages/salaries in replacement earnings. Additionally, employers often "topped up" the money to varying percentages of women's usual earnings. Women typically took the full 27 weeks of leave.

5. All of the names are fictitious.

6. During the first interview, we asked some of the participants a battery of questions that measured attitudes toward gender.

7. In an unusual case, one man (Sam) was home nearly full-time for the entire year: he was still in school, and clearly giving priority to things other than occupational success; his unusual position was possible because he and his partner owned a house and the latter had credentials that enabled her to find high-paying contract work.

8. See Glenda Wall (2001) on the promotion of breastfeeding by various authoritative sources. Only one woman in the study did not breastfeed her baby; another woman stopped after several weeks of trying.

9. See Diane Eyer's (1992) *Mother–Infant Bonding: A Scientific Fiction* for a discussion of the myths around the notion of "bonding."

10. Many researchers have made the point that men's involvement in infant care is related to what is going on in their relationships with their partners (Backett 1987; Lamb and Lewis 2004; Walzer 1998).

11. This section is based on Christa Kelleher's observation that the women were often protecting their husbands, in the days and weeks after the birth.

12. See Martha McMahon (1995) on how middle-class

women typically feel they have to accomplish certain things before they are ready to be mothers. A good relationship is the most important requisite, but financial stability is also important.

13. Charles remained involved in infant care for the next year as well. I interviewed this couple when their first baby was two years old, and they had two children.

● References

Backett, Kathryn. 1987. "The Negotiation of Fatherhood," in *Reassessing Fatherhood*, eds Charlie Lewis and Margaret O'Brien (London: Sage), 74–90.

Beaujot, Rod. 2000. *Earning & Caring in Canadian Families* (Peterborough: Broadview Press).

Bianchi, Suzanne M., John Robinson, and Melissa A. Milkie. 2006. *Changing Rhythms of American Family Life* (New York: Russell Sage Foundation).

Blum, Linda. 1999. *At the Breast: Ideologies of Breast-feeding and Motherhood in the Contemporary United States* (Boston: Beacon Books).

Bobel, Chris. 2002. *The Paradox of Natural Mothering* (Philadelphia: Temple University Press).

Brodie, Janine. 1996. "Restructuring and the New Citizenship," in *Rethinking Restructuring: Gender and Change in Canada*, ed. Isabella Bakker (Toronto: University of Toronto Press), 126–40.

Budig, Michelle, and Paula England. 2001. "The Wage Penalty for Motherhood," *American Sociological Review* 66, 2: 204–25.

Calliste, Agnes. 2001. "Black Families in Canada: Exploring the Interconnections of Race, Class, and Gender," in *Family Patterns, Gender Relations*, 2nd edn (Toronto: Oxford University Press), 401–19.

Coltrane, Scott. 1996. *Family Man: Fatherhood, Housework, and Gender Equity* (New York: Oxford University Press).

Cowan, Carolyn, and Philip Cowan. 1992. *When Partners Become Parents: The Big Life Change for Couples* (New York: Basic).

Crittenden, Ann. 2001. *The Price of Motherhood: Why the Most Important Job in the World Is Still the Least Valued* (New York: Metropolitan Books).

Currie, Dawn. 1988. "Rethinking What We Do and How We Do It: A Study of Reproductive Decisions," *Canadian Review of Sociology and Anthropology* 25, 2: 231–53.

DeVault, Marjorie. 1991. *Feeding the Family: The Social Organization of Caring as Gendered Work* (Chicago: The University of Chicago Press).

Dunne, Gillian. 2000. "Opting Into Motherhood: Lesbians Blurring the Boundaries and Transforming the

Meaning of Parenthood and Kinship," *Gender & Society* 14, 1: 11–35.

Eyer, Diane. 1992. *Mother–Infant Bonding: A Scientific Fiction* (New Haven: Yale University Press).

———. 1996. *Motherguilt: How Our Culture Blames Mothers for What's Wrong with Society* (New York: Random House).

Feeney, Judith, Lydia Hohaus, Patricia Noller, and Richard Alexander. 2001. *Becoming Parents: Exploring the Bonds between Mothers, Fathers, and Their Infants* (Cambridge: Cambridge University Press).

Fox, Bonnie. 2001. "The Formative Years: How Parenthood Creates Gender," *Canadian Review of Sociology and Anthropology* 38, 4: 373–90.

———. 2006. "Motherhood as a Class Act: The Many Ways in Which 'Intensive Mothering' Is Entangled with Social Change," in *Social Reproduction: Feminist Political Economy Challenges Neo-liberalism*, eds Kate Bezanson and Meg Luxton (Montreal & Kingston: McGill-Queen's University Press).

———. 2009. *When Couples Become Parents: The Creation of Gender in the Transition to Parenthood.* (Toronto: University of Toronto Press).

Furstenberg, Frank. 1996. "The Future of Marriage," *American Demographics* 18.

Gerson, Kathleen. 1993. *No Man's Land: Men's Changing Commitments to Family and Work* (New York: Basic).

———. 1997. "The Social Construction of Fatherhood," in *Contemporary Parenting*: Challenges and Issues, ed. Terry Arendell (Thousand Oaks: Sage).

Hartmann, Heidi. 1981. "The Family as the Locus of Gender, Class, and Political Struggle: The Example of Housework," *Signs* 6, 3: 366–94.

Hays, Sharon. 1996. *The Cultural Contradictions of Motherhood* (New Haven: Yale University Press).

Hill, Shirley. 2005. *Black Intimacies* (CA: Altamira Press).

Hochschild, Arlie. 1989. *The Second Shift: Working Parents and the Revolution at Home* (New York: Viking).

Kelleher, Christa. 2003. "Postpartum Matters: Women's Experiences of Medical Surveillance: Time and

Support after Birth," unpublished doctoral dissertation, Sociology, Brandeis University.

———, and Bonnie Fox. 2002. "Nurturing Babies, Protecting Men: The Unequal Dynamics of Women's Postpartum Care giving Practices," in *Childcare and Inequality: Rethinking Care Work for Children & Youth* (New York: Routledge), 51–64.

Lamb, Michael, and Charlie Lewis. 2004. "The Development and Significance of Father–Child Relationships in Two-parent Families," in *The Role of the Father in Child Development,* 4th edn (New York: John Wiley), 272–306.

Lewis, Charlie. 1986. *Becoming a Father* (Milton Keynes: Open University Press).

Lupton, Deborah, and Lesley Barclay. 1997. *Constructing Fatherhood: Discourses and Experiences* (London: Sage).

Luxton, Meg. 1980. *More Than a Labour of Love: Three Generations of Women's Work in the Home* (Toronto: The Women's Press).

MacDermid, S., T. Huston, and S. McHale. 1990. "Changes in Marriage Associated with the Transition to Parenthood: Individual Differences as a Function of Sex-role Attitudes and Changes in the Division of Household Labor," *Journal of Marriage and the Family* 52: 475–86.

McMahon, Anthony. 1999. *Taking Care of Men: Sexual Politics in the Public Mind* (Cambridge: Cambridge University Press).

McMahon, Martha. 1995. *Engendering Motherhood: Identity and Self-transformation in Women's Lives* (New York: Guilford Press).

Miller, Tina. 2007. "'Is This What Motherhood Is All About?' Weaving Experiences and Discourse through Transition to First-time Motherhood," *Gender & Society* 21, 3: 337–58.

Nelson, Fiona. 1996. *Lesbian Motherhood: An Exploration of Canadian Lesbian Families* (Toronto: University of Toronto Press).

Ornstein, Michael, and Glenn J. Stalker. 2012. "Canadian Families' Strategies for Employment and Care for Preschool Children," *Journal of Family Issues* 22, 10: 1–32.

Perkins, Wesley, and Debra DeMeis. 1996. "Gender and Family Effects on 'Second-shift' Domestic Activity of College-educated Young Adults," *Gender & Society* 10: 78–93.

Ranson, Gillian. 1998. "Education, Work, and Family Decision-making: Finding the 'Right Time' to Have a Baby," *Canadian Review of Sociology and Anthropology* 35, 4: 517–34.

Rexroat, Cynthia, and Constance Shehan. 1987. "The Family Life Cycle and Spouses' Time in Housework," *Journal of Marriage and the Family* 49: 737–50.

Richardson, Diane. 1993. *Women, Motherhood, and Child Rearing* (New York: Macmillan).

Rosenberg, Harriet. 1987. "Motherwork, Stress, and Depression: The Costs of Privatized Social Reproduction," in *Feminism and Political Economy: Women's Work, Women's Struggles,* eds Heather Jon Maroney and Meg Luxton (Toronto: Methuen), 181–96.

Sanchez, Laura, and Elizabeth Thomson. 1997. "Becoming Mothers and Fathers: Parenthood, Gender, and the Division of Labor," *Gender & Society* 11, 6: 747–72.

Townsend, Nicholas. 2002. *The Package Deal: Marriage, Work, and Fatherhood in Men's Lives* (Philadelphia: Temple University Press).

Waldfogel, Jane. 1997. "The Effects of Children on Women's Wages," *American Sociological Review* 62: 209–17.

Wall, Glenda. 2001. "Moral Constructions of Motherhood in Breast-feeding Discourse," *Gender & Society* 15, 4: 590–608.

———. 2004. "Is Your Child's Brain Potential Maximized? Mothering in an Age of New Brain Research," *Atlantis* 28, 2: 41–50.

———, and Stephanie Arnold. 2007. "How Involved Is Involved Fathering? An Exploration of the Contemporary Culture of Fatherhood," *Gender & Society* 21, 4: 508–27.

Walzer, Susan. 1996. "Thinking about the Baby: Gender and Divisions of Infant Care," *Social Problems*: 43, 2: 219–34.

———. 1998. *Thinking about the Baby: Gender and Transitions into Parenthood* (Philadelphia: Temple University Press).

Chapter 14

A number of researchers have examined why so many women who are home full-time with babies or young children feel socially isolated, overwhelmed by their responsibilities, and stressed by the high demand of full-time mothering and the low level of control over the timing of that demand. They have concluded that the fact that mothers almost single-handedly hold the responsibility for their children for most of the day is at the heart of these problems. This conclusion is not a new one. Early in the twentieth century, a number of feminists (such as Charlotte Perkins Gilman) argued that private nuclear-family living was a problem, and especially that it was a chief source of women's subordination to men. They thought that the position of homemakers was especially problematic because they did housework and child care alone. Some of those feminists proposed the design of multi-family housing that would include communal kitchens, dining rooms, laundries, and child care centres, as well as private dwelling units. The proposals of these visionary women were never realized. But today co-operative housing in Canada involves some communal space as well as collective management. As a result, such housing has the potential to create less private definitions and experiences of family life and the work that sustains family. In this chapter, Diana Worts reports on her research involving in-depth interviews with women living in housing co-ops in Toronto. She describes the differences that living in co-operative housing can make for women raising children.

"Like a Family":
Reproductive Work in a Co-operative Setting

Diana Worts

> There's a bond with the people across the street because they're also in the co-op. . . . It's ki-i-ind of like a little bit of [an] extended family community. And sometimes it's really made a big difference. (Karen)

Introduction

Nuclear families raise a number of concerns for gender scholars. One of these is that this family pattern goes hand in hand with the *privatization* of "reproductive work"—or the myriad everyday tasks involved in tending to the health and well-being of others.[1] Moreover, privatization combines with a gendered division of labour in marriage that assigns this work *to women*. Thus, while caregiving work benefits society as a whole, privatization ensures that the bulk of it is performed by individual women, as an unpaid "labour of love" for family members. Privatization also establishes a less-than-optimal context for family work—a context that virtually guarantees its isolation, invisibility, and devaluation. As a result, those who carry responsibility for these tasks risk a variety of problems, including depression, physical exhaustion, and family violence—and if they choose to leave, poverty (Dobash and Dobash 1979; Goldberg and Kremen 1990; Oakley 1974; Rosenberg 1987). Importantly, the difficulties associated with the organization of caregiving work are magnified if and when women become parents, as the workload in the home increases dramatically at this time while the gendered division of labour loses much of its flexibility. Indeed, studies have found that parenthood can transform a marriage in which roles are relatively fluid to one in which the woman is the primary caregiver and the man the primary breadwinner (Cowan and Cowan 1992; Fox 1997). Thus, it is to *women raising children* that the critique of the privatization of family life in Western societies most obviously applies.

But the organization of caregiving work is not uniform across Western nations. Research comparing social policies in different countries demonstrates that governments vary widely in their approach to child care and other reproductive work. While policies and programs in the US and most of Canada are organized around the assumption that this work is a private family responsibility, those in many European nations (and to some extent, Quebec) are based on the notion that the work should be *socialized*—or that *society as a whole* should bear a large share of the costs. Thus, in Sweden, for example, state-funded child care, extended parental leaves, and high-quality part-time work are readily available; and as a result, women do not suffer the same consequences as their North American counterparts, despite the fact that they do the bulk of the reproductive work in their families (Daly 1994; Sainsbury 1994).

Moreover, research on poor American communities also identifies alternative ways of organizing caregiving tasks. For example, studies highlight the fluid boundaries of poor black women's households in past decades, showing the variety of ways "family" may be constructed, and—for better or for worse—the lack of economic dependency on a single (male) partner these relationships often entail (Collins 1990; Stack 1973). This research directs attention beyond a focus on the division of labour in marriage, and suggests, instead, a need to look at how "domestic" tasks may become the concern of the *entire local community*.

In the US and Canada, as well as many other countries, the organization of caregiving work bears a direct connection to the organization of *housing*. The home is the material and symbolic base of family life; and domestic work is typically carried out within private households or on behalf of individuals who live (or have lived) under the same roof. In a nation where few institutional means exist for socializing the burden of care, settings where housing is organized collectively are of interest. They offer an opportunity to examine whether alternative ways of organizing shelter can foster alternative ways of carrying out family work.

In Canada, *co-operative housing* is such an alternative. A form of social housing (i.e., government-owned, non-equity), it is funded in part by the Canadian welfare state. While the primary aim is affordability, one means by which affordability is achieved is a unique organizational structure known as "collective self-management"; and this feature distinguishes the co-operative model from other social and rental housing. Co-ops are like private rental or ownership accommodation in that they consist of single-family houses and apartments and each unit is self-contained; however, they are not individually owned or rented but are leased at cost from the co-operative corporation. More important, in contrast to both private housing and other forms of social housing, decisions about their operation and maintenance are made and carried out *collectively* by the *community of residents.* Thus this form of housing introduces an element of collectivism into the very basis of family life—the home.

In large part because they are affordable, co-ops are attractive to women (and men) raising children. As a result, they are more likely to house children than the private housing market (Burke 1994). Co-ops are especially appealing to women parenting alone. A primary reason is affordability, but secondary reasons include central location, reliable maintenance, security of tenure, protection and mutual support, and control over the housing environment (Selby and Wilson 1988; Spector and Klodawsky 1993; Weckerle and Novac 1989). At least some of these drawing cards can be seen to "substitute" for the advantages that might accompany marriage and home ownership. Co-ops are also attractive to women raising families in two-parent households. In many cases the economic and social advantages are less obvious than they are for women raising children alone. However, housing costs are often considerably lower than they would be in the rental market, and there is the added benefit of having access to rent-geared-to-income (RGI) should the need arise (Cooper and Rodman 1992).[2] Moreover, the advantages of community support, and of gaining some control over housing costs and the local environment (particularly in cases where the alternative is long-term renting), can make co-ops attractive to partnered women as well (Cooper and Rodman 1992; Selby and Wilson 1988).

This study makes use of in-depth interview material to investigate the organization of caregiving work in co-operative settings. It draws on the experiences of 25 women living in housing co-ops in and around the city of Toronto. The women represent a total of 18 different co-ops, and at the time of interview

they had been co-op residents for anywhere from 3 to 25 years. All the women interviewed were parents. All had at least one child who had spent a substantial part of their growing-up years living in co-op housing. In addition, three of the women had spent a part of their own childhood in a co-op. At the time of interview, 11 of the women were living with a male partner, while 14 were raising children alone.

The analysis is organized around the notion that, as members of housing co-ops, these women gained access to a variety of resources *beyond the household* that assisted them in carrying out family work. Access to these resources was, moreover, structured in unique ways by the setting itself. The analysis identifies and describes two broad "channels" through which community-level resources flowed to members of co-op communities: (1) *affordability* in housing, and (2) *ties to other members.* The discussion focuses on the kinds of resources the women in this study received through each of these channels. It shows that affordability delivered a variety of more or less tangible resources that helped them provide adequately for their children's physical and socio-emotional needs. The ties to other members offered a wide range of both tangible *and* intangible support. This support assisted women, on both the practical and the socio-emotional level, with the work of raising a family.[3] The conclusion draws out the consequences of each resource channel for the organization of family life. It suggests that the first channel, by itself, served primarily to shore up the privatized family household—and (women's) personal responsibility for caregiving work. The second channel, on the other hand, challenged the private nature of family life and began, in small ways, to shift the burden of responsibility for child rearing away from the household and toward the local community.

Affordability as a Resource Channel

Affordability served as a resource channel for these women in several ways. It was important in itself because it gave them *access* to an essential resource—housing. But beyond this, it often improved both the *quality* of their accommodation and its *location*. These affordability outcomes had quality-of-life implications for the women and their families.

Housing Access

The most obvious product of affordability was the housing itself. In fact, the majority of women in the study cited their need for affordable housing as the primary reason they had originally chosen to live in a co-op. The significance of affordability was, moreover, linked to personal (i.e., privatized) responsibility for children. Especially among the single women, responsibility for children was both the reason their living arrangements mattered, and the reason their financial resources were strained. Marilyn explained: "On your own . . . you can live with a friend or do something [temporary]. But not with two kids." Similarly, Anne-Marie described herself as having been a "free spirit" prior to becoming a parent, but observed that, "Everything's different now that I've had my daughter, because of financial needs and realities [that have] just taken a role in my life that they never did before."

For many of these women, the problem was that the time and energy required to care for their families limited their ability to generate income, and so pushed them into the realm of need. Karen, whose older child was chronically ill, explained that, "There's no way [I could work full-time]. I would be stressed out of my mind . . . at work and at home. And

there's no way I'd be able to look after my kids." Irene added that, "I've lived on a housing subsidy for many years. . . . And I'm *very* grateful for that opportunity to do so. It's meant that I could raise my kids, you know, in the way that I wanted to raise them." So, the state support that makes this type of housing affordable was a major means by which women with limited means managed to keep a roof over their families' heads while *also* continuing to care for their children. As Karen observed, "It's made all the difference in the world. . . . It kind of ameliorates the effects of poverty, being there. Just softens it."

Affordability was most important to the low-income single mothers in this study. For these women, rent-geared-to-income programs were a critical component of affordability, and several had been paying RGI for extended periods of time. However, both single and married women also used RGI as a "backup" system in the event that personal or household incomes dropped unexpectedly for a short period of time. Indeed, several women with moderate household incomes had initially chosen co-op housing because it offered this kind of safety net to members. Elizabeth, for example, worked part-time while her partner worked short-term contract positions. She commented that,

> I guess when we moved in we knew [my husband's] income . . . there were no guarantees when it would come in. . . . And I was at home with [my older child] at the time. So . . . we really needed a place that was affordable. And we had that security [of RGI] if we needed it. So that seemed like a good thing for us.

Thus, for women (both married and single) whose household-level resources were limited or uncertain, the knowledge that RGI was there provided a sense of security they would not otherwise have had. As Elaine put it, "Yeah, there've been times when I've used the subsidy pool. It's been great! It's got me through."

RGI also served as a kind of safety net for women whose marriages were unstable. Julia reported that the possibility of getting a subsidy gave her "the security of knowing if . . . something happened [to my marriage] and I couldn't make it on my own I'd be able to get some kind of assistance." And Barbara recalled that RGI had enabled her to keep a roof over her own and her children's heads, while also getting back on her feet and caring for her children, after her first marriage dissolved.

> I mean it was bad enough being separated; and it was bad enough, you know, having very low income. But I can't imagine doing it in a regular rental market. . . . [With RGI] I was able to stay in university. [And because I was working at home] I was able to be more accessible to my kids when they were young and [I was] going through a divorce.

So RGI meant women, single or married, were less dependent on the economic protection marriage can provide. Thus they were in a stronger position to provide care for their children both within a financially insecure marriage and, if necessary, on their own.

Regardless of how they used it, though, a major benefit of RGI was that it gave women and their families *stability* in housing. When household incomes changed, whether through the loss of a partner or the loss of employment, housing costs were adjusted accordingly. Thus families were spared the search for less expensive accommodation at a time when they were already under considerable strain. The single women interviewed were especially aware of

how important this kind of protection was to their families' well-being. Anne-Marie commented that the stability RGI had brought to her daughter's life was "*totally* important; it's the most important thing in my life, basically." And Hannah echoed the sentiment. "At this point I think [living outside the co-op with my kids] would be quite difficult, just because of the financial situation. . . . I don't have the confidence that I could set up something that would feel, you know, really stable."

Affordability was also important to women not receiving RGI. The combined effects of co-op housing's non-profit status and members' volunteer labour ensured that even the non-subsidized costs were lower than those in the surrounding private rental or ownership markets. This was sometimes a factor, both in the choice to move into co-op housing, and in the decision to remain there over the long-term. As was the case for many of the women who relied on RGI, affordability was important to women paying unsubsidized rents, not only as a means of keeping a roof over their families' heads but also for its impact on their ability to care for their children.

> Affordability gives you . . . some freedom to have a family life. . . . I can work three days a week, or three and a half days a week, and still pay my rent and . . . have a little bit of money leftover. So that's important—'cause I'd rather be with [my baby and toddler] than at work all the time. (Monica)

For Victoria, affordable housing left enough in the budget to enrich her daughter's life. "Even though my income didn't allow it . . . my kid had the advantages. She had the classes. She had the trips. She had all the same things as her [middle-class] friends." Thus, for these women, too, affordability served not only to keep a roof over their own and their families' heads but also to let them raise their children in a way that made sense to them.

Housing Quality

Another resource available through affordability was better *quality* housing. Women who were, or had been, lone parents were most likely to observe that their co-op home was an improvement over the private housing they had been able to afford. And housing quality, like access, was linked to the ability to care for their children. Alice, who had a long history of living in "slummy households all over the city," recalled that her first reaction to finding her co-op was a huge sense of relief because, in contrast to her previous arrangements, "it look[ed] neat—nice, neat and clean," and "like a nice place for a kid to grow up in."

Equally important to low-income women was the fact that their home was not readily identifiable as "social housing." Thus they escaped the stigma so often attached to other forms of affordable accommodation. Once again, this was important largely for its impact on their children's well-being.

> I don't think my daughter thinks of it as a single mother's ghetto or anything like that. . . . See, living in [identifiable social housing] you can't fail to feel some kind of stigma, right? . . . Whereas we live in a little enclave, you know, and we're not really very identifiable as anything. I think that's really quite important. Yeah. Really, *really* important, in fact. . . . We just blend in. We're not very noticeable. (Anne-Marie)

> I get . . . a lot of really positive responses about living in [my co-op]. . . . So I'm

hoping that, because of that, [my son's] going to have more of a positive experience with growing up. And not have that stigma attached to him, of, "You live in low-income housing," and stuff like that. 'Cause . . . it's really hard for a kid to hear that. (Norma)

So, affordability helped these women meet the needs of their children. Moreover, it helped them do so in ways that went beyond the basic requirement for shelter. The quality of housing it delivered also meant their children had a better chance of growing up with a healthy sense of self-worth.

Housing Location

Affordability also connected these women to resources available outside the co-op. This was especially important for women raising families alone, as they were able to live closer to the downtown core, and/or in a better quality neighbourhood than they otherwise could. Central location was important because it placed households within easy reach of facilities and services not available in outlying areas. Most single mothers in this study relied on public transit, so proximity to high-quality daycares, schools, medical services, and their place of employment was often crucial to their ability to juggle multiple responsibilities. For Lucy, location was the primary reason for moving into her co-op. It put her within easy reach of a high-quality daycare and school, a large park and playground, and her place of employment. This, she said, made juggling her daily tasks "much more manageable" than it had been in her previous suburban apartment.

Location not only simplified these women's lives; it also helped them provide opportunities for their children. For example, living downtown could mean children were exposed to a broader range of experiences than they would have been in other similarly priced housing.

> On the weekend I don't have to range far with my kids to find something interesting that's happening. . . . And 'specially, being a person with limited income and no car, I find that tremendously beneficial for my kids. . . . Because the reality of Toronto is that, like I said, for [what I pay here], where am I going to live? The edges of Scarborough? . . . I mean, just the reality, I think, for a lot of, especially single moms, is when you have to live in the middle of nowhere and you're an hour-and-a-half bus ride away from anything enjoyable, or especially [anything] free [of charge], you're not going to go do it. (Monica)

For single women who had lived downtown even before moving into a co-op, the significance of location was less that it gave them access to facilities and services than that it improved the quality of the surrounding neighbourhood. These women had often lived in areas that were unsafe and/or otherwise not "family friendly," simply because this was all they could afford. By improving the quality of their neighbourhood, affordability made parenting a less risky undertaking for these women. Karen recalled that the rental units she had lived in with her older son "were places where I would have to escort my son to the door, they were so unsafe." Her younger son had grown up in a co-op, and this, she said, had "made all the difference in the world, between . . . life for my [older] son and life for my [younger] son."

For these single women, affordability did not, in itself, challenge the notion of maternal responsibility for their children's well-being.

For the most part, they drew on the resources available to them through their housing to sustain their personal responsibility for child rearing. In fact, a significant minority of women who had received RGI over the long-term remained quite isolated from their local community. From this perspective, then, affordability *per se* served to shore up privatization and not to redistribute the burden of care beyond the household.

Ties to Other Members as a Resource Channel

The same is not true, however, of the second channel through which these women gained access to the resources needed to raise a family—their ties to other members of the community. Ties to neighbours gave the women in this study various types of practical help with the work of raising a family. But they also provided another resource that could be equally, or sometimes more, important—the socio-emotional support that nourished them on a more personal level and at times made the local community come to resemble an extended family.

Practical Support

Many women received small, but important, assistance with general household tasks through their ties to other co-op members. So, for example, members sometimes picked up groceries or emergency items, or ran errands, for each other; or they borrowed or loaned vehicles, equipment, or supplies. Several women also exchanged clothes and/or toys with neighbours; and in at least one co-op, members had organized a more formal clothing exchange that operated out of their laundry facility. Meal preparation was sometimes shared, most often in emergency situations such as a serious illness or injury, or following a birth or death in the family; occasionally, though, members who were especially close engaged in this type of exchange on a more regular basis. Skills exchanges (e.g., haircutting, sewing, gardening, or providing "alternative" health care) were important in a few cases; and child care exchanges—mostly on an irregular basis, but occasionally more formally organized—also occurred between women who were close, or whose children were close. All these exchanges took some of the work of raising a family beyond the boundaries of the household, and therefore off the shoulders of individual women.

One of the most frequently mentioned forms of practical support, however, indicates something unique about this kind of setting. Especially in co-ops with shared outdoor space, women described being able to spontaneously call on other members to watch preschool-aged or young school-aged children in the co-op yard while they "r[a]n into the house to start dinner" or did other small tasks or errands. In fact, 16 of the 25 women made spontaneous reference to this kind of exchange being (or having been) a regular part of their life. This includes nearly all of those who lived in co-ops with shared yards, and a few other women as well. As Fiona explained, "There's a community of moms. And we watch each other's kids." Elizabeth echoed the sentiment. "You know your neighbours' children; they know your children; so we tend to look out for each other that way."

Similarly, women with older school-aged children, while not feeling their children needed full-time supervision, nevertheless found relief in the knowledge that they lived in a community with "many eyes watching" as their children played outside on co-op property. These women's experiences suggest that

a kind of *collective responsibility for children* can and does develop in this setting. Monica put it this way: "After school and on the weekends and stuff, people keep their eyes on all the kids around here. You don't see kids messing around without some adult going, 'Hey,' you know, 'I know your parents.'" This aspect of co-op life stands in contrast to the notion of personal/familial responsibility associated with the privatization of family life.

Where it existed, the sense of collective responsibility for children was especially important to women (generally single women) whose household-level resources were strained, or women whose children were unusually vulnerable for any reason. Carmen, a single mother of two, had serious health challenges that placed her at risk of being unable to care for her children. Living in a co-op she found, to her great surprise and relief, that other members treated her children like their own, and so eased some of the frightening burden of sole responsibility.

> When I didn't live in the co-op I was constantly very scared. . . . I realized, what happens if something happen[s] to me? What happens with my kids? . . . So when I came here . . . I immediately became more relaxed about it, knowing that my kids could go any place, any neighbour's, because they knew them, they talked to them. . . . They knew my situation.

Kathleen, whose son had a learning disability, took comfort in the knowledge that he was surrounded by people who understood him and were therefore more inclined to treat him with compassion.

> It's been really good to know that the kids that he plays with on the street, that their

parents know him. They know that he's a lot younger [mentally] than he appears to be. They know, they just know the situation, and I don't have to, sort of, worry.

The sense of collective responsibility for children came to Gillian's aid when her older daughter suffered a serious illness that permanently changed the child's life. Neighbours "watch[ed] out for her" because they cared about her well-being. Moreover, this caring was important to Gillian because it signified their ability to see "beyond" the young woman's difficulties, and affirmed her daughter's continuing value in the eyes of others. "People knew her before. And they still know her now. And that's really important for me." The kind of ongoing commitment in the face of challenges that Carmen, Kathleen, and Gillian described is akin to what *family* members are typically expected to provide for one another.

For all these women, then, the sense of collective responsibility for children that developed in this setting resembled the kind of "caring" generally associated with family. Because this attitude extended to the entire local community on some level, their children were better cared for, and/or the women themselves were less overworked, than would have been the case in a privatized setting where children have only their parent(s) to turn to.

Socio-emotional Support

Ties to other members of the co-op also provided a more personal form of support to women engaged in family work. They were the source of ongoing socio-emotional exchanges that helped these women face the challenges of raising children. These exchanges consisted primarily of talking, but sometimes included "just being there" in times of need. They grew directly out of the fact that these women had regular contact with one another in the course of their daily activities. Moreover, this contact was especially likely to occur when the women's daily activities were based in the home—the very circumstance that leads to isolation in a more privatized setting.

For example, Fiona commented that living in a collective setting kept her from feeling alone while she was at home with an infant.

When she was really little and I'd be feeling a little stir-crazy I would just walk out into the courtyard, go around the block. I'd run into someone, have a nice conversation about something, and I'd go back home feeling a lot better. And that's been really important, for sure. . . . It saved me, a few times, from . . . feeling overwhelmed or sad.

Likewise, some women who had lived outside their co-op during at least one child's infancy regretted not having moved in sooner for just this kind of reason. Elaine described the first two years of her daughter's life, living in a suburban townhouse, as a time of feeling "disconnected" and "very isolated." And Victoria recalled a similar experience during her daughter's infancy in a suburban apartment building. "It was the most horrendous year, probably, of my entire life—well, *definitely*, of my entire life. . . . I was so isolated. I was so lonely. . . . The next move was basically because I was *so* unhappy there." Hannah, who had spent her first two children's infancy in private housing and her third child's infancy in a co-op, remarked on the difference between the two settings. "You know, when you have a baby, and the kind of isolation that can go on when you have a baby. You don't have that here. Or you're less likely to have that here, because you can just step outside [and find someone to talk to].” So, having others nearby for social contact and emotional support was especially important for women at home with an infant. During this period of heavy demands these women did not feel they coped alone; and this stood in contrast to their experiences in private housing.

The socio-emotional support they received through their ties to other members was also important to women at home with preschool-aged and young school-aged children. The reasons were similar to, though less pronounced than, those of women with infants. Julia, whose partner worked very long hours, had sole responsibility for her school-aged children. She had been at home with them until her youngest entered school; and with little money and no car, leaving the house had been difficult. She explained how living in a collective setting had allowed her to connect with other mothers of young children without really having to leave home.

> Living in a co-op brings people together. . . . Whereas if you weren't living in a co-op . . . you'd have to go out and join something to get that. . . . But when you're in a co-op . . . the whole point is that you're *supposed* to be doing things together. . . . So, even if you don't consciously plan it that way, you're setting up a situation where you're in a group of other parents who are in the same situation.

Women with teenaged children often continued to value the socio-emotional support of other members as their children entered adolescence. This was especially true of single women who had lived in the co-op through their children's younger years. Marilyn, a lone parent with a teenager and a grown child, had gone through a difficult period with her daughter during the young woman's early teens. She explained, after a long pause that suggested it was painful to recall, what living in a co-op community had meant to her during this emotionally trying time.

> And then, of course, when [my daughter] left home for that period of time, I had a lot of support. And there were people I knew I could just phone. And people . . . —two in particular—I became very close friends with. We would sit over coffee after [co-op] meetings and just *talk*. . . . It was great. . . . It was a *lifesaver*.

Similarly, Alice, a single parent of a grown child, had turned to fellow co-op members for moral support during her daughter's teenage years.

> [Living in a co-op has made being a single parent] easier because there are more people. There are more people who have either been there [or can offer] moral support. . . . I mean, what do I do with my horrible [teenager], you know? And you find out . . . other people have lived through it. . . . And you don't feel quite so bad.

Once again, the ties between neighbours that developed in this setting expanded the boundaries of home and family, so that women felt less alone in the challenges of raising children.

The feeling that a shared concern for children's well-being existed among members of the local community was, however, much less common for women with teenagers than it was for women with younger children. In fact, several women stated that their older children were somewhat alienated from the co-op community. Patti, for example, commented that her co-op was very supportive of young children, but that it often failed to address the needs and concerns of teenagers. "It's a wonderful, wonderful place for raising kids. . . . People take care of the kids. People really do. It's just the youth and up they get a little stitchy about." This suggests that the socio-emotional support women with teenaged children received in this setting was most often directed toward the women themselves, not toward their children.

Sometimes, however, socio-emotional support did come through older children's contact with other adult members of the community. Women who referred to this phenomenon all had children who at the time of interview were in their early twenties, but who had grown up in the co-op. These women described feeling validated as parents because other members, having been a part of their children's growing up, were genuinely interested in these young adults as individuals in their own right.

> As [my daughter] goes through the courtyard, people stop and ask how she is, what she's doing. They are . . . genuinely interested in her life. . . . It's a really nice feeling to hear from someone else that they've talked with your child. . . . That's a very affirming thing as a parent, to have other people interested in your child separately from you. (Victoria)

Gillian echoed the sentiment: "There is, for me, a sense of validation in that [experience] . . . as a parent. And also . . . there's a really nice sense that other people have been part of [my children's] growing up." Once more, these women's comments suggest that they did not feel alone in an aspect of parenting that generally follows from being a close family member—the genuine valuing of the child that develops in the context of regular ongoing contact.

The socio-emotional support women received from fellow members was also important during the sometimes lengthy process of getting back on their feet following a marital breakup.

> I guess the one thing that stood out [during my early time as a single parent] is . . . there were a couple of women who were in the same situation as me, who were staying focused. You know, they weren't falling apart. . . . We would touch base from time to time, you know, call on the phone, get together, maybe go out for a drink or something like that. And that was a real, sort of, solidarity. . . . That was comforting. (Barbara)

> [When my first marriage broke up] I knew . . . other single moms in the co-op, and was able to get some support from them. [That] was a really great source of comfort to me in all those questions—you know, "Have I done the wrong thing? It's better to stay together for the kids," and all that stuff. (Kathleen)

So, these women drew on the socio-emotional support of members of the local community to help them sustain their families during periods of high demand, in which supports within the household were absent or in short supply.

On the most general level, the practical and socio-emotional support women received through their ties to other co-op members led to a sense of being supported in their child rearing at a level beyond the household. As Victoria said, "[The co-op community] has been the underpinning, in some ways, of my parenting, for the last [18] years. . . . [It's given me] a feeling that there was a constant that I could depend on." For Hannah, it was "a really good feeling to know that there are people—and quite a few of them, actually—who would be there for you. And for your kids. . . . [It's a] sort of safety net, actually." Carmen added that, "[I feel that] I'm not the only mother. There's also the mothers of the others, looking [out] for all the children. So that [is] something I find amazing. You know, I don't have to take care of my children alone." In other words, for these women, raising a family was in some respects a community rather than a private household concern. Although as mothers they retained primary responsibility for their children's well-being, they clearly felt they had strong "backing" in their role as a parent through their ties to other members of the local community. The result, as Julia explained, was that living in a supportive community "makes me a better mother."

One final form of socio-emotional support women gained through their ties to members of the local community was a sense of physical safety, for themselves and their children, in the knowledge that they were surrounded by "familiar" others. Several women contrasted this feeling with the fear and insecurity they had experienced in previous housing.

> I've had a couple of pretty lousy incidents with men when I was little, and as an adult, when I was [in our previous apartment]. So I'm pretty sensitive about that. [But] I always felt safe here, being surrounded by people who, you know, know me and would hear if something strange was going on. (Gwen)

> It's safer. It's absolutely safer for my kids [here]. . . . There's a bond with the people across the street because they're also in the co-op. . . . It's ki-i-ind of like a little bit of [an] extended family community. And sometimes it's really made a big

difference. Safer. My younger son [raised in the co-op] feels more secure. (Karen)

As Karen's comments suggest, the ties to neighbours that developed in this setting could create the kind of comfort normally associated, at least on the ideological level, with family. Thus this sense of physical safety is another measure of the extent to which the boundaries around the family household were expanded in this setting, to incorporate the local community.

Co-op Networks as Extended Family

Indeed, women raising families in co-op housing often indicated that they thought of their ties to other members as constituting a kind of *extended family*. Ten of the 25 women in the study spontaneously named other co-op members as part of what Gillian called "chosen family," or "spiritual family"—that is, people who were not related by blood or marriage, but who could be counted on to "be there" in times of need.

> I always think there's your blood family . . . and the ones that you choose as well. And I think of them as more my spiritual family. And there are people in the co-op that I would say that of. I just know that, you know, even if one of us moves, that we'll always be a part of each other's lives. (Gillian)

Similarly, Hannah thought of members of her co-op as "family" "in the sense that . . . I could rely on them . . . if I needed anything for my kids." Kathleen also experienced her co-op as something of an "extended family." In part, this feeling grew out of her personal history. She had first lived in the co-op as a teenager in her parents' household, and later had moved to her own unit in the same co-op where both her parents and brother had separate residences. The blood relatives had since moved away, but Kathleen felt the co-op community as a whole had "*become* a family." Similarly, Carmen commented that "[When] you are 18 years in the same place and with the same people, it's your family, and you create a family." Other women used family terminology to refer to specific neighbours with whom they were especially close. Monica, for example, spoke of three of her neighbours as being "like a sister." And Victoria described how one of her neighbours, "just sort of walks in [to my place]. She goes through the cupboards and gets what she wants. And I think she feels like she's part of our family here." Elizabeth talked about a teenaged neighbour who felt "like an adopted daughter, or a niece, maybe," and who was "like a big sister to my kids." Julia referred to a neighbouring couple as "my kids' honorary grandparents," while Gillian thought of one of her neighbours as her daughter's "guardian angel." Still other women described a kind of pride in association generally reserved for family or very close friends. Irene, for example, referred to the "family pride" she and many of her fellow members felt in connection with several well-known former co-op residents—writers, artists, and political figures who had made a name for themselves in the world at large. "We always feel when somebody's sort of getting their name out there, apart from the co-op, there is a family sort of feeling here." And Freda, Hannah, and Gillian all talked about the connections they felt to children from other co-op households they had watched grow from babyhood or childhood into young adulthood.

I know all the kids here. I know all the teenagers. You know? All of the kids that have grown up here. If I see them on the street in another part of the city they say hello. . . . I think that's big. (Freda)

Not only do you have your own kids, but you have all these other children out there. And you're just watching this whole community grow. You watch these kids grow up. (Hannah)

[With a couple of young women in the co-op I've] had conversations that don't have to do with [their] parents' concerns. [It's] just between the two of us. And that is . . . for me, a real privilege, to have the opportunity of being able to talk with, you know, a young woman [I've watched grow up]. (Gillian)

All of these examples suggest that the meaning these women attached to their ties to members of the local community resembles the meaning attached to "family." Thus, for many women living in this setting, the boundaries of family life were, in this less tangible but still very real sense, expanded to include the local community.

The sense of belonging to a unit larger than the family household was most important to the women who needed more resources than their own households could supply. Single women, for example, were especially inclined to see the community as extended family. Victoria talked about how, living in the same community for many years, she had become "part of the web." And Hannah referred to the general sense she had, in her co-op, that other members were "there for you," and that there was always a "safety net" to fall back on in times of need. The sense of being surrounded by extended family was also very important to women who had weathered a crisis during their time in the co-op. Freda, whose youngest child had been born with a physical disability, put it matter-of-factly: "I don't think I would have been able to raise my [youngest child] without the support I've found here." And Carmen described how, during and following her own near-fatal illness, her neighbours had come through for her. She said, "The neighbours, you should see the neighbours. The solidarity. . . . It's a family. It was like a family. They . . . came forward; they [looked after everything]. It was incredible. My neighbours—what they did!" Victoria had weathered three separate health crises with the help of neighbours. During this time she had received everything from in-home medical attention, through personal care, to care for her daughter. And when Gillian's daughter had suffered a permanently crippling illness, the family had received support from neighbours ranging from financial aid, through assistance with day-to-day tasks, to emotional support. In every case, these women felt they had received aid that went far beyond what they would have expected from neighbours. Instead, they felt it mimicked what they would have expected from family members.

Women not only experienced this extended family feeling directly; they also experienced it through their children. That is, many of them felt that their children also "belonged" to a unit larger than their own household. Membership in such a unit is implied by the sense of collective responsibility for children that often developed in this setting, and the way other adults often took an interest in grown-up co-op children as individuals. But beyond this, many women also felt their children had developed special bonds with other children in the co-op. As Karen explained, "You know, it's a co-op, and the kids share that bond." Indeed, these women sometimes maintained that their children's ongoing contact with other co-op children came to resemble sibling interactions.

There's also kids a little older, a little younger so, you know, [my daughter] can get a range of experience. . . . She has the experience of a brother through [one of those] relationship[s]. . . . Because we've done so much back and forth . . . they are that close. (Freda)

You go out there [into the shared yard], and whoever's out there is the person you play with. If they're four, if they're nine, if they're 16 . . . It's a great thing because, you know, if you don't have older brothers and sisters—and there's a lot of only kids—they have a tremendous benefit of getting close to both boys and girls who are older and younger. (Gillian)

There is an obvious link between viewing the co-op community as extended family and feeling that some measure of collective responsibility for children exists in this setting. Given that the sense of collective responsibility was the source of such important benefits, it is no surprise to find that women sometimes fostered the sense of extended family in their children. One of the ways they did this was by encouraging their children to think of the entire co-op as "home." Fiona recounted a conversation between her daughter and the mother of her daughter's friend (who lived in private housing), in which this approach is evident. The child's friend had recited her street address and the friend's mother had then asked Fiona's daughter, "Do you know where you live?" As Fiona recalled, "[My daughter] said, 'Yeah, I live at [the co-op].'" And so [the mother] said, "But what number?" Her daughter had had no answer because, as Fiona had explained to the other woman, "*It doesn't matter*. If she turned up at the co-op someone would bring her home." Fiona interpreted this incident as evidence of her daughter's sense that the co-op community was a kind of extended family—a unique "social set" that reached beyond the family household, and one to which the little friend did not have access.

> [My daughter] has a sense of something that a lot of other kids don't, which is her community—her immediate community. And so when you say to her "the co-op" it *means* something to her. . . . It's a whole other, sort of, social set that most people don't have. . . . And she sometimes feels sad for people who don't live in co-ops. That's what she says.

Freda described an incident that demonstrated that her daughter, too, had learned to think of the entire co-op as "home." Although the child had misunderstood the location of its boundaries, she had not misunderstood the message that the co-op as a whole was her "home turf."

> A couple of weeks ago we had a funny thing. We couldn't find the kids.[4] . . . And then my one friend said, "Well, I found . . . my granddaughter two doors up from the co-op, with a little friend there." . . . And I went and got [my daughter] and I brought her back, and I was very upset, and [told her], "You can't leave the co-op." And she says, "Well, I didn't know that wasn't part of the co-op."

Encouraging their children to think of the entire co-op as "home" (and the community as "family") released both parents and children from an overly tight grip on each other's time and energies. It gave children a freedom of movement they might not otherwise have had, and at the same time relieved parents of some of the pressure associated with being "on duty" at all times.

> [My daughter] comes home and has a snack after school, and goes out. And, you know, I don't see her until suppertime. . . . And because we . . . have the fencing along the streets and so on, the property is very well defined. And, you know, as long as they stay within its boundaries, I can make two phone calls and find her. (Freda)

Patti described feeling similarly released from perpetual vigilance when the children from her first marriage were young. "[Living in a co-op with a shared yard], I could keep the kids sort of 'corralled,' and I wouldn't have to be looking at them every two minutes of the day."

The freedom of movement that came from living in a community where everyone knew each other, and where people looked out for each other's children, relieved women in another sense. It meant children always had easy access to playmates, which took some of the pressure off their parent(s) to plan social activities for them. As Gwen put it, "I think the advantages [to living in a co-op] are the kids. They have direct access to a whole group of other children out there. You know, you don't have to go looking for it." Freda and Fiona both made similar comments:

> We didn't do kindergarten with [my daughter]. . . . I never felt that there was difficulty with that, because there were so many other children here—so that she could gain the experience of peer group. (Freda)

> [The courtyard is] a really great, giant front yard full of kids [my daughter's] age. And so they all just toddle out there. (Fiona)

So, the sense that the local community was a kind of extended family released both women and children from some of the constraints that accompany a more privatized approach to family life.

Shared Values

There was an important underpinning to this extended family feeling—the sense that members, or at least a core group of them, shared a similar set of values. The content of these shared values was not necessarily explicit, and likely varied from one group to another; but the sense that they were among "like-minded others" was a theme that ran through the interviews of women with strong ties to other members. Carmen felt "at home" in her community because, "In terms of . . . the philosophy of the co-op, it was great [to move here], to understand that, in a way, I was really in a place close to my values that I came with." And Freda, who had raised her older children mostly in private housing, described her early parenting as a time that "really pushed me over the edge" because there was no support for the kind of "left-wing politics" she had been involved in before having a family. By contrast, she felt comfortable in her current environment because it was what she referred to as "an *alternative* co-op." She explained that, "because we're an alternative kind of housing . . . then alternative people tend to situate themselves here." As a result, Freda found support for her own political activism and involvement in alternative health care.

The significance of shared values was not only that it validated women personally; it also created an environment in which they felt that their children would be nourished in much the same way as they were at home. Usually, the values cited in this connection were linked in some way to a sense of collective responsibility for people and/or the environment. Women felt that living in a collective setting encouraged their children to practise those ideals in their daily lives in a way that living in private housing could not. For example, several women spoke with pride of how their children participated in collective clean-up days, or shovelled snow or picked up garbage in the co-op on a regular basis. They felt that this fostered in their children a sense of responsibility toward a unit larger than their own household—a sense that would not have developed as easily and naturally in a private rental or ownership situation. Barbara described it this way: "Because we live in a co-op, they can get the sense of the bigger picture that, you know, you don't just stop at the edge of your grass. You know, if there's a piece of garbage on the road, that you pick it up. . . . You know, this belongs to *all* of us." Carmen echoed the sentiment. "[Being involved in shared activities meant] they grew up feeling that we have a responsibility, you know. And this is wonderful. . . . So they grew up with different values about the place they live. They have to share more." Likewise, several women were pleased to see their children learning to think and act collectively as they shared a play area with other children in the co-op. As Carmen noted, "[All the] children play together, and they're very caring [toward] each other." Gillian elaborated on children's experience growing up in a cooperative setting.

> Kids who've grown up here, they [teach] the younger kids. . . . So there is a modelling on that level as well. . . . [And] the sense of who gets to play is very different [from private housing]. It's not "who's in, who's out." [If] you're here, you're in.

At least as important as the *content* of the values to which children were exposed in this environment, though, was the feeling that members of the community *shared* them. This was important because it meant parents' belief systems were reinforced outside the household. Hannah explained that living in a co-op underscored for her children "life values that, you know, you hope would be passed on to your children." As a result, the job of raising a family fell less heavily on the shoulders of parents themselves. As Gillian put it, "[When kids] see their parents' values lived out in other households, among other adults, it bears much more weight." Thus, living in a community where values were shared gave these women a feeling that there was support beyond the household for their children's social development.[5] This, in turn, laid the foundation for a shift in the way they conceptualized reproductive tasks. Rather than seeing this work as only a private matter, women living on co-op housing were able to turn often to the local community, and to find a surprising range of supports for child rearing located there.

Conclusion

This study has highlighted the phenomenon of access to community-level resources in a co-operative setting. It has identified and described the range of resources available, and shown how that access was structured. It has argued that the resources available to women raising families in this setting were both tangible (material and practical) and intangible (socio-emotional). It has argued, further, that women's access to resources in this environment could be seen as a system comprising two distinct channels—affordability and ties to other members. The distinction between the two resource channels corresponds in some ways to the distinction between the two resource types; however, the correspondence

is not absolute. Although one channel (affordability) ostensibly provided only a material resource and the other (ties between members) was rooted in socio-emotional resources, the interview material demonstrates that at least the second channel actually delivered a range of tangible and intangible resources. The goal of conceptualizing access to resources in this manner is, however, more than descriptive. Ultimately the aim is to tease out the consequences for the organization of family life and caregiving work. With that in mind, several general points can be drawn from the analysis.

Regarding affordability, two points can be made. First, this resource had a number of quality-of-life implications for these women that went beyond the basic problem of securing shelter. Whether by freeing up parental time and money or by reducing family members' exposure to risk or stigma, affordability made the challenges these women faced raising their children more manageable. The second general point that can be made about affordability is that it bore a mixed relationship to the organization of family life. On the one hand, it decreased economic dependency on marriage. In this respect it seemed to challenge the assumed (nuclear family) context for child rearing. Yet, the provision of affordable housing did not, by itself, challenge the notion of women's *personal responsibility for children*. Access to affordable housing may have made the job more manageable but it did not fundamentally change the nature of the work.

With regard to the second resource channel, again, two general points can be drawn from the analysis of the interview material. First, like affordability, ties to other members delivered a variety of types of support. And like affordability, too, the significance of this support was often that it enabled women to better fulfill family roles and responsibilities.

So, for example, members may have exchanged services and thereby simplified their daily routines; but they remained ultimately responsible for seeing to their family members' needs. Yet the second point that can be made about ties to other members is that the resources available through this channel did differ in important ways from those available through affordability; and where they differed there were important ramifications for the organization of family work. These ties could involve shared values, a sense of extended family, and perhaps most important of all, a sense of *collective responsibility for children*. To the extent that they involved these elements, ties to other members began to dissolve the boundaries of the family household. In this respect, they went some distance toward remaking reproductive work as a community rather than only a private familial matter.

Notes

1. The terms "family work," "caregiving work," "domestic tasks," "reproductive work," or simply "family life," are used interchangeably here to describe this form of labour.
2. RGI is the term for a group of government-funded programs that provide housing charge assistance to co-op households, based on need and availability. They are administered at the co-op level, but in accordance with government regulations that determine eligibility. Charges are set as a proportion of total household income, and the difference between the cost to the household and the actual cost of the unit is covered by government funds.
3. For the purposes of this discussion, practical support refers to help with family-related tasks and with meeting material needs, while socio-emotional support refers to talking, sharing experiences, and "just being there" through tough times.
4. Notice that Freda referred to both parents and children in the collective sense ("we couldn't find *the kids,*" not "I couldn't find *my daughter*"). She clearly saw herself as connected to, and in some sense jointly responsible for, individuals beyond her own household.
5. This chapter focuses on the advantages of collectivism for women with family responsibilities. These advantages were identified by the majority of the women interviewed for this study. However, a small minority of study participants (all of whom desperately needed the affordable housing) were quite alienated from their co-op communities and thus did not benefit from the collective aspect of their surroundings. Indeed, this feature of co-op life actually proved costly to such women. It added an additional layer to their family work—the tasks involved in "defending" family privacy in a setting that supported fluid boundaries (Worts 2005).

References

Burke, M.A. 1994. "People in Co-operative Housing," in *Canadian Social Trends* (Toronto: Thompson Educational Publishing).

Collins, P.H. 1990. *Black Feminist Thought: Knowledge, Consciousness, and the Politics of Empowerment* (New York: Routledge).

Cooper, M., and M.C. Rodman. 1992. *New Neighbours: A Case Study of Co-operative Housing in Toronto* (Toronto: University of Toronto Press).

Cowan, C.P., and P.A. Cowan. 1992. *When Partners Become Parents: The Big Life Change for Couples* (New York: Basic Books).

Daly, M. 1994. "Comparing Welfare States: Towards a Gender-friendly Approach," in *Gendering Welfare States*, ed. D. Sainsbury (Thousand Oaks, CA: Sage Publications).

Dobash, R.E., and R. Dobash. 1979. *Violence against Wives: A Case against the Patriarchy* (London: Open Books).

Fox, B.J. 1997. "Reproducing Difference: Changes in the Lives of Partners Becoming Parents," in *Feminism and Families: Critical Policies and Changing Practices*, ed. M. Luxton (Halifax, NS: Fernwood).

Goldberg, G., and E. Kremen. 1990. *The Feminization of Poverty: Only in America?* (New York: Praeger).

Oakley, A. 1974. *The Sociology of Housework* (London: Martin Robertson).

Rosenberg, H. 1987. "Motherwork, Stress, and Depression: The Costs of Privatized Social Reproduction," in *Feminism and Political Economy*, eds H.J. Maroney and M. Luxton (Toronto: Methuen).

Sainsbury, D. 1994. *Gendering Welfare States* (Thousand Oaks, CA: Sage Publications).

Selby, J.L., and A. Wilson. 1988. *Canada's Housing Co-operatives: An Alternative Approach to Resolving Community Problems* (Vancouver: UBC School of Community and Regional Planning).

Spector, A.N., and F. Klodawsky. 1993. "The Housing Needs of Single Parent Families in Canada: A Dilemma for the 1990s," in *Single Parent Families: Perspectives on Research and Policy*, eds J. Hudson and B. Galaway (Toronto: Thompson Educational Publishing).

Stack, C. 1973. *All Our Kin* (New York: Harper & Row).

Weckerle, G.R., and S. Novac. 1989. "Developing Two Women's Housing Co-operatives," in *New Households, New Housing*, eds K.A. Franck and S. Ahrentzen (New York: Van Nostrand Reinhold).

Worts, D. 2005. "'It Just Doesn't Feel Like You're Obviously In': Housing Policy, Family Privacy, and the Reproduction of Social Inequality," *Canadian Review of Sociology and Anthropology* 42, 4: 445–65.

Chapter 15

As Kath Weston wrote years ago, lesbians' and gays' families are "chosen" in a way that the families of heterosexual couples often are not. Weston was describing the fact that many lesbians and gays had been rejected by their families of origin when they "came out," and that they worked hard to create new families based on friendship and caring. Because lesbian and gay couples must carefully plan and arrange to have children, their families are chosen in yet another sense. In this chapter, British sociologist Gillian Dunne describes the variety of ways in which lesbians in the 1990s organized their families and their child care differently than heterosexual parents. These couples' family patterns provide all parents with guidelines for handling their responsibilities in ways that do not involve gender inequalities.

Opting into Motherhood: Lesbians Blurring the Boundaries and Transforming the Meaning of Parenthood and Kinship

Gillian A. Dunne

The extension of educational and employment opportunities for women, together with widening experience of the "plastic" nature of sexualities (Giddens 1992: 57), has enabled increasing numbers of Western women to construct independent identities and lifestyles beyond traditional marriage, motherhood, and indeed, heterosexuality (Dunne 1997). As contemporary women's identities expand to incorporate the expectations and activities that have been traditionally associated with masculinity, there has not been an equivalent shift of male identity, let alone practice, into the traditional domains of women. Exceptions notwithstanding (Blaisure and Allen 1995; Doucet 1995; Ehrensaft 1987; VanEvery 1995), a distinctly asymmetrical division of labour remains the majority pattern (Berk 1985; Brannen and Moss 1991; Ferri and Smith 1996; Gregson and Lowe 1995; Hochschild 1989). The intransigent nature of the gender division of labour means that women continue to perform the bulk of domestic work and that mothers bear the brunt of the social and economic penalties associated with caring for children. Men's relative freedom from the time constraints and labour associated with the home and parenting enables them to be more singleminded in the pursuit of employment opportunities and retain their labour-market advantages.

The perceived contradiction between employment success and motherhood has led to a growth in the numbers of women opting into a paid-working life and out of motherhood (Campbell 1985: 5–8; Morell 1994: 11). Changing patterns of household and family formation have stimulated debates in Europe and North America as to whether there has been a decline in the importance of kinship and family life (Popeno 1988; Scott 1997). Given the way that motherhood represents a core signifier of femininity, and the powerful social pressure on married couples to have children, academic interest is turning to voluntary childlessness (Campbell 1985; Abshoff and Hird 1998; McAllister and Clarke 1998; Morell 1994).

While women's decisions to remain child-free can be framed in terms of resistance in the context of heterosexuality (Abshoff and Hird 1998; Morell 1994), we need to remember that other groups of women are perceived to be excluded from the procreative equation (see Silva and Smart 1996). In common with gay men, lesbian women are popularly represented and viewed as barren (Weston 1991). At one level, lesbians, by virtue of their sexuality, represent a vanguard of women who escape social pressure to become parents. Indeed, this freedom to "construct their own biographies" (Beck and Beck-Gernsheim 1995) without reference to children is understood by many as a major advantage of their sexuality (Dunne 1997). Differences in lesbian women's and gay men's relationship to reproduction and their families of origin have stimulated some fascinating North American (Weston 1991) and British (Weeks, Donovan, and Heaphy 1998) research on the recasting of kinship along lines of friendship.

While contemporary women begin to see the demands of motherhood as conflicting with their newly won bid for autonomy, there has been a recent shift in attitudes toward parenting among the lesbian population. A rising awareness of alternatives to heterosexual reproduction has led to the growing recognition that their sexuality does not preclude the possibility of lesbian and gay people having children. In Britain and in the United States, we are witnessing the early stages of a "gayby" boom, a situation wherein lesbian women and gay men are opting into parenthood in increasing numbers. According to Lewin, "The 'lesbian baby boom' and the growing visibility of lesbians who became mothers through donor

insemination constitute the most dramatic and provocative challenge to traditional notions of both family and of the non-procreative nature of homosexuality" (1993: 19). In this article, I want to address this apparent contradiction between childlessness as resistance and lesbian motherhood as provocative challenge by showing that the mothering experiences that lesbians are opting into are qualitatively different from those that some women seek to avoid.

I take the view that sexuality is socially and materially constructed and that heterosexuality plays a central role in reproducing gender inequality (Dunne 1997, 1998d, 2000). The dominance of heterosexuality is the outcome of institutional processes that render alternatives undesirable and/or unimaginable (Dunne 1997; Rich 1984) and that construct gender difference and gender hierarchies (Butler 1990: 17; Rubin 1975). Consequently, there is a crucial relationship between gender and sexuality. As Butler (1990: 17) and Rubin (1975) argue, social processes that construct gender as a meaningful category are deeply implicated in the construction of sexual preferences (Dunne 1997; 1998b). Gendered experience is mediated by sexuality in a number of other ways. For example, the existence of material constraints that usually limit women's ability to be financially self-reliant suggests that the capacity to lead a lesbian lifestyle is an economic achievement (see Dunne 1997, 2000). Additionally, we can extend the more interactive conceptions of gender formulated by Fenstermaker, West, and Zimmerman (1991) to show that the gender of the person who one does gender for and/or to and who does it to us makes a difference (see Dunne 1998b). The way that gendered action is mediated by sexual identity has important implications for the performance of household tasks and caretaking. For example, I argue (Dunne 1998b) that Berk's (1985) insightful observation about the domestic division of labour being about linking the "musts" of work to be done with the "shoulds" of gender ideals is somewhat dependent on the work being allocated between women and men. However, the unfortunate division of labour within the academy between those interested in sexuality and those interested in gender inequalities has meant that the implications of these important insights have not been fully developed in mainstream feminism (Dunne 2000).

I wish to support and extend Lewin's observations on single lesbian mothers by drawing on my work on lesbian couples who have become parents via donor insemination. I argue that an attentiveness to the gender dynamic of sexuality illuminates additional challenges that arise when women combine with women to rear children—the possibility of showing what can be achieved when gender difference as a fundamental structuring principle in interpersonal relationships is minimized (see Dunne 1997, 1998a). I suggest a complex and contradictory situation for lesbians who have opted into motherhood via donor insemination. By embracing motherhood, lesbians are making their lives "intelligible" to others—their quest to become parents is often enthusiastically supported by family and heterosexual friends. However, their sexuality both necessitates and facilitates the redefinition of the boundaries, meaning, and content of parenthood. When women parent together, the absence of the logic of polarization to inform gender scripts, and their parity in the gender hierarchy, means that, to borrow Juliet's words, "We have to make it up as we go along." Their similarities as women insist on high levels of reflexivity and enable the construction of more egalitarian approaches to financing and caring for children. In this way, some of the more negative social consequences

of motherhood can be transformed. Although not unique in their achievements, nor assured of their success, women parenting with women have a head start over heterosexual couples because of their structural similarities and the way that egalitarianism is in the interests of both partners.[1]

In an important study of divisions of labour, Berk concludes that gendered patterns of task allocation are so ingrained and taken for granted that they "hamper our ability to imagine other ways of organizing work" (1985: 199). This leads her to suggest, in a footnote, that science fiction may represent a medium for the exploration of alternative arrangements. This conclusion, however, reflects the heterosexual framework that dominates mainstream theorizing about gender, work, and family life. I contend that beyond the constraints (gender, emotional, and sexual) of heterosexual relationships, there are spaces for creative thinking about the organization of work, parenting, and the involvement of men and extended kin in children's lives. A focus on lesbian experience offers a marvellous opportunity to explore the limits and possibilities of egalitarianism without recourse to science fiction (see Dunne 1998a, 1998b). The solutions women together find to solving the problem of finding time for children and time to earn a living may provide models for feminists regardless of how the women define their sexuality. Greater knowledge of how egalitarianism can be operationalized may also help raise people's expectations in relation to notions of fairness and encourage change.

I shall now introduce the study and summarize some findings in relation to the respondents' parenting circumstances. I will then focus on the stories of three couples to illustrate some of the ways that these women negotiate and transform the shifting boundaries of parenthood and kinship. I have chosen these couples because their experiences are not atypical and because their stories touch upon and bring to life many of the themes that emerged in the larger study of lesbian couples.[2]

The Lesbian Household Project

The Lesbian Household Project draws on the experience of 37 cohabiting lesbian couples with dependent children.[3] It is a detailed investigation of the allocation of work and parenting responsibilities between women that aims to provide empirically grounded theoretical insights into divisions of labour more generally. Using a snowball technique, the sample was recruited from across England through a wide range of different sources. The only selection criterion was that partners be living together with at least one dependent child: all who contacted me agreed to participate and were interviewed. The majority live in the inner-city neighbourhoods (usually with high ethnic-minority populations) of three northern cities and three southern cities. The sample includes several Irish women, a Greek, an Iranian, and at least five Jewish women; all are white. As anticipated, respondents tend to be educationally and/or occupationally advantaged.[4] The majority work for public-sector employers or are self-employed. They are usually professionals, managers, technicians, or administrators in "female" occupations such as teaching, social work, local government, health, and counselling, and 70 per cent hold degrees or professional qualifications (see Dunne 1999). The sensitivity of the topic together with the invisibility of lesbians in the population means that no study of this nature can make claims of representativeness. However, there is no reason to assume that the

sample is particularly unrepresentative, especially in relation to couples who have experienced donor insemination.

A number of methods, both qualitative and quantitative, innovative and conventional, were used to illuminate respondents' employment, domestic, and caring strategies (see Dunne 1999). After the completion of a background questionnaire, both joint and individual in-depth interviews were carried out, time-use diary data were collected, and participants were contacted again two years after first contact. To help establish context and to situate the couple within their wider social environment, the first interview began with a discussion of their pathways to parenting. Respondents were then asked to map out their social and kinship networks.

Parenting Circumstances

The sample includes eight households where children were from a previous marriage, one household where the children were adopted, and 28 (75 per cent) where they had been conceived by donor insemination. In the majority of households (60 per cent), there was at least one child younger than five; and in 40 per cent of households, co-parents were also biological mothers of older, dependent, or non-dependent children. The research revealed a fairly unique and important opportunity for women parenting together—the possibility of detaching motherhood from its biological roots through the experience of social motherhood. Interestingly, 15 women in the study expressed a longstanding desire to mother as a social experience but a strong reluctance to experience motherhood biologically. These women had often taken responsibility for siblings in their families of origin and for the children of others usually featured in their lives and occupational choices. This social–biological separation also meant that motherhood is not necessarily ruled out for women who have fertility problems. Parenting was depicted as jointly shared in 30 households (80 per cent). As we will see in the three case studies, in contrast to men who share mothering (Ehrensaft 1987) yet remain happy with the identity of father, the singularity and exclusivity of the identity of mother represented a major problem for women parenting together.

Contrary to media representation in Britain, almost all of the women who had experienced donor insemination organized this informally—they rarely used National Health or even private fertility services. Respondents tended to want to know the donor, and in 86 per cent of households, this was the case. A wide range of reasons was given for this preference. A common feeling related to wanting to know that a good man, in terms of personal qualities, had a role in creating their child. Sometimes more specific ideas about biogenetic inheritance came up in discussions, and for Jewish women there was a preference for Jewish donors. Some employed the metaphor of adoption—the idea that children should have the option of knowing their biological father at some stage in the future. Commonly, donors were located through friendship networks or by advertising. Occasionally, they made use of the informal women's donor networks that exist in many British cities. When organized informally, children were always conceived by self- or partner insemination, and the majority became mothers in their current lesbian relationship.

Lesbian motherhood undermines a core signifier of heterosexuality and challenges heterosexual monopoly of and norms for parenting. The social hostility toward those parents and children who transgress the sanctity of heterosexual reproduction is such that the decision to become a mother by donor insemination can never be easily made. Typically, respondents described a lengthy period of soul-searching and planning preceding the arrival of children. For some, this process lasted as long as seven years. Unlike most women, they had to question their motives for wanting children, to critique dominant ideas about what constitutes a "good" mother and family, and to think about the implications of bringing up children in a wider society intolerant of difference. Informing this process was much research—reading the numerous self-help books that are available on lesbian parenting, watching videos on the topic, and attending discussion groups. I would suggest that lesbian parenting via donor insemination is the "reflexive project" par excellence described by Giddens (1992: 30). For respondents in partnerships, a central part of this process was the exploration of expectations in relation to parenting, for example, attitudes to discipline, schooling, and if and how far responsibilities would be shared. Key considerations related to employment situations. Respondents did not expect or desire a traditional division of labour, and thus timing was often influenced by their preference to integrate child care and income generation. In the meanwhile, potential donors were contacted. Respondents described a fairly lengthy process of negotiation with donors that focused on establishing a mutuality in parenting expectations and, if he was previously unknown to the couple, getting to know each other and developing confidence. While recognizing the generosity of potential donors, some were rejected because of personality clashes or concerns about motives, but more usually, rejection was because a donor wanted too much or too little involvement.

Men featured in the lives of most of the children, and it was not unusual for donors to have regular contact with their offspring (40 per cent of households); in three households, fathers were actively co-parenting. This involvement was usually justified in terms of providing children with the opportunity to "normalize" their family arrangements by being able to talk to peers about doing things with father. Donors were usually gay men—and all male co-parents were gay. This preference appeared to be based on three main assumptions. First was the respondents' perceptions of gay men as representing more aware, acceptable, and positive forms of masculinity. Their desire to involve men (donors or other male friends) in the lives of children, particularly boys, was often described as being about counteracting dominant stereotypes of masculinity. Second, because of the particularities of gay men's lifestyles, respondents believed that they would be less likely to renege on agreements. Third, they thought that should a dispute arise, a heterosexual donor (particularly if he were married) had greater access to formal power to change arrangements in relation to access and custody. That none expressed any serious difficulties in relation to father and/or donor involvement attests to the value of the careful negotiation of expectations before the arrival of children. It also says much about the integrity and generosity of the men concerned, although it must be noted that most had preschool-aged children, and conflicts of interests may come as the children mature.

In situations where children had been conceived in a previous marriage or heterosexual relationship, there was more diversity and conflict regarding fathers' involvement. In several cases, the father had unsuccessfully contested custody on the grounds of the mother's lesbianism. Indeed, two had appeared on daytime television arguing that their ex-wives' sexuality conflicted with their capacity to be good mothers. There were also examples of good relations between mothers and ex-husbands. While there were several examples of fathers having lost contact with their children, in most cases, respondents suggested that the child or children had more quality time with their fathers after divorce than before. Despite tensions and possible conflict between mothers and ex-husbands, these respondents suggested that they worked hard to maintain their children's relationships with the fathers. Thus, ironically, in this group as well as in the donor insemination group of parents, there are examples of highly productive models of co-operation between women and men in parenting.

The role of fathers and/or donors and other male friends in children's lives reminds us that lesbian parenting does not occur in a social vacuum. While generally hostile to the idea of the privatized nuclear family, respondents were keen to establish more extended family networks of friends and kin. Often, respondents described the arrival of children as bringing them closer to or helping repair difficult relations with their families of origin. Typically, they described a wide circle of friends (lesbian "aunties," gay "uncles," and heterosexual friends) and kin supporting their parenting.

I now want to illustrate some of these themes by drawing on the voices of respondents in three partnerships where parenting was shared and where men were involved.

Vivien and Cay's Story

We do feel lonely and unsupported and isolated at times, but we also feel very confident and excited about the way that we've carved out our family and the way that we go forward with it and the way that we parent. So although it's kind of a lonely path because there's not a lot of us to kind of reflect on each other, I don't see that as, oh, poor us. I see that more as, well, we're trying something out here and we've just got to get on with it. (Vivien)[5]

It was not uncommon to find a woman who had been married and had grown-up children who was starting over again with a partner who wanted to have children herself (*n* = 4). Women parenting together was understood as offering the opportunity to experience parenting in new and exciting ways that were tempered by the wisdom that comes from already having raised children. Cay and Vivien are fairly typical of these households. Vivien, age 44, has a grown-up son, Jo, who lives independently. Cay, age 32, is the biological mother of two boys, Frank, age four, and Steve, age two. When we first met, they had been living together for six years in a small terraced house in inner-city Birmingham. Cay, born in North America, is a self-employed illustrator of children's books who supplements her income by working as a cleaner. Vivien, of Irish-Greek descent, recently completed a degree and acquired her "first real job" as a probation officer. Cay told me that she had always wanted to have children and that her sexuality had not changed this desire. Vivien was enthusiastically supportive of the idea although she did not want to go through a pregnancy herself.

Like the vast majority of respondents, Vivien and Cay organized donor insemination informally. They had little difficulty in locating a willing donor—John, an old friend of Vivien's.

> Vivien: It worked out well. He's my oldest friend, and we've known each other since we were teenagers, and he has the same kind of colouring and stuff, he could be my brother in terms of colouring and looks.

Originally we asked one of my brothers to donate, and he felt he would maybe want more of an involvement, more of a say in the children's lives, and we wanted somebody who would let us have the responsibility and would take on a sort of a kindly uncle role. And John agreed to do that.

The description "kindly uncle" was frequently used by respondents to describe what was a fairly limited yet enthusiastic relationship between a donor and his child or children. Respondents almost always wanted to retain responsibility for bringing up their children. Like most of the couples in the study, Vivien and Cay regard these responsibilities as shared.

> Cay: It can't be anything but joint I think. The way we've approached it is that if it's not totally agreeable between both of us, it couldn't have really gone forward, given the kind of relationship we have. We've seen other people, you know, where one parent has said, "Well, I want a child and that's it." But the other one says, "Yes, you can have one, but I don't want to have lots of responsibility." That's not our way.

When respondents described their parenting as jointly shared, they meant that each partner took an active role in the routine pleasures, stresses, and labour of child care. In comparing current arrangements with her experience when married, Vivien described some of the advantages of the lack of demarcation around mothering:

> I can enjoy the mothering in a new and exciting way that I hadn't been able to before, because even though I was married I didn't have the freedom and sharing that I have in this relationship. I had

the weight of the responsibility for the child squarely on my shoulders. So I felt I couldn't allow myself much time to actually enjoy just being a mother, which I can do now because I know that even if one—sometimes I just play with them, and Cay can come in and put them to bed or do something else. Whereas I wouldn't have expected that before.

Like Vivien, respondents took great pleasure in child care, and this was reflected in their ordering of priorities. Cay suggested that because she and Vivien had joint responsibility for housework, they were less subject to the tyranny of maintaining high domestic standards—a sentiment reflected across the sample. This, together with their shared approach to doing tasks, she believed, gave them more fun time with their children—this was supported in the time-use data across the sample. For example, comparison of respondents' time use with trends for married parents with young children revealed that regardless of the employment status of married mothers, because they did the bulk of routine domestic work, it occupied far more of their time than child care, while the reverse was the case for respondents (Dunne 1998a).

Vivien and Cay described their roles before and after the arrival of children as interchangeable; earlier, Cay had been the main earner when Vivien was a student. Routinely, birth mothers and co-parents alike spoke of seeking integrated lives—valuing time with children, an identity from the formal workplace, and the ability to contribute financially. Within reason, they were prepared to experience a reduced standard of living to achieve the kind of quality of life desired. Thus, there was an unusually wide range of partner–employment strategies in the sample. Like

Vivien and Cay, some took turns in who was the main earner, while others (a quarter of the sample) opted for half-time employment for both parents. Rather than the polarization of employment responsibilities that characterizes married couples' parenting experiences, particularly when children are young,[6] few households had extreme partner differences in employment hours, and being the birth mother was a poor predictor of employment hours. Gartrell et al. (forthcoming), in their longitudinal study of donor insemination lesbian parents with young children in the United States, also note a tendency for both partners to reduce their hours of employment. Analysis of employment trends for married couples (even those with higher education) reveals that it is rare for partners to share care by both working part- or halftime (see Dunne 1998a; 1999). The experiences of women parenting together (and feminist-inspired, heterosexual couples) (Ehrensaft 1987; VanEvery 1995) raise thorny questions about the role of consumption in limiting egalitarianism in more affluent heterosexual partnerships. Increasingly, we are finding that a preferred solution for the achievement of equality is for both parents to prioritize their economic activities over mothering and pass caretaking and domestic work onto women with less power (Ehrensaft 1987; Gregson and Lowe 1995).

While Vivien and Cay describe themselves as the boys' mothers, in common with most respondents, they struggle over terminology to describe and symbolize that relationship. Because of the singularity and exclusivity of the label *mother* or *mum* and/or their feminist critique of the way the term can eclipse other important aspects of identity, respondents often preferred to encourage the use of first names, special nicknames, or the word *mother* borrowed from another language.

Vivien: Yes, [we are the boys' mothers] absolutely, yes. Very much so.

Interviewer: What do they call you?

Vivien: By our names. . . . They very rarely use the word *mother*.

Cay: In fact [Frank] never used the word *mother* until he started going to school, and then, hearing the other kids saying it, it was just a kind of copying thing.

Here we catch a glimpse of some of the everyday pressures toward social conformity and the dilemmas experienced by parents and children as they negotiate a world hostile to difference. Just as this motivated some to involve donors in their children's lives so that they had the option to pass as relatively "normal" in school, many respondents relented and used the term *mother* to describe the biological mother.

Cay's parents live abroad and are described as proud grandparents. Because John, the boys' father, is not out about his sexuality to his parents, they have no knowledge about the boys. Vivien's parents are dead, but her immediate kin are actively involved in supporting them.

Vivien: My brothers are thrilled, though. My brothers treat the children as if they were their own kids. They don't separate them, you know, they don't see them as any less their kids. And their cousins that they're totally unrelated to just are their cousins, and in fact Tom looks like one of my cousins in Ireland. He doesn't look like any of Cay's.

However, the very positioning outside conventionality that enables the construction of more creative approaches to organizing parenting brings also the problem of lack of recognition and validation from the outside world. Vivien speaks for many in the study:

I think we have to acknowledge that within this house we can sit down and we can talk about the equality that we feel and the experiences that we have and the confidence that we have in our relationship and in our parenting. But very little outside of this house tells us that those things that we're talking about tonight are actually true. We don't get a lot of affirmation outside of our own house that we are good parents, there is not that acknowledgement of the equality and negotiation that goes on within the relationship. And I think heterosexual friends that we have tend to probably see our relationship in their own terms. . . . I don't think they've got an insight into how much we really do work together. . . . You know, we have to work at it all the time, we have to forge links with the school, we have to forge links with this and forge links with that, we have to work hard at being good neighbours and making contact with the neighbours so that as the children come along they're not surprised and they can adjust. We're doing the work, we're doing the outreach, we're doing the education, and what we get back is the right to be ourselves, sort of, as long as we're careful.

Again, their experience underscores the difficulties associated with challenging the normative status of heterosexuality in relation to reproduction and the organization of parenting roles. Constantly, these pioneering women feel obliged to justify their alternative families and approaches to parenting to a wider society that cannot see beyond the constraints of heterosexuality and that is informed by media representations that vilify lesbian parents. Their struggle for validation was not confined to the heterosexual world.

> Vivien: Other lesbians I think may see us as trying to repeat some sort of heterosexual relationship, and that's not what we're trying to do. So we have to kind of justify it to our heterosexual friends and justify it to our lesbian friends.

The contradiction illuminated here between being a lesbian and being a mother serves to remind us that while it can be argued that assisted conception is an important expression of the ideologies supporting compulsory motherhood, it is less easy to apply this thinking to lesbian mothers. Within lesbian culture, the absence of children within a relationship does not constitute failure. In fact, research (Sullivan 1996) supports much of what respondents said about their decision to have children going against established societal norms, specifically those of the lesbian and gay community. Until recently, this community, particularly the radical or revolutionary wing, has been suspicious of motherhood because of fears of constraints on women's autonomy and the importation of oppressive family arrangements (see Green 1997).

Thelma and Louise's Story

> I think we go about things in our own way, we don't have the role definition. We get the best of both worlds really. We get to continue along the road with our careers and also to spend time as a family and to enjoy the time with the children. Disadvantages? We could earn more money I suppose if we worked full-time,

but then it takes away the point of having children I would say. (Thelma)

It was not unusual for both partners to have experienced biological motherhood as the result of donor insemination while in their relationship. At the time of first contact, four couples were in this situation (this number had risen to seven at the follow-up stage two years later). In these households, children were brought up as siblings, and parenting was equally shared. The experiences of Thelma and Louise are not atypical of mothers in this situation. They have been living together for seven years in an apartment that they own in inner-city Manchester. They have two daughters, Polly, age four, and Stef, age two. Thelma works in desktop publishing, and Louise is a teacher. Like many in the sample, Thelma and Louise operationalize shared parenting by reducing their paid employment to half-time. They both wanted to have children; their decisions about timing and who would go first were shaped by emotional and practical considerations. Thelma needed to build up sufficient clientele to enable self-employment from home, and Louise wanted to gain more secure employment.

> Louise: I was a year younger and I wasn't really sorted out work-wise and you were.

> Thelma: There were very pragmatic as well as emotional reasons for why I should go first. It was when I started freelancing at this place and then I ended up freelancing because I got pregnant. But that seemed okay anyway. . . . I mean it was all right to take a break. I knew that I could get work.

> Louise: And I hadn't got there. And there was time to save up as well. During that

time we managed to save up quite a lot, to get over the small baby time. Before getting out to work again.

By the time Louise was pregnant, two years after Thelma, she was in a much stronger position at work, having undergone retraining. She had secured a permanent position in teaching and, after maternity leave, arranged a job share with a friend. Like women more generally, respondents' careers had rarely progressed in a planned linear manner. Instead, their job histories have a more organic quality (see Dunne 1997)—moving across occupations and in and out of education or training. However, in contrast to married women more generally, where the gender division of labour supports the anticipation of financial dependence on husbands when children are young (Mansfield and Collard 1988), an important consideration in the timing of the arrival of children for most biological mothers in this study was the achievement of certain employment aims that would enable greater financial security and allow time to enjoy the children. Their gender parity and this approach to paid employment meant that there were not major earning differentials between partners. This helps to explain why respondents have greater scope in operationalizing shared caregiving, as their options had not been foreclosed by earlier decisions. Although both partners working part-time brings a reduced standard of living, it also brings the advantage, as Thelma remarks, of enabling both to continue in their careers.

After several miscarriages with an earlier donor, Thelma finally got pregnant. Again, they used their friendship networks to locate a donor who then took on a "kindly uncle" role.

Louise: He was just living with a friend of ours, it was just brilliant.

Thelma: Yeah, and ended up being a really good friend as well. . . . I got pregnant the first go really.

Interviewer: And then did you have any views on how much involvement he should have?

Thelma: I think we both wanted a known father and yes, if they wanted some involvement, that was fine. The clearly defined lines were, we're the parents of the children—or of the child at that time—and so any kind of parenting decisions would always be ours.

Interviewer: And what will Polly call her donor?

Thelma: His name—and she calls him Daddy Paul. So I mean she doesn't ever really call him Daddy. Either she calls him Paul or Daddy Paul.

Louise: He is a bit like an uncle [to them both] she'd see now and again, you know, he'd be like this kindly uncle figure, who'd take her to the pics and take her to the zoo and that kind of thing. Give her treats.

They originally planned that Paul would be the donor for Louise; however, there were difficulties in conception, so a new donor was found. Hugh, a gay friend of Thelma's brother, who was temporarily living in England, agreed. While Thelma and Louise both wanted to experience motherhood biologically, they viewed parenting as shared, and this situation was legally recognized in their gaining of a joint parental responsibility order.

Louise: We don't just happen to have a relationship and happen to have two children. We always thought joint, that's why the court thing was important to us. They are sisters and I defy anybody to question that. That's very important to us and we also made it clear that if we ever split up, if I depart with Stef into the horizon and Thelma with Polly, that we have joint care for them.

Again, their interpretation of shared parenting brought them up against the limitations of language to describe a social mother's relationship to a child.

Thelma: They both call us Mum.

Louise: It started off that you were going to be Mum and I was going to be Louise, and then coming up to me giving birth to Stef, it just got a bit kind of funny, so we thought it's not really going to work any more because if they're sisters how come?—it just all didn't work, so now we're both Mums. And they just call us Mum.

Thelma: Stef says Mummy Louise or Mummy Thelma.

Louise: And Polly mostly calls us Louise and Thelma doesn't she?

Thelma: Yeah she does. She calls us both Mum when she wants to, but mostly she calls us by our names.

Louise: The last couple of years she's started calling me Mum.

Some of the immensity of the creative project in which lesbians engage is revealed in the tensions in the last two extracts and in the next. While they describe the children as having

two mothers, Louise reminds us of the contingent nature of this. The rule of biological connection is unquestioned in the assumption that in the event of a breakup each will depart into the horizon with her own child. This next extract illustrates other practical difficulties faced by the couple as they engage with the wider society.

Louise: It's a lot easier now because we've both had a child. I don't think I had any role models in terms of being a non-biological mum. There's a thing that if you want to be acknowledged as a parent, you just had to "come out." It's the only way to explain that you're a parent. And even that is a very hard way to explain you're a parent. My inner circle at work would know and it's funny—I nearly wrote it down one day—because it was just like some days I'd be a parent and some days I wasn't. So it would depend on what day of the week it was and who I was talking to. I think I made it harder for us by me not being called Mum [in the early stages]. Because as soon as people found out you weren't the mum, then they'd just—it was like "who the hell are you then?"

Such is the power of ideas about the singularity and the exclusivity of the identity of "Mum" in a social world structured by heterosexual norms that polarize parenting along lines of gender. Respondents had a store of both amusing and uncomfortable stories about other people's confusions about who was the mother of the child or children or the status of social mothers.

Again, the family has interesting and extensive kinship networks. The children have two fathers. Paul was not out to his elderly parents so they did not know about his child.

However, Hugh, who comes to England several times a year to see them, had told his mother.

Louise: I think Hugh was terrified of telling his mother—he's an only child—had a very close relationship with his mother and he was terrified of telling her. And she was absolutely delighted with it—"I'm the children's grandmother"—she's Stef's grandmother biologically, but she's also Polly's socially. So she's just been this incredible grandmother.

Thelma: Paul's parents don't know. His parents are quite old, they're in their late eighties and they don't know he's gay and I don't think he'd ever tell them. So for him that one's a secret. But his sister knows.

Louise: I think we'd be more worried by it, but I just guess by the time the kids are old enough—I think you've got to start coming out very confidently once you've kids, you can't be messing around really. And it would worry me I think if—if Paul explained to them [the children], that he's not been able to tell his parents. I'm just hoping that by the time it comes up, they won't be around any more.

This discussion illustrates several important themes that featured across the sample. First, respondents were keen to avoid keeping secrets from their children about their conception. Second, they articulated high levels of positivity about being lesbian[7]—this was seen as essential for supporting their children in their dealings with the outside world. Third, all expressed the desire to have their social bonds recognized by friends and kin as being equivalent to blood ties. Finally, kinship was calculated in a remarkable variety of ways. Kin

appeared highly flexible in this, with countless examples like Hugh's mother. This next discussion illustrates respondents' strength of feelings with respect to recognition.

Louise: And family that we see, all of them without exception treat both children equally. That's the deal basically, they're not allowed to pick and choose.

Thelma: It was the same with Grandma.... Part of the deal was that Stef and Polly are sisters and if she took one of them, then she had to, by definition, take on the other.

Louise: We were quite assertive with her—and that's why I'm not seeing my dad, it's because he's still kind of learning to do that, until he really gets his head around it. He can't just send one of them a present and not the other. Actually it looks like he's getting there, doesn't he? He's just about cracked it.... My sister, when Polly was born, my sister just said I'm auntie [name], without any—obviously she isn't biologically, but in all senses of the word, she is.

Interviewer: And they wouldn't distinguish between the children?

Louise: No. Nobody who we see regularly would. Even school and things like that—Stef is Polly's sister. . . . the kind of entry through schools is if you're a sibling and that's kind of a high priority and Stef has entry into that school now, because she's Polly's sister. Although biologically they're nothing.

Without exception, respondents believed that they approached and experienced parenting in ways that were very different from the heterosexual norm. They were redefining the meaning and content of motherhood, extending its boundaries to incorporate the activities that are usually dichotomized as mother and father. Going against prevailing norms was never without difficulties and disappointments. In joint and individual interviews, respondents usually singled out the ability and commitment to communicate as crucial. They spoke of arrangements being constantly subject to negotiation and the need to check in regularly with each other so that routines that may lead to taking the other for granted could be rethought and sources of conflict discussed.

Bonnie and Claudia's Story

We've had a lot of interest and a certain amount of envy from a lot of heterosexual couples who had babies at the same time, because they just haven't had the breaks that we've had from the baby. They've had breaks, but they've felt guilty, whereas we don't particularly feel guilty because we know that Peter's with Philip and they both want to be together. (Claudia)

In three partnerships, donors were actively co-parenting from separate households—becoming a "junior partner in the parenting team" as one father described himself. In two cases, the father's parenting was legally recognized in a joint residency order. Bonnie, Claudia, and Philip share the care of Peter, age two. Bonnie and Claudia have lived together for nine years in a terraced house in inner-city Bristol. Bonnie, Peter's biological mother, works full-time in adult education, and Claudia has a half-time teaching post. They describe and contrast their feelings about wanting to have children:

Claudia: Well, I think it was something that I was looking for when I was looking for a relationship. So I think it was a more immediate thing for me. You were interested in principle. And I knew the father—this is Philip—although not with the view to having children. So you got to know him after we met really. And then the subject came up.

Bonnie: I think for you it had always been like a lifelong thing.

Claudia: I always wanted a baby. I wanted us to have about two.

Bonnie: She was just obsessed with babies, weren't you? Whereas, I wasn't really like that, I come from a big family and I like having lots of people around me. It was more for me that I didn't want to have not had children. It's different, because I didn't want to look back and think, Oh Christ, I didn't have any children. But I tend to get very caught up in whatever I'm doing, and I was busy doing my job and having this relationship and our friends. So in a way it was Claudia's enthusiasm and sense of urgency about it that actually pushed us to making a decision, taking some action. And the only reason I ended up having the baby was that Claudia had a whole series of fertility problems. We just always decided, didn't we, that if one of us had a problem the other one would.

Their experience illustrates another fairly unique advantage for women who want to become mothers in a lesbian relationship—if one partner has fertility problems, the other may agree to go through the pregnancy instead. There were three other examples of partners swapping for this reason, and several others expressed their willingness to do so. As mentioned earlier, I was struck by the fact that many respondents desired to be mothers but felt reluctant to experience motherhood biologically. As there is no reason to believe that this feeling is confined to the lesbian population, it must pose a real dilemma for some heterosexual women. The advantage of the possibility of detaching motherhood from biology via social motherhood in lesbian relationships helps explain why co-parenting is so eagerly embraced—there were several examples of women who had advertised their desire to meet other lesbians, specifically mentioning a preference for women with children.

In their negotiations with Philip over the four years that preceded the birth of Peter, they came to the decision that he would be an actively involved father.

> Claudia: Philip wanted a child, and he, I think, was also looking for a kind of extended family relationship, wasn't he?— with us and the children. But he also wants his freedom, I suppose, his lifestyle, a lot of which he needs not to have children around for. Yes, so it fits in the sense that what we get is time without Peter, to have a relationship that needs its own sort of nurturing and stuff, and he gets special time with Peter and a real bonding. I mean he's seen Peter every day since he's been born. So he has become part of the family, hasn't he?—in a sense, or we've become part of his. But we live in two separate homes. People sometimes don't realize that.

Claudia's words alert us to another underlying reason for respondents' confidence in fathers and/or donors retaining a more minor role in children's lives—routine child care does not usually fit in with the lifestyles of most men, gay or heterosexual. The masculine model of employment that governs ideas of job commitment and what constitutes a valuable worker is based on the assumption that employees are free from the constraints of child care.

After extended maternity leave, Bonnie returned to her successful career in adult education. At this point, Claudia, despite being the higher earner, reduced her employment hours to half-time so that she could become Peter's main caregiver. Men's superior earnings are often described by egalitarian-minded heterosexual couples as ruling out opportunities for shared parenting (Doucet 1995; Ehrensaft 1987). However, women parenting together, without access to ideologies that polarize parenting responsibilities, bring fresh insights to this impasse, which supports gender inequalities.

> Bonnie: We started in a completely different place [from heterosexual couples]. I think we feel it's just much easier to be co-operative and to be more creative in the way that we share out paid work and domestic work, because that's how we look at it. We're constantly chatting about it, aren't we, over the weeks, and saying, "How does it feel now? Are you still thinking about staying on part-time?" and we've talked about what it would be like if I went part-time as well, and could we manage on less money?

> Claudia: Yes, and I think the thing that's part of the advantage is that in a conventional setup, although it may be easier to start with, everyone knowing what they are supposed to be doing, but the men don't know their children so they miss out. . . . I'm having a balanced life really.

Bonnie: I think that's why we've got the space to enjoy our child in a way that a lot of heterosexuals perhaps don't. It's so easy to fall in—the man earns slightly more so it makes sense for him to do the paid work, and women have babies anyway. Because we could potentially each have had the child it's all in the melting pot. Nothing is fixed.

Claudia: And I don't think a lot of women [enjoy mothering]. They think they're going to, but they get isolated and devalued, and lose their self-confidence and self-esteem.

It was not unusual to find the higher earner in a partnership reducing her hours of employment to share care or become the main caregiver. In contradiction to the dictates of rational economic models, this was often justified on the grounds that a person in a higher paid or higher status occupation has more power and may be less penalized for time out than someone in a more marginal position (Dunne 1998a). I would argue that their rationale (like the part-time/part-time solution) can actually make good long-term financial sense. It also illuminates masculine assumptions in relation to value—the idea that market work is superior to caring.

As in the vast majority of households (Dunne 1998a), routine domestic work was fairly evenly divided between Claudia and Bonnie. Their guiding principle was that "neither should be running around after the other." Like most respondents, they spoke of the advantage of the absence of gender scripts guiding who should do what (see Dunne 1998b).

Bonnie: Well, I think one of the main advantages [of being in a lesbian relationship] for me is that unlike heterosexual couples there are no assumptions about how we are going to divide things up and how we're going to cope. Because I know that it's perfectly possible for heterosexuals to do things differently and some share tasks more than others and all the rest of it. But they're still all the time having to work against these kind of very dominant set of assumptions about how things should be done in heterosexual households, whereas we don't have that.

For heterosexual couples, gender difference not only shapes contributions but provides a lens through which they are judged (Baxter and Western 1998; Berk 1985; Dunne 1998b).

Peter goes to a private nursery three days a week (the costs are shared with Philip), and the rest of his care is divided between Claudia, Bonnie, and Philip.

Bonnie: Philip lives in the next street, and so he can just come round every day after work or pick Peter up from nursery and bring him back and do his tea, bath, and things, and then we'll roll in about 6:30 or whenever, or sometimes one of us is here anyway.

Claudia: Yes, we try to work that one of us is always home, either with him or working at home. . . . He's the only one of us who works locally and he's got a bleep [beeper] as part of his job and it's ideal because the nursery can call at any time if there's an emergency.

Interviewer: It strikes me you've got the most ideal situation!

Bonnie: Yes, we think so! [laughing] We're the envy of the mother and toddler group.

Their experience with Philip provides a radical alternative model of co-operative parenting between women and men, based on a consensual non-sexual relationship with a father who is interested in being actively involved in his child's life. In effect, Philip is prepared to engage in mothering,[8] and in doing so, he shares some of the social penalties associated with this activity—all three parents collaborate in balancing the demands of employment and child care, and the result is the lessening of its overall impact. While Bonnie and Claudia were aware that it was difficult to keep Philip abreast of everyday decision-making, they were keen to involve him in major ones. This seemed to work well in practice.

> Bonnie: [It's worked] extremely well. We keep being surprised. I mean we keep thinking . . . we're going to have a fundamental disagreement about something. But I don't think there has been really.

In this discussion, we can see some of the risks associated with involving biological fathers in children's lives—the potential for disagreement and conflict. While respondents generally seemed to have exercised high levels of control in relation to the terms and conditions of donor access to children, and arrangements were working well, the gradual extension of legal rights to biological fathers (see Smart and Neale 1999) increases the mothers' dependence on the integrity of these men.

Again, finding the right words to describe their parenting relationship was difficult. Bonnie expresses a common feminist critique of the label *mummy*, which is hostile to ways that it can be employed to subsume other aspects of a woman's identity.

> Bonnie: I've always been quite keen that Peter should know what our names are anyway. I think there's something completely depersonalizing about the way women sit around and talk about a child's mummy as if she's got no identity. It's fine if there's a baby in the room and it's your child, but everyone will say, "Ask Mummy, tell Mummy." But you become this amorphous mummy to everybody. All women are sort of mummy, they don't have their own identity. So I've been quite keen that he should grow up knowing that people have roles and names, and that you should be able to distinguish between the two.

Yet, her radicalism is tempered by her recognition and desire to celebrate her special connection with the child, and she becomes swayed by arguments for the best interests of the child.

> Bonnie: But I also feel completely contradictory, that there is something very special emotionally about having your own mummy.

> Claudia: And then Philip had very strong feelings about it all, didn't he? He'd always been clear that he wanted to be Daddy, and while we went on holiday together last summer, he made it very clear that he thought that in some sense you needed to be recognized as Peter's mother, that that was important, an important thing in terms of what the relationship meant, and that it would be wrong to deny Bonnie that. . . . Yes, he [also thought] that Peter would, if we started him calling both of us Mummy, sooner or later he'd be ridiculed by some of the other children, and then he would have a terrible conflict of loyalties—does he go with the crowd or does he protect us? And that we shouldn't put him in that position. So we went for

Mummy, Daddy, and Claudia. And then he started calling me Mummy anyway. But now he calls me Addie. [laughter]

This Mummy, Daddy, and Claudia configuration that then evolved into Claudia being called Mummy or the nickname Addie is potentially very undermining of the co-mother. Other couples specifically avoided involving biological fathers to this extent because of such complications of status and role. Claudia's confidence in her relationship with Peter was affirmed through her experience of mothering as main caregiver and, hopefully, by their capacity to be aware of the issues, as the discussion above appears to indicate. Philip's desire for recognition as Daddy is at one level less problematic. He earns this validation through his active involvement in parenting, and because he is not attempting to share fatherhood with a partner, there are no additional complications in relation to exclusion. However, the gender dynamics of this are interesting. While much of the social aspect of Philip's parenting involves the activities of mothering, he is content with the identity of dad. Conversely, in common with the rest of the sample, rather than draw upon dominant polarized heterosexual frameworks—mother/father—respondents extend the meaning of motherhood to include so-called fathering activities such as breadwinning. This raises the wider question: What exactly is a father?

Once again, their parenting is supported by a complex network of kin who have been encouraged to recognize and act upon social as well as biological ties. As they map out the main people supporting their parenting, Bonnie and Claudia discuss the input of kin:

Bonnie: That's my sister Holly and her partner Vickie, who is dyke as well, which

is very nice, and they live round the corner as well. So in a sense they are part of our community, very much so, and Vickie was around for the birth. So they lead a different sort of lifestyle in the sense that they haven't got any children, so they're definitely sort of aunts that come in and do babysitting and things. They're sort of busy but they're important, and we promote the relationship actually, don't we?

Interviewer: What about Philip's parents? Do they have any . . . ?

Bonnie: Yes, there's Philip's mum and dad. They see him two or three times a year—it's only been a year and a half, but they've made a lot of effort. They came down just after his birth.

It is no simple act, however, for extended family to claim kinship ties in these nontraditional situations that require coming to terms with a relative's sexuality. While part of being lesbian and gay is about learning how to come out to self and others, I think we have given scant attention to the work involved when heterosexual family members, particularly elderly parents, claim kinship ties that require coming out on behalf of others. For Philip's parents, it was easier for them to explain his entry into fatherhood to other family members by inventing a complicated story about Philip and Bonnie being or having been lovers.

Claudia: They told all their family that Bonnie and Philip have a kind of relationship.

Bonnie: His parents lied, basically.

Claudia: [The story being that] They're not

living together any more because Bonnie is already living with this other woman who is a nurse and has got a mortgage and it would be too complicated to change things.

Bonnie: They absolutely want Peter to be their grandson and they love that, and I think in their own head they're dealing with it, they're very nice to us both, aren't they? They send us joint cards and progress reports.

Claudia: We even slept in a double bed in their house once.

Bonnie: Yes, they accept it, you can see, on one level. But obviously they can't fully accept it, they can't tell their friends. So that's how that goes.

As Claudia had been adopted, her family was used to the complexity of kinship relations.

Claudia: [My family is] all interested and very supportive but there's no one nearby to pop in. . . . They all only see him about twice a year. Family get-togethers, isn't it?

Bonnie: And you made an effort to go and visit and show Peter off.

Claudia's biological parents were described as treating Peter similarly to their other grandchildren, all of whom receive scant attention. Interestingly, in the case of her adoptive parents, in common with many other respondents, the arrival of children helped rebuild bridges after earlier estrangement over issues of sexuality.

Claudia: Well, [my adoptive parents] have much more difficulty with me being a

lesbian than my parents do. And they've virtually rejected me really. Not immediately when I came out but later on. And then [my adoptive mother], since she found out that I was trying to get pregnant, has been completely supportive. I think [my adoptive father] finds it more difficult.

Interviewer: And she thinks of Peter as your son?

Claudia: Yes. And she describes herself as his adoptive grandmother.

Bonnie's mother could see distinct advantages in her daughter's parenting arrangements:

My mum is Peter's grandmother. She's very, very involved with Peter, totally supportive of this relationship, and thinks that—why hadn't anyone ever mentioned it before? It seems a great way to bring up children. Having brought seven children up without the help of my father, she now thinks it's wonderful not only to have a supportive woman partner but a father involved who lives up the road. It's great. Peter sees more of his father than most children probably do. So she's good.

Aside from a wide circle of friends, Bonnie, Claudia, and Philip had support from parents and siblings, with their son Peter looking forward to presents from four sets of grandparents.

Conclusion

These three stories illustrate many common themes that emerged across the sample, particularly the creativity and co-operation that appear to characterize much of the parenting experience of lesbian couples. I have focused on the involvement of fathers and/or donors and on the complexity of kinship to show how like and unlike these families are to other sorts of family formations. I could equally have looked at the important friendship networks that supported their parenting, the presence of lesbian aunties and heterosexual friends. Lesbian families are usually extended families, supported by elaborate networks of friends and kin.

In common with single lesbian mothers in the United States (Lewin 1993: 9), kin occupy an important place in respondents' accounts of their social interaction. My focus on couples in shared parenting situations reveals other interesting dimensions of kinship: the complexity of these relations and the importance respondents placed on having non-biogenetic ties recognized and validated by family of origin. Demanding recognition of kinship ties in a same-sex context represents an extremely radical departure from the economy of sexual difference underpinning conceptions of kinship more generally (see Butler 1990: 38–43). Considerable effort was involved in achieving this end by all parties. One reason for their usual success in this respect, I believe, is that the presence of children helps make intelligible a lifestyle that can appear strange and "other" to heterosexual observers. This is supported, I think, by the way that often quite strained or difficult relationships between respondents and their parents were transformed as daughters became mothers and their parents became grandparents. Many respondents experienced high levels of enthusiastic support from heterosexual friends in their quest to become, and their experience of being, parents.

Regardless of whether parenting was shared, mothering was usually carried out in a context where mothers experienced a great deal of practical and emotional support from their partners, where routine domestic responsibilities were fairly evenly shared, and where there was a mutual recognition of a woman's right to an identity beyond the home. Beyond the confines of heterosexuality, they had greater scope to challenge the connections between biological and social motherhood and fatherhood. By depriviliging the biological as signifier of motherhood (although this appears to be contingent on the relationship remaining intact) and the capacity to mother, many were actively engaged in extending the meaning, content, and consequence of mothering to include both partners (or even fathers) on equal terms.

Lesbians opting into motherhood in a hostile world have to engage in an extended period of planning: nothing can be taken for granted. The pleasure they experienced in spending time with their children and the high value they attached to mothering are often reflected in the employment strategies of both parents. Thus, biological motherhood was a poor predictor of differences in income and employment hours within partnerships. They were advantaged by their structural similarities as women and their positioning outside conventionality. In resolving the contradiction between time for children and the need to generate income, their options had not usually been foreclosed by earlier employment choices shaped by the anticipation and/or experience of a gender division of labour (Dunne 1997, 2000). They consequently have greater scope to operationalize their egalitarian ideals in relation to parenting. The high value they attached to nurturing, together with their desire to be fair to each other, meant that within reason they were prepared to experience a reduced standard of living (see Dunne 1998a). Their views about what constitutes shared parenting were less distorted by ideologies that dichotomized parenting along lines of gender in such a way that men can be seen and see themselves as involved fathers when they are largely absent from the home (Baxter and Western 1998; Ferri and Smith 1996). Consequently, their solution to the contradiction was to integrate mothering and breadwinning.

In their everyday lives of nurturing, housework, and breadwinning, respondents provide viable alternative models for parenting beyond heterosexuality. While our focus is on lesbian partners, anecdotal evidence suggests that lesbians are also founding parenting partnerships on the basis of friendship—with gay men or other lesbians. By finding a way around the reproductive limitations of their sexuality, they experience their position as gatekeepers between children and biological fathers in an unusual way. Ironically, we find examples of highly productive models of co-operation between women and men in bringing up children. Unhampered by the constraints of heterosexuality, they can choose to include men on the basis of the qualities they can bring into children's lives. It is no accident, I believe, that respondents usually chose to involve gay men. These men were seen as representing more acceptable forms of masculinity, and their sexuality barred them from some of the legal rights that have been extended to heterosexual fathers.

Their positioning outside conventionality and the similarities they share as women enable and indeed insist upon the redefinition of the meaning and content of motherhood. Thus, when choosing to opt into motherhood, they are anticipating something very different from the heterosexual norm. Some felt that their gender parity and commitment to egalitarianism enabled a conscious recognition and articulation of the power that was perceived to derive from the actual bodily experience of creating another human being. Within the gender context that frames their arrangements, they felt safe to identify and celebrate this special biological and psychological connectedness with a child because it did not ultimately lead to polarization within the partnership in relation to access to other sources of social reward.

At one level, motherhood bridges the gap between the known and the unknown. It represents a common currency where we can predict the routines, pleasures, and concerns of parents, and sexuality can be sidelined. At another level, however, we have seen that their experience of motherhood seems quite different from that of most heterosexual mothers. Importantly, by building bridges in this way, friends, colleagues, and extended family bear witness to these differences, and their experience reflects back into the lives of others. These alternative reference points may help to reinforce women's confidence in their critique of conventional assumptions shaping heterosexual practice. Much recent scholarship on sexuality, for example, queer theory, sees a radical future in subverting gender categories through practices of parody (Butler 1990). To this end, the influential philosopher Judith Butler asks us to rethink the transformational potential of practices such as "drag, cross-dressing, and the sexual stylization of butch/femme identities" (1990: 137). However, my concern is that in our contemporary preoccupation with these exotic and exciting aspects of sexual radicalism, we ignore the challenge that ordinary lesbian women and gay men pose to the status quo through their prioritization of egalitarian ideals. Central to the reproduction of the social order (institutional heterosexuality, gender inequality) are ideological processes that reify and legitimize current arrangements by rendering invisible or stigmatizing alternatives. The visibility of lesbian parents in the mainstream as they negotiate with schools, health workers, neighbours, employers and co-workers, and heterosexual parents helps to make intelligible the unimaginable to others. They create a cognitive dissonance that may enable others to evaluate and move beyond the taken-for-grantedness of heterosexuality. As women together, they renegotiate the boundaries, meaning, and content of parenthood. By doing so, they undermine much of the logic shaping conventional divisions of labour, for

example, that specialization is the most efficient and effective way to finance and run a household and care for children, that prioritizing the career of the higher earner makes long-term financial sense, and that biological motherhood is the precursor of the capacity to mother. They challenge conventional wisdom by showing the viability of parenting beyond the confines of heterosexuality. Rather than being incorporated into the mainstream as honorary heterosexuals, by building bridges between the known and the unknown, their lives represent, I believe, a fundamental challenge to the foundation of the gender order.

● Notes

I would like to dedicate this article to the memory of Linda Edwards, who graciously shared her story of mothering with me during the last few days of her struggle with breast cancer. Her courage and humanity was an inspiration throughout the study. My thanks to all participants in the Lesbian Household Project and to the following for their helpful comments on this article: Shirley Prendergast, Nina Hallowell, Ginny Morrow, Shelley Sclater, Beth Schneider, and the anonymous reviewers, particularly the one who raved!

1. Both VanEvery (1995) and Ehrensaft (1987: 20) mention that women are the driving force in the quest to achieve and maintain egalitarianism. Both comment on the extent to which structural factors, such as men's superior earnings, and wider social expectations mediate success in this respect.
2. See the extended version of this article for additional case studies (Dunne 1998c).
3. I am grateful to the Economic and Social Research Council for funding this recently completed three-year project (reference number R00023 4649).
4. See Dunne (1997, 2000) for exploration of the link between the capacity to move beyond heterosexuality and economic self-reliance.
5. To maintain confidentiality, the names of participants and their children and their geographical

location and occupations have been changed. To give some sense of their employment circumstances, I have assigned similar kinds of occupations.
6. While British mothers are more likely now than in the past to be employed full-time, it is mothers rather than fathers who balance the demands of paid work and child care. It is very unusual for mothers and fathers to have similar lengths of paid workweeks, even when mothers are employed full-time (Dunne 1998a; Ferri and Smith 1996).
7. I was struck by the almost unanimous confidence of the sample in their sexuality—respondents saw their lesbian identity as a great source of advantage. Their identification as lesbian rather than gay was also evidence of their usually feminist inclinations. In a previous life-history study of lesbians who were generally not mothers (Dunne 1997), there were more examples of ambiguity in this respect. I suspect respondents' self-assurance is related to a combination of factors including historical period, being in fulfilling relationships, their achievement of motherhood, and the process of soul-searching that preceded this.
8. Silva (1996) draws a useful distinction between motherhood, a uniquely female experience, and mothering, which, although usually a female practice, can be performed by either gender.

● References

Abshoff, K., and M. Hird. 1998. "Subverting the Feminine: The Case of Child-free Women," paper presented at the Annual Meeting of the British Sociological Association, University of Edinburgh.

Baxter, J., and M. Western. 1998. "Satisfaction with Housework: Examining the Paradox," *Sociology* 1: 101–20.

Beck, U., and E. Beck-Gernsheim. 1995. *The Normal Chaos of Love* (Cambridge, MA: Polity).

Berk, S.F. 1985. *The Gender Factory: The Apportionment of Work in American Households* (New York: Plenum).

Blaisure, K., and K. Allen. 1995. "Feminists and the Ideology and Practice of Marital Equality," *Journal of Marriage and the Family* 57: 5–19.

Brannen, J., and P. Moss. 1991. *Managing Mothers: Dual Earner Households after Maternity Leave* (London: Unwin Hyman).

Butler, J. 1990. *Gender Trouble: Feminism and the Subversion of Identity* (New York: Routledge).

Campbell, E. 1985. *The Childless Marriage* (London: Tavistock).

Doucet, A. 1995. "Gender Equality, Gender Difference and Care," PhD diss., Cambridge University, Cambridge, UK.

Dunne, G.A. 1997. *Lesbian Lifestyles: Women's Work and the Politics of Sexuality* (London: Macmillan).

———. 1998a. "'Pioneers behind Our Own Front Doors': Towards New Models in the Organization of Work in Partnerships," *Work Employment and Society* 12, 2: 273–95.

———. 1998b. "A Passion for 'Sameness'? Sexuality and Gender Accountability," in *The New Family?*, eds E. Silva and C. Smart (London: Sage).

———. 1998c. "Opting into Motherhood: Lesbian Experience of Work and Family Life," London School of Economics, Gender Institute Discussion Paper Series 6.

———. 1998d. "Add Sexuality and Stir: Towards a Broader Understanding of the Gender Dynamics of Work and Family Life," in *Living "Difference": Lesbian Perspectives on Work and Family Life*, ed. G.A. Dunne (New York: Haworth).

———. 1999. "Balancing Acts: On the Salience of Sexuality for Understanding the Gendering of Work and Family-life Opportunities," in *Women and Work: The Age of Post-feminism?*, eds L. Sperling and M. Owen (Aldershot, UK: Ashgate).

———. 2000. "Lesbians as Authentic Workers? Institutional Heterosexuality and the Reproduction of Gender Inequalities," *Sexualities*.

Ehrensaft, D. 1987. *Parenting Together: Men and Women Sharing the Care of the Children* (New York: Free Press).

Fenstermaker, S., C. West, and D.H. Zimmerman. 1991. "Gender Inequality: New Conceptual Terrain," in *Gender, Family and Economy, the Triple Overlap*, ed. R.L. Blumberg (London: Sage).

Ferri, E., and K. Smith. 1996. *Parenting in the 1990s* (London: Family Policy Studies Centre).

Gartrell, N., et al. Forthcoming. "The National Lesbian Family Study 2: Interviews with Mothers of Toddlers," *American Journal of Psychiatry*.

Giddens, A. 1992. *The Transformation of Intimacy* (Cambridge, MA: Polity).

Green, S. 1997. *Urban Amazons: The Politics of Sexuality, Gender and Identity* (Basingstoke, UK: Macmillan).

Gregson, N., and M. Lowe. 1995. *Servicing the Middle-classes: Class, Gender and Waged Domestic Labour* (London: Routledge).

Hochschild, A.R. 1989. *The Second Shift* (New York: Avon).

Lewin, E. 1993. *Lesbian Mothers* (Ithaca, NY: Cornell University Press).

McAllister, F., and L. Clarke. 1998. *Childless by Choice: A Study of Childlessness in Britain* (London: Family Policy Studies Centre).

Mansfield, P., and J. Collard. 1988. *The Beginning of the Rest of Your Life: A Portrait of Newlywed Marriage* (London: Macmillan).

Morell, C. 1994. *Unwomanly Conduct* (London: Routledge).

Popeno, D. 1988. *Disturbing the Nest: Family Change and Decline in Modern Societies* (New York: Aldine).

Rich, A. 1984. "On Compulsory Heterosexuality and Lesbian Existence," in *Desire: The Politics of Sexuality*, eds A. Snitow, C. Stansell, and S. Thompson (London: Virago).

Rubin, G. 1975. "The Traffic in Women: Notes on the 'Political Economy' of Sex," in *Towards an Anthropology of Women*, ed. R.R. Reiter (London: Monthly Review Press).

Scott, J. 1997. "Changing Households in Britain: Do Families Still Matter?," *Sociological Review* 45, 4: 591–620.

Silva, E. 1996. "The Transformation of Mothering," in *Good Enough Mothering?*, eds E. Silva and C. Smart (London: Routledge).

———, and C. Smart, eds. 1996. *Good Enough Mothering?* (London: Routledge).

Smart, C., and B. Neale. 1999. *Family Fragments* (Cambridge, MA: Polity).

Sullivan, M. 1996. "Rozzie and Harriet? Gender and Family Patterns of Lesbian Co-parents," *Gender & Society* 10, 6: 747–67.

VanEvery, J. 1995. *Heterosexual Women Changing the Family: Refusing to Be a "Wife"* (London: Taylor Francis).

Weeks, J., C. Donovan, and B. Heaphy. 1998. "Everyday Experiments: Narratives of Non-heterosexual Relationships," in *The New Family?*, eds E. Silva and C. Smart (London: Sage).

Weston, K. 1991. *Families We Choose* (New York: Columbia University Press).

Chapter 16

In this culture, many people might assume that women are suited to the care of children in ways that men simply are not, whether because of biology or socialization. The fact that women typically feel wholly unprepared to care for their first baby, and rely on information and instructions provided in popular books written by "experts," may do little to challenge these beliefs. Andrea Doucet interviewed 118 fathers who defined themselves as primary caregivers for their children: some were single fathers, more were at home full-time with their children, and a few were home on parental leave. Her main question was whether men who do much of the child care in their families provide the kind of care for their children that mothers do—whether they mother. This chapter, from her book *Do Men Mother?* examines whether and how men who care for their children, as a primary activity, take on the responsibility for their emotional well-being, as is expected of mothers. Her findings both challenge any assumption that men are not suited to do mothering and highlight the importance of cultural expectations that men display their masculinity.

Fathers and Emotional Responsibility

Andrea Doucet

A mother's attachment to her baby is beyond the universe. You know yourself. I mean you'd rip your body apart if it was to save your children. I'm sure a father would, but the fear isn't there as much. When Gary mentioned how he worries, that's a very learned thing. When you become a new mother, you can either spend your life worrying about whether they're going to outlive you, or you can just push that aside and realize you have very little control over it, that it's a waste of energy . . . So, you have to push that away. But sometimes if it creeps in, you can get a little crazy. A man wouldn't worry because he knows he will survive if something happens to his kids. I don't know if I would. *I would survive, but I would be a different person. It would scar me for life.* I *would never hit a happy plateau like I hit every day now. There would always be this hole* as *big* as *the house.* Just hearing about it—I heard someone lost their child, just a few weeks younger than Oliver, to crib death. I mean, I go through a half an hour of "Oh my God! How are those people surviving?" (Kathy, interviewed with her husband, Gary, stay-at-home father of three children, October 2002)

I think that mothers care for their children differently. When my son has something going wrong emotionally, [my wife] has the emotional reaction that stems from the first moment that he was born. And I know that she has that connection with the physical act of childbirth and it is kind of a continuum. And I think that is a unique thing.

I was there at the birth. I was there for all three of them. And I had a connection with them. But she had her body transformed. I don't think we can undermine the fact that women are connected to their children in that very physical, that very primordial sense. Then every time he cries or she gets upset—and especially him, because it was a very difficult birth—she'll think about that, and I think that *she's more inclined to go the extra mile to be emotionally connected to him,* whereas my response, in contrast, is to look at it for what it is. (Tom, stay-at-home father of three, speaking about his wife, Natasha, July 2002)

Introduction

It was the end of summer in 2002 and Denise's ten-month maternity leave was coming to an end. She found herself sleepless in Ottawa, filled with worry. She wasn't concerned about leaving her son, Nathan, but rather about the fact that her son's daytime caregiver would be Martin, her husband. Denise was especially anxious about the bond being formed between Martin and Nathan, a deep bond that would intensify as the two spent days together while she was at work. Night after night, she wrestled with several recurring qualms: would Nathan become closer to his father, than to her? Who would he go to for comfort? Perhaps the most vexing question for her was, Who would Nathan call out for in the middle of the night? As she explained to me in the joint couple interview I conducted with them in October of that year, "I felt threatened when we first decided that Martin would stay home . . . If he had wanted Daddy in the night instead of me, I would probably have fallen apart . . . *I wanted to be the mommy.* I wanted to be the one he calls in the middle of the night."

While Denise lay awake worrying about whose name Nathan would call in the dark of night, fathers in other households throughout the city were waking to their children's cries while their wives lay undisturbed beside them. In Richard and Aileen's home, seven-year-old Sarah would walk around to the far side of the bed where her father lay sleeping. Greg, a joint-custody father of a five-year-old girl explained to me, "I've always said I have mother's ears. My ex would have never heard that baby cry in a hundred years." Archie, who used to be the one who slept soundly through the nighttime cries, found that after a few months of being at home he was getting up with their infant son, Jordan: "A really interesting thing happened when I started staying home. Up until that point, I would . . . do the night feeding and then go to bed. If the baby woke up after that point, Jean would hear it and would get up with Jordan. After two months of me staying home, she no longer heard when he woke up. It was *me* getting up. It was really bizarre and I still can't account for it."

There is something about responding to a child's tearful cries in the middle of the night that cuts to the heart of parental protection and care. The parent who wakens and lovingly responds to the child's cries—or the parent whose embrace is sought by the sleepy child—is a metaphoric encapsulation of *nurturing.* As beautifully rendered in a traditional lullaby, "Hush, my darling, don't fear, my darling, the lion sleeps tonight," the parent who brings "hush" and calm to the "darling," child embodies emotional bonds and connection.

Denise's profound worry and Archie's noting of a "bizarre" and unaccountable shift in his behaviour exemplify what Sara Ruddick, in *Maternal Thinking,* has termed "preservation" or "protective care": "it simply means to see vulnerability and to respond to it with care, rather than . . . indifference, or flight" (1995, 19). This state of mind and the sets of practices associated with it are also well captured in several decades of feminist scholarship on "care" and the "ethic of care"[1] as including qualities of attentiveness, competence, and responsiveness (Fisher & Tronto, 1990; Gilligan, 1982; Graham, 1983; Noddings, 2003; Tronto, 1989, 1993, 1995). As evinced by the political theorist Joan Tronto in her description of caring, emotional responsibility involves skills that include "*knowledge* about others' needs" which the caregiver acquires through "an *attentiveness* to the needs of others" (Tronto, 1989, 176–8; my emphasis). In wanting to denote both the tasks of caring and the responsibility for caring, I have used the term *emotional responsibility* to capture the essence and work of protective care and the responsibility for its enactment (that is, the "response-ability")[2] (Doucet, 2000, 2001b, 2004).

Fathers and Emotional Responsibility

While there has been some debate on the character, quality, and enactment of care with distinctions drawn between levels and kinds of caregiving (Tronto, 1993), between care as *love* ("caring about") or *labour* ("caring for") (Graham, 1983; Ungerson, 1990, Tronto, 1993), and whether care is a feminine or feminist practice (Larabee, 1993; Tronto, 1993; Noddings, 2003), the issue of the *gendered* quality of care is less a matter of debate. International research has demonstrated that most of the work and responsibility for protective care and emotional responsibility for children rests with women. Nevertheless, it has also been shown that men can and do take on the work of care. In this vein, Sara Ruddick's assertion that "men can mother" is supported by a large body of research attesting to men's successful efforts

with the maternal tasks of "preservation" and "protective care." That is, many studies on fathering have argued that fathers have the desire and the capacity to be protective, nurturing, affectionate, and responsive with their children (Coltrane, 1996; Dienhart, 1998; Doucet, 2004; Dowd, 2000; Lamb, 1981, 1987; Lupton & Barclay, 1997; Parke, 1996; Pleck, 1985; Pruett, 2000; Snarey, 1993).

Given that my research is on self-defined primary-caregiving fathers, it is not surprising that these findings about fathers' capable nurturing are strongly confirmed in my research. Cameron, a stay-at-home father of two preschool children as well as a foster parent of a mentally challenged teenager, tells me, "*I often find myself even ahead of them. I know what they want before they even express it.*" When asked to describe his fathering, Jerome, a stay-at-home father for ten years of two school-age children in rural Nova Scotia, chooses only the following words: "*Kind and gentle. Lots of hugs, Protective.*" A final example is with Manuel, the comment of his wife, Julie, that he is so tremendously in tune with the children:

There was a little thing on the radio the other day. Some engineer has decided there are five different kinds of cries from a baby—you know, tired, hungry, uncomfortable . . . And he has found that most babies fall into the categories of those five cries. He's developed a monitor that will tell you what that cry is. We were listening to this on the CBC, and I said to [our daughter] Lyn, "You know what? Your dad was like that. Just wonderful. Well, I have never seen anybody who just knew [for instance] that that baby needed a sweater taken off. That this little squirm meant that." I tell them things like this and they go, "Oh he is so wonderful!"

All these statements by and about fathers hint at connection, hugging and holding the child, and knowing intuitively what the child wants. But do fathers' stories about caregiving add anything *new* to our understanding of nurturing and emotional responsibility?

In addition to confirming that fathers are indeed nurturing, my research confirms that fathers shed a light on *other* kinds of protective care. While preservation and protective care are usually related to closely holding and looking after children, fathers also specialize in the following kinds of nurturing: fun and playfulness; a physical and outdoors approach; promoting children's considered risk taking; and encouraging children's independence. These findings emerge from fathers' descriptions of their typical daily and weekly routines with their children, their reflections on differences between mothers' and fathers' care, as well as from the 14 couple interviews, where mothers' views on the differences and similarities between the parents' care were directly discussed. Findings on recurrent patterns of fatherly nurturing are discussed below.

Fun and Playful:
"A Bouncing, Rollicking Time"

Many cross-cultural longitudinal studies have demonstrated that fathers use play to connect with their children (Coltrane, 1996; Lamb, 1987; Parke, 1996; Pruett, 2000; Yogman, Cooley & Kindlon, 1988). This finding is also evident in the fathers' narratives in this study and is repeated across social class and ethnicity and for both heterosexual and gay fathers.

The women in my study also concur with this view. In the couple interviews, where couples place little pieces of paper on their co-constructed Household Portrait, the response is overwhelmingly consistent along distinct gendered lines when they come across the piece of paper that denotes play. Craig, a stay-at-home father of twins says, "My immaturity has come into this in a big way. I can get on the floor and find myself watching their TV programs with them." Kathy places the "play" task slip in Gary's column, indicating this as his domain: "They like playing with their dad. To say I play with them would be a gross exaggeration. I do games and that sort of thing, but Gary's a lot of fun. He's all of about ten years old."

Several fathers use the example of cooking to contrast their approach with their female partners." Kyle says, "I teach the kids more about cooking than Carol does. Probably because I take the approach that cooking should be fun, and Carol takes the approach that cooking should be perfect." William, who has run fathering groups, offers a similar view: "It is less the practices and more the style. Feeding a kid is feeding your kid. With fathers, there is more fun associated with cooking, more adventure, flexibility, and getting the kids involved in doing it themselves."

Bernard, a 42-year-old father who shares custody of a son with two lesbian mothers, notes that the style of parenting that four-year-old Jake receives is different between the moms' house and Dad's house. He evokes an approach to fathering similar to that of most heterosexual fathers:

> When Jake and I are at my house, it's a different pace. They do more domestic stuff at the moms' house. I say, to heck with all that. We are out there doing things, spending time together. Moms' place is domesticated: There are books, photos, a computer, a playroom. He sees that his moms work and that they spend time with female friends—some guys but mainly female friends. He doesn't see

them do much outside of that. At my place he sees photos of himself and my family. He sees books. Sports trophies. My golf clubs, my bowling ball. He comes to my bowling group. He sees all this guy stuff. When I go out into the community, he sees a lot of males. It's a *testosterone world here, an estrogen world there.*"

This does not mean that mothers don't use fun and play as a way of responding to their children but rather that fathers and mothers highlight this as a dominant *paternal* pattern in relating to infants and young children. Carl, for example, mentions that though they both take turns putting their two preschool daughters to bed, there is a slight difference, with his style being more a "big, bouncing, rollicking time," whereas hers is "very much a cuddle kind of time."

Physical Activities and the Outdoors: "I Get Them Out as Much as Possible"

The majority of fathers in my study talk about making it a point to get their children outdoors as much as possible, to do lots of physical activities with them, and to be very involved with their children's sports (Brandth & Kvande, 1998; Doucet, 2004; Plantin, Sven-Axel & Kearney, 2003). Three examples illuminate this theme in the fathers' narratives. Robert, a former sign maker who lives in rural Quebec and is home with two boys, talks about his typical daily routine: "I like to spend time outside with them. Spring, summer, winter, fall, if the weather is nice, we're gallivanting outside all over the countryside. I get them out as much as possible . . . to get them away from the routine in the house. It re-energizes me."

Peter, a part-time graphic designer and stay-at-home father of two boys for the past

six years, speaks about preferring being outside with his sons to going to community playgroups: "If we have a choice between going to playgroups or going to the river to throw rocks, we will always go down to the river. We like to go to the parks that are wilder so we can be out in nature."

James, a gay divorced father who took a four-month paternity leave with his son, sums up his time at home this way: "We got out every day. We'd be out of the house by ten. He had an afternoon nap, so we would get back at about one-thirty . . . I saw it as an 18-month adventure. People used to comment on how adventurous we were. I would put him on the back of the bike and we would bike to museums, to the island, everywhere."[3]

Mitchell, a former naval officer and a stay-at-home father of three children under the age of six (including twins), reflects that it may be personality and not gender that leads him to be out with the kids. Nevertheless; he adds, concurring with most of the other men's narratives, that he prefers to be outside with them: "I think it has more to do with personality than whether you're male or female. I think if I enjoyed something like painting or more arts and crafts type thing, I'd probably spend more time doing that with the children. But I prefer being outside running around and going to the park."

Can the valuing of physical and outdoor activities be part of nurturing and emotional responsibility? I would argue that, indeed, they represent ways of responding to the physical and developmental needs of children. Fathers reason that being outdoors and engaging in physical exertion is good for children; they get fresh air and exercise, sleep better, and have the opportunity to explore parks and nature trails. Indeed, fathers' encouragement of activity and exercise with young children and recreational sports for school-age children can be seen as having positive physical and mental developmental outcomes (Beauvais, 2001; Kremarik, 2000).[4]

Measured, Practical Reactions: "My First Response Is to Fix the Problem"

Many fathers also remark that their response to emotionally charged situations is to fall back into what is often viewed as masculine ways of being. When Peter's youngest son was severely ill in the hospital, he found himself acting with what would be considered stereotypical masculine responses focused on *doing* rather than on *being*: "My typical male characteristics are lack of emotion or the deferring of emotion, which I found out when we had a very sick child. My first reaction would be action rather than an emotional response."

In a joint interview, Alistair, a writer, and his wife, Claire, a researcher and doctoral student, reflect on how they respond to the children. Her approach is to "make her feel better" and to "get her to tell me," whereas his response is more "measured" and more oriented to trying "to fix the problem." Alistair says, "I think if [our daughter] Georgia is upset, my first response is to try to identify and fix the problem. Whereas your initial response [turns to Claire] is, How can I make you feel better?"

In response to Alistair, Claire notes that at certain times, his more measured and patient response is what is required, particularly as the children grow older and may not always be willing to open up quickly to their parents. She says, "With Georgia, I can see that she's sad. I'll get her to tell me. It won't come pouring out of her. If she's ready to talk, he's there to listen. And he gives an even, measured response. So they will draw on that too." Claire's noting that "they will draw on that too" reminds us that *connection*, strategically disguised here as *distance*

or strategic *indifference*, can nevertheless act as a form of protective care in certain contexts.

Promoting Risk Taking: "I Am Quite Willing to Let These Kids Fail"

Fathers' narratives are also replete with evidence that they encourage risk taking. Whether it is on the play structure in the park, exploring, or learning through physically falling or intellectually failing, most fathers claim to be more likely to facilitate their child's trying things out on his or her own. A couple of examples illustrate fathers' comfort with judicious risk taking.

Bernard, mentioned earlier as a gay father who shares custody of his son with two lesbian mothers, talks about his approach to his son's outdoor play, which contrasts to the child's two mothers. His relaxed attitude resonates with many fathers in the study: "I do consider his safety. I help him to make a decision. If he was climbing a tree, the mothers would be sitting back and watching him and then yelling that that was far enough . . . They would be more careful. I would be close by him helping him to make the decision about how far he can go; I would guide him through that decision."

A different kind of risk taking comes from Kyle, an Italian-Canadian father of two daughters who is married to Carol, a German Canadian. They live in a rural area and both work part-time, Kyle as a local city councillor and Carol as a librarian. In speaking about their daughter Emma, a gifted child who is home-schooled and who often has difficulties adjusting to social situations, Kyle refers to his wife's approach as "setting up structures, lectures, long heart-to-heart talks late at night," while his is best characterized as "more sink or swim. Push her into a situation and then talk to her later about it. I am quite willing to let these kids fail."

Encouraging Children's Independence: "You Guys Can Make Your Own Lunches"

The issue of risk taking and letting children learn in an independent manner is a more narrow articulation of the wider issue of promoting their independence. This fourth aspect of fathers' emotional *connection* with children is, ironically, their role in facilitating processes of *autonomy* in children. That is, most fathers in this study indicate that they play a strong role in promoting the children's physical, emotional, and intellectual independence. Recurring examples in fathers' accounts include strongly encouraging the kids to be involved in housework, to make their own lunches, engage in independent play, tie their own laces (shoes or skates), and carry their own backpacks to school. As Alistair says, "I might be less likely to go out of my way to help the kids if it's something they can do themselves."

Jacob, a sole custodial father of three young children, also captures this particularly well in noting that "I have always had them help out with chores" and that all three children (eleven, nine, and seven) make their own lunches: "This year I said, 'you guys can make your own lunches.' I lay the ground rules: 'You need a sandwich, or sometimes soup, then fruit and vegetables and a snack.' They can do it with a little guidance—even Pippa [the youngest]."

Versions of this story were repeated by the majority of men interviewed. Initially, this telling of events puzzled me. Is the promotion of children's independence the opposite of protective care, or a fundamental part of it? As I worked laboriously through the reams of interview transcripts, my first interpretation was that this was an example of the father letting go of the child, in contrast to dominant understandings of nurturing and protective care that

suggest that the parent is connected to (or holds on to) the child. Gradually, however, I came to view this behaviour as an integral part of nurturing. That is, the protective care of children with its qualities of attentiveness, responsiveness, and competence, involves both holding on and letting go—and it is the careful letting-go that fathers demonstrate particularly well.

Understanding Fathers' Narratives of Emotional Responsibility

In examining fathers' caregiving, my research reveals several dominant paternal patterns. What are the sources of such differences? Why do they appear so prominently in fathers' narratives? Drawing from both fathers' and mothers' narratives, I have developed six points to assist us in making sense of gendered differences in approaches to, and the enactment of, the emotional responsibility for children. First, both mothers and fathers remark on the residue of gendered upbringing as key factors accounting for differences in caring. Second, there are the strong beliefs by fathers—as well as many mothers—that mothering and fathering are inherently different—as identities and as *embodied* experiences. Third, many fathers speak further about embodiment issues, specifically the social taboos around men and physical touching, both with boys and girls in the preteen and teen years. Fourth, fathers note the leading role played by mothers in determining the balance of emotional responsibility within households. Fifth, fathers' narratives are marked by **hegemonic masculinity**, evidenced, mainly in their devaluation and concurrent distancing from the feminine. Finally, I consider what we learn more broadly about nurturing and parenting by looking at differences in fathering narratives on emotional responsibility. Is it possible that fathers develop a concept of nurturing that incorporates both traditionally feminine and masculine qualities and, indeed, exists *between* maternal *equality* and paternal *difference?*

Growing Up Male: "I Grew Up as a Guy"

It should not be surprising that most fathers exhibit more traditionally masculine qualities in their caregiving, given that most boys grow up in cultures that encourage sport,[5] physical and emotional independence, and risk taking (see Connell 1995, Mac an Ghaill, 1994; Seidler, 1997).[6] Alistair says he learned on the playing fields (and arenas) of boyhood that the rules of the sports take precedence over attention to somebody getting hurt: "We were out playing ball hockey and Vanessa got hurt. It's the kind of accident that happens in ball hockey. Someone gets hurt, and you kind of stand around like a bunch of male apes and you kick them gently and say, 'Well, can you play or not?' We're not a great nurturing bunch. Because you're learning certain things when you're playing ball hockey. There was my daughter and she was hurt in the face, and, you know, I was concerned. But also *this* is *ball hockey,* and you learn certain things when you do that."

Devon, a technician and a sole-custody father of a seven-year-old son notes that danger is just part of "what little boys do": "I grew up as a guy. We did dangerous things, That's what little boys do. A father thing is, should I let him go up the tree? Yeah, but then a little skepticism is there."

In contrast to Devon, as well as to her own husband, Peter, Linda takes a more cautious parenting approach, rooted partly in "having grown up as a girl": "I don't know if boys take more physical risks than girls. I suspect that they do.

Having grown up as a girl, I saw boys on the highest bars at the park, or riding their bikes on one wheel. I think that has some bearing on it."

Most sociologists view statements like ones given above as evidence of socialization. Yet it is more than this. As Patricia Yancey Martin has recently written, gendering processes are deeply ingrained so that they "become almost automatic": "Gendered practices are learned and enacted in childhood and in every major site of social behaviour over the life course, including in school, intimate relationships, families, workplaces, houses of worship, and social movements. In time, like riding a bicycle, gendering practices become almost automatic" (Martin, 2003, 352).

Within such automatic gendering processes, there remains the question of how active fathering affects their daughters. That is, will fathers' daughters who "are learning certain things when . . . playing ball hockey" or "riding a bike on one wheel" also grow up to exhibit these traditional masculine qualities? The long-term impact of fathers actively caring for their daughters will, however, only be revealed if and when the daughters become parents.

Embodied Differences between Mothers and Fathers: "A Longer and Tighter Hug"

A second factor that underlies gendered differences in fathers' narratives is their profound belief in distinct differences between mothering and fathering as identities and as embodied experiences. Even where fathers are left literally holding the baby as their ex-wives or ex-partners leave home, or where they express little feelings towards their ex-wives or partners, the majority of fathers still noted that mothers are more protective, nurturing, and emotionally connected. While admitting that his ex-wife is not nurturing, Jack, a sole-custody father living in New Brunswick, nevertheless says, "I still think in general that the most common situation is that women feel that attachment to the children . . . because she's the mother, right?"

Fathers express great confusion over the origins of this special bond. Is it based in biology (hormones, birthing, and breastfeeding), or is it a result of culture and socialization? Some fathers did implicate the latter. For example, Lorne, a papermill foreman and sole-custody father of three in a northern Ontario town, says, "It's the way we programmed ourselves," especially the fact that "boys are not allowed to get emotional in public." A few fathers reiterate these sentiments, but most suggest an embodied basis for the differences between mothers and fathers. Alistair, who stayed home for over a year with his first infant daughter, is aware of the physical connections associated with pregnancy, birth, and breastfeeding, and also of women's overall emotional involvement, especially with young children: "I think you are *so physically* involved as a mother, from the beginning. Nine months of pregnancy—such a commitment—and then into the breastfeeding. And then normally mothers are much more involved with taking care of very small babies. There is a tremendous bond right there. Even when I was taking care of Georgia at home, I didn't have the same physical bond as Claire did with this baby. I think women are more sensitive and more inclined to be emotionally involved."

Gary, a carpenter and stay-at-home father of three boys, succinctly captures many of the fathers' views on this matter when he speaks about how his wife, Kathy, relates to the kids: "Well, like I said, men do nurture. We do give them a hug tell them it's okay, sit them on our knee. But I just find with the mother they do it more or longer. They give a tighter hug."

Embodiment: "I Am Very Nervous about That Kind of Thing"

It may be that a mother's hug is longer and tighter because there are different social perceptions of fathers' and mothers' acceptable physicality with children. Although the early years—with infants and preschool children—provide fathers with ample opportunity to hug and hold their children, many fathers of preteen and teenage boys and girls noted that they were more closely scrutinized by society in general. Brandan, a self-employed sole-custodial father of four, draws links between hegemonic masculinity and homophobia (Connell, 1987, 1995; Kaufman; 1999; Kimmel, 1994) when he says, "I hug and kiss them, but it's not the same. And frankly I'm not as comfortable hugging the big guys as the little guys, Like, the older guys go, 'Hey, man . . .' I mean, we're not homophobic, but it's something you're raised with."

Similarly, most of the single fathers of preteen and teenage girls say that, in some way, public displays of close physical affection can easily be misinterpreted. Henry, a sole-custodial father of two, currently unemployed, says he is always aware that his actions may be misinterpreted:

As a single dad, all I have to do is breathe at the wrong time, or say the wrong thing in front of the wrong person. I am very conscious of that. For example, one of my daughter's favourite rants is "You can't touch me! You can't hit me!" because she has been taught at school about violence and stuff like that. I don't use that against her any more at 12 years old. A couple of years ago, she would get a smack if she needed one. But I am very conscious of the fact that if she screamed that out in public it's like "whoh!" They could be taken away on a moment's notice. Just on suspicion. So I am very nervous about that kind of thing.

Even several fathers living with female partners relay a subtle sense of unease in embodied father–daughter relations. Alexander, a university professor who took parental leave to be with two of his three daughters and is now a joint-custody father, reflects on how things changed when his daughter reached puberty: "When puberty arrives, the entire dynamic changes. You don't think much of the physical thing that goes on with your kids until then. Embracing and hugging. I am trying to think about the parallel with a mother and son. Obviously the same thing happens to a degree, yet far less starkly."

Fathers Rely on Mothers: "You Can Never Replace the Mother"

References to gender differences in parenting also appear throughout fathers' narratives partly because fathers *rely* on mothers to take on the overall primary care of children (see also Daly, 2002; Stueve & Pleck, 2003). That is, the role and influence of mothers on the processes of fathers *becoming* and *enacting* their caregiving is highly significant within these narratives. In two-parent households, or even in joint custody households where parents live apart, the father *expects* that the mother will take on the emotional responsibility for the children. Sasha, an African Canadian, a dance instructor, and a joint-custody father, says, "I think it is a spiritual thing. They were with their mom before they came to earth. That is what men do not have, that extra, extra-special thing with the children."

Luke, a stay-at-home father of two girls for 12 years who now works night shifts in a home for mentally challenged adults, says, "You have to recognize that [even] as a stay-at-home father you can never replace the mother. Don't even think about it."

Narratives of Hegemonic Masculinity and Difference: "We're Still Men, Aren't We?"

Fathers also explicitly and deliberately draw attention to differences in mothering and fathering because they want to distance their fathering from mothering and indeed from any feminine associations attached to it. Archie says that fathers in general respond to children "in a less feminine way. If a kid falls and hurts himself, women would probably rush over more than men. I say, 'Come on, toughen up.' I think there are more differences there. I am not sure how to characterize it."

Indeed, many fathers express confusion about this issue because they simply do not want to equate what they do with the work that women do. As Maurice says when I ask him about housework, "I like to cook. But I wouldn't want to call this women's work."

Theoretical assumptions that can initially assist us in making sense of these processes are those that highlight the way men distance themselves from and devalue the feminine (Bird, 1996; Chodorow, 1978; Connell, 1987, 1995, 2000; Johnson, 1988; Thome, 1993) as well as theoretical work related to the concept of hegemonic masculinity (Coltrane, 1994; Connell, 1987, 1995, 2000; Kimmel, 1994; Messner, 1997). Although there have been varied discussions of the meaning and relevance of the concept hegemonic masculinity, one of the authors who coined it, Connell, has recently boiled it down "the opposite of femininity" (Connell, 2000, 31). The fathers' narratives touched on in this chapter are filled with inchoate contradictions that illuminate how fathers distance themselves from the feminine. Yet, as explained below, some also admit that being a primary-caregiving father allows them the opportunity to find, as one father, Roy, put it, the "feminine in me."

Between Equality and Difference, between Masculine and Feminine

What seems to occur for fathers entering into female-dominated terrain is that by crossing into an area where they have not been traditionally equal to women, they move both between equality and difference and between the stereotypically feminine and masculine. In seeking to find ways of becoming equal or symmetrical to women in their caregiving efforts, men also have hegemonic masculinity at their backs, reminding them that they are men operating in traditional female worlds. Most men, even sole-custody fathers, thus cling to the view that in spite of their most ardent efforts, they can never be mothers or replace the *mothering* done by women. Rather than *duplicate* the maternal terrain travelled, fathers *alter* it to incorporate differences, which could be viewed as more traditionally masculine traits such as independence, autonomy, and sporting interests.

It is notable that most of the gay fathers in this study recognize the need to consider both masculine and feminine in mothering and fathering and to emphasize the importance of traditionally feminine qualities in fathering, particularly in the raising of sons. A good example of these qualities is found in Bernard's narrative. While drawing borders between the moms' house and his own and between "an estrogen world there" and "a testosterone world here," he also points out that he is aware of the need to demonstrate some traditionally feminine qualities in his parenting and to allow Jake to develop his own feminine qualities:

I do some things that are typical of fathering. I throw a ball and play catch, mini golf, take him on the roller coaster, watch movies, play sports. But I also do non-typical things. I let him cry; I am physically demonstrative. I want to break that generational cycle. I let him play with dolls, watch women superheroes like the Power Puff Girls. He plays with girls and boys. I want him to experience things that he is interested in . . . If boys were allowed to be whatever they are, I think that would mean they would become fathers who are extremely close to their children. More expression. Less inhibiting . . . There is male and female in all of us, but the female is pressured out of boys more. The inhibiting of the feminine. Like the censoring of boys' emotions.

Bernard is in fact remarking on the setting-up of borders between girls' and boys' activities and identities and the potential for breaking down some of these borders through the recognition of the "male and female in all of us." This provides a good entry point into using the lenses of *borderwork* and *border crossings* to assist us in seeing and theorizing men's caring work and the "Do men mother?" question. In the final two sections of this chapter, I intersperse men's narratives of care through the metaphors of borderwork as the setting-up of boundaries between men and women and the simultaneous crossing of these same borders through the recognition of "the fluctuating significance of gender in the on-going scenes of social life" (Thorne, 1993, 16).

Borderwork

. . . [M]y work draws on the concept of *borderwork* as developed in the work of Barrie

Thorne, sociologist and ethnographer of children in schools. The concept draws attention to the way context matters greatly in gendered interactions. It also provides a way of describing spaces and times where gender boundaries or borders are instigated between the genders. Like the childhood games that pit girls against boys and create the illusion of irreconcilable and permanent opposite sides, there are parallel moments and sites where gender borders divide mothers and fathers.

There are many instances of borderwork in the narratives collected on mothering and fathering, two of which will be highlighted here. The first one is the overwhelmingly different reactions from mothers and fathers to an anecdote discussed in the individual interviews with fathers as well as in the couple interviews, that of how each parent responds when their child is hurt or has fallen down. Second, there is the constantly reiterated belief in the close embodied connection between mother and child, a connection that most fathers believe they cannot replace or duplicate.

Gendered Responses to the Child's Falling Down: "Oh, Get On with It"

When they speak about their daily routine with children, the, most recurrent example that fathers give as a difference between mothering and fathering is the promotion of children's independence and, more specifically, how parents react to the child's falling down or hurting himself in physical play or solo exploration. This example came up on its own in so many of the first interviews that I started using it as an anecdote and having fathers as well as mothers comment on it. Denise gives the example without being asked: "If Nathan falls down and hurts himself, I am more likely to go and pick him up right away."

Shahin, an Iranian-Canadian cabinet-maker and a stay-at-home father of one son, says, "My wife would be much gentler with my son about how you throw a basketball into a hoop and is willing to put up with mistakes, whereas if my son misses once, I would say, 'Oh get on with it' or 'Get off your tush!' If my son falls, my wife immediately hugs him—whereas I would immediately go there and say, 'No cut, no bruises, you're okay.'"

I ask Harry, a rural poultry farmer and stay-at-home father of two sons, whether he thinks mothering and fathering are different. After a long silence, he responds: "I don't know how to describe it. It's like when they fall and get hurt, we both tell them that everything is going to be all right. But the boys get a different feeling about it from me than from my wife, I'm sure. She is all over them, and from me, well, 'You're all right; let's get on with it.'"

The articulation of a "different feeling" of mothers is related, in turn, to the way fathers narrate a larger story of another emotional connection of mothers and fathers to children.

The Connection between Mother and Child: "It's Something I Will Never Understand"

As described earlier in this chapter, fathers' narratives are marked by a strong belief in fundamental differences between mothering and fathering. These beliefs are so consistent across the study that I came to view them as a second form of borderwork in emotional responsibility. Although there is considerable confusion over just where these differences come from, the majority of women and men nevertheless take the position that mothering and fathering differ in relation to the propensity for connection with their children. As Matthew, an electronics technician on parental leave, says,

"It's not the same. She holds the baby more to her body; she rocks the baby more. I love her and everything, but I don't hug her as much. She's not part of me as much."

Shahin's narrative includes many of the explanations that fathers offer for mothers' greater connection with their children. In one fell swoop, referring to birthing, psychological factors, hormones, and Mother Nature's way of "making sure that the child is protected," he says, "In my opinion, women have an edge in parenting, whether you say psychological or hormonal or whatever, in terms of being able to cope with certain things. I think the bond is vaster in women. Whether it's Mother Nature's way of making sure that the child is protected or not, I think they're willing to put up with a lot more. I think in general that society has made women better workers, or at least those expectations are there. I could never be a woman—I would die of exhaustion!"

Similarly, in a joint interview Nina and Mitchell concur that there is a different connection between the mother and the child, that it may be a spiritual one and of another "nature," as well as something that, as Mitchell says, he may "never understand":

Nina: I think there is more to being a mother than just being a stay-at-home parent. I think there is a difference in terms of what it means to be a mother, what it means to be a father . . . I think part of it has to do with certain early connections with the child. I think the mother is connected just by being the vessel that the child is carried in. You're much more connected.

Mitchell: I'm sure there's a spiritual connection there. It's something I will never understand.

Nina: You know, talking to the child, feeling the child move around inside of you, I always found an incredible experience. I mean, I didn't have great pregnancies, but I just thought it was so neat . . . I think it makes a difference. I don't think that means that fathers can't be connected to their children, but I think that it starts earlier on for the mother. And it changes the nature of the connection.

Like heterosexual fathers, the majority of the gay fathers (seven out of nine) also espouse fundamental differences between mothering and fathering and a belief in the greater significance to the role of the mother, even though they are admittedly uncertain about it. Jean Marc expresses this well. A 43-year-old gay and divorced father of seven-year-old twin boys, he took a four-month parental leave when his twins were infants. He says, "Frankly I am perplexed about the fathering role. I think there is a mothering instinct that goes way beyond what a father feels for his children."

These articulated instances—reacting to a child's falling down and parental reflections on the close bond between mother and child—demonstrate remarkably consistent gendered responses in both mothers' and fathers' narratives and, indeed, "a magnetism of gender-marked events for observers and participants in the realms of memory" (Thorne, 1993, 64). Borderwork thus occurs in specific times, usually the early months and years of parenting when children require a great deal of physical and emotional nurturing. It is also articulated in particular spaces, notably the embodied space between parent and child as most often expressed through the metaphor and empirical reality of the hug. In these moments and sites, gender borders are drawn through the expressed belief that mothering and fathering are oppositional sets of practices and identities.

Crossing Borders

In spite of such borderwork sites and moments, there are also spaces and times in the flow of mothers' and fathers' lives when gender boundaries are relaxed to the point that they are barely noticeable. Then mothers and fathers are side by side and difference in roles is largely indistinguishable. That is, "although the occasions of gender separation may seem more dramatic, the mixed-gender encounters are also theoretically and practically important" (Thorne, 1993, 36). Several such moments are highlighted below as examples of the dismantling or crossing of gender borders.

While fathers acknowledge deep-seated differences between mothers and fathers in their caregiving styles and their perception that mothers have a greater propensity for emotional connection, what emerges in the daily practice of care and emotional responsibility is not so stark. While working through the interview transcripts generated from my interviews with fathers and mothers, I repeatedly attempted to group couples into tidy categories of various kinds of emotional responsibility according to, for example, their protectiveness or the promotion of independence. Yet these efforts were confounded by the way, for each person, and especially in the couple interviews, individuals and couples move back and forth in their views as to *who* was more nurturing, in which contexts, and at which times. That is, these shifts in emotional responsibility are deeply rooted in the changing ages of the children, specific spatial and time-bound contexts, cultural contexts, arid what is occurring in these complex balancing acts between working and caring at

particular points in time. Metaphorically, the back-and-forth movements resemble something of a dance (see also Dienhart, 1998), or the ebb and flow of moving water (Hamilton, 2005; Hekman, 1999). As one mother, Claire, expresses it, *"Looking back over all these years, there is movement and flow."* Six factors are flagged here as important generators of an increased sense of connection and protectiveness on the part of men and the breaking-down of gender borders between mothers and fathers in relation to emotional responsibility.

The Impact of Passing Time and Children's Changing Ages: "Movement and Flow"

Examples of movement and flow over time for two-parent mother/father households is well illustrated by Richard, a stay-at-home father of three young children, and his wife, Aileen. Initially, they point out that their two-year-old son, Jean-Philippe, goes mainly to Aileen when he is upset or tired. When considering why this is the case, Richard notes that Jean-Philippe "gets more sympathy" from his mother, which, in turn, generates a discussion of the changes over time as the children mature:

> Aileen: I think it has changed. It changes through the child's life because when Elizabeth was born, the first—what, two years . . . ?
>
> Richard: Two—three years . . .
>
> Aileen: For two years she didn't want to have anything to do with Richard . . .
>
> Richard: Not to that point . . . but if she got hurt she would go to her mother.

Aileen: She wanted me. And then when she was about two, she changed. And it had to be Richard.

Later in their interview, however, they reverse this view and argue that "Mommy's not as sympathetic." They both agree that Aileen now encourages greater separation from the children while Richard feels more connected to them. Aileen's words have resonances of a traditional fathering model seeking more time and space from his children. When I ask them to whom seven-year-old Elizabeth turns to when she is upset, their joint interview elicits the following responses:

Richard: She will come to me.

Aileen: Mommy's not as sympathetic.

Richard: She'll walk right by her and even ask her where I am. Come and find me . . . in the garage or wherever.

Aileen: That's because you let her come out of her room two or three times every night—me, that's it!

Richard: I don't let her, I mean . . .

Andrea: Are you fine with that, Aileen? You know, the fact that Elizabeth goes to him?

Aileen: Oh, yeah [laughs]. The more they go to him, the more time I have for myself.

Mother Moving Over: "Oh Wow, I Get to Try This"

A second factor that helps to account for changes in the movement and flow of emotional responsibility between men and women is the shifting presence of mothers into and out of the emotional domain of parenting. In spite of the reliance on mothers for emotional responsibility as well as mothers holding on to this as their domain, what is also particularly striking in fathers' narratives is that when mothers are not available or they let go of caring for brief or long periods, fathers do come to take on emotional responsibility for children. When Denise went away for a business trip, for example, Martin came to take a bit more of an emotional role with four-year-old Nathan. In his joint interview with his wife, Denise, he says, "I don't know how to describe it. He is certainly more emotional with Denise, whereas with me, we get out, we wrestle. We still read and cuddle. But not as much. When Denise was away, he got into our bed in the middle of the night, and he was surprised that she wasn't there. But he had a cuddle with me."

William, who set up one of the first series of father-only playgroups in Ottawa over 15 years ago, illustrates that the absence of women in father-centred spaces increased fathers' confidence in their ability to respond to children: "I thought it was very interesting that men learned from other dads. When the wives are there, the men may step aside and let the woman take over."

Dean, who used to be a stay-at-home dad and is now a joint-custody father, "discovered" that he "got to function in areas that [his ex-wife] Carly wouldn't allow [him] to function in before." In his words, "She used to be the listening ear for the girls, sitting with them at night before they went to bed. She would go in and tell a story. Suddenly I got to do some of that. But mostly I would go in and listen to the radio. Get my little earplugs. "They just needed a body in the room. I would be there. And they would chat, you know, and ask, 'Are you still there?' 'Yeah, I'm still here.' And they would fall asleep. This was a ritual that we did with all the children. When she left, it was like, oh wow, I get to try this."

Fathering without a Mother: "I Get Lost in the Nurturing"

Perhaps what is most revealing about the permeability of the line between motherly and fatherly nurturing is at the time that mothers have effectively moved out of parenting. This is the case for the 25 sole-custody fathers in my study who were parenting with only minimal participation by the mother (and the two widowers). In their interviews with me, many of these fathers visibly and audibly struggle with the way to express these thoughts but find themselves admitting that they have become different kinds of father as a result of being on their own with their children. Roy, a military technician and sole-custodial father of a four-year-old boy, speaks about how, when he has a difficult time raising his son, he cannot rely on the child's mother to take care of things. Thus, he grapples with his own inner struggles and reasons that he has become a "soft father" because he is fathering without a mother: "And because he doesn't have that mother side in the house, a mother to turn to me and say, "Would you just go away?" And for her to turn around and take care of things. I'm like, Now what do I do now? If I had to try and fit myself somewhere into the equation, I probably would try to give him more of a soft father than anything else. But a soft father who wants him to learn not just have fun."

Golin, an African-Canadian sole-custody father of four school-age children, finds that nurturing can become all-encompassing: "There is this big cultural background, which

does not escape me, so I draw on that a lot, partly Nigerian, but partly my own family where I grew up. So the nurturing comes from there. I always have to remind myself to set boundaries because I get lost in the nurturing."

Particular Cultural Contexts: "There Are Very Different Expectations"

Ethnicity and gender intersect to create even more issues for fathers to deal with, ones that do not play out in straightforward ways, however. For example, the experience of being a Latino father is related to the length of time he has spent in Canada, his level of education, and the social networks that surround and affect his parenting. That is, a university education in Canada and living among friends and colleagues who espouse symmetrical parenting can greatly mute the effect of ethnic tradition on parenting approaches and beliefs. This is the case with two Latino fathers in the study, Eduardo and Manuel, whose university education and marriages to feminists have led them to shed some ideas on fundamental gender differences that they had absorbed from their Latin-American upbringing. A similar situation occurs for Shahin and Mohammed, two Muslim fathers from Iran whose education levels and marriages to working mothers have encouraged them to question deeply rooted beliefs in gender difference in parenting. As Shahin puts it, "If anything, my background probably would have told me that I shouldn't be doing this [being a stay-at-home father] because I come from a rather chauvinistic country. And then on top of that I was raised with a very strict, very disciplined and harsh father. I never saw a father who raised the kids practically in my life. It was always a mother."

While particular cultural ideas might promote a very specific parenting style and affect gender roles more generally, these influences can be mediated by social networks, choice of marriage partner, or education. What is notable is that for immigrant fathers who remain embedded in their particular cultural community in the larger Canadian society, parenting ideas are more likely to change slowly. Thus, the five Somali immigrant fathers in this study hold to the view that mothering and fathering are different because these are strong cultural ideas retained by both men and women in their community and neighbourhood. Dalmar, for example, is clear that his opinion on the importance of the mother's role with younger children comes from his Somali background. A 52-year-old father of four children and a part-time university lecturer, he finds that neither his high level of education nor his marriage to a social worker have transformed his deeply held cultural views. In a focus group with other Somali fathers, he says, "In Somali culture, the perception is that the mother is important, especially with young children. Just as boys and girls are raised differently, fathers and mothers are not the same. Boys and girls are still treated differently in Somali families. There are very different expectations."

Moments of Crisis and Challenge: "I Guess Because We Lost John . . . "

The crossing of gendered borders in emotional responsibility can also occur as a result of emotional crises that enable, or force, men to shift emotionally. Such severe crises can include one's own childhood traumas, a child's serious illness, losing a child, or the responses to a child with developmental delays or difficulties. Craig speaks about becoming more protective after the death of one of their infant triplets: "I guess because we lost John, I'm an overprotective parent. When I have Zachary in my arms, I am on Michael all the time to stay with me and not to move. The thing is that, if he is going to take off,

I've got Zachary in my arms, and I am not going to be able to catch him as fast as I want do. That is always in the back of my mind."

Some fathers mention moments of crisis or challenge that occurred in their family of origin and that marked the way they cared for others. Kyle, for example, says that his caring for his ill mother was a formative experience in the development of his "female side" and of himself as a shared caregiver of two children: "I think I'm more in touch with my female side than most men are. That may have to do with my upbringing. I had to deal with caring for, in a palliative kind of way, an aging and dying mother for a very long period of time."

Similarly, Luke's vivid story of becoming a caregiver early begins with a traumatic incident that marked him. When I asked him about his own parents, he stumbled with his words as he worked around the edges of the question: "There was not real nurturing from my father, but my mother was a really nurturing person." As I probe to learn more, he admits that "both my parents were alcoholics." Luke describes an accident that marked the beginning of his own emotional and caring capacity: "I had two sisters that were older than I am, but when I was three they died tragically in a bus accident. It was in 1963. They got out of the bus and there was a big steep grade. This transport that was behind the bus tried to stop and let them cross, but he jackknifed, and my two sisters, six and nine years old, and this other girl were killed . . . I don't remember them . . . I don't remember anything in that era. But I do remember I was given the caring role after that."

Being There: "Because of What Has Transpired in My Life . . . "

Gender borders are also taken down by shifts in feelings and behaviour that occur for fathers caring for a child on their own for long periods without having a female partner to rely on. This occurs for fathers parenting alone and for stay-at-home fathers who have had long periods of time alone with their children. Two examples can be provided here.

After his wife left, Ron, a sole-custody father of two school-age children, moved his computer business into his home so that he could balance work and caring for his children. He reflects on how having this "forced on me" led to remarkable changes in his emotional life with his children. In his words, "Because of what has transpired in my life, I have a paternal feeling. And I have a maternal feeling, whatever that means. All I know is that you totally love them to the best of your ability. You protect them . . . There are differences in men and women, but as a parent, the same heart chord can be struck."

Frank, a stay-at-home father of two young children, says that he is now the more protective parent as a result of being at home and that his experience has generated the awareness of his nurturing side: "I have changed from being at home . . . I see this at the park. The kids are running all over the equipment and they're having fun, but I think they're going to fall . . . From my own experience, it's brought out some nurturing side of me. I mean, I knew it was there, but I didn't know to what extent."

Conclusions

In this chapter I have explored, in Sara Ruddick's terms, the first maternal demand or preservation or protective care, which is at its core an ability to know and attentively respond to the needs of one's children. My own naming of this maternal, or paternal, responsibility is that of *emotional responsibility*. The question "Do men mother?" can be answered, at least partially, by asking, Do fathers take on the preservation and protective care of children? Do they resemble mothers in their approach to emotional responsibility?

At first glance, the answer is an affirmative one. My research on primary caregiving fathers joins a large body of scholarship produced over the past two decades that argues that fathers can be just as nurturing and responsive with their children as mothers are. It is well documented that fathers who are actively involved with their children can develop skills that enable them to partake in this task of preservation.

On second glance, the answer to the question, Do men assume emotional responsibility and partake in the task of preservation? is also negative, in the sense that fathers widen our current understandings of protective care, preservation, and ultimately that of emotional responsibility. My research also uncovers some unique dimensions that fathers bring to our understandings of protective care. In examining fathers' caregiving, my work highlights their emphasis on fun and playfulness, especially with infants and young children, physical activities, an outdoors approach, an emphasis on the practical sides of nurturing, and the promotion of independence and risk taking with older children. This occurs for the majority of fathers cross social class, income levels, occupations, ethnicity, and sexuality. While all these dimensions of caring are not normally part of what we consider nurturing behaviour, my argument is that all these elements are important aspects of the emotional responsibility for children. For example, physical and outdoor activities can lead to positive physical and mental developmental outcomes (Beauvais, 2001), which represent, in turn, unique ways of responding to children's needs. Similarly, while the promotion of independence and of risk taking are rarely included in discussions of nurturing, encouraging autonomy in children can be seen as a form of long-term protection and ultimately of connection.

The roots of these strong patterns in fathers' narratives of nurturing can be traced to several key elements in men's lives. This chapter went back to their boyhood, to the embodied experiences of fathers as they move on female-dominated terrains of parenting, to the reliance on mothers, and to the role of hegemonic masculinity. The latter was evident in men's apparent need to emphasize gender differences through the distancing of themselves from the feminine connotations tied up with the work and identities of caring for children.

This chapter has also detailed where and how embodiment figures into the ways that both fathers and mothers accord greater significance to women's emotional connection to children whether symbolically or in practice. In particular, fathers and mothers draw on embodied aspects of early parenting by reference to the physical, emotional, and symbolic experiences of pregnancy, birth, breastfeeding, and post-childbirth recovery. Men and women refer to all the "messy empirical realities of actual flesh and blood bodies" (Monaghan, 2002, 335) and the differing gendered locations of women and men in relation to the passage of children into the world. What remains striking is the belief in the mysterious and symbolic power of *mothering* as something that the majority of men and women inexplicably uphold. Many are perplexed by the strength of this belief, and indeed most are at a complete loss to explain it, but it nevertheless emerges as a dominant theme from fathers' and mothers' narratives. Fathers also draw attention to the way bodies can matter in the physical touching between fathers and preteen/teen daughters, as well as in noting the tensions of men kissing and touching boys in a society where homophobia thrives.

This chapter has also highlighted that though fathers' and mothers' narratives indicate strong beliefs in gender differences in emotional responsibility, there is a fair degree of ebb and flow within households and ultimately some disjunction between beliefs and practices. Following the work of Barrie Thorne, I have named this ebb and flow as the crossing of gender borders and the breaking-down of some of the binary distinctions between mothering and fathering. Notably, the passage of time and children's maturing affect the ebb and flow, as do particular cultural contexts, men's previous experiences of caring, and the effects that family crises have on fathers' beliefs in their nurturing capacities. Perhaps more than anything else, the movement and flow within daily domestic practice is very much led by mothers. That is, the role of the mother is a key factor in determining the ways in which fathers take on the care and emotional responsibility of children. While some theorists within the sociology of the family (i.e., Allen & Hawkins, 1999) have called this "maternal gatekeeping," implying that women exclude men and do not want to give up this area of power and expertise, my research suggests that many fathers also expect mothers to take this on.

Yet, though men do rely on women to take on emotional responsibility, what happens in everyday practice can contradict such expectations. When mothers are not available, or have let go of caring for brief or long periods, fathers do fill the powerful and protective space where emotional responsibility is taken on. There are times when women are unavailable, involved in other activities, or simply need to let go. The mother moves over and the father nudges gently into this space. They will, as Julie says of

Manuel, "father like a mother." If the mother leaves or is a fleeting presence in the daily lives of the children, the father will sometimes take on emotional responsibility in a manner that combines both protection and promotion of independence. As Golin says, "I get lost in the nurturing," and as Roy says, "I'll be a soft father."

To conclude this chapter, the comments of two fathers are apt descriptions of perceived gender difference in emotional responsibility. Ed, a stay-at-home father of two living in rural Ontario comments, "We certainly do look at things differently—housework and activities for the children. I tend to be more concerned about *doing things* with the children rather than making sure the house is perfect. Instead of playgroups, we'll go to the park and walk through the forest."

Archie remarks that in the everyday practical care of children "the broad strokes" remain somewhat different: "Some of the stuff by definition is the same. When you have smaller children, the getting through the day is by definition the same—the feeding, the changing have to be the same. Once you start getting into the non-physical, non-life-sustaining, you do get different practices between women and women. Men are going to be outside more, and more physical. But not always. I think in broad strokes, you will find that women tend to be more emotional and supportive."

As explored in this chapter, these "broad strokes" of parenting where fathering is linked with being "outside more and more physical" while mothering is linked with being "more emotional and supportive" are also related to the larger gendered worlds of women and men. This includes growing up male, issues of embodiment around mothering and fathering, relational narratives of "doing gender" and hegemonic masculinity as revealed mainly in the devaluation of the feminine.

● Notes

1. Perhaps the most well known instigator of this debate is Carol Gilligan (1982) and her book *In a Different Voice*. It is astounding that nearly a quarter-century after its first printing, it is still amply cited in scholarship on care or other aspects of female-dominated practice. Two decades of scrutiny, critique, and appreciation of this work is rooted in Gilligan's claim that there is a moral orientation, "a different voice," which is often associated with women. This "care voice" or "the ethic of care" is characterized by a commitment to maintaining and fostering the relationships in which one is woven (Gilligan, 1982, 19) and an ethic that emphasizes "attachment, particularity, emotion, and intersubjectivity (Cole & Coultrap-McGuin, 1992, 4–5). In contrast, the "justice voice" or the "ethic of justice"—associated mainly with the work on moral development by Gilligan's colleague and mentor, Lawrence Kohlberg, as well as with the work of the liberal political theorist John Rawls—emphasizes individual rights, equality, autonomy, fairness, rationality, a highly individuated conception of persons, and a concept of duty that is limited to the perception that *different* implied *women,* Gilligan's work initially caused a "storm of controversy" (Jaggar, 1990, 249) around the problematic equation of women with care and the associated dangers of essentializing women's caregiving. Gilligan, in response, consistently maintained that though the care voice is heard most often in women, it can also be heard in men (Gilligan, 1986).

2. I am grateful to Carol Gilligan for pointing this out to me.

3. All but one of the gay fathers felt that they parented in a mainly masculine way, drawing on similar patterns of behaviour to heterosexual fathers—emphasizing sports and play, outdoor activity, risk taking, and the promotion of independence.

4. The pattern is also in evidence for the nine gay fathers in the study. Three fathers indicate that they are not really sports oriented, whereas the other six

are. Of the three who claim not to be interested in sports, the one with an infant says that he nevertheless plays with children at playgroup more than the mothers do.

5. Sport itself also needs to be socially and historically located (Burstyn, 1999). According to Michael Messner, "[M]odern sport is a 'gendered institution' in that it is a social institution constructed by men, largely as a response to a crisis of gender relations in the late nineteenth and early twentieth centuries. The dominant structures and values of sport came to reflect the fears and needs of a threatened masculinity. Sport was constructed as a homosocial world, with a male-dominant division of labour that excluded women. Indeed, sport came to symbolize the masculine structure of power over women" (Messner, 1992, 16).

6. Recent literature on boys in school highlights how these processes begin in boyhood, when exhibiting signs of emotion marks boys as wimps (Pollock, 1987) and as "polluting the male ideal" by "conveying qualities of softness, emotion, and embodiment that are dangerously feminine" (Prendergast & Forrst, 1998, 167).

● References

Allen, S.M., & Hawkins, A.J. (1999). Maternal Gatekeeping: Mothers' Beliefs and Behaviors That Inhibit Greater Father Involvement in Family Work. *Journal of Marriage and the Family*, 61, 199–221.

Beauvais, C. (2001). *Literature Review on Learning Through Recreation (Discussion Paper No. F-15)*. Ottawa: Canadian Policy Research Network.

Bird, S.R. (1996). Welcome to the Men's Club: Homosociality and the Maintenance of Hegemonic Masculinity. *Gender & Society*, 19(2), 120–32.

Brandth, B., & Kvande, E. (1998). Masculinity and Child Care: The Reconstruction of Fathering. *The Sociological Review*, 46(2), 293–313.

Chodorow, N. (1978). *The Reproduction of Mothering: Psychoanalysis and the Sociology of Gender*. Berkeley and Los Angeles: University of California Press.

Coltrane, S. (1989). Household Labor and the Routine Production of Gender. *Social Problems*, 36(5), 473–90.

Connell, R.W. (1987). *Gender and Power*. Cambridge: Polity Press.

———. (1995). *Masculinities*. London: Polity Press.

———. (2000). *The Men and the Boys*. Berkeley: University of California Press.

Daly, K. (1993). Reshaping Fatherhood: Finding the Models. *Journal of Family Issues*, 14, 510–30.

Daly, K. (2002). Time, Gender, and the Negotiation of Family Schedules. *Symbolic Interaction*, 25(3), 323–42.

Dienhart, A. (1998). *Reshaping Fatherhood: The Social Construction of Shared Parenting*. London: Sage.

Doucet, A. (2000). "There's a Huge Difference Between Me as a Male Carer and Women": Gender, Domestic Responsibility, and the Community as an Institutional Arena. *Community Work and Family*, 3(2), 163–84.

———. (2001). You See the Need Perhaps More Clearly than I Have: Exploring Gendered Processes of Domestic Responsibility. *Journal of Family Issues*, 22(3), 328–57.

———. (2004). Fathers and the Responsibility for Children: A, Puzzle and a Tension. *Atlantis: A Women's Studies Journal*, 28(2), 103–14.

Dowd, N.E. (2000). *Redefining Fatherhood*. New York: New York University Press.

Fisher, B., & Tronto, J. (1990). Towards a Feminist Theory of Caring. In M.K. Nelson (Ed.), *Circles of Care: Work and Identity in Women's Lives* (pp. 35–62). New York: State University of New York Press.

Gilligan, C. (1982). *In a Different Voice: Psychological Theory and Women's Development*. Cambridge, MA: Harvard University Press.

Graham, H. (1983). Caring: A Labor of Love. In D.A. Groves (Ed.), *A Labor of Love: Women, Work and Caring* (pp. 13–30). London: Routledge and Kegan Paul.

Kaufman, M. (1999). Men, Feminism, and Men's Contradictory Experiences of Power. In J.A. Kuypers (Ed.), *Men and Power* (pp. 59–83). Halifax: Fernwood Books.

Kimmel, M.S. (1994). Masculinity as Homophobia: Fear, Shame and Silence in the Construction of Gender Identity. In M. Kaufman (Ed.), *Theorizing Masculinities* (pp. 119–41). Thousand Oaks, CA: Sage.

Kremarik, F. (2000). Family Affair: Children's Participation in Sports. *Canadian Social Trends (Statistics Canada)*, Autumn 2000, 20–4.

Lamb, M.E. (Ed.). (1981). *The Role of the Father in Child Development*. New York: John Riley.

———. (Ed.). (1987). *The Father's Role: Cross-cultural Perspectives*. Hillsdale NJ: Erlbaum.

Larrabee, M.J. (Ed.). (1993). *An Ethic of Care: Feminist and Interdisciplinary Perspectives*. New York and London: Routledge.

Lupton, D., & Barclay, L. (1997). *Constructing Fatherhood: Discourses and Experiences*. London: Sage.

Mac an Ghaill, M. (1994). *The Making of Men: Masculinities, Sexualities, and Schooling*. Buckingham: Open University.

Martin, P.Y. (2003). "Said and Done" Versus "Saying and Doing": Gendering Practices, Practicing Gender at Work. *Gender and Society,* 17(3), 342–66.

Messner, M.A. (1997). *Politics of Masculinities: Men in Movements.* Thousand Oaks, CA: Sage.

Monaghan, L.F. (2002).. Hard Men, Shop Boys and Others: Embodying Competence in a Masculinist Occupation. *The Sociological Review,* 50(3), 334–55.

Noddings, N. (2003). *Caring: A Feminine Approach to Ethics and Moral Education* (2nd edn). Berkeley: University of California Press. .

Parke, R.D. (1996). *Fatherhood.* Cambridge, MA: Harvard University Press.

Plantin, L., Sven-Axel, M., & Kearney, J. (2003). Talking and Doing Fatherhood on Fatherhood and Masculinity in Sweden and England. *Fathering,* 1(1), 3–26.

Pleck, J.H. (1985). *Working Wives, Working Husbands.* London: Sage.

Pruett, K. (2000). *Fatherneed: Why Father Care Is as Essential as Mother Care for Your Child.* New York: Broadview Press.

Ruddick, S. (1995). *Maternal Thinking: Towards a Politics of Peace* (2nd edn). Boston: Beacon.

Seidler, V. (1997). *Man Enough: Embodying Masculinities.* London: Sage.

Snarey, J. (1993). *How Fathers Care for the Next Generation: A Four-Decade Study.* Cambridge, MA: Harvard University Press. .

Stueve, J.L., & Pleck, J.H. (2003). Fathers' Narratives of Arranging and Planning: Implications for Understanding Parental Responsibility. *Fathering,* 1(1), 51–70.

Thorne, B. (1993). *Gender Play: Girls and Boys in School.* Buckingham, UK: Open University Press.

Tronto, J. (1989). Women and Caring: What Can Feminists Learn about Morality from Caring? In S. Bordo (Ed.), *Gender Body/Knowledge: Feminist Reconstructions of Being and Knowing* (pp. 172–87). New Brunswick and London: Rutgers University Press.

———. (1993). *Moral Boundaries: A Political Argument for an Ethic of Care.* New York and London: Routledge.

———. (1995). Care as a Basis for Radical Political Judgements (Symposium on Care and Justice). *Hypatia,* 10(2), 141–49.

Ungerson, C. (1990). The Language of Care: Crossing the Boundaries. In C. Ungerson (Ed.), *Gender and Caring: Work and Welfare in Britain and Scandinavia* (pp. 8–33). New York: Harvester Wheatsheaf.

Yogman, M.W., Cooley, & Kindlon, D. (1988). Fathers, Infants and Toddlers: A Developing Relationship. In C.P. Cowan (Ed.), *Fatherhood Today: Men's Changing Role in the Family* (pp. 53–65). New York: Wiley.

Section 3

The Work of Sustaining Families

Chapter 17

There are many reasons why the division of household work based on gender has been resistant to change. The low status of care work in a capitalist economy and the fact that this kind of work is seen as "women's work" are important cultural causes. The differences in the bargaining power of men and women, which in large part reflect their different positions in the paid labour force, are important structural causes. The fact that upper-middle- and upper-class couples have been able to employ women from Third World countries to do the work that they have no time for is an important cause as well.

In this chapter, Sedef Arat-Koç reviews the history of government policy that has continually chosen to enable couples with money to meet their child care needs by shifting much of the work to the shoulders of a woman whose poverty and migration status give her no other work options. As well, Arat-Koç examines the situation of these workers, and the factors that make them vulnerable to exploitation. Finally, she explains what it means for these domestic workers to leave their own families behind.

The Politics of Family and Immigration in the Subordination of Domestic Workers in Canada

Sedef Arat-Koç

Despite the sustained labour-force involvement of a majority of women, neither the availability and the quality of socialized child care arrangements nor the division of household work between men and women appear to have changed radically. The structure, demands, and pressures of the labour market in Canada allow for little flexibility in the accommodation of family needs and responsibilities. Under these circumstances, housework and child care remain private problems to be shouldered mainly by women, who must either work double and triple days or find substitutes.

In this context, the employment of live-in domestic workers has been a solution to the burdens of housework and child care among high- and middle-income groups. Yet the way domestic service is organized in capitalist society in general, and the specific conditions of the majority of live-in domestic workers (98 per cent of whom are women), make this type of work particularly oppressive.

In discussing the implications of the domestic service "solution" to the housework and child care problem, I will document and analyze the structural and historical conditions of live-in domestic workers in Canada. My primary focus is on foreign domestic workers with temporary work permits. The conditions of this group best demonstrate the complex articulation of gender issues with those of class, race, and citizenship.

The Crisis of the Domestic Sphere

There has been a very significant increase in women's participation in the labour force in

Canada since the 1960s. What is interesting is that the change has been most dramatic for women with children. The employment rate for women living with partners whose youngest child was under three years of age rose from 36 per cent in 1976 to 70.5 per cent in 2009; the employment rate for those whose youngest children was three to five years old rose from 45.5 per cent to 79.2 per cent in the same period (Statistics Canada 2012: 1). The percentage of two-parent families with only one income earner declined from 37.2 per cent in 1976 to 14.4 per cent in 2007. By 2007, about 85 per cent of two-parent families had two income earners (Vanier Institute 2010: 83).

The response of society and the state to these changes in women's employment has been negligible. First, women continue to do significantly more housework and child care than men, although men are now doing more housework and child care than they used to (Marshall 2006). Even in dual-earner couples in which both partners work full time women do considerably more household work than men (Marshall 2006: 13). Moreover, women continue to hold the responsibility for the household work that needs to be done every day.

Second, the child care situation in Canada has been in a state of crisis for some time. Rather than keeping up with the need for adequate, affordable, and quality spaces, child care in Canada in the 1990s had become, as Susan Prentice put it, "less, worse, and more expensive" (Prentice 1999). There has been no substantial change since then because neither federal nor provincial governments have committed to providing child care to every child who needs it (Mahon 2007). A very large percentage of children receiving non-parental care are in unlicensed arrangements, the quality and dependability of which are unknown. In 2006, only about 17 per cent of children under

the age of 13 had access to regulated child care centres in Canada (Friendly, Beach, Ferns, and Turiano 2007). And access to regulated child care varies tremendously by province, from almost 35 per cent in Quebec to less than 6 per cent in Saskatchewan (Friendly and Prentice 2009: 42). The OECD has reported that access rates to regulated daycare for Canadian children three to six years of age is less than a quarter of the rates for children in most European countries (Friendly and Prentice 2009: 63).

A third factor that contributes to a crisis of the domestic sphere has to do with the inflexibility of work arrangements. Canadian employers and the state have provided little accommodation for the family responsibilities of working people. Except for an extended parental-leave system, Canada lacks official recognition of recent changes in the labour force. Without the rights to refuse shift work and overtime and to work reduced hours or flexible workweeks (rights that are almost commonplace in Europe), working parents in Canada find that even privatized solutions fail to meet their needs (The Task Force on Child Care 1986).

As a result of the squeeze on working parents from pressures in the public and private spheres, there are signs that employment of domestic servants, a rare practice since the 1920s, has become widespread again. Decades ago, several governmental and mass-media sources mentioned the employment of domestic workers as a solution to the need for child care (Royal Commission on the Status of Women 1970; Hook 1978; Vanstone 1986). There was evidence then that the employers of live-in domestic workers were overwhelmingly dual-career couples with small children. For 71.4 per cent of employers in the 1980s, the major reason for hiring a domestic was to "free both spouses for the labour market" (The Task Force on Immigration Practices and Procedures 1981:

35–45). While the majority of employers have been in upper-middle to upper-income categories, there is a possibility that the demand for live-in domestic servants among middle-income families will continue to rise. An important reason for this is that user fees—as opposed to municipal, provincial, or national government financing—constitute a high proportion of child-care costs and middle-class families cannot get subsidies for such services in Canada. The fees parents pay for regulated child care in large cities can be as high as $2000 a month; it is not uncommon to pay nearly $1000 a month in many places—except in Quebec where the parent fee for child care for an infant or toddler is only $154 a month ($7 a day) (Friendly and Prentice 209: 63). It has been suggested that especially for parents with two or more preschool children, the employment of a live-in nanny costs significantly less than sending children to a daycare centre or hiring live-out help (Vanstone 1986: 51; Walmsley 1989: 129).

While the demand for domestic workers rises, the conditions of domestic service in general and live-in service in particular are so undesirable that it is very difficult to find Canadians willing to do the job. As a result, the Canadian Department of Immigration has devised mechanisms to bring in domestic workers, usually from the Third World, on temporary status. Most (96 per cent) of these workers are in live-in service (The Task Force on Immigration Practices and Procedures 1981: 53).

Although foreign domestic workers have certainly provided some solution to the pressures their employers face in meeting the demands of work and family, this solution is very questionable when one considers the working and living conditions of the workers involved. This paper starts with a short history of domestic service. The discussion of the conditions of domestic workers is divided into four parts. The first part examines the labour process in domestic service and analyzes what the domestic worker shares with the housewife. The second part focuses on the ambiguous status of the domestic as a special type of worker who is neither a member of the family nor an employee in the public sphere, enjoying some advantages of socialized work. In the third part, the citizenship status of foreign domestic workers in Canada is analyzed as a major factor contributing to, as well as perpetuating, the oppressiveness of their conditions. Finally, the status of domestic workers as mothers is briefly described.

History of Domestic Service

The emergence of domestic service, service provided by non-family members in the domestic sphere, is relatively recent, corresponding to the public/private split that came about with industrialization. Although servants were very widely employed in feudal Europe, the nature of their work and their status differed significantly from those of later domestic servants.

In feudal Europe, the labour requirements of most households—including those of most peasants and artisans—necessitated, at least during certain phases of their family cycle, the employment of servants. Servants were the children of poorer families and/or the children of families in different phases of their family life cycle. Social historians like Flandrin (1979) and Mitterauer and Sieder (1982) have clearly demonstrated that in an era when "family" was synonymous with household, servants were very much a part of the patriarchal family, owing the same obedience to, and expecting the same protection and guidance as would, any family member, especially a child. In households that combined productive and reproductive work, servants performed unspecialized work alongside other family members, little of which had to do with the creation and maintenance of a comfortable domestic environment (Fairchilds 1984: 23–4).

With industrialization, the types of work performed by the family were divided and assigned to separate and gendered spheres. As the middle-class home sought to become a "haven" in the competitive and harsh environment of early industrial society, the very purposes and nature of servant-keeping were transformed to serve the new emphasis on domestic comfort. Changes in the structure of society and the family in this period affected domestic service in more ways than one. Parallel to servants' work becoming exclusively "domestic" for the first time was the "feminization" of the occupation. As the home was defined to be women's sphere and housework to be women's work, domestic servants as well as their employers became predominantly female.

Another change that characterized this period of transformation was the increased social distance between master and servant. Two factors contributed to this. One was the increased privatization of the family, which defined it as a nuclear unit of parents and children and excluded servants as "strangers" (Fairchilds 1984: 13–17; Rollins 1985: 33–6). Second, unlike the situation in feudal peasant and artisan households, where masters were direct producers, some of the bourgeois mistresses of the new domestic servants began to separate themselves from manual work. While the majority of middle-class women who could only afford one servant had to work side by side with them to keep up with highly demanding housework, upper-class women, committed to an ideology of domesticity, nevertheless began to maintain a clear distinction between their own managerial and supervisory roles in the

home and the physical drudgery that servants undertook (Dudden 1983).

The history of domestic work in both Canada and the United States has been closely connected to histories of racial and ethnic relations and immigration, as well as to industrialization and urbanization. During the colonial period in the United States, domestic service was performed mainly by convicts, **indentured** servants, and black slaves. In this period, the low status and indignities that servants suffered were common in both the south and the north (Rollins 1985: 49).

From the American Revolution until about mid-nineteenth century, the exploitative and degrading treatment of black slaves in the American South coincided with relatively egalitarian master/servant relationships in the northern United States and Canada. The term *help* was used for the native-born whites in the American North, who partially replaced the foreign or black servants of the colonial period (Rollins 1985). Generally employed by farmers and small shopkeepers, the "help" co-operated with the employer in the hard work of the household economy. The relationship of "help" to their employers was quite egalitarian in the sense that they shared the conditions and the tables of the families for whom they worked. Also distinguishing the "help" from past and future groups of domestic workers was the fact that theirs was less an occupation and lifelong status than an activity that allowed casual, temporary, and/or part-time employment (Dudden 1983). These conditions contrasted sharply with relations in bourgeois households in the cities, where the social distance between employers and employees was growing.[1]

From around the middle of the nineteenth century to the 1920s, the kinds of changes in domestic service that occurred in Europe as a result of industrialization and urbanization also prevailed in North America. As the urban middle-class family became more privatized, its emphasis on domestic comforts and luxury increased and therefore it became more dependent than ever on outsiders to actualize its standard of a private haven. While this substantially increased the demand for domestic workers, changes such as the decline in the general status of the domestic sphere, the "bourgeoisification" of servant employers, and the distinction drawn between the family and non-family members precluded better working and living conditions for domestic workers.

Further contributing to a decline in the status of servants—or, in certain regions, the persistence of their low status—was the availability of groups of vulnerable workers. In the northeastern United States, immigrants like the Irish—many of them single women—were fleeing economic desperation in their own countries. Finding almost no alternatives to domestic work, they were particularly vulnerable. The term *servant,* which was rarely used in the democratic atmosphere of the post-revolution era in the American North, was reintroduced in this period (Steinberg 1981: 159; Rollins 1985: 51–2). In regions where there were large concentrations of people of colour, it was usually the women of the oppressed racial/ethnic groups who had to take domestic service positions.

> Despite differences in the composition of the populations and the mix of industries in the regions, there were important similarities in the situation of Mexicans in the southwest, African Americans in the south, and Japanese people in northern California and Hawaii. Each of these groups was placed in a separate legal category from whites, excluded from rights and protections accorded to full citizens. (Glenn 1992: 8)

Since the turn of the twentieth century, changes in the labour market as well as changes in the household have led to a decline in domestic service. First, alternative avenues of female employment opened up, as industrialization proceeded and some white-collar occupations were feminized. So, women rejected domestic service in favour of better working conditions elsewhere. Even when net wages from clerical, shop, or factory work were lower, women left domestic work to enjoy the relative independence of private life after work (Barber 1985). The demand for domestic workers also began to fall with improvements in household technology, falling birth rates, and the market production of goods previously produced in the household (Leslie 1974: 74). Since the beginning of the twentieth century, increased access to electricity, running water, and sewage systems; mechanization of heating, refrigeration, laundry; the development of food processing; and increased use of ready-made clothing meant for middle- and upper-class women that one person alone (in this case, the housewife) could do all the housework (Fox 1980; Luxton 1980). To the extent that domestic service survived, living-out became more widespread (Rollins 1985: 54).

In Canada, despite women's unwillingness to enter domestic service, employers were remarkably successful in maintaining a large supply of servants until World War II. Organized around church groups, YWCA, and other women's clubs and organizations, women seeking domestics were greatly helped by the Immigration Department (Leslie 1974; Roberts 1979). As domestic service in urban Canada became so undesirable that no native-born whites would do it, and as industrialization diverted women into other occupations, the Immigration Department became increasingly and more directly involved in ensuring a supply of domestics.

Although the demand for domestic workers decreased from the early part of the twentieth century until the late 1960s, it has always exceeded the supply. This has especially been the case for live-in jobs. As a result, the Department of Immigration developed new schemes in the post-war period to bring domestic workers to Canada, and to keep them doing domestic work.

The Material Conditions of Privatized Household Work

The geographic, economic, social, and ideological separation of the public work sphere from the home, which developed with socialized commodity production under capitalism, has led to a decline in the status of domestic labour—whether done by a housewife or a servant. One of the causes of this decline is the physical, economic, and ideological invisibility of domestic labour. Physically, what makes domestic labour "invisible" is the service or maintenance nature of the work whose products are either intangible or consumed very quickly. The domestic labourer is at a disadvantage compared to the factory worker in this regard:

> The appropriate symbol for housework (and for housework alone) is not the interminable conveyor belt but a compulsive circle like a pet mouse in its cage spinning round on its exercise wheel unable to get off . . . (Williams, Twart, and Bachelli 1980: 114)

Also, domestic labour is performed in private, and perhaps is more isolated than ever before in human history. As the production of goods as well as services (such as education and health care) moved out of the home, as the husband and children left, and as the development of household technology made collaboration in certain tasks with other women less necessary, the household worker faced increased isolation, loneliness, and invisibility.

Economically, domestic labour is invisible because it is not part of capitalist production that utilizes wage labour to produce commodities (for the market) and profit. When performed by the housewife, domestic labour is unpaid; it produces use value and no profit. The work is more visible when carried out by a domestic servant because it is paid. As one domestic servant stated, however, it still can remain invisible, even in the eyes of the female employer:

> You know how housework is; you could tidy up the house and wash the dishes 20 times a day. At the end of each day, especially with three growing boy child, the house look like a hurricane pass through it, so when she is in a bad mood she wants to know what I do all day. (Noreen in Silvera 1983: 25)

Domestic labour involves physical and mental work, which goes into the reproduction of labour power and of the labour force. This is indispensable for the economy. Intertwined as it is with intimate, personal relations, however, domestic labour is considered a private matter, a "labour of love." As such, it is ideologically invisible as a form of real and hard work, a status that is hard to change even when it is paid.

Domestic labour generally does not appear on paycheques or in GNP figures; it is not considered "real work," and is defined as "nonproductive." Yet it involves very long working hours.[2] It is work that never ends. Especially for caregivers of young children who must be always on call, there is no clear boundary between work and leisure. For the housewife and the live-in domestic servant, the place of work is also the place of leisure. A domestic does not go to work, but wakes up to it. This makes her "leisure" vulnerable to interventions and her work hours stretchable to 24 hours a day, seven days a week.

Contrary to its image as a place of comfort and safety, the home is a hazardous and stressful workplace for the domestic labourer. Besides working with dangerous chemicals and being involved in several activities that are accident prone, the domestic worker also experiences stress. Stress is typical for occupations that involve high demand and low control (Rosenberg 1986; 1987). In domestic work, the need to adjust the work to the different schedules of family members, and to juggle conflicting demands of housework and child care, create stressful conditions. Being her own boss is largely a myth for the housewife. It is probably more so for the domestic worker whose schedule and standards of work are controlled by the employer.

Unlike wage labour which is—at least theoretically—changeable, the labour of the housewife is a lifelong, or at least marriage-long, commitment. Compared to the housewife, the domestic servant should fare better in this respect. This is only the case when we consider the free labourer, however. Domestic servants in Canada have very often been restricted in their ability to change employers, or even to decide whether or not to sell their labour power.

Although domestic labour under capitalism assumes several universal characteristics such as invisibility, isolation, and low status, the way these are experienced by individuals performing domestic labour may vary significantly by class, race, and citizenship. In the case of foreign domestic workers, the isolation

and resulting loneliness imposed by the privatized nature of housework and child care are perpetuated by racial, cultural, and linguistic barriers. Likewise, the invisibility of domestic labour and the low status attached to it are further reinforced by the powerlessness of domestic labourers when they are visible-minority women from the Third World on temporary work permits, who lack basic political rights.

Neither a Wife Nor a Worker: The Contradictions of the Domestic Worker's Status

While sharing with the housewife many of the material conditions of privatized housework and child care, the domestic worker also has an ambiguous status: she is neither a wife nor a full-fledged worker with corresponding rights and privileges. Squeezed between the private and public spheres, she belongs to neither one nor the other, and probably experiences the worst aspects of both.

With the historical privatization of the family, the domestic worker has been excluded from membership in, or close bonding with, the employing family. Lost are the co-operation and companionship apparently characteristic of relations between "help" and employers in rural America. The domestic worker today is like a stranger, "being in the family, but not of it" (Leslie 1974: 87). She is involved in the work of a house, but not the pleasures and intimacies of a home. Positive aspects that are rightly or wrongly attributed to the private sphere—love, intimacy, nurturance, companionship—are not even part of her realistic expectations.

> I feel as if this is my home. It is my home, this is where I live. It's not like I come to work for them and then evening time I leave and go home. When you are living

with them, they make you feel as if you really don't belong, and where the devil do you really belong? It's a funny thing to happen to us, because it make us feel like we don't know if we coming or going. This live-in thing really puts us in a funny situation. (Gail in Silvera 1983: 113)

Potentially, lack of intimacy with the employing family is liberating. Since class differences turn close employer–employee relationships into paternalistic ones, many domestic workers actually prefer maintaining a business-like professionalism. Professionalism in relations, however, is not possible for the domestic worker, since it requires relative power in social, political, and legal terms. Historically, the social construction of domestic work in Canada has deprived domestic workers from these forms of power.

In losing the close relationship to the family and becoming an employee, the domestic worker has not been compensated by the advantages other employees enjoy. The isolation of domestic service makes the organization of workers, as well as the standardization and regulation of working conditions, very difficult. This difficulty is greater for live-in workers for whom there is no separation between home and work. The result is generally a vulnerable and often exploited worker whose conditions are at the mercy of the employer:

Wages are too often regulated by the employer's bank account, hours of service by his personal caprice, and moral questions by his personal convenience. (Salmon, cited in Leslie 1974: 112)

Labour standards legislation—which is under provincial jurisdiction in Canada and therefore not uniform—either does not apply or only partially applies to domestic workers. As of the mid-1980s, domestic employees in private homes were totally excluded from labour standards legislation in Alberta, New Brunswick, Nova Scotia, the Northwest Territories, and the Yukon. In other provinces they were only partially covered—in many, only with provisions providing lower than the general minimum wage, longer than the 40-hour workweek and rarely any overtime pay (The Task Force on Immigration Practices and Procedures 1981: 74–8; Estable 1986: 51–3).

In Ontario, which has about two-thirds of all domestic workers in Canada, the Employment Standards Act was extended finally to domestics in 1984. It set daily and weekly rates of pay based on a standard workweek of 44 hours. This change, however, was almost meaningless for live-in domestic workers because they were not covered by the hours of work and overtime pay provisions of the Act. Since it is not uncommon for live-in domestic workers to work or be on call 60 to 80 or more hours per week, the actual hourly wage can in many cases fall substantially below the minimum wage. Working very long hours and having little or no time off are actually some of the most common complaints of live-in domestic workers:

I want something where I can go home to my house at night, close my door and pray to my God in peace. I want to know that when I go to bed at night, I don't have to listen out for people shouting at me to come and look after their food or come and change diapers. (Noreen in Silvera 1983: 26)

It took two years of negotiations with the Ontario government, and a Charter of Rights case against it (filed by the Toronto Organization for Domestic Workers' Rights, INTERCEDE) before Ontario acquired labour regulations (in October 1987) that gave live-in domestic workers the right to claim overtime pay after a 44-hour work-week.[3] Whether or not this provision is enforced depends on how much de facto bargaining power domestics have in relation to their employers. So far, even when protective legislation exists, governments have generally failed to enforce it. In practice, especially when they are dealing with vulnerable workers who have no choice but to remain in their jobs, employers are free to set work hours, duties, and pay rates.

In Ontario, provincial governments have not only failed to enforce existing legislation but also have prevented domestic workers from defending their rights in an organized, collective way. The Ontario Labour Relations Act denies the domestics employed in private homes the right to unionize. The same Act also denies domestics access to an impartial tribunal for unfair practices (Estable 1986: 51).[4] In the early 1990s, the NDP government in Ontario symbolically recognized the right of domestic workers, along with other groups of previously non-unionized workers, to unionize—but did not provide solutions for the practical difficulties of organizing from the private sphere. After the Conservative Party came to power in 1995, however, even this symbolic right was taken away (Fudge 1997).

In some cases, existing regulations may even sanction abuse. One serious problem domestic workers face is the lack of clear job definitions. The Canadian Classification and Dictionary of Occupations (which the Immigration Department used until 1997 in connection with employment authorizations), for example, added to the problem. In this system *babysitter* was defined as someone who, besides doing other work, "ke[pt] children's quarters clean and tidy" and "cleans other

parts of home." The definition of *maid/domestic*, on the other hand, included, "may look after children" (The Task Force on Immigration Practices and Procedures 1981: 76). The specific combination of the class status of the domestic worker and the fact that domestic service takes place in the private sphere creates the potential for a very peculiar relation of domination between the employer and the domestic worker, especially if there is a live-in arrangement—which is compulsory for foreign domestic workers on temporary work permits.

There are social–psychological dimensions to the subordination of a domestic worker that make it different from the subordination of housewives (who also do domestic work) and workers (who also stand in an unequal class relation to their employers). While a factory worker experiences subordination and control during work, when she leaves her job at the end of the day she is a free person in relation to her employer. The live-in domestic worker, on the other hand, cannot leave her workplace and her employer's supervision. Sharing private space with the employers, and yet not being part of their family, the domestic finds it difficult to create her own private space and private life:

> Some domestics have to share a room with the children in the household or have their room used as a family room, TV room, sewing room, etc. One woman had to keep her door open at all times in case the children started to cry; others say their employers do not respect their privacy and walk in without knocking. In one case the piano was moved into the domestic's room for the children to practice on! (Epstein 1983: 26)

Living in the employer's home, it is also difficult to invite friends over. Other specific complaints about lack of privacy refer in certain cases to the domestic's mail and phones being watched, personal belongings searched, and inquiries into her activities after days off (Silvera 1981; 1983). Because live-in domestic service creates the possibilities of total scrutiny over both the work and the lives of domestic workers, it probably is not an exaggeration to call it a "total institution" (Cock 1980: 58–60; Fairchilds 1984: 102–4).

Clearly, during its historical development, domestic service lost only some of the elements of the child-like status it had in earlier patriarchal households. Gone are the protection, security, and bonding to the family that were typical of service in feudal society; remaining are the supervision and the personal nature of the authority relationship that strip the domestic worker of full adult status. Linguistic practices are often reflective of this. For example, it is very common for both employers and domestics themselves to refer to domestics as "girls," regardless of their age. It is also common for domestic workers to be called by their first names while they are expected to address their employers as Mr. or Mrs. (Hook 1978: 63; Rollins 1985: 158).

Besides demanding physical work, domestic service involves a personal relationship with the employer. Unlike factory work, which requires completion of clearly defined tasks in clearly defined ways, domestic service is very unstructured. Especially in live-in arrangements, a domestic is not just hired for specific tasks, "but for general availability; above all, a servant ha[s] to take orders as well" (Leslie 1974: 83). Consequently, the deference, obedience, and submissiveness that the domestic is supposed to display can sometimes be as important or a more important part of her job than the actual physical work.[5] The domestic worker, therefore, is hired not for her labour

alone but also for her personality traits.

Also unique to the employer–employee relationship in domestic service is that both the domestic and the mistress are designated, on the basis of gender, as responsible for domestic work. In different studies, all the female employers interviewed have indicated that they needed the domestic worker to help them because their husbands would not (Kaplan 1985; Rollins 1985). Employment of a domestic worker has enabled these women to avoid a confrontation with their husbands about sharing domestic work. In this sense, the presence of the domestic worker "emphasizes the fact that women—all women—are responsible for cleaning the house, at the same time that it releases the housewife to become a lady of leisure or a career woman" (Kaplan 1985: 17). Given the gendered division of labour in the household, the labour of the housewife and the domestic worker are interchangeable: the domestic worker is employed to replace an absent full-time housewife; but when the domestic worker can't work, the housewife must. Given social degradation of domestic work and the class inequality between the domestic worker and the mistress, however, their shared subordination does not often lead to solidarity:

> the domestic represents the employer in the most devalued area of the employer's activities. . . . Any identification the employer has with the domestic is a negative identification. (Rollins 1985: 185)

Rather than solidarity, shared subordination can lead to "housewife power strategies" through which "many housewives seek to maintain class and race privileges vis-à-vis their domestics" (Kaplan 1985). Often, what characterizes servant–mistress relationships is deference from the worker and maternalism from the employer.

Good Enough to Work, Not Good Enough to Stay: Implications of Citizenship Status for Foreign Domestic Workers

From the nineteenth century on, the Canadian state has been very active in recruiting and controlling a domestic labour force (Leslie 1974; Barber 1986; Lindstrom-Best 1986). The amount of planning and energy that has gone into these activities tells us a great deal about the importance of domestic service for the Canadian economy and society. The low status and unfavourable conditions of the workers involved, however, stand in stark contrast to the attention their recruitment and control have received. In fact, the conditions have been so undesirable that not only has it been difficult to find Canadians interested in the job, but the only way of keeping immigrant domestics in domestic work has sometimes been through indenturing them.

Active state involvement in recruitment and control of domestic workers started in the late nineteenth century when industrialization diverted women into other occupations and it became difficult to find enough Canadian-born women interested in domestic service. This involvement ranged from making the immigration of domestics easier by sending immigration employees to England and Scotland to select domestics, to encouraging and even enforcing the so-called "assisted passage" agreements that bonded servants to their employers for a certain period of time (Leslie 1974: 95–105). Bonding became such a necessary part of controlling the domestic labour force that the Department of Immigration sometimes evaded legislation in order to fulfill its policing function. For example, around the turn of the century, most provinces enacted master and servant legislation aimed to protect servants from an exploitative contract that they might have signed in order to immigrate. According to this legislation, contracts signed outside the province were not legally binding. The Immigration Department, however, in order to enforce bonded status, avoided this legislation by having immigrant domestics re-sign their contracts upon arrival in Canada (Leslie 1974: 122, 79ff).

Immigration of British and Scottish domestic workers in the late nineteenth and early twentieth centuries shared with later domestic immigration the practice of bonding. What made immigration practices in this period different from later periods, however, was that recruitment of domestics from abroad was closely linked to Canada's nation-building efforts. Until the 1920s, the middle-class women and social reformers involved in female immigration work voiced racist, nationalist, and moralistic concerns that went beyond a simple interest in meeting demands for the domestic labour force. Through their efforts in selecting, protecting, and supervising domestics, the organizations involved in female immigration wanted to make sure that the recruits would become more than servants—that these women of the "right" national and racial stock and character would, in the long run, constitute the "pure and virtuous mothers of the ideal Canadian home and the foundation of the moral Canadian nation" (Roberts 1979: 188–9). While these expectations were certainly restrictive for domestic workers, they also conveyed the message that these women "belonged" in Canadian society, a message that would be missing in later immigration practices.

The West Indian Domestic Scheme

Although the demand for domestic servants has decreased since the early part of the twentieth century, it has still exceeded the supply. This has especially been the case for live-in jobs. As a result, the Department of Immigration has developed new schemes in the post-war period to bring domestic workers to Canada and to keep them doing domestic work. In 1955, for example, the Domestic Worker Program was started to import domestic workers from the Caribbean region (primarily from Jamaica). Under this scheme single women of good health, between 18 and 40 years of age, with no dependants and of at least Grade 8 education, were allowed into Canada as landed immigrants on the condition that they would spend at least one year as domestic servants before being free to choose other types of work (Arnopoulos 1979: 26). Through this program, between 1955 and 1960 an average of 300, and between 1960 and 1965 around 1,000 domestic workers were admitted per year (Bolaria and Li 1985: 178).

Even though the West Indian Domestic Scheme brought in domestics as landed immigrants, it involved special "administrative controls" which were missing in previous immigration schemes involving white European domestics. Any domestic who broke her contract or was found "undesirable" (e.g., upon becoming pregnant in her first year) would be deported to her country of origin at the expense of the Caribbean government. Also, unlike preferred domestics from western and northern Europe, West Indian domestics were not eligible to apply for interest-free travel loans from the Canadian government under the Assisted Passage Loan Scheme (Calliste 1989: 143).

The Introduction of Temporary Status

In the late 1960s, the demand for domestic workers started to increase in Canada. This was due to women's increasing participation in the labour force and the underdeveloped child care system they faced. In this period, the Department of Immigration started to see the Domestic Worker Program as an inadequate solution to the labour shortage in domestic service because most women who came as domestics found their working conditions unacceptable and left service for other work once they fulfilled their one-year obligation. Rather than providing the mechanisms to improve the conditions of domestic work and make it attractive for people to stay in—by extending and effectively enforcing labour standards and human rights legislation to domestic workers, for example—the Canadian state opted for a solution that would force people to stay in domestic work.

In the 1960s and the early 1970s—in spite of the high and rising demand for domestic workers—immigration authorities arbitrarily lowered the rating for domestic work within the occupational demand category (Bakan and Stasiulis 1992). In 1973, the government started issuing temporary work permits that would only let these workers stay in the country for a specified period of time (usually a year), doing a specific type of work, for a specific employer. The temporary employment authorization system is a new version of indenture. From 1973 to 1981, foreign domestic workers could only come to Canada as **"guest workers"**—instead of immigrants. As guest workers they had no rights to stay in Canada or claim social security benefits. Although foreign domestics could be allowed to change employers with special permission from immigration authorities, they could not leave domestic service without also having to leave Canada. Extension of the employment visa beyond the first year was possible and common, but the foreign worker inevitably had to leave Canada. Under this new scheme, increasing numbers of domestic workers were brought into Canada every year. The numbers of employment visas issued to domestics rose consistently from around 1,800 in 1973 to more than 16,000 in 1982 (Silvera 1983: 15; Bolaria and Li 1985: 178).

The official purpose of the employment visa system was to meet the urgent and temporary needs of Canadian employers to fill jobs that cannot be filled domestically without threatening the employment opportunities of Canadian residents (Wong 1984: 86). When we consider the case of domestic service, however, both the unwillingness of Canadians to take live-in work, as well as the century-long efforts of the Canadian state to import domestic workers from abroad, suggest that neither the need nor the solution has been temporary. Despite the persistence of a high-demand/low-supply situation, domestic workers have, since the 1970s, only been accepted to Canada with temporary status. Until recent years when the numbers and categories of temporary migrant workers in Canada have expanded exponentially, domestic workers have been the only occupational group besides foreign agricultural workers—who do seasonal work—to whom temporary work permits applied on a permanent basis.

When we look into Canada's immigration practices since the mid-1970s, we see an increasing tendency to resort to temporary employment visas as opposed to permanent immigration to meet labour demands not only in domestic service but also in several other job categories. Since 1975, the annual number of people entering Canada on temporary employment visas has consistently exceeded the number of landed immigrants destined for the labour force (Epstein 1983: 237; Wong 1984: 92). Migration to Canada, therefore, has changed in part from a movement of people to a movement of labour power. The benefits of this to Canada as a labour-importing country are enormous. As the literature on migrant workers in western Europe, South Africa, and California has demonstrated, recipient countries benefit not only by avoiding the costs of developing a young and healthy labour force but also by avoiding a commitment to supporting them during old age, sickness, and unemployment (Gorz 1970; Castles and Kosack 1980; Burawoy 1980). "Behind the term "guest worker" [is] a belief that such workers [are] like replaceable parts. Like cogs in a machine, for every part that breaks down, there [is] a seemingly endless supply of replacements" (Rist 1979: 51).

There are also significant political advantages to employing workers without citizenship rights. Lacking electoral and political rights and freedoms, and dependent on their employers not only for wages but also for their continued stay in the country, workers on employment visas are expected to create a docile and acquiescent labour force. Historically, the presence of migrant workers has also frequently been associated with racist and xenophobic divisions in the working class. "Canadians have the feeling that we are coming here to rob them, to take away their jobs, yet we are the ones who clean up their mess, pick up after them. We take the jobs they wouldn't take and yet they hate us so much" (Primrose in Silvera 1983: 100). One significant ideological implication of temporary work permits is that designation of a group of workers as temporary and foreign encourages a desensitized attitude toward their conditions. Hannah Arendt argues that with the development of nation-states and national sovereignty, basic human rights and freedoms were thoroughly implicated with the rights of citizenship (1966). In liberal democratic societies, where emphasis on formal equality has become a part of popular political discourse, separation of people into "citizen" and "noncitizen" categories, into "insiders" (to whom rights apply) and "outsiders," serves to legitimize inferior conditions and lesser rights for the latter group.[6]

The major effect of Canada's employment visa system on domestic workers has been the creation of a captive labour force, which has guaranteed that the turnover in domestic service would remain low no matter how bad the working and living conditions. Unable to leave domestic service without losing their rights to stay in Canada, foreign domestics have also found it difficult, in practice, to change employers. Under some of the migrant worker programs introduced since the 1970s, a foreign worker's status in Canada would change to that of visitor if she left or lost her job. While workers have been generally given a period of two weeks to find a new employer, the decision to issue a new employment visa was at the discretion of the individual immigration officer who judged whether the working conditions with the previous employer were in fact intolerable (The Task Force on Immigration Practices and Procedures 1981: 26–7).[7] Besides the hassle given by individual immigration officers, there was a regulation under the Foreign Domestic Movement (FDM) of the 1980s that required workers on employment visas to have a "release letter" from the former employer before changing employers (Toughill 1986).[8]

Unlike other workers who enjoy the basic freedom to leave a particular job or employer, the only freedom that the foreign worker on an employment visa has is to return to her country of origin. In the case of many Third World women who come to Canada out of conditions of economic desperation, there is no choice but to stay in Canada. As Nancy Hook reported, compared to Canadian workers, foreign domestic workers on employment visas were more likely to live in the homes of their employer, to work more days per week, more overtime without pay, and receive a smaller hourly wage (Hook 1978: 107–8).[9]

Even though their status in Canada has by definition been temporary, domestic workers on employment visas have been required to pay Canada Pension Plan, Unemployment Insurance premiums, and income tax (about one month's earnings a year) without being able to claim benefits.[10] The nature of the employment visa has made access to unemployment insurance benefits impossible because the worker either has to find a new employer or leave the country if she loses a job. Benefits from Canada Pension Plan have also been inaccessible because the "guest worker" is expected to retire in the country of origin (The Task Force on Child Care 1986: 121). For services that they do not expect to receive, foreign domestics have paid a very high price. Revenue Canada has calculated the total of revenues from CPP and UIC premiums collected from foreign domestics between 1973–79 to be more than 11 million dollars (The Task Force on Immigration Practices and Procedures 1981: 70).[11]

The Foreign Domestic Movement (FDM) Program

In 1981, a federal task force was established to study the conditions of domestic workers on temporary work permits. Its report recommended that the Temporary Employment Authorization system be continued provided that opportunities for landing be broadened (The Task Force on Immigration Policies and Procedures 1981). The Foreign Domestic Movement (FDM) program which came into effect in November 1981 has enabled foreign domestics who have worked in Canada continuously for two years to apply for landed immigrant status without having to leave the country. While this was a progressive step, it failed to solve the problem of foreign domestic workers in Canada. First, the FDM continued to impose a two-year period of bonded service that the domestic had to fulfill before applying. In some ways, the practice of indenturing was strengthened by the entrenchment in the FDM of a mandatory live-in requirement for all participants in the program. Domestic workers who insisted on live-out arrangements would not only lose their rights to apply for landed immigrant status but would not even receive extensions on their employment authorization (Employment and Immigration Canada 1986: 17–18).[12]

Another problem with the FDM program has been that it gave no guarantee that landed immigrant status would be granted. Applicants needed to meet Immigration assessment criteria and demonstrate a "potential for self-sufficiency."[13] Reflecting societal notions about domestic labour in general, these women continued to get very low points for both the Specific Vocational Preparation category and, ironically, the Occupational Demand category (The Task Force on Immigration Practices and Procedures 1981: 18–21).[14] As a result, immigration officers required domestic applicants (again without any guarantees to grant them landing) to take upgrading courses (with high foreign student fees), to demonstrate adaptation and integration into Canadian society (through volunteer work in the community), and to prove financial management skills (through showing evidence of savings, etc.)—all special requirements applying to domestic

workers only. For live-in foreign domestics, it has been difficult to afford both the time and the money to meet these requirements. Another problem has been that domestics with children (in the home country) and older domestics have faced special discrimination during assessment for immigrant status.[15]

> They say Immigration say any woman over 45 soon can't clean house and will be just a burden on the government, and woman with over two children will bring them into the country and take away the opportunities other Canadian children have. (Noreen in Silvera 1983: 29)

So-called "rationalized" immigration policies, oriented toward the demands of the market, aim to import labour power rather than people. It is not, therefore, surprising to see dependants being treated as "superfluous appendages" of the labour market (as they were called in South Africa).

The overall effect of the 1981 changes in the Temporary Employment Authorization Program has been to create the possibility for *individual* upward mobility of some domestic workers while providing no *structural* solution to the problems of domestic service or foreign domestic workers in general. Indeed, it is ironic that to accumulate enough points to get landed immigrant status, a domestic has had to move out of domestic service altogether. The implicit message that immigration policies and practices give is that domestic workers, as domestic workers, are "good enough to work, but not good enough to stay" in this country. This message surely tells us a great deal about the status of domestic labour in general.

Furthermore, it is interesting to note the parallel between the modern attitude of the Canadian government and the historical treatment of domestic workers. Domestic servants did not receive legal equality and citizenship rights until the late nineteenth or early twentieth century. In France and England, for example, because they were considered to be too dependent on their masters to be recognized as civil persons, domestics (together with women) were the last groups to be enfranchised. Many of the basic workers' rights and freedoms we take for granted and often associate with capitalist society are, in fact, connected to citizenship rights. With the alleged attempt to meet the temporary labour requirements of the Canadian economy without threatening the jobs of Canadians, the employment visa system has created a *permanent* temporary workforce without citizenship rights.

By treating both the need and the presence of foreign workers as *temporary* the Canadian government has done nothing *permanent* either to improve significantly the conditions of workers or to find other solutions to problems of housework and child care. As long as it has been able to maintain a captive labour force without citizenship rights to do live-in domestic service, the Canadian government has found little incentive for improving conditions for domestic work. Changes in immigration policy since the early 1990s also demonstrate this point.

The Live-in Caregiver Program (LCP)

In April 1992, the Ministry of Employment and Immigration introduced several changes to the previous FDM program and renamed it the "Live-in Caregiver Program" (LCP). Today, except for small changes in its provisions, domestic workers and caregivers entering Canada are still regulated by this program in effect since 1992. According to the original provisions of the LCP introduced in 1992,

women intending to do domestic work would be admitted to Canada on the basis of the education and training they have related to the care of children, seniors, and the disabled. Specifically, this would involve the successful completion of the equivalent of Canadian Grade 12 education plus proof of six months of full-time formal training in areas such as early childhood education, geriatric care, and pediatric nursing (CEIC 1992; *Domestics' Cross-cultural News* 1992). These new criteria were contested by domestic workers' advocacy organizations which argued that many potential applicants from Third World countries would not qualify under the new program. In many countries, basic schooling only goes to Grade 10 or Grade 11 and formal training in areas of child, elderly, and disabled care does not exist (DeMara 1992; *Domestics' Cross-cultural News* 1992). The government responded by revising the requirements to a high-school diploma and a minimum of one year work experience in caregiving (in the three years preceding their application), which would be counted as equivalent to six months of formal training.

The program introduced in 1992 lifted some of the extra requirements the earlier FDM placed on foreign domestics for landed status (i.e., doing skills upgrading, demonstrating successful adaptation by doing volunteer community work, and demonstrating financial management skills by having to show savings). To become a landed immigrant, a foreign domestic worker now had to demonstrate a minimum of two years employment as a full-time live-in domestic worker within 36 months after her arrival in Canada. Also, domestic workers no longer needed to obtain a "release letter" from their employer in order to change employers. To receive a new employment authorization from immigration officers, domestic workers would instead have to get a "record of employment" from their employers showing how long they were employed and a statement of their earnings (CEIC 1992).

Despite limited improvements on freedom of movement and the conditions for landed status, the LCP continues in the tradition of immigration policies regarding domestic workers by imposing the kind of status and conditions on workers that lead to abuse and an unfavourable working environment. Under the LCP, the temporary work permit system and the mandatory live-in requirement still prevail, while women have to prove higher qualifications to work as domestic workers. The new program has "enable[d] Canadian employers to obtain higher qualified labour for less pay" (*Domestics' Cross-cultural News* 1992) while doing little to help domestic workers to improve their conditions.

The conditions and status of foreign domestic workers have hardly changed since the 1970s. Politically, there is also less hope for change in the short term. Compared to the 1970s, 1980s, and part of the 1990s, there is no longer a strong women's movement in Canada to take up the issue of domestic labour (in general and in its racialized forms) and struggle for change. With the withdrawal of support by the federal government to women's groups, some of the specific organizations which did advocacy and service work for domestic workers, such as INTERCEDE (Toronto Organization for Domestic Workers' Rights) which had been active since the 1970s, have also vanished. Economic restructuring and neoliberalism have also led to significant changes in employment norms, increasing precarious forms of work and reducing workers' protections and security. As importantly, the new political and ideological climate is different from the one of the 1970s, 1980s, and part of the 1990s

when the conditions of domestic workers were seen as an anomaly. Today, with expansion of precarious work and increase in numbers of temporary migrant workers, it seems that their conditions are increasingly normalized rather than being challenged.

The category of temporary worker has become more widespread in Canadian immigration and the numbers of migrant workers have grown exponentially especially since the early 2000s. In 2002, the federal government introduced a Foreign Worker Pilot Program which started to issue temporary visas to foreign workers in any occupation with a "labour shortage." In September 2007, the applications from employers under the program were expedited and the program further expanded, especially in Alberta where the economy has experienced a boom and in British Columbia when the Olympics created employment in several sectors. Since 2007, the number of temporary migrant workers have consistently exceeded the number of permanent residents entering Canada. As economic restructuring has pushed precarious work into the mainstream in the labour market, and changes in immigration policies continue to shift the status and conditions of migrant workers from anomaly to near normativity, the present situation presents more difficult challenges. But it also presents potentially positive possibilities for migrant domestic workers. On the one hand, in an environment where most workers experience a "race to the bottom," changing the working and living conditions of domestic workers has become increasingly challenging, short of radical systemic changes. On the other hand, neoliberalism and economic restructuring mean that conditions that have applied to migrant domestic workers are not only conditions for a highly racialized and gendered occupation that other workers can distance themselves from. Thus, we can also interpret current conditions as creating the possibility of potential solidarity among different sectors of labour.

Temporary Status and Transnational Families

According to research I have done in collaboration with Fely Villasin, one of the most negative implications of temporary immigration status and the living-in requirement for domestic workers is that women must come to Canada alone, having left their own families behind (Arat-Koç with Villasin, 2001). All the immigration programs for domestic workers since the early 1970s have been built on the premise that foreign domestic workers who arrive in Canada are—or should live as—single people. In reality, a significant percentage of domestic workers have children.

Canadian immigration regulations as well as individual employers assume that there is an incompatibility between this type of employment and parenting responsibilities of the worker. During interviews Fely Villasin and I conducted in 2000, a domestic worker explained how her employer did not allow her daughter, who was visiting her in Canada, to stay in her house; the employer warned her, "don't forget you are working." Sometimes the worker herself internalizes the notion of incompatibility between worker status and parenting that is imposed by the state and the employers. One of the respondents to our questionnaire replied to the question "If you have children, did they come to Canada with you?" in the negative, explaining that she "did not come to Canada as an immigrant but as a worker" (Arat-Koç with Villasin 2001: 21, 22).

Even though recent immigration programs for domestic workers allow them to apply for permanent resident status after two or three years of live-in service under temporary work permits, the time it takes for domestic workers to sponsor their families is, from the time of their arrival in Canada, on average, three to five years, and often longer. Moreover, for many domestic workers, Canada is not necessarily the first country they go to on a temporary work permit. When several years of work abroad are combined with an average of three to five years, and sometimes up to seven years of waiting in Canada, the experience and the impacts of separation are profound for domestic workers and for their families.

Several factors made the experience of family separation very painful for domestic workers. In addition to a profound sense of responsibility for the well-being of their children and feelings of guilt that they may be neglecting them by having to take employment abroad, domestic workers also suffer a sense of deprivation of intimacy and support. During the interviews, one domestic worker regretted being separated from her husband. She said that the deprivation of "emotional and physical contact" caused her loneliness and depression. Another domestic worker summarized the effects of separation from her common-law spouse as a feeling of "emptiness in the sense that [there is] no one who would comfort you when you have a problem or giving reassurance when you are down" (Arat-Koç with Villasin 2001: 29).

For most migrant domestic workers with children, the decision to leave their children was an extremely painful one. In addition to handling practical questions regarding whom to leave their children with and whether the children would be safe, well-cared for, happy, and healthy, domestic workers had to deal with heart-wrenching feelings during separation from their children. During her interview, one domestic worker described the time she bid her children goodbye and boarded the bus to Manila as follows: "I could not walk up the bus, the driver had to carry me up. I was so weak and faint—leaving my kids and not knowing how long it would be before we could be together again" (Arat-Koç with Villasin 2001: 26).

Even though migrant workers were very aware of the significance of their remittances for their children's upkeep and future, they experienced a profound sense of guilt, anxiety over the well-being of the children, as well as a sense of sadness, loss, and loneliness. As one worker told us, "My life will not be complete. A part of me will always be missing, wondering about how my child is doing" (Arat-Koç with Villasin 2001: 26). The mothers we interviewed constantly worried about their children. They tended to blame themselves when the children were maltreated, got into trouble, or did badly in school. Even when there were no apparent problems, there was anxiety about the unknown. One domestic worker said that her biggest regret was that she would "not know what is going on inside them" and that she could not "share their troubles and triumphs" (Arat-Koç with Villasin 2001: 27). Most mothers tried to maintain a good long-distance relationship with their children by spending large amounts on telephone bills.

Our surveys and our interviews with domestic workers as well as professionals dealing with immigrants' health revealed serious physical and mental health problems associated with separation from family. Complaints ranged from chronic stomach pain, muscle tension (specifically in the neck and shoulders), sleep problems, and frequent headaches, to severe anxiety and depression. Describing the effects of separation, one of the respondents to the questionnaire wrote about "a gap, depression, frustration, and loneliness." Another

domestic worker dealt with similar feelings by "always wanting to keep [herself] busy because [she] always felt sad if [she was] not doing something" (Arat-Koç with Villasin 2001: 27).

Mothers often assumed that the separation affected the children negatively, that they "felt as orphans," deprived of the love of their parents. As one woman said, "the effect of separation on my children was overwhelming. [They] felt insecure and unprotected while I was away. The trust on me as a parent was totally diminished by the time we got together in Canada" (Arat-Koç with Villasin 2001: 28). Some children were too young when the mothers left to know or remember them. Some older children were angry and resentful toward the mother, who, they thought, had betrayed them. Some children appreciated the economic necessity and the sacrifice but had deep feelings of longing and sadness. Other studies confirm this. Rhacel Salazar Parrenas (2003), who interviewed children of migrant domestic workers in the Philippines, reports on the profound sense of loss. When she asked Ellen, who was 10 when her mother left, how she felt about the children in her mother's care in New York, the girl responded:

> Very jealous. I am very, very jealous. There was even a time when she told the children she was caring for that they are very lucky that she was taking care of them while her children back in the Philippines do not even have a mom to take care of them. It's pathetic, but it's true. We were left alone by ourselves and we had to be responsible at a very young age without a mother. Can you imagine? (Parrenas 2003: 42)

Even as she experienced a sense of loss, Ellen was not unaware of her mother's dedication and commitment:

I realize that my mother loves us very much. Even if she is far away, she would send us her love. She would make us feel like she really loved us. She would do this by always being there. She would just assure us that whenever we have problems to just call her and tell her . . . And so I know that it has been more difficult for her than other mothers. She has to do extra work because she is so far away from us. (in Parrenas 2003: 43)

Parrenas's research makes it clear that the children of transnational mothers who had positive surrogate parental figures and open, regular communication with their mothers were able to resolve the emotional challenges and focus on school. Even the well-adjusted, though, suffered the loss of family intimacy (Parrenas 2003). It was not unusual for some children to deal with feelings of loss and longing by emotionally withdrawing from the mother. Two of the respondents to our questionnaire who were still separated from their children said: "I think they do not miss me any more or I don't exist. They don't care if I call or write to them." "They hardly know me . . . Even in my vacation in the Philippines, I could feel the gap between us" (Arat-Koç with Villasin 2001: 28, 29).

Problems did not end if/when families were reunited. When children met their mothers in Canada, they often met as strangers. Most mothers found it very hard to help their children get over feelings of abandonment. They also found it hard to undo the distance that had developed between themselves and their children. As one woman said, "The children I take care of give me a hug as soon as I come to work, and hug me goodbye when I leave. They are much more affectionate than my own children who have joined me" (Arat-Koç with Villasin 2001: 33–4).

In addition to problems in establishing trust, love, and intimacy, mothers also found it difficult to establish authority over their children. As mothers tried to fulfill their maternal role, some children resented, resisted, and rejected this, questioning where she had been all these years and what right she had to control their lives (Arat-Koç with Villasin 2001: 34).

The difficulties in re-establishing parent–child ties sometimes lasted many years, sometimes never ended. In addition to the challenges of re-establishing authority, intimacy, and trust, mothers were confronted with the anger of children who were having difficulties adjusting to life in a new country. Feeling powerless about imposed emigration, the children tended to blame their difficulties on the person who seemed to be responsible for making this decision. One domestic worker related a moving story of how her kids were "brainwashed" against her and how she has often "fe[lt] alone against the world," despite all the efforts she put into providing for them and sponsoring them to move to Canada. It took five years before her children even "began to understand" her. Still, she admitted, "It is really hard for us to get reunited with them after a long time of separation" (Arat-Koç with Villasin 2001: 34).

As a result of the difficulties during separation, as well as the challenges faced after reunification, most migrant domestic workers in our research experienced forced family separation as a form of emotional abuse that emotionally scarred those involved for a long time, if not permanently.

Conditions of Domestic Work and the Role of the State

In Canada, the state has played a contradictory role in the organization of paid domestic work. It has underregulated working conditions while overregulating the workers. While the provincial labour standards laws, respecting "the sanctity of the home," have either completely ignored or at best unequally treated the home as a workplace, the federal government, which has jurisdiction over immigration, has overregulated the workers (Luxton, Rosenberg, and Arat-Koç 1990: 15). In Canada, therefore, it has not simply been the generally low status of housework, or even the availability of a supply of foreign workers, that have created the conditions of domestic workers' vulnerability. As Castells (1975: 54) put it: "immigrant workers do not exist because there are "arduous and badly paid" jobs to be done, but, rather, arduous and badly paid jobs exist because immigrant workers are present or can be sent for to do them."

It is ironic that the consistently high and increasing demand for domestic work has corresponded with a deterioration of workers' conditions. This is due to the active role the state has played in structuring and controlling not only the volume but also the conditions of these workers. There is a striking contrast between the laissez-faire approach the liberal state has taken that favours private solutions to problems in the domestic sphere and its rigid intervention in the provision, organization, and control of "help" for that sphere. Given the specific combination of state policies in areas of child care provision, labour legislation, and immigration, domestic service is not simply a private but a politically constructed solution to the crisis of the domestic sphere.

The positions put forward by both the federal and provincial governments in child-care policy for the last three decades indicate the persistence of a clear preference for privatized solutions—with little concern about the quality and conditions for either children or caregivers. The absence of a universal child-care program or even a political commitment to

increasing child-care spaces means that parents are left with no choice but to make private arrangements. While the pressures that many parents face in relation to child-care needs constitute a real and serious problem, the assumption in most legislative and policy debates and proposals has been that domestic workers should subsidize the inadequacy of the social child-care system through their underpaid and overworked conditions.

Current domestic-service arrangements bring the interests of employers and employees into conflict. Given the pressures on budget and time that many middle-class working couples face, a domestic-service relationship may turn into a zero-sum game in which the improvements in the pay and working conditions of domestic workers mean losses for the employers. As a relationship between female employers and workers, domestic service emphasizes most clearly the class, racial/ethnic, and citizenship differences among women which stand in the way of gender unity.

Feminism and Domestic Service

The domestic-service question is a feminist question, not just because 98 per cent of domestic workers are women, or because it potentially may create divisions among women that feminism needs to solve to make "sisterhood" a reality. It is also a feminist question because it is so closely implicated in the privatized nature of domestic labour in our society. Domestic service, as it is organized in Canada, is not just a question of human and workers' rights. It is a question of women's oppression and liberation. Women's liberation has been defined by some as the upward *mobility* of individual women *out of* some subordinate positions and occupations. According to this definition, "women's liberation" can be compatible with a general devaluation of the subordinate positions and occupations many women hold.[16] If we choose, instead, to define women's liberation as a collective and transformative struggle—in addition to being one of individual liberation—that deals with class and racial inequalities and aims to restructure society to eliminate subordinate positions, live-in domestic service becomes a very backward "solution" for the crisis of the domestic sphere.

Women's liberation is a multi-dimensional project which needs to involve challenging capitalism and the state as well as gender relations in the home. A domestic-service "solution" to the crisis of the domestic sphere means that neither the gender division of labour in the household nor the existing demands of the workplace, which refuse to address tensions between paid work and family responsibilities, are challenged. When adopted by wealthy and middle-class women, this "solution" also leaves the state relieved of pressures and responsibility for providing collective solutions for people's needs. It leaves housework and child care as women's work—still isolating, of low status and low value. Rather than solving the problem of gender inequality, it adds class and

racial dimensions to it. Instead of housework and child care being the responsibility of *all* women, it becomes the responsibility of *some* with subordinate class, racial, and citizenship status, who are employed and supervised by those they liberate from direct physical burdens.[17] Reinforcing divisions of mental and manual labour, this may perpetuate low status and pay for domestic service.

The domestic service "solution" is also backward because it does not solve the problems posed by the separation of spheres. Given the availability of a cheap source of vulnerable workers, it discourages a struggle for socialized services and more flexible work arrangements.[18] Rather than easing the public/private split in society, therefore, this solution polarizes and deepens it with added class and racial dimensions. The crisis of the domestic sphere necessitates a search for creative solutions and an honest, open debate around each solution and its gender, class, and racial implications. In the absence of such a debate and a vision of concrete, constructive alternatives that would emerge from them, individualized ad hoc solutions may bring more harm than good to both individual women and to the struggle for the emancipation of all women.

● Notes

This is a revised and partly updated version of a paper originally published in *Studies in Political Economy* 28 (Spring 1989) and M. Luxton, H. Rosenberg, and S. Arat-Koç, *Through the Kitchen Window*, 2nd edn (Toronto: Garamond, 1990). I am grateful to Pramila Aggarwal, Michal Bodemann, Bonnie Fox, Charlene Gannage, Roberta Hamilton, Mustafa Koç, Meg Luxton, Barb Neis, Lynne Phillips, Ester Reiter, Harriet Rosenberg, Jane Ursel, and Fely Villasin for ideas and useful comments on different versions of the paper.

1. *The Canadian Settler's Handbook* advised immigrant domestics that they would enjoy "social amenities" in rural Canada and that "no lady should dream of going as a home-help in the cities, for there class distinctions (were) as rampant as in England" (cited in Lenkyj 1981: 10).

2. According to one study, in Sweden, 2,340 million hours are spent in housework annually, as compared to 1,290 million hours in industry (cited in Rowbotham 1973: 68).

3. Although these regulations may be a progressive step in recognizing the principle of overtime for domestic workers, they do not necessarily provide standard overtime protection since it is the

employers who are given the option to negotiate with their employees to take the overtime in time off rather than in money for actual overtime worked. In this respect, regulations covering domestic workers still deviate from provisions of the provincial Employment Standards Act.

4. There is also the "Subversive Activities" provision in the 1977 federal Immigration Act which, through its vague wording, provides an intimidating message to all non-citizen residents in Canada that engaging in union activities may become grounds for deportation (see Arnopoulos 1979: 41–5).

5. It is wrong, however, to confuse this appearance with real thoughts and feelings of the worker. Responding to Lockwood who referred to the domestic worker as the "most socially acquiescent and conservative element" of the working class, Jacklyn Cock emphasizes the need to differentiate between deference and dependence. While the domestic recognizes her dependence on and powerlessness in relation to her employer, her deference is only "a mask which is deliberately cultivated to conform to employer expectations, and shield the workers' real feelings" (Cock 1980: 104–6).

6. Here I have drawn on an argument made by Gerda Lerner in a different context. Commenting on the origins of slavery, Lerner has suggested that the process of marking a group of people as an outgroup and "designating th[is] group to be dominated as entirely different from the group exerting dominance," have been essential to the mental constructs involved in the institutionalization of slavery (see Lerner 1986: 76–7).

7. The criteria for tolerability used by immigration officers could sometimes be very flexible. Silvera reports the case of a domestic from the Caribbean who wanted to leave her employer for reasons of sexual assault. Because the assault was less than sexual intercourse, her complaint was not found legitimate and she was deported from Canada (see Silvera 1981: 58).

8. Although Employment and Immigration spokespersons have on a number of occasions announced that the practice of requiring release letters would be ended, a survey conducted among foreign domestic workers in Toronto suggests that it is very common (Arat-Koç and Villasin 1990: 12).

9. Research also shows that there is a very strong relationship between living-in (a requirement for foreign domestic workers) and working very long hours. According to a survey among 576 domestic workers in Toronto, only 35 per cent said they worked a standard workweek of 44 hours. Forty per cent worked for an average of 45 to 50 hours a week. Eighteen per cent worked 50 to 60 hours and 6 per cent worked more than 60 hours a week. Among the live-in domestics who did overtime work, only 34 per cent received the legal compensation. Twenty-two per cent said they received some, but less than the legal rates of compensation. An overwhelming 44 per cent of those doing overtime work stated that they received no compensation whatsoever! (Arat-Koç and Villasin 1990: 6).

10. In 1987 Canada had international agreements with only six countries (the United States, Jamaica, Italy, Greece, Portugal, and France) whose nationals could combine CPP contributions in Canada with pension contributions in their own countries (INTERCEDE 1987: 12).

11. Since 1986 the immigration department has been imposing fees for issuing, extending, and renewing employment authorizations. In addition to being underpaid and overtaxed in a society that offers them no privileges and freedoms of citizenship, domestic workers are now being asked to "take the burden off the Canadian taxpayer" and pay the costs of their own processing and policing.

12. The enforcement of the live-in requirement has been so strict that some domestics who lived-out have been threatened by deportation—even if their employer didn't have room and agreed with the arrangement (see "Patriarch of the Month" 1992).

13. Many domestic workers who have had years of experience supporting themselves (and others) find it very offensive to have to prove such potential: "I supported five children *before* I came here, and I've supported five children since I came here, and they want to know if I can manage on my own?" (Mary Dabreo, cited in Ramirez 1983/1984).

14. A point needs to be made about conceptions of the value of different occupations that immigration partly borrows from Canadian Classification and Dictionary of Occupations. CCDO has a rigid and static conception of skill as a "thing" that is largely determined "objectively" by the time spent in formal education. As Gaskell (1986) has argued, however, "skill," far from being "a fixed attribute of a job or a worker which will explain higher wages

or unemployment," is a result of a political process determined by the relative power (through supply/demand advantages, organizational capabilities, etc.) of different groups of workers.

15. The 1978 case of "seven Jamaican women" was fought on the basis that discrimination against women with children was discrimination on the basis of gender. Seven Jamaican women filed a complaint with the Canadian Human Rights Commission after being ordered deported for having failed to list their minor children in their applications to come to Canada. They won their case on the ruling that no married man had ever been deported for having to list his children (cited in Timoll 1989: 57).

Although explicit and direct discrimination against women with dependent children has been eliminated, the practice still survives because those women who express their intention to stay in domestic service and also sponsor their dependents to Canada often fail to meet Immigration criteria on the grounds that they would not make enough income to make their families "self-sufficient."

16. This is Betty Friedan's position on housework. She approvingly cites others in *The Feminine Mystique* who think housework can be done by "anyone with a strong enough back (and a small enough brain)" and find it "peculiarly suited to the capacities of feeble-minded girls" (Friedan 1963: 206, 244).

17. With the emergence of surrogate motherhood, the same potential also applies to child-bearing. The employment of surrogate mothers of working-class backgrounds may indeed become the solution upper-class and career women opt for to avoid the time and inconvenience a pregnancy would cost.

18. During the 1920s, in the southern United States where there were more servants, the growth of commercial bakeries and laundries lagged behind such developments in the north and west (see Katzman 1978: 275).

● References

Arat-Koç, S, and F. Villasin. 1990. "Report and Recommendations on the Foreign Domestic Movement Program," prepared for INTERCEDE, Toronto Organization for Domestic Workers' Rights.

——, with F. Villasin. 2001. *Caregivers Break the Silence: A Participatory Action Research on the Abuse and Violence, Including the Impact of Family Separation, Experienced by Women in the Live-in Caregiver Program* (Toronto: INTERCEDE).

Arendt, H. 1966. *The Origins of Totalitarianism* (New York: Harcourt, Brace and World).

Arnopoulos, S.M. 1979. *Problems of Immigrant Women in the Canadian Labour Force* (Ottawa: Canadian Advisory Council on the Status of Women).

Bakan, A., and D. Stasiulis. 1992. "Foreign Domestic Worker Policy in Canada and the Social Boundaries of Citizenship," unpublished paper.

Barber, M. 1985. "The Women Ontario Welcomed: Immigrant Domestics for Ontario Homes, 1870–1930," in *The Neglected Majority: Essays in Canadian Women's History,* eds A. Prentice and S.M. Trofimenkoff (Toronto: McClelland & Stewart).

——. 1986. "Sunny Ontario for British Girls, 1900–30," in *Looking into My Sister's Eyes: An Exploration in Women's History,* ed. J. Burnet (Toronto: The Multicultural History Society of Ontario).

Bolaria, B.S., and P.S. Li. 1985. *Racial Oppression in Canada* (Toronto: Garamond Press).

Burawoy, M. 1980. "Migrant Labour in South Africa and the United States," in *Capital and Labour,* ed. T. Nichols (Glasgow: Fontana).

Calliste, A. 1989. "Canada's Immigration Policy and Domestics from the Caribbean: The Second Domestic Scheme," *Socialist Studies* 5.

Castells, M. 1975. "Immigrant Workers and Class Struggles in Advanced Capitalism: The Western European Experience," *Politics and Society* 15, 1: 33–66.

Castles, S., and G. Kosack. 1980. "The Function of Labour Immigration in Western European Capitalism," in *Capital and Labour,* ed. T. Nichols (Glasgow: Fontana).

CEIC. 1992. *Immigration Regulations,* 1978, as amended by SOR/92-214, P.C. 1992-685 (9 Apr.).

Childcare Resource and Research Unit. 2000. *Early Childhood Care and Education in Canada: Provinces and Territories 1998* (Toronto: Childcare Resource and Research Unit, University of Toronto).

Cock, J. 1980. *Maids and Madams: A Study in the Politics of Exploitation* (Johannesburg: Ravan Press).

DeMara, B. 1992. "New Immigration Rules Racist Domestic Workers Rally Told," *Toronto Star,* 3 Feb.

Domestics' Cross-cultural News. 1992. Monthly newsletter of the Toronto Organization for Domestic Workers' Rights, June.

Dudden, F.E. 1983. *Serving Women: Household Service in Nineteenth-century America* (Middleton: Wesleyan University Press).

Employment and Immigration Canada. 1986. *Foreign Domestic Workers in Canada: Facts for Domestics and Employers,* pamphlet (Ottawa: Supply and Services, Cat. No. MP23-61/1986).

Epstein, R. 1983. "Domestic Workers: The Experience in BC," in *Union Sisters: Women in the Labour Force,* eds L. Briskin and L. Yanz (Toronto: The Women's Press).

Estable, A. 1986. *Immigrant Women in Canada: Current Issues,* a Background Paper for the Canadian Advisory Council on the Status of Women, Mar. (Ottawa: Supply and Services).

Fairchilds, C. 1984. *Domestic Enemies: Servants and Their Masters in Old Regime France* (Baltimore: The Johns Hopkins University Press).

Flandrin, J.L. 1979. *Families in Former Times* (Cambridge: Cambridge University Press).

Fox, B. 1980. "Women's Double Work Day: Twentieth Century Changes in the Reproduction of Daily Life," in *Hidden in the Household: Women's Domestic Labour under Capitalism,* ed. B. Fox (Toronto: The Women's Press).

Friedan, B. 1963. *The Feminine Mystique* (New York: Dell Publishing).

Friendly, M., J. Beach, C. Ferns and M. Turiano. 2007. *Early Childhood Education and Care in Canada 2006.* (Toronto: Childcare Resource and Research Unit).

Friendly, M. and S. Prentice. 2009. *About Canada Childcare.* (Halifax: Fernwood Publishing).

Fudge, J. 1997. "Little Victories and Big Defeats: The Rise and Fall of Collective Bargaining Rights for Domestic Workers in Ontario," in *Not One of the Family: Foreign Domestic Workers in Canada,* eds A.B. Bakan and D. Stasiulis (Toronto: University of Toronto Press).

Gaskell, J. 1986. "Conceptions of Skill and the Work of Women: Some Historical and Political Issues," in *The Politics of Diversity,* eds R. Hamilton and M. Barrett (Montreal: Book Centre).

Glenn, E.N. 1992. "From Servitude to Service Work: Historical Continuities in the Racial Division of Paid Reproductive Work," *Signs* 18, 1.

Gorz, A. 1970. "Immigrant Labour," *New Left Review* 61.

Hook, N.D. 1978. *Domestic Service Occupation Study: Final Report,* submitted to Canada Manpower and Immigration, Jan.

Human Resources and Development Canada. 1997. *Status of Daycare in Canada 1995 and 1996: A Review of the Major Findings of the National Daycare Study 1995 and 1996* (Ottawa: Author).

INTERCEDE. 1987. *Know Your Rights (A Guide for Domestic Workers in Ontario)* (Toronto: Oct.).

Kaplan, E.B. 1985. "'I Don't Do No Windows,'" *Sojourner* 10, 10 (Aug.).

Katzman, D.M. 1978. *Seven Days a Week: Women and Domestic Service in Industrializing America* (New York: Oxford University Press).

Keung, N. 2008a. "Guest Labour Program Raises Troubling Questions," *Toronto Star,* 15 Mar.

———. 2008b. "Tories to Shake up Immigration," *Toronto Star,* 14 Mar.

Lenkyj, H. 1981. "A 'Servant Problem' or a 'Servant–Mistress Problem'? Domestic Services in Canada, 1890–1930," *Atlantis* 7, 1 (Fall).

Lerner, G. 1986. *The Creation of Patriarchy* (Oxford University Press).

Leslie, G. 1974. "Domestic Service in Canada, 1880–1920," in *Women at Work, Ontario, 1850–1930* (Toronto: The Women's Press).

Lindstrom-Best, V. 1986. "'I Won't Be a Slave!'—Finnish Domestics in Canada, 1911–30," in *Looking into My Sister's Eyes: An Exploration in Women's History,* ed. J. Burnet (Toronto: The Multicultural History Society of Ontario).

Luxton, M. 1980. *More Than a Labour of Love* (Toronto: The Women's Press).

———, H. Rosenberg, and S. Arat-Koç. 1990. *Through the Kitchen Window: The Politics of Home and Family,* 2nd edn (Toronto: Garamond Press).

Mahon, Rianne. 2007. "Challenging National Regimes from Below: Toronto Child-care Politics," *Politics and Gender* 3: 55–78.

Marshall, K. 2006. "Converging Gender Roles," *Perspectives* (July), Cat. No. 75-001-XIE (Ottawa: Statistics Canada).

Mitterauer, M., and R. Sieder. 1982. *The European Family* (Chicago: University of Chicago Press).

National Council of Welfare. 1999. *Preschool Children: Promises to Keep: A Report by the National Council of Welfare* (Ottawa: Author).

Parrenas, R.S. 2003. "The Care Crisis in the Philippines: Children and Transnational Families in the New Global Economy," in *Global Woman: Nannies, Maids and Sex Workers in the New Global Economy,* eds B. Ehrenreich and A.R. Hochschild (New York: Metropolitan Books).

"Patriarch of the Month." 1992. *Herizons* 6, 3 (Fall).

Prentice, S. 1999. "Less, Worse and More Expensive: Childcare in an Era of Deficit Reduction," *Journal of Canadian Studies* 34, 2 (Summer).

Ramirez, J. 1983/1984. "Good Enough to Stay," *Currents* 1, 4.

Rist, R. 1979. "Guestworkers and Post-World War II European Migrations," *Studies in Comparative International Development* 15, 2: 28–53.

Roberts, B. 1979. "'A Work of Empire': Canadian Reformers and British Female Immigration," in *A Not Unreasonable Claim: Women and Reform in Canada, 1880s–1920s,* ed. L. Kealey (Toronto: The Women's Press).

Rollins, J. 1985. *Between Women: Domestics and Their Employers* (Philadelphia: Temple University Press).

Rosenberg, H. 1986. "The Home is the Workplace: Hazards, Stress and Pollutants in the Household," in *Through the*

Kitchen Window: The Politics of Home and Family (Toronto: Garamond Press).

———. 1987. "Motherwork, Stress, and Depression: The Costs of Privatized Social Reproduction," in *Feminism and Political Economy,* eds H.J. Maroney and M. Luxton (Toronto: Methuen).

Rowbotham, S. 1973. *Women's Consciousness, Man's World* (Harmondsworth, UK: Penguin).

Royal Commission on the Status of Women. 1970. *Report of the Royal Commission on the Status of Women* (Ottawa: Supply and Services).

Silvera, M. 1981. "Immigrant Domestic Workers: Whose Dirty Laundry?," *Fireweed* 9.

———. 1983. *Silenced, Talks with Working Class West Indian Women about Their Lives and Struggles as Domestic Workers in Canada* (Toronto: Williams-Wallace Publishers).

Statistics Canada. 2007. <http://www40.statcan.ca/01/ cst01/ labor05.htm>

Statistics Canada. 2012. <http://www.stat.can.gc.ca/pub/89-503-x/2010001/article/11387/tbl/tbl004-eng.htm>

Steinberg, S. 1981. *The Ethnic Myth: Race, Ethnicity, and Class in America* (Boston: Beacon Press).

The Task Force on Child Care. 1986. *Report of the Task Force on Child Care* (Ottawa: Supply and Services).

The Task Force on Immigration Practices and Procedures. 1981. *Domestic Workers on Employment Authorizations, Report* (Apr.).

Timoll, A.L. 1989. "Foreign Domestic Servants in Canada," unpublished research essay, Department of Political Science, Carleton University, Ottawa.

Toughill, K. 1986. "Domestic Workers Praise Rule Change," *Toronto Star,* 22 Sept.: C2.

Vanier Institute of the Family. 2010. *Families Count: Profiling Canada's Families.* (Ottawa)

Vanstone, E. 1986. "The Heaven-sent Nanny," *Toronto Life* (Apr.).

Walmsley, A. 1989. "Can a Working Mother Afford to Stay Home?," *Chatelaine* (Nov.).

Williams, J., H. Twart, and A. Bachelli. 1980. "Women and the Family," in *The Politics of Housework,* ed. E. Malos (London: Allison & Busby).

Wong, L.T. 1984. "Canada's Guestworkers: Some Comparisons of Temporary Workers in Europe and North America," *International Migration Review* 18, 1: 85–97.

Chapter 18

In this chapter, Meg Luxton examines the source of stress felt by many adults today because of the incompatibility of the demands that our jobs or careers place on us and the needs of family members for our care. First, she situates dual-earner couples in a historical context that highlights the economic need most households have for two incomes. Then, relying on interviews with adults living in Toronto in 1999 and 2000, Luxton describes the kinds of dilemmas that employed people face when close family members need special attention and care. Finally, she reviews the different strategies that families and individuals might use to handle the joint demands of earning a livelihood and caring for family. In so doing, she pushes us to think about the relationships among families, the economy, and the state.

Family Coping Strategies: Balancing Paid Employment and Domestic Labour

Meg Luxton

Since the early twentieth century, the majority of families in Canada have made a living by combining paid employment and unpaid domestic labour.[1] To ensure an income, one or more family members sell their capacity to work, or their labour power, to an employer. On the job their labour power is consumed and they earn its monetary recompense, a wage or salary. In consumer markets and in their homes, people use those earnings and their unpaid labour to obtain and produce the goods and services that make up the means of subsistence for themselves and their families. Each day, the means of subsistence are prepared and consumed and family subsistence, including the capacity to work again, is produced. This labour of social reproduction ensures the survival of both individuals and the society as a whole (see Chapter 1). A man explained how this cycle of production and consumption played out in his daily life:[2]

> I like my job. It's interesting and it pays pretty good. I go to work every day, come home, and you know how it is, some of the money you make has to go to food and the mortgage and stuff you need for every day. So you have to keep working just to have enough money to live on. And you hope that maybe you can make a bit more than you need for every day. If you're lucky, maybe you do. (M A#27 1/00)

This particular form of family economy imposes conflicting demands on people whose livelihood depends on it. A young mother with two preschool children described her situation:

> I have to work and so does my husband. Without both incomes we wouldn't get by. But we have two little kids. So who is supposed to look after them? If I quit work, I could stay home with them, but we wouldn't be able to pay the bills. If we pay someone else to look after the kids, it takes almost all of my pay. Like it's almost impossible! I think maybe people won't be

able to have families soon, unless something changes. (F A#26 1/00)

As her description implies, while such family livelihoods depend on both paid employment and domestic labour, the organization of the two different labour processes mean that the demands of one are at odds with the demands of the other. An office worker explained how she saw the issue:

> At my workplace they call it "family friendly" policies and talk a lot about helping us employees "balance work and family." Mostly it just means you can come in a bit earlier and leave earlier, or it's okay to take unpaid time off occasionally if your kids are sick or that it's okay to have your kids call you at work. And though they call it "family," they really mean women 'cause the guys never have to worry about that stuff. And it doesn't really help with the fact that if you're at work, you can't be at home looking after things. And if you stay home, you don't get paid. (F A#30 1/00)

As the comments of these two women indicate, the massive entry of women into the paid labour force has made it harder for individual families to manage their domestic responsibilities. As people struggled to find ways of improving the conditions of their lives, a range of social policies and practices have developed, some of which have made paid work and domestic labour a bit more compatible. These include universal services such as education and health care and a range of policies designed to ensure minimum income and employment standards, access to housing, child care, and care of dependent adults (Ursel 1992). However, most social policies

assume that individuals and their families are primarily responsible for personal caregiving and that women remain primarily responsible for managing the competing demands of the two labours necessary for family subsistence (Eichler 1988; 1997). A woman explained how this worked:

> My husband was injured at work. He was in hospital for weeks and we thought he was going to die. So I took time off work to stay with him. Then I had to go back to work. When he got out of hospital, he needed full-time care. Everyone—the doctors, the social workers, the nurses—they all assumed I would take care of him. When I said I couldn't, they acted like I was a monster! Surely if I was a good wife I would do anything for him. Like who was going to pay the bills? I said, he needs care, he should get it. That's what health care is for. Or, he was injured at work, the company should pay someone to care for him. It was a big struggle. I spent hours fighting to get him the care he needed. They really tried to make me do everything but I said I can't, I have to work. I felt terrible, but he understood. (F M#16 12/99)

Changing Patterns of Paid Employment

In the early twentieth century, the tensions between the two labours were mediated by the predominant family form, a heterosexual nuclear family, and its conventional divisions of labour based on gender and age. According to prevailing norms, adult men were "breadwinners" whose primary responsibility was to earn an income for the family while adult women were "housewives" whose primary responsibility was running the family home and caring for its members.[3] In practice, the higher the man's income and the more secure his employment, the less income other family members had to provide. Whether income-earning men were available or not, women were primarily responsible for domestic labour, and their participation in paid employment was always negotiated in relation to the needs of family members, especially when children were young or when there were family members who needed regular care related to illness, disability, or aging. Where necessary, many women augmented family incomes by intensifying domestic labour—making preserves, clothing, and other items for household use or engaging in a variety of home-based income-generating activities such as taking in laundry or sewing or renting rooms to boarders. Children were typically expected either to attend school as part of a strategy to strengthen their future employment chances or to get paid employment and contribute to the family economy by either contributing their earnings to the family household or reducing its expenses by moving away to set up their own household. Where necessary, older girls were expected to contribute to domestic labour, especially where there were a number of younger children or where their mother had income-generating work that made it difficult for her to handle all the domestic labour (Bradbury 1993).

This strategy, widely accepted as the norm, was idealized as the appropriate way to organize family life and naturalized in economic and social policies as diverse as wage rates and welfare regulations (Ursel 1992; Armstrong and Armstrong [1978] 1994). From the early twentieth century until the 1970s it was the dominant family form and division of labour (Armstrong and Armstrong [1978]

1994: 84–5). However, as Dionne Brand (1994) and Linda Carty (1994) have shown, African-Canadian women have a history of higher-than-average labour-force participation rates. Indigenous or Aboriginal women have had lower-than-average labour-force participation rates but have worked in mixed economies since colonization (Abele 1997). Immigration policies have permitted particular categories of women workers to enter Canada to fill certain types of labour needs (Stasiulis 1997; Preston and Giles 1997). Patterns of class, race, ethnicity, national origin, region, religion, and other cultural differences shaped the ways in which different populations both were located in the labour market and related to prevailing norms and the economic and social policies that presumed specific family forms and divisions of labour. A woman described her mother's experience as an immigrant:

> She came here in the fifties, as a domestic worker. She came because she had two daughters and in Jamaica she couldn't make enough to support us. The Canadian government wouldn't let her bring us so for years she sent money home and our grandmother raised us. (F A#13 11/99)

Another woman described how the prevailing norm of the income-earning husband and the homemaker wife created problems for her family in the 1960s:

> I remember how ashamed I used to feel because my father was unemployed—for years—and my mother went out to work. The worst was when teachers would tell me my mother should come to help at some school event, and I would have to explain that she couldn't. They would look at me and I always felt like scum of the

earth. In those days, fathers worked and mothers stayed home and anyone who didn't conform was obviously of a lesser sort. (F A#15 1/00)

Never a satisfactory resolution, this strategy excluded those who did not live in heterosexual nuclear families and created pressures on people to marry. It depended on the man's ability to earn enough money to support a dependent wife and children, something few men actually achieved. It put pressure on men as the sole-income providers while isolating women in a demanding low status and unpaid job. It made women economically dependent on their husbands which left them vulnerable, especially if the relationship broke down (Luxton 1980). While it encouraged economic independence on the part of young-adult children, in low-income households it easily pitted parents and young-adult children against each other in struggles over family unity versus individual independence.[4] Parents might urge children to leave school to earn a living and contribute to the family household whereas children often preferred to stay in school or set up their own households. Parental demands often undercut girls' chances for staying in school by expecting them to help out at home.[5] This strategy also depended on families' capacities to make ends meet by expanding unpaid labour in the home to reduce expenses, something that became difficult as household expenses were increasingly monetary, such as mortgage payments and taxes—demanding income rather than useable goods (Parr 1999: 101–18).

Throughout the century, the participation rates of women in the formal labour force steadily increased, dramatically changing family economics and divisions of labour (see Table 18.1). Among cohabiting male–female couples in 1961, almost 70 per cent relied on the man as the single-income provider. By 1991 only 19 per cent did so, a number that has remained fairly constant since. In the majority of cohabiting male–female families (61 per cent), both adults had paid employment and, in 5 per cent, women were the sole-income providers (Oderkirk, Silver, and Prud'homme 1994). By 1997 women were the higher-income earners in 23 per cent of couples and the sole-income provider in about 20 per cent of couples (*Globe and Mail*, 21 Feb. 2000: A2). Most dramatically, the labour-force participation rates of married women with young preschool children increased from 49.4 per cent in 1981 to 69 per cent in 1991. By 2000, the vast majority of mothers with young children remained in the labour force.

There were many reasons for such changes. The growth of the service sector in the 1960s and 1970s created a particular demand for women workers (Marchak 1987). Birth rates have declined as women had fewer children, and as a result women spent less of their adult lives in active child care. In 1961 the average number of children born per woman was 3.84 (Grindstaff 1995); by 1997 it was 1.6 (Statistics Canada 2000: 7). Changing gender ideologies, fuelled by the revitalization of the feminist movement, reflected women's interest in paid employment, as protection from the vulnerability of dependency on men, to augment their families' incomes, and because they liked the income, sociability, and status that paid employment secures. The potential consequences of women's economic dependency on men were revealed by a 1997 study which showed that men gained financially when their marriages ended; their incomes went up 10 per cent. In contrast, women and children did poorly; women lost about 23 per cent of their incomes. The only way women could regain their former financial status was by remarrying (*Toronto Star*, 10 Apr. 1997).

Table 18.1 Canadian Labour-force Participation Rates of All Men, All Women, and Married Women, 1901–1995

Year	All Men	All Women	Married Women	Women as a % of the Total Labour Force
1901	78.3	14.4	n.a.	13.3
1911	82.0	16.6	n.a.	13.3
1921	80.3	17.7	2.16	15.4
1931	78.4	19.4	3.45	16.9
1941	85.6*	22.9*	3.74	24.8
1951	84.4	24.4	9.56	22.0
1961	81.1	29.3	20.7	29.6
1971	77.3	39.4	33.0	34.4
1981	78.7	52.3	51.4	40.8
1991	75.1	58.5	61.7	45.4
1995	72.5	57.4	61.4	45.1

* Includes those in active service
Population 15 years of age and over

Sources: Leacy, F.H., ed., in *Historical Statistics of Canada*, 2nd edn, eds M.C. Urquhart and K.A.H. Buckley (Toronto: Macmillan, 1965), 107–23; Statistics Canada, *Historical Labour Force Statistics 1995*, Cat. No. 71-201; *Labour Force Annual Averages*, Cat. No. 71-529; *Women in Canada*, Cat. No. 89503E, p. 78; 1961 Census 94-536.

Men's earnings since the 1980s typically have been insufficient to support a family. The average earnings of men over 35 years of age have remained relatively unchanged while younger men's earnings have declined (Best 1995; Morissette 1997). The importance of women's earnings to total family income is reflected in the percentage of families whose income would fall below the Low Income Cut-off if women's earnings were not available.[6] In 1992, the average family had to work 77 weeks per year just to pay the bills. Since there are only 52 weeks in a year that meant either families had to go deeply into debt, or they had to rely on more than one income (*Toronto Star*, 7 Feb. 1998). In the same year, 4 per cent of dual-earner families had low incomes; if wives' earnings were deducted, this number would have increased to 16 per cent (Statistics Canada 1995b: 88). Between 1991 and 1996,

average family incomes for all husband–wife families in Canada declined. Where the wife had no income, family income declined by 6.9 per cent, compared to families where the wife was employed whose incomes declined by 1.9 per cent (Statistics Canada 1998b: 3).

But, like men, most women seek paid employment for more than just financial benefits. A 1995 Statistics Canada survey found that 64 per cent of adult women said that having a paid job was important for their personal happiness and 55 per cent agreed that having a paid job was the best way for a woman to be an independent person (Ghalam 1997: 16). A mother who had stayed home for two years after her first child was born, refused to do so again. She explained why:

When I stayed home, I hated it. I only did it because I really thought it was the best thing for the baby. I missed going to work, I was bored at home and I don't think it was so great for the baby to have me moping around. With what we're paying for child care, it isn't financially worth our while me working, but a job is more than money. (F A#19)

By the early twenty-first century, women had become an integral part of the paid labour force and women's paid employment was an essential part of their household's livelihood. Employers depended on women's labour-force participation. In 2000, 54.8 per cent of women 24 years of age and over had paid employment and women were about 45 per cent of all paid workers (*Globe and Mail,* 21 Feb. 2000).

However, while women are increasingly in the paid labour force for most of their adult lives, their relationship to paid work continues to be quite different from men's. Jobs remain significantly sex segregated with women clustered in jobs that are typically low paid. Even when they do the same work, women often get paid less than men. In 1996 the top 10 jobs for men were (in descending order) truck drivers, retail sales, janitors, retail trade managers, farmers, sales reps and wholesale trade, motor vehicle mechanics, material handlers, carpenters, construction trade helpers. For women they were retail sales, secretaries, cashiers, registered nurses, accounting clerks, elementary teachers, food servers, general office clerks, babysitters, receptionists (*Toronto Star,* 18 Mar. 1998). Women's attachment to the labour force continues to be shaped by their responsibilities for domestic labour. Under pressure to manage things at home, they often take part-time or home-based employment. They are about 70 per cent of all part-time workers, 47 per cent of home-based employment (Ghalam 1993) and 29 per cent of all self-employed workers

(Nadwodny 1996: 17). They are far more likely (62 per cent) than men (27 per cent) to have employment interruptions "stopping working for pay for a period of six months or more" (Fast and Da Pont 1997: 3). The combination of job ghettos, reduced work time, work interruptions, and discriminatory pay rates means that women continue to earn less than men (Drolet 1999).

But just as domestic labour responsibilities shape women's attachment to paid employment, paid employment shapes men's and women's relationship to domestic labour. The assumption that men are income earners and do not have responsibility for domestic labour is central to the way most paid work is organized and fundamental to most male-dominated occupations (Luxton and Corman 2001). While employers need workers, they have no immediate interest in how their workers live, whether they support anyone else with their earnings, nor whether their workers have children or are responsible for caring for other people. Some employers have implemented "family friendly" policies, and the labour and women's movements have won important policies such as paid maternity and parental leaves or unpaid personal leaves, but, for the most part, paid employment is organized on the principle that during working hours, workers are available for work and undistracted by other concerns. Typical male occupations usually assume that workers can do eight-hour shifts or longer, can be counted on to do overtime or travel, and don't expect time off for the birth of a child or to care for people who are sick or elderly. Many men assume that if they provide their family's main income, they have met their familial responsibilities and cannot be expected to take full responsibility for domestic labour as well.

As more women with young children and other pressing domestic responsibilities entered the paid labour force, they confronted directly the problems arising from the way paid employment fails to accommodate domestic labour. Caregiving to children, elderly, ill, or disabled people requires attention and energy, often unpredictably. The more dependent the person, the more likely their lives may depend on immediate care, regardless of the paid work responsibilities of the caregiver. A mother described how this played out in her life:

> I got a phone call at work. My supervisor came to tell me and he was pissed off. He said I was not ever to get calls at work again but he let me go. We're paid piece work so I don't know why he was so mad. He wasn't paying me when I stopped working. It was my daughter's teacher. She'd fallen and hurt her head and the ambulance was taking her to the hospital. I told the supervisor I had to go to the hospital. He said if I didn't go straight back to work I was fired! Well, I had no choice did I? (F M#14 12/99)

Changing Strategies for Managing Domestic Labour and Paid Employment

As the homemaker wife/income-earner husband strategy became increasingly less of an option, families developed a variety of other strategies to cope with the competing demands of domestic labour and paid employment. Where both partners have paid work, the responsibility for income generating is shared, providing the household with some protection from the insecurities of the labour market. A man explained:

> I got laid off with no warning. We showed up for work one night and the place was padlocked. They'd gone bankrupt and the owners had disappeared. Well, if it had happened two years earlier, we would have been in deep trouble, but as it was, my wife was working so we managed. (M A#19 12/99)

This arrangement not only reduces the onus on men to provide incomes for their families, it also reduces women's dependence on their husbands:

> I never thought about it before, but after I started working, I realized how much it meant to me not to have to ask him for every penny. I love having my own money. (F A#22 1/00)

However, with no one available to do domestic labour full-time, it is harder to get it done, caregivers for dependants have to be found and the relationships managed. There are additional expenses as well as complications arising from scheduling, coordinating, and planning. A woman with two school-aged children described her arrangements:

> I work 11–3 Mondays to Wednesdays and 3–9 on Thursdays and Fridays. My husband works rotating shifts so one week he's on days 7–3, then afternoons 3–11, then nights 11–7. So the way we do it is, if one of us is home, no problem. If it's a Thursday and my husband can't be there, the kids can go to a neighbour's after school and she will keep them till I get home. It's a bit late. They don't get to bed till 10 p.m. which means it's a struggle to get them up in time to go to school the next morning. If it's a Friday, either my girlfriend comes over to stay with them or I hire a babysitter—one of the kids from the local high

school. Well, you can imagine how many phone calls it takes each week to make sure everything works! (F A#17 12/99)

Women's Strategies for Coping with the Double Day

Women who make the transition from being either childless employees or full-time mothers at home to being employed mothers often begin their new double day by trying to do both jobs so that neither detracts from the other. A woman with two preschool children described how she presented herself at work:

When I came back to work after my maternity leave, I knew I had to act like I did before I had children, as if I had no kids. My workplace had been really good to me—no fuss about maternity leave either time. They gave me really nice showers for both babies. But I knew enough was enough. They expected me to leave anything to do with the kids at home and I couldn't let it come up at work. Occasionally my boss will ask how my children are, but he does it to be friendly. He doesn't really want to know. So I make sure, no matter what is happening, no one at work ever sees me dealing with family stuff. (F M#16 11/99)

Many women try to continue their domestic labour as if they had no other demands on their time and energy (Luxton 1990: 43). A woman recalled her efforts, when she first started her job, to maintain what she considered appropriate standards at home:

I was running from morning till night, and late into the night at that. My house was spotless, my kids took home baking

to parents' night, I made their Halloween costumes myself, and I made sure we ate home-cooked meals every night. That lasted for about a year. Then I collapsed. I just couldn't keep it up and I stopped feeling like I should. (F M#18 1/00)

Few women can keep up such intensity for very long. While some maintain reduced involvement in paid employment, working part-time or trying to work from home, most end up relinquishing their exacting standards for domestic labour in order to reduce the amount of time they have to spend. The more hours women spend in paid employment, the more they cut back on household labour (Frederick 1995; Luxton and Corman 2001). They tolerate lower standards of cleanliness and tidiness, rely more on take-out foods, and as one woman put it:

just focus on what's important and let the rest go hang. What matters is spending time with the kids. If we do it in a messy house, so what? If I buy the snacks when it's my time to contribute to school lunches, so what? (F A#22 1/00)

It is much more difficult for most women to cut back on the amount of time and energy they put into caregiving. A mother described the difficult changes she had to make when her employer changed the time she had to start work:

My shift used to start at 10 a.m. That was very good. I got the children up and took them to the daycare. We had a lot of time. We could sing and tell stories and I didn't have to rush them. Mornings were a very good time. Now I have to be at work at 7 a.m. I let the children sleep until 5:30. Then I must wake them. It is very hard.

They are so tired and do not want to get up and then I have to rush, rush, rush. My employer, he says if we are late three times we get fired so I am very mean to my children in the morning now. It makes me very sad. (F A#28 1/00)

The less time and energy mothers have available to them, the less they can attend to their children. One mother captured an important effect of time constraints and stress on her parenting:

Mostly for me it isn't the time per se. My kids know I am busy and they're fine with it. It's when I am so stretched and stressed that I lose my sense of delight in their lives. I get snappy. I'm short with them. My [15-year-old] son said the other day, "Mom, when you're not here or you're upstairs working, and I don't see you, it's okay because I know you love me. But when you scream at me, I don't feel loved." He's right. But sometimes I just lose it. I can't cope. (F M#18 11/99)

Women who are already stretched by employment and child care responsibilities may find it impossible to care for others, imposing cruel choices on them. A single mother, struggling to manage on two part-time jobs, felt she had too little time for her three children, when her mother was suddenly taken ill:

I just cry all the time. I am too tired. I can't give my kids the attention they need. I am terrified I will lose my job and now this! My mama's in hospital and she needs me. Yesterday I didn't even get to visit her! But my youngest didn't come home from school so I went looking for him. I felt like God was making me choose between my mama and my son! (F M#25 3/00)

This strategy imposes serious strains on women. A national survey found that more than 28 per cent of women and slightly less than 16 per cent of men in relationships where both were employed full-time felt severely time crunched (Frederick 1993: 8). "Nearly 50 per cent of full-time . . . mothers reported they would like to spend more time alone. The proportion for men never rises much above 25 per cent" (Frederick 1995: 58).

Sharing Domestic Labour with Men

As more and more women took on paid employment, there was a widespread assumption that their male partners would take on more domestic labour. Since the 1970s, popular media and academic studies alike have proliferated, claiming that men are beginning to increase their involvement in household labour, especially child care (McMahon 1999). Public opinion polls in Canada show that since the 1970s there has been an increase from about 50 per cent to over 80 per cent of adults who agree that husbands should share domestic labour (Luxton 1990; Wilson 1991: 56). However, extensive studies of the impact of women's employment on domestic labour actually show that household labour remains sex segregated and that women do the bulk of it (Nakhaie 1995). As McMahon (1999: 13) documents, hundreds of studies from Australia, Europe, the United States, and Canada reveal that women's employment has a minimal impact on men's involvement in domestic labour, and men's domestic labour-participation rates remain consistent, regardless of race or social class differences across various countries: "there are no significant cross-cultural and cross-class differences in men's performance of domestic labour."[7]

A 1983 Canadian study of a national sample of 2,577 people investigated the extent to which men were taking on more tradition-ally female household tasks. In dual-earner couples, on average, women performed over 76 per cent of feminine-typed tasks, while men did less than 30 per cent (Brayfield 1992: 25). The 1992 General Social Survey found that even among young people "young women did more unpaid work than young men and spent more time on the 'traditionally female' chores such as cooking and housekeeping" (Frederick 1995: 14).[8] Only 10 per cent of men in dual-earner households claimed to have primary responsibility for domestic labour and an additional 10 per cent said they fully shared responsibilities (Marshall 1993). Since October 1990, fathers in Canada have been entitled to take a paid 10-week parental leave for a new baby. Of the 31,000 parents who have taken leave at the birth or adoption of a new baby, about 1,000 were fathers. Fathers as a percent-age of all parents on leave have been about 3 per cent annually since 1991 (*Globe and Mail*, 29 Mar. 2000).

The 1996 census in Canada, which included questions on unpaid work for the first time, confirmed that there continued to be significant gender differences in the amount of time spent on unpaid work. Asked if they had spent time in the previous week doing housework or home maintenance, 25 per cent of women and 8 per cent of men said they spent 30 hours or more. Among those with full-time employment (30 hours or more), 51 per cent of wives reported spending 15 hours or more doing unpaid housework, compared with 23 per cent of husbands. Among men and women with full-time employment and children, 64 per cent of women and 39 per cent of men spent at least 15 hours a week on child care. If at least one child was a preschooler, the num-bers increased: 80 per cent of women and 49 per cent of men spent at least 15 hours a week

on child care. For those with no children under six, the proportion dropped to 51 per cent of women and 29 per cent of men (Statistics Canada 1998a: 17–18).

While survey research demonstrates gen-eral trends by comparing women and men, it does not investigate intra-household divi-sions of labour. Case studies based on inter-views with both partners in a household, and especially longitudinal studies which trace domestic patterns over time reveal the inter-personal dynamics behind the time-use pat-terns. Typically, where households can afford to pay for services, they do so. Where house-hold income is insufficient, men are drawn into domestic labour in limited ways, usually fill-ing in while their wives are at their paid work (Luxton and Corman 2001). A majority of par-ents have organized their child care by ensur-ing that parents work different shifts so that one of them can always be home. But while men may be providing care for their children, parenting is not gender-neutral, so the type of care fathers and mothers provide continues to be different. Women often talk about having to do additional work to compensate for men's approach to child care. One couple's comments about their divisions of labour illustrate such gender differences at work. The man described his after-work routines:

> I get home before she does so I pick the kids up from the sitter and bring them home. I usually start dinner, then when she gets home we finish getting it ready together. We both put the kids to bed. (M A#16 11/99)

His wife elaborated:

> We both look after the kids. He picks them up and they usually get home about

half an hour before I do. When I get in, it's crazy. The kids are hungry and squabbling so we rush to get dinner ready. Then we play a bit and do homework and read stories, then it's bath time and to bed. (F A#16 11/99)

She went on to explain the difficulties she had with their arrangement:

He's great with the kids. He really is, but I wish he would be a bit more on top of things. Like, he never thinks to give them a snack when he comes home. He says it's too much bother and makes a mess and it will spoil their appetite for dinner. He'd rather just concentrate on getting dinner ready. But it means they are so cranky and strung out. I always have to break up fights and calm them down when I come in. And he never will get them doing their homework before dinner. He says they need time to play but it ends up I have to be the heavy saying "homework now!" (F A#16 11/99)

He offered a different assessment:

She's always fussing. She thinks I should make them do their homework after school but I don't like to pressure them. They need time to relax and I don't want to be always nagging them. Then she thinks I should give them snacks and play with them, but if I did that, dinner would be late. I don't like to eat late. (M A#16 11/99)

In effect, while he spent more time than she did, and both did the evening cooking and child care together, he was ensuring that the basic work got done, while leaving the responsibility for emotional well-being and discipline to her.

There are a variety of explanations for why men have not taken on more responsibility for domestic labour. Prevailing cultural norms about and representations of domesticity, ranging from gender-specific toys such as dolls and play kitchens to ads for household products, typically assume that men are not involved in domestic labour. Men get little public validation or support for their involvement in domestic labour and may be subject to ridicule for doing "women's work" (Luxton 1990: 50). A man described the reaction of his employer when he asked for reduced working hours to allow him to care for his elderly father:

The request obviously threw him for a loop. He didn't want to say no outright but it made him uncomfortable, even though several women in the office have taken time off or reduced time to look after families and he had no problem with that. In fact, he is proud to say he is an enlightened employer. When I asked for the same thing, he hesitated, then he asked if my wife couldn't get time off her job. I said I wanted to look after my father. He was almost squirming but he finally agreed I could work four days and leave early two of those days. But he kept asking me if I really wanted to be doing it. It was like he couldn't believe I really wanted to do it. It was hard not to feel like a freak. (M M#23 1/00)

Even fewer men than women have paid jobs that in any way help workers accommodate family responsibilities, and in workplaces that are predominantly male, work practices typically have evolved to seriously preclude any such possibilities (Luxton and Corman 2001).

Existing sex-based differences in income reinforce sexual divisions in the home. In most households where both partners are employed, men are still typically the higher-income earners. If the woman's paid time is worth substantially less than her husband's, it makes sense financially for her to quit work in order to take care of a newborn or an elderly relative while her partner keeps his job. This apparently sensible coping strategy increases the pay gap between them, for in moving in and out of the labour force more frequently, her earning potential is diminished. The more continuous employment record of the man is rewarded with promotions, seniority, training opportunities, and so on. This strategy also reproduces gender differences because it reinforces women's involvement in caregiving while undermining men's possibilities of increasing theirs:

> Before the baby was born we agreed we both wanted to share child care. But after she was born, I was home all the time so I just got better at caring for her and she knew me. He helps out a lot but it's not like what I do. (F A#24 1/00)

When men are the higher-income earners, both women and men can readily justify subordinating domestic demands to the requirements of his employment. Whether this means moving to accommodate his transfer and promotion, keeping the children quiet during the day while a shift worker sleeps or a professional works at home on the weekend, or accepting men's prolonged absence from the home as they work overtime to meet their job's expectations, most women accept the demands of men's paid employment as a legitimate reason for men's lack of domestic labour:

> He often stays late at work so how can I expect him to come home after such a

long day and start housework. That's just too much. (F M#18 1/00)

The importance of economic earnings in shaping domestic divisions of labour is underscored by evidence that suggests that men's participation in domestic labour may increase in relation to the strength of their wives' labour-force attachment. The longer women are in paid employment and the greater the women's income is as a proportion of total household income, the more likely men are to do domestic labour (Luxton 1981; Marshall 1993).

But the power that accrues to most men who are income earners plays out in other ways as well. When so few men do domestic labour, those who do are often highly praised for even minimal contributions, a practice that can easily reinforce the notion that domestic labour is not expected of men. A woman conveyed her confusion about how to assess her husband's contributions:

> Everyone tells me that he is so terrific around the house. They tell me I am so lucky to have a husband who does so much. All my friends are forever telling me they wish their husbands were half as helpful. So then, I feel so mean when I want to say he doesn't do nearly enough. Maybe I expect too much? And sometimes when we fight over it, he says, "Well all your friends say I do more than my share. So what's your problem?" I don't know. (F M#19 1/00)

In the context of marriage and a commitment to making it work, many women hesitate to escalate their demands that men do more. They risk undermining their important and valued sense that their relationship is based on love and mutual caring if they challenge their partners to do more, and lose. If they force a serious confrontation about the distribution of domestic labour, they run the risk of provoking a major fight. In the interests of domestic harmony and of maintaining their sense of the value of their marriage, many women concede. Conversely, some women decide that struggles over the redistribution of household labour and responsibilities are not worth it. Growing numbers of young women and men are not marrying, more women are choosing to remain childless, and more women are having children without marrying (Oderkirk 1994: 5). Married women who are frustrated by their husbands' resistance may opt to leave the marriage. Charles Hobart (1996: 171) argues that one explanation for contemporary divorce rates is that:

> paid employment has greatly reduced the time available to wives for domestic work, and having paycheques has empowered them, giving them increased influence and independence. Conflict has resulted, over (1) husbands' reluctance to share the domestic work fairly and (2) wives' refusal to be traditionally subservient.

The strategy of redistributing domestic labour between women and men is thus difficult to implement, both because the material conditions of social life work against it, and because, typically, men have the power in their own households to resist. It is not in their interests to take on more, unpaid, work, especially if their wives continue to do it if they refuse. Women's efforts to encourage men to do more are hampered by the private nature of family life. Their struggles are rarely understood as part of major changes in social divisions of labour; instead they are experienced as private conflicts between the individuals involved. Unlike struggles to change the occupational segregation of the paid labour force, where collective action by unions, legal challenges, and public campaigns have provided support for the workers involved, efforts to change household divisions of labour remain private, the interpersonal struggles of the couple involved.

Finally, systemic sexism means that not only do most men resist changing domestic divisions of labour, but there is little social recognition of the problem and widespread resistance to feminist efforts to make a political issue of the inequality. As McMahon (1999: vi) has argued, "the central role men's material interests play in their motivation to defend the gendered status quo" has been "systematically obscured or marginalized in both popular and academic discussion" because men have deeply vested interests in keeping the discussion of the existing inequalities in the gendered division of labour in the home "blandly apolitical."

Paying for Domestic Labour

One solution, for those who can afford it, is to hire replacement labour such as cleaners, babysitters, nannies, or nursing care, or to pay for services such as restaurant meals, nursery schools, or nursing homes. A wife's sole responsibility for housework and a husband's "propensity for doing housework" both decline as each individual's income increases (Marshall 1993). The more money people have available to them, the more they are able, and inclined, to purchase services and labour instead of doing the work themselves (Brayfield 1992: 28). A lawyer described what she did when her mother was released from hospital needing full-time care:

> For the first few days, she came to my home and I hired round-the-clock nursing care. But it was very unsatisfactory. I

couldn't rely on them. They kept phoning me to ask questions and I didn't really trust them around the house. So I contacted one of these services and got them to locate a good nursing home. It costs the earth, but I don't have to worry. (F M#15 11/99)

There are at least four problems with this solution. The first was identified by the same lawyer who was satisfied with the care her mother received but regretted her lack of personal involvement, a lack imposed by her need to work long hours in order to make enough money to pay for the care:

I could afford it. That wasn't the problem. But I felt terrible. I want to be more involved, you know. If she could have stayed at home I could have seen her more often and been much more involved in her care every day. As it is, I go to visit early in the morning on the way to work and I pop in briefly at night. But it's not the same. (F M#15 11/99)

The second problem is that it makes no economic sense for families to pay more for services than the earnings of their lower earner. That means in effect that relatively low-earning women hire other women at even lower earnings or pay for services that are affordable only because the employees are paid low wages. Such dynamics perpetuate low-wage employment and trap immigrant women who come to Canada under government, foreign domestic worker plans in terrible working conditions (Giles and Arat-Koç 1994; Bakan and Stasiulus 1997). As Sedef Arat-Koç notes (1990: 97–8), they also pit women against each other:

Current domestic service arrangements bring the interests of employers and employees into conflict. Given the pressures on their budget and time that some middle-class working couples do indeed face, a domestic service relationship may turn into a zero-sum game in which improvements in the pay and working conditions of domestic workers mean losses for the employers. As a relationship between female employers and workers, domestic service emphasizes, most clearly, the class, racial/ethnic, and citizenship differences among women at the expense of their gender unity.

A woman who had hired a foreign nanny described how such differences had a devastating effect on her children:

At first we got along fine and the children loved her. She was always terrific with them. Gradually things got tense. If I was late getting home, she would be mad. Then she wanted more money and I just couldn't afford it. It was too uncomfortable and I was so relieved when she left but the children were devastated. They cried for months for their "other mother." (F M#13 12/99)

Strategies that involve purchasing services are attractive to many people because they are relatively straightforward and do not require people to engage in lengthy and complicated political negotiations to change legal and social policies. However, as they depend on maximizing individual family incomes, they encourage competition among people in a society. They generate tendencies for individuals to want higher pay and lower taxes even when reductions to government revenues mean cuts to the social services available to everyone. A unionized worker described the impact such views had on collective bargaining in her local:

> Up to now, we have always had a commitment to ensuring those at the lowest pay got the most. But recently, more and more members are saying they don't care about making pay rates more fair. They just want more money for themselves. It's very divisive. (F M#25 2/00)

A parent involved in his daughter's daycare centre made a similar point, showing how such practices increase inequalities:

> I'm on the board at our daycare centre. We are part of a large coalition of groups who have been fighting for a national child care plan for Canada. We want the federal and provincial governments to fund great child care centres everywhere. Economists have done the calculations. We could afford it. But so many people are calling for tax cuts. If governments have less money, they won't fund child care. But the tax cuts won't give individual people enough money to buy child care. They will just mean the rich get richer and the poor get less money and no services. (M A#25 2/00)

The most important problem with hiring or purchasing alternatives is that most households simply cannot afford to do so. The costs of child care in a regulated centre, for example, were in 2000 about $9,000 a year for infants (*Toronto Star,* 11 Sept. 1999: A1, A30), a hefty chunk out of the average full-year full-time earnings for women of $31,506 per year (Drolet 1999: 25). The majority of households cannot sustain such expenditures over any length of time.

Changing Paid Employment—"Family Friendly" Workplaces

Another strategy for coping with the conflicting demands of paid employment and unpaid domestic labour has focused on changing the organization of paid work. As individuals, community activists, and union members, employees have struggled to make workplaces more accommodating of employees' personal lives (de Wolff 1994). They have fought for maternity, parental, and caregiving leaves (Heitlinger 1993; Mishra 1996). They have argued for flexible working hours that allow workers to coordinate their time more effectively with family demands. Employers have responded unevenly to such demands (Duxbury et al. 1992). Most are reluctant to implement such policies unless they see an obvious advantage to the success of their enterprise. Policy analyst Judith Maxwell (2000) argues that even though there is a tension between short-term goals of immediate growth in earnings and long-term goals of the viability of the enterprise and future productivity, business leaders have an interest in promoting more effective policies:

> Employers also have an immediate role to play in the way they support today's employees in their role as parents. Employers should ask these parents what working conditions they need to be the best that they can be at work, and still do their best for their children.

Workers who have access to such policies readily acknowledge that even limited programs help. However, they do not always work in ways that policy analysts expect. A study by Statistics Canada found that while such policies were originally intended to support women workers, typically men have benefited more from them (Frederick 1997). And the limits to such policies leave many people in crisis. A woman whose husband was hospitalized for three weeks said that her employer allowed her to have one week paid "emergency" leave and two weeks unpaid leave. She was deeply grateful and made full use of both:

> It was so wonderful. I could just stay at the hospital and not have to even think about work. My company was really good to me. (F M#21 1/00)

However, her husband's illness lasted more than the time allowed her. She had to go back to work just when he was sent home, still too ill to care for himself. Like so many others in her situation, she found that existing policies are insufficient:

> I was in a state of panic for weeks. It was so difficult. I went to work, but how could I concentrate? I was frantic with worry about what was happening at home. (F M#21 1/00)

The more a workplace relies on women workers and the more skilled those workers are (and therefore harder to replace), the more likely the employer is to implement and permit workers to make use of such policies. Unionized workers have been more successful than non-unionized employees in winning such benefits. In a study of 11 workplaces that implemented policies intended to help employees mediate their paid employment and family responsibilities, Laura Johnson (1995: 63) concluded that: "Employers and employees have provided ample opinion that they benefit from family friendly programs."

Changing State Policies

Closely tied to efforts to reorganize working conditions in the paid labour force are struggles over government policies. Throughout much of the twentieth century, most government policies were based on the premise that women were wives and mothers with husbands to support them (Eichler 1988; 1997). A range of social policies provided some modest support for families in general, such as the family allowance, initiated in 1945 as a universal benefit to assist families with the costs of child rearing (Baker 1995: 128). Policies were developed for women, especially mothers, who did not have income-earning husbands to support them (Ursel 1992; Baker 1995). However, from the 1980s on, governments turned to neoliberal economic policies aimed at reducing government provision of social services while fostering private for-profit businesses. The resulting government policies increasingly embodied a major ambivalence about the role of women in families and the labour market. In all areas of policy—from taxes, social assistance, legislated maternity and parental leaves to the absence of a national system of early child care—governments reluctantly recognized that caregivers could not participate in the labour force without some government support. The policies that were developed, however, put pressure on individuals to provide as much care for themselves and others as possible (Armstrong 1996; Brodie 1996). As Chow, Freiler, and McQuaig (1999: 1) note: "Not knowing whether to support women as mothers, workers, or both has led to a form of policy paralysis and an underdeveloped system of support to families with children."

In the current context of limited assistance from certain policies and haphazard access to other services, families develop coping strategies that enable them to manage the competing demands of paid employment and domestic labour as best they can. A man described the decision-making process he and his wife went through after the birth of their first child. His comments indicate how vital even the limited support available was for them:

> My job wasn't very secure. I was afraid if I asked for time off I would get fired, so we weren't going to mess around there. My wife really liked her job. She could get maternity leave paid and even take some unpaid time too. So we did that. But then when it came time for her to go back, we weren't sure we could find child care that wouldn't cost more than she was making. And we weren't sure what we thought about her being home with the baby—people say sitters or child care are okay but how do you know? But she liked her job and didn't want to give it up. Once we found this daycare centre—it's great! Then we were set. (Values A#23)

What's at Stake? The Politics of Social Reproduction

A mother of two preschoolers tried to understand why unpaid domestic labour is such a problem:

> I really don't understand why it's so difficult to get men to do their fair share in their own homes or why employers and governments don't just see that it's in everyone's interests to ensure children get good care and parents can go to work secure in knowing their kids are having a wonderful time at daycare. It's almost like a conspiracy—it's just cheaper to get women to do everything for free. Do you

think they just want women to carry the burden? (F M#17 12/99)

The United Nations (1991) estimates that women's unpaid work internationally is worth about $4 trillion annually. The General Social Survey indicates that in 1992 people in Canada performed at least 25 billion hours of unpaid work, 95 per cent of which was domestic labour—looking after children and caring for the home. Statistics Canada estimates that this labour is equivalent to about 13 million full-time jobs, is worth about $234 billion, equals about 40 per cent of Canada's gross domestic product and that women did two-thirds of it (Statistics Canada 1992; Chandler 1994; Statistics Canada 1995a).[9]

More importantly, this labour is the main source of caregiving for all children and for many dependent adults. As the labour that ensures households' livelihoods, it is critical for the personal well-being and daily survival of most people in Canada. If women were actually paid for all that work (especially at good wage rates), the wage bill would be enormous.[10] Conversely, if men had to take on even half of the work women do, they would add enormously to their workload; their leisure time would be seriously eroded. Employers and governments understand that provision of universal quality services by well-paid employees is expensive. They are typically resistant to reducing profits or spending public revenues unless there is widespread public support for doing so.

In countries where there has been a demand both for women's participation in the paid labour force and for increased birth rates, there have been well-developed policies to mediate the demands of both labours. Women have benefited by having long paid maternity leaves, as well as the right to have their former job back and retraining when they return to the job (Heitlinger 1979). In countries where there are public commitments to reduce wealth inequalities, and to ensure that all people have adequate care and decent standards of living, there are welfare state provisions available to all. Women and men have benefited from a range of policies and services that relieve the pressure on individuals and particularly women, such as lengthy parental leaves, free or low-cost, high-quality child care centres, or home care for the ill and elderly.

Canada has never had a strong welfare state and since the late 1970s, the neoliberal economic policies that federal, provincial, and territorial governments have implemented dramatically cut government provisions of social services and other measures that foster greater equality among people and between women and men (Brodie 1996). Jane Jensen and Sharon Stroick (1999: 3) describe what such changes have meant for parents and children:

> As Canada has done in the past, many countries pay family allowances or allow tax exemptions or credits for all children, whatever their parents' incomes may be. In Canada, recognition of this universal dimension of family life began to disappear in the 1970s, when targeting of social programs became popular. . . . [H]aving and raising a child was, in effect, treated as a "private consumption decision" of adults, as if parents did not have legal or moral obligations to spend money on child care.

A woman described the impact of such changes on her life as an employee:

> I used to work for a government agency as a home care provider. They privatized the agency, so I lost my job. Later I got another job in a private agency but

it wasn't unionized and I make about half what I made before. And all they care about is making their money so we actually don't provide care to people any more. We go in and get out as fast as we can. I feel terrible about it. (F A#13 11/99)

Another woman described the impact on her unpaid domestic responsibilities when her husband was injured:

> So on top of my regular job I now have almost a second job, at home, looking after him. I have to get up with him at night, sometimes three or four times. I have to make sure he gets his medication at the right time. Sometimes if I get stuck in traffic on the way home I get so scared because he has to get his injections right on time and if I'm late, it's just so much a problem. (F M#16 12/99)

What these examples illustrate is the way most women, as the main people responsible for the work of social reproduction, maintain the standards of living for their household through their unpaid labour. When neoliberal economic policies impose even more unpaid work on private family households, they rely on women's ability to increase their unpaid work, and in effect, force women to absorb the social costs.

While individual women and men engage in whatever strategies they can to get by, organized groups in the women's movement and the labour movement continue to struggle for policies that will redistribute more of the wealth in society to the majority of families, reduce the conflicts between paid employment and domestic labour, reduce the burdens on women and improve the quality of caregiving and the standards of living for the majority of the population. In 1995 at the United Nations Fourth

International NGO Conference on Women at Beijing, China, Canadian delegates were among the 30,000 women from over 185 countries at the NGO Forum who identified prevailing neo-liberal policies as detrimental to most women around the world. Instead, they called for a new political orientation that took account of the needs of the majority of the world's people. In the years since then, Canadian feminist and labour groups have identified a range of policies that would help families secure their standards of living and improve the conditions of women's unpaid domestic labour.

In 2000, as part of an international campaign to eliminate women's poverty and violence against women, the main national labour organization, the Canadian Labour Congress (CLC), and the largest national women's organization, the National Action Committee on the Status of Women (NAC) demanded (among other things) a right to social security, equality at work, child care, and an end to violence against women:

We demand full access to welfare and income security, fully-funded public health care and education, social housing, and adequate pensions. Working women demand improved labour standards, including a minimum wage above the poverty line—$10 an hour; the right to unionize; we want effective and enforceable pay and employment equity legislation; we need sexual, racial, sexual orientation, and personal harassment protection; and we demand the restoration of unemployment insurance to 1996 levels at a minimum. Women demand access to non-profit, state-funded child care, paid maternity leave, parental leave, family leave, dependent care leave. (Canadian Women's March Committee 2000)

These demands illustrate what is at stake in the politics of social reproduction and show that negotiations between individuals in family households over how to balance paid employment and domestic labour are part of much larger struggles over standards of living, allocations of social resources and, ultimately, over the kind of society Canada will become.

● Notes

1. This focus on the majority pattern tends to obscure the fact that capitalist class households acquire their income from investments and can hire workers to do all their domestic labour for them. Some households based on farming, fishing, arts and crafts, or other kinds of self-employment generate incomes by selling the products of their labour. Those who receive government transfer payments such as employment insurance, workers' compensation, or other forms of social assistance have to fight to ensure they receive enough to get by while those who have no secure sources of income typically live in precarious poverty.

2. The quotes cited in this paper come from interviews that are part of a study, "Care Giving and Support among Family, Friends, Neighbours and Communities," a sub-project of a larger project funded by the Social Sciences and Humanities Research Council Grant # 410-94-1502, "Rethinking Families: Canadian Social Policy and International Commitments to Conceptualize, Measure and Value Women's Family Work." The interviews were conducted between September 1999 and January 2000. The identification in brackets indicates the sex (F or M), the situation they were interviewed about—either A for adult children living with their parents or M for people who had experienced an unexpected medical emergency, ID number of the speaker, and the date of the interview. The people interviewed lived in the Greater Toronto Area.

3. The term *breadwinner* with its assumption that bread is the main dietary staple illustrates the cultural specificity of this norm. Although it remains a popular term, I have used the culturally neutral term *income earner* instead.

4. Bettina Bradbury (1993: 119–27) documents for the late nineteenth century how parents and children negotiated and struggled over the competing dynamics of schooling, household needs for additional incomes, and children's commitment to contributing to their parental household or establishing their own. Similar struggles continued for working-class and low-income households throughout the twentieth century.

5. For poignant personal accounts of the impact on their lives of taking on family responsibilities when parents either needed help or were unavailable, see Campbell (1973), Crean (1995: 11), Joe (1996).

6. Statistics Canada identifies families or individuals as "low income" if they spend on average at least 20 per cent more of their pre-tax income than the Canadian average on food, shelter, and clothing (Statistics Canada 1995b: 86).

7. As McMahon points out: "Men's performance of domestic labour is one of the few sociological phenomena of which this can be said" (1999: 12).

8. The 1992 General Social Survey done by Statistics Canada (1992) was based on interviews with more than 9,000 people and was designed to find out about the amount and range of unpaid work done in Canada.

9. There are several different ways of calculating the economic value of unpaid work: replacement costs (what it costs to pay someone to do the work), opportunity costs (what the worker would earn if she or he were employed instead of doing domestic labour), or input/output costs (calculating the market equivalents to determine the price of household output) (Goldschmidt-Clermont 1993; INSTRAW 1995).

10. A 1992 study based on Statistics Canada data and using very low rates of pay as comparators calculated that the average annual cost of unpaid household work was between about $12,000 to $16,000 per year, per household. (Chandler 1994; Luxton 1997: 437).

● References

Abele, F. 1997. "Understanding What Happened Here: The Political Economy of Indigenous Peoples," in *Understanding Canada Building on the New Canadian Political Economy,* ed. W. Clement (Montreal and Kingston: McGill-Queen's University Press).

Arat-Koç, S. 1990. "Importing Housewives: Non-citizen Domestic Workers and the Crisis of the Domestic Sphere in Canada," in *Through the Kitchen Window: The Politics of Home and Family,* 2nd edn, eds M. Luxton, H. Rosenberg, and S. Arat-Koç (Toronto: Garamond Press).

Armstrong, P. 1996. "Unravelling The Safety Net: Transformations in Health Care and Their Impact on Women," in *Women and Canadian Public Policy,* ed. J. Brodie (Toronto: Harcourt Brace and Co.), 129–49.

———, and H. Armstrong. [1978] 1994. *The Double Ghetto: Canadian Women and Their Segregated Work,* 3rd edn (Toronto: McClelland & Stewart).

Bakan, A., and D. Stasiulis, eds. 1997. *Not One of the Family: Foreign Domestic Workers in Canada* (Toronto: University of Toronto Press).

Baker, M. 1995. *Canadian Family Policies: Cross-national Comparisons* (Toronto: University of Toronto Press).

Best, P. 1995. "Women, Men and Work," *Canadian Social Trends* 36 (Spring): 30–3.

Bradbury, B. 1993. *Working Families: Age, Gender, and Daily Survival in Industrializing Montreal* (Toronto: McClelland & Stewart).

Brand, D. 1994. "'We Weren't Allowed to Go into Factory Work until Hitler Started the War': The 1920s to the 1940s," in *We're Rooted Here and They Can't Pull Us Up: Essays in African Canadian Women's History,* eds P. Bristow et al. (Toronto: University of Toronto Press).

Brayfield, A. 1992. "Employment Resources and Housework in Canada," *Journal of Marriage and the Family* 54: 19–30.

Brodie, J. 1996. "Canadian Women, Changing State Forms, and Public Policy," in *Women and Canadian Public Policy,* ed. J. Brodie (Toronto: Harcourt Brace and Co.), 1–28.

Campbell, M. 1973. *Halfbreed* (Halifax: Goodread Biographies).

Canadian Women's March Committee. 2000. *An Open Letter to Canadian Women,* 24 Jan. 2000.

Carty, L. 1994. "African Canadian Women and the State: 'Labour Only, Please,'" in *We're Rooted Here and They Can't Pull Us Up: Essays in African Canadian*

Women's History, eds P. Bristow et al. (Toronto: University of Toronto Press).

Chandler, W. 1994. "The Value of Household Work in Canada," *1992 Canadian Economic Observer,* Statistics Canada, Cat. No. 11-010 (Apr.).

Chow, O., C. Freiler, and K. McQuaig. 1999. "A National Agenda for All Families: Reframing the Debate about Tax Fairness," paper submitted to the Finance Sub-committee, Federal Government, 12 May.

Crean, S.G.H. 1995. *A Woman for Her Time* (Vancouver: New Star Books).

de Wolff, A. 1994. *Strategies for Working Families* (Toronto: Ontario Coalition for Better Child Care).

Drolet, M. 1999. "The Persistent Gap: New Evidence on the Canadian Gender Wage Gap," Statistics Canada, Income Statistics Division (Ottawa: Industry).

Duxbury, L., C. Lee, C. Higgins, and S. Mills. 1992. *Balancing Work and Family: A Study of Canadian Private Sector Employees* (Ottawa: Carleton University).

Eichler, M. 1988. *Families in Canada Today: Recent Changes and Their Policy Consequences,* 2nd edn (Toronto: Gage Educational Publications).

———. 1997. *Family Shifts: Families, Policies, and Gender Equality* (Don Mills, ON: Oxford University Press).

Fast, J., and M. Da Pont. 1997. "Changes in Women's Work Continuity," *Canadian Social Trends* 46 (Autumn): 2–7.

Frederick, J. 1993. "Tempus Fugit . . . Are You Time Crunched?," *Canadian Social Trends* 31 (Winter): 6–9.

———. 1995. *As Time Goes By . . . Time Use of Canadians* (Ottawa: Industry).

———. 1997. *Statistics Canada* (Ottawa: Industry).

Ghalam, N. 1993. "Women in the Workplace," *Canadian Social Trends* 28 (Spring).

———. 1997. "Attitudes Toward Women, Work and Family," *Canadian Social Trends* 46 (Autumn) 13–17.

Giles, W., and S. Arat-Koç, eds. 1994. *Maid in the Market: Women's Paid Domestic Labour* (Halifax: Fernwood).

Goldschmidt-Clermont, L. 1993. "Monetary Valuation of Unpaid Work," paper presented at the International Conference on the Measurement and Valuation of Unpaid Work, Statistics Canada, Apr.

Grindstaff, C.F. 1995. "Canadian Fertility, 1951 to 1993," *Canadian Social Trends* 39 (Winter): 12–16.

Heitlinger, A. 1979. *Women and State Socialism: Sex Inequality in the Soviet Union* (Montreal: McGill-Queen's University Press).

———. 1993. *Women's Equality, Demography and Public Policy: A Comparative Perspective* (London: Macmillan Press).

Hobart, C. 1996. "Intimacy and Family Life: Sexuality, Cohabitation, and Marriage," in *Families Changing*

Trends in Canada, 3rd edn, ed. M. Baker (Toronto: McGraw-Hill Ryerson), 143–73.

INSTRAW (International Research and Training Institute for the Advancement of Women). 1995. Measurement and Valuation of Unpaid Contribution Accounting Through Time and Output, Santo Domingo, Dominican Republic.

Jensen, J., and S. Stroick. 1999. "Finding the Best Policy Mix for Canada's Kids," *Perception* 23, 3 (Dec.): 3–5.

Joe, R. 1996. *Song of Rita Joe: Autobiography of a Mi'kmaq Poet* (Charlottetown, PEI: Ragweed Press).

Johnson, L. 1995. *Changing Families, Changing Workplaces Case Studies of Policies and Programs in Canadian Workplaces for the Women's Bureau,* Human Resources Development Canada (Ottawa: Supply and Services).

Luxton, M. 1980. *More Than a Labour of Love: Three Generations of Women's Work in the Home* (Toronto: The Women's Press).

———. 1981. "Taking on the Double Day: Housewives as a Reserve Army of Labour," *Atlantis* 7, 1 (Fall): 12–22.

———. 1990. "Two Hands for the Clock: Changing Patterns in the Gendered Division of Labour in the Home," in *Through the Kitchen Window: The Politics of Home and Family,* 2nd edn, eds M. Luxton, H. Rosenberg, and S. Arat-Koç (Toronto: Garamond Press).

———. 1997. "The UN, Women, and Household Labour: Measuring and Valuing Unpaid Work," *Women's Studies International Forum* 20, 3: 431–9.

———, and J. Corman. 2001. *Getting By in Hard Times: Restructuring Class and Gender in Hamilton, Ontario 1980–1996* (Toronto: University of Toronto Press).

McMahon, A. 1999. *Taking Care of Men: Sexual Politics in the Public Mind* (Cambridge: Cambridge University Press).

Marchak, P. 1987. "Rational Capitalism and Women as Labour," in *Feminism and Political Economy: Women's Work, Women's Struggles,* eds H.J. Maroney and M. Luxton (Toronto: Methuen).

Marshall, K. 1993. "Dual Earners: Who's Responsible for Housework?," *Canadian Social Trends,* Cat. No. 11-008E (Spring/Winter): 11–14.

Maxwell, J. 2000. "We Must Invest in Our Kids," *The Globe and Mail,* 24 Feb. 2000: A21.

Mishra, R. 1996. "The Welfare of Nation," in *States Against Markets: The Limits of Globalization,* eds R. Boyer and D. Drache (London: Routledge), 316–33.

Morissette, R. 1997. "Declining Earnings of Young Men," *Canadian Social Trends* 46 (Autumn): 8–12.

Nadwodny, R. 1996. "Working at Home," *Canadian Social Trends* 40 (Spring): 16–20.

Nakhaie, M.R. 1995. "Housework in Canada: The National Picture," *Journal of Comparative Family Studies* 26, 3 (Autumn): 409–25.

Oderkirk, J.C. 1994. "Marriage in Canada: Changing Beliefs and Behaviours, 1600–1990," *Canadian Social Trends* (Summer): 2–7.

——, C. Silver, and M. Prud'homme. 1994. "Traditional-earner Families," *Canadian Social Trends* 32 (Spring): 19–25.

Parr, J. 1999. *Domestic Goods: The Material, Moral, and the Economic in the Postwar Years* (Toronto: University of Toronto).

Preston, V., and W. Giles. 1997. "Ethnicity, Gender and Labour Markets in Canada: A Case Study of Immigrant Women in Toronto," *The Canadian Journal of Urban Research* 6, 2 (Dec.): 135–59.

Stasiulis, D. 1997. "The Political Economy of Race, Ethnicity, and Migration," in *Understanding Canada: Building on the New Canadian Political Economy*, ed. W. Clement (Montreal and Kingston: McGill-Queen's University Press).

Statistics Canada. 1992. Initial Data Release from the 1992 General Social Survey on Time Use (Ottawa: Author).

——. 1995a. "Unpaid Work of Households," *The Daily* (20 Dec.).

——. 1995b. *Women in Canada: A Statistical Report* (Ottawa: Industry).

——. 1998a. *The Daily*, Cat. No. 11-001E (17 Mar.).

——. 1998b. *The Daily*, Cat. No. 11-001E (12 May).

——. 2000. *Canadian Social Trends*, Cat. No. 11-008, 56 (Spring).

United Nations. 1991. *The World's Women, 1970–1990: Trends and Statistics* (New York: United Nations Social Statistics and Indicator, Series K, No. 8).

Ursel, J. 1992. *Private Lives, Public Policy: One Hundred Years of State Intervention in the Family* (Toronto: The Women's Press).

Wilson, S. 1991. *Women, Families, and Work,* 3rd edn (Toronto: McGraw-Hill Ryerson).

Part IV

Families Negotiating Change

In Canadian culture, a solid, loving relationship is usually assumed to be the essential foundation on which to build a family—although single adults are increasingly raising children. The situation of single parents makes clear that this society is organized around the assumption that there are two adults in families, as two adults are needed to do the essential work of earning and caring. What is less apparent is that families also need more than two healthy, loving adults. The situations of First Nations communities, recent immigrants to Canada, and families who struggle to pay their bills and put food on the table reveal how critical are access to good jobs and safe housing, as well as supportive social services (health care, education, child care, and assistance of various kinds). Families need supportive social environments as well as hard-working and caring adults who are committed to each other and their children. In Canada, state support of citizens' social security was never as strong as in Europe, and two decades of neoliberal policies have meant a weakening of social services.

The chapters that follow examine how families change as their social environment changes. Immigration, the colonial erosion of First Nations traditions, a weakened economy and tighter labour market, and divorce all present new situations for families. These chapters also explore how individuals, including children, react to changes in their situations and take action to sustain family livelihood and family relations.

Section 1

Immigration

Chapter 19

Change is a constant feature of family life, if for no other reason than that family members age. But many Canadian families have experienced much more significant change than the aging of their members. The profound upheaval of immigration changes families in innumerable ways and, in the process, highlights both the impact of material and cultural context on families and people's agency in making (and remaking) their families.

In this chapter, Guida Man summarizes what she has learned of the changes that women from Hong Kong have experienced in their move to Canada. In explaining those changes, Man makes clear how profoundly family and gender relations are shaped by the organization of the communities in which people live. Her findings question the common assumption that gender relations become more equal in couples who move to Canada from cultures that are clearly patriarchal.

From Hong Kong to Canada: Immigration and the Changing Family Lives of Middle-class Women from Hong Kong

Guida Man

The Canadian government has historically adopted an approach characterized by pragmatism and economic self-interest in regard to immigration. Its immigration policies toward the Chinese have in the past been discriminatory in terms of race, gender, and class and continue to be partial to people from middle- and upper-class backgrounds. Hence, the entry of Chinese women and consequently the formation of Chinese families in Canada have been hampered by these restrictions.

The Canadian government's expansionist economic strategy toward immigration, and the way in which race, gender, and class operate as social relations, determine at any historical moment whether the Chinese are allowed into Canada and what category of Chinese are permitted. During the early periods of Chinese immigration, many racially discriminatory measures such as the head tax and the Chinese Exclusionary Act were imposed on the Chinese, but not on western European immigrants (see Abella and Troper 1982; Baureiss 1987; Hawkins 1988; Li 1988). And although some Chinese labourers were admitted into Canada to work on the railroad and the mines, the Canadian government prohibited Chinese women from entering Canada.[1] This measure effectively reduced the reproductive activities of the Chinese, and hence the formation of Chinese families.

While the head tax was imposed from 1885 to 1923, to prohibit Chinese labourers and their wives from entering Canada, affluent Chinese merchants and their wives were permitted entrance and an exemption from the head tax during the period 1911 to 1923 (Sedgewick 1973: 129; Wickberg 1982: 94, Man

1998: 120).[2] These wealthy merchants were useful in procuring trade for Canada, and therefore were accorded preferential treatment vis à vis their poor counterparts. Even during the exclusionary period between 1923 and 1947, when no Chinese was officially admitted, special privileges were granted to an elite class of Chinese who would otherwise have been prevented from entering Canada due to their race.[3] But the number of women who belonged to the elite class was minuscule; hence, the population of Chinese women in Canada remained very small.[4] Consequently, the number of Chinese families was low even as late as 1951.[5]

The pivotal shift occurred in 1967, when the Canadian government adopted a universal point system to select immigrants. The point system allowed the Chinese to be admitted under the same conditions as other groups (Hawkins 1988). The new initiative supposedly eliminated the racial and gender discriminatory elements of the Immigration Act, but the class discriminatory measures remained. The 1967 point system (and its subsequent revisions in 1978 and 1985) inevitably privileges people from middle- and upper-class backgrounds who have the opportunity to acquire the "appropriate" educational, vocational, and language skills required by the Canadian government.

The 1967 revision of the Canadian immigration policy, coinciding with riots in Hong Kong triggered by skirmishes on the Chinese border, resulted in a large influx of Chinese immigrants from Hong Kong. Many of the Chinese who were admitted were middle-class professionals such as physicians and engineers. They were highly educated, cosmopolitan, with professional or technical skills, and proficient in either French or English. Many of the Chinese women who came into Canada at the time were sponsored by their husbands and relatives. But the selection policy also attracted some middle-class Chinese women professionals who had the educational and occupational skills to come in as independent applicants. By 1971, 83 per cent of the Chinese in Canada were recorded as belonging to a census family household (Statistics Canada 1971).

The universal point system of the 1967 immigration policy emphasized the educational and vocational skills of the new immigrants. Consequently, the 1986 census data gave a very positive picture of Chinese immigrant women's educational level (see Table 19.1) and their participation in the labour market (see Table 19.2), in comparison with their male counterparts and other Canadians. The data show that a higher percentage (12.8 per cent) of Chinese immigrant women ("foreign-born") have obtained a university degree than other immigrants, both female and male (7.9 per cent and 11.2 per cent respectively). However, fewer Chinese immigrant women than immigrant men and native-born women were able to enter the highly coveted managerial and professional occupations (14.4 per cent, as opposed to 25.4 per cent and 25.2 per cent respectively). At the same time, native-born Chinese Canadians are more likely to hold university degrees than other Canadians, both female and male (19.3 per cent and 20.6 per cent respectively), and also have higher participation rates in managerial and professional occupations (25.2 per cent and 26.7 per cent respectively).

In response to the transfer of government from British to Chinese sovereignty in Hong Kong in 1997, and the anticipated political, social, and economic uncertainty under Chinese rule, the 1980s saw a second wave of Chinese immigrants from Hong Kong to Canada. The Canadian media responded to the new immigrants by focusing on the wealthiest of the business immigrants. They

Table 19.1 Level of Schooling for Foreign-born and Native-born Chinese Canadians and Other Canadians by Sex, 15 Years of Age and Over, 1986

Level of Schooling	% Chinese Canadians				% Other Canadians	
	Foreign-born		Native-born			
	Female	Male	Female	Male	Female	Male
Some High School or Less	50.4	38.8	26.7	30.8	45.5	43.1
Completed High School	11.6	10.0	15.0	10.0	14.3	11.3
Trade Certification or Diploma	0.6	0.9	0.5	0.8	2.1	4.2
Non-university without Diploma	5.3	6.0	7.4	6.2	7.0	6.6
Non-university with Trade or Diploma	9.2	9.4	17.2	9.5	14.5	14.6
Some University	10.1	12.7	13.9	22.1	8.7	9.0
University with Degree	12.8	22.2	19.3	20.6	7.9	11.2
TOTAL %	100	100	100	100	100	100
TOTAL SAMPLE	2,520	2,401	367	389	198,139	188,864

Source: Compiled from 1986 Public Use Microdata File on Individuals, a product of the 1986 Census of Canada. These data are based on a sample of 500,000 individuals, representing approximately 2 per cent of the population.

Table 19.2 Occupations by Foreign-born and Native-born Chinese Canadians and Other Canadians by Sex, 1986

Occupations	% Chinese Canadians				% Other Canadians	
	Foreign-born		Native-born			
	Female	Male	Female	Male	Female	Male
Managerial, Administrative, and Related	4.5	9.0	7.4	12.1	4.5	10.1
Professional and Technical	9.9	16.4	17.8	14.6	12.4	10.3
Clerical and Related	17.3	6.0	31.3	12.6	20.1	5.5
Sales	4.7	6.4	8.2	10.3	5.8	7.1
Transport: Equipment Operating	0.0	1.7	0.3	2.8	0.4	4.8
Processing, Machining, and Construction	2.3	15.4	1.3	6.9	4.1	22.7
Service	13.7	21.4	10.1	12.3	10.2	8.2
Farming and Other Primary	0.6	0.4	0.5	1.8	1.7	6.8
Other	2.2	3.7	1.1	4.1	1.5	5.6
Not applicable	34.8	19.6	22.0	22.5	39.3	18.9
TOTAL %	100	100	100	100	100	100
TOTAL SAMPLE	2,520	2,401	367	389	198,139	188,864

Source: Compiled from 1986 Public Use Microdata File on Individuals, a product of the 1986 Census of Canada. These data are based on a sample of 500,000 individuals, representing approximately 2 per cent of the population.

are dubbed "Gucci Chinese" (Cannon 1989) or "yacht people" (*Calgary Herald*, 14 Feb. 1988: D3) by the media—in contrast with their poor Vietnamese cousins, the "boat people." Hence, a particular image of the immigrants has been created: that of affluent businessmen, driving Mercedes-Benzes and living in monster homes (*Halifax Chronicle Herald*, 25 Jan. 1988: 15; *Vancouver Sun*, 26 May 1989: B4; *Maclean's*, 7 Feb. 1994: 30). In fact, this image typifies only a small minority, and is far from the actual "lived experiences" of most Chinese immigrants, particularly Chinese immigrant women.

Although the media image of the Hong Kong Chinese immigrants does not include women, since 1987 the number of Chinese immigrant women from Hong Kong has exceeded that of their male counterparts. For example, in 1992, 20,102 females versus 18,829 males immigrated to Canada from Hong Kong, and in 1993 the numbers of females and males were 18,800 and 17,685 respectively (EIC 1992, 1993). Despite their numbers and their contributions, Chinese women's experiences have remained invisible. This is congruent with the fact that the study of women was not legitimized as a topic of discourse, and that women's perspective has largely been ignored in academic research until fairly recently (Eichler 1985). Moreover, women's labour has almost always been incorporated into the family, or into their husbands' work (Luxton 1980). Consequently, their experience is seen to be either subsumed under that of men (Jacobson 1979) or tied to that of their male counterparts, and therefore they are perceived as not having a separate reality.

Theoretical Framework and Methodology

More recently, feminist theorists have ruptured the silence of women's experience. Hence since the 1980s, we have seen the emergence of studies on immigrant women in general (see, for example, Ng and Estable 1987; Boyd 1990; Ng 1998; Thobani 1998; Lee 1999), and on Chinese women in particular (see, for example, Nipp 1983; Adilman 1984; Yee 1987). Nipp's and Adilman's studies shed light on the historical accounts of Chinese immigrant women in Canada, while May Yee and the Chinese Canadian National Council's (1992) book project illuminated Chinese women's lives by making space for Chinese women to voice their stories from their own perspectives. These studies have found Chinese women to be actors who toiled and laboured alongside their male counterparts, and who were involved actively in political and community organizing.

Research on immigrants has typically derived its theoretical perspectives from work centred around the concepts of "adaptation" and "adjustment." Such analyses assume that the onus is on the individual immigrant to adjust. The immigrant's failure to assimilate is seen to be her or his own fault. Studies based on these theoretical perspectives often focus only on microstructural processes (i.e., on the individual and the immediate family). Their analyses seldom go beyond the individual to investigate the interaction between her or him and the macrostructure, to look at how socially constructed opportunities and limitations rooted in institutional and organizational processes shape individual immigrants' lives. In my research, I have adopted a feminist methodology (Ng 1982; Hartsock 1983; Haraway 1985; Smith 1987; Hill-Collins 2000) which places women as "subjects" of the study and takes into account both structural processes and individual negotiations. This methodology has enabled me to investigate how individual Chinese immigrant women as subjects account for their situations, and how their stories are as much their subjective experiences as they are shaped by objective structures in the form of organizational and institutional processes. Organizational and institutional processes are in fact interconnected. I have delineated them in order to obtain clarity in my exploration.

As mentioned previously, the Chinese come from diverse backgrounds and locations. I will focus on exploring the experiences of middle-class women in Chinese families that have recently immigrated from Hong Kong, and I will attempt to explain how their experiences in Canada have been transformed as a result of the difference in the social organization of the two societies. I have artificially categorized their experiences into topics: employment opportunities, housework and childcare, relationships with husbands and children, and social life. In actuality, people's everyday lives are not neatly delineated into categories. Human experiences and interactions with others occur in dialectical, rather than in linear relations. Events and feelings diverge and converge. Similarly, these categories overlap each other.

The Sample

The data for this study were generated through in-depth interviews with 30 recent middle-class Chinese immigrant women from Hong Kong. The women were all married, with at least one child. They had immigrated to Canada between 1986 and 1990. The majority of them (26 out of 30) came as dependants of their husbands. Five of them were living in Vancouver at the time of the interview, and the rest were living in Toronto. A snowball-sampling method was used to locate the interviewees. In other words, friends and colleagues were asked to refer women with the requisite characteristics. Women who were interviewed were then asked to suggest other women for inclusion in the study.

Each interview lasted between one and a half hours to three hours. An interview schedule was used as a guideline. All questions were open-ended. Interviewees were encouraged to talk freely about their experiences in Canada and in Hong Kong. Most of the interviews were conducted in Cantonese (a Chinese dialect spoken by most people in Hong Kong), interspersed with some English phrases—a mode of speaking favoured by most "Chyuppies."[6] Two interviewees preferred using the English language, and the interviews were conducted in English interspersed with Chinese phrases.

Institutional Processes

Institutional processes here refer to those processes and practices that are embedded in government, law, education, and professional systems. Such processes can engender and perpetuate social injustice in our society. In the previous section, I described how the institutionalized discriminatory process and practice of the Canadian immigration policies regulated the entrance of Chinese women into Canada. In this section, I will show how their opportunities for employment were restricted by institutionalized processes.

Employment Opportunities

Most of the women in this study came to Canada as dependants of their husbands who were the principal applicants under the "Independent Class"[7] as "business" or "other independent" (professionals such as engineers, accountants, etc.) immigrants. These women therefore need not have high educational levels to score entry points. Due to their middle-class background, however, on the whole, their education is quite high. The majority have university degrees or post-secondary education. Their qualification is even higher than that of the average immigrant from Hong Kong. Despite the fact that these women were classified as "dependants" by the immigration policy, and were therefore supposedly not destined for the labour market, many of these women had worked as professionals in Hong Kong. Although not all of these women actively sought employment when they first arrived, those who did were either underemployed or unemployed. Institutionalized practices in the form of the requirement of "Canadian experience," and the lack of an accreditation system to calibrate their qualifications, have made it difficult for them to obtain employment commensurate with their qualifications. Consequently, some women found themselves economically dependent on their husbands for the first time in their lives. At the same time, immigrant men are subjugated to the same institutionalized discrimination.

The experiences of the husbands of these women were not unlike the experiences of other Chinese immigrants from Hong Kong. A study conducted in 1991 by the Alberta Career Development and Employment Policy and Research Division, the Hong Kong Institute of Personnel Management, and the Canadian Employment and Immigration Commission found that of 512 Hong Kong immigrants between the ages of 30 and 39 who entered Canada after 1980, 23 per cent reported no change in income, 46 per cent recorded a drop, and 31 per cent reported a rise in income. The majority (62 per cent) also experienced a drop in occupational status, 25 per cent experienced no change, and only 13 per cent had acquired a higher status (*Canada and Hong Kong Update* 1992: 7).

Another survey conducted in 1989, which focused specifically on Chinese immigrant women's needs in Richmond, BC (SUCCESS 1991), found that whereas 70 per cent of the women surveyed had worked prior to immigrating to Canada, fewer than 50 per cent were employed when surveyed. Of those who were employed, there was a significant degree of frustration and loss of self-esteem as a result of underemployment, low salaries, and limited opportunities for advancement. Nearly one-quarter of the respondents stated that their foreign education was not recognized in Canada. Over 46 per cent of these women had completed secondary education, and 41.2 per cent had post-secondary education which included college/university or professional training.

Chinese Canadians are concerned about the upsurge in racism. They feel that they are disadvantaged when it comes to getting jobs and being promoted—a "glass ceiling" keeps them from advancing to management ranks. In a survey conducted for the Chinese Canadian National Council, 63 per cent of survey respondents from Chinese-Canadian organizations and 59 per cent from non-Chinese-Canadian social service organizations reported their belief that Chinese Canadians are being discriminated against (*Globe and Mail*, 26 Apr. 1991: A7).

These findings concur with my interview data. One of the women I interviewed, who has a postgraduate degree, and has worked as a translator and teacher in Hong Kong, got so exasperated with her job search that she gave up the idea of entering the labour force altogether. She lamented,

> It's a Catch-22. I cannot get a job because I don't have Canadian experience, and yet I don't see how I can possibly get Canadian experience without being hired in the first place!

Her frustration is echoed by other Chinese immigrant women.

A common strategy many immigrant women I interviewed adopted is what Warren (1986) terms a "positive and pragmatic bridge" attitude toward their new positions. As one woman who worked as a Chief Executive Officer supervising over 300 employees when she was in Hong Kong rationalized:

> In terms of my employment here when I first arrived, I couldn't work as a manager as I didn't have Canadian experience; I couldn't work as a secretary because I was told I was overqualified. I was lucky to get a job with this company. They wanted to do business with Hong Kong. . . . That's why they hired me. They wanted someone to start the HK market. I was hired as an assistant. . . . They paid the B.Comm. graduates $1,200 a month. They paid me $1,500 a month. So they really respected me. . . . Either you don't work for someone, but if you work for them, you have to do your best, doesn't matter what the pay is. I kept telling myself that they were paying me to learn. I was in a new country. I didn't have a choice. I was paving my way for the future.

These women are cognizant of the futility of hoping for changes in processes that are institutionalized and embedded in the social system. Since they could not transform the macrostructure, they therefore resolved to change their own attitude toward their situations.

Organizational Processes

Organizational processes refer to the differences in the way societies are organized. Immigrants are often judged by their ability to "adjust" to the host society. What is neglected, however, is an investigation into

the differences between the social organization of the society from which the immigrant has come and the one to which she or he has immigrated. By uncovering how the individual woman's experience is shaped by the larger socio-economic structure, we can begin to understand the problems which seemingly dwell only on the micro level. The differences in the ways societies are organized determine the different ways people get their work done, conduct their lives, and relate to other people. In the following, I have attempted to demonstrate how Chinese immigrant women's everyday lives have been transformed because of the different organization of Hong Kong and Canadian societies.

Relationships with Husbands and Children

Being in a new country may change the relationships these women have with family members. The effects of their transformed relationships with husbands and family members vary depending on their labour-market participation and that of their husbands. Apart from the institutional processes that hamper immigrants' opportunities to enter the Canadian labour market, the differences between the social and organizational structures of Hong Kong and Canadian societies also contribute to new immigrants' unemployment and underemployment.

Under British colonial rule, Hong Kong adopted what economists consider a pure capitalist system. With an industrious workforce, this system created, on the one hand, a very low unemployment rate (around 3 per cent); on the other hand, it engendered a wide disparity between the rich and the poor, between professionals and low-level blue-collar workers. As well, unions have a relatively low profile, and workers enjoy few benefits. Although the Hong Kong economy has always been robust, the absence of a guaranteed minimum wage and the lack of an adequate social safety net (Cheng and Kwong 1992) make life extremely difficult for the poor and the unemployed. For the middle-class citizens, however, the situation is promising. The low unemployment rate, coupled with the brain drain due to emigration, allows professionals, whether men or women, to enjoy good salaries and excellent benefits.

In Canada, the situation is quite different. The relative strength of unions means that many workers, whether white- or blue-collar, are protected. The wage gap between blue-collar workers and mid-level professionals is relatively narrow. Compared to Hong Kong, the average low-level worker in Canada fares better. Workers generally enjoy fairly good employee benefits, and comparable wages. But while there is a guaranteed minimum wage, the high cost of living has kept some people on welfare. And while the government strives to provide a social safety net for its citizens, the unemployment rate has remained high (hovering around 10 per cent). The continuing economic recession further exacerbates the situation. Competition for jobs is keen, and employers can be discriminatory about whom they hire. This does not provide an ideal situation for a new immigrant looking for work.

The changes these couples experience in their economic situation either improve or worsen their relationships. Some middle-class immigrant women professionals, who became unemployed or underemployed as a result of immigration, have found themselves economically dependent on their husbands for the first time in their lives. Such dependency has put some Chinese women in relatively powerless relationships with their husbands. Other women, however, have more positive experiences. They have found that their relationships with their husbands have improved because of their husbands' diminished career demands in Canada, which allows more time with their spouses. Their husbands have become underemployed or have reduced their business activities because of the lack of business connections and opportunities in a country with a less favourable economic environment. These women reported greater intimacy with their husbands. Spouses were drawn closer to each other by their common struggle to overcome obstacles in the new country, and to comfort each other when they were overwhelmed by feelings of isolation and alienation. As one woman whose husband used to be part owner of a manufacturing business in Hong Kong told me:

> My relationship with my husband has improved since we've emigrated. We are now much closer to each other. . . . In Hong Kong, my husband needed to entertain his clients, so he was out in the evenings a lot. He also used to travel back and forth to China quite often. So, even though we were living together, we led separate lives. Here, we only have a small business. He doesn't need to entertain any clients. Also he doesn't know that many business contacts, so he's home every evening. And because we are still struggling with the new business, I now help out in the store quite a bit, so we are together a lot. I'm really enjoying this togetherness. It's brought a new dimension to our marriage. We've discovered a renewed intimacy in our relationship. Now that we are together a lot, he really appreciates my help. He consults everything he does with me, something which he had never done when we were in Hong Kong. He used to consult with his

mother, but not with me. They have a very close relationship, you see.

There were others, however, who found the isolation of being new immigrants and the stress of unemployment heightened their incompatibility and lack of communication, leading to marriage breakdown. One of the women I interviewed complained about her situation:

> My husband has been unemployed for over a year now. He had a very good position as an administrator with lots of benefits when he was in Hong Kong. The first year we were here, he found a job as a clerk. He was getting less than half of what he was making before. . . . But then the company went bankrupt, and he was unemployed. He's so depressed now that he is making me down too. He also kept blaming me for making him come here. We've had a lot of fights, and I'm not sure what will happen next. We talked about separating. I'm just living day-to-day at the moment.

Some of the husbands of the interviewed women who were either unable to complete the transfer of their businesses from Hong Kong to Toronto in time for their departure, or were afraid of relinquishing all their business contacts in Hong Kong, ended up spending half of the year in Hong Kong and away from their families in Toronto. These men are known among the Hong Kong immigrants as "astronauts."[8] This phenomenon also occurs among other immigrants who are reluctant to forgo their high-status, lucrative professional jobs in Hong Kong to face possible unemployment in Canada.[9] This long-distance arrangement has varying consequences for the wives. One astronaut's wife lamented the burden and the loneliness of maintaining the household on her own. She confided, "I can't wait for the time when my husband can stop travelling back and forth. I'm tired of being here alone with the kids." Her dissatisfaction is like that of women in the same situation in another study who expressed considerable worries stemming from their husbands' absence (SUCCESS 1991).

Another astronaut's wife in my study, in contrast, marvelled at her newfound independence, and attributed her heightened communication with her husband to his frequent absences. Interestingly, her positive reaction was similar to the findings of studies on dual-career commuting couples, which showed that some couples' relationships improved because of their time apart (Gerstel 1984; Man 1991; 1995). Here is what she told me:

> The first year when he [the husband] was still spending a lot of time in Hong Kong, he used to call me long distance all the time. We also wrote love letters to each other regularly. We were missing each other very much. We hadn't been that close together since we were married. And every time he came back to visit, it is like reliving our honeymoon again. It was really the sweetest year we have had for a long time.

One woman reported that she had been having problems with her two teenage children since they immigrated to Canada. What appear at first to be this family's adjustment problems due to immigration in fact have a concrete, material base. As this woman confided to me:

> Mothering is of course a lot easier in Hong Kong than here. There, the kids can be a lot more independent. My kids usually just hop on a cab right after school, and go to their respective tennis or music lessons. Afterwards, they just hop on

a cab to go home. By the way, cabs are really cheap in Hong Kong. Also, Hong Kong is such a small place, you can go to any place within half an hour. I never had to worry about my children's transportation. The situation here is very different. It is too expensive for my kids to take cabs every day, and the public transportation in my area is not very good. I have to dovetail my work schedule with that of my children.

This woman now works late every night, so she can go straight after work to pick up her teenage son from his extracurricular activities. By the time she gets home, finishes making dinner, and cleans up, she is usually so exhausted that she just goes straight to bed. Her relationship with her children has become strained. Her son resents his loss of independence because he now has to wait for his mother to pick him up; and her daughter is annoyed that her mother cannot spend quality time with her. It is clear that what seem to be this woman's private, personal problems with her children in fact originate from external factors. The differences in social organization in Canada and the home country, such as the size of the city, the transportation system, and the high cost of living, have tremendous impact on the individual woman, affecting her everyday life, and the relationships of family members.

Housework and Child Care

In advanced capitalist societies such as Canada and Hong Kong, housework and child care are privatized. Rather than acknowledging child care as a public issue and allocating funds to establish child care facilities, these governments have shifted the responsibility onto private households—that is, onto women (see Chapter 17). Despite the fact that economic demands have pushed many married women into the labour market, the unequal division of labour in the home has relegated women to primary responsibility for housework and child care.

Feminist debates have located the family as the site of oppression for women, creating for housewives "the problem with no name" (Friedan 1963); and housework as "more than a labour of love" (Luxton 1980). Feminist research has also focused on the interconnectedness of housework and paid work (Connelly 1978; Armstrong and Armstrong 1984; Luxton and Reiter 1997; Man 1997; Hill-Collins 2000), and on how women must negotiate the conflicting demands of paid work and family responsibilities (Duffy, Mandell, and Pupo 1989).

Many upper-class women, and increasingly some middle-class women, try to "resolve" the demands and pressures of juggling paid work, housework, and child care by employing paid domestic help. Such a solution, however, inevitably creates a division among women along class lines, and threatens to undermine the collectivism within the feminist movement.

Although the gendered division of household labour is in some ways similar in Hong Kong and Canada, the differences in family structures and the social organization of these societies transform the situation of Chinese immigrant women, making their day-to-day living vastly different in Canada than in Hong Kong.

While the nuclear-family structure is prevalent in Hong Kong, many Chinese families (whether in Canada, Hong Kong, or elsewhere) retain vestiges of the extended-family form.[10] In such cases, three generations typically reside in the same residence. This extended-family arrangement is as much an adherence to the Confucian ideal (which stresses one's duty to care for the old) as a pragmatic arrangement in response to the high cost of housing and the shortage of state-subsidized homes for the aged. Very often, the arrangement is mutually beneficial for all parties. The grandparent (typically the grandmother) or the unmarried aunt is provided for; in return, they are able to help with housework and child care. In cases where families adopt the nuclear-family structure, the small geographical area of the colony enables relatives to live in close proximity to each other, and thus promotes the development of close-knit support networks.

Regardless of whether the household in Hong Kong consists of a nuclear family or extended family (i.e., whether members of the extended family live together under one roof), the organization of the society enables members of the extended family to interact regularly and to lend support to each other if they so wish. The definition of family advocated by Fox and Luxton (see Chapter 1) urges ignoring household and focusing on personal support networks. It is evident that for Hong Kong Chinese families, who is in the household is less important than who interacts and helps each other to meet the needs of family members (see also Eichler 1988: 8–18). As one woman described her situation in Hong Kong:

> When we were in Hong Kong, my mother-in-law used to live with us. She did the cooking and the cleaning. She also picked up my oldest son after school so I didn't have to rush home right after work. My mother, on the other hand, lives close to my youngest son's school, so she used to pick him up after school and looked after him until I got to her place to pick him up after work. That's why my oldest son is very close to his maj-maj (paternal grandmother), and my youngest one is attached to his paw-paw (maternal grandmother)!

> You see, I had a lot of support in Hong Kong. Here, I have to do everything myself.

Beyond assistance in housework and child care from members of the extended family, the class privilege of these middle-class Chinese women permitted some of them the luxury of hired help when they were in Hong Kong. This support system enabled them to pursue their career interests and allowed them free time for recreational or creative activities. Many of these women have taken this support system for granted.

Transplanted to Toronto, these women experience, first, a loss of support from the extended family (since many older parents are reluctant or unable to emigrate); and second, a decrease in their earning power due to the women's underemployment or unemployment, making it no longer economically feasible for them to have hired help. The extra burden of domestic labour is almost always assumed by the woman as her sole responsibility. Those women who tried to cope with a dual workload of housework and paid work often felt exhausted at the end of the day. Their predicaments are echoed by Chinese immigrant women in another study who described problems in child care, household maintenance, and transportation (SUCCESS 1991). One woman described to me her typical day:

> I usually get up at seven, prepare breakfast for my kids and my husband, then take the TTC to go to work. It takes me at least one hour to get to work by public transit. We're a one-car family. I don't usually get to drive the car except when my husband is not around. Depending on where I work, I don't usually get home until six-thirty or seven, make dinner, clean up, and if I'm lucky, I get to watch a bit of television before going to bed. But

usually, I need to do the ironing, washing, and mending, etc. I really don't have time to do much else. My husband and kids, though, they watch a lot of television.

A few women managed to recreate in Canada the support system they had in Hong Kong. Unlike other women, these women did not experience a drastic change in household duties, and were therefore able to maintain the balance of work and family responsibilities. Lily, whose parents had immigrated to Canada a few years prior, described how she maintained this mutually supportive network with her parents:[11]

When I came here in 1987, I told my parents that I've brought money with me to buy a house. But I promised them that we'll live close by. . . . So we bought a house very close to theirs, so close that my younger daughter could go there after school. And we now eat dinner at my parents' place every night. . . . It's not only because of the fact that I don't know how to cook, but my mother felt that since my husband and I had to work, it would be better that we eat at their place. She told me that it's the same cooking for two people as cooking for six. At least this way, we get to see them every day. If we weren't eating there, I don't think we'd be driving there to see them every day. Also, because my younger daughter's school is very close to my parents' house, it's very convenient for my daughter as well. . . . So this is how my parents help us out. My mother cooks for us Monday to Friday, and on the weekends, I take them out for dinners. This way, my mother gets to have the weekends off. So, we take care of each other. . . . Also, it gives my mother

something to look forward to every night when we go over there.

While in Hong Kong, many of these middle-class women did not actually engage in the physical labour of doing housework (cooking and cleaning), but rather the management of it. But since they clearly identified the management and control of the household as domestic labour, and as such an important task, they were proud to define themselves as capable housewives, in addition to being successful career women. For these women, power lies very much in the management and control of every aspect of family life. Nor is this image contradictory to their commitment to participation in the labour market in Hong Kong. These women were able to juggle the dual or triple workload of housework, paid work, and child care because of the household support system they had when they were in Hong Kong. There, many Chinese husbands took for granted that their wives would share the breadwinner role, as well as managing the household. Domestic harmony was maintained even though wives went out to work, because the husbands' daily sustenance was provided. Dinner still appeared on the table on time (although not prepared by the wife); shirts and pants were washed and ironed, ready to be worn the next morning (compliments of the mother or the hired help); and household maintenance chores were taken care of (by the hired workman). All this, however, did require skillful management by the wives. Husbands were relieved of virtually all of these tasks when they were in Hong Kong.

When asked whether her husband shared the housework in Canada or not, one of my interviewees laughed,

No way! He had never lifted a finger all his life. Before we got married, he used to live at home, and his mother did everything for him. I would never dream of asking him to help me with housework. Besides, Chinese women don't do that. To ask your husband to help you with housework is to admit that you are incapable of being a good wife! It is a loss of face on the woman's part!

Since many of the husbands had never done housework before, they did not offer to help their wives after they immigrated to Canada. Nor do these women seek their help. As one woman explained:

> I feel that if I can manage it myself, I wouldn't ask. Furthermore, if my husband really wants to do it, he can offer to help. But he hasn't! As for my children, I would rather they spend their time studying or having fun. I don't really want them to waste their time on housework.

Some women, however, did get help from other family members, particularly with cleaning and grocery shopping:

> There's a lot of work. Fortunately, my husband and sons do help me with vacuuming. They also do the yardwork and cut the grass. Grocery shopping is very convenient here. There are also many Chinese supermarkets close to where we live. My husband loves to go grocery shopping. Usually, we just pick up some grocery on our way home from work. We shop several times a week because it's so convenient.

For some women, galvanizing the help of family members, with lots of planning and organization, were the keys to "getting things done" in Canada:

First of all, domestically, I have a lot of help. But I also have to be organized. My daughters are now older, so it's not like they would dirty up the walls, etc. Also being daughters they are much tidier than boys. I plan my schedule carefully. We only do laundry once a week. Every Friday night, we do the laundry. We also take turns ironing, me and my daughters usually. Sometimes my husband would offer to help. . . . Actually, there aren't too many things we buy that need ironing. I do everything the easy way; e.g., in terms of flowers, I buy pots of cactus. I change them only once every one or two months. . . . Also, there's not much dust here, so we only dust once a month. Once in a blue moon, we'll do a spring cleaning. Vacuum cleaning is my husband's responsibility. So is changing light bulbs, fixing the water faucet, gardening. He really enjoys gardening. We call him "the gardener."

Although cheaper housing costs allowed families to have bigger residences in Canada, these increase the amount of housework for women. Here is a comment from an interviewee:

> There seems to be more housework here. One reason could be that our house here is more than twice as big as our apartment in Hong Kong, so there's a lot more space to clean. As well, in Hong Kong, people usually have parquet floors, or tiled floors. Here, we have carpeting, which needs vacuuming more often.

In regard to doing other, more "male-oriented" types of housework, Mabel revealed her and her husband's ignorance about this kind of work:

Oh, he [husband] had never even used a hammer . . . and I'm definitely not handy myself either. I don't know how to fix a lock, or even to put up a nail. Most Canadians know how to do these things, but I never had to do it, so I didn't know how to do it at all. In the winter, I didn't know that I had to put caulking on my window. All these are little things, but they all add up. . . . In Hong Kong, services are so easily available people never think of doing anything themselves. You call up a handyman even just to put up a picture, or screw on a light bulb. It sounds ridiculous, but that's the reality there.

Both Mabel and her husband are highly educated professionals. They are capable and motivated people. However, they felt totally inadequate when they first came to Canada because they were not able to do small household maintenance chores like "other Canadians." This is due to the fact that the way in which the labour market is organized in Hong Kong is quite different from Canada. Until 1980, because of a constant flow of legal and illegal immigrants from China (Wong 1992), there had been a stable supply of cheap labour in Hong Kong, and services were relatively inexpensive. This in turn alleviates maintenance chores in middle-class households where both spouses participate full-time in the paid labour force. In Canada, because of the high cost of services, people are compelled to learn to do many household maintenance chores out of necessity.

In cases where the children are young, or when they participate in extracurricular activities which require the wife to chauffeur them back and forth, the women carry a triple burden of paid work, housework, and child care. The way in which a society organizes its child care facilities can have a tremendous impact on women who work full-time for pay. Kathy, a social worker, voiced her criticism of the inadequacy of daycare in Canada:

I have a five-year-old and a two-year-old. I'm finding that daycare is a serious problem. Daycare is not flexible enough to accommodate working parents. Their hours of operation doesn't fill our gaps. We have to choose between quality or service. Sure, there are a few daycare centres now which run from 7 a.m. to 6 p.m. They are all privately run. They offer the service, but not necessarily the quality. So sometimes you don't want to put your child at risk. I have to choose very carefully. I have now found a very good quality daycare, and I can trust them very much . . . they have a lot of educational activities, lots of good materials which enable my children to learn a lot. On the other hand, they don't provide the service—i.e., their hours of operation are limited. So I have to juggle with my time to put my kids there. I am always dashing about like a mad woman. . . . I have no social life at all.

Most of the women I interviewed choose to live in areas within close proximity of friends and relatives, and which have easy access to Chinese grocery stores. However, the actual location of the houses is almost always determined by their children's schools and husbands' workplaces. Their own work location was not a determining factor in their initial decision. This can be attributed to the fact that children are considered the wives' responsibility. In order not to cause the women any more time loss in chauffeuring the children to and from school, it makes perfect good sense that homes be located close to schools.

Social Life

The immigrant women I interviewed have frequent interactions with other Hong Kong immigrants. Socializing with people who have common backgrounds and experiences creates for them a sense of continuity and is a stabilizing force in their new country (Warren 1986). Agnes, a secretary turned housewife, commented,

> I feel we have more in common with each other. We often get together and reminisce about our lives in Hong Kong. We also laugh about our ignorance of Canadian culture, and the little faux pas that we get ourselves into. Other times, we exchange information about schools, dentists, and other practical knowledge. Or we marvel at the high price we now pay for little things such as cooking wares and stockings. I have a feeling of solidarity when I talk to these people. They understand where I'm coming from.

Some women, however, also have friends from different ethnic groups. Usually, these friends are neighbours or parents of their children's friends, and occasionally friends they have met at work. This is in contrast to their lives in Hong Kong, where most working women customarily socialize with their colleagues. As well, social life there is more spontaneous. As one woman puts it succinctly, "We usually just get together after work for movies and dinners; it's never planned."

Although it is common and economically feasible for most people to organize frequent dinner parties at restaurants in Hong Kong, the astronomical cost of dinner parties at restaurants in Canada forces many to have small dinner parties at home, and only occasionally. This kind of change is seen by some as having positive effects. One woman expressed it this way:

> Life is comparatively quieter here. On the other hand, I now feel closer to my few friends. Our conversation is more personal and more meaningful, whereas before, I was always with a big crowd, and the conversation was usually superficial.

Nevertheless, women who have to juggle paid work, housework, and child care typically are too exhausted at the end of the day to have much social life (Bernardo, Shehan, and Leslie 1987; Duffy, Mandell, and Pupo 1989). A mother of two who has a demanding career explained:

> I don't have any time for social life at all. Even if someone invites me for dinner on the weekend, I find it tiring to go. I don't know how everybody else does it here. There's no time for social life here at all. I have a lot of friends here, but I never have time to see them.

In Hong Kong, her situation was quite different:

> I was a member of a pottery club, calligraphy club, and an alumni choir. Here, I don't have any extracurricular activities. I simply don't have the time or energy. It seems foolhardy to drive an hour to go to a class when I don't even have enough time to manage my household chores. On the other hand, I really need this kind of outlet. But I don't have the kind of time and energy.

It is clear that the differences in social organization between Hong Kong and Canada, in terms of the household support system and the size and spread of the city, transform this woman's everyday experience.

Conclusion

Many migration studies have previously assumed that migration involves moving from a less developed to a more developed country, and from a rural to an urban area. It is further assumed that the entry of female migrants into the host labour market will lead to a rejection of their traditional roles and subjugated positions. These studies argue that the economic independence migrant women acquire through their engagement in waged work will assure them a higher status and a more equitable position in the family. Hence, migration has the positive effect of engendering equality of the sexes, as well as generating beneficial changes in domestic relations (Schwartz-Seller 1981; Morokvasic 1981).

I found that these migration theories are not applicable to middle-class Chinese immigrant women. Many of these highly educated, urbanized women do not necessarily enjoy a "liberating" or "less oppressive" experience when they settle in Canada. Because of the differences in the social organization of Hong Kong and Canada, these women's daily experiences have been transformed. While in Hong Kong, many of these middle-class women had help with their housework and child care from either members of the extended family such as mothers or mothers-in-law, or hired help. This kind of support system enabled the women to pursue their career interests, and allowed them free time for social life and recreational activities.

Transplanted to Canada, these middle-class women lost the support system they had in Hong Kong. The lack of a support system

exacerbated the workload of these middle-class women, making their struggle to negotiate the conflicting demands of family and career even more difficult. Furthermore, the physical spread of Canadian cities, and the lack of transportation systems in suburbia—where most of the Hong Kong immigrants reside—heighten children's dependency on their mothers, intensifying women's workloads. Consequently, some of them experience an intensification of traditional roles, unequal distribution of household labour, and gender and sexual oppression in the home. This, compounded with institutionalized discrimination which renders their previous work experience obsolete and the absence of an adequate accreditation system, has subjected some of them to unemployment and underemployment. These states, in turn, force them to become economically dependent on their husbands, who are themselves subject to the same discrimination.

Although some of the women I interviewed experienced improved family relations with their husbands after immigration, there were others who suffered communication problems, and marriage breakdowns. For some women, their power and status inside and outside the home deteriorated after they immigrated to Canada. Moreover, those who had professional careers in their home country experienced a loss of economic power through unemployment or underemployment (although some of their husbands also experienced such losses). They also experienced diminished buying power, and a general lack of opportunity.

● Notes

1. Adilman (1984) made reference to the discussions of the immigration of Chinese women found in the

Debates of the House of Commons (1923, v. 3, pp. 2310, 2311, 2314, 2318, 2384, and 2385); and in the

Debates of the Senate (1923, pp. 1121–4). It is evident from these debates that the central concern in regard to the immigration of Chinese women into Canada was the proliferation of the Chinese population in Canada. In prohibiting Chinese women from coming into Canada, the government intended to effectively prevent the Chinese from settling permanently in Canada.

2. According to Sedgewick (1973), Immigration Policy at the time "allowed merchants and their families exemption from the head tax and freedom to move in and out of the country" (136). However, the qualifications for "merchant" status were not clearly defined. Hence, some labourers were able to immigrate in the guise of merchants.

3. According to Wickberg (1982: 141), the Chinese Immigration Act of 1923 contained the following provisions: abolition of the head tax; students below university age were no longer admitted; and only four groups of immigrants could enter Canada. All were categorized as temporary settlers. They were:
   (i) university students;
   (ii) merchants—(term was changed so as to exclude operators of laundries and restaurants, retail produce dealers, and the like). Merchant status was defined as "one who devotes his undivided attention to mercantile pursuits, dealing exclusively in Chinese manufactures or produce or in exporting to China goods of Canadian produce or manufacture, who has been in such business for at least three years, and who has not less than $2,500 invested in it. It does not include any merchant's clerk, tailor, mechanic, huckster, peddler, drier or curer of fish, or anyone having any connection with a restaurant, laundry or rooming-house.";
   (iii) diplomatic personnel;
   (iv) native-borns returning from several years of education in China.

4. For example, in 1911, the ratio of Chinese men to Chinese women in Canada was approximately 28:1; in 1921, it was 15:1; and in 1931, it was still 12:1. Even as late as 1951, the ratio was 3.7:1 (see Li 1988: 61, Table 4.2).

5. As late as 1941, there were 20,141 "separated" families in the Chinese community, whereby the husbands resided in Canada, while the wives remained in their home country. In the same year, there were only 1,177 "intact" Chinese families in Canada in which both the husbands and wives resided in Canada. By 1951, the situation only improved slightly, and the discrepancy still remained very high: 12,882 "separated" families versus 2,842 "intact" families (see Li 1988: 67, Table 4.4).

6. Chinese yuppies.

7. "Independent Class" immigrants are immigrants that are selected on criteria which are tied to the economic needs of Canada. They include skilled workers, also known as "other independents," and "business immigrants," which include entrepreneurs, investors, and the self-employed (see Margaret Young, *Canada's Immigration Program*, Library of Parliament, Research Branch, July 1992).

8. Some immigrants took advantage of an immigration clause (Immigration Pt. III, Ch. I-2, p. 17, 24 [2]) which allowed a permanent resident to be outside of Canada for 183 days in any one 12-month period without losing their permanent residency status, by continuing to conduct business between Hong Kong and Toronto. In fact, one husband I interviewed started his first year of immigration by conducting his business this way; and another husband was still commuting between Hong Kong and Toronto at the time of the interview.

9. For an in-depth study of the astronaut phenomenon, see Guida Man, "The Astronaut Phenomenon: Examining Consequences of the Diaspora of the Hong Kong Chinese," in *Managing Change in Southeast Asia: Local Identities, Global Connections, Proceedings of the 21st Annual Conference of the Canadian Council for Southeast Asian Studies* (University of Alberta, 1995).

10. This, however, is not to be conflated with the popularized stereotypical image of Chinese families being largely patriarchal extended families with several generations living under the same roof. Ho et al. (1991) has reported empirical evidence which shows that the average size of the Chinese households has always been small, even prior to industrialization. The average size ranged from less than six from AD 755 to approximately five for the first half of the twentieth century. This is as much because of economic reasons as due to the social customs of the time. The majority of the Chinese were poor peasants who subsisted on meagre means, and could not afford to support more than their immediate family members.

Poverty and hunger governed the lives of these peasants. The idealistic Confucius conception of extended families were the entitlement of the few aristocratic gentry who numbered fewer than 10 per cent of the Chinese population.

11. The names mentioned here are pseudonyms, since the interviewees were assured anonymity. Most Chinese (especially the baby boomers and post-baby-boomer generation) who were brought up in the British educational system in colonized Hong Kong find themselves adopting English names over and above their Chinese names. Many Chinese in Hong Kong use their English names at school, at work, and for everyday use, but kept their Chinese names for official documents. In Canada, most Chinese maintain the same practice.

● References

Abella, I., and H. Troper. 1982. *None Is Too Many: Canada and the Jews of Europe* (Toronto: Lester & Orpen Dennys).

Adilman, T. 1984. "Chinese Women and Work in British Columbia," BA thesis, University of Victoria, Apr.

Armstrong, P., and H. Armstrong. 1984. *The Double Ghetto: Canadian Women and Their Segregated Work* (Toronto: McClelland & Stewart).

Baureiss, G. 1987. "Chinese Immigration, Chinese Stereotypes, and Chinese Labour," *Canadian Ethnic Studies* 19, 3: 15–34.

Bernardo, D.H., C.L. Shehan, and G.R. Leslie. 1987. "A Resident of Tradition: Jobs, Careers and Spouses' Time in Housework," *Journal of Marriage and the Family* 49: 381–90.

Boyd, M. 1990. "Immigrant Women: Language, Socioeconomic Inequalities and Policy Issues," in *Ethnic Demography: Canadian Immigrant Racial and Cultural Variations*, eds S. Halli, F. Trovata, and L. Driedger (Ottawa: Carleton University Press).

Canada and Hong Kong Update. 1992. No. 7 (Summer).

Cannon, M. 1989. *China Tide* (Toronto: Harper & Collins).

Cheng, J.Y.S., and P.C.K. Kwong, eds. 1992. *The Other Hong Kong Report* (Hong Kong: The Chinese University Press).

Chinese Canadian National Council (CCNC), The Women's Book Committee. 1992. *Jin Guo: Voices of Chinese Canadian Women* (Toronto: The Women's Press).

Connelly, P. 1978. *Last Hired, First Fired: Women and the Canadian Work Force* (Toronto: The Women's Press).

Duffy, A., N. Mandell, and N. Pupo. 1989. *Few Choices: Women, Work and Family* (Toronto: Garamond Press).

Eichler, M. 1985. *On the Treatment of the Sexes in Research* (Ottawa: Social Sciences and Humanities Research Council of Canada).

——. 1988. *Families in Canada Today: Recent Changes and Their Policy Consequences* (Toronto: Gage).

Employment and Immigration Commissions (EIC). 1992, 1993. Immigration Statistics. Quarterly Statistics.

Friedan, B. 1963. *The Feminine Mystique* (New York: Dell Books).

Gerstel, N. 1984. "Commuter Marriage," PhD diss., Columbia University.

Haraway, D. 1985. "A Manifesto for Cyborgs: Science, Technology, and Socialist Feminism in the 1980s," *Socialist Review* 80.

Hartsock, N. 1983. "The Feminist Standpoint: Developing the Ground for a Specifically Feminist Historical Materialism," in *Discovering Reality*, eds S. Harding and M.B. Hintikka (Boston: D. Reidel), 293–310.

Hawkins, F. 1988. *Canada and Immigration: Public Policy and Public Concern*, 2nd edn (Kingston and Montreal: McGill-Queen's University Press).

Hill-Collins, P. 2000. *Black Feminist Thought* (New York: Routledge).

Ho, Lok-sang, et al. 1991. *International Labour Migration: The Case of Hong Kong* (Hong Kong: Hong Kong Institute of Asia-Pacific Studies, The Chinese University of Hong Kong).

Jacobson, H. 1979. "Immigrant Women and the Community: A Perspective for Research," *Resources for Feminist Research* 8, 3 (Nov.): 17–21.

Lee, J. 1999. "Immigrant Women Workers in the Immigrant Settlement Sector," *Canadian Women Studies* 19, 3.

Li, P.S. 1988. *The Chinese in Canada* (Toronto: Oxford University Press).

Luxton, M. 1980. *More Than a Labour of Love: Three Generations of Women's Work in the Home* (Toronto: Women's Educational Press).

——, and E. Reiter. 1997. "Double, Double, Toil and Trouble . . . , Women's Experience of Work and Family in Canada 1980–1995," in *Women and the Canadian Welfare State: Challenges and Change*, eds P.M. Evans and G.K. Werkele (Toronto: University of Toronto Press).

Man, G. 1991. "Commuter Families in Canada: A Research Report," report presented to the Demographic Review Secretariat, Health and Welfare Canada, Sept.

——. 1995. "The Astronaut Phenomenon: Examining Consequences of the Diaspora of the Hong Kong

Chinese," in *Managing Change in Southeast Asia: Local Identities, Global Connections* (Edmonton: University of Alberta), 269–81.

———. 1997. "Women's Work Is Never Done: Social Organization of Work and the Experience of Women in Middle-class Hong Kong Chinese Immigrant Families in Canada," in *Advances in Gender Research*, Vol. II (Greenwich: JAI Press), 183–226.

———. 1998. "Effects of Canadian Immigration Policies on Chinese Immigrant Women (1858–1986)," in *Asia-Pacific and Canada: Images and Perspectives* (Tokyo: The Japanese Association for Canadian Studies), 118–33.

Morokvasic, M. 1981. "The Invisible Ones: A Double Role of Women in the Current European Migrations," in *Strangers in the World*, eds L. Eitinger and D. Schwarz (Bern, Stuggart, Vienna: Hans Huber).

Ng, R. 1982. "Immigrant Housewives in Canada," *Atlantis* 8: 111–17.

———. 1998. "Work Restructuring and Recognizing Third World Women: An Example from the Garment Industry in Toronto," *Canadian Women Studies* 18, 1: 21–5.

———, and A. Estable. 1987. "Immigrant Women in the Labour Force: An Overview of Present Knowledge and Research Gaps," RFR/DRF 16, 1 (Mar.).

Nipp, D. 1983. "Canada Bound: An Exploratory Study of Pioneer Chinese Women in Western Canada," MA thesis, University of Toronto.

Schwartz-Seller, M. 1981. *Immigrant Women* (Philadelphia: Temple University Press).

Sedgewick, C.P. 1973. "The Context of Economic Change Continuity in an Urban Overseas Chinese Community," PhD diss., University of Victoria.

Smith, D. 1987. *The Everyday World as Problematic: A Feminist Sociology* (Toronto: University of Toronto Press).

Statistics Canada. 1971. Census of Canada.

———. 1986. Census of Canada, Public Use Sample Tape, Individual File.

SUCCESS, Women's Committee Research Group. 1991. Chinese Immigrant Women's Needs Survey in Richmond (Vancouver: SUCCESS).

Thobani, S. 1998. "Nationalizing Citizens, Bordering Immigrant Women: Globalization and the Racialization of Women's Citizenship in Late 20th Century Canada," PhD diss., Simon Fraser University.

Warren, C.E. 1986. *Vignettes of Life* (Calgary: Detselig Enterprises).

Wickberg, E., ed. 1982. *From China to Canada: A History of the Chinese Communities in Canada* (Toronto: McClelland & Stewart).

Wong, S.L. 1992. "Emigration and Stability in Hong Kong," *Asian Survey* 32, 10 (Oct.).

Yee, M. 1987. "Out of the Silence: Voices of Chinese Canadian Women," RFR/DRF 16, 1 (Mar.).

Young, M. 1992. "Canada's Immigration Program," background paper, Library of Parliament, Research Branch, July (Ottawa: Supply and Services).

Chapter 20

This chapter discusses general findings from a study of immigrant families living in and around Vancouver. Gillian Creese, Isabel Dyck, and Arlene McLaren draw on the results of focus groups and interviews to provide an overview of the changing experiences of the immigrants they talked to, and the multiple effects of immigration on them and their families. In so doing, they make clear that the impact of immigration is different for women and men; youth, adults, and children; and different racial groups. But for all, immigration unsettles and changes family relations.

This research explores the variety of ways immigrants adapt to their new environment. It finds that as these immigrants create networks of support, they blur and extend family boundaries, locally and transnationally, as they negotiate ways to solve the problems they encounter in finding employment and procuring good education for their children.

Gender, Generation, and the "Immigrant Family": Negotiating Migration Processes

Gillian Creese, Isabel Dyck, and Arlene Tigar McLaren

Academic research tends to view the immigrant family in two quite different ways. The dominant view for many years has been that "the immigrant family" is a naturally bounded, unified whole. For example, it has been assumed that one can analyze "the Greek-Canadian family," "the Polish-Canadian family," and "the Chinese-Canadian family" as if they were uniform entities (Ishwaran 1980). According to this idea, the immigrant family undertakes a linear journey to integration, moving from the home culture to the new culture. Such a model of immigration assumes the existence of two original, distinct cultures and a unidirectional process of adaptation; it also assumes that the primary dynamic exists between host and immigrant culture, ignoring dynamics within immigrant cultures as well as across them.

The notion that the two cultural poles of home and new culture are fixed or monolithic is difficult to sustain (Kibria 1997; Pizanias 1996). How can we say, for example, what is the Canadian family, when it can best be typified as diverse and in flux (Eichler 1997)? Or what is the "Asian" family, differing as it does according to country, region, social class, ethnicity, religion, and so forth? Such monolithic visions are fictional families, bearing an uneasy relationship to people's daily experiences. Further complicating any definition of "the immigrant culture" is the time of immigration, as well as processes of restructuring and globalization, and the emergence of diaspora cultures that stretch across national boundaries (Kibria 1997). Finally, such a model of immigrant family integration privileges cultural values and treats them as separate from everyday practices and social relations in families (including their power dynamics), discourses (including racist ideas), and structural constraints that provide barriers to integration.

A second way to understand immigrant families is to see families as fluid and constantly being negotiated and reconstituted both spatially and temporally (e.g., Lawson 1998). This view considers ways in which immigrant families are unfixed categories that are not discretely located in space. Families may adopt spatially extensive survival strategies incorporating multiple members in diverse places who remain part of a single income-pooling unit, or who continue to exercise influence over dynamics in the same household. As such, families may be situated in the home country, the new country, and elsewhere—the family is redefined as transnational (Hyndman and Walton-Roberts 1998). Moreover, boundaries between such transnational families can blur with local, national, and international networks that include kin, friends, and contacts. According to this second perspective, immigrant families (like other families) are heterogeneous, multiply positioned, and stratified—they differ in their composition, their social positions according to social class, ethnicity, race,[1] and locality, and in the experiences of various family members, especially in relation to gender and generation (e.g., Das Gupta 1995). Thus we cannot speak about the immigrant family because this denotes a far too static picture of what is a shifting set of complex social relations, with unpredictable outcomes.

Our research suggests that the second view of immigrant families as fluid and heterogeneous is the more fruitful way to understand migration processes, and families. Such processes may have more than a single country of origin and take place through a web of daily practices—within and between households—connected to immigration policy, neighbourhood, social networks, housing, the labour market, consumption, leisure, health,

schooling, and so forth. Some immigrants celebrate this fluidity. In one of our focus groups, a woman from Poland, recently divorced (since coming to Canada) and a mother of a 13-year-old daughter, observed: "The family here looks different." She likes how the family looks in Canada: "for me it's absolutely right that immigration changes the picture of the family." In contrast, others voiced deep concern over the reconstitution of family dynamics. For example, a grandfather from India spoke about his disappointment over "the breaking of the family" in Canada. These different views reflect the variety of family, gender, and generational anxieties and struggles that emerged as themes in our research and provide preliminary insights into different ways that people negotiate immigration and settlement.

Our study is based on 16 focus groups that we held in five districts in the Greater Vancouver region,[2] and multiple interviews with families in two of these neighbourhoods. We selected the five districts on the basis of their different residential type and unique history and profile of immigrant settlement: East Vancouver, Westside Vancouver (including Kerrisdale, Oakridge, and Shaughnessy), Richmond, North Surrey-Delta, and Tri-cities (Coquitlam, Port Coquitlam, and Port Moody). East Vancouver is an inner-city residential area that has long been a reception area for diverse groups of immigrants; Vancouver's affluent Westside, until recently largely British in ethnic origin, now has a large Chinese-origin population; Surrey is an outer suburb with a diverse immigrant mix, including a significant South Asian population; and Tri-cities is an outer suburb that has only recently begun to attract new immigrants among its residents. The focus groups varied in their composition. In all districts, we conducted focus groups with recently arrived immigrants. In most districts we also carried out focus groups with service providers, second-generation young adults, and women-only groups. And in one district, we organized a focus group with members of the "host" community. The focus groups served as a preliminary stage of research to help familiarize ourselves with immigrant issues and as preparation for an in-depth longitudinal study of immigrant families in some districts. Over a five-year period, from 1997 through 2002, we interviewed 25 families (in most cases three or four times) in two neighbourhoods, East Vancouver and the Tri-cities. This paper draws largely from the focus groups with illustrations extracted from the family interviews. A more detailed analysis of the longitudinal family interviews is discussed elsewhere (Creese, Dyck, and McLaren 2006). These overlapping case studies, we believe, shed light on the complex connections between the everyday practices of immigrant families and how these interact with locality and larger regions.

Although talking about family in the public setting of focus groups is difficult, we were often struck by the animation of the discussions. In the focus groups, participants also discussed employment issues and relations with native-born people, which we have reported on elsewhere.[3] Our longitudinal interviews with families provided a more intimate portrayal of the complex and shifting nature of family relations. In this paper, we have chosen to report on three broad themes to do with the daily practices of family life that arose in the focus groups: network making; the dynamics of gender, generation, and racialization; and the negotiation of educational and employment opportunities. These themes—which we briefly illustrate—highlight the struggles, contingencies, heterogeneity, and fluidity of the everyday practices of immigrant families in a variety of localities.

1. Network Making

Immigrants may use informal networks of friends, relatives, or associates to help them settle into a new location; these may be used on their own or in conjunction with institutional service provision. Most immigrants are faced with a vast array of information that has to be accessed and processed in the first months of settlement as they attempt to find housing, jobs, and schools, and to negotiate everyday needs. This is often complicated by lack of English language ability, or French for those first settling in Quebec. Some immigrants have friends, relatives, or other contacts through ethnic affiliation who may be able to help; others have fewer resources in place when they arrive.

As some research has shown, immigrant families interact in various ways with local, national, and international networks (e.g., Hyndman and Walton-Roberts 1998). What struck us in the focus groups is the vast differences among networks, which vary from being densely organized (containing many people), and operating transnationally, to being thin (with few people) and confined to the localized context. For some immigrants, they are non-existent. Furthermore, such networks may extend, blur, and otherwise problematize the boundaries and meanings of family. For example, an Indo-Canadian participant from Surrey described a migration process including marriage and extended-family reunification that involved buying land, building houses together, setting up jobs for one another, and working together. He said, "And that is where we all stayed together just like a network, like support mechanisms and everything, housing, food, set up a job, and those kinds of things. We always move together."

Reciprocal support within families and across generations was important to some. The reunification of families allowed grandparents to support adult children, including those pursuing studies in Canada, through participation in the running of a household or caring for young children (see also McLaren's [2006] study of South Asian elderly women who were sponsored by their families to come to Canada and who contributed to running the households, caring for children, and providing family income from farm labour and other sources). Others from the Punjab mentioned common village origin (rather than just blood and marital relatives) as an important dimension of chain migration and available support on arrival in Canada, which expands notions of family in the new country. In our longitudinal interviews, we observed extensive shifts in family over time as in the case of chain migration in which individuals sponsored family members to join them in Canada. Two South Asian sisters, who had recently entered Canada as independent immigrants, applied to sponsor siblings, spouses, parents, and in-laws. All together for a period of time, seven adult family members of the extended family shared the accommodation of a two-bedroom basement suite and pooled resources. One of the sisters later moved to a suite nearby with her husband and baby.

In contrast to densely organized chain migration, a woman from Poland living in the Tri-cities talked about networks contingent upon changing family structure, migration, and different locales. When she first arrived in Toronto with her husband, they relied heavily on extended family and the Polish community for help in gaining crucial information: "They were like the sailboat by this ocean of new information." Later, after divorce and a move with her child to British Columbia, she profoundly missed the benefits of the large Polish community in Toronto. She deliberately sought Polish contacts, partly activated

by links to Toronto that she maintained regularly through telephone and e-mail contact, to help her find housing and health service providers. Thus, she extended a network that had begun with family connections. Since then she has developed non-ethnically based social networks through volunteer work and through her daughter's school friends and sports activities. Friends made through her volunteer work have been helpful in providing her with job information and developing her career plans.

Such fluidity and blurred boundaries of families and networks, as illustrated in these examples, suggest that network making is far more complex than is captured in the often-used simple distinction between nuclear- and extended-family networks. The meaning of family structure and networks, how they operate and the purposes they serve, may be transformed as they interact with different spatial and social patterns. For example, Hong Kong's small geographical area enables nuclear families to be in close proximity to relatives not living in their households, a situation amenable to developing a close-knit family network that is in effect an extended family. Such an extension of family beyond the household may not be possible (or work in the same way) in more spatially stretched locations such as large Canadian cities (Man 1996). In our family interviews, a household from Hong Kong consisted of elderly parents, a son and daughter and their spouses, and another son who eventually married. Over time, the young couples began to migrate from their suburban location to another location with a greater concentration of Chinese immigrants, and they planned to move their parents to join them. On the other hand, immigrant families who lack the support networks of the extended family that were available to them in their home country (Man 1996; Pizanias 1996) may attempt to replicate them by symbolically adopting friends as relatives (Dhruvarajan 1996). In other words, networks may include a variety of family structures and contacts; these may change over time, and may extend beyond a specific neighbourhood to cross a sprawling city, a nation, or international borders. How families construct support networks is a critical element of the everyday practices of immigrant settlement.

2. The Dynamics of Gender, Generation, and Racialization

The fluidity of immigrant family life is perhaps nowhere more apparent than in the dynamics of gender, generation, and racialization. Immigration unsettles family relations in multiple ways and may give rise to new forms of independence, dependence, and identity. Recent research has shown, for example, how immigration policy, procedures, and discourses produce women's "dependence" within families and other sites of interaction, including employment, by frequently categorizing family men as independent applicants and women as their dependents (Agnew 1996; Boyd 1997; Ng 1988; Vanderbijl 1998; McLaren and Black 2005). As Satzewich (1993) argues, immigration policy reinforces the myth of women's dependency (i.e., by categorizing them as if they were unemployable when in fact immigrant women have a high rate of employment) and promotes their marginalization (i.e., the stereotypes of dependency make it difficult for immigrant women to find decent employment). Thobani (1998) and Ng (1990) further argue that immigrant women are racialized. The very term "immigrant women" connotes women who are racialized as non-white. White immigrant women more easily slough off their immigrant status whereas women of colour,

whether immigrant or Canadian-born, may continue to be treated as immigrants, who really "belong somewhere else" and who are a drain on Canada's resources. Immigration can, therefore, be understood as an ongoing process that in many ways promotes the marginalization of women of colour and those for whom English is a second language.

While immigration procedures may frequently inscribe women as dependent upon their husbands, focus group narratives revealed processes that were more complex and contradictory. A prominent narrative in the focus groups emphasized the independence from family that immigrant women may acquire in Canada. Participants from a variety of backgrounds talked about the position of women in the family as more equal in Canada, with its laws that protect them better than in their places of origin. As a woman from Hong Kong argued: "I am better protected here. The laws in Canada are protecting the women." Another participant, the woman from Poland who had divorced since coming to Canada, commented on the greater freedom that women enjoy in Canada, while acknowledging that new expectations placed additional stress on family relations:

> The woman has more freedom here. . . . For example, in my country still is this tradition to treat woman as the family person . . . the women are growing faster than the men . . . they are going to ask for some bigger freedom, some bigger partnership between them.

Women's improved social status was often double-edged, however, causing some participants to worry about increased conflict between spouses, the prevalence of divorce in Canada, and limited social support in the absence of extended kin nearby. Participants in a focus group linked to Tri-cities, for example, suggested that domestic violence is widespread and particularly exacerbated by women's vulnerability in the sponsorship process. Immigration to Canada can mean less independence and freedom for women, especially for those who are mothers.

Our family interviews suggest that greater "freedom" for women was often not borne out in everyday practices, which are constrained both by the "privatized" nuclear-family form in Canada (where parents are solely responsible for their children), and the systematic marginalization of immigrants—including skilled professionals—in the local labour market. Both downward mobility and the intensification of domestic labour were experienced by all the families we interviewed, with the brunt of additional work and stress borne by mothers. Women commonly put their own career aspirations on hold to look after children and to prioritize their husbands' (usually unsuccessful) attempts to remake their careers. This was particularly difficult for women who were professionals prior to migration. A former teacher from Iran, for example, talked about the health problems she experienced, which were related to isolation, marginal employment, and loss of her professional identity.

Our family interviews included some in which men adjusted to increased domestic demands by contributing more to domestic work in Canada. For example, a father from Uganda worked nights so that he could care for his children after school and cook dinner for the family while his wife attended classes in the evening. But most men left the bulk of domestic work to their wives, creating a source of marital friction and additional stress for many women.

Some women were surprised to find just how difficult it was to care for children in Canada and, at the same time, pursue other activities. As a young woman from Latin America argued in a focus group, in Canada jobs are more essential to have yet more difficult to find, and mothering and employment harder to combine than in her country of origin where extended female kin shared child-rearing responsibilities. Many of the women were primarily responsible for negotiating child care and, as a result, suffered severe isolation and often a sense of danger. As a single mother living in the outer suburban area of Tri-cities poignantly remembered:

> It is such a difficult time when you are landed, the language skills mostly are very crude during this time and the family, the child mostly—everything is your responsibility—and you don't have the communication skills, you don't have the knowledge about the country. Everything is strange, everything is danger almost. You have to do everything by yourself. It is really stressful and almost killing as an immigrant.

Some mothers feared that if they ever left their child unattended in Canada (as they had done in their country of origin) they could be accused of neglect. Generally, caring for children could be so time-consuming that it prevented women from being involved in the community, even though such involvement may be necessary for mothering and settlement more generally. As a woman living in East Vancouver commented:

> If you come as an immigrant woman you get that blockage whereby your children become your focus, and you have some hours when children are in school, which you can use to explore what it is about the community, because how do you know

who [to go to] unless you have connections in the community?

Helping to organize other women in her community is now a central part of her life.

As these illustrations suggest, how mothers interact with the community is a vital issue for understanding settlement following immigration. Very little research, however, examines immigrant mothers' networks. Several writers (e.g., Boyd 1989; Pedraza 1991) note that research on social networks and migration has tended to be indifferent to gender. In focusing on immigrant families and the significance of social networks in providing various resources, Zhou (1997), for example, treats this process as if it were undifferentiated by gender, and ignores the specific requirements of mothering. Some studies examine the significance of mothers' networking as family and gendered strategies of providing for their children's well-being (e.g., Bell and Ribbens 1994; Dyck 1992), but few look at how mothers who have immigrated construct personal networks and make use of them. Our research attempts to understand how mothering, which is located spatially both within the home and outside it, is central to sustaining and transforming social relations (Dyck 1992) and the ways that mothers extend their practices beyond the household in ways that vary over time and space. For example, a young woman who had just arrived from India at the time of our first family interview had few connections with the local South Asian community (which she considered too conservative compared to her cosmopolitan upbringing in India) until after her daughter was born four years later; she then began to attend local Punjabi events and joined a Punjabi mother's group with her daughter.

As Man (1996; see Chapter 19) suggests, women's independence and control over their lives may be limited by the organization of Canadian cities, including the proximity of services, relatives, and transportation. In our research, the neighbourhood interacted in various ways to form new relations of dependence and restricted movement. A young woman from Hong Kong living in the Tri-cities, for example, commented on her dependence on her sister and father to get to school and visit friends until she got her driver's licence. At the same time, her mother, who did not speak English, was now dependent on her and her sister to get out. Both the young woman and her mother resented these new forms of dependence, feeling constrained in their activity. The same young woman expressed a strong sense of loss accompanying the geographical and social dislocation of immigration: "I felt like I lost my whole life, my own space."

As a great deal of research suggests, immigrant family experiences can differ considerably according to generation (e.g., Maykovich 1980). Many participants, for example, suggested that parents struggle during migration while younger children adjust quickly and the second generation integrates more easily than the first. Not all agreed, however, that children adjust easily. Some participants talked about the isolation that many immigrant children feel, especially those who arrived in their teens. A woman expressed anxiety about teenaged children who often face greater difficulties than adults: "I see a lot of the newcomers, immigrants, where the children are just sitting at home and they don't know what to do" and suggested "the newcomers' children are mostly outsiders from our society," especially those in families with limited financial resources to pay for community activities. Other women talked of the feeling that children weren't welcome in Canada. One woman, for example, concluded from her difficult search to find housing that "many people didn't like children." And several participants, particularly in our family interviews, complained about their own children's behaviour as they adopted "Canadian ways" of interacting that did not demonstrate appropriate respect for elders and deference to parental authority.

Two focus groups with second-generation young adults who grew up in the Lower Mainland—Chinese Canadians in Kerrisdale and Indo-Canadians in Surrey—highlighted the complex interaction of changing immigration policy, different family migration strategies, and changing settlement geographies in generating distinct and shifting generational identities and intergenerational relations. Conversation in these focus groups turned to young adults' feelings of being a racialized minority while growing up, often one of only a few Chinese- or Indian-origin children in their schools and neighbourhoods. Some expressed a sense of fragmented identities: "All my friends were white and I thought of myself as white except when I got home I was Chinese. You don't notice until you look in the mirror that you are different." As this comment illustrates, fragmented identities can be confusing and painful. The family interviews provided examples of the variability of identity, with youth who largely identified with their Canadian peers (for example just "Canadian" for the teenage sons of a family from Uganda), those who identified as hyphenated Canadians (for example "Spanish-Canadian" for the teenage children of a family from Guatemala), and those who identified primarily by their country of origin (including a teenage daughter from Iran who wished to return "home" to raise her own children).

Unlike the diversity of identities evident among youth in the family interviews, most of the young men and women in the second-generation focus groups expressed an appreciation of their ability to move between cultures, to form, as it were, situational identities. This greater ease of moving between cultures and identities may be linked to the density of the local communities—Chinese-Canadian and Punjabi-Canadian—from which the youth focus groups were drawn. One young woman commented on speaking English at Pacific Centre (a downtown mall) and Chinese in areas of Chinese business concentration. In both cases decisions about language were tied to notions of what was appropriate in a specific place, and possible sanctions for contravening conventions. Similarly a young Indo-Canadian woman from Surrey commented: "we all had a school personality and a home personality." Yet this separation of school and home was not constant, but, according to participants, depended on the community in which the family lived—how white, multicultural, or Indo-Canadian it was—and how liberal, as several emphasized, the father was.

Second-generation participants also identified issues of parenting that set them apart from their peers. One may take for granted that parents, especially perhaps immigrant parents, should stress the importance of education and the need for scholastic achievement. However, some participants who had gone to school in the Lower Mainland reflected critically upon their parents' emphasis on scholastic achievement and the necessity to excel and work hard at school as a factor that inhibited their "integration" with their white peers. Young Chinese-Canadian men and women in Kerrisdale, for example, mentioned that these family attitudes and expectations about education, such as attendance at Chinese school, limited their opportunities to make friends with white children. One commented: "It was always 'get the highest mark that you can.'"

The importance of education for this Chinese-Canadian group was further reflected in comments on how the family would support the children through school and university, and how this family lifestyle acted as a source of division between themselves and white students who were not supported in the same way.

Some young adults had lived through changes in immigration patterns, which meant the increased density of some Chinese-Canadian communities. This change made many participants feel less "alone," and in some cases helped bridge the cultural/generation gap that existed between some children and their parents. As a participant said: "In terms of my relationship with my parents, I can communicate so much better now. I talk to my friends in Chinese a lot now, so I'm a lot more articulate with my Chinese now than before." For some Indo-Canadian participants, in contrast, strong patterns of family chain migration and extended-family settlement strategies produced early residential concentration and strong community ties. This was sometimes double-edged—especially for the young women who experienced support but also strong social pressure from the broader Indo-Canadian community which monitored their behaviour, even when parents were willing to allow them to become more "Western." In this context the boundaries of family that were not fixed and intact in the first place, became even less fixed and more permeable as the influence of community members filtered through the boundaries to control the behaviour of family members.

Overall, participants in our research identified ways that immigrant families were shaped by dynamics of gender, generation, and racialization. As immigrants, women and men had different experiences and, therefore, spousal relations often shifted in unsettling ways. There was no consensus, however, about whether or not coming to Canada meant that women improved their social position. But this was a topic of considerable interest to many participants. Despite the rhetoric that North American society promises more freedom for women, many participants suggested that immigration may lead to new dependencies and greater isolation. Mothers, for example, may face new constraints (e.g., legal, linguistic, spatial) while they take on the onerous responsibilities of settling themselves and their families in their new country and community. The social position of both men and women deteriorated after migration in terms of economic opportunities, but women also bore the brunt of the intensification of domestic labour as family strategies often prioritized men's quest for economic improvement. Generation was also a dimension that made for different experiences. Some parents, for example, became more dependent on their more linguistically able children, and many lamented the more permissive and child-centred milieu in Canada. Finally, racialization was a theme that second-generation participants were particularly concerned about, especially because it changed over time. These concerns were expressed, for example, in comments about changes in identity, ambiguous feelings of belonging, tensions with white residents, and ways that the increased density of communities of origin (particularly Chinese and South Asian) redefined daily life in Vancouver.

3. Negotiating Educational and Employment Opportunities

As countless research attests, education and employment are primary sites in which immigrants must negotiate their "integration" into local neighbourhoods. More than any other topic, people in the focus groups told us over and over again how worried they were about employment issues. They also talked passionately about education. The disjuncture between hopes and actual experiences of schooling and employment often meant a fragile sense of the future and of family settlement in Canada. Many participants worried about their own opportunities as well as those of their spouses and children. But they were also hopeful. As a participant from Surrey commented, "If children can pursue their education fully, they will have no problems in Canada."

Research has not fully recognized the extent to which education and employment become family projects in which women, particularly as mothers, play a central role involving strategies that occur over time and space and that shift as negotiation takes place. Mothering practices are often shaped by the issue of their children's schooling and, because of recent changes in the labour market, a sense of educational urgency presses mothers more fully into the pursuit of educational opportunities for their children (Reay 1998).

Many of the parents in our focus group talked about coming to Canada because of the educational opportunities they thought this country promised their children. Families often pin their hopes for the future on their children's education. As a Kerrisdale focus group participant commented, "the most important thing is the children's future." At the same time, some family interviews raised concerns about Canadian education. For example, a woman from Poland argued that her daughter would not be able to keep up to her peers if she were to return to school in Poland, thereby constraining her choice of whether to stay or leave Canada.

The focus group participants talked in ways that suggested that obtaining educational and occupational opportunities were central family projects varying from family to family. How families were able to support their children's education, for example, was dynamically related to their resources. A young woman suggested that due to differences in age of arrival and parents' financial security, her older brother had far fewer advantages than she did:

> I think my brother had a hard time. He is a smart guy. He would have liked to go to university and stuff but because of my parents' immigration process, I think it was hard for them to put him through university. So he started driving a taxi because my dad had a taxi at the time. He didn't have the same opportunities that me and my sister did.

Some parents who had adequate economic resources and knowledge about the local school chose to settle in specific neighbourhoods. Some had resources that allowed them to provide their children with tutoring, either paid or provided by members of their family or social network. Furthermore, some parents, especially those from Kerrisdale (a wealthy area of Vancouver), were knowledgeable about local schooling issues and talked about the ways that schools should be changed to reflect their interests (see Mitchell 2001 for an account of Chinese immigrant parents' attempts to change school curricula and pedagogy in a suburb of Vancouver). Some felt, for example, that schools kept children too long in English-as-Second-Language classes, and did not have enough Chinese-origin teachers relative to the student body. Overall, the research participants had mixed opinions about the quality of Canadian schools, pointing to how Canadian education is less rigorous, but also less stressful and more creative, than in their countries of origin.

Family strategies intersected with education, both locally and internationally, illustrating again the spatial fluidity of families. Some parents with adult children wanting to study in Canada migrated to support their children, in one case to provide child care for grandchildren. In other families, parents maintained economic and residential ties with their country of origin while their children attended school or university in Canada. In one instance, a young woman who was pursuing a master's degree at a university in Vancouver had come to the realization that this education might not lead to good employment opportunities in Canada. She was considering the possibility of returning to Hong Kong, where her brothers were still living: "I want a job that I can make progress [in] instead of just working as a cashier or helper. Because I'm young, I don't have a family myself, I want to develop my own career." The importance of having a job is summed up by her statement: "If you don't have a job you cannot see the future."

Several participants talked of the transnational mobility and choice they had in employment due to their family resources, and some accounts referred to the phenomenon of the "astronaut family," where the husband in a family goes back to Asia to pursue business. Family costs were attached to this strategy. For example, a Taiwanese woman perceived that such spatial separation of the family was a threat to family cohesion and encouraged marital discord. This spatial stretching of the family household can lead women to experience family life as lone parents, taking on the local responsibilities of child raising (see also Waters 2002).

Others without the choice to return to their countries of origin talked of stresses, discouragement and little income for family members who were unable to find paid employment. As they faced restricted employment opportunities, many participants adopted a family strategy that looked to the next generation for greater success—expected because of their locally attained education and potential to speak English fluently. At the same time many parents' desire for their children's integration was double-edged, simultaneously wanting it and fearing the loss of cultural identity that might result from it. Those who explicitly wanted their children to "mix with other races" as one Kerrisdale participant put it, were also poignantly mindful of the many barriers that made this difficult. These barriers included living in a neighbourhood peopled by a specific cultural group which could inhibit acquiring fluency in English, and taking ESL classes which might unintentionally reinforce such networks.

Conclusion

Depictions in most texts of the immigrant family are strangely silent on the permeable nature of families as they experience dislocation and resettlement. To stress "the unit of intimate partners," as do some texts, fails to capture the divisions and tensions within immigrant families and the shifting boundaries of their everyday experiences. Our research points to the inadequacy of normative views of nuclear and extended families, with examples of households with fluid and fluctuating social boundaries and whose physical boundaries may span several single-family dwellings and indeed several national borders. The use of networks in finding jobs, housing, and information about schools and other services appears to be a common, but not universal, strategy. Such networks take many forms that extend or blur the boundaries and meanings of family and also disrupt notions of a linear immigration process. As part of the process of immigration, family households are constituted and reconstituted in diverse ways that may involve complex and changing forms of dependence and renegotiation of family life. This renegotiation may also involve conflict and anxiety along the fault lines of gender, generation, and ethnic/racialized communities.

⬤ Notes

1. We acknowledge the social construction of all categories of ethnicity or race, whether in the census, research, or everyday language. Some researchers choose to signify this by using scare quotes around social categories such as "Indo-Canadian," "Chinese," or "White." We have chosen not to do this for consistency and stylistic reasons. The terms used by participants are preserved in quotations.

2. This paper is based on research that was conducted by a team of researchers who are part of the Vancouver RIIM Centre of Excellence: Gillian Creese, Isabel Dyck, Dan Hiebert, Tom Hutton, David Ley, Arlene Tigar McLaren, Geraldine Pratt. As well, the following researchers assisted us in our research: Wendy Mendes-Crabb, John Rose, Hugh Tan, Ann Vanderbijl, Margaret Walton-Roberts, and Priscilla Wei. We would like to thank the following agencies and their members for their participation in and help with the focus groups: City of Port Moody Parks, Recreation and Cultural Services; Coquitlam Leisure and Parks Services; Coquitlam School District; Vancouver and Lower Mainland Multi-cultural Family Support Services Society; Coquitlam Women's Centre; Greater Coquitlam Volunteer Centre; ISS; LINC; MOSAIC; Multicultural Family Centre; Progressive Intercultural Services; Richmond Police Department; Richmond Planning Department; Richmond Public Library; Richmond School District; Storefront Orientation Services; SUCCESS, Richmond Office; Surrey Delta Immigrant Society; Surrey Planning Department; Vancouver Community College; Vancouver Planning Department. We especially thank the focus group participants.

3. See Dan Hiebert, "Immigrant Experiences in Greater Vancouver: Focus Group Narratives" <http://www. riim.metropolis.globalx.net>.

⬤ References

Agnew, V. 1996. *Resisting Discrimination: Women from Asia, Africa, and the Caribbean and the Women's Movement in Canada* (Toronto: University of Toronto Press).

Bell, L., and J. Ribbens. 1994. "Isolated Housewives and Complex Maternal Worlds: The Significance of Social Contacts between Women with Young Children in Industrial Societies," *The Sociological Review* 42: 227–62.

Boyd, M. 1989. "Family and Personal Networks in International Migration: Recent Developments and New Agendas," *International Migration Review* 23.

——. 1997. "Migration Policy, Female Dependency and Family Membership: Canada and Germany," in *Remaking the Welfare State*, eds P. Evans et al. (Toronto: University of Toronto Press).

Creese, G., I. Dyck, and A.T. McLaren, 2006. "The 'Flexible' Immigrant: Household Strategies and the Labour Market," Vancouver Centre of Excellence, RIIM, Working Paper Series No. 06-19.

Das Gupta, T. 1995. "Families of Native Peoples, Immigrants, and People of Colour," in *Canadian Families: Diversity, Conflict and Change*, eds N. Mandell and A. Duffy (Toronto: Harcourt Brace & Company), 141–74.

Dhruvarajan, V. 1996. "Hindu Indu-Canadian Families," in *Voices: Essays on Canadian Families*, ed. M. Lynn (Toronto: Nelson Canada), 301–28.

Dyck, I. 1992. "Integrating Home and Wage Workplace: Women's Daily Lives in a Canadian Suburb," in *British Columbia Reconsidered: Essays on Women*, eds G. Creese and V. Strong-Boag (Vancouver: Press Gang), 172–97.

Eichler, M. 1997. *Family Shifts: Families, Policies and Gender Equality* (Toronto: Oxford University Press).

Hanson, S., and G. Pratt. 1995. *Women, Work and Space* (London: Routledge).

Hyndman, J., and M. Walton-Roberts. 1998. "Migration and Nation: Burmese Refugees in Vancouver," *The Bulletin* 11: 1–5.

Ishwaran, K., ed. 1980. *Canadian Families: Ethnic Variations* (Toronto: McGraw-Hill Ryerson).

Kibria, N. 1997. "The Concept of 'Bicultural Families' and Its Implication for Research on Immigrant and Ethnic Families," in *Immigration and the Family*, eds A. Booth et al. (Mahwah, NJ: Lawrence Erlbaum Assocs), 205–10.

Lawson, V.A. 1998. "Hierarchical Households and Gendered Migration in Latin America: Feminist Extensions to Migration Research," *Progress in Human Geography* 22: 39–53.

McLaren, A.T. 2006. "Parental Sponsorship—Whose Problematic? A Consideration of South Asian Women's Immigration Experiences in Vancouver," Vancouver Centre of Excellence, Research on Immigration and Integration in the Metropolis (RIIM), Working Paper Series No. 06-08.

———, and T.L. Black. 2005. "Family Class and Immigration in Canada: Implications for Sponsored Elderly Women," Vancouver Centre of Excellence, Research on Immigration and Integration in the Metropolis (RIIM), Working Paper Series No. 05-26.

Man, G. 1996. "The Experience of Middle-class Women in Recent Hong Kong Chinese Immigrant Families in Canada," in *Voices: Essays on Canadian Families*, ed. M. Lynn (Toronto: Nelson Canada), 271–300.

Maykovich, M.K. 1980. "Acculturation Versus Familism in Three Generations of Japanese-Canadians," in *Canadian Families: Ethnic Variations*, ed. K. Ishwaran (Toronto: McGraw-Hill Ryerson), 65–83.

Mitchell, K. 2001. "Education for Democratic Citizenship: Transnationalism, Multiculturalism, and the Limits of Liberalism," *Harvard Educational Review* 71, 1: 51–78.

Ng, R. 1988. *The Politics of Community Services: Immigrant Women, Class and the State* (Toronto: Garamond Press).

———. 1990. "Immigrant Women: The Construction of a Labour Market Category," *Canadian Journal of Women and the Law* 4, 1: 96–112.

Pedraza, S. 1991. "Women and Migration: The Social Consequences of Gender," *Annual Review of Sociology* 17: 303–25.

Pizanias, C. 1996. "Greek Families in Canada: Fragile Truths, Fragmented Stories," in *Voices: Essays on Canadian Families*, ed. M. Lynn (Toronto: Nelson Canada), 329–60.

Reay, D. 1998. "Engendering Social Reproduction: Mothers in the Educational Marketplace," *British Journal of Sociology of Education* 19, 2: 195–209.

Satzewich, V. 1993. "Migrant and Immigrant Families in Canada: State Coercion and Legal Control in the Formation of Ethnic Families," *Journal of Comparative Family Studies* 24: 315–38.

Thobani, S. 1998. "Nationalizing Citizens, Bordering Immigrant Women: Globalization and the Racialization of Citizenship in Late 20th Century Canada," unpublished PhD diss., Simon Fraser University.

Vanderbijl, A.E. 1998. "The 'Immigrant Family'," paper presented at the Western Association of Sociology and Anthropology Meetings, Vancouver, BC, 15–16 May.

Waters, J.L. 2002. "Flexible Families? 'Astronaut' Households and the Experiences of Lone Mothers in Vancouver, British Columbia," *Social & Cultural Geography* 3: 117–35.

Zhou, M. 1997. "Growing up American: The Challenge Confronting Immigrant Children and Children of Immigrants," *Annual Review of Sociology* 23: 63–95.

Chapter 21

For many people, family consists of more than parents and siblings. Relations with family across generations and beyond both the nuclear unit and the household are often very important in the lives of men, women, and children. Migrants to Canada often receive ongoing support from family in their countries of origin, as they build new lives here. In addition to benefitting from that support, new Canadians often hope to maintain their cultural traditions, and especially to pass them on to their children. And family "back home" are central to that project. In this chapter, Kara Somerville describes some of the ways that women migrants from India rely on and cultivate ongoing relations with family who live outside Canada, as they care for their families in Canada. Their ongoing transnational interactions enable them to create families here that reflect both cultures.

Making and Sustaining Transnational Families

Kara Somerville

Making and sustaining family, especially one with young children, involves considerable work, as well as commitment. Social researchers have examined who does homemaking and child care, and the time spent on doing household work. They have paid less attention to the symbolic value of this work. Some sociologists argue that daily housework produces not only meals, clean clothing, and orderly rooms, but also family. When American sociologist Marjorie DeVault (1991: 13) examined the work that women do to feed their families, she argued that in doing this cooking, serving, and orchestrating of family meals, "women quite literally produce family life." For immigrant families, the symbolic value of cooking family meals may involve not only the creation of a sense of collective family identity but also identification with traditions common to the country they left and a sense of ethnic identity and connection to a family that extends across two countries.

This chapter examines how Indian immigrants to Canada feed their families and meet their health-care needs, both of which are work critical to the well-being of family members. I argue that these two kinds of work are embedded in networks of family members extending across national borders and that the process of doing this work entails a daily flow of information, advice, and products between migrant women in Canada and their kin in India, which cements the emotional connections of those involved. These exchanges help to reproduce and maintain family relationships and enfold family members in a sense of family. I also find that women are more involved in the mental, manual, and emotional work central to sustaining their families than men. While men traverse borders regularly, and do so as frequently as their wives, via email, phone calls, and air travel, there is a gender difference in the work of reproducing family. Women are the ones who use the transnational space to draw on resources that enable them to do this important caring work for their nuclear-family members.

The chapter is based on a larger study of Indian immigrants to Canada, and the ongoing relationships they maintain with kin in their country of origin. Such relationships constitute what sociologists call "transnational families." Transnational families "live some or most of the time separated from each other, yet hold together and create something that can be seen as a feeling of collective welfare and unity, namely 'familyhood,' even across borders" (Bryceson and Vuorela 2002: 3).

I argue here that making family meals and addressing family members' health-care needs are tasks performed by women across national borders. Among migrant women in Canada, homemade food and health-care products and services that are acquired through kin networks in India come to be viewed as authentic family creations. The preparation of family meals and the work involved in acquiring health care, and the authentic ingredients in both endeavours, are based on the mobilization of transnational social networks. Acquiring what is necessary to good health and cooking homemade food from India forges a connection between kin in India and Canada. The food and the act of consuming this food are imbued with important meanings that help to create families across national borders. The home remedies, doctors' visits, and medical advice from kin also serve to forge transnational families. Both products and their acquisition become permeated with a sense of family togetherness. This chapter argues, then, that feeding the family and meeting the family's health-care needs are both physical and symbolic forms of caregiving that create and maintain transnational families.

Literature Review

In arguing that the social-reproductive work that Indian migrant women do on a daily basis produces transnational families, this chapter adds to both gender scholars'

research on domestic labour and migration scholars' research on transnational families. Feminist scholars have shown the importance of the daily household work involved in bearing and caring for the next generation and sustaining the well-being (and ability to work) of adults—work that has been women's responsibility (Kaplan Daniels 1987; Laslett and Brenner 1989; Luxton 1980; Luxton and Corman 2001). This work of social reproduction involves acquiring the goods necessary to do the work—shopping, in other words. It involves doing all the work essential to meet family members' physical needs, as well as to maintain the home. And it involves addressing the emotional needs of family members, which partly rests on building and nurturing relationships among family members. Feminist scholarship has not only highlighted this work, which was virtually invisible in family sociology until the women's liberation movement, it has also argued that this domestic labour is shaped by the economy and important to it. Looking at the work of "feeding the family," Marjorie DeVault (1991) added to these arguments about the social importance of housework by highlighting its cultural importance. She argued that in bringing family members together to eat the same food and orchestrating conversation among everyone around the table, women who prepare and serve family meals are creating family. That is, feeding the family is work that creates a sense of collective belonging and identity at the heart of family. Moreover, as homemakers encourage their children and their spouse to talk about their daily experiences, while they eat dinner, they nurture close relationships among them.

Scholars have also studied caregiving that extends across national boundaries (see Parreñas 2005). Because mothers of young children are employed in large numbers outside the household, middle- and upper-class families have increasingly relied on hiring women from debt-ridden developing countries to help care for their children. Research on these paid domestic workers (or nannies) has shown that many are mothers. Forced to leave their children behind, these women engage in "transnational mothering." Often separated for many years, they stay in frequent phone contact with their children, send home money sufficient to meet their material needs, and rely on extended family members to provide their daily care (Arat-Koç 2006, see also Chapter 17 of this text; Hondagneu-Sotelo and Avila 1997; Parreñas 2001, 2003, 2005).

Researchers who study transnationality have found that separated families remain linked despite their physical separation; migration does not dissolve family relationships, but it can redefine and challenge the ways they are organized (Bernhard et al. 2005). There is an enormous amount of physical and emotional care work that is required to maintain family relations across space (Bernhard et al. 2005; Viruell-Fuentes 2006), which ranges from sending money to care for family members in the country of origin (Goldring 2004; Landolt 2001; Levitt 2001; Mahler 1995; Schmalzbauer 2005), to providing kin work and communicating about children's upbringing (Aranda 2003; Da 2003; Levitt 2001; Schmalzbauer 2004). Many researchers comment on the ways family relationships change as a result of spatial separation (Da 2003; Ho 2002; Hondagneu-Sotelo 1994; Hondagneu-Sotelo and Avila 1997; Parreñas 2001; Sorensen 2005). For example, Hondagneu-Sotelo and Avila (1997: 557) argue that transnational mothering rearranges mother–child interactions and reshapes the meanings of appropriate mothering. The studies on transnational families contribute to an understanding of the creative ways that family members stay connected across global spaces, often highlighting the intense loneliness, isolation, and emotional struggles that result from separation. As a result, many of these studies serve to warn against romanticizing transnational motherhood.

Context: South Asian Immigration to Canada

A significant proportion (19.8 per cent) of the Canadian population is composed of immigrants, with recent immigrants from Asia making up the largest proportion of newcomers to Canada (Statistics Canada 2008). South Asians in Canada represent one-quarter of all visible minorities of the total population, and the number of South Asians is predicted to increase, making it the most populous visible minority group in Canada by 2017 (Statistics Canada 2006). "South Asian" is an umbrella term that encompasses a large grouping of nationalities,[1] with India ranking as the highest source country among them. Toronto is the major gateway for immigrants in Canada, and India is currently the top source country for recent immigrants to Toronto (Statistics Canada 2008). This research sampled a small group of individuals from within this large community. Given the small sample of immigrant men and women from Karnataka, India, this study does not claim to be representative of Indian immigrants.

Methodology

To examine transnational interactions, the study on which this chapter is based used a qualitative research design. The sample for this study included 35 immigrants from Karnataka, India, residing in the Greater Toronto Area,[2] out of which 21 were men and 14 were women. Women and men with children formed the majority of the sample, but married women and men with no children also participated.[3] Participants' ages ranged from 28 to 62, with an average age of 47 years. Nineteen of the participants were permanent residents in Canada and the remaining 16 are Canadian citizens. All of the participants were Hindu, and spoke English in addition to various Indian languages. Every participant in this study had at least completed post-secondary education, with 14 also completing post-graduate degrees. This sample is part of a larger study on transnational practices among Indo-Canadian migrants. The larger study interviewed more than 50 first- and second-generation Indo-Canadians to understand the daily flows of people, goods, and information across national borders.

I recruited participants through a variety of methods: notices in Indian newspapers with Toronto distributions, announcements made at cultural and religious events, emails to members of various cultural and religious organizations, and snowball sampling. These recruitment strategies provided for a wide range of experiences. Engagement in transnational practices was not a criterion for recruitment or participation. Instead, I set out to determine whether transnational practices existed and were prevalent among these migrant families and, if so, to examine their gendered dimensions.

I engaged in individual semi-structured in-depth interviews. This yielded rich narratives about men's and women's experiences and their physical and symbolic transnational ties. The interviews lasted one to three hours and were all conducted in English. I began analysis as the data were being collected. Once the interviews were transcribed verbatim, I engaged in a content analysis using a framework of key concepts and themes derived from the data. This allowed both the extraction of significant statements from the transcripts and a thematic analysis to emerge from the narratives.

Findings

Bryceson and Vuorela (2002) have noted that the existence of transnational families rests on keeping kin ties alive and maintained in spite of great distances and prolonged separations. Contemporary transnational families are sustained within a globalized world in which access to communication technologies facilitates ties to the homeland. International telephone service enables families to talk easily and cheaply on a daily basis; videos and webcams can keep family members actively engaged in the daily lives of their loved ones in another country; email provides fast access to information, photographs, and correspondence; and airlines make it possible for family members to visit one another and have meaningful face-to-face interactions. These relatively new forms of transnational communication provide avenues for practical and emotional care, which alter the practice of caregiving among migrant families.

These flows are multidirectional in the sense that the people, information, and products flowing through are initiated and received in both the sending and receiving countries. Among this sample of migrants, 100 per cent of participants phone India at least weekly; 94 per cent email India at least weekly; and 80 per cent visit India on a yearly basis. The purpose of these phone calls, emails, and visits is twofold: first, it enables migrants to maintain a feeling of connectedness with their family members in India; second, it enables migrants to mobilize resources to facilitate the daily care of their families in Canada. It is within the social environment created by these cross-border connections that these women migrants are able to sustain their families, physically and emotionally, while engaging in forms of transnational caregiving.

The following findings demonstrate the ways family networks that span national borders facilitate migrant women's health care and feeding of their families. Physical trips to India are made to obtain medicines, recipes, herbs, or food items; transnational networks are established so products can be picked up by whomever visits India; and communications are maintained so advice in India can be sought, and kin can be consulted. Through these strategies, it becomes apparent that families are sustained through networks of relations and resources that are located in both India and Canada.

Feeding the Family Transnationally

The women in this study all emphasize the importance of acquiring food and nutritional products from India. While sitting in a kitchen in Toronto, a woman named Aadarshini[4] who emigrated from India almost ten years ago explains: "any day you could come to my house [in Toronto] and have sweets, and you would taste something my mother prepared in India." This statement was made with pride—pride of the authentic Indian foods she had available in her home, and pride that her mother was still baking sweets for her immigrant daughter's family. She went on to explain: "We get very specific things from India: spices, baby stuff, soap, homemade sweets, recipes, gardening, curry powders. We have to be careful with the border but we need these things to survive in this country. And we send dark chocolate, nail-polish remover, intensive-care cream, soaps, and perfumes." Family survival means something different in a transnational context. No one actually needs baby soap or homemade sweets to survive, but this woman explains that she needs these items to feel alive and to feel that her children are being adequately cared for. This necessitates acquiring specific products from family members in India.

Similarly, another woman, named Ashna, summarized the daily importance of transnational caregiving. "Everything I do every day involves things from India—whether recipes, the clothes I'm wearing or the people I'm talking to." Likewise Padma explains, "We have taste buds that are very demanding. Whenever somebody goes [to India] we try to ask them for a favour to bring things back." Her demanding taste buds are able to recognize a difference between Indian foods acquired from India and Indian foods purchased in Canada. Another woman discusses the same reliance on getting certain foods from India. "For me food is key . . . We definitely have to get pickles and chutneys and snacky things from my mom in India. It is not the same taste here. There are all the goodies that we still get sent from India." Putting food on their families' tables in Canada necessitates cross-border acquisition of foods and spices. Whether phrased as a form of survival, a need, or a desire, all of these women share their experiences of acquiring food products directly from family in India.

Not only are products crossing borders, but advice is also flowing between Canada and India to ensure that meals are prepared in an authentic manner. Vedha, who immigrated to Canada at the age of 29, relies heavily on her mother in India when she is cooking for her family. "I call my mom a lot. She's a great cook. The food sometimes tastes different here and I call her to ask 'mom, why didn't this work?' I think it is because the vegetables and stuff are different here. My mother is a godfather for cooking." Women like Vedha, Ashna, and Padma use a variety of transnational methods to achieve their goals of providing culturally authentic food for their families. On a daily basis, the meals they put on their families' tables are produced by learning that extends across borders.

Shresthi was born in India yet raised in Canada. Several years before our conversation, she had married an Indian man who was living in India at the time of their courtship. She explained the importance of learning to cook from someone living in India, and described the process of learning to cook from her mother-in-law. "I never really cooked before I got married. I would make little things like pasta and stuff, but I would say I learned to cook Indian food from my mother-in-law because I wanted [my husband] to like the food here [in Canada]. So she taught me how to cook when I was staying there." These transnational exchanges reaffirm and further nurture family relationships and notions of family togetherness. In this way, the processes involved in transnational cooking highlight their symbolic characteristics.

The creation of family meals requires considerable effort, for which women do the bulk of the work, and through which they symbolically create family. Indian food is very important to all the participants in this study. Participants enjoy Indian dishes, and most of the meals they cook at home involve Indian foods or spices that are acquired through family networks in India. This food has a symbolic importance that food bought in Canada does not. Having food sent or brought by family in India provides an important link to the family that was left behind. Therefore, choosing Indian foods directly from India is about more than taste alone—it is also about personal connection and the meanings associated with family closeness and shared family meals. Cooking and eating have become social events that symbolically bring families together across nation states, not only across kitchen tables.

Migrant women make a conscious effort to obtain provisions (pickles, chutneys, spices, etc.), recipes, and advice from their family in India. Cooking meals the same way they did in India, with the same spices and with the same results, provides a cultural and familial authenticity that cannot be achieved outside of their transnational network. It provides these women with a connection to family in India, who can be in a position to provide them with what is necessary for their survival and, more importantly, their comfort in Canada. In this way, there is a difference between simply supplying a food product and providing a symbolic connection to family through food. Even though migrants consume these foods with their families in Canada, the presence of these foods on the table symbolically reminds them of their connection to family in India, which embeds these migrants in a larger sense of transnational "familyhood."

Keeping Families Healthy Transnationally

Not only are food products important, but so too are medicines. Women migrants use their transnational networks as a source of social capital, and health-care resources are generated within transnational families. Whenever someone in the participants' migrant network is going to India or arriving in Canada, they ask them for medicines. A woman migrant named Sadashaya explained: "Every time if I go back to India I am going to bring the whole sort of medicine stuff from India." In this way, resources are mobilized to sustain family life across national borders.

Shriya, a female migrant in her forties who has been in Canada for 16 years, still relies on alternative medicines from India to treat her health problems.

For chronic colds and cough, and swelling of the feet, they give you this alternative medicine in India. Very often antibiotics wear you down, and these are small things and they don't have any side effects. I get spices and powders sent from India which I use to make these medicines for my family.

Shriya relies on a network of friends and family in India to meet her health-care needs. Rani, who came to Canada with her husband and two children seven years ago, showed me a selection of ointments, pills, and herbs used by her and her family, which came directly from India.

I had my friend mail me ointment. Doctors here couldn't diagnose a skin reaction so I described the symptoms to my friend in India and he diagnosed it properly and sent me this ointment . . . I use a lot of home remedies [from India] for my family too . . . The thing is we can get everything here. But herbal remedies, because of our culture, are very important. We have tried to avoid drugs as far as possible. If there is a natural way to treat health problems we have chosen that route first. We bring natural products from India, and occasionally we have to get it from the local store here.

In order to obtain these products migrant women mobilize their networks in India to make sure that they are acquiring culturally appropriate health-care products for their families.

Familiarity, trust, and comfort lead many migrant families to meet their health-care needs by moving back and forth between their countries of origin and settlement. Rakasha immigrated to Canada with her husband and daughter when she was 41, and explains how much she relies on her Indian network.

Last year I suffered with a cold. I was coughing and coughing. I suffered for three months and I went to the doctor in Canada and they gave me antibiotics and antibiotics—it was killing me. Three months on antibiotics—just imagine my state. Finally, my mom in India got worried and then what happened is she said, "Okay, I'll give you a family doctor number in India, and call him." So I called him up and told him all of the symptoms that I had and all the antibiotics these people gave me. Then luckily, one of my husband's friends was already in India, in Bangalore, and so when the doctor told me that these are the medicines you have to take, these are the dosages and after a week you call me and tell me how you are. He said, "If I'm not wrong it should be cured in three days' time." So the friend in India brought them and I started the medicine and on the fourth day I stopped coughing.

Rakasha's story indicates how she uses a transnational network of friends, family, and professionals to meet her health-care needs. Through telephone conversations with her mother in India, she is referred to a medical professional in India who sends her medicines through a friend from Canada who is visiting in India.

It is not just medicine, but also medical advice, that flows across national borders. Pushpa, who immigrated in her early forties, explains how she relies on medical advice from relatives in India.

[India] has a lot of home remedies. Knowing a lot of these things work, to remedy a situation we'd try home remedies. If we need to know more about them we would contact ancestors or elders in India. If what they suggested doesn't work, then we would see a physician.

For Pushpa, her first course of action is consultation and advice from family in India; Canadian medical professionals are a last resort. Her ties to India provide her with the medical advice she needs to combat her family's everyday ailments.

Migrant women are part of transnational social networks involving themselves, their migrant relatives and friends in Canada, their relatives and friends in India, and medical professionals in India. They are meeting their medical needs through an informal transnational kin network. By relying on ties with people in India and taking advantage of cross-border travel by themselves and others, these women are part of a network practising transnational health approaches.

Choosing to provide caregiving to their families through the mobilization of transnational networks has symbolic roots. Although some of the women in this study describe Indian health care as cheaper, more accessible, or superior than that offered in Canada, a more nuanced understanding of their narratives reveals that the foremost reason for transnational health care is not economic or practical, but symbolic. Neepa immigrated to Canada with her husband three years ago. She explains why she uses Indian health care despite being able to access Canada's health-care system. "I always get medicine and health care there [in India]. My family has always seen the same doctor, and so my children in Canada should too." The reason why migrant women want themselves and their children to use India's health-care services and products has more to do with a symbolic sense of family than a biomedical explanation of care.

The medical care they receive in India symbolically recreates home in the host society. Migrant women feel more comfortable with the style of health care offered in India. Participants describe the medical experience in India as "homely"; they do not associate this word with the more common definition of "unattractive" but instead use the word to refer to something that is familiar and reminds them of home. Indian health care symbolizes their homeland and their family still residing in India. Shivani, who is married and has one daughter, explains, "If I get sick in Bangalore I go to the next door doctor. If he is not there, I go to the third door doctor. It is very homely there . . . Whenever my children go to India they get treated there." Migrants feel a connection to people in India by experiencing the same medical processes as family members who never left. Therefore, much like travellers wait to get home from a vacation before seeing a doctor, many Indian migrants wait to vacation in India before seeking treatment for their ailments.

Calling friends and family in India allows these women migrants to feel as though their family is still involved in their daily lives and their daily care, in a way that would not be possible if they relied exclusively on Canadian health care for diagnoses, advice, and medicines. Calling family in India when their child is sick helps these women feel connected to, and actively engaged with, their families in the homeland. Lavanya explains, "When my son is sick I call my mom [in India]. Anything that happens in life the first person I talk to is her . . . The only person I talk to regarding my family's health is my mom and the doctor in India." There is an emotional connection to family in India that these women rely on to feel they are adequately caring for their children. Another mother, named Rupa, explained: "They are more emotional and sentimental in India. I call up everybody. When my daughter is sick and I call home [to India] I feel connected and homely and encouraged. I feel relieved."

Gendered Dimensions of Transnational Caregiving

Findings indicate that transnational caregiving is a highly gendered process. Transnationalism extends women's gendered caregiving by providing them with an opportunity to meet their families' needs in Canada while simultaneously incorporating the traditions, products, and people in their country of origin. Both men and women contact family and friends in India; however, women generally mobilize these networks for care of themselves and their families, whereas men are generally concerned with less personal needs. As a result of women's roles as mothers and caregivers, they more frequently use transnational ties to ensure the daily care of their families.

Regularly phoning family in India was common among both men and women in this study. All of the women and 96.6 per cent of the men phoned India weekly. Although this was a small percentage difference in the frequency of contact, there was a very important gendered dimension when we examined the length and content of the communication. First, participants indicated that women's phone calls generally lasted longer than men's. Second, women were more likely to use phone communication to discuss personal family matters, whereas the men were more likely to discuss business, sports, or engage in small talk with family. One woman explained the differences when asked who stays in touch:

It is generally me making all of the social contacts; you know, I make a conscious effort. I think generally it is women who keep track of birthdays and such, and I think this extends into social contacts. Even with friends, like I speak with my girlfriends far more than he does with his friends. He talks to them about some game and such but we keep in touch.

Another woman indicated: "My husband calls a lot, that's true, but his calls are so short, and he passes the phone to me after he speaks briefly with his mother. I fill her in on the children and their activities and keep her in touch with what we are doing here." The phone calls that women conduct with family and friends living in both Canada and India involve a lot of effort. This effort leads to qualitative, if not quantitative, differences, in communication across national borders.

In terms of health care, many of the men in this study discuss the importance of acquiring medicines and herbal remedies from India; however, it is their wives who do most of the work associated with the acquisition of these products. One man describes how his family relies on trips to India to obtain Indian herbs for home remedies, but his experiences reveal the gendered dimensions of this family reliance. Although he begins to talk about "we," he quickly adjusts his language to more accurately reflect his wife's crucial role in transnational health care; his wife is the migrant family member who decides what is needed and ensures they have adequate supplies: "We call either her mother or my mother in India [to get herbs]. We bring our ingredients from India, but now we have exhausted everything *my wife* brought, so now *she* has to go to the Indian store [in Canada]" [emphasis added]. Women are the ones who contact their own mothers or their husband's mothers in order to ensure that their families have access to doctors, specialists, and elders in India, and make certain that their home is supplied with herbal remedies and spices sent directly from family in India. Therefore, it is through women-centred networks that transnational caregiving is performed.

Similarly, in terms of feeding their families, findings indicate that men deem it very important to eat authentic Indian foods, but they do not engage in the daily activities required to feed their families. Abhijay explained that he expresses his Indo-Canadian identity through food. Although, like Abhijay, many of the men discussed how they express their identity and their ethnicity through the foods they eat, they do not prepare the meals, and do not engage in transnational cooking. Abhijay goes on to describe how he values South Indian vegetarian food; however, the work involved in reading labels, obtaining ingredients, and cooking these meals involves a lot of work on behalf of his wife:

> I am a vegetarian and I find a lot that I stick to those values that I have. But it is very hard to be a vegetarian here. If you go to the grocery store, *my wife* has to take a long time to read the labels, and know which salts are made with bones and all that. So *she* tries to get a lot of things from India. [Vegetarianism] is a value I don't want to give up. [emphasis added]

Similarly, Musuri explains how Indian food prepared in Canada is an important way for his son to develop his identity, which is based on Indian heritage on his father's side, and Sri Lankan on his mother's side. "My *mother* has provided my *wife* with spices [from India], because I want my son to get used to both forms of cooking, and to identify with both sides" [emphasis added]. Ensuring the salience

of India by acquiring spices from women kin in India reveals the work involved in ensuring that care is embedded in a transnational social field. Male migrants provide insights into the importance of culturally authentic cooking performed by the women in their lives. Although the men in this study identify the importance of transnational cooking, they are generally not the ones who are engaged in the act of obtaining spices or preparing meals.

Women are the ones who ensure that their families are eating authentic Indian foods, and using medicines that are obtained directly from family in India. Women keep track of the spices they have available and what needs to be purchased, arrange for shipments of products, and prepare the meals or remedies that their families require. This exemplifies women's transnational social reproduction. It is this qualitative difference that illuminates the gendered dimensions of health care and food provision among these Indo-Canadian families. By regularly keeping in touch with friends and family in India, women are mobilizing networks to provide not only products but also an important cultural link that enables their care work to be symbolically constitutive of their Indian family.

Conclusion

This chapter has discussed the transnational caregiving practices of migrant women from Karnataka, India. Through in-depth interviews with women and men living in Toronto, Canada, it has revealed the complex ways in which families are being created and sustained across national borders. My analysis shows that the social relationships through which family is created and maintained are shaped by the larger social context, specifically the transnational space in which they are embedded. The migrants in my research are fostering transnational family ties through physical visits to India, and ongoing email and phone communication. By staying in touch, migrants are able to foster family ties and a sense of belonging that enables them to develop and sustain a crucial connection to family in India.

Focusing on social reproduction highlights the ways transnational families are created by migrant women. This study has therefore argued that the relations that sustain families are gendered. Women see their transnational networks as alternative social spaces in which to develop their caregiving strategies and nurture their families. Women play a key role in the creation and maintenance of their families through their reproductive activities which are occurring transnationally. Caring work involves connecting households and individuals transnationally. Through these connections, women migrants are creating a sense of family togetherness. The transnational spaces that women navigate therefore reveal the ways they fulfill their caregiving responsibilities.

This chapter has shown how there are important symbolic meanings associated with the ways women are using their transnational space to create their families. The symbolic expressions of transnationalism are important because they enable women migrants to mobilize their resources in meaningful ways. This provides women and their families with a sense of belonging and permits them to carry out their daily caregiving in ways that nurture their transnational family bonds. The symbolic and affective value of food and health care acquired through family in India creates a meaningful anchor to the homeland, which becomes important in the creation of transnational families in Canada. Family identities thus result directly from the transnational meals and health-care work being performed by migrant women.

Other researchers have pointed out how the daily lives of transnational families complicate the understandings of traditional caregiving. My study has expanded this argument through an analysis of two specific caregiving activities: feeding the family and meeting family members health-care needs. I have highlighted the emotions and resources that women invest in the provisioning, preparing and eating of food, as well as in the provision of health-care diagnoses and remedies. Women migrants from Karnataka, India, translate their labour and knowledge of cooking and health care into a transnational strategy to create and maintain their families in Canada. Through these daily activities of social reproduction, women are creating new ways of sustaining their Indian families in a transnational space.

● Notes

1. South Asian includes individuals from Bangladesh, Bhutan, India, Maldives, Nepal, Pakistan, and Sri Lanka.

2. The Greater Toronto Area (GTA) is the largest metropolitan area in Canada. In addition to the City of Toronto, it includes four surrounding regional municipalities—York, Halton, Peel, and Durham. The census enumerated 2 320 200 immigrants in Toronto in 2006, accounting for almost half of the area's total population.

3. Caregiving for families includes caregiving for spouses, so three women with no children were interviewed as part of this sample (one of whom was pregnant at the time of our interview).

4. All names used in this paper are pseudonyms to protect the anonymity of participants.

● References

Aranda, Elizabeth M. (2003). "Global Care Work and Gendered Constraints: The Case of Puerto Rican Transmigrants," *Gender & Society* vol. 17, no. 4, pp. 609–26.

Arat-Koç, Sedef. (2006). "Whose Social Reproduction? Transnational Motherhood and Challenges to Feminist Political Economy," in *Social Reproduction: Feminist Political Economy Challenges Neo-Liberalism*, eds Kate Bezanson and Meg Luxton. McGill–Queen's University Press, pp. 75–92.

Bernhard, Judith K., Luin Goldring, and Patricia Landolt. (2005). *Transnational Multi-local Motherhood: Experiences and Reunification Among Latin American Families in Canada*. LARG (Latin American Research Group).

Bryceson, Deborah, and Ulla Vuorela. (2002). "Transnational Families in the Twenty-first Century," in *The Transnational Family. New European Frontiers and Global Networks*, eds D. Bryceson and U. Vuorela. New York: Oxford, pp. 3–30.

Da, Wei Wei. (2003). "Transnational Grandparenting: Child Care Arrangements Among Migrants from the People's Republic of China to Australia," *Journal of International Migration and Integration*, vol. 4, no. 1, pp. 79–103.

DeVault, Marjorie L. (1991). *Feeding the Family: The Social Organization of Caring as Gendered Work*. Chicago: University of Chicago Press.

Goldring, Luin. (2004). "Family and Collective Remittances to Mexico: A Multi-dimensional Typology," *Development and Change*, vol. 35, no. 4, pp. 799–840.

Ho, Elsie. (2002). "Multi-local Residence, Transnational Networks: Chinese 'Astronaut' Families in New Zealand," *Asian and Pacific Migration Journal*, vol. 11, no. 1, pp. 145–64.

Hondagneu-Sotelo, Pierrette. (1994). "Latina Immigrant Women and Paid Domestic Work: Upgrading the Occupation," *Clinical Sociology Review*, vol. 12, pp. 257–70.

Hondagneu-Sotelo, Pierrette, and Ernestine Avila. (1997). "'I'm Here, But I'm There': The Meanings of Latina Transnational Motherhood," *Gender and Society*, vol. 11, no. 5, pp. 548–71.

Kaplan Daniels, A. (1987). "Invisible Work," *Social Problems*, vol. 34, no. 5, pp. 403–15.

Landolt, Patricia. (2001). "Salvadoran Economic Transnationalism: Embedded Strategies for Household Maintenance, Immigrant Incorporation, and Entrepreneurial Expansion," *Global Networks: A Journal of Transnational Affairs*, vol. 1, no. 3, pp. 217–41.

Laslett, Barbara, and Johanna Brenner. (1989). "Gender and Social Reproduction: Historical Perspectives," *Annual Review of Sociology*, vol. 15: 381–404.

Levitt, Peggy. (2001). "Transnational Migration: Taking Stock and Future Directions," *Global Networks: A Journal of Transnational Affairs*, vol. 1, no. 3, pp. 195–216.

Luxton, Meg. (1980). *More Than a Labour of Love: Three Generations of Women's Work in the Home*. Toronto: Women's Press.

Luxton, Meg, and June Corman. (2001). *Getting by in Hard Times: Gendered Labour at Home and on the Job*. Toronto: University of Toronto Press.

Mahler, Sarah. (1995). *American Dreaming: Immigrant Life on the Margins*. New Jersey: Princeton University Press.

Parreñas, Rhacel Salazar. (2001). "Mothering from a Distance: Emotions, Gender and Intergenerational Relations in Filipino Transnational Families," *Feminist Studies*, vol. 27, no. 2, pp. 361–90.

———. (2003). "The Care Crisis in the Philippines: Children and Transnational Families in the New Global Economy," in *Global Woman: Nannies, Maids and Sex Workers in the New Economy*, eds Barbara Ehrenreich and Arlie Russell Hochschild. New York: Metropolitan Books Henry Holt and Company, pp. 39–54.

———. (2005). *Children of Global Migration: Transnational Families and Gendered Woes*. Stanford, CA: Stanford University Press.

Schmalzbauer, Leah. (2004). "Searching for Wages and Mothering from Afar: The Case of Honduran Transnational Families," *Journal of Marriage and Family*, vol. 66, no. 5, pp. 1317–31.

———. (2005). *Striving and Surviving: A Daily Life Analysis of Honduran Transnational Families*. New York: Routledge.

Sorensen, Ninna Nyberg. (2005). "Transnational Family Life Across the Atlantic: The Experiences of Colombian Dominican Migrants in Europe." Paper presented at the International Conference on Migration and Domestic Work in a Global Perspective, Wassenar, The Netherlands. May 26–29.

Statistics Canada. (2006). Census. Catalogue No: 11-008. Ethocultural Diversity on Canada: Prospects for 2017. Canadian Social Trends by Alain Belanger and Eric Caron Malenfant. Accessed September 3, 2008 from: http://www.statcan.ca/English/freepub/11-008-XIE/2005003/articles/8968.pdf

———. (2008). Census. Catalogue No: 11-008-X. Census snapshot – Immigration in Canada: A portrait of the

Foreign-born Population, 2006 Census. April 22, 2008. Accessed September 9 from: http://www.statcan.ca/english/freepub/11-008-XIE/2008001/article/10556-en.pdf

Viruell-Fuentes, Edna A. (2006). "'My Heart Is Always There': The Transnational Practices of First-Generation Mexican Immigrant and Second-Generation Mexican American Women," *Identities: Global Studies in Culture and Power*, vol. 13, pp. 335–62.

● Acknowledgements

This research was supported by the Social Sciences and Humanities Research Council. I thank the men and women migrants who agreed to take part in this study and generously shared their time and experiences with me; without them this chapter would not have been possible. I also thank Bonnie Fox for her helpful feedback on an earlier draft. Her detailed suggestions contributed greatly to the final version of this chapter.

Section 2

Economic and Other Stress

Chapter 22

In this chapter, Jo-Anne Fiske and Rose Johnny take up the story begun in the selections from Eleanor Leacock's work (in Chapter 3) about the damage done to the families of First Nations people in Canada by colonialism, integration into a capitalist economy, and government policies. Life in the First Nations community in BC that they discuss traditionally featured co-operation, sharing, and generalized reciprocity among kin, which constituted a powerful survival strategy. With access to rich ancestral land, these foragers traditionally enjoyed a communal way of living that was based on co-operation in procuring food and generosity in sharing food. Because individuals depended on the group and not a spouse or parent, they—men, women, and children—experienced considerable personal autonomy.

Fiske and Johnny describe the ways government policies have affected First Nations family organization and social relations. Rose Johnny's life experiences, as a member of the Lake Babine First Nation, are woven into this account.

The Lake Babine First Nation Family: Yesterday and Today

Jo-Anne Fiske and Rose Johnny

Introduction

> What happened to this "one big family" that the village once was? Our ancestors used to help each other and share with each other. My dad speaks of gatherings when he was young. Everyone shared the moose or the thousands of fish caught.

Family and kinship relations lie at the heart of community organization and personal identity in First Nations communities. It is often said that a First Nations community is "one big family." This not only signifies an assertion of communal purpose and shared responsibility, but also indicates the intricate kinship ties that exist as a result of frequent village endogamy. The *extended family,* therefore, is often seen to be the basic unit of social identity, economic support, and psychological nurture. The importance of family and kin relations takes precedence over all other emotional and social ties in most, if not all, First Nations communities. Family organization marks a significant cultural distinction from other sociocultural groups in Canada, most dramatically from the Euro-Canadian majority who stress an autonomous *nuclear family* organization and for whom other social relations may be equally if not more significant than family ties.

To understand cultural differences in family and kinship relations, we must always be critically aware of the way they are represented. Scholarship on family and kinship is grounded in the language and norms of the dominant society. For example, "extended family" is a term used to describe family organizations that embrace three or more generations and ties to other relatives. However, the notion of "extension" makes sense only if a smaller unit, the nuclear family, is taken as the norm. The assumption of a normative unit, the patriarchal nuclear family, has shaped colonial relations in Canada for centuries. Fur traders and Christian missionaries were the first Europeans to impose foreign forms of family organization on the original peoples of North America. Many did so because they disapproved of any marriage or family relations that differed from their own; specifically, they opposed polyandry and polygyny, and scorned maternal leadership (Leacock 1980; Anderson 1991). Christian missionaries insisted that marriage was a holy sacrament and refused holy rites to men or women with more than one spouse. Children who were born "out of wedlock" were labelled *illegitimate,* a European category unknown in Aboriginal North America.

The power of European settlers and later of the Canadian government and dominant society to impose foreign family structures and values on the original peoples of North America has its roots in the ethos and practices of colonialism. Central to colonial relations between First Nations and the Europeans was a perception of cultural and moral superiority. When France and Britain entered what is now Canada they wanted more than the natural resources and land, they wanted to change forever the people of these lands by assimilating them into the Euro-Canadian society. To do so meant changing family values and structures and gender relations to mirror those of the dominant society (Bilharz 1995; Byrne and Fouillard 2000; Stevenson 1999). The colonial governments of New France and the British colonies were supported in their efforts to change First Nations families by Christian missionaries; with the Canadian confederation of British colonies in 1867, the Canadian government assumed unto itself these rights

and powers and continued to deploy Christian missionaries to this end.

This power continues today and is understood as *internal colonialism;* that is, power relations between First Nations and the dominant society remain ones of subordination marked both by ideological and political subordination (Frideres 1988). Historically, colonialism is characterized by deliberate deployment of ideological, political, and economic strategies to exploit and expropriate the resources held by the colonized population and to undermine, if not eradicate, their world views, family and kinship organization, cultural practices, and religion.

Colonialism, however, is not just a historical practice of early settlement; it is a persistent power relation that shifts its facade and ideology with changing social dynamics and moral values. Internal colonialism refers to the power relations that emerged in the twentieth century, and most particularly in the last 60 years. In this era, colonial relations endure within a rhetoric of equality and social justice. In fact, as Frideres makes clear, equality is more a myth than a lived experience. The myth of equality provides the rationalization to continue what the early colonizers began: eradication of social and cultural uniqueness and denial of inherent rights of the First Nations (267).

The overall outcome of European settlement has been an overpowering of all aboriginal peoples. They have steadily lost the political autonomy they knew before colonization, suffered economic constraints through loss of land and resources, and endured massive cultural change not of their choosing. From the time of early European settlement to the present, the dominant Canadian society and government have intruded on First Nations family relations in myriad ways, some subtle and some overtly oppressive, some intended and others not. By means of the *Indian Act, 1876* (which has been amended several times), the federal government assumed control over First Nations and their lands. The *Indian Act* also divided communities into "status" (registered Indians who receive government benefits) and "non-status" Indians, and denied First Nations peoples rights enjoyed by other Canadian citizens. It enforced changes in family relations ranging from marriage practices, adoptions, and residence rights to an inability to bequeath property according to established custom.

Provincial governments interfered more recently. Social welfare and child protection policies and practices directly and indirectly affected the daily lives of all First Nations peoples. For instance, family ties were severed when social workers apprehended infants for adoption into non-aboriginal families.[1] Exportation of infants to the United States signified to the bereft mothers and their kin incomprehension of, if not outright contempt for, aboriginal family practices. Less obvious, but none the less damaging, were a profusion of economic and political encroachments that altered the daily and seasonal economic activities of communities. As we shall see, capitalist expansion, changes in resource management laws, and educational policies have all had a radical impact on First Nations families.

Although broad similarities of changing family relations and structures exist for all First Nations families, clear differences prevail as a result of specific First Nations cultural and legal traditions, particular adaptations to Euro-Canadian influences, and distinct effects of provincial policies. In this account, we offer a glimpse into the contemporary Lake Babine Nation family. We weave reminiscences of Rose Johnny and the history of the Lake Babine Nation into the context of Canadian colonial history, highlighting major historical

crises that have shaped family and community. We place Rose's recollections and perspectives within the concept of a changing political economy in which the Canadian government foisted paternal practices upon the Lake Babine Nation, usurped their traditional lands and resources; rendered them dependent upon government funds; and subjected them to debilitating policies and practices. We examine colonial strategies of family disruption: *Indian Act* definitions of "Indian"; removal of children to residential schools, imposed patriarchal family relations, and apprehension of children and infants.

The Lake Babine First Nation Family

The Lake Babine First Nation (also known as the Nedu'ten) is one of several nations known to us as the Yinkadinee or Carrier, who are related by language (an Athapaskan dialect), political and legal structures, and cultural traditions.[2] The First Nations of central British Columbia were among the last in Canada to encounter the full effects of the process of colonization. Europeans did not settle in Lake Babine First Nation territories on the shores of Lake Babine in large numbers until the middle of the twentieth century. Because the Lake Babine First Nation was more isolated than many First Nations, their family structures have retained culturally distinct features that have supported the people through periods of acute social disruption and personal stress.

Europeans first arrived permanently in Lake Babine First Nation territory in 1822, when the Hudson's Bay Company established its first trading post on Lake Babine. The men of the trading post had an immediate effect on Lake Babine First Nation family relations. Traders and the subordinate "company men" entered into "country marriages" with Lake Babine First Nation women, who were often left behind when their men were transferred to another post or were retired from the company. Few records remain of these European–Lake Babine First Nation marriages but, judging from other studies of "country marriages," it is safe to assume that considerable hardship emerged for many of the women and their children (Brown 1980; Van Kirk 1980). Frontier marriage relationships were marked by ambiguity and contradictions. First Nations women were condemned for sexual behaviours alleged to be promiscuous and adulterous, even while European men were exonerated for parallel conduct. The newcomers interpreted *polygyny* (the practice of having several wives) and mourning practices—which included painful rituals at the time of the deceased spouse's cremation and long periods of mourning marked by *affinal servitude* (services performed for relatives by marriage)—as signs of women's subjugation.[3] They also understood onerous work and trading that took women from their home communities to indicate a miserable existence for women. At the same time, the traders' own practices devalued women's autonomy and defined arduous domestic labour as the natural lot of women. Interracial marriages on the trading frontier often forced wives, even if temporarily, into dependence upon their foreign husbands and alienated them from their own kin and thus from the economic and personal autonomy they would have known as participating members in their extended families.

Although the Lake Babine First Nation was and remains a matrilineal people—that is, one that traces descent, membership, inheritance rights, and so on from the mother's side—the Lake Babine First Nation family soon became influenced by European patrilineal practices and patriarchy, and by principles of European marriage as a legally binding monogamous lifetime relationship. The Oblates of Mary Immaculate, a Catholic order from France, were regular visitors to the Lake Babine First Nation. The priests reviled Lake Babine First Nation practices of divorce and attempted to prevent marriage between Catholic converts and adherents of traditional sacred practices. They boldly separated couples united by custom and forced marriage arrangements against the will of principals and family, instilling fear of eternal damnation and denying the sacraments to those who resisted. As Betty Patrick, a band member and researcher for the Lake Babine First Nation, commented upon reading a missionary's account of his own interventions and the people's staunch resistance, "No wonder the people were so confused and had such a hard time!"

Conversion to Catholicism brought an entire new social order to the Lake Babine people, one marked by new notions of authority and punishment for social and sacred transgressions. Missionary priests introduced new forms of all-male village councils, which they authorized to administer corporal punishment, commonly whipping, to adults who broke church laws; to enforce a curfew for adults and children alike; and to intervene in family conflicts and interpersonal tensions. The priests discredited the traditional matrilineal family, in which authority over children was assumed by the mother's kin in harmony with complementary obligations and authority resting in the father's family, in favour of patriarchal authority of the husband over wife and children.

Conversion also required baptism and Christian naming, a practice that ended the use of traditional names and introduced the use of the *patronymic* (the family name inherited from one's father). Prior to this practice, family names did not exist. Rather, matrilineal ties were indicated by membership in the House, a matrilineal kin group who shared common resources and who displayed clan and House crests to symbolize social identity and personal entitlements. The Lake Babine people are divided into four matrilineal clans, which are further divided into the Houses. Individual identity is derived from clan and House membership, not from the father's line. Nonetheless, the father's House did, and continues to, perform important functions throughout a person's lifetime, most particularly in times of personal conflicts and economic stress, and at death.

Missionaries' hostility toward Lake Babine First Nation marital practices was rooted in concepts of morality. The priests firmly believed that matrilineal societies existed because of rampant promiscuity and female immorality. They also abhorred principles of matrilineal clan organization because Lake Babine people valued co-operative labour and communal ownership over private ownership. In the priests' eyes, communal principles constituted a derogatory state and an impediment to "civilization," which was presumed to rest upon private ownership and accumulation of wealth. Compounding their antipathy toward the Lake Babine First Nation and the other Yinkadinee nations was their attitude toward the *bah'lats* or "potlatch," which was the cornerstone of social organization and cultural identity.

The seat of government and legal order, the *bah'lats* was a ceremonial feast of public witnessing. All important community and intercommunity affairs were decided at a gathering of community members, all of whose interests were represented through the hereditary clan and House chiefs. Witnesses assumed an important role; they could be called upon to validate any decision or transaction, and for this they received presentations

of gifts and food corresponding to their social rank and responsibilities. The potlatch or feast, an institution shared in various forms with other First Nations of the Pacific region, could not be eradicated or even altered without disruption of every social relationship. At the heart of society, *bah'lats* regulated membership in matrilineal clans and Houses, relations between maternal and paternal kin, succession to seats of honour and leadership, hereditary chieftainship, and virtually every aspect of resource access, management, and distribution. In the inseparable world of the sacred and the profane, the *bah'lats* was, and remains, sacred; all social relations and obligations of the *bah'lats* have spiritual significance, and all teachings of elders and hereditary chiefs are steeped in esoteric knowledge and wisdom.

In a matrilineal society, a balance of rituals and services is needed to reinforce paternal ties. The *bah'lats/clan complex* protects these relationships. At all rites of passage, from birth to death, an individual's father's House (now generally called the "sponsoring clan") performs necessary services and rituals. **Exogamy**, marriage between clans, was and remains the rule; matrilineal succession to seats of honour and resource territories the law. In the past, ethnographers tell us, a man succeeded his mother's brother to important positions in the potlatch and with them gained specific rights to resource territories (Jenness 1943; Morice 1889). Today, other maternal relationships grant similar rights; a woman will follow her maternal aunt or grandmother, for instance, or a man will succeed a brother. Each individual has membership in her or his mother's House, which was the primary productive unit and which remains the primary social unit.

For myriad reasons colonizing powers, representing the government and corporate enterprises as well as the church, reviled the *bah'lats,* and in 1884 the practice was criminalized by means of amendments to the *Indian Act* that became known as the "potlatch law." Although criminalization did not eradicate the *bah'lats* as was intended, Lake Babine First Nation families endured considerable stress as they sought to retain the social and legal customs upon which family life depended.

The twentieth century wrought further radical changes. Colonial education was introduced by the Catholic missionaries. Initially children attended day schools in their home community. In 1922, the Lejac Residential School opened. Now children were taken more than 150 kilometres from home for 10 months a year. As in the other residential schools across North America, students were forbidden to speak their language, interact with children of the opposite sex, or maintain cultural traditions (Deiter 1999; Knockwood 1993; Milloy 1999). For a few hours each day, the children studied the Bible and learned the rudiments of literacy and arithmetic. The main thrust of the school, however, was toward agricultural training and the school's own economic self-sufficiency. Boys toiled in the fields and raised livestock, while girls worked at domestic chores in preparation for a life as dependent wives. The intent was to eradicate traditional gender roles and to instill in the girls a sense of bodily shame and a Christian view of the sinful nature of sexuality. For some girls, this meant remaining in school until they were of marriageable age (15 to 16), when under the auspices of the "church chief"—an appointee of the priest—and kin they entered into arranged marriages.

Although relatively few Lake Babine children attended Lejac for any length of time compared to children in other Yinkadinee communities, the consequences were devastating for the entire community. Parents had no influence over the curriculum or even the staff, who were members of foreign missionary congregations. Few could spare the several days needed to travel to the school for visits with their children. Moreover, when day schools on the reserves did operate, they offered a similar curriculum and also excluded parents and community leaders from the administration and routine practices. As has been well documented elsewhere, residential school life was harsh, frequently abusive, and dangerous (Fiske 1991; Knockwood 1993; English-Currie 1990). Contagious diseases took lives and left survivors weak and vulnerable.

Not only were families torn by death and absence, intergenerational alienation emerged with cultural loss. Traditions surrounding puberty and the special preparation of young girls for motherhood and adult female responsibilities were seriously disrupted. Traditions of lengthy menstrual seclusion, with accompanying sacred and practical instruction from female kin and uninterrupted periods of intense craft work, were condemned by missionaries. School residence, of course, made such practices impossible, and so valued teachings were lost or at least diminished for many Lake Babine First Nation women and girls. By the 1970s, rituals honouring the onset of womanhood had been altered. Some families no longer passed on the ancient teachings or did so only in a truncated manner.

"Oh my God! I'm bleeding!" As I sat there fearful, thinking I was going to die, I kept asking myself, "Why me?" All of a sudden Mother grabbed me and dragged me into the room. She immediately put covers over the window and a blanket all around my bed. I sat there stunned and shocked, but was too scared to speak. The only ones that were allowed into this small, dark room were Mom and my sisters. I was forbidden to look at Dad and my brothers, let alone speak to them. "What have I done?" I kept wondering. Mom brought me my meals, and she gave me a small pail to urinate in. This went on for a whole week. I was going nuts. On my last day Mom double-checked to see if I was still bleeding. Thank God I wasn't! I never thought I'd be so happy to see school again.

Mom later explained to me what was going on. I was becoming a woman. Our tradition was that when a female bleeds for the first time, she is to have no contact at all with any of the males in the family or the village. This was considered bad luck for the male hunters. I freaked out. "Would I have to do this every month?" I asked. Thank God, that was only during a female's first period. I don't think I could have lasted if I had to do this ritual once a month.

Unfortunately, I was the second oldest. By the time my younger sister became a woman this ritual was no longer practised.

Not only did residential schools teach girls to be ashamed of their bodies, they taught all the children to be ashamed of their language and culture. When the children left the colonial institution, many found it difficult to speak their language; others were ashamed to do so. Recognizing the need for English to get jobs in the dominant society, some parents discouraged their children from learning their own language. Communication became difficult between children and parents, as was the case for Rose and her relatives.

My parents were raised when the residential schools were in. I think they were totally brainwashed; therefore, they were not able to teach us the language. It did not help [that] when they did speak the language, they did it in two different dialects. Yet I do understand most of the language.

Harsh schooling practices have left a bitter legacy for First Nations families. Residential schooling has had an intergenerational impact. Anxious to have a better life for their children, parents encourage academic success, yet cannot do so with confidence. Their own painful experiences, coupled with the racism their children still experience, sabotage the determination of many. Others, whatever the odds, refuse to diminish their aspirations. For non-status parents, the challenges are aggravated by lack of the community and financial support enjoyed by their status kin. Notwithstanding the hardships they endured, Rose's parents enabled her to finish her schooling even as she resisted.

Another thing that my parents taught me about was *style*. I had no use for it. While my friends had the latest trends, I was wearing hand-me-downs. I'd only receive new clothes for Christmas or for my birthday. Wanting to be like the others or wanting the same clothes was not going to get me anywhere in life. The only thing important to my parents was that we had food on the table and a home to live in.

Except for education. I had to have that in order to get ahead. I remember one day I decided I wasn't going to go to school any more. Being the brave girl I thought I was, I told my parents. Talk about explosive! My dad hit the ceiling, mumbling at the same time. He grabbed me and made me pack my clothes. In between smacking me, he yelled, "Go ahead! Let's see how far you go without an education!"

I pleaded through my tears and was terrified. Where was I going to go? Finally

I told him I would continue my schooling. Believe me, after that I did my homework every night right up until I graduated. I did not realize it then, but I should've been honoured that I was the only Indian to graduate in my class.

Colonial schooling did more than hasten cultural disruption; it also separated generations of children and parents. A primary motivation for developing schools away from the children's community was to limit contact between children and parents in the hopes that children would internalize the moral and religious values of Europeans and structure their adult lives so as to fit into the capitalist political economy either as wage labourers or as small-scale agriculturists (Miller 1996; Milloy 1999). As a consequence, girls and boys who remained in the system for long periods reached adulthood with little knowledge of how to be effective parents and how to form and sustain close emotional relationships. School discipline was harsh, often seemingly capricious, and was premised on alien codes of ethics and morals that failed to respect the children's parents or their spiritual values. Whereas in the past Lake Babine parents and grandparents had shared child rearing and fostered feelings of affection while leaving children free to learn by experience and subtle teaching, a new parenting style emerged that was patterned after the harsh routines and physical punishments introduced by missionaries and was forged to meet crippling social and economic constraints. As Rose explains, respect for parents remained strong even as the younger generations struggled for more autonomy and pursued new ways to adjust to their changing world.

One month after I graduated I began working. My parents were still strict with me. I felt as though I never really grew up. Here I was, 21 years old, sitting in the bar and my dad would come in after me. I would quickly run out the other door. This went on until I was 23. My friends would tease me, and it did not help that they were younger, much younger than I. My parents had this power over me. I was brought up never to speak back or to disobey them. Then my mother died of cancer. I waited a couple of years before I moved out on my own.

Economic transformation also affected family structure and kin relations. In the 1920s the provincial government required First Nations peoples to "register" trap lines, essentially huge tracts of land possessed and used by the matrilineal kin groups for trapping, hunting, fishing, gathering, and other purposes. In keeping with state paternalism, rules for registering the trap lines were rigid and left little opportunity for community or personal discretion in management of ancestral lands and resources. This new form of legal resource regulation brought with it the government's expectations of patrilineal, nuclear-family relations. Applying sexist practices, the government did not countenance female possession or inheritance, except in the case of widows who could hold land for sons until they reached adulthood. Earlier on, the federal government, through the Department of Indian Affairs, had assumed control over "Indians and the lands reserved for them." Among other intrusions, this meant government interference with personal estates, and, accordingly, matrilineal inheritance of traplines (for example, from brother to sister's son or from sister to brother) and collective ownership by a clan or Bouse were denounced and often denied in favour of father-to-son inheritance. The once undisputed role of the matrilineal kin group comprising the House as the owner/manager of a bounded resource territory was undercut and came to compete with patrilineal membership within a trapline "company." In this way, the government was able to coerce families into accepting a new family order, a process that further undermined the collectivity of the extended family and the authority and dignity of the House.

Colonial undermining of the traditional family relationships continued into the mid-twentieth century as the federal government persisted in its efforts to assimilate First Nations into mainstream society. In particular, the Department of Indian Affairs sought ways of moving former trappers and hunters into wage labour. For the Lake Babine people, this meant working in the rapidly expanding forestry industry at manual jobs. In the 1950s many Lake Babine families were removed from their traditional village of Old Fort, an isolated community that could be reached only by boat, to Pendleton Bay on the opposite shore of Lake Babine, where the men were employed in small sawmills. A temporary village emerged, one without the services and facilities that could ease the burden of homemaking. Adolescent girls were routinely responsible for helping with heavy housework. They carried water from the lake for washing and emptied chamber pails each morning. Women boiled water for laundry and housecleaning and cooked meals on the wood-burning range. Hard physical work at the mills and in the home strained parents' patience and this, coupled with the growing acceptance of physical punishment learned from the missionaries, often led to family tensions and conflicts as parents struggled to teach the values of hard work, self-discipline, and respect. Even an unfortunate accident or the mischievous behaviour of children could provoke unanticipated and misunderstood punishment, as Rose discovered the day her brother tripped her as she went to empty the family's chamber pail.

I get shivers just thinking about it today. Anyways, I went tumbling down. I smelt so bad that a skunk would run away from me. I sat there on the ground, crying. Then Mom came along. Boy, was she ever angry. I thought to myself, "Good for you George, now you're going to get it." Then to my surprise she came charging at me. I'm telling you, I got the spanking of my life. What was going on? She ordered me into the house to change. "I just finished doing laundry, you little. . . . " You see, we had to wash our clothes in a tub with a washboard. As I was sobbing, I looked up. I could see my brother George just killing himself laughing.

"After you change, I want you to clean up this mess," she yelled. I was so angry at my mother. What she had just done did not make any sense to me.

The transformation from a trapping economy to mill work created new family stresses. Economic hardship pressed upon parents and children alike; food could not be wasted. Since time immemorial salmon, which appears in Lake Babine each summer, has been the traditional staple of the Lake Babine First Nation diet. Families at Pendleton Bay netted salmon and then dried and canned it in amounts large enough to last all winter. Dry staples, purchased at the Hudson's Bay Company stores in the traditional villages or from a small store at Pendleton Bay, supplemented the traditional bush foods. For most families these goods were relatively expensive, and for parents as concerned about their children as Rose's parents were, waste was a major concern.

I learned very quickly how to cook. There was an incident when I burnt the rice. I remember how angry my dad was. "Do you know how much food costs?" Let's just say that against my will I have acquired the taste for burnt rice. Yes, I had to eat the whole thing. My parents did not believe in wasting food.

It was difficult for children to understand the tensions felt by their parents. Rose's experiences were by no means unusual, for nearly everyone in the community faced the same constraints and had been influenced by Euro-Canadian notions of punishment and self-discipline. Children and adolescents were attracted to popular culture, which created further tensions between themselves and their parents and grandparents.

We weren't allowed to watch too much television. Our bedtime was at 8:00 p.m. But on the weekends, and some weeknights, we were able to stay awake later than that. I remember my sisters and I used to get up on the table and pretend we were go-go dancers, especially when the *Ed Sullivan Show* was on. We used to say that we would be stars one day. We would name off the stars that we wanted to be like.

Rose, like her peers, felt a range of mixed emotions toward her parents. They delighted, as all children do, in the freedom of playing together when their parents left them alone.

I used to love it whenever they went out to socialize. They used to take us along and leave us in the car. Our treat was pop and chips. We used to play tag and hide-and-seek in the streets.

Rose did not attend the residential school, but a Catholic school in the village of Burns Lake. Her school experience granted greater opportunities than the schooling of her parents' generation. By the time she was a teenager, Rose was busy with her peer group, independently contributing to her family and her community through volunteer work and social events.

I enjoyed my teen life. For that is when a group of us got together and started a youth group. When the Immaculata School was in existence, the white people used to hold balls for every occasion. We would dress up as waitresses and serve drinks and food. We also used to hold concessions at the bingo every Friday. Bingo was only held once a week. With the money we raised, we would go on trips. We also had fun with bake sales, car washes, garage sales. We used to sing as a group in choir every Sunday. We were too exhausted from all of that hard work to run around at night. Not that we were allowed to, anyways.

With maturity, misunderstanding and resentment disappeared and ambivalent feelings deepened into understanding and respect. Rose understood the values of hard work and appreciated the care and training that underlay the strict discipline.

I really hated my parents and tried to figure out why they treated me so badly. I finally realized why Mom and Dad were so hard on me. I feel that I would not be here if it wasn't for them.

The community at Pendleton Bay did not remain for long; by the mid-1960s centralization of the logging industry and new harvesting technology forced many small mills to close. The Department of Indian Affairs, aware that Pendleton Bay mills would soon disappear, planned a second move for the Lake Babine First Nation, this time to Burns Lake, a small village lying outside Lake Babine First Nation traditional lands. The move, the government officials thought, would bring new prosperity to the people—jobs for the men, improved schooling for the children. Reluctantly, the people left the forests and lakes that had nurtured their ancestors. But the promises proved to be false; today unemployment remains high, social integration difficult, and educational achievement, while steadily improving, remains minimal.

The residential and reserve schools did not prepare parents for active involvement in their children's education. Nor has the contemporary integrated school met the community's vision of an appropriate education. Like the residential schools of the past, the curriculum of today is directed to non-aboriginal Canadians, while the schools themselves remain under non-aboriginal authority. Few opportunities to speak and study the language are offered in these schools; little is taught about traditions, and even less is experienced. Cultural differences in learning styles have not been transcended. Migration to Burns Lake has exacerbated intergenerational misunderstanding; grandparents pine for their traditional homelands, while young adults and their children settle into a village lifestyle removed from traditional economic rounds and opportunities to enjoy the lakes and forests. This has led to sadness and tensions in families and the elders' fear that the young generations have lost both respect for and understanding of time-honoured practices that made the Lake Babine family and

community strong. Central to the traditions of the past were ceremonies that celebrated womanhood and taught adolescent girls their maternal, social, and spiritual duties, all of which had been ridiculed by the missionaries as superstition or primitive. The consequences for Rose were disturbing.

Today, a girl's first menstruation and other traditions are not fully practised by any family, which perhaps explains the radical change within today's generation. Children are having children today. The schools are teaching the young ones about sex. If we ever thought about a boy it was confession on Sunday. The same with swearing. I remember [I was made to eat] soap and wanting to vomit. After that, I didn't even want to think about that swear word.

Today's children are the lost generation. White society has taken over and manipulated us. There is no curfew for the children. It has been tried, but they rebel. The children today stay up late. Many are in trouble with the law, and started to do drugs and alcohol. We even have teenagers getting pregnant at a very early age now. Where did things go wrong?

I remember attending the potlatch when I was young and before my mother died. We had to sit there for hours and hours. All of the children sat quietly listening to what was going on. Today that is not so. The children are tearing about the place.

Integration into the economic and social institutions of the dominant society also brings changes in cultural practices. Rose laments recent changes in the mourning traditions and rituals she knew as an adolescent 20 years ago, practices that later sustained her during the loss of her mother. Today, funeral and mourning rituals blend Lake Babine traditions of the *bah'lats* with Catholic practices. At death, the deceased is brought home to rest in the chapel on the reserve. The father's clan performs all the necessary rituals for caring for and watching over the body, the burial, and other necessary routine tasks. Following the funeral, the deceased's maternal clan hosts a *bah'lats*; the father's clan is repaid for its services as all the seated guests of the remaining clans witness the transactions. Traditionally, the entire community mourned; parties, bingos, and other entertainments were suspended. As communities have grown and developed economic institutions integrated into the regional political economy, cultural practices are adapted to a new sense of time and social obligations.

When a member of the family passed on, we had to wear black all year round. We did not have the TV or radio playing. There were a few times that I had to stay up late with my parents. I got a big smack across the back of my head if I was ever caught sleeping. My parents embedded into my head that I do not cry at another family's funeral, especially if they were not related to me. This was pretty hard for me, seeing that I am very emotional. I guess you could say that I was being constantly corrected.

Now a few of the families do not mourn for the whole year. Today it is all right to simply wear a tiny black ribbon on the arm. A female or a male used to be shunned for playing bingo before the year was up. But that does not stop them now.

The shift to a cash economy has accentuated individualism, which in turn introduces new perceptions of generous distribution of gifts and money at the *bah'lats*. Communal

production of food and other items from the traditional lands has dramatically declined, altering the tenor of extended-family relations. Reciprocal exchange of goods and services is no longer as obvious, nor is communal pooling of staple foods that elders recall from their youth. Significant obligations performed by the father's clan were traditionally honoured at the *bah'lats* by payments of articles harvested from the clan's land; more recently payment has been made in cash and goods. These goods, given generously, symbolized respect for the hereditary chiefs and appreciation for the mutual exchange of services and goods that unite the four clans into a strong community.

Today, however, other services are also paid for as clans and Houses take on new obligations for one another. Participation in the reciprocal exchange of services and goods can become expensive. In consequence, tensions within and between families rise as they juggle multiple obligations. The people can no longer rely on resources of their ancestral lands to carry out their mutual obligations. Resolution of these tensions is not easy. The demand for cash and consumer goods is, after all, the driving force of a capitalist society that coerces us all to be consumers. As Rose explains, consumerism and the personal accumulation of commodities violate the principles of family co-operation she learned from her parents.

Money has taken over the lives of the Indians. Everybody wants to get paid for something. We must get out of that trap. If your sister wants you to babysit or asks you to take her somewhere, you should not charge her. If your cousin or any relative needs a lift into town to purchase food you should not ask them for any money. If you catch a lot of fish, you should not sell it to your in-laws or your nephews.

Lake Babine First Nation resistance to the economic intrusions of colonialism reaches beyond idealistic statements about past practices. Their resistance to colonial impositions has been steadfast and is perhaps best symbolized by their responses to the *Indian Act,* which affected virtually all aspects of family relations. Sexist determinations of who constitutes a "status" or state-recognized Indian have been the most damaging.[4] Prior to 1985, Indian status and band membership rules (that is, registration in an Indian band as defined by the state) were sexually discriminating. Women, but not men, lost status when they married a spouse without status, whether their husbands were non-aboriginal or aboriginal. Patrilineal rules prevailed, so that these women could not transfer Indian status to their children. Status could pass only from the father to the children. Therefore, non-status women and women of any other racial origin gained status when they married a status man, and so did all the children of that marriage. Loss of status meant banishment from the First Nation community; when they lost status women were compelled to leave their home community and to give up any personal property on the reserve. They were denied access to family resources and refused the right of burial with their kin for themselves and their children.

The hardship thrust upon First Nations families by the sexist provisions of the *Indian Act* cannot be overstated. With the forced removal of some of their sisters, siblings found themselves alienated from one another and from nieces and nephews. The economic relations of extended families were weakened when Canadian law denied resource rights to the women stripped of their Indian status. The Lake Babine First Nation, for example, is one of many nations that rely on salmon as their staple food. Women of the matrilineal group commonly share the work of netting and preserving a year's supply; where the government enforced its ruling, smaller groups found it difficult to preserve adequate salmon, and, of course, the non-status sisters could not contribute through their own labour. Men were also enfranchised—that is, were stripped of Indian status and granted Canadian citizenship either because they so chose or because of several rules of the *Indian Act* regulating their place of residence and rights to education and professional careers.

Children who grew up away from their kin were deprived of their language and culture as well as the companionship and support offered by the extended family. Often they were rejected by white Canadians and unwelcome in their home communities.

> Life was not any better at school. You see, I was considered non-status. According to the government I was not an Indian. Talk about confusion. The white kids called me down and laughed at me for being Indian. Then the Indian [status] kids would taunt me and accuse me of acting white. Most of my school years were spent going home crying. I tried to seek comfort from my father. He finally explained that the government was very smart. They made up this rule that if anyone Indian was off the reserve for more than one year, he/she was automatically off the band list. This happened to my father. He was so angry. You see, there were no jobs on the reservations then. The men had to work off-reserve in another town. So, when Mom married Dad, she lost her status. Nobody had any answers as to why they were following the white man's rules.

First Nations women across Canada protested the sexist provisions of the *Indian*

Act that divided families and robbed women of their identity. Eventually, two women in eastern Canada took their complaints to the courts, which ruled against them. In 1980 Sandra Lovelace of Tobique, New Brunswick, turned to the international courts for justice. Realizing that it could not win, the Canadian government instigated changes to eradicate the offensive measures. Its first gesture, in 1981, was to issue a Governor General's proclamation allowing First Nations the right to opt out of the discriminatory provisions. The Lake Babine First Nation was the first to do so.

In 1985, the *Indian Act* was amended;[5] women who had lost status through marriage became eligible for reinstatement of status and band membership, and their children for status and band membership contingent upon their mother's band agreeing to recognize them. For the Lake Babine First Nation this meant a long-awaited reunification of many of their families. But it also meant greater demands upon their dwindling resources. State promises for adequate support proved illusory as the federal government retreated from social programs in fear of the burgeoning public debt and as popular sentiment shifted to a neoliberal ideology that rejects "special rights." Like all other First Nations, Lake Babine First Nation also faces the dilemma of not being able to freely define its own membership. Revisions to the *Indian Act* in 1985 did not eliminate the state's power to refuse the transmission of Indian status but merely redefined the conditions. Today, under a rule known as the "second-generation cutoff," children of mixed status–non-status parentage are unable to transfer status to their own children, which creates new tensions for the community. Families continue to be divided as resource-strained community governments face the dilemma of accepting residents for whom they cannot offer social and cultural services.

The struggle now is one of gaining self-government grounded in the traditional laws of the Nation, which place extended family relationships at the heart of Lake Babine society. The nation stands at a new threshold in family relations as the colonial legacy of patriarchy and paternalism is being confronted and resisted in new ways. An impressive housing program in the 1990s allowed many families to return to their home villages. Social and administrative services were expanded shortly afterward: social assistance, child welfare, and health programs are now under the Nation's own administration. The courts have recognized the jurisdiction of customary family law, which provides greater power to the Nation in determining how and when to intervene in individual families' lives. When the BC Court of Appeal affirmed legal plurality in 1993, customary adoption laws were affirmed, thereby re-establishing the legal and moral strength of traditional family relationships. Clearly some steps toward decolonization have been successful.

Nonetheless, the journey of Lake Babine families toward decolonization is not without its pitfalls. In 2002 the British Columbia government held a "treaty referendum," ostensibly to gather public direction regarding treaty negotiations. This controversial exercise posed eight questions as to what British Columbians as a whole would be willing to negotiate regarding self-government, treaty rights, resource rights, and so on. Although only a little more than one-third of the voters returned their ballots, the Liberal government took the results as a strong endorsement to curtail the powers of self-governance to "municipal powers." Should the provincial government succeed in this goal, Lake Babine Nation—along with all other First Nations in BC with the exception of the Nisga'a, which signed a treaty prior to the Liberal victory in 2001—will face continuing status as internal colonies in their own lands. The impact of political setbacks is exacerbated by the current decline of the region's resource-based economy. Unemployment, inflation, and withdrawal of provincial services are having a negative impact on the people as once again families look elsewhere for work and social opportunities.

Conclusion

C. Wright Mills argued in *The Sociological Imagination* that a historical perspective is indispensable when analyzing structural relations of power. Feminists assert that in order to conjoin "personal troubles" and "public issues," as Mills urges us to do, historical narratives must move beyond the history of the nation to the personal histories of the people of the nation. In this paper we have sought to do both. By linking the national history of the

racist and sexist colonial regime to the stories of Rose Johnny, we have attempted to explicate the colonial legacy that burdens First Nations people, in particular the women.

Rose's life experiences illuminate the intergenerational impact of colonial policies and practices that intrude into the very core of family relations. Personal narratives reveal the pain of colonial exploitation and the degradation of aboriginal families and thereby illustrate the *connections* between the political and the personal. Analysis of the specific colonial mechanisms that intruded upon the lives of Rose and her family—loss of traditional lands, removal from the homeland, residential schools, and the *Indian Act*—not only demonstrates the racist, sexist ideology that underlies assimilationist practices, but also portrays the strength of families coping with and resisting new intrusion into their way of life.

● Notes

1. For a personal account of life as a foster child see Leanne Green, "Foster Care and After," *Canadian Woman Studies/Les cahiers de la femme* 10 (2, 3); for a comprehensive survey of the consequences of welfare policies see Patrick Johnston, *Native Children and the Child Welfare System* (Toronto: Canadian Council on Social Development, in association with James Lorimer, 1983).
2. The family life of the Saik'uz whut'enne, a Yinkadinee nation to the east of the Lake Babine First Nation, has been described in several publications. See, for example, Bridget Moran, *Stoney Creek Woman: The Story of Mary John* (Vancouver: Tillacum Library, 1988); Bridget Moran, *Judgement at Stoney Creek* (Vancouver: Tillacum Library, 1990); Jo-Anne Fiske, "Carrier Women and the Politics of Mothering," in Gillian Creese and Veronica Strong-Boag, eds, *British Columbia Reconsidered: Essays on Women* (Vancouver: Press Gang, 1992).
3. Several European observers described the mourning rituals of widows and their condemnation of

these rituals, but apart from Father Adrian Morice failed to mention the restrictions placed upon widowers at the time of the wife's death and for a period of at least a year thereafter.
4. Several studies have been made of the impact of these provisions upon First Nations women and families. See, for example, Kathleen Jamieson, *Indian Women and the Law* in *Canada: Citizens Minus* (Ottawa: Advisory Council on the Status of Women/Indian Rights for Indian Women, 1978); Janet Silman et al., *Enough Is Enough: Aboriginal Women Speak Out* (Toronto: The Women's Press, 1987); Shirley Bear et al., "Submission for the Standing Committee on Indian Affairs and Northern Development. Bill C-31: A Comment on the Elimination of Sex-Based Discrimination in the Indian Act by the Women of Tobique Reserve" (unpublished manuscript, 1985); Lilianne Ernestine Krosenbrink-Gelissen, *Sexual Equality as an Aboriginal Right: The Native Women's Association of Canada and the Constitutional Process on Aboriginal Matters, 1982–1987*

(Saarbrucken, Germany: Breitenbach Verlag, 1991).

5. The amendments are popularly known as Bill C-31. Far from resolving the discriminatory issues, new ones were created for most First Nations, not the least of which has been the emerging practice of calling reinstated women "Bill-C31s," an expression that denigrates and implies a lack of legitimacy to their claims for full First Nations citizenship.

⬤ References

Anderson, Karen. 1991. *Chain Her by One Foot: The Subjugation of Native Women in Seventeenth Century New France.* New York, London: Routledge.

Bilharz, Joy. 1995. "First Among Equals? The Changing Status of Seneca Women." In Laura F. Klein and Lillian A. Ackerman, eds, *Women and Power in Native North America.* Norman, OK: University of Oklahoma Press.

Brown, Jennifer, S.H. 1980. *Strangers in Blood: Fur Trade Company Families in Indian Country.* Vancouver: University of British Columbia Press.

Byrne, Nympha, and Camille Fouillard, eds. 2000. *It's Like the Legend: Innu Women's Voices.* Toronto: Gynergy Books.

Deiter, Constance. 1999. *From Our Mother's Arms: The Intergenerational Impact of Residential Schools in Saskatchewan.* Toronto: United Church of Canada.

English-Currie, Vicki. 1990. "The Need for Re-evaluation in Native Education." In Jeanne Perreault and Sylvia Vance, eds, *Writing the Circle: Native Women of Western Canada.* Edmonton: NeWest.

Fiske, Jo-Anne. 1991. "Gender and the Paradox of Residential Education in Carrier Society." In Jane Gaskell and Arlene McLaren, eds, *Women and Education,* 2nd edn. Calgary: Detselig.

Frideres, James S. 1988. *Native Peoples in Canada: Contemporary Conflicts.* Scarborough: Prentice Hall.

Jenness, Diamond. 1943. *The Carrier Indians of the Bulkley River: Their Social and Religious Life.* Washington, DC: Smithsonian Institution, Bureau of American Ethnology; Anthropological Papers No. 25.

Knockwood, Isabelle. 1992. *Out of the Depths: The Experiences of Mi'kmaw Children at the Indian Residential School at Shubenacadie, Nova Scotia.* Lockeport, NS: Roseway Publishing.

Leacock, Eleanor Burke. 1980. "Montagnais Women and the Jesuit Program for Colonization." In Eleanor Leacock and Mona Etienne, eds, *Women and Colonization: Anthropological Perspectives.* New York: Praeger.

Miller, J.R. 1996. *Shingwauk's Vision: A History of Native Residential Schools.* Toronto: University of Toronto Press.

Milloy, John S. 1999. A *National Crime: The Canadian Government* and *the Residential School System 1879 to 1986.* Winnipeg: University of Manitoba Press.

Mills, C. Wright. *The Sociological Imagination.* Oxford, 1959.

Morice, Adrien G. 1889. "The Western Denes, Their Manners and Customs." Proceedings of the Canadian Institute, 3rd Series, Vol. VII, No. 1.

Stevenson, Winona. 1999. "Colonialism and First Nations Women in Canada." In Enakshi Dua and Angela Robertson, eds, *Scratching the Surface: Canadian Anti-racist Feminist Thought.* Toronto: Women's Press.

Van Kirk, Sylvia. 1980. *"Many Tender Ties": Women in Fur Trade Society, 1670–1870.* Winnipeg: Watson & Dwyer Publishing Ltd.

Chapter 23

Neoliberal dynamics in the economy—especially companies moving their jobs (and capital) overseas, but also the changing nature of jobs and conditions of employment and the weakening of protections on wage levels—have made for worse material conditions for making and sustaining families. Meanwhile, Canadian governments' neoliberal approach to policy, especially since the early 1990s, has weakened the social safety net in this country.

In this article, Kate Bezanson briefly reviews what neoliberalism has meant in the economy and for social policy. Then she examines what it has meant for families. To provide some sense of this, she describes several families who participated in one of two studies that involved interviews over time with samples of Ontario families, paying attention to the key problems they were dealing with when supporting themselves and their loved ones. What Bezanson's descriptions indicate is how some people negotiate difficult conditions ranging from poverty and daily economic insecurity to "care crises" (family members' needs for care when adults are not in a position to provide it). Bezanson examines how people draw on whatever resources and support they can find in their personal networks—including family and friends—and the consequences of relying on loved ones for help over extended periods of time.

Putting Together a Life: Families, Coping, and Economic Change, 1997–2008

Kate Bezanson

Putting together a life—a job, a family, a home, or a sense of community and belonging—happens in many ways and changes over time. People lose and find work; children are born and move away; marriages begin and end. Although each life that is joyfully put together or painfully comes apart is unique, it exists in particular circumstances that affect how people react, whom they turn to for support, and how they get what they need to survive. A huge number of factors in people's lives influence their chances of getting a good education, living a healthy life, being safe and free from harm, and having a sufficient income. In Canada, our lives are nested inside a range of policies, laws, services, and practices that make it easier or harder to buy homes, get income when unemployed, or get support for the work of caregiving. Our lives also depend on an economy that creates jobs from which taxes are paid and services delivered. So putting together a life, a seemingly individual act, happens within the confines of the social, economic, and political world.

In the mid-1990s and again in the mid-2000s, a team of researchers and I interviewed members of families living in Ontario about their experiences of putting together their lives. In the 1990s, major changes were taking place in Ontario under the Conservative government of Premier Harris. In the mid-2000s, a newly elected federal Conservative government under Prime Minister Harper also began to transform the social-policy landscape. Both periods were economic boom times, yet both periods were marked by significant changes in public spending and social policy. What is striking about these two periods is that, despite a booming economy, many families struggled to manage their work and personal lives. The cumulative changes in social, political, and economic policies and regulations made it harder for many families to put together a life.

This chapter describes the context in which people put together a living by exploring a broad economic process termed "neoliberalism." I review the kinds of changes in social supports and protections that have taken root since the 1990s. I then move to the stories of a variety of families that show what putting together the necessities of life looked like at different points in time. Finally, I turn to a discussion of what the future holds for families as economic recession lingers in Canada.

I. Economic Processes: Confronting Change[1]

The economic crisis that began in the fall of 2008 was devastating for many nations, and for many families. Jobs disappeared, industries were wiped out, houses were repossessed, and countries like Greece and Spain faced bankruptcy and massive unemployment. Governments responded by bailing out companies on the verge of bankruptcy and by attempting to stimulate the economy by pumping money into mainly public-works projects. These actions meant that governments generated public debts and now must confront paying them down by cutting services and public-sector jobs and/or raising taxes.

The crisis that unfolded in 2008 was predictable. Scholars and commentators generally agree that an economic approach that began to spread in the early 1970s and accelerated in the

1990s and 2000s was a root cause of the crisis (McNally 2011; Harvey 2010). This approach is called neoliberalism. As we explore the experiences of families living through social and economic change in two different periods, we will see some of the ways in which this approach came to be applied to public and private life. In order to identify its features in the stories of families, we must first give it shape.

Neoliberalism is an approach that elevates the free market and advocates individualism and individual rights over any collectivism or group rights. The kind of neoliberalism that we must grapple with in trying to understand the experiences of families is one rooted in the ideas of scholars associated with what has been called the Chicago School (see Braedley and Luxton 2011; Connell 2011). These thinkers were opposed to government intervention in the economy. They were anti-regulation in the sense that they argued that constraints on markets distorted them. They generally rejected the kinds of regulations developed in response to the current crisis, like banking and credit oversight. And they linked the neoliberal approach with democracy and silenced important public debates about market liberalization (see Lott 2007). Those who pointed to the effects of such markets on workers, communities, and cultures were often characterized as being against freedom and democracy. The ideas associated with neoliberalism came to be seen as common sense, and it became harder for people to question their logic or effects.

What made neoliberalism such a risky approach, leading to dislocation and eventually, crisis? Neoliberalism is about re-regulation, not de-regulation or self-regulation. Certain regulations—keeping wages low and making work more insecure, or making it easy to move capital out of countries—are a main part of the neoliberal project, but regulating *how* capital moves and how credit systems are overseen is generally viewed as constraining. As a result, almost everywhere, neoliberal policies were imposed by crisis and/or by force.

The basic neoliberal approach proceeded as follows through much of the 1980s, 1990s, and 2000s. A nation, say an African or a Latin American one, suffered an economic recession or crisis (there were many throughout this period). An international agency—usually the International Monetary Fund—would advance loans, tied to conditions. We can conceptualize these conditions as a form of neoliberalism in action because they hemmed in the choices available to governments and created markets that usually did not serve the needs or interests of the country receiving the loans. The conditions included cutting social spending (reducing government and social services), reducing regulations on industry and trade, usually focusing on export-led growth (producing and selling products on the world market, rather than encouraging local production of necessities for the local population), and generally discouraging policies and practices that were social investments (aside from infrastructure like roads for business purposes). Privatization—not collective ownership—was central to the conditions of the loans, so water, hydro, and sometimes education came to be delivered by for-profit companies as ways to put short-term cash into government coffers.

Beginning in earnest in the 1990s, many governments, including the Canadian and Ontario governments, promoted the idea that neoliberal policies would create better lives for most people. The stories of families in one Canadian province living in a period when these kinds of changes were unfolding, first in the 1990s and again in the 2000s, present a snapshot of how people manage the complexities and crises they face as social services

are cut, the nature of their work lives changes, incomes do not keep up with the cost of living, and processes of de- and re-regulation take hold.

II. Neoliberalism and the Welfare State in Canada

In Canada, in the 1990s in particular, the logic of neoliberalism was embraced as the federal and provincial governments faced a recession and began to privatize industries, cut social spending, and change labour laws. Government transfers and entitlements were cut: family allowances were eliminated; Employment Insurance was made less accessible and worth less money; and transfers to provinces for housing, welfare, health, and education were altered significantly (see Rice and Prince 2000). Provinces like Ontario cut by almost one-quarter the amount of monthly support for those receiving social assistance or welfare; amalgamated school boards, hospitals, and municipalities; and significantly weakened the rights of workers and trade unions (Bezanson 2006). Federally, there were some positive developments, such as the creation and expansion of the Canada Child Tax Benefit (Battle 2006, 2008), but there was virtually no sustained movement on child care and early learning (see Mahon 2006). In 2006, Canadians elected a minority Conservative government under the leadership of Prime Minister Harper. Despite inheriting a large budget surplus, this government spent this money in its first two years on a variety of cuts, including cuts to sales taxes and eliminating government agencies. Also eliminated were the agreements between the federal and provincial governments to create a system of national daycare. During the same period, the Ontario government, now under Liberal leadership, attempted to address the fact that child care was abandoned by beginning to roll out full-day kindergarten for four- and five-year olds.[2]

In people's work lives, a neoliberal logic also played out. We now live in what one sociologist called a "political economy of insecurity" (Beck 2000). The labour market of the 2000s was very different than the one of the 1970s and 1980s. Non-standard work—a term referring to work that does not match the post–World War II norm of a 40-hour per week full-time, full-year job—became increasingly common (see Stanford 2011; Vosko 2009). Beaujot (2000:129) asserts that by the mid-1990s, "only one-third of workers ha[d] what might be considered to be a typical pattern of one job, 35–48 hours per week, Monday to Friday during the day, working on a permanent basis for an employer at one place of work." The labour market in Canada since the 1990s has been characterized by significant increases in multiple job holding; part-time, temporary, casual/on-call jobs; and self-employment (Vosko 2000). In its important review of labour law, the Law Commission of Canada (2004:5) reflected on the problems with the rise of non-standard work:

> Among the problems associated with non-standard work are the following: poor pay, little job security, a lack of access to important statutory benefits and protections (such as Employment Insurance, employment standards protections, workers' compensation, the right to collective bargaining) and a lack of access to employer provided benefits such as dental, life and disability insurance.

As governments weakened labour-market protections and supports—making work lives more precarious—and as globalization altered the kinds of jobs and sectors in which people in Canada worked (increasing the service sector especially), the conditions under which most families were able to put together a living became more challenging. Moreover, women entered the labour market in record numbers, with 73 per cent of all "women with children less than age 16 living at home . . . part of the workforce" in 2009 (Ferrao 2010:10). About 73 per cent of employed women work full time, and women's and men's overall employment rates are similar (58.3 per cent for women and 65.2 per cent for men) (Ferrao 2010). At the same time, there remain huge inequalities in the labour market, and many of these have intensified during this period of neoliberal restructuring. Women and people of colour in particular are concentrated in low-wage, insecure, and often part-time work (Statistics Canada 2007; Galabuzzi 2006).

In Canada, two-earner families are the norm. In 2008, 68 per cent of couples were dual-earners (Marshall 2009:12). Yet the distribution of caregiving in the home is not equal (Duffy 2011). A dual-earner, female-carer model prevails (Bezanson 2006). What is particularly striking about this arrangement is that Canada has an abysmal record of investment in early childhood education and care (see OECD 2006). In 2008, for every 100 Canadian children ages 0–12 requiring daycare, there were regulated spaces for just over 18; in Ontario, there were regulated spaces for 13.6 (Beach et al. 2009). In terms of early childhood services, Canada ties with Ireland for last place among economically advanced countries (see Table 23.1). Further, the combined effects of the gutting of social welfare supports like Employment Insurance and the neoliberal push to get more people working have meant that work–life conflicts are especially high for women. Economic

Table 23.1 Early childhood services among economically advanced countries 2008

Benchmark	Number of benchmarks achieved	1 Parental leave of 1 year at 50% of salary	2 A national plan with priority for disadvantaged children	3 Subsidized and regulated child care services for 25% of children under 3	4 Subsidized and regulated child care services for 80% of 4-year-olds	5 80% of all child care staff trained	6 50% of staff in accredited early education services tertiary educated with relevant qualification	7 Minimum staff-to-children ratio of 1:15 in pre-school education	8 1.0% of GDP spent on early childhood services	9 Child poverty rate less than 10%	10 Near universal outreach of essential child care services
Sweden	10	✓	✓	✓	✓	✓	✓	✓	✓	✓	✓
Iceland	9		✓	✓	✓	✓	✓	✓	✓	✓	✓
Denmark	8	✓	✓	✓	✓		✓	✓	✓	✓	
Finland	8	✓	✓	✓		✓	✓	✓			✓
France	8	✓	✓	✓	✓	✓	✓	✓		✓	
Norway	8	✓	✓	✓	✓	✓		✓		✓	✓
Belgium (Flanders)	6		✓	✓	✓		✓			✓	✓
Hungary	6		✓		✓	✓	✓	✓		✓	
New Zealand	6		✓	✓	✓	✓	✓	✓			
Slovenia	6	✓	✓	✓		✓		✓			✓
Austria	5		✓		✓	✓		✓		✓	
Netherlands	5		✓		✓	✓	✓	✓			
United Kingdom*	5		✓	✓	✓	✓	✓				
Germany	4		✓				✓	✓	✓		
Italy	4		✓		✓	✓	✓				
Japan	4		✓		✓	✓					✓
Portugal	4		✓		✓	✓	✓				
Republic of Korea	4		✓			✓	✓				✓
Mexico	3		✓			✓	✓				
Spain	3			✓		✓	✓				
Switzerland	3				✓				✓	✓	
United States	3			✓			✓		✓		
Australia	2			✓			✓				
Canada	1						✓				
Ireland	1						✓				
Total benchmarks met	**126**	**6**	**19**	**13**	**15**	**17**	**20**	**12**	**6**	**10**	**8**

*Data for the United Kingdom refer to England only.

Source: UNICEF, "The Child Care Transition", Innocenti Report Card 8, 2008. UNICEF Innocenti Research Centre, Florence.

insecurity was already widespread even in the pre-2008 economy. The logic of the neoliberal restructuring of work and the welfare state meant that more work was shifted onto families, and usually onto women within them. When services, like home care for the ill, were downloaded to lower levels of government or cut entirely, the need for the care did not disappear, but was usually absorbed by women's unpaid work. As British economist Diane Elson (1998) has argued, this assumes that women's unpaid labour is infinitely elastic and can expand to meet needs given various states of social investment. The result is not simply much greater stress, anxiety, and imbalance in people's lives, but also a marked deterioration in the most important relationships in people's lives (see Bezanson 2006; Luxton 2006). Relying on loved ones for care can strain these relationships. Some carework simply does not get done, and the consequences are dire. The processes of neoliberalism as they unfolded in Canada in the 1990 and 2000s, then, left many families in a precarious and stressed position before the market crash.

III. Case Studies: Putting Together a Life

Two different studies, involving repeat interviews with members of families in Ontario, illustrate the ways in which families put together their lives in the context of changing economic climates, social supports, and employment conditions. The first study, called *The Speaking Out Project (SOP),* was a longitudinal study that tracked 41 families over almost four years (from 1997 to 2000), as the effects of neoliberal policies took hold in the province of Ontario. Almost all of these participants were interviewed four times.[3] A team of researchers generated a sometimes

joyful but often heartbreaking picture of the ways in which the series of changes in social, economic, and political policies piled on top of one another and often compounded problems in people's lives. In 2006, with a team of different researchers, I began longitudinal interviews with participants from 49 households, again in Ontario, with significant paid work and caregiving responsibilities.[4] These participants were interviewed twice. The study, called *Ensuring Social Reproduction (ESR),* aimed to uncover the gaps and tension in social and labour market policies and how these played out in people's day-to-day lives. *Ensuring Social Reproduction* began interviewing members of families shortly after the election of the Harper government, and captured some of the effects on families of early economic and social policy changes, as well as some changes in provincial social policy. Both studies were attentive to the realities that many families have multiple sources of income (wages, tax benefits, student loans, and so on) and tracked changes to income sources beyond wages. Both studies also attended to the ways in which people transformed their incomes into the necessities of life.

The *SOP* oversampled low-income households, while the *ESR* study oversampled middle-income households. About half of the members of families interviewed for the *SOP* resided in the Greater Toronto Area, with the remainder drawn from a wide spectrum of regions in the province. For the *ESR*, participants were selected from four locations in Ontario: Niagara (17), the Greater Toronto Area (18), Central-north Ontario (13), and Eastern Ontario (1). In both studies, we made efforts to include rural as well as urban households. A brief description of each study follows, then we move to the stories of those interviewed.

Speaking Out Project 1997–2000[5]

The *SOP* involved a diverse sample of households, representing a range of family forms, income backgrounds and income sources, locations, and characteristics (Neysmith, Bezanson and O'Connell 2005; Bezanson 2006). As Table 23.2 below shows, many lived in two-parent households. Sixty per cent of the households in this study were low income, 37 per cent were middle income, and only 2 per cent were high income.[6] The primary source of income for 60 per cent of these households was from employment, while the remaining 40 per cent drew their income from sources such as Employment Insurance, student loans, or social assistance. In this study, as in Canada in general, single mothers, visible minorities, and Aboriginal peoples were overrepresented in the low-income category (Bezanson 2006:13). Twenty per cent of participants self-identified as members of non-white racialized minorities, 8 per cent identified as Aboriginal, 6 per cent as having a disability, and 8 per cent identified as GLTBQ. Almost 13 per cent stated that their first language was not English.

Table 23.2   Household Type, 2000

Household Type	Number	Percentage (rounded)
Two-parent	16	39
Lone-parent	10	24
Single, no children	7	17
Mixed generation	3	7
Couples (opposite and same sex), no children	3	7
Housemates, no children	2	5
TOTAL	41	99

Source: Adapted from Bezanson (2006:18).

Ensuring Reproduction Study, 2006–2008

Using a snowball sampling technique, we selected participants who lived in 49 households from a range of income backgrounds, household structures, geographic locations, ethnic/cultural origins, and caregiving types. We oversampled people with children under age six, and women who were pregnant so that we could track them as they made decisions about parental leaves and child care. We also interviewed people who were providing significant elder care.

Of the 49 households, 30 had significant child care responsibilities, 16 had significant elder care responsibilities, and 3 had both significant child and elder care responsibilities. The structure of the households also varied. As Table 23.3 below shows, most lived in two- parent households. Income varied from very low to very high. Table 23.4 shows the income distribution for the 49 households, for 2006. As a point of comparison, in Canada in 2006, average income after tax for families was $67 500 (Statistics Canada 2009).

Participants self-reported their ethnic and cultural heritage. Twelve per cent identified as having Aboriginal ancestry, 6 per cent identified as French Canadian, 5 per cent as African, 6 per cent as South Asian, with 6 per cent listing

Table 23.3 Household Structure, 2006

Household Structure	Number	Percentage (rounded)
Two parent	34	69
Lone-parent	4	8
Multigenerational	9	18
Other	2	4
Total	**49**	**99**

Table 23.4 Household Income, 2006[7]

Income Range	Number of Households	Percentage (rounded)
Below LICO[8]	9	18
Marginally above LICO (within $5000 per annum)	5	10
Middle income (> $5000 above LICO to $100 000 taking into account community and household size)	25	51
High Income (>$100 000)	10	20
Total	**49**	**99**

other identifications such as Jewish or Anglican. Fourteen per cent identified as "Canadian," 6 per cent as "Caucasian," 6 per cent did not respond, and the remaining participants (a little over 38 per cent) cited Eastern, Southern, or Northern European ancestry.

IV. Living through Social and Economic Change: Stories from the Studies

The collection of stories reveals a mixed and layered picture of love and devotion to children, parents, or friends alongside stress, sleeplessness, and worry. They depict the kinds of crises, such as finding and keeping good child care, that can make or break paid-work decisions and options. They also reveal that control over paid work is a crucial element for women in particular in order to meet caregiving roles.

Social supports, especially extended kin providing assistance with unpaid work, were very significant in managing multiple roles. To illustrate how families cope, we explore four quite different stories.

We begin with Ashley and Rosa, a multigenerational household in Toronto who faced near-constant want, and whose relationship was the casualty. Jade and her family's story gives a glimpse of the challenges of putting together a living in the Niagara region while on maternity leave and, subsequently, re-entering the labour market with a small child in need of care, two school-aged children, and two careers. Monica and Randy, in a mid-sized southern Ontario city, struggled with a life-altering workplace injury that left them and their children vulnerable and insecure. They adapted by sharing a home with Monica's mother, opening a home daycare and trying to see the opportunities in the midst of crisis. We conclude with Tamara and Tony, a couple in Eastern Ontario coping with health crises of older parents, while maintaining two careers and providing support to children and grandchildren. All of the stories show fragility and strength, but they also reveal how social supports and social policies can bolster or undermine the capacity to put and hold together the necessities of life.

Ashley and Rosa (*SOP* 1997–2000)[9]

Ashley, an African-Canadian woman in her mid-fifties, and Rosa, her 33-year-old daughter, moved in together in order to pool finances. While not well off, both Ashley and Rosa had full-time jobs in Toronto. Their situation deteriorated after Rosa became pregnant and, because of complications with her pregnancy, could no longer work. Ashley also lost her job due to funding cutbacks at a community agency. Rosa applied for social assistance and was enrolled in a full-time upgrading program while Ashley continued to look for full-time employment. Ashley volunteered for a seniors group, a community association, and for arts organizations.

Both Ashley and Rosa tried to conceal their financial difficulties. This often meant isolating themselves from others, including other family members, making them more dependent on each other. The labour market in Ontario in the mid-1990s was just beginning to improve, and when we first met, many social service agencies were experiencing cuts in their funding. Ashley and Rosa talked of having their utilities cut off, of buying cheaper cuts of meat and produce, and of "going without" to make ends meet. As their financial situation worsened, mother and daughter began to share personal belongings, such as winter

boots. While they were each other's primary source of support, they reluctantly had to ask for help from family and friends.

Mother and daughter talked of feeling indebted and ashamed at having to accept the family's charity; at times they felt resentful of the judgments that sometimes accompanied this support. They both sensed that the mood of the province was changing to one of less compassion for those who fell on hard times, Rosa commented:

> During the day I won't listen to [radio stations] 640 or 1010. Why should I listen to something that's going to be bashing me? It's like buying the *Sun* paper. Why am I going to buy a paper that's going to give me more concern, anxiety? I just don't. Things that drive me nuts, I just try and cut myself off from.

Ashley and Rosa were heavily indebted as a result of student loans and other debts, and found the household carrying costs were becoming impossible to maintain. Both believed they had sunk as low, financially and emotionally, as they could. Rosa commented:

> You always have this feeling of anxiety, of some type of doom and gloom going to happen immediately. You can see yourself being okay in the future, but the immediate thing is just waiting for something to fall apart. Every time somebody rings that doorbell, what next?

Frustrated with their financial situation and overwhelmed by their debt load, Ashley and Rosa's relationship began to fray. The mutual support they provided to one another began to unravel. By the third interview, Ashley and Rosa were no longer living together, and each was accusing the other of not carrying her own weight. The financial hardship that brought them together ultimately drove them apart. Ashley described the final days of their shared living arrangement as strained:

> I told Rosa, I said, "I just, I can't take it any longer," and I couldn't. We were just arguing and it was like very tense. She wasn't paying her fair share. All of my money was going, all of the food I was buying. I ended up paying most of the hydro bill and the cable bill. I didn't have the money . . . I just said, "this is ridiculous." From about the sixth of the month, I would pay all the food from there. Where the heck was her money? I don't know, I was paying all of it, and I'm not going to not buy food. I spoke to my eldest daughter . . . "Why don't you just take Rosa and Mary [Rosa's daughter]?" And she said, "I'll think about it."

Rosa also attributed their break-up to strained finances:

> It's almost like a married couple. When money and stuff comes into play, that's the big, that's one big argument. Do you know what I mean? And it gets worse, money always gets worse. The payments, it was just like trying to dodge, and trying not to get caught—give them a rubber cheque. I think that was the proverbial straw.

After a bitter parting of ways, Rosa rented the basement of her sister's home. While the arrangement proved to be mutually beneficial in terms of reciprocal child care, Rosa was unhappy. She continued to pay market rent and hide her financial situation from her sister. Her sister was oblivious to Rosa's frequent use of local food banks or her strategy of pawning personal possessions to make the rent. Her sister was so unaware of Rosa's financial situation that she asked Rosa to act as co-signer for a mortgage. Rosa was less successful in hiding her poverty from her daughter. Rosa talked of how difficult it was trying to maintain a facade that everything is fine:

> Something [my daughter] said just totally broke my heart, "Mommy, how come you never have any money?" And I was just like, oh God, it's the last thing you want to put your kid through.

Now on their own, mother and daughter felt increasingly less able to cope with daily pressures. For Rosa this meant she stopped taking an interest in herself:

> If I could see my way out, then [it's worth it] but it's when you have no light some days. Like I said, I don't care. Like going to the doctor and stuff, and just looking normal. I don't care if I have dandruff anymore, it's good enough—you don't have to sit beside me, you don't have to talk to me. That's how I feel about this.

The daily grind of poverty continued to wear them down, and it seemed as though things would continue to get worse:

> I feel like I'm going to explode walking around with ten cents in my pocket, but I just do it, I do it because I have to do it. It's my job to do it. If I was by myself I could do crazy things, but I don't, I can't do that to my daughter.

Ashley moved back to her home town and applied for social assistance. Income security continued to be her biggest preoccupation.

Since her falling-out with Rosa, familial relations were fraught with conflict and, for a period of months, Ashley did not have any contact with her children. She felt even more cut off because she couldn't afford to have telephone service. Ashley enrolled in an Employment Insurance–funded business program and began a plan to start her own business. While she doubted that she would be able to earn a decent living from the business, she enjoyed what she was doing and felt she was making a worthwhile contribution to her community. She continued to look for full-time work.

Since separating from her mother, Rosa was determined to become more financially independent. She successfully sought child-support payments from her daughter's father and dropped out of the upgrading courses offered through social services when they yielded no work opportunities. Rosa approached a temporary agency and was soon working short administrative stints in offices across Toronto. Luckily, one of these short-term placements became a full-time job. Rosa was able to move off of assistance and out of her sister's home. By the end of the study she and her daughter were living in a one-bedroom apartment in Toronto. She remained hopeful that her job and housing situation would be stable.

Jade[10]

In 2006 when we first met, Jade, a white woman in her thirties, was living with her husband, two sons (7 and 9 years of age), and infant daughter. Jade was on maternity leave from a permanent, full-time retail position. Jade had an arrangement with her employer in which she worked part-time while on maternity leave to, as she put it, "bank hours" because she anticipated that she would need days off to

care for sick children and go to appointments when she returned to work. She began banking hours when her daughter was four weeks old. Her job had no benefits and she did not get paid for sick days. Her husband also worked in the service sector full time, 40 to 60 hours per week. He had no dental or health benefits associated with his job and Jade said that his job was not terribly secure. Their combined household income for a family of five was about $60 000 for 2006. Jade had enough paid work hours to qualify to Employment Insurance (EI) while on maternity leave. EI covered 55 per cent of earnings up to a maximum of a little over $400 per week. For Jade, this meant that for her year of leave, she received about $10 000. She decided to take the leave herself instead of sharing it with her spouse because she considered her job to be more secure and because her husband earned more money. While on leave, she worried and tried to plan about what she would do for child care when she returned to work full time.

> . . . just for [the baby], the only person I know is like 30 bucks a day, and that's a lot. My pay cheque is only . . . under four hundred dollars a week . . . I'm gonna do about half of it in child care. Just over a hundred and fifty a week, just for her, and then there will be something for the boys for after-school care.

The year she gave birth to her daughter, the Harper government was elected. They eliminated the proposed national system of child care and replaced it with a *taxable* monthly cheque worth $100 per child under six. Jade said the money—after taxes about $60 for her household—was handy for diapers. It could not help cover the cost of child care much less allow her not to work for pay.

By the second interview in 2007, Jade had changed jobs. Her employer, for whom she had been banking hours, did not have a full-time position for her because the business was not doing well. She took a position in another company that paid a bit more and had benefits and daytime hours that more easily accommodated child care. She continued to work on Saturdays at her previous job, extending her workweek to six days. Her spouse stopped working on Saturdays to provide child care, but often worked 12-hour days until 8 pm to make up for lost work time. So Jade managed pick-ups, sports, homework, meal preparation, and bedtime. Getting child care for her one-year-old was very hard, as most centres don't have spaces for children under 18 months of age, despite the fact that maternity leave lasts 12 months. When she did find a space for her daughter with a home-based provider, she lamented that her prediction about the cost of child care was accurate: "Half of my paycheque every week . . . goes to child care," she said. On days when her daughter was sick, she had to pay for daycare her daughter was not attending *and* hire a sitter to care for her daughter, thus using her entire paycheque for the day. She reflected that despite this she needed to work. During her maternity leave, she told us:

> I had to borrow money from my aunt because our gas was disconnected. Twice. Which was hard . . . Christmas was stressful until we had the flood . . . that helped actually . . . because a lot of the things that we got paid [from the insurance company], like that got damaged, we didn't replace. [Borrowing money was] embarrassing. Stressful. Hard. Very hard. Because my income wasn't a lot to begin with, so when it's cut in half, it was nothing every two weeks.

Even with two adults working full-time, they live paycheque to paycheque. Jade recounted a story of her husband not getting a paycheque one night when it was expected and not being able to buy groceries.

Jade does the bulk of the household work, manages the household finances, and arranges child care. She barters and trades household items and clothes, and worries constantly about meeting expenses. She notes that despite their total household income, she cannot pay all the bills each month so she alternates and carries household debt. She finished the last interview saying that "I wish we could be like Quebec and have . . . $7 a day child care . . . That is under an hour's worth of work, paid for me. . . . I'd actually *make* some money, instead of just squeak[ing] by."

Randy and Monica (*SOP,* 1997–2000)[11]

Randy and Monica were a white couple in their early thirties who lived in a medium-sized community with their three children. At the time of the first interview, their ages were 14, 7, and 5 (the eldest was Monica's child from a previous relationship). They lived in Monica's mother's home, which had an apartment in the basement. Monica ran a home daycare business. This housing arrangement was central to their ability to manage on their modest household income. When we first met, Randy had returned to school to finish grade 12 and was receiving Workers' Compensation for a back injury that left him with a permanent disability. Money was their biggest concern throughout the four rounds of interviews.

The crisis of Randy's injury, and his subsequent depression, was a transition in the lives of the members of this household. Randy had done physical labour. After his accident, he did not work for pay for three years. Their children were very small at that time. Randy had applied for Workers' Compensation Benefits (WCB) shortly after his injury, but the processing of his claim took some time. Monica explained that they applied for social assistance in the intervening period:

> We were waiting for his compensation to come in. We kept calling and calling Compensation and asking "When is the cheque going to be sent?" We finally got this one lady that talked to us very nicely, and didn't say, "It's in the mail." She said, "I don't know." I said, "Look, we have no money, we have three kids, we've got to do something here," and she said, "If you call your social services, there is an emergency welfare thing that they do." So I called and they said, "Oh yeah, no problem." A lady came down and talked to us, and she said, "That's what it's there for."

Randy's recovery period dramatically changed this couple's relationship. Randy noted that up until his injury, his expectation was that his wife would do most of the work of maintaining the home and raising their children. He was working long hours and was "money-focused." "I always saw myself as the bread-winner," he said. "I support my family and if I can't, that makes me feel bad . . . me not being able to has made us closer than we were before I hurt my back." After his accident, during his convalescence, he spent most of his time caring for his kids. He felt that this was a major life shift for him; later he tried to organize his paid work around spending time with his family. He explained the change in the household division of labour after his accident, noting that he had to adjust to Monica being the primary wage earner:

It's sort of changed over the last three years since I've been off. I've always encouraged Monica to be home to raise our kids. Because she had in-home day-care, we saw the kids take their first steps, say their first words and I didn't want us to miss that for our kids. When I hurt my back, Monica ended up going to take a job in a factory and I did the cooking and cleaning, the laundry, the housework, whatever. Well, our son Shawn did a large part of it because whatever I couldn't bend down and get, he picked up.

While receiving WCB, Randy completed his grade 12 equivalency. He spent a lot of time doing homework with his kids and, despite the fact that he felt limited and frustrated by his disability, he saw it as something of a blessing because it put him on a new path with his family and his life.

Monica's perspective on the situation was somewhat different. Having a full house, with Randy around when he was not working, was stressful for Monica. She explained that Randy was much easier to be around when he was doing some paid work:

> He's the happiest person on the earth when he's working, and he's okay for the first day or two when he's not working. But after that he gets cranky. He nit-picks at everything. He's yelling at the kids. Nothing is done right. I think, "Just go away! This house has been like this for years, and like now all of a sudden it's not right and the house is a pig-sty." He goes on and on. It's because he's getting frustrated, so he takes it out on everybody else, which isn't fair to the kids.

Although his attitude was positive about his accident, money was a significant concern.

In 1997, Randy received about $14 000 from WCB, while Monica made between $6000 and $8000 per year from her home daycare business. Randy's benefits were terminated in 1998; later that year he received a settlement. Randy would have preferred to receive substantial training that would equip him to get work in a new field. He drew on racialized stereotypes to explain his position, asserting that services and supports were hard to access for white men like himself:

> I'm not receiving any benefits. They give you six months after your training to find a job, and then your benefits are done. My main concern is they didn't give me any training. I went back to school and got my Grade 12. And so did everybody! I'm competing with these people. I can't do excessive bending, lifting, sitting, twisting, so everything that I enjoy doing I can't do. That's why I've accepted this job at a call centre. I tried to get free training through compensation; they basically told me if I didn't speak English and I worked in a factory my whole life then they would be willing to put me through university for four years. They told me that to my face.

Randy had a great deal of difficulty at the call-centre job because of his back, as he could not sit for long periods of time. Also, the hours were such that he did not see his kids very often. In 1998, he quit the call-centre job and began doing summer work in landscape design. He also worked part-time in a small business to earn some additional money.

The biggest challenge for Monica in providing home daycare was getting the parents of the children who pay her privately to pay her on time, or at all. Although there was slightly more predictability in her work, because she was considered self-employed, Monica did not have a great deal of security: "If I got sick for a long time [like Randy], I would lose all my [daycare] kids."

Monica found it hard to draw a line between her paid work and her home life. Her hours were very long and the schedule was hectic. Living in the same home as Monica's mother was also a source of both support and tension. Though Monica and Randy maintained a separation in their lives between themselves and her mother, the proximity of living quarters meant maneuvering so as not to get in each other's way. Despite a certain lack of privacy, both Randy and Monica acknowledged that they could not have managed without this kind of housing arrangement. They paid for upkeep, utilities, and property taxes. In addition, Monica ran her business from the home, which had a large yard and lots of room. Because the big-ticket item of housing was covered, their biggest expense was food, including food for the daycare children.

In the final interview Monica and Randy said that they were feeling more secure financially. Randy explained their situation: "Monica's getting a couple of extra kids in her daycare. My business is increasing a little. We're getting by. We're the working poor again."

Tamara and Tony, *ESR* 2006–2008

Tony and Tamara's story is one of managing a series of health-care crises, and coping with resultant physical, social, and emotional dislocation. This couple, who were in their sixties, were in an enviable financial and professional position, yet they were still overwhelmed by the work of caring for Tony's parents. To get the kind of care Tony's father needed after a stroke, they had to draw upon their friends and contacts in the health-care field to get the quality and type of support needed.

Tony and Tamara are a high-income, professional couple, with three adult children and several grandchildren. They live in a medium-sized city in southern Ontario, and have unionized, salaried positions with employee benefits. They both have a good deal of control over their working conditions and working time, though both work very long hours. At the time of the interviews, they provided child care for their grandchildren once or twice a week. In the first interview, they were coping with Tony's father's major health crisis, the hardship of trying to provide care and support while travelling long distances, and the subsequent chaos of moving both of his parents from their home community to theirs in order to get better care and to be able to assist his mother. In the first interview, Tony and Tamara described what happened with Tony's father:

Tony: The situation this summer, to give the background, [was that] my father had an operation in May. And they live up in [a small city in Northern Ontario], so it wasn't . . . regular day-to-day contact to maybe have a good assessment for what his state was. And he was to have this operation and he had one that was supposed to be, quote "easy," in fact the surgeon's comment was, "Oh this'll be a piece of cake." Any surgeon says that from now on, get off the table, put your clothes on, run, get out of the hospital. He obviously . . . had success for 180 operations before this one, so I guess he had some expectation, but things went badly on the table. My father had a major heart attack the next day. And about a week later . . .

Tamara: About a week later he had a stroke. . . .

Tony: . . . He went from being somebody who was capable of doing things for himself, to effectively, well, we're not sure even now, but he may be at best, wheelchair bound . . .

Tamara: And he will have short-term memory loss permanently . . . and then there are issues of eating . . . his swallowing and his speech.

The two had been driving more than five hours each way, every weekend for several months, in order to care for Tony's father and his mother, who was unable to cope with his father's health crisis. They both used all of their vacation and sick time, and their own health began to suffer. Finally, through contacts and connections—"pulling some strings" as Tamara put it—they were able to get Tony's father into a residential health-care facility that was well equipped to manage his multiple health-care needs. Tamara reflected on what happened next:

We got him [Tony's dad] down here. We thought we had your mom's approval, she seemed to be very excited about it, and so then the whole deal was that she would move down here [to our area] as well, because they were talking about doing this for five years and never did . . . and, now we find out after having moved here that she's *extremely* unhappy and it was the worst thing that's ever happened to her.

They found an apartment for Tony's mom that was close to her husband's facility, and walking distance to all amenities. Tony's mother's depression and despair seemed to increase over the course of the interviews: she barely fed herself, she was overwhelmingly negative, and she paid little attention to self-care. Tony and

Tamara, in addition to daily and sometimes multiple trips per day to care for Tony's father, took on the tasks of managing Tony's mother. They handled everything from groceries to meal preparation to self-care. It was clear to Tony and Tamara that Tony's mother would not be able to provide care for Tony's dad if he recovered sufficiently to return home, so they began the work of looking at nursing homes for him.

Tony and Tamara knew that they were good at handling problems. They were both first-born children, and reflected on the fact that they were often called on to solve problems and crises. Their competence came at some cost to them, however. Tamara said that she never thought she would feel so relieved to go to work; it seemed like a break in comparison to the constant caregiving she had been providing. Tony wished that there were resources to make it easier to cope with such problems. He said:

> Nobody advertises "caring for elderly parents, they're getting difficult, call 1-800." There are 1-800-beat-cancer and 1-800-heart-disease and things like that . . . but, in terms of caregiving for elderly people who are just getting old and frail . . .

Both Tony's and Tamara's health was of concern, and the emotional stress they were under exacerbated these problems. Tony took blood pressure medication, and his nurse practitioner cautioned him to watch his blood pressure closely "because of what's going on," Tamara relayed. "[The nurse said] 'you could be setting yourselves up for strokes yourselves.'"

Between the first and second interviews, Tony's father took a turn for the worse, and died. Tony's grieving took a back seat to caring for his mother and dealing with his father's estate. Tamara said:

> It's very overwhelming. . . . Tony's been very, very patient with her [his mum] and been really the person to handle all of this stuff with her agreements for things in terms of the banking . . . getting address changes done, things changed from his name to her name and all that kind of stuff . . . it's draining for the person who's bereaved.

His mother continued to deteriorate. She was increasingly angry, volatile, and fragile. She refused to accept help from "strangers," such as meals-on-wheels, and resisted social engagement. Although she exhibited physical and to some extent, mental health needs, she asserted that she would not see doctors because, as she said, "doctors will kill you." Tony was candid in his assessment of his mother's state. He said that he didn't know if "she's at the point where she realizes that she needs to make changes and learn how to live, or if she's simply [going to] give up and die."

Tony and Tamara were emotionally drained in our last interview. Tamara reflected that they needed to take some time for themselves. She drew an analogy between her son's allergies as a child and the stress that they have coped with:

> Our son had allergies and they used to say that you could handle grasses or you could handle mould but you put the two of them together and you would cross the threshold of your tolerance. You can't deal with it, it's too much, and I think we were getting to that point. That stress levels were getting really high.

Tamara said that she had pulled back from providing support to Tony's mother.

It's mostly Tony [now]. . . . I found that in order for me to not get upset about things, it was better for me, the way I could reduce stress was to back off sometimes from some of these things and realize that he [Tony] needed to be doing stuff for his mum but we didn't need to get tension between us about how much time was going [to her]. . . . When I was there [with his mum] all the time, and I heard [her negativity], Tony and I would bicker about it or rehash it. In some ways, I'm letting him be thoughtful about how much I can handle of the stress. . . . In order to help him, I need to not be too stressed . . . so he does the majority [of his mother's care].

At the end of the last interview, Tamara reflected on the fact that her own parents were beginning to require care. She said that she is not fretting about it, and that she has learned that they need to take time for themselves and to relax.

V. Conclusion

Policies and regulations circulate through each of the stories profiled in this chapter. The kinds of work people have, how much it pays, and how flexible or reliable it is shape the quality and character of people's non-work lives. Their work lives also shape their access to other supports: maternity leave, employment insurance, extended benefits, and so on. Jade's family's story, for example, is a typical one for those interviewed with middle incomes in the sense that concerns about money and balancing work with caregiving are all being juggled at once. Despite their financial challenges and difficulties with child care, however, they fared better than many middle-income households and most low-income households. Because

self-employment rose considerably since the 1990s in Canada, fewer Canadian women and men had insured earnings under the EI system and thus *did not qualify* for EI benefits for maternity/parental leaves. Jade had health benefits at her new place of employment, which offset some household costs. Jade and her spouse also both had full-time hours mostly at one place of employment, though both worked very long hours to make enough money to meet their five-person family's needs. Their work was more *standard looking* than many Canadians' work, but it was characterized by Jade having two jobs and her husband working 12-hour days so that she could work a 6-day week. The supports that they needed—quality, affordable child care, well-paid parental leaves, more flexible work arrangements—were not available to them. The legacy of neoliberal welfare restructuring and the effects of the last decade or so of changes in labour markets due to globalization left this family without a strong safety net as the economy teeters.

For other households, like Ashley and Rosa, or Monica and Randy, low income, injury, inadequate support from public assistance, and precarious labour market attachment, resulted in them turning to family for support. In Ashley and Rosa's case, relying on one another so heavily for so much tore apart their relationship. All internalized guilt and shame for their economic hard times. Those who had any experience with social assistance felt that they had to distance themselves from it and the public stereotypes that surrounded it; the discourse of individual responsibility so resonant in neoliberal politics penetrated deeply into these lives. In these stories and in most of the interviews conducted with parents of young children in both studies, high-quality, affordable child care stood out as critical to both child well-being and employment success.

Tony and Tamara stand out among those profiled here as their high income and significant control over their own working conditions and hours made it easier for them to weather the storm of the health-care crises they confronted. Yet this household still felt the effects of cuts to health care and health-related supports, and still needed to "pull strings" to get needed resources.

After decades of retrenchment of the Canadian welfare state and increased flexibility and precariousness in the labour market, Canadians faced the most recent economic recession with the lowest level of protection in the last century (Yalnizan 2009). One of the key features leading to the crash of 2008 was record levels of household debt. This debt load compounds and makes even more intractable the economic risks families face. Recent federal and provincial budgets underline the continuing crisis: wage freezes, layoffs, cuts in public spending, and privatization are all on the menu.

One of the questions that has emerged in Canada as this particular recession has taken hold is about the future of families. Many of the job losses since 2008 have been in traditionally male jobs. Some have gone so far as to call this a "he-cession" (Pelieci 2009). Will men, some wonder, become stay- at-home dads, and will roles reverse? While it may be the case that some men will do this, there are several problems with this logic and the question is too optimistic given the weight of evidence on the subject. This is the first recession in which women, and especially women with children, are already in the labour force in record numbers and most households rely on two incomes (Yalnizan 2009). In past recessions, women often were called *into* the labour market to offset income shortfalls. Women are already in the labour market and thus this kind of buffer is reduced. It may be more likely that youth are called into the labour market in greater numbers, returning to a family model of work more characteristic of the early part of the last century. Further, the weight of evidence from economics, sociology, and anthropology indicates that during periods of economic downturn, men do not in significant numbers take on a greater share of social reproduction (Scott 2008; Elson 1995). It would appear that without any real investment in child care, and given that the current session of Parliament has already seen the Harper government make significant changes to EI, the depth of the effects of income insecurity and family stress is only beginning to become plain. Successive neoliberal governments, who gutted income supports and labour regulations and failed to invest in care work and to regulate risky credit markets, have left families facing a fraught future in what remains a neoliberal political economy of insecurity.

● Notes

1. A version of the material presented in sections I and II appeared initially in Bezanson, Kate. (2011). "Neoliberalism, Families and Work–Life Balance," in N. Pupo, D. Glenday and A. Duffy (eds), *The Shifting Landscape of Work*. Toronto: Nelson.

2. Both the 1990s government of Mike Harris in Ontario and the 2006 onward federal Harper government used a variety of methods to limit public debate about changes in legislation and spending (Bezanson 2006; 2010). One of the first acts of the Harper government was to cut funding to equity-seeking agencies, such as court challenges and Status of Women Canada. These changes made it harder for people to challenge the logics of welfare state retrenchment.

3. Only two participating households dropped out of the study over the three-year period, but the number of

participant household units increased (from 38 in 1997 to 41 in 2000) because relationships ended and household units split (Bezanson 2006:16).

4. The funding for the 2006–2008 study came from SSHRC grant 410-2004-1786.

5. With permission from Fernwood Press, the material for this portion of the chapter is drawn from Neysmith, S., K. Bezanson, and A. O'Connell. (2005). *Telling Tales: Living the Effects of Public Policy.* Halifax: Fernwood.

6. Statistics Canada's Low Income Cut-Offs (LICOs) were used to define income categories. For 1998, they ranged from $11 839 for a single person living in a rural area to $45 634 for a family of seven in a large urban centre (Bezanson 2006:186, note 20). For this study, high income was defined as those households with more than double the average family income, while middle income fell between the LICO and the high income threshold (Bezanson 2006:186, note 20).

7. We followed Statistics Canada's definition of economic family in determining household categories, with

several deviations based on how people identified the composition of their households and the pooling of resources.

8. We used the 2006 Statistics Canada LICOs, which take into account community size and household size to determine low income.

9. Excerpted from Neysmith, S., K. Bezanson, and A. O'Connell. (1995). *Telling Tales: Living the Effects of Public Policy.* Halifax: Fernwood. With permission from the publisher.

10. Excerpted from Bezanson, Kate. (2011). "Neoliberalism, Families and Work–Life Balance," in N. Pupo, D. Glenday, and A. Duffy (eds), *The Shifting Landscape of Work.* Toronto: Nelson. With permission from the publisher.

11. Excerpted from Neysmith, S., K. Bezanson, and A. O'Connell. (1995). *Telling Tales: Living the Effects of Public Policy.* Halifax: Fernwood. With permission from the publisher.

● References

Battle, K. (2006). "Modernizing the Welfare State." *Policy Options*, April–May 2006: 47–50.

———. (2008). *A Bigger and Better Child Benefit: A $5,000 Canada Child Tax Benefit.* Ottawa: Caledon Institute of Social Policy.

Beach, J., M. Friendly, C. Ferns, N. Prabhu, and B. Forer. (2009). *Early Childhood Education and Care in Canada 2008.* Toronto: Childcare Resource and Research Unit.

Beaujot, R. (2000). *Earning and Caring in Canadian Families.* Peterborough, ON: Broadview Press.

Beck, U. (2000). *The Brave New World of Work.* Cambridge: Polity.

Bezanson, K. (2006). *Gender, the State and Social Reproduction.* Toronto: University of Toronto Press.

Braedley, S., and M. Luxton. (2011). "Introduction," in S. Braedley and M. Luxton (eds), *Neo-Liberalism and Everyday Life.* Montreal and Kingston: McGill–Queen's University Press.

Connell, R.W. (2011). "Understanding Neoliberalism," in S. Braedley and M. Luxton (eds), *Neo-Liberalism and Everyday Life.* Montreal and Kingston: McGill–Queen's University Press.

Duffy, A. (2011). "The Lengthening Shadow of Employment: Working Time Re-examined," in N. Pupo, D. Glenday, and A. Duffy (eds), *The Shifting Landscape of Work.* Toronto: Nelson.

Elson, D. (1995). *Male Bias in the Development Process.* Manchester: Manchester University Press.

———. (1998). "The Economic, the Political and the Domestic: Businesses, States and Households in the Organization of Production." *New Political Economy*, 3(2).

Ferrao, V. (2010). "Paid Work," in *Women in Canada: A Gender-based Statistical Report, 2010–11.* Ottawa: Statistics Canada.

Galabuzzi, G. (2006). *Canada's Economic Apartheid: The Social Exclusion of Racialized Groups in the New Century.* Toronto: Canadian Scholars Press Inc.

Harvey, D. (2010). *The Enigma of Capital.* New York: Oxford University Press.

Law Commission of Canada. (2004). *Is Work Working? Work Laws that do a Better Job.* Ottawa: Law Commission of Canada.

Lott, J.R. (2007). *Freedomnomics: Why the Free Market Works and Other Half Baked Theories Don't.* Washington: Regnery Publishing Inc.

Luxton, M. (2006). "Friends, Neighbours and Community: A Case Study of the Role of Informal Caregiving in Social Reproduction," in K. Bezanson and M. Luxton (eds), *Social Reproduction: Feminist Political Economy Challenges Neo-Liberalism.* Montreal and Kingston: McGill–Queen's University Press.

McNally, D. (2011). *Global Slump: The Economics and Politics of Crisis and Resistance.* Oakland: PM Press.

Mahon, R. (2006). "The OECD and the Reconciliation Agenda: Competing Blueprints," in J. Lewis (ed.), *Children in Context: Changing Families and Welfare States.* London: Edwin Elgar.

Marshall, K. (2009). "The Family Work Week," *Perspectives on Labour and Income*, April 2009, Ottawa: Statistics Canada.

OECD. (2006). *Starting Strong: Early Childhood Education and Care*. Paris: OECD.

Pilieci, V. (2009). "'He-cession' Hits Men's Jobs Harder." *Winnipeg Free Press*, April 11, 2009. Retrieved online April 20, 2009 at: http://www.winnipegfreepress.com/business/he-cession-hits-mens-jobs-harder-42843302.html.

Rice, M., and J. Prince. (2000). *Changing Politics of Canadian Social Policy*. Toronto: University of Toronto Press.

Scott, J. (2008). "Paid and Unpaid Work: A Retreat in Gender Role Egalitarian Attitudes." Paper presented at the annual meeting of the American Sociological Association Annual Meeting, Sheraton Boston and the Boston Marriott Copley Place, Boston, MA. Available online 2009-05-23 from http://www.allacademic.com/meta/p242289_index.html

Stanford, J., A. Di Caro, and C. Johnston. (2011). "Canada's Labour Movement in Challenging Times: Unions and Their Role in a Changing Economy," in A. Duffy, D. Glenday, and N. Pupo, *The Shifting Landscapes of Work*. Toronto: Pearson.

Statistics Canada. (2007). *Women in Canada: Work Chapter Updates*. Ottawa: Statistics Canada.

———. (2009). "Average Income After Tax by Economic Family Types 2003–2007," *The Daily*. June 2, 2009. Ottawa: Statistics Canada.

UNICEF. (2008). *The Child Care Transition*. Florence, Italy: UNICEF Innocenti Research Centre.

Vosko, L. (2000). *Temporary Work*. Toronto: University of Toronto Press.

———. (2009). *Managing the Margins: Gender, Citizenship, and the International Regulation of Precarious Employment*. Toronto: Oxford University Press.

Yalnizan, A. (2009). *Exposed: Revealing the Truths About Canada's Recession*. Ottawa: Canadian Centre for Policy Alternatives.

Section 3

Divorce and Its Aftermath

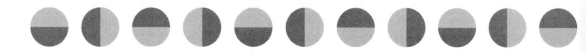

Chapter 24

Divorce rates are high in Canada, with nearly 4 in 10 marriages expected to end in divorce. This chapter contains some of what Catherine Riessman found in the 1980s, when she interviewed 104 American women and men about their divorces. Her focus here is on the stories these people created to make sense of the trajectory of the troubles in their relationships. These stories tell us something about what men and women expect of marriage.

According to Riessman, women and men have somewhat different expectations about marriage. Those differences are rooted primarily in gender differences in roles and responsibilities in families—especially that men are responsible for income earning and women are primarily responsible for children and home-making. Shortage of space precluded inclusion of Riessman's findings on women's criticisms of their ex-husbands' failings as providers and men's criticisms of their ex-wives' homemaking (and even, in some cases, the energy they spent in their paid jobs), as well as women's upset about the inequality in their former marriage. But these omitted findings—which indicate very different expectations of spouses, depending on their gender—might be a bit dated, given the widespread acceptance of (and need for) women's employment, the increased involvement of men in child care and housework, as well as the decline in good, stable jobs that enable men to provide financially for their family.

Mourning Different Dreams: Gender and the Companionate Marriage

Catherine Kohler Riessman

> How is it possible to bring order out of memory?
> –Beryl Markham, *West with the Night*

Jennifer is a graphic artist who has been separated for a few months. She has two small children. The large house that has been her marital residence is up for sale, and her living room is cluttered with boxes as she packs; she is moving into a small apartment. As she tries to make sense of her divorce, she uncovers a contradiction—a personal myth about what the "good" life is that is at odds with the reality of her experience:

> That there's a daddy and a mommy and the children and the house. And I know that that myth, for me anyway, was terrible. And the life that I've created beyond that myth is a million times better. But there's still . . . this longing for the completion of the original unit. (C004)

Other divorcing women and men describe similar myths and similar longings for this "original unit." Gloria—an educational consultant separated a year longer than Jennifer—mused about the specifics of this notion of marriage:

> We really had a lot of things going for us. We were professionally interested in the same field . . . and the dream was to have a very satisfying couple life and a

professional life where . . . he would be . . . working more than I am, but I would be working and I would enjoy that. But I would maintain my home as a first priority. And we could do a lot of things together . . . work things together, fun together, travel together. . . . I felt Keith and I were very close friends when we married. Very close friends. (C012)

In this "dream," Gloria tells us a great deal about what individuals expect from modern marriage—an exclusive "couple life" in which to realize emotional intimacy, companionship, and, as she says elsewhere in the interview, sexual fulfillment. She links these core components to a set of institutionalized roles; her primary commitment is to the domestic sphere and her husband's is to work outside the home. At the same time that marital roles are different, her choice of the metaphor of friendship suggests she expects equality with her husband and mutual respect.

Both Gloria and Jennifer were sorely disappointed. Jennifer's husband was incapable of the kind of emotional intimacy she wanted, and Gloria's husband was sexually unfaithful. To explain what went wrong and to make sense of her separation, each constructs a lengthy account, legitimating the divorce by noting how the dream had been betrayed. Gloria describes the repeated infidelities of her husband, a minister:

That's where the most pain is. I guess that's where the dream ended . . . We'd been married about eight years . . . and we were in the parish and Keith began having an affair with a former parishioner—25 years his junior—who he claimed to be a counseling case for six months. Until I got wise and asked him and he said yes,

he was having an affair, but he was trying desperately to end it. Two years later he was still having it. And that nearly drove me literally nuts. . . . And when we left that parish and he decided to go to Greenville, I thought, Oh, good, maybe this will all end. . . . And I remember when we bought our first house—we'd lived in . . . parsonages before—he was still seeing Bea and I said, "Damn it, if you take that black mud pot of a relationship into our new home it will kill me." And he took it, for the first four or five months. And it was very difficult but I kept thinking, Maybe, maybe with Greenville and [if] he gets into something he really likes, maybe that'll take care of it. Except that [when] he went to Greenville he started up another one. And that's still going on. I have become aware of two or three others, all of whom I know. I know all these people. (CO12)

Gloria's husband not only betrayed her dream of what marriage ought to be but personally betrayed and humiliated her by having affairs with people she knew. Gloria continues her account by saying she went into therapy where, over a period of time, she came to define the problem and decided to leave the marriage. Like others, she took charge of her divorce by reconstituting the meaning of what had occurred, and an important step in this process of understanding was the construction of an account, an interpretation of what happened and why.

Constructing an Account: The Ideology of the Companionate Marriage

In making sense of divorce, individuals recall and reinterpret the events of their marriages, bringing "order out of memory." They construct accounts that make sense, both to themselves and others, out of nonsense—images, memories, random happenings. Accounts develop in particular historical and cultural contexts: for example, there are socially acceptable reasons for ending a marriage in the 1980s that might have been unacceptable in past decades or are still unacceptable today in some parts of the world. There is a link between these private and social understandings, particularly concerning gender. The divorce accounts reveal an essential paradox: women and men construct heavily gendered definitions of what marriage ought to be, but at the same time they mourn these gender tensions and blame their divorces on them.

The major cultural theme that both women and men use to create divorce accounts is the ideology of the companionate marriage—the belief that husband and wife should be each other's closest companion at the same time that they are expected to retain gender-specific roles. This belief, whose roots I will discuss below, is an essential piece of each individual's "tool kit" in accounting for divorce. Although this ideal vision of marriage—the "dream" that Jennifer and Gloria refer to—has failed them, women and men nevertheless affirm it by justifying their divorces on the grounds that particular core elements of the companionate ideal—emotional intimacy, primacy and companionship, and sexual fulfillment— were missing from their marriages. They find fault with their spouses' performance of the institutionalized roles that are part of the companionate ideal. They describe how the preconditions for the companionate marriage—role differentiation and yet equality—have not been met in their particular cases. Women and men differ in the aspects of this ideal vision they select as justification for divorce, however, and there are social class variants in themes within gender groups, as well. Even when they

identify the same missing elements, on closer examination women and men seem to mean different things by them.

Women's Constructions of Emotional Intimacy

To explain why they divorced, individuals often use the phrase "lack of communication," and in doing so they are making sense of private experience by drawing on an ethic and vocabulary of love that is particular to contemporary American culture.[1] Women, more than men, identify this interpersonal aspect as missing in marriage. Nearly two-thirds say they did not get the kind of emotional intimacy they expected from their husbands. Closer examination of their talk suggests women are referring to a special kind of emotional intimacy: "feeling really in touch, communicating deeply and closely" (C002), "inner connectedness" (N025), "warmth and sharing" (C042), "getting down to gut feelings" (C033).

Deep Talk and Small Talk

Talk with a spouse is how women think emotional intimacy ought to be realized. At the same time that they want to talk about both "deep" topics and everyday events, they also want communication that goes beyond words, and that is reciprocal. As women construct it, a spouse should "know them" in some all-encompassing way. This ideal of romantic love, however, is tempered by the twentieth-century American belief in the value of "struggle" in relationships.[2] Women want to talk with husbands about negative feelings as well as positive ones. A salesclerk says:

> We never fought. If I became angry, I could scream and yell and even throw

things and get no feedback. None. Nothing. (L008)

Yet, though women want complete communication with a spouse, they appear to hold somewhat contradictory ideas about how it should be displayed. On the one hand, women expect intuitive understanding—to be understood without a lot of words. A clerical worker expresses this expectation:

> If you love me, you should know where I'm coming from, why and how I reacted to such and such . . . different things he should pick up on, what I had to say before the incident occurred, and give way sometimes and recognize what my need was. I think that when there is love you do that. (N025)

On the other hand, women want talk. They constantly complain that husbands were silent about their feelings, both positive and negative, as this proofreader describes:

> I had, for so many years, beaten my head against the wall and cried and screamed and said, "Talk to me. Tell me how you feel." And he'd go upstairs and read a book and leave me sitting down here with a bottle and nine million cigarettes, snuffling. (L013)

Not only do women want to talk about emotions, they also want "small talk"—about mundane things that happen during the day at the job or at home. They especially want verbal interaction about work—their own as well as their husbands'—but, as they construct it, their husbands are at fault because they will not talk about these topics, at least with them. Women typically do not understand that the problem may have to do with the different kinds of work women and men do, and resultant absence of similar activities to talk about. Instead, as they see it, the problem is in husbands' characters. One woman, whose husband was a factory foreman, defines the issue:

> I remember I would ask Nick questions when he would come home from work. . . . He was tired a lot so we would have deadening conversations where I'd say, "Well, tell me what happened today?" And he'd say, "Nothing much." And I'd talk about what happened to me and then I'd wonder if he could tell me anything 'cause I felt so out of his life. Maybe he didn't think I wanted to really know. I don't know. I think it was difficult because I had the college education and he (voice trails off). I think I'm a competitive person, very competitive and this may have been hard for him, maybe he just didn't want to compete at all. But we gradually had nothing to say to each other. (C014)

She constructs the problem psychologically—his lack of "competition" in comparison with hers. Yet she also notes that she has a college education (and a middle-class job), whereas he works in a factory—two very different contexts to come home and discuss at night. We know from other research that working-class men are more likely to talk to their buddies than to their wives about their daily lives at work.[3] Women like Lynn, a clerical worker, lament this gender division:

> I would talk but I don't think he ever listened. I think actually I bored him. And I would ask him, "What did you do today?" and he'd say, "Oh, nothing." Somebody else would walk in and he would say, "Oh,

you wouldn't believe what I saw today." (C022)

A particularly vivid example of the importance of talk for women and the conflict it creates in marriage is given by Betty, who took extreme action in order to get her husband to talk to her:

> George was not the greatest conversationalist. I used to do things to bug the guy and the thing is, I did it on purpose. If I felt like he was not paying enough attention. You see, he was not playful at all. I mean, most people can put a smile on their face sometimes and he very seldom did. . . . There was no child in him at all and there's a lot in me. You know, I like to play.

She continues by telling a story about a particular incident:

> Well, one time he was sitting here reading his newspaper (points to chair in living room). I just wanted to talk, walk over and say, "Hi, I remember you," you know, anything. I set his newspaper on fire to get attention. I did that once and boy did he get mad. See, playing is so important to me, you don't know how important, especially after being married to someone who was not playful. Yeah, there was a lot of times when I felt like I was being crazy and I was being crazy all by myself. (C013)

It is significant that Betty—a full-time homemaker during her marriage who became a construction worker after her separation—explicitly states that she wanted "attention," in the form of talk with her husband. Her rather dramatic action—setting his newspaper on fire as he was reading it—is an effort to get him to talk to her. . . . Her closing statements express how it felt to try to be "crazy" and "playful" in the context of a companionless marriage, where emotional intimacy, as she defines it, could not be realized.

The Expectation of Reciprocity

Women expect reciprocity in verbal exchanges but, as they look back on their marriages, too often they see "one-way love." A clerical worker describes the norm of reciprocity:

> I guess it's called "give and take." Just recently I was thinking about it . . . and I thought what a cliché, give and take. I was wondering what it really meant and I've come to the conclusion that it should mean that there is one person that is supposed to take first, and the other then gives, and then the other person takes and then you give. It's like giving way to what their need is. And there was none of this that occurred either by me or him. I consider that love. There was no love. (N025)

Others also spoke about reciprocity as love, calling it by other names: "giving and getting" (N013) or "emotional exchange" (C008).

Although women are more alike than different in referring to the absence of talk and reciprocity in marriage, women in contrasting economic circumstances use distinctive vocabularies to describe the emotional barrenness of their situations. Poor women use imagery that is rooted in the material conditions of their lives, specifically the metaphor of money:

> I felt like I was talking to a bank president, you know, who was telling me about a loan I was defaulting on. I was just so discouraged. There was no compassion.

There was no hug. And it reminded me of other times I had cried and how he always turned to stone. (C042)

These women invoke images of bank presidents, wallets, and loans to signify the emotional distance of husbands. The language that women in middle-class occupations use, in contrast, is more abstract, reflecting psychological understandings. A physician says:

There was a deadness [in the marriage], there was no life. All we could talk about were impersonal things and there was no ability to deal with what was behind things. We couldn't talk about things at an emotional level. (C010)

Women of all social classes often make reference to friendship in explaining what emotional intimacy ought to be like. An academic puts it this way:

There wasn't such a strong bond [in my marriage]. I mean, I didn't see it then, but I see it in contrast to my relationship with Tim [current boyfriend], like the person was your friend in a way. . . . There just wasn't that tie. (N004)

A woman on welfare looks back on her marriage and invokes the same image, saying, "My husband was never a friend to me, we were like bedmates" (C017). Friendship, women of all backgrounds suggest, entails talking and listening, giving and getting, equality not hierarchy.

Primacy and Companionship for Women

A common explanation for divorce in the accounts of both women and men is that they had "nothing in common" with their spouses. This reflects the belief about modern marriage that the conjugal relationship is the primary relationship, one that takes priority over all others. Joint activities and shared leisure are expected, because they vivify the bond between the spouses. More than half of those in the sample make sense of their divorces in the context of problems with companionship and its corollary complaint—that the commitment to the marital tie was not primary enough. Women interpret the relationship between primacy and companionship differently than men do, and women in different social circumstances see the issues in contrasting ways, as well.

Women do not expect husbands to relinquish ties to kin and friends nearly to the extent that men expect this from women. Women usually do not fulfill this expectation. Repeatedly, women note that their husbands were resentful when they wanted to spend time with close friends. Often, but not always, conflicts arose when women were needed by friends or family members in crisis, as this salesclerk describes:

My mom was going to have a mastectomy. And I told him I was going home. And he never wanted anything to do with my family. I was his and no one else's. As soon as he found out I wanted to go home, [he said], "No, you are not going," to which I replied, "I am going, she is my mother, if you don't like it, too bad." And I went. (C024)

"I was his and no one else's"—this lament is echoed implicitly or explicitly by many women. As women construct it, they do not expect this exclusivity from husbands. They do not define the marital relationship as emotionally exclusive, relegating kin and friends to a marginal position. Certainly, they resent some of the types of friends and the "male" activities husbands pursue with them—drinking and gambling, for example. One solution women see to these problems, however, is to incorporate men's friendships into the family, perhaps in an effort to control their husbands' behaviour. A case in point is this clerical worker:

> Well, on the one hand, some of his friends I really couldn't accept. They were mainly interested in going out and having a good time, drinking and gambling. Things like that. From my point of view it was a men's thing to do and the women were not included. . . . We didn't have friends that were family. Like husband and wife and children, let's get together and do something. Most of his friends were men. They were married, but we never associated on that level. They would come over for a brief period and have a drink, leave, and I always kept to myself, just extended whatever was the polite thing to do. Receive them at home and talk a little. . . . I tried many times to have his friends over, [asking], "Why doesn't he bring his wife over or children? We could do things together." (N025)

Rather than keeping husbands to themselves, women seek to integrate the family into a larger social world of kin and friends, and sometimes they even use these ties to buffer and preserve the troubled marriage.

Women do not expect primacy nearly to the extent men do, but they still expect companionship in marriage—to "do things together." Women's ideas of what these joint activities ought to be differ markedly from men's. An office manager describes one of the hopes she had when she married that was never realized:

> We got married in April and the first Christmas, I mean, see, I always have these dreams and everything has to go with the way the dream is. . . . I wanted to go to midnight Mass with my husband, only he didn't want to go. . . . It used to bother me going to Christmas alone, church alone. (N023)

"Going to Christmas alone"—this woman's slip of the tongue reveals the loneliness of a companionless marriage.

As women construct it (especially women whose husbands had working-class occupations), "male" leisure pursuits get in the way of doing things together. A clerical worker interprets her resentment this way:

> See, the type of recreations he had were, like I say, more male oriented. Like, "Let's go to the bar, or Hialeah, or the dog races," things like that which I didn't care to attend. And he didn't want me to come anyway. It's like there were two worlds and there was no way of putting them together. (N025)

This woman makes explicit the link between gender and lack of companionship, for it is the "male-oriented" nature of her husband's recreational interests that excludes her, not his overt exclusionary behaviour or his ties to male friends. In her mind, bars, Hialeah, and the dog races are "male" settings. According to her report, her husband invited her to join him in these places ("let's go"), but she wasn't interested ("I didn't care to attend"), interpreting his invitation as his lack of sincerity ("he didn't want me to come anyway"). In her mind, separate spheres pivot on tacit theories of "appropriate" settings and activities for women as opposed to men. These beliefs, in turn, produce tension in marriage, where companionship is expected.

Women in professional occupations complain less than do poorer women about the lack of shared leisure (almost half of poorer women saw it as a problem). Professional couples expect and do take time together, but even here some women recall "two worlds" of sex-typed leisure. A physical therapist highlights the differences:

> I enjoyed going to plays and theatre and things like that, where he hated it. If we went, I could see him doing it, just *doing* it, maybe falling asleep. (C016)

Her husband, like many others, had a major interest in sports and was what she called "a TV freak." For many wives this was a bone of contention, particularly as they began to develop interests on their own, as the college administrator did:

> We stopped sharing daily lives. First our friendship started to sort of split apart and I found I didn't want to watch the Bruins and I didn't want to go to softball. I began to assert what I wanted to do rather than saying, It's all right, I'll join Nick in what he likes to do. . . . He also watched a lot of TV and I . . . dislike TV and what it did to conversation. (C014)

Women's accounts suggest that they have strong feelings about where and how joint leisure ought to occur in marriage that, in turn, reflect gender divisions. Women, particularly those in working-class occupations, speak over and over again of wanting to "go out," intimating that the home is no place to spend time that is not focused on household chores and child care. A woman who has children and is on welfare puts it this way:

> He did not mind dedicating a lot of time toward sports, his friends, the softball league, and things like that. If I asked just like to go to a movie with the children or go out to dinner at a restaurant—just one day—he couldn't understand why I wanted to do that when I could do it at home, just sitting down and watching TV. Or just have a family dinner, which [he thought] would be the same as going to a restaurant. (N013)

As this woman goes on to explain, one difference between having dinner in a restaurant and at home is that "you don't do the dishes afterwards."[4] Women want to "go out" and "be sociable" because their workplace is the private sphere of the home; men, in contrast, are "out" all day at their jobs. Even if wives are also employed outside the house, they do not define the home as a space for leisure because it is associated with chores, demands, and responsibilities—a "prison" rather than the "haven" it is for men.[5] In women's minds, there is no "free" time for them at home.

Women's Views about Sex in Marriage

Sexual gratification for both wives and husbands is a core aspect of modern marriage, something taken for granted. It is closely related to the other expectations, because in addition to providing physical release, marital sex may be a way to realize emotional intimacy, primacy, and companionship. Given the high value placed on sex in American culture, it is not surprising that sexual issues figure in nearly 60 per cent of the divorce accounts. Women and men interpret sexual events in distinctive ways, however.

Sexual infidelity was mentioned in 34 per cent of the accounts.[6] Women take this action very seriously and interpret it as evidence of betrayal or as the catalyst for divorce. For Gloria, for example, whose account of her husband's repeated affairs with women she knew opened this chapter, discovering the affairs was significant to her because they were proof that her husband could not be trusted. In this construction (which other women share), it is not only the sexual behaviour itself but what it signifies about the spouse's character that is disturbing to the wife. This deeper discovery—that the husband is not the person the wife thought he was—is especially troubling, because it compromises her ability to love in return, thereby contradicting her beliefs about reciprocity in emotional expression. Gloria makes this point clear:

> Although I still had the love, the freedom to love him just got absolutely slammed shut. Even though we had a relationship after that [discovery of the first affair]. Not with my heart in it. (C012)

For another group of women, affairs mean something different Although these women still view affairs as very serious and as key turning points in the decision to divorce, they believe that the marriage was "over" in an emotional sense by the time that the affair occurred. In this construction, the affair is the catalyst for separation, but the web of explanation for the problem goes deeper. After a lengthy description of a series of marital problems, a news reporter concludes:

> We just sort of withdrew into our separate worlds. Then, as luck would have it, he met someone that he fell in love with and that was the catalyst. As soon as he met her and had real feelings about her, he wanted out. So the final ending was very sudden. (L003)

Not only do women see their husbands' infidelities as the catalyst; they define their own in this way as well. A recurrent plot exists in some women's accounts: their marriage existed "in name only," they then "met someone" and fell in love, and this provided the "push" needed to end the marriage. The academic speaks directly about the emotional logic, which was also implicit in several other women's explanations, behind this scenario:

> It really took meeting somebody else before I could leave. I might have left anyway, but I think it would have taken a lot longer. . . . I think it might have taken meeting somebody else because I'm so afraid of being alone. That's really a big, that's my big problem. . . . I was so terrified and I think, really, I think it's possible I wouldn't have done it unless I'd met somebody else. (N004)

The fear of being alone keeps these women in "empty" marriages, and they rationalize moving quickly to another relationship after they have an affair. A few women even define being "mentally unfaithful" as incompatible with marital vows. Several women described how they began to be attracted to someone else toward the end of their marriage. The proof-reader says:

> I eventually started to feel like I liked Vince much better than I liked my husband. And if I was going to be mentally unfaithful, I might as well leave him. (L013)

By making sense of infidelity in these ways, women are drawing on a gendered belief that sex and emotional closeness go hand in hand—that sex and love cannot be separated.[7]

In this belief system, women's sexual infidelity is justified in the absence of deep emotional ties to a spouse. Similarly, husbands' affairs are legitimate cause for ending a marriage because they mean that the husbands are giving away their love—to the women they are sleeping with, rather than to their wives. Even if it is also clear at some level to their wives that this is not the case, they cannot continue to give their love freely if their husbands betray them and thus challenge the expectation that sex and love are one. Women have deeply held beliefs about the rules that should govern the relationship between sexual and emotional intimacy, and these influence how they interpret sexual infidelity. (Interestingly, though the joining of sex and intimacy is a woman's theme, it is voiced by both women and men to explain marital failure. Several men in their accounts describe their wives' sense of betrayal when they—the men—were sexually unfaithful. Once discovered, they were never forgiven.)

In women's talk about sexual gratification there is additional evidence that women tend to link sex and intimacy. A number of women raise the issue of marital sex while talking about emotional closeness in their marriage. As closeness began to wane, so did sex. A factory worker talks explicitly about the connection between physical and emotional intimacy:

> To me, sex isn't just sex. It doesn't bother me not to have sex. To not have a relationship would bother me more than not having sex. In a close relationship, in a close feeling with someone, of sharing and confiding, and being together and cuddling, to me sex is a natural thing. Without that I don't want it. Consequently, there were many times we had problems [and] he wanted to have sex and I wasn't interested. (C033)

In her view, sex is "natural" when it flows from emotional closeness. When this condition was lacking in her marriage, she withheld sex. As she later states, when her husband wanted sex, she'd say, "I'm sorry, if you can't give me what I need then I don't see why I should give you what you need" (C033). The giving and withholding of sex is an exercise of power—one of women's major weapons, it appears, in the face of husbands' failure to live up to wives' standards of intimacy. It is not surprising in this context that a number of women comment on the decline in frequency of sex as the marriage became emotionally strained. Paradoxically, the absence of sex then becomes a justification for ending the marriage, As a factory worker says, "What kind of a marriage is this when you don't sleep together?" (N026)

. . .

Men's Constructions of Emotional Intimacy

Like women, some men blame divorce on "lack of communication"—a phrase that is commonly used to explain a flawed relationship. When men elaborate, saying "we weren't real close" (C003), there was a lack of "emotional support" (L009), or "I had love to give but wasn't getting it back" (C037), at first glance they sound like their female counterparts. But there is a difference. Only one-third of the men (as opposed to two-thirds of the women) say they did not get the emotional intimacy they expected from marriage. The comments men make about the topic tend to be brief in contrast to women, who go on at length about it. Closer examination of men's talk suggests they are defining "closeness" in distinctive ways.

In their accounts of their marriages, men blame themselves for not living up to women's standards of intimacy. As they construct it, they were the silent partners in marriage, not giving wives enough "love and understanding" (C02l). When they talk about specifics, however, it is clear that their style involves less talk and more action. As a physical therapist says bluntly, "I'll act and she'll feel." At the same time he subtly considers himself at fault for his way of relating in the marriage:

> I'm a very private person. . . . I think that was the problem in the marriage, that my wife felt I didn't talk enough, I keep things very much to myself and I'll act and she'll feel, like, "Where in the hell is this coming from because there's never been any prelude to this, we never discussed this, we never talked about this and all of a sudden, he's done something." In my own mind, I've worked it out, just seemed like the best course of action or whatever at that time. But I'm not the type of person to sit down and discuss things with people at any length. (N036)

Although this man admits he is not "the type of person" to talk things out, he nevertheless believes that his style "was a problem in the marriage." He appears to accept women's view that shared introspection is a good thing. The modern cultural ethos of communication holds sway over both sexes, and this man feels the worse for it.

In men's definitions of emotional closeness, talk is not the centrepiece. Rather, men expect wives to be there for them in much fuller ways. Lillian Rubin argues that it is physical proximity that is desired, but the men in my sample suggest this is only one aspect.[8] Men want a variety of physical and other concrete demonstrations of intimacy. A factory worker vividly depicts what was missing in his marriage:

> When you come home from work at night . . . just to have somebody greet you at the door with open arms, you know, kiss and ask, how you are, or how your day went. I never received that. (C037)

To be greeted at the door by a wife with open arms—this image recurred with remarkable regularity, particularly in the accounts of working-class men, just as the wish for reciprocal talk about emotions with a husband recurred in the accounts of women from all social backgrounds. As this man says, he wants talk to a certain extent—he wants his wife to ask about his day—but this is just one small part of what he expects. It is just as important that his wife be at the door, with "open arms" and a kiss—physical manifestations of caring. Note that his expectations for intimacy here are unidirectional. Like a number of other men, he complains that he did not "receive" love. In his view, marriage is a kind of haven, a place to retreat to, where he can be tended by a wife, away from the pressures of alienated work. In exchange for her emotional support of him, he expects to support her financially. This is reciprocity as many men understand it.

Other men voice similar understandings of the importance of physical, not verbal, manifestations of emotional intimacy. Joe, a corrections counsellor with a master's degree, is one of four men who discuss the absence of intimacy in marriage at length. He says:

> I don't think I was ever as close to Jackie [former wife] as I am to Sue [current girlfriend]. . . . Part of it is, I tend to be somewhat of an emotional person. I grew up in a very close family, I grew up in an extended family. My grandmother and my aunts and uncles and cousins on the

top floor. And summers, we had a summer house, it was a collective summer house with aunts and uncles, cousins, and so we spent every summer together. And then I'm a very affectionate person and Jackie's very cold, came from a very staunch New England family that didn't show emotion, you know. Her mother frowned on us holding hands together when we first met. . . . I show emotion. I think that was the hardest thing. Jackie never really felt that, you know . . . if I put my arm around her in public, she'd shun it or kissed her in public, she'd—even after we'd been married for ten years—she felt that someone might see it. I used to ask her, "Who cares? I really don't care." Sue is very affectionate and I like that. (N012)

Although emotional intimacy is a topic of obvious importance to Joe, he does not offer it as a reason for his separation. Instead, he discusses it in another context in the interview, after a question about how his relationships have changed since divorcing. When asked about the "main causes of his separation," he describes how he and his wife "grew in different directions" and how work stress undermined the marriage. Women who speak about the absence of emotional closeness, in contrast, tend to define it as causally related to the end of the marriage.

Joe's description of his emotional nature can also be seen as a type of justification.[9] He needs to account for his nature, because it is deviant in our culture for a man to be so affectionate; he explains that he got that way because of his early family experiences. No woman in the sample needed to justify the importance of emotional expression.

Most obviously, Joe defines emotional closeness as physical demonstrativeness.

Talking about feelings and problems does not figure in his construction of what being "an emotional person" is. He wants to express his love physically, not talk about it. His understanding of emotional intimacy is markedly different from what women describe it to be.

Primacy and Companionship for Men

Men assume that they will have easy access to their wives when they marry. They expect that the marital tie will be the primary tie for them and for their wives—that the couple will be self-contained. Consequently, men count on spending considerable time with their wives—alone together, as a couple.

Men's central complaint (nearly half mention it) is that wives are not "there" for them because they are not emotionally exclusive. In their minds, their wives' other relationships limit the time the couple can spend alone together and undermine the primacy of the marriage. Continuing bonds and obligations to kin are often seen as the problem. One man recalls, "she would show more attention, you know, to her family than she would to me" (N017). Wives' involvements with relatives, and sometimes even with the couple's children, are seen as usurping time and energy that husbands want. Wives' friendships with other women are seen similarly. Women, as noted earlier, have their own language for this problem—"I was his and no one else's."

Men in middle-class occupations are more likely than those with working-class jobs to complain about wives' kin ties. Joe, though he has mentioned growing up in a large, close extended family, wanted a different sort of life with his wife. He described in a vivid way the variety of relationships that occupied his wife and, even more, took over their home:

Jackie was like a little old lady in the woods who lives with 64 cats. Anytime something wandered to the back door that was injured, which is fine, I mean, if an animal is injured, I took it in too and I played doctor. But I didn't want to keep them and she ended up gradually building up to a whole house full of animals. We had five cats in a two-bedroom apartment. Plus her brother came to live with us and I felt that I was supporting him and putting him through school as well as putting myself and her through school. And he lived with us for three years. He lived in the other bedroom in a two-bedroom apartment, and I just felt the lack of privacy, even though he and I are friends. I felt that he wasn't contributing to the house—he never did any cleaning, I had to clean up after him as well as pay for the food, he never really contributed to the food and never paid us rent, so I didn't feel that obligation. Maybe she felt a strong obligation to him, but I didn't feel it and that was a source of arguments, that was one of the problems. (N012)

Cats, brothers, sisters, mothers, and the obligations wives feel to them—men echo this lament over and over. As men see it, wives' overinvolvement in the lives of others interferes with marital "privacy," especially when wives respond to others' trouble by giving them a temporary home. They perceive, often correctly, that wives take care of others even when they don't want to, that obligations to others are a burden for women. Wives need to learn to say "no," to stop "overdoing it" (N012), and to tend to the immediate family instead.

When relatives get too involved, moreover, men feel a husband cannot fulfill his mission—to be a good provider for the family. Relatives use up scarce material goods that men have worked hard for, as this apartment superintendent describes:

> Her father was living with us, her brother just moved in with us, without any help. I mean, it's not that they were bad people, but they were sponging off me, I felt. And, you know, I'd be working all day, they'd be eating all the groceries and stuff. (N017)

Beyond these concrete sources of resentment, wives' ties to others are also directly responsible for the demise of the marriage in some men's minds, because wives can turn to others for help in difficult times and are not solely dependent on their husbands or on themselves:

> I have these strong feelings that if her mother didn't help her she would have been forced to try to make things work. She didn't have to just come home. (N039)

A handful of men resent the time and attention that children require from their wives. This is especially true if the children are from the wife's previous marriage, because they acutely compromise the primacy of the couple relationship. As one man says, "We were right off the bat a family." In his account (heavily influenced, one suspects, by the family therapy literature), this prevents the "formation of the spouse subsystem" (C041). Another man is more direct, calling his wife's children "an intrusion in the marriage" (C026).

Men want the home to be their haven from work. Children and relatives (particularly if they move in) severely diminish peace and quiet at home and interfere with easy access to emotional support. Husbands have a hard time enjoying their wives and getting what they need from them with so many others around.

Under these conditions, men feel that they have to compete—that there is not enough attention to go around. They believe that the home should *their* space, for they have worked hard to get it, and that they should not have to share it. (For some, having a wife and children is similarly their accomplishment, evidence of their lineage.) A lawyer speaks of his resentment of the collectivity of his wife's women friends, who, as members of a consciousness-raising group, invaded his home on a regular basis:

> My own feeling is that it [the separation] was rather heavily influenced by the explosion of the women's movement and my wife's participation in it and her changing expectation. My inability to understand what was going on. . . . Women developed support groups which met often, in fact, they were meeting in *my* house and it became simply stated that I was not welcome to even be in *my* house at the time that these meetings were taking place. And I felt extremely resentful about that. In fact, angry. And so the whole notion of the support group became a very big conflict between us because I felt that there were other people who were discussing my own personal affairs. . . . And there was developing this movement among women that had very little . . . understanding about how this was all going to impact on males and as a male, I had no way of dealing with that. There were no male support groups and I wouldn't have participated in one even if there were because I didn't like the notion of them. And I think that it was very bothersome for me because I felt that all of the changes that were happening in my own house were coming from this whole movement over which I had no control.

Or no input. And it was totally mystifying to me. (C027)

As this man formulates the problem, he lost the privacy of his relationship with his wife and the privacy of his home, as her ties to women and the women's movement usurped his place and changed the rules of marriage. (There may also be another issue here, one that may not be as gender-linked: is the marital home his, hers, or theirs? His account is reminiscent of the remarks of the woman quoted earlier who disappeared whenever her husband's friends came over to the house.) Bob, a factory foreman, constructs the problem that women's friendships pose to a marriage a bit differently, emphasizing his wife's time away from home:

> Bob: When Lisa was going out a lot with her friends, you know, I felt lonely and I felt responsible for a lot of that, too. I could have made her stay home or whatever and just let her go out once in a while, but I let her have everything at once.
>
> Int.: Sounds like you feel that was a mistake.
>
> Bob: Yeah, I do. [If I had it to do over again] I'd let her go out maybe once a week with her girlfriends or whatever. I feel everybody should have at least one free night in a week. (C031)

Both men feel they lost control over their wives and link this loss to their wives' deep involvement in friendships. But they are suggesting something more. We know from other research that men depend on a spouse for connection and emotional support much more than women do; wives are men's primary, often only, confidant.[10] If their spouse is not available, men feel they have nobody. It makes sense, then, that men expect the marital relationship to be primary, exclusive, private, and to take precedence over all other relationships.

Men do not always put marriage first, of course, and some tended to realize this in their retellings. A number of men spoke of their overinvolvement in work:

> Within our marriage, my job was more important than my family. That was one of the things that kind of, it wasn't *the* thing, but it was certainly one of the things that contributed to the breakup of the marriage. (N032)

> I used to spread myself really thin. I spent as much time with my social life and my friends in the Biology Department [his job] as I did with Cindy and that probably wasn't a good idea. (C035)

> I had a partner [in the insurance business], so I was spending all my time with my partner. Not paying enough attention to my wife's needs. (L012)

> I got so wrapped up in some of those things [politics, work], I got lost in priority of what was important in my life. I didn't really pay that much attention to my wife, I guess. When I look back at it. (N019)

It is no coincidence that all these men have solidly middle-class occupations and thus jobs they can "lose themselves" in, to the exclusion of family. No man with a working-class job makes such a statement. But all these men, working and middle class, are making the same point in different ways: If they had the marriage to do over they would have made the relationship more central in their lives. In their accounts the marriage failed, at least in part, because they did not make it emotionally exclusive and primary.

A related ideal of modern marriage that both men and women prize is doing things together with a spouse, enjoying companionship when not working. Husbands expect easy access to their wives for leisure activities but, as they experience it, their wives are either too busy or do not want to do what they want to do. Tension over different leisure interests is especially characteristic of marriages that working-class men describe. Free time is especially important for these men, who have little control over their work, yet working-class marriages (more than middle-class ones) tend to be sex-segregated, and consequently, men's leisure interests are often different from women's. An X-ray technician complained that he and his wife "did not do things together" and expressed his sadness that she did not join him in doing things that were important to him:

> I don't think she ever rode my motorcycle, which is no big deal, but I thought she should try it. It's not that big a thing, but enough things like this add up. (N034)

His words recall those of the woman office manager who spoke in a similar vein about having to go to midnight Mass alone. Company at midnight Mass or on a motorcycle—both speakers are remembering separate spheres of leisure in marriage; both exemplify how far apart women and men in working-class marriages are in the activities they value and want to share with a spouse. Although women and men can and do go to church and ride motorcycles, in practice both of these activities tend to be gender-linked. . . .

Although men with professional occupations complain less about lack of shared leisure with wives, when they do it is almost as if the existence of contrasting interests constitutes "proof" that the marriage is not viable. These men reason that if a marriage does not provide companionship, it offers nothing at all. Leisure and planning for leisure occupy a large part of middle-class life, and men work hard in order to be able to provide for family recreation. "Doing things together" solidifies bonds, and if men cannot have good times with wives at these moments, they sense there is no basis for marriage. A physical therapist sums up his recollections of his marriage:

> I think we had a relationship that was a strong physical relationship, but I don't believe we really had a real commonality of interest. We kind of would make things do, that we could share, that neither of us was terribly excited about. She might humour me by going to see a play or something that I wanted to see and I might see a ballet or something that she wanted to see. But there were no real common interests. Like I like to run, I like to play tennis, I like to be physically active and play golf. Judy would go out to play golf and walk through holes, sit down in the shade and say, "To hell with this." She took some tennis lessons, but she's never developed any interest or any aptitude for it. So you had two people who really cared a lot about each other but I don't think we really had the commonality of interest in the relationship. (N036)

Men's Views about Sex in Marriage

As mentioned earlier, both women and men in the sample complained about sex in marriage but, as others have found, the men tended to be more dissatisfied with it than did the women. The men's responses suggest why this might be so. Instead of viewing sex as women tend to—as a way to express intimacy already established by talking and sharing—men expected to become intimate with their wives through sex. In their minds, if the sexual aspect of a marriage is working, that is proof that good communication is taking place.[11]

Because wives see sex so differently, it is no wonder that many men are dissatisfied with the sexual aspects of marriage and that the bedroom becomes a major battleground in the modern family. Some men describe conflict over the frequency of sexual intercourse and corroborate women's remarks cited earlier that indicate women exercise power in marriage by withholding sex. A high school teacher says:

> I was . . . sick of fighting about sex, and when to have sex. Having to, you know, almost beg for it at times. (C023)

Wives try to enforce their definitions to how sex ought to occur. Because men cannot feel intimate if they do not have sex, a consequence of the downward spiral of marital sex is extreme loneliness. . . .

Because sex is a major way to achieve intimacy for men, the absence of sex creates a kind of loneliness for them that women never describe. As a way of managing their disappointment, some men blame their wives by defining the problem as "frigidity." (The women's accounts suggest that the problem may have been otherwise.) Several men, at the same time that they admitted that their sexual style was different from their wives," retrospectively understood that their wives wanted emotional intimacy before physical intimacy. An academic says:

She would be much more desirous of tenderness, affection, you know, apart from a sexual relationship, and I'd be much less available, let alone initiating of that with her. (C041)

Another man, a pharmacist, talking about his difficulties in "communication" with his wife, describes his approach:

I went in with the wrong point of view. I went in from the sexual point, I thought, tried more stimulating new approaches and stuff. That wasn't where she was coming from. That's where I thought things were. That's what was bothering me. I found out later that [other] things were bothering her and she just withdrew. (N019)

. . .

Private Meanings for Social Troubles

Neither the women nor the men interviewed, whether working class or middle class, questioned the ideology of the companionate marriage. It was the failure of their particular partners to live up to the ideal that was defined as the problem, not the dream itself. One might argue that there are serious flaws in contemporary beliefs about marriage. Most obviously, it is an idealized image of what a relationship can provide. Few marriages can sustain its core elements, in proper ratio, over time. Given that the essential ingredients of the companionate ideal have different meanings for husbands and wives, a shared consensus is even less likely. Yet personal fulfillment through marriage has become a central preoccupation

of American culture—the perpetual quest for the perfect relationship. Paradoxically, these "great expectations" create the very conditions for disappointment and divorce.[12]

How individuals make sense of divorce tells us something, as well, about what people expect when they marry again, for individuals recreate the social order of marriage in the explanatory schemas they invoke to explain its demise. Women and men create very different marital "realities" in their tellings and, by this process, participate in constructing a gendered social world. By holding up the expectation that men should be the primary providers and women should be the caregivers, for example, both women and men reflect and, in turn, reproduce the division of labour that is so consequential for inequality between women and men. In their accounts, they both experience and produce their culture.[13]

There are also inherent strains within the ideal of modern marriage. The realization of the core ingredients of the companionate marriage—emotional intimacy, primacy and companionship, and mutual sexual fulfillment—depends on equality between husbands and wives. Yet institutionalized roles call for differentiation. . . .

In their accounts, women and men seek explanations in their personal situations and psychologies and for the most part eschew structural and political explanations. As Mills reminds us, social problems are often mistaken for individual issues in an individualistic society. The love myth is so powerful precisely because it promises to resolve contradictions; it offers to heal both sides of a duality.[14] Paradoxically, marital difficulties pivot on a duality—gender difference—essential to the definition of marriage itself.

● Notes

1. Ann Swidler, "Love and Adulthood in American Culture," in *Themes of Work and Love in Adulthood,* eds N.J. Smelser and E.H. Erikson (Cambridge: Harvard University Press, 1980), 120–47. For a somewhat different analysis of the history of love and gender differences, see Arlie Russell Hochschild, "Attending to, Codifying, and Managing Feelings: Sex Differences in Love," in *Feminist Frontiers: Rethinking Sex, Gender, and Society,* eds L. Richardson and V. Taylor (Reading, MA: Addison-Wesley, 1983), 250–62.

2. On the value of struggle, see Swidler, "Love and Adulthood." Others have also found similar assumptions about communication in women's talk about relationships. See Francesca Cancian, *Love in America: Gender and Self Development* (New York: Cambridge University Press, 1987); Lillian Rubin, *Intimate Strangers: Men and Women Together* (New York: Harper & Row, 1983).

3. David Halle, *America's Working Man: Work, Home, and Politics Among Blue-Collar Property Owners* (Chicago: University of Chicago Press, 1984), 34–73.

4. For a fuller discussion of this Hispanic woman's account, especially the ways in which it is different in its organization from a white middle-class woman's account, see Catherine Kohler Riessman, "When Gender Is Not Enough," *Gender and Society* 1 (1987): 172–207.

5. Lillian Rubin, *Worlds of Pain* (New York: Basic Books, 1976), 95.

6. This study's figure of active infidelity, 34 per cent, is slightly lower than the incidence of self-reported extramarital sex in other studies of the divorced. Graham Spanier and Linda Thompson, in *Parting: The Aftermath of Separation and Divorce* (Thousand Oakes, CA: Sage Publications, 1987) report that 38 per cent of their sample (about equal percentages of women and men) reported engaging in extramarital coitus during the marriage. Differences between their findings and the findings here can be explained methodologically.

I coded the frequency from qualitative data—its mention in the account; they specifically asked about affairs during the marriage.

7. For an analysis of how this belief operates in women's extramarital affairs, see Annette Lawson, *Adultery: An Analysis of Love and Betrayal* (New York: Basic Books, 1988); for more on women's tendency to link sex and love, see Cancian, *Love in America;* Rubin, *Intimate Strangers.*

8. Rubin, *Intimate Strangers,* 76.

9. See Marvin B. Scott and Standford M. Lyman, "Accounts," *American Sociological Review* 33, 1(February 1968): 46–62.

10. Deborah Belle, "Gender Differences in the Social Moderators of Stress," in *Gender and Stress,* eds R.C. Barnett, L. Biener, and G.K. Baruch (New York: Free Press, 1987), 257–77.

11. On men's dissatisfaction with sex in marriage, see Theodore Caplow et al., *Middletown Families: Fifty Years of Change and Continuity* (Minneapolis: University of Minnesota Press, 1982), 177. Lawrence Stone generalizes that in Western societies, "Men have tended to find it easier than women to separate the purely physical pleasures of sex from emotional commitment." He relates prostitution, and massage parlors in the modern period, to this male predilection. See Lawrence Stone, "The Road to Polygamy," *New York Review* (March 2, 1989):12.

12. Elaine Tyler May, *Great Expectations: Marriage and Divorce in Post-Victorian America* (Chicago: University of Chicago Press, 1980).

13. Michael Moerman, *Talking Culture: Ethnography and Conversation Analysis* (Philadelphia: University of Pennsylvania Press, 1988). For a different theoretical perspective, see Aafke Komter, "Hidden Power in Marriage," *Gender and Society* 3 (1989): 187–216.

14. C.W. Mills, *The Sociological Imagination* (Oxford: Oxford University Press, 1959), 12. For more on the love myth as the resolution for contradictions, see Swidler, "Love and Adulthood."

Chapter 25

Too often, sociologists think of children only in terms of their dependence on adults, and their needs for care. Very rarely, for example, do studies of who does the housework and who provides care for young children consider that some of this work might be done by older children in the family. Similarly, when we think about divorce, we worry about its effects on children, but fail to consider them as active in how relationships and arrangements unfold in the months and years after their parents separate.

Researchers have found that children whose parents divorce have more problems than do children who grew up with both parents. Even so, they also find that only a minority of children who have lived through divorce have problems, and that these problems may be due as much to conflict between the parents (before as well as after the divorce) as to the divorce itself.

This chapter by British sociologists Carol Smart, Bren Neale, and Amanda Wade offers an insightful look into the ways children actively negotiate the changes they live with when their parents divorce. Their research shows that children not only have agency but also that their actions may affect their parents' ongoing relationship with each other. Moreover, aside from potential and real problems caused by divorce, parents' separation may have some positive effects for children as well as adults.

"Doing" Post-divorce Childhood

Carol Smart, Bren Neale, and Amanda Wade

> While marriages can be cancelled and remade, families cannot; they live on in the persons of the children who move quietly across the boundaries of new partnerships and families.
> —Beck and Beck-Gernsheim, 1995: 149

Introduction

This quotation from *The Normal Chaos of Love* is quite remarkable for its myopic, adult-centred understanding of the nature of post-divorce family life. While we would not dissent from the idea that families are not coterminous with marriage, we question whether the essence of family resides in the children who, it seems, flit about in a quiet fashion between the newly formed relationships generated by adults. The children in this evocative image are rendered quite passive and docile. The impression given is that they do their parents' bidding while at the same time being the receptacles of the meaning of "family" because they inertly embody the generative product of the adults' previous union. In our two linked studies we did not find any children who could be said to move *quietly* between their parents' new relationships or households. They moved noisily, or sadly, or angrily, or joyfully, but not exactly quietly. Moreover, they did not embody the meaning of family. . . . They acted out their own interpretations of family, including some people and excluding others. Some even exercised their choice not to visit one parent at all, or drove out their parents' new partners when they were sufficiently motivated to do so.

Even the children who were perfectly happy did not fit this docile image: They had their own demands and wishes and were capable of making them known.

Unlike Beck and Beck-Gernsheim, we suggest that children play an active part in restructuring relationships after divorce and in redefining the meaning of family after separation. In this reading we explore the challenges that children face in this renegotiation and in sustaining relationships with parents across separate households. This includes the ways in which the dislocations of space and the experience of parental absence implicit in post-divorce family life impact upon children's lives. We will examine changes in involvement with and connection to parents, and children's and young people's responses to the changes that occur over time as parents re-establish their lives, renegotiate relationships with former partners, and enter into or disengage from new partnerships or other forms of relationship. At the heart of this chapter is a concern with the contributions which children themselves make to the maintenance of relationships and to the complex business of living in a reorganized family. Hence our title refers to "doing" post-divorce childhood. We start with the ontological assumption that children are sociological actors rather than passive symbols of family life. Finally, we begin to consider whether the establishment of family practices which are not coterminous with the single-household, nuclear family means that new forms of childhood are emerging in the twenty-first century.

Orienteering for Children

Giddens (1991) has argued that, in post-traditional societies, individuals are increasingly obliged to work out their own solutions and moral maps when they face major transitions in their personal lives. He has suggested that this means that individuals are increasingly engaged in a reflexive project of the self in which they write their own biographies rather than following custom or tradition. With regard to the family, the transformation of traditional family forms gives rise to pioneering a new social territory and constructing innovative forms of intimate relationships. We have referred to this elsewhere (Smart, 2000) as a process of "orienteering" without a compass in which individuals find themselves in a new cultural and moral space and need to devise a new etiquette of kinship. Following these ideas, we have been concerned to explore the extent to which this process applies to children who are increasingly navigating different forms of post-divorce family life. Even more than their parents, they have no modern cultural tradition[1] to rely on to help them find their way in the new terrain. They may have to learn to live with strangers in the form of their parents' new partners and their children, or even new half-siblings. Their expectations of their parents may have to be revised, and they may see them behaving in new and unaccustomed ways; perhaps distressed or lonely, or perhaps loving a new sexual partner, or stepparenting "strange" children. There are no external normative frameworks available to help them with the task of forging these new relationships, and we need to understand more about how they rise to this challenge and "do" childhood under these new conditions. . . .

The children in our linked studies lived in widely varying circumstances. Not only was there a complex pattern of family structures, kinship, lifestyles, and social and economic circumstances across the samples, but even where we found a close resemblance in children's backgrounds and family arrangements, their responses to and perceptions of these frequently varied. Indeed, siblings could have very different attitudes towards parents and new family members despite sharing the same pattern of residence and contact. Notwithstanding this, a number of distinct themes on the subject of the renegotiation of family relationships can be discerned in the children's accounts. Below we explore some of the key elements in "doing" post-divorce childhood before returning to the more speculative theme of whether childhood is itself changing in certain ways.

Dealing with Separation

At the core of children's and young people's renegotiation of their relationships with parents after divorce or separation is the experience of absence. Although some parents who establish civil relationships with each other may continue to do certain things as "a family," such as spending Christmas, birthdays, or holidays together, these parents' lives do basically disengage and diverge. "Doing" separation therefore becomes an inherent feature of children's lives; being with one parent involves them in being apart from the other. The ways in which separation is managed by children can differ widely and are affected by such things as the quality of relationships; the nature, length, or frequency of the separation; its causes and predictability; the sense that children make of it; and the resources they have for responding to it.[2] We found that children with unreliable contact with a parent who seemed to make little emotional or practical investment in them could feel extremely unhappy. Yet even children with reliable contact could speak of "missing" the parent from whom they were apart. This could be a matter of sadness even though both parents were fully involved in their lives. At the other end of the spectrum, children with an oppressive or abusive parent could find relief in never having

to see that parent again. Similarly, some co-parented children, such as those having daily opportunities to see each parent and whose residence arrangements had been in place for a number of years, expressed little sense of having lost something precious as a result of their parents separating. Separation from a parent is therefore not always a problem for children; it can constitute either a loss or a gain.

These different scenarios are evidenced in the experiences of the children and young people we discuss below. Louise (9) recalled that her father's presence had caused her sadness and fear, and she was quite clear that she was happier without him around. She had made it plain to the Court Welfare Officer who interviewed her that she would not see her father under any circumstances, and as a result he was advised to drop his application for contact. Louise could be said to have been empowered by her strong stance as she stated quite firmly that no child should have to "put up with" unsatisfactory or abusive fathers. . . . In contrast, Maya felt rejected by her father and was preoccupied by his apparent lack of love and concern for her:

> *Maya (15):* I don't know whether [my father] is alive or dead . . . He was horrible, really horrid because he was beating my mum . . . and he hated children. Once my mum had me he just didn't want me. . . . I think about him a lot, I suppose . . . I don't feel whole really, you know, being without a father, even though I don't like that father . . . There's sort of like a space missing . . . I've always thought that I wish I had a different father, you know, not him but a proper father.

Maya only knew her father through her mother's accounts. His absence appeared to be disempowering, although what she regretted was not so much the loss of this relationship *per se* but that she had never had a proper father. Nor did she have other supportive relationships in her family that she could rely on. Maya and Louise therefore represent two ends of a continuum of parent–child separation: One had rejected her father and the other felt he had rejected her.

For other children parental absence was not necessarily absolute even if contact was rare, and this could give rise to the opportunity of transforming a fairly minimal relationship into something more substantial. Hector, for example, saw his father only once or twice a year because he lived abroad. Their contact was tenuous and sporadic and such meetings as they had lasted at most a matter of a few hours. During his interview Hector's most strongly voiced wish was for a closer relationship with his father:

Hector (10): [My father] phoned me but my mum picked it up and there was a big argument—again. Well, not a big argument but it was a pushy argument and sort of, "I don't see why you shouldn't come up [here]" and "Well, it's further for me and I don't have a car." "Well, you should get one then, you should make more effort." I'd like to spend a bit more time with my dad really . . . not always just two or three hours, that's not very good. I barely know him. I've told mum I'd like to see my dad more and she said she'd like that too, and he said he'd like that too, but she says it's very hard and then he says "Well, why doesn't she move?," and she says, "Well, why doesn't he move?"

Hector described trying to bring about improvements in his contact with his father

through the medium of email.[3] He also planned to travel independently so that he could visit his father rather than remaining dependent on his father's rare visits to Britain. At the same time, it was apparent that Hector was aware that his attempts to bring about a more satisfying relationship with his father might fail. He did not disguise from himself that contact visits appeared to be a low priority for his father, but he still wanted to improve their relationship. Hector's experiences provide an example of children's agency and how they may, on occasion, take the lead in trying to forge decent relationships.

The children we have discussed so far were dealing with long-term absence and with parents who created problems for them. But even children who had two unambiguously loving parents whom they saw regularly had to manage the emotional and physical transitions between households which can be demanded of children of divorced parents. While some grew accustomed to living in this way and became used to parting from one or other parent routinely, others experienced it as a series of separations whose repetition did little to diminish their upsetting impact:

Lisa (8): [When I began to be co-parented] I thought I might miss [my mum and dad] terribly and I wouldn't want them to go, and I still don't want them to go. The boys aren't that bothered, they say, "OK, bye," but I still make a big fuss about it. . . . [If I miss my mum and dad] I just try to get on with something nice. But it never works really because you miss the parent and you can't really stop missing them until you see them again.

Lisa faced the choice between managing these regular transitions creatively or seeing one of her parents less often. Thus where children had good relationships with their parents that they wanted to preserve, they often had to devise strategies for coping with their feelings. These involved practical measures, such as having changeovers on a school day to create a neutral territory or to interpose a diversionary activity between leaving one home and joining another. Or they might telephone one parent to exchange news while they were still staying with the other. These were strategies that parents could initiate and help to maintain, but it was striking how self-sufficient many of the children were in recognizing and dealing with their feelings. Lisa was not alone in being able to give an explicit account of the way in which she coped. Other children spoke, for example, of immersing themselves in a book as a way of entering an absorbing, imaginary world for a time, and so distracting themselves and allowing their feelings to subside. Or they spoke of the practical ways in which they dealt with their situation. While some children could turn to adults for support, it was not always available to them, and in some instances they felt that it was not appropriate to ask. In these situations children could become resilient and competent in finding their own ways to cope:

> *Chelsea (8):* When I go on holiday with each parent it's funny because I always miss the other one and you don't really, you can't really tell your mum and dad 'cos to them they think, "Oh well she just wants to be with her dad or mum." So I keep it to myself. But I send them postcards. And I normally take a picture of one of them [with me] when it's [going to be] a long time.

> *Sabrina (10):* If I'm upset usually I'd just either ring dad or . . . I just go and sit in

the dining room or sit in my bedroom and find something to do. . . . I'd just go to my room and think, think about something else and it would stop me being upset.

These strategies for coping should not necessarily be seen as burdens on children as for the most part they preferred to manage their emotions in these ways than to see less of a parent. When they did become too burdensome, however, some children did decide to opt out. . . .

Dealing with Parents

Just as children's self-sufficiency and competence can be underestimated, so too their position as "dependants" can mask their contribution to the work of sustaining relationships with other family members after divorce. This activity, which might be termed "caring," is one of [our] central themes. . . . The theoretical debate on the ethic of care, and the question of whether children can be said to subscribe to such an ethic, are [our] subjects [elsewhere]. In what follows we limit ourselves to an examination of the ways in which some children spoke of their feelings towards their parents after divorce and how this then led them to act. Finch and Mason (1993) and Mason (1996) have suggested that caring is to do with thought, feeling, and interpersonal connection as well as with activity (labour), and arises less from the structural position and kin relationship of the individuals concerned than the quality of the bond between them and the feelings of commitment which this engenders. We wanted to explore whether this proposition could be said to hold true for children and, when they were attentive to their parents' needs and circumstances, whether they acted in this way voluntarily or from a sense of obligation.

What was interesting about the accounts of the children and young people we spoke to was how many of them voiced a belief that divorce had intensified their appreciation of their parents, and their desire actively to help them. They suggested that, as a result of the divorce or separation, they no longer took their parents for granted or saw them simply as an accustomed backdrop to more immediate concerns of their daily lives. Instead, they had become more consciously aware of their attachment to their parents, perceiving the intimacy that they shared with them as potentially vulnerable, and therefore as something to which they wanted to give time and commitment.

Selina (16): I think I've probably got closer to mum and dad just because of the situation. . . . Like, my friends will take their parents for granted, [and say things] like "Mum's always there when I get home" or "Oh god, mum was moaning last night" kind of thing. But I don't 'cos when they're there I know it's only for a short time and I like appreciate them a lot more, I think. . . . My friends don't understand . . . [they'll say] "Oh, are you coming out on Sunday?" or something and I'll be like "Oh no, I can't because I'm going . . . " "Oh, go on!" "Well, no, because I won't see them for a week" kind of thing.

In some cases children simply spoke of developing a close and companionate relationship with their parents and of enjoying time spent in activities with them, or discussing subjects of mutual interest. Often, however, as in Selina's case, it was apparent that they made time to talk to their parents, and that this was an activity in which they chose to engage in preference to another.

We also found children who spoke thoughtfully about the demands made on their parents by post-divorce family life and who displayed considerable attentiveness to their feelings and circumstances. Some children, for example, recognized that their parents had to undergo regular transitions which might also be difficult. So, where a parent had not re-partnered, children could express sympathy for the one who had half a week full of children and half a week alone. Other parents might face different demands. Some, with new partners and children, for example, had to cope with a constantly shifting population of children. Emma's mother was one such parent. As well as having Emma (10) and her baby brother Rory, she had a child by another former partner, and was a part-time stepmother to her current partner's son Josh. Additionally, she worked as a childminder, taking in as many as six children a day. Emma described her mother as "Such a busy mum, always doing anything and everything for everybody." She also said, "She's like my best friend" and "I don't mind sharing her though 'cos she's so wonderful." Emma's interview illustrates how she and children like her did not simply care *about* their parents (were solicitous for them) but cared *for* them, meaning that their attentiveness was translated into active support. She demonstrated this through acting as a second mother to Rory and entertaining him when her mother was busy. Her account suggested that the ways in which she contributed towards the family were entirely voluntary and there was no suggestion that she was burdened by her responsibilities; rather, she was matter of fact about which tasks she could and could not take on. Of course, parents could make it clear that they wanted children to contribute to the running of a shared household. Clare was another elder daughter in a large reconstituted family. She was slightly less enthusiastic about caring in a practical way:

Clare (11): [Mum]'s just so busy. Because she's got four children and it's just really, really hard. Sometimes I feel sorry for her. . . .

Q: *You're the oldest aren't you? Are there things that you have to do to help?*

Clare: Well, I do help, I don't exactly have to, but I do. . . . I get things for mum if she needs them, I go up to the shops if she needs something like milk. . . . I don't exactly like doing it, I'm usually like, "Oh, I don't want to, I'm tired." I'm just making excuses, but I usually go up there.

Clare's comments on the way she helped her mother were not volunteered, as were Emma's, but came in response to a direct question. She did not disguise her lack of enthusiasm for household tasks and she did not rush to offer her "domestic services" to her mother. At the same time, she was alert to the amount of work that her mother had to do even if she did not particularly want to share in it.

We also found instances where boys could be just as thoughtful as girls.[4] David, for example, like many of the children and young people in our study with a parent who had not re-partnered, was concerned that his mother might be lonely and so provided a degree of support and companionship:

David (15): I worry about mum . . . I think my relationship with my mum has been affected because I try to speak to her more and be with her more, because she's . . . got no immediate partner. . . . I'll go and put the tea on and I'll try and stay in so that we can all sort of eat together.

At times, of course, children could be faced with a parent who was not coping and who was extremely needy. Parents could be vulnerable at the point of divorce and behave in ways that children found unpredictable and out of character. They could make excessive or unrealistic demands on their children for help and support. Nevertheless, in the context of ongoing family life we found that most children did not find being supportive of parents an onerous, anxiety-laden or burdensome activity, but regarded it as an everyday family practice and expression of relatedness. Interestingly, children often spoke of parents in affectionate terms that mirrored those of a parent speaking of a child. They expressed concern about whether a parent was eating properly (especially in the case of fathers living alone) and whether they were taking proper care of themselves.

Beth (14): My dad will just let people walk all over him which I'm a bit worried about. Which is probably why I'm a bit worried about leaving him when I move out, but, I don't know, he's a grown man, he should be able to look after himself by now. [laughing]

Q: *Do you ever have any worries about your mum?*

Beth: I think my main worry at the moment is that in like five years' time her and Ian will end up splitting up or something and then she'll be really upset. I don't really worry that much about her though. She can stand up for herself. She can sort herself out. She's got a good head on her shoulders, she'll be OK.

Most of the strategies for dealing with parents that we have outlined here are "positive" in nature. But sometimes children resorted to anger and confrontation when they felt that their parents were behaving poorly or without sufficient sensitivity to their own feelings. In these cases the children were clear that they would not put up with unacceptable behaviour on the part of a parent and were not afraid to say so:

> *Pele (10):* Sometimes we [argue] with dad, if we know he's in the wrong. . . . We made a deal that his wife wouldn't come to Quentin's bar mitzvah.

> *Quentin (13):* I didn't want her there because it was my day and it wasn't right to have my mum and step-mum. But the day before he rang up to say she was coming to the "do" afterwards.

> *Pele:* He went back on his word and changed at the last minute.

> *Quentin:* I felt very annoyed. He picked me up from school and we just sat in the car park and talked for an hour and I shouted at him. . . . I think he's got the message that we don't want her and he can at least tell the truth from the start—at least we'd know then.

Other children, in a complete antithesis to Beck and Beck-Gemsheim's image of children moving quietly, metaphorically kicked and fought to get their views across:

> *Rachel (16):* I had a difficult relationship with my dad for a while. I tried to move out and stuff, but that was really a bluff, I suppose. Me and my dad are both really stubborn. And we'd argue about things and it just got too much. So I packed up all

my stuff and came to mum's, but I phoned him and went back the same night and sorted it out. So it may not have been the best way to go about it, but it changed after that. I have a much better relationship with him now.

And although some children came to appreciate their parents more, others were less enchanted. Their reactions could be uncomfortable for some parents, and many children were prepared to voice their anger or irritation. In other cases they might withdraw from a parent rather than shouldering the uneven struggle of trying to keep a poor relationship going.

Monitoring and Managing the Relationship between Parents

Children were very interested in how their parents regarded each other after their separation because they could feel implicated in or worried by the dislike or hatred one parent might feel towards the other. They might also experience conflicts of loyalty. The children and young people we interviewed were quick to discern whether expressions of friendship were real or simulated for their benefit. Parents might have been willing to discuss these matters with their children, volunteering the information they thought they needed or would benefit from, but children also adopted their own strategies for testing out such information. They closely observed their parents' social interactions and noted changes in their relationships with new or established friends, or partners. Children acknowledged that this monitoring could be a form of surveillance.[5] They listened in on conversations (sometimes putting a glass to the wall), observed what letters arrived, and noted what photographs a parent carried. They were especially alert to the nuances of parents' behaviour towards each other, wanting to know "what was going on," not only at the time of the separation but also subsequently. Given that this process of observation and evaluation was continuous, they sometimes found themselves revising their initial impressions or conclusions:

> *Joey (15):* Mum and dad used to really not get on and it used to be a really sort of tight-lipped situation and now, I don't know, just gradually, and there have been times when they first started to get on it felt really strange and I sort of thought, well was dad trying to "get back in" maybe, or is he trying to do anything. But now it just feels as though, I mean it seems to be much easier and it's just so much better. I mean he comes up at Christmas sometimes and it's just much better for them to get on and for everybody to get on as a family, because when they didn't get on it felt as if maybe we would have to take sides and I didn't want to do that. . . . I think mum sometimes used to feel as though dad and Antony and Nick and I would go off and chat because we hadn't seen each other and mum would be left in the kitchen, and sometimes she'd get quite upset about it, but now we can all get along as a family.

Joey was attentive to his mother's feelings. He also closely scrutinized the shifts in his parents' relationship and was concerned to detect whether there was a hidden agenda in his father's behaviour. Additionally, he felt relief in the re-establishment of a cordial, and possibly even friendly, relationship between them. He made it clear how much he disliked feeling caught in the middle between two alienated parents and was relieved when he no longer had to feel conflicting loyalties.

Not all parents could be civil of course, and where one (or both) parent(s) continued to be abusive, manipulative, hostile, or violent children faced very difficult situations. We acknowledge outright manipulation of children in parental conflicts . . ., but even in quite ordinary situations children could feel caught in the middle:

> *Matt (15):* [The arguments are] just relentless. I wish they would stop it.

It is important to recognize, however, that for some children it was their parents' divorce that allowed them to escape from the war zone:

> *Nick (14):* It's almost made it easier though, our mum and dad not living together, because before there were arguments and things like that and it was difficult really to live. But now that they've moved apart they're both much happier and much more relaxed. Like my mum, she comes in tense from work just 'cos her work's like that, but she comes home and she'll relax rather than before she would have come home and there probably would have been an argument about something completely stupid and irrelevant, 'cos they argued for the hell of it basically.

Both Matt and Nick tried to ignore their parents' quarrels, but sometimes children tried to act as peace makers and pacifiers.

> *Nina (11):* Sometimes if dad doesn't like [the arrangements] then he can get me to change mum's mind.
>
> *Q: What happens?*
>
> *Nina:* He just moans, and then I talk to him on the phone and try to cheer him up.

Q: How?

Nina: I just talk to him for a while and have a joke and then it makes it easier for my mum.

Andrijka (10): Sometimes dad gets a bit angry, well, not angry, but he doesn't like the way things are between the houses because they're so far away, so sometimes he tells me what he feels and I wouldn't say that in front of mum because I don't think dad would tell her how he felt, so I don't really want to tell things that dad didn't want her to know, really. . . . It's a bit upsetting because sometimes he's sort of making mum out to be a bad person when she's not and sometimes it's just, he's not actually talking about her, he's talking about the position of the houses and I feel a bit the same way about that.

The children developed a strong sense of diplomacy but also became skillful in managing difficult situations and their parents' moods. These examples reveal very clearly the emotional complexity of post-divorce childhood and extent to which children become fluent in new narratives of tact and sensibility.

Dealing with New Partners

[Elsewhere] we discussed how children new partners and how this was linked to whether they operated within a model of family with closed or open boundaries. But the children could also experience their parents' re-partnering as a form of loss in that they often found they enjoyed less parental attention than previously. This meant that they could dislike partners out of jealousy rather than because were intrinsically unlikeable:

Thomas (11): I don't like mum's new partner, not overly fond of what he did to us and like . . . the principle's bad, just taking someone else's isn't exactly the best thing to do is it? . . . Now, when we go out he's always like right next to her and my brother's on the other side of her and I'm walking behind or in front of all of them and I don't get much attention now. And they're thinking of having a baby and if that happens I'll only get like a quarter of the attention and so I'm going to say that I'm going to spend a lot more time with my dad if they have a child.

Hope (14): When mum got together with [her new partner] there were some problems at first, like I had my nose out of joint a bit having to share her, which was difficult. But we've got round that now, he's not there so much as he used to be, so we've still got our time together, which is really useful.

In some cases children acted to rid of themselves of these unwelcome intruders:

Chelsea (8): Mum had a boyfriend and he always was like always really grumpy . . . I don't think I could ever like him because he was always grumpy. Whenever he came my mum always used to cook him a special, well a different, dinner than we used to have, but it was always special and I thought she liked him best but she always said, "I don't." But once when they were together I wrote a letter and I asked my mum to sign [it] if she loved me, so she signed. And I wrote on the letter,

Dear Bill,

I think it's time we split up now and got somebody else.

But my mum found out about it.

And Alex, who was 12, left notes lying around his home in prominent places which said "JIM MUST GO." Both he and Chelsea managed to get across to their mothers their dislike of the new men and in Chelsea's case her mother ended the relationship. In Alex's case, she agreed to see him mostly when Alex was with his father.

. . . [M]any children could form close attachments with new partners and saw them as friends or family members, if not as parents. But even where this was impossible some children were aware that even though they did not like the new partner, he or she might make their parent happy. Hope, above, for example, commented of her mother's relationship, "They've been together for about a year and they're really close. It's really good for her." Similarly, Beth, who spoke at length about her dislike of sharing her home with her mother's partner, when asked what wish she would like to make for her family and herself said:

> *Beth (14):* I'd want my mum and Ian [partner] to get on really well and stop arguing altogether. When I was little I used to be happy they argued except for the fact Ian shouted a lot, because I thought "Oh, they might split up this time." But I'd want them to get on well.

Clearly, re-partnering is a complex issue and some children did not feel "free" to like a new partner because they were aware that their other parent was still alone or simply very unhappy. They could feel uncomfortable with one parent's happiness if it seemed to be based upon the other one's misery:

> *James (12):* I haven't always liked [my dad's partner] 'cos my mum felt really

unhappy. But I like her now. . . . It's okay having her there I'm used to it now, and I just—well, dad's—happy and everything, dad's happy, and I suppose that's okay.

A major part of "doing" post-divorce childhood seemed to involve coming to terms with the fact that parents too need happiness and that this could be valued and valuable, even if the child or young person did not much like the situation. By and large they saw the family as a network of relationships in which the needs, wishes, and interests of each member had to be recognized. They knew that their feelings of dislike might not be shared by others and some recognized that their antipathy was born of jealousy rather than being based on an "objective" evaluation of the new partner. Hope, above, described herself as initially being acutely jealous of her mother's new partner and as only beginning to acknowledge this after reaching a point in her arguments with her mother where she ran off to her father. James could only allow himself to like his father's new partner after a passage of time. What we are suggesting, therefore, is that re-partnering is a major event that prompts children to think about their families in new ways and that gives rise to a variety of strategies of management and negotiation.

An Altered Self?

So far we have talked about the ways in which divorce can alter children's relationships. However, there is also a sense in which it separates or distances children from their parents. If divorce changes parents, it also can make children aware that they too have to change:

> Q: *Do you think [your parents' separation] has changed you at all?*

Tom (12): Don't know really. Maybe. . . . I'm very sort of cautious about criticism from people now, [more] than I would have been I think. . . . And I think I sort of get in major stresses now and again which I don't think I used to before.

Q: Do you think it's changed you at all, living in a family like yours?

Charmaine (11): Yes, I think it's maybe made me a bit more mature. Yes, I think it's got me a bit more used to dealing with things that maybe I didn't want to happen.

What stands out for a number of children was that they felt they had become more independent of their parents. Selina, for example, recognized that she had, of necessity, become less dependent upon her parents:

Selina (16): It was really funny when we went to Holland on the hockey tour. A couple of my friends were really missing their mum and dad. We were only there for ten days and . . . I didn't like, miss either [of my parents] because . . . well, every week I'm without one of them. In a way . . . I don't miss them at all because . . . I'm used to not having them around. . . . I suppose, due to everything, I'm a lot more independent than a lot of [my friends]. . . . And Nat's [brother] the same. We're very independent and we had to grow up a lot faster than a lot of other people. . . . Because we've had to manage really.

This newly acquired sense of independence was not restricted to the emotional sphere but could extend to the social sphere as well. Children often felt they had more autonomy and were less subject to parental oversight,

even where they were making a great deal of effort to spend time with both parents. When parents lived in separate households they were not always well positioned to oversee children's day-to-day lives and could find it difficult to impose a routine or sometimes discipline. Some children experienced very different routines and/or attitudes in each home and could, as a consequence, enjoy a greater sense of freedom:

Ryan (10): I think my mum probably worries about me being at my dad's 'cos he lets me do loads of things that she wouldn't let me do.

Q: What sorts of things?

Ryan: Well, things that are more dangerous and stuff like that [physical activities such as climbing and sledding]. He lets me stay up later . . . like at weekends [mum] makes me go to bed at like ten past ten on Friday and he lets me stay up 'till about two o'clock on Saturday.

. . .

Q: If you could have a wish for the future, for you and your family, what wish would you make?

Ryan: I wouldn't wish 'em to get back together 'cos I wouldn't really like that anyway, but probably [live] a bit closer to friends and stuff like that.

Q: When you said you wouldn't like it if they got back together, what wouldn't you like?

Ryan: Well, my mum would be there to tell me not to do things.

Q: Yes? So, some of the things that you're able to do when you're at dad's house, you wouldn't be able to do?

Ryan: No.

Moreover, new partners did not always diminish this greater sense of freedom because they did not have the same authority as a parent:

> *Beth (14):* It means you can get away with more, I think . . . because both my parents work late and there's only Ian [mum's partner] and he couldn't tell me what to do if he wanted to, well, he can tell me "Please will you make your . . . why can't you wash up?" or something, but he couldn't like say, "Right, that's it, you're staying in, you're not going out."

Q: Right, so that's not part of his role in the house?

Beth: No, he can't like, boss me about, tell me how to live my life.

The post-divorce family is clearly very much a new terrain for children in which they can actively negotiate new norms and/or new styles of relationships with both parents and new partners. They are faced with new opportunities (whether welcomed or not) and in this process can change themselves and can challenge previous assumptions about how children and adults should relate. Some children began to question their parents' attitudes, values, and expectations—perhaps before they might otherwise have done so as a normal part of growing up. In this sense they are clearly engaged in a form of "orienteering" through a landscape of intimate relationships.

Changing Childhoods?

Selina's belief that she had had to grow up faster than her friends (Weiss, 1979) was echoed by several of the children we interviewed, and the way they articulated their feelings demonstrates this. Divorce confronts children with experiences which make them think differently about their family practices and re-evaluate their relationships. This process gives them the opportunity to take an active, independent stance and to experience themselves as autonomous persons. Sometimes reassessing their families in this way led them to the conclusion that they did not like one parent very much, or it encouraged them to try to sustain contact with a parent. In these cases children exercised the choice which they felt they had about their family ties and could increase, reduce or even sever contact. Other children came to place more value on their parents than they once did. They became attentive to the feelings and circumstances of other family members and were responsive to opportunities for contributing to the well-being of those for whom they cared. As we have seen, they might make tea for a tired parent, offer companionship or, where parents were involved in ongoing conflict with each other, they acquired skills in empathy or mediation.

Once children begin to think for themselves about their place in their family it is not surprising that they should want to have more say in matters that affect them. Moreover, children with parents who live apart are almost invariably aware of having choices available to them about where and how they live. Some, of course, have more scope than others for negotiating the structure of their family arrangements or the nature of their day-to-day activities. Parenting styles, and the personal and social resources upon which they are able to draw, are important factors in increasing or diminishing their ability to exercise choice. Nevertheless, for many, divorce can be said to open up new areas of social experience which can offer (or demand of) children enhanced independence and autonomy. They may have to manage emotional transitions between two separate households, get used to travelling long distances to maintain contact with a parent, adapt to living intimately alongside new adults and children, or adapt to not seeing one parent at all.

It does not require a divorce for children to become active practitioners of family life who negotiate individualized relationships with different family members, value their parents, or balance caring for others with their own self-interests. Doing family life in the context of divorce, for some children at least, will not be substantially different from doing family life in co-residential families. Indeed most contemporary children may be growing up a little faster in a context where both parents may work outside the home and where attitudes towards children and parenting are beginning to change. Many of the children in our study, particularly those who were living substantially in one home, spoke of their family lives with some complacency, indicating that they were not constantly acting against a background concern about the contingency of relationships but were getting on with their perfectly ordinary childhoods.

Jake (11): It seems ordinary now, this pattern, because it's been happening like this for a long time. Basically I take things as they come and I just get on with it.

Pele (10): You get on with your life and then when something comes up, just try and cross that bridge when you come to it.

If divorce alone does not bring about this process of changing childhoods and changing families, it does contribute in quite specific ways and is probably one of the most significant catalysts in bringing into being new forms of childhood. It necessarily alters children's perception of "family" and the relationships that this entails and, crucially, makes it impossible for children to take family ties for granted. As we discussed [elsewhere] kinship in the UK has always been substantially personal, flexible, and affective (Finch, 1997) in that it is based more on the degree of liking and affection between kin than the positional relationships which exist between them. The ties between children and parents have, however, always been regarded as an exception to this and have been seen as less flexible and less voluntaristic than those between other kin. Changes in family structures and attitudes seem, however, to be bringing about more optionality in the parent–child relationship—at least for some children.[6] It is noticeable how often the children and young people in our samples spoke of "liking" or "not liking" individual parents. They may have felt that their hold a unique position in their lives which could not be taken over in any absolute sense by adults, but they no longer felt bound to them in the same way. We found that respect and liking significantly influenced the commitment as well as the closeness they felt towards them. In facing up to the restructuring of their family lives and being confronted by the contingent nature of contemporary human relationships, it seems some children may now be thinking much more explicitly about their relationships and what "family" means to them. . . .

● Notes

1. Of course children do have access to fairy stories and children's literature, and the increasingly popular soaps. Much traditional literature is rather negative when it comes to children's experiences of stepparents, however, and even the immensely popular Harry Potter books are negative about the experiences of living with kin who are not biological parents. One has only to think of the dreadful Dursleys and their ghastly son Dudley who had poor Harry living in a cupboard under the stairs for nearly 11 years to be reminded that children get rather negative images of life apart from their biological parents.

2. For example, as early as 1980 Wallerstein and Kelly made the point that parental absence which was chosen by a child was quite different in its consequences and psychological impact to parental absence chosen by an adult who appeared to the child.

3. The use of this new technology to improve father–son relationships is very interesting; we found an instance of this in our research for *Family Fragments?* (Smart and Neale, 1999).

4. We raise this because there is a strong assumption following Gilligan (1982) that it is really only girls who do this kind of emotional work. We were not attempting to test this hypothesis in this research, but we certainly found many examples of boys being attentive and caring.

5. As Rachel (16) said, "I always knew quite a lot about what was going on between mum and dad because I've always made it my business to know quite a lot about everything. Which can be a bit annoying sometimes—Ha!—for other people."

6. It is important to acknowledge that not all children can take advantage of these developments. . . .

● References

Beck, U., and E. Beck-Gernsheim. 1995. *The normal chaos of love.* Cambridge: Polity Press.

Finch, J. 1997. *The state and the family.* Lecture to inaugurate the annual theme of the Institute of International Social Sciences, University of Edinburgh, 30 October 1996. Edinburgh: Institute of International Social Sciences.

Finch, L., and J. Mason. 1993. *Negotiating family responsibilities.* London: Tavistock/Routledge.

Giddens, A. 1991. *Modernity and self-identity.* Stanford, CA: Stanford University Press.

Gilligan, C. 1982. *In a different voice.* Cambridge, MA: Harvard University Press.

Mason, J. 1996. Gender, care, and sensibility in family and kin relationships. In J. Holland and L. Atkins (eds), *Sex, sensibility, and the gendered body.* Basingstoke: Macmillan.

Smart, C. 2000. Divorce and changing family practices in a post-traditional society. In *Family matters.* Melbourne: Australian Institute for Family Studies.

Smart, C., and B. Neale. 1999. *Family fragments?* Cambridge: Polity Press.

Weiss, R. 1979. Growing up a little faster: The experience of growing up in a single parent household. *Journal of Social Issues* 35: 97–111.

Chapter 26

About one in every eight Canadian families involving a couple with children are blended families. They are families with at least one adult who is divorced. Usually, they also involve children from a former marriage of one of the adults. This composition often means that both children and adults had to adjust to having only the divided attention of a parent or a partner as the family was formed. If there are children from former marriages, one or both of the adults—as well as the children—likely also have some kind of ongoing relationship with an ex-spouse or a parent living in another household.

These families involve complexity that is unlikely in other kinds of nuclear families. As a result, there is a tendency in sociological research, as well as popular culture, to regard blended (or reconstituted) families as inherently problematic. In this chapter, however, Elizabeth Church indicates the positive potential embodied in blended families. She does this after identifying the challenges and potential problems that they face—in part due to cultural ideals about nuclear families.

Kinship and Stepfamilies

Elizabeth Church

Introduction

The number of stepfamilies in North America has rapidly increased over the last 30 years. In the United States, half of all current marriages are remarriages for at least one of the partners; one-third of American children will live in a stepfamily at some point before they become adults, while 40 per cent of adult women will be part of a stepfamily (Coleman, Ganong, and Fine 2000). The numbers are less dramatic in Canada, where the rates of divorce and remarriage are lower. Nevertheless, by the early 1990s only about one-third of Canadian children were born into "traditional" families where there were two married parents who had not lived together prior to marriage (Juby, Marcil-Gratton, and Le Bourdais 2001). Twenty-six per cent of men and 15 per cent of women who had been married more than once identified themselves as

stepparents (Ram 1990). The 1994–95 National Longitudinal Survey of Children and Youth, which looked at the family histories of 22,831 Canadian children, found that 8.6 per cent of Canadian children under age 12 lived in a stepfamily (Marcil-Gratton 1998). The actual number of stepfamilies may also be underreported because researchers often only count families where couples are legally remarried, while the reality is that couples with children are increasingly cohabiting without marriage (Bumpass, Raley, and Sweet 1995; Coleman, Ganong, and Fine 2000; Juby, Marcil-Gratton, and Le Bourdais 2001; Vanier Institute 1994).

. . .

Divorce and Remarriage

Although there has been a recent rapid increase in the number of stepfamilies in North America, historically there were about as many stepfamilies as there are now. Historians and scholars (Gordon 1978; Ihinger-Tallmart and Pasley 1987; Stone 1977) estimate that between the sixteenth and nineteenth centuries in England and the United States about 20 to 30 per cent of families were stepfamilies. The anomalous period in terms of the numbers of stepfamilies is thus the time from about the end of the nineteenth century, when maternal mortality rates decreased, to about 30 years ago when divorce rates rose.

The main difference between stepfamilies then and now is that the earlier ones were formed as the result of the death of a parent. Today's come about primarily through divorce. In the United States, it was only by the 1950s that stepfamilies created by divorce became more prevalent (Ihinger-Tallman and Pasley 1987). In Canada, the divorce rate rose significantly between 1972 and 1976 following the 1968 *Divorce Act,* which made divorce more easily accessible in all provinces (Dumas and Péron 1992). Since then, the number of stepfamilies in Canada has also increased.

There is little research comparing stepfamilies following the death of a parent and those as a consequence of divorce, even though there are obvious structural differences. In a stepfamily formed after the death of a parent, the children generally live with the surviving parent and the stepparent and there is only one household. When both parents are living, there are usually two households, and the children may move from one to the other. Household boundaries with the latter group are often more permeable than those formed after death. In her study of 60 Canadian adolescents living in stepfamilies, Penny Gross (1985) found that a third had changed residence at least once. In my study of stepmothers, 35 per cent of the stepmothers had had at least one stepchild move in or out of their residence at least once. For example,

when one stepmother, Amy (all the names and some details have been changed in this example and any other references to stepmothers in my study), started living with Peter, his three children (Eric, Rebecca, and Melanie) lived with their mother and her new husband and visited their father on weekends (the "traditional" arrangement for stepfamilies). When Eric was 14, he decided he wanted to live with his father and moved in with Amy and Peter. Rebecca was having problems with her stepfather so she moved in as well, but returned to her mother's house after two years. None of these changes was recorded through the courts, so that Peter's ex-wife was still legally recognized as the custodial parent (the one with custody of the children). Each move made significant changes in each household. Amy, for example, had initially expected that she would have fun and relaxed weekend visits with her stepchildren. Instead, she found herself disciplining two teenagers as well as cooking and cleaning for them.

Even with the prevalence of divorce, it still carries a *stigma,* or negative label. When college students rated hypothetical situations about parents and children from intact nuclear families, single-parent families, and stepfamilies, they considered children from divorced families less stable and secure than children from non-divorced, nuclear families (Coleman and Ganong 1987). The popular press also emphasizes the negative aspects of divorce. Expressions such as "broken home" are still common, and studies showing that divorce has a harmful effect on children are given a lot of attention in the media (Whitehead 1993). Divorce is expected to cause problems. This attitude may be in part because society is still generally oriented toward first marriages, where there is only one household and the family configuration is constant. Any departure is seen as deviant or harmful.

Another way to conceptualize divorce is to recognize it as a normal part of many people's lives. For many, divorce is part of a developmental life cycle. In the United States, "serial marriage," where people marry and divorce a number of times, has become increasingly common (Coleman, Ganong, and Fine 2000). Some writers (Stone 1977) speculate that there is a natural duration to marriages. Now that people are living longer, divorce has become the way to maintain that length. Seeing divorce as a part of life for many people is not to deny that divorce and remarriage can cause significant upheaval in people's lives. Both can be painful and difficult events with long-term effects. It is not all bad news, however. In a review of research on the effects of divorce on children, Amato (2000) found that, while children with divorced parents score lower than children with married parents on measures such as academic success, psychological adjustment, and social competence, the differences are fairly small. In assessing the impact of parental divorce on children, we need to consider multiple factors such as conflict between the parents, post-divorce economic hardship, and support from peers, and not assume that divorce is the main variable.

In North America, although women remarry less often than men, both men and women remarry frequently and fairly quickly after divorce. In Canada it is estimated that 76 per cent of men and 44 per cent of women who divorce will remarry (Ram 1990), and 75 per cent of them will do so within three years of divorce. In the United States, half the men and women remarry within three years of their divorce, and 84 per cent of men and 75 per cent of women eventually remarry (Cherlin 1988). Women's and men's rates of remarriage are linked with their economic status. Following divorce, the standard of living for many women and children drops (and child-support payments do not make up the difference), while on average most men's standards of living increase (Maccoby and Mnookin 1992). After remarriage, most women's financial situations improve, while men's worsen (Ganong and Coleman 1994). Women who are highly educated and financially and occupationally independent tend to remarry less often, while the opposite pattern occurs with men, so that high-income men remarry more frequently than low-income men (Crosbie-Burnett, Skyles, and Becker-Haven 1988; Ihinger-Tallman and Pasley 1987). It may be that some women remarry to get themselves out of difficult economic circumstances.

Kinship

In our society, *kinship—family* relations—is based on the *marital dyad,* or married couple (Firth 1956; Johnson 1988; Mead 1970; Schneider 1980). In other societies kinship may be established by the relationship between brothers and sisters or the links to the wife's or husband's family. If a marriage ends in a society where kinship links are through brothers and sisters, kinship bonds are often strengthened rather than weakened (Johnson 1988). In our society, however, the breakup of a marriage can cause a great deal of instability. Without an extended family to act as a support, divorce may lead to a situation where people feel they are floating around without an anchor. The emphasis on the marital relationship and the lack of an extended-kin network may also account for some of the effects of divorce on children, because children may also lose their family through their parents' separation. Margaret Mead, an anthropologist who was herself a stepmother, made these observations about the American family:

We are a society in which the union of a male and female institutes a new social unit . . . Neither the father's kin nor the mother's kin have any legal responsibility for the children, as long as the parents are alive . . . Each American child learns, early and in terror, that his [sic] whole security depends on that single set of parents who, more often than not, are arguing furiously in the next room over some detail in their lives. A desperate demand upon the permanence and all-satisfyingness of monogamous marriage is set up in the cradle. (Mead 1970, 113)

Because we do not have a strong extended-family structure, we depend heavily on the marital relationship to provide support and nurturance for children. When the marital relationship collapses, this causes more chaos than might occur in an extended-kin network.

One reason for the high rate of remarriage in our society may be that men and women lose their family through divorce and thus seek to fill this vacuum quickly. Johnson (1988) found that women who became closer to their parents after divorce—that is, created a kin network with their parents—were less apt to remarry, while men and women who decreased contact with their parents tended to become involved in relationships more frequently and faster.

Generally, the remarried couple forms the centre of a new stepfamily. This emphasis on the marital couple does not work as neatly in the stepfamily, however, as it does in nuclear, non-divorced family. Relationships predating the marriage, such as the parent–child relationship, may be stronger than the newly married dyad's bond. People not living with the new family, such as non-residential parents, will usually have an impact on the stepfamily.

People in stepfamilies may also have diverse ideas about what it means to be part of this kind of family. In my study of 104 stepmothers, I discovered that these women conceptualized kinship—whom they considered part of their family—in five distinct ways (Church 1999b). One group was what I called *nuclear stepmothers*. These women adopted the nuclear family as their model for the stepfamily. They defined their family as themselves, their partners, stepchildren, and biological children. They often wanted to sever contact with non-residential family members, such as ex-spouses and in-laws. All assumed a mother role with their stepchildren, which led them to feel in competition with their stepchildren's mother. A second group was the *extended stepmothers*. They also considered their stepchildren kin, but did not view themselves as a mother. Their view of kinship was elastic and they welcomed remarriage as an opportunity to expand their network of connections. In describing their families, they often included extended kin, such as their ex-partner or their partner's ex-wife's family. The *couple stepmothers,* by contrast, focused on their relationship with their partner and saw this as the centre of the stepfamily. They did not consider their stepchildren part of their family, as they believed their stepchildren already had enough parenting from their biological parents. Their ideal relationship was to be a friend to their stepchildren. A fourth group was the *biological stepmothers*, who divided family along biological lines. They saw two families living in the same house: the stepmother and her children as one family and her partner and his children as the other. Finally, there were the *no-family stepmothers*. They felt alone in the situation and regarded themselves as outsiders to the stepfamily, which they considered their partner and his children. They were the most unhappy stepmothers and generally had very poor relationships with their stepchildren. Of course, I was talking to only one member of the stepfamily. It is probable that others, such as biological parents and stepchildren, have a different perspective on their family.

Multiplicity of Roles in Stepfamilies

The number and variety of relationships are much greater in stepfamilies than in nuclear, non-divorced families. In order to give an idea of how relationships multiply in stepfamilies, let me give you an example of one stepmother from my study. Her story is typical of many others. Hazel was originally married to Kurt, with whom she had two children: Alice and Bob. Within this family, Hazel had three different relationships: as a wife to Kurt, a mother to her daughter Alice, and a mother to her son Bob. After nine years of marriage, she and Kurt separated. Two years later she met George, who had been married to Laura and had two children, Kathleen and Noel. Hazel and George formed what is called a *complex stepfamily,*

because both brought children from a previous relationship. Hazel's ex-husband Kurt subsequently married Ann, and they had a daughter, Elizabeth, and a son, Jesse. George's ex-partner Laura met Ravi and they began living together. It may help to chart all these relationships on a genogram (see Figure 26.1). A genogram is a graphic way to represent family relations and is an easy way to grasp the relationships in a family structure as complicated as this one. It is often used to trace families back through generations. (For more information about how to construct genograms, see Monica McGoldrick and Randy Gerson's [1985] book.)

As a result of living with George, the number of Hazel's kin relationships has radically increased. She now has nine (instead of three): with her current partner, George; with her former husband, Kurt; with her daughter, Alice; with her son, Bob; with her stepdaughter, Kathleen; with her stepson, Noel; with her partner's ex-wife, Laura; with her ex-husband's current wife, Ann; and with her partner's ex-wife's current partner, Ravi. Similarly, Hazel's daughter Alice has also tripled the number of

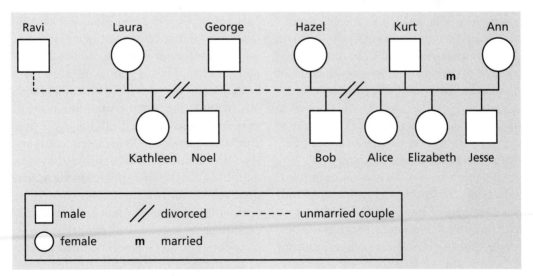

Figure 26.1 Genogram of Hazel's Family,

kinship links she had in her original family. In charting this family, I have stayed within two generations and have not even considered the mushrooming of other extended kin. Alice, for example, has acquired two more sets of grandparents as the result of her parents' new relationships. The multiplication of potential relationships in stepfamilies is staggering.

One sign that we, as a society, have not acknowledged the complexities of stepfamilies is that we have no terms for some of the relationships. Hazel, for example, has no names for three of her nine roles. She can call herself a partner, an ex-wife, a mother, and a stepmother, but what does she call herself in relation to her partner's ex-wife Laura; her ex-husband's current wife Ann; and her partner's ex-wife's current partner Ravi? Lacking a way to describe these relationships may leave people unprepared to deal with them. In my study, many stepmothers said they had no idea of the complications that the new stepfamily would bring. While they had recognized they were adding their partner and his children to their lives, they usually did not anticipate the impact of their partner's ex-wife, or their partner's ex-wife's current partner. In Hazel's case, she and Ann (her ex-husband's current wife) have worked together to develop a homework schedule for Alice, who has school difficulties. In order to plan last summer's vacations, she had to work around many people's work schedules—including Ravi's (her partner's ex-wife's current partner), whom she has rarely met.

There are few societal models for the multiplicity of relationships created by stepfamilies. Members of stepfamilies often struggle with how to act and interact with these new people. From the start, Hazel was very uncomfortable with the constant presence of Laura, her partner's ex-wife, in her life:

When I first started living with George, Laura would come over after school to visit with the children [Hazel's stepchildren, Kathleen and Noel] during the times the children were living with us. I felt really uncomfortable about having her in the house when I wasn't home, but I didn't think I could say anything because she and George had had this arrangement before I came on the scene. But I would sit at work imagining that she was going through my kitchen cupboards, and it bothered me so much that George told Laura he didn't want her in the house unless we were there. So then she got mad and refused to come into the house at all and would stay in the car and honk the horn for Kathleen and Noel to come out. They got angry with me and told their father that I was unreasonable . . . I ended up feeling like the wicked stepmother.

One way some people deal with the ambiguity of relationships in stepfamilies is to exclude non-residential members. Following divorce, non-residential parents often lose contact with their children. Frank Furstenberg (1988) found that 44 per cent of children had no communication with their non-residential parent in the previous year, while 21 per cent visited their non-residential parent less than once a week. The 35 per cent of non-residential parents who saw their children more than once a week tended to have more recreational than instrumental contact; that is, they were more likely to take their children to the movies than help them with their homework. There are multiple reasons why non-residential parents do not maintain their connection with their children. Some non-residential parents in Furstenberg's study said they felt "awkward" visiting their children, or that it was too "emotionally painful." Our model of kinship, where so much hinges on the marital relationship, may contribute to this awkwardness. When a marriage ends and one parent, usually the father, moves out, he has to renegotiate a new relationship with his children, one not based on day-to-day living. Since we have few models for how non-residential kin can be involved with children in an "instrumental" way, these parents may be unsure how to establish a new footing with their children.

As well, if the residential parent—usually the mother—wants to recreate a nuclear family, she may perceive the non-residential parent as intrusive. Similar to my finding that some stepmothers attempt to recreate a nuclear family, Burgoyne and Clark (1984) found that over half the families they interviewed tried to forge a nuclear, non-divorced family. These stepfamilies usually wanted the non-residential parent out of the picture. If your ideal is the nuclear family, you may not see a way to incorporate the new family relations that spring up with remarriage. One solution is to cut off people outside the household.

With joint custody, however, it becomes more difficult to maintain the fiction that a stepfamily can be a nuclear family. When children move regularly between two households, how do we decide which is their "primary" house and who is the residential and who the non-residential parent? As the number of joint custody situations increases in Canada, and kin do not disappear after divorce and remarriage, a new model of the extended family may emerge.

The Assumption That Household Equals Family

In our society we tend to merge the concepts of household and family. If we see a man and a woman living in the same house with children, we assume that these individuals are a family. This equating of household with family is very much tied to our ideology about kinship (Rapp 1992), which is dominated by the ideal of the nuclear family. This equation does not hold true for the stepfamily in at least three ways: (1) members of stepfamilies who live together may not feel related; (2) people in stepfamilies use a variety of criteria, in addition to household ties, to determine who is part of their family; and (3) household boundaries in stepfamilies are more fluid than they are in nuclear families.

1. Members of stepfamilies who live together may not feel related. The relationship of stepparent and stepchild is that of in-laws: they are related by marriage. In our society in-laws, or **affines**, do not usually live in the same household (Bohannan 1984). We do not generally expect that people will love, or even like, their in-laws—the popularity of mother-in-law jokes bears witness to this. We do expect, however, that residential stepparents, just because they live with someone who has children, will take on a parental role with their stepchildren. Just as we may not like or love in-laws who live outside the household, there is no reason to assume we will like or love the ones we live with. Researchers (Furstenberg 1987; Hetherington and Clingempeel 1992) have found that children in stepfamilies were less likely to feel close to stepparents or to want to be like them when they grew up. This is not to say that all stepparent–stepchild relationships are negative. The majority of stepchildren in Furstenberg's study expressed "benign" if "distant" feelings about their stepparents. What Furstenberg's study demonstrates is that just because stepparents and stepchildren live in the same household, we cannot assume that they will have a close relationship.

In my study of stepmothers, even those stepmothers who got along well with their stepchildren saw significant differences between their relationships with biological children and stepchildren. Often they described themselves "walking on eggshells" with their stepchildren, while they felt more "natural" with their biological children. Gina has been stepmother for 13 years and is very close with her stepdaughter, Jane, but there is a reserve in her relationship with Jane that has never existed with her biological daughter:

> I still don't think of her [the stepdaughter] as a daughter. I still think of her as a stepdaughter. I've only known her since she was a teenager, while with my daughter who's three and a half I have a completely different relationship. I have a completely organic kind of relationship that grew from the ground up. We will have a history, and I know everything about her and she knows everything about me, and I'm completely comfortable with her. To this day I don't feel like that about Jane.

The barrier of not having a common history was a frequent theme in my study. In stepfamilies, some people share a history while others do not. This can lead to people feeling like outsiders. To return to Hazel (whose family was charted on the genogram), her struggles with her partner's ex-wife Laura stem in part from joining a family that already has its own patterns. When George and Laura separated, he kept the family house and Laura found another place. Hazel and her children later moved into George's house. One reason Laura felt comfortable rummaging through Hazel's kitchen cupboards is that this was once her kitchen. For Hazel, however, Laura's presence was an unwelcome symbol of Laura's history with George.

One consequence of assuming that a household equals a family is that a stepfamily is regarded as a full-fledged family from the moment the couple marries (here again is the tyranny of the ideology of the marital couple). The assumption is that members instantly feel part of a family. Unlike a non-divorced family, which typically starts with the couple having time alone together and then has nine months of pregnancy to adjust to the idea of becoming parents, a stepfamily couple immediately plunges into life with children. Although stepfamilies may look like instant families, most go through a developmental process to become a family. Becoming an integrated stepfamily takes time. Some families take about two to four years (Visher and Visher 1988), others as long as 12 years, while some stepfamilies never gel as a family (Papernow 1993).

One factor affecting the development of the stepfamily is that, for some of its members, the stepfamily is their third type of family structure. Initially, they were part of a nuclear never-divorced family, then they were in a single-parent family, and now they are in a stepfamily. Not all people in stepfamilies go through this sequence (some exceptions are stepparents who do not have children from a prior relationship, and parents and children who were always in single-parent families), but the majority of members in new stepfamilies have experienced these three types of families. In the example that was charted on the genogram, Hazel was first part of a nuclear family with her husband Kurt and two children, then she formed a single-parent family, and now she has become part of a stepfamily with her new partner George and his children. Each of these types of families tends to have different patterns of interacting, which means members of a new stepfamily have to learn the "rules" of stepfamily life.

This means there has also been the loss of two earlier families. These events are often painful for children, who have little choice about their parents separating and re-partnering. Although there has been a great deal of attention to the effects of divorce on children (the loss of the original nuclear family) (Amato 2000; Hetherington 1987; Hetherington and Aratesh 1988), there has been less research on the effects of ending a single-parent family (Hetherington and Jodl 1993). Children and parents in single-parent families often develop very close bonds, and children may feel pushed aside when their parents become involved in a new adult relationship (Martin and Martin 1992; Visher and Visher 1988).

Forming a new stepfamily also often means bringing together families with different traditions and ways of behaving, from the kinds of foods eaten to how children are disciplined, how birthdays are celebrated, or even which television shows are watched. These patterns derive from cultural and religious backgrounds, experience in one's own family of origin, and the individual family's development over time. In general, remarried couples are less similar to each other in demographics—age, education, religion—than first-married couples (Ganong and Coleman 1994), so a remarrying couple may be bringing together two quite dissimilar families.

Building a stepfamily often means integrating differences and evolving new rules and rituals. This can be a slow process. One stepmother in my study, Angie, had children from her previous marriage, as did her husband, Ernesto. When they tried to decorate their first Christmas tree, the two sets of stepsiblings ended up squabbling about whose decorations would go on the tree. Angie's solution was to have two trees, one for each family:

The first couple of years after we got married, we had two Christmas trees, one in the living room and one in the rec room. Once they [Angie's biological children and stepchildren] got older, 1 could say to them, "It's really a big hassle," but the first couple of years, there was so much decoration and everybody wanted everything: My kids wanted this because we had always had it on our tree, and the other ones wanted that because they had it on their tree.

Eventually the family was ready to share a Christmas tree, but the children needed the transitional time in order to feel their own Christmas traditions would be preserved.

2. People in stepfamilies use a variety of criteria, in addition to household ties, in deciding who is part of their family. Stepfamilies are spread over at least two households. People may feel stronger ties to people living outside their household than to those with whom they live. A child may live with her mother and stepfather, and this will be called her family, but her strongest attachment may be to her father whom she visits on weekends. In the National Survey on Children done in the United States, children were asked: "When you think of your family, who do you include?" A third of children in stepfamilies did not mention a stepparent, while only 10 per cent left out a parent, even if that parent was absent or saw the child infrequently (Whitehead 1993). For some people in stepfamilies, the biological bond takes precedence over the household bond. In the non-divorced family these two bonds are not at odds, because the household contains biologically related kin. In the stepfamily, in-laws live with one another and biologically related kin live apart.

Who, then, is the stepfamily? Many writers about stepfamilies include only those families where the children live full time, not recognizing the strong loyalties between non-residential parents and children. The reckoning about who is part of a stepfamily depends on who is talking. When I charted Hazel and her family on the genogram, I focused on only one dimension: the relationships among the various kin. Let us now add another dimension: their households (see Figure 26.2). Bob lives with his mother, Hazel, and his stepfather, George, while his sister Alice lives with her father, Kurt, her stepmother, Ann, and her half siblings Elizabeth and Jesse. George's two children from his previous marriage, Kathleen and Noel, live half-time with him and their stepmother, Hazel, and half-time with their mother, Laura, and her partner, Ravi. We can add this dimension to the genogram by enclosing households within dotted lines.

When I asked Hazel whom she considered part of her family, she included her two biological children, her current partner, George, and her stepchildren, Kathleen and Noel, but she did not mention Kurt, her ex-husband. By contrast, if I had asked her son Bob who his family was, he probably would have included

Kurt, who is his father, as well as his mother and his sister Alice. He might also have mentioned his stepfather (George), depending on his relationship with him. Bob's sister, Alice, might also count her stepmother, Ann, her half sister, Elizabeth, and her half brother, Jesse, because she lives with them. Thus, each of them would draw their family differently. If I had asked Hazel, Bob, and Alice whom they considered their family when they were still part of their original nuclear family, they all would have probably listed the same people.

In her study of 60 Canadian adolescents living in stepfamilies, Penny Gross (1985) asked them who was part of their family. Based on their answers, she developed a typology of four ways of defining remarried families. The most common type was *retention,* where the adolescents included both the residential and non-residential biological parent but excluded stepparents. The second type was *substitution,* where the non-residential biological parent was excluded and a residential stepparent replaced that parent. In the third type, *reduction,* one residential parent was omitted and a

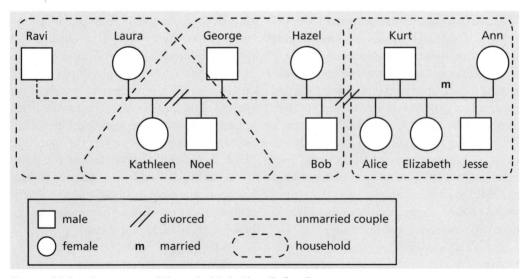

Figure 26.2   Genogram of Households in Hazel's Family,

stepparent was not added in, and in the fourth type, *augmentation,* the adolescents included both biological parents and at least one stepparent (usually the residential one) as part of their family. When Gross looked at how the adolescents determined who was part of their family, she found they used four dimensions: *procreative,* based on blood or biological ties; *residential,* whom they lived with; *emotional,* whom they felt close to; and *social,* whom they interacted with or spent time with. Thus, people in stepfamilies use a variety of criteria to decide whom they consider kin. Gross attended only to the parental level. The adolescents in her study also inherited lots of other kin through remarriage, such as stepsiblings, half siblings, step-grandparents, and step-uncles and -aunts.

There is also a large degree of choice in deciding who is part of one's family. In my study stepmothers often picked and chose whom they considered relations. Often they felt related to those people whom they liked or to whom they felt close. Paula, for example, had children from her previous marriage, as did her current husband, Barry. Both her parents and Barry's parents had disapproved of their remarriage and refused to acknowledge their respective step-grandchildren. Through her stepchildren, Paula got to know Barry's ex-wife's parents (her stepchildren's maternal grandparents), who were very encouraging of Paula's efforts to create a new family life for the two sets of children. They invited Paula and Barry and the children to spend summer vacations at their cottage and became so close to all the children that Paula's children started calling them "Grandma" and "Grandpa," even though there are no biological or legal ties. Paula now considers her husband's ex-wife's parents kin because they supported her when her own family did not.

Some writers (Popenoe 1993; Whitehead 1993) see the looser ties in stepfamilies as negative and harmful to children. Rather than considering the advantages of an extended-kin network, they focus on how the stepfamily is, to its detriment, not like the nuclear family. When we think about stepfamilies, we need to think more expansively. Although few would deny that becoming part of a stepfamily can create stresses (and I will discuss some of them in the next section), there are also potential benefits—for instance, that remarriage may increase the number of people who care for the children.

3. Household boundaries in stepfamilies are flexible. Boundaries are more fluid in stepfamilies and stepfamilies tend to be less cohesive than non-divorced families (Visher and Visher 1988). There are a number of reasons for this. First, children move around more. They may move between households weekly or biweekly, or they may make more permanent moves—for example, when a child changes his or her principal residence to live with the other parent. It is not always clear who is, and is not, part of the household.

Second, adolescents from stepfamilies are more likely to leave home earlier and live on their own than adolescents from non-divorced families (White 1993; White and Booth 1985). It is unclear from these studies whether the adolescents left on their own or were encouraged to leave, but it appears that looser structures in stepfamilies mean that adolescents become independent more quickly.

Third, the boundaries between people tend to be fuzzier in stepfamilies. Who one is in relation to others in a stepfamily is often unclear. My daughter may marry a man with two children so that I am now a step-grandmother. What should my relationship be with these children? Should I act like a grandmother? A friendly, concerned adult? An uninvolved, distant adult? Each decision I make will affect other relationships. If I give my step-grandchildren birthday presents, will their maternal grandparents feel usurped? Will my biological grandchildren feel jealous? Will my daughter feel I am slighting her children? On the other hand, if I don't give them presents, will my son-in-law be upset?

Although the flexibility of boundaries in stepfamilies may give members of the stepfamily more freedom and choice, it also can lead to less stability and more stress. The divorce rate for remarriages is higher than for first marriages (Cherlin and Furstenberg 1994; Ganong and Coleman 1994; White and Booth 1985). The reasons for this are still not completely clear. Some researchers have found that remarriages with stepchildren living in the household are more likely than those without stepchildren to end in divorce, and that the presence of stepchildren placed strain on the marital relationship (Hobart and Brown 1988; White and Booth 1985). Other studies have not shown this effect (Ganong and Coleman 1994). It may be that the presence of children creates problems for only some stepfamilies. The looser boundaries in stepfamilies may also lead some to resolve conflict by changing the composition of the family and dissolving the marriage.

How then are children living in stepfamilies affected by decreased stability and cohesiveness? The popular opinion (Whitehead 1993) is that stepfamilies are negative environments for children. The research findings are more complex, however. In their thorough review of recent research on stepfamilies, Coleman, Ganong, and Fine (2000) found that, while stepchildren were generally at greater risk of problems such as lower school achievement and depression than were children living with two biological parents, the differences between the two groups were small. There is no simple answer to the question about the effect of remarriage on children. Multiple factors must be considered: for example, the age and sex of the children at the time of divorce and remarriage, the stepfamily's financial situation, the type of parenting, the complexity of the stepfamily, and so on. In their longitudinal studies on children's development in remarried families, Hetherington and her colleagues (Hetherington and Jodl 1993) found that about one-quarter to about one-third of children in stepfamilies experienced serious emotional and behavioural problems, compared to about one in ten children in non-divorced families. The longer the children lived in their stepfamilies, the smaller the number with serious problems. It appears that, after an initial difficult adjustment period, most children do fine in stepfamilies (Hetherington and Aratesh 1988; Hetherington and Jodl 1993).

Stepparent and Gender Roles

Just as stepfamilies are expected to function like non-divorced families, so too are stepparents expected to take on the role of parents. Not only is this imposed from without, but stepparents themselves often believe that they should be parents to their stepchildren. As part of my interviews with stepmothers, I asked them to define a "good stepmother" (Church 1994). The majority believed a good stepmother should act and feel exactly the same as a good mother. That is, they collapsed together the roles of mother and stepmother. This ideal often created a conflict for them, however, because in their daily life they rarely could act as a mother to their stepchildren.

There are a number of reasons why stepparents cannot, and perhaps should not, attempt to be parents, particularly at the beginning. First, the biological parents are often already involved in the children's lives and may resent what they see as the stepparents' interference. Second, children often do not want a replacement parent and will reject stepparents if they try to discipline or direct them. Third, especially at the beginning, stepparents are the "outsiders" (Smith 1990) to the family and need to take time to find a way in. Fourth, stepparents' traditions and expectations about families may be quite different from, and conflict with, patterns and rules already present in the stepfamily. And fifth, stepparents have no legal status in relation to their stepchildren. This lack underlines their tenuous position in the stepfamily. In most places in North America, for instance, stepparents cannot sign a medical release form if a stepchild needs emergency medical help.

Although stepparenting is often difficult for both men and women, stepmothers seem to find it more stressful than do stepfathers (Ahrons and Wallisch 1987; Ambert 1986; Santrock and Sitterle 1987). This gender differential is very much tied to our differing expectations about how men and women should act in families. Stepmothers are more likely to take on the household work than are stepfathers (Ambert 1986; Coleman, Ganong, and Fine 2000). Even though they are not the biological parent, stepmothers often have primary responsibility for the household tasks and child care (Ganong and Coleman 1994), become the mediator for family relationships (McGoldrick 1989), and expect themselves to be more involved than do stepfathers (Crosbie-Burnett, Skyles, and Becker-Haven 1988).

Stepparents' difficulties in defining their place in the stepfamily mirror the dilemma faced by the stepfamily as a whole. Just as paradigms for stepfamilies are based on non-divorced families, models for stepparents are often derived from the biological parent role. And, some stepmothers believe that if they cannot achieve being the good mother, then they must be a wicked stepmother (Church 1999a; Morrison and Thompson-Guppy 1985).

Smith (1990) found that the more flexibly and broadly stepmothers conceptualized their role, the more satisfied they were. It may be that, just as we need to broaden our thinking about stepfamilies, stepparents may benefit from a more expansive understanding of their relationships with stepchildren.

Class, Ethnicity, and Sexuality

One major limitation to the research on stepfamilies is that it has focused primarily on white, middle-class, heterosexual, married families with a residential mother and stepfather. Although we know that couples with lower socio-economic status divorce more frequently than those with higher socio-economic status (Ganong and Coleman 1994; Stone 1990), we know very little about how different economic situations affect the dynamics and development in stepfamilies. Research on non-divorced North American families has shown that the working class, middle class, and upper class define kinship in distinctive ways (Schneider and Smith 1973). It makes sense that stepfamilies from different classes will vary as well. Similarly for cultural background—little attention has been paid to how cultural factors play a role in stepfamilies, yet they likely are significant. One of the stepmothers in my study was from India, as was her partner. She said that her stepchildren easily accepted her presence, because they were surrounded by quasi-kin:

> In India it's different. Like everybody's relative is called an aunt or an uncle. "Uncle" doesn't just mean the mother's brother or father's brother. You could call even a close friend of your parents "Auntie." And if someone was your father's aunt or your mother's uncle, they would be like grandparents.

If stepfamilies are somewhat invisible, in our society gay and lesbian stepfamilies are almost completely unseen. Gay and lesbian stepfamilies are often reluctant to identify themselves publicly because of possible discrimination. In the United States, the majority of lesbian families with children are formed after one or both of the partners leave a heterosexual relationship in which they have had children and then start a new lesbian partnership (this pattern is changing somewhat as alternative insemination is becoming more common) (Hare and Richards 1993). That is, lesbian families are often stepfamilies. There is some evidence to show that non-biological parents act more like stepparents with children from a previous relationship and more like biological parents with children born in the current relationship. Even when they take on a parental role with their stepchildren, many gay and lesbian stepparents feel they are given even less recognition and support for their work than are heterosexual stepparents (Miller 1989).

Conclusion

As long as we continue to hold up nuclear non-divorced families as the ideal for families, we do a disservice to stepfamilies as well as to other kinds of families. When nuclear families are the sole model, stepfamilies look dysfunctional. As we have seen, there are stresses associated with being part of a stepfamily. The initial adjustment is often very difficult and remarried couples are more likely to separate than never-divorced couples. I believe that part of the stress in stepfamilies results from the lack of positive models. People of stepfamilies rely on structures and norms derived from non-divorced families that are often inappropriate.

If we accept stepfamilies as distinct, viable forms of families, we may also expand many of our received notions about families. The fluidity of movement between households, the large extended-kin network, and the multiplicity of roles in the stepfamily mean that a group of people can be a family without being bound by household limits, biological ties, or traditional parental and gender roles. As well as potentially creating a less stable situation, the stepfamily can also offer more choice of kin and greater freedom in defining roles. Perhaps, rather than nuclear families always setting norms for stepfamilies, we can turn our thinking around and use stepfamilies to help challenge some of our unexamined beliefs about how families should act.

● References

Ahrons, C.R., and L. Wallisch. 1987. "Parenting in the Bi-nuclear Age: Relationships between Biological and Stepparents." In K. Pasley and M. Ihinger-Tallman, eds, *Remarriage and Stepparenting: Current Research and Theory.* New York: Guilford Press.

Amato, P. 2000. "The Consequences of Divorce for Adults and Children." *Journal of Marriage and the Family* 62: 1269–87.

Ambert, A.-M. 1986. "Being a Stepparent: Live-in and Visiting Stepchildren." *Journal of Marriage and the Family* 48: 795–804.

Bohannan, P. 1984. "Stepparenthood: A New and Old Experience." In R. Cohen, B. Cohler, and S. Weissman, eds, *Parenthood: A Psychodynamic Perspective.* New York: Guilford Press.

Bumpass, L., K. Raley, and J. Sweet. 1995. "The Changing Character of Stepfamilies: The Implications of Cohabitation and Nonmarital Childbearing." *Demography* 32: 425–36.

Burgoyne, J., and D. Clark. 1984. *Making a Go of It: A Study of Stepfamilies in Sheffield.* London: Routledge & Kegan Paul.

Cherlin, A. 1985. "Remarriage as an Incomplete Institution." In J. Henslin, ed., *Marriage and Family in a Changing Society,* 2nd edn. New York: The Free Press.

——, ed. 1988. *The Changing American Family and Public Policy.* Washington, DC: Urban Institute Press.

Cherlin, A., and F. Furstenberg. 1994. "Stepfamilies in the United States: A Reconsideration." *Annual Review of Sociology* 20: 359–81.

Church, E. 1994. "What Is a Good Stepmother?" Paper presented at the annual conference of the National Council on Family Relations, Minneapolis, MN.

——. 1999a. "Stepmothers as Anti-mothers: Witches or Heroines?" Paper presented at the Conference on Mothers and Education: Issues and Directions for Maternal Pedagogy, St. Catharines, ON.

——. 1999b. "Who Are the People in Your Family? Stepmothers' Diverse Notions of Kinship." *Journal of Divorce and Remarriage* 30: 83–105.

Coleman, M., and L. Ganong. 1987. "The Cultural Stereotyping of Stepfamilies." In K. Pasley and M. Ihinger-Tallman, eds, *Remarriage and Stepparenting: Current Research and Theory.* New York: Guilford Press.

Coleman, M., L Ganong, and M. Fine. 2000. "Reinvestigating Remarriage: Another Decade of Progress." *Journal of Marriage and the Family* 62: 1288–307.

Crosbie-Burnett, M., A. Skyles, and J. Becker-Haven. 1988. "Exploring Stepfamilies from a Feminist Perspective." In S. Dornbusch and M. Strober, eds, *Feminism, Children and the New Families.* New York: Guilford Press.

Dumas, J., and Y. Péron. 1992. *Marriage and Conjugal Life in Canada: Current Demographic Analysis.* Ottawa: Statistics Canada.

Firth, R. 1956. *Two Studies of Kinship in London.* London: Athlone Press.

Furstenberg, F. 1987. "The New Extended Family." In K. Pasley and M. Ihinger-Tallman, eds., *Remarriage and Stepparenting: Current Research and Theory.* New York: Guilford Press.

Furstenberg, F. 1988. "Childcare after Divorce and Remarriage." In M. Hetherington and J. Aratesh, eds, *Impact of Divorce, Single Parenting, and Stepparenting on Children.* Hillsdale, NJ: Erlbaum.

Ganong, L., and M. Coleman. 1984. "The Effects of Remarriage on Children: A Review of the Empirical Literature." *Family Relations* 33: 389–496.

Ganong, L., and M. Coleman. 1994. *Remarried Family Relationships.* Thousand Oaks, CA: Sage.

Gordon, M., ed. 1978. *The American Family in Social-Historical Perspective,* 2nd edn. New York: St. Martin's Press.

Gross, P. 1985. "Kinship Structures in Remarriage Families." Unpublished doctoral dissertation. Toronto: University of Toronto.

Hare, J., and L. Richards. 1993. "Children Raised by Lesbian Couples: Does Context of Birth Affect Father and Partner Involvement?" *Family Relations* 42: 249–55.

Hetherington, E.M. 1987. "Family Relations Six Years after Divorce." In K. Pasley and M. Ihinger-Tallman, eds, *Remarriage and Stepparenting: Current Research and Theory.* New York: Guilford Press.

Hetherington, E.M., and J. Aratesh. eds. 1988. *Impact of Divorce, Single Parenting and Stepparenting on Children.* Hillsdale, NJ: Erlbaum.

Hetherington, E.M., and W. Clingempeel. 1992. "Coping with Marital Transitions: A Family Systems Perspective." *Monographs of the Society for Research in Child Development* 57. Hetherington, E.M., and K.M. Jodl. 1993. "Stepfamilies as Settings for Child Development." Paper presented at the National Symposium on Stepfamilies, Pennsylvania State University, University Park.

Hobart, C., and D. Brown. 1988. "Effect of Prior Marriage Children on Adjustment in Remarriage: A Canadian Study." *Journal of Comparative Family Studies* 19: 381–96.

Ihinger-Tallman, M., and K. Pasley. 1987. "Divorce and Remarriage in the American Family: A Historical Review." In K. Pasley and M. Ihinger-Tallman, eds, *Remarriage and Stepparenting; Current Research and Theory.* New York: Guilford Press.

Johnson, C.L. 1988. *Ex Familia: Grandparents, Parents and Children Adjust to Divorce.* New Brunswick, NJ; Rutgers University Press.

Juby, H., N. Marcil-Gratton, and C. Le Bourdais. 2001. *A Step Further in Family Life: The Emergence of the Blended Family. Report on the Demographic Situation in Canada 2000.* Statistics Canada.

Maccoby, E., and R. Mnookin. 1992. *Dividing the Child: Social and Legal Dilemmas of Custody.* Cambridge, MA: Harvard University Press.

McGoldrick, M. 1989. "Women through the Family Life Cycle." In M. McGoldrick, C. Anderson, and F. Walsh, eds, *Women in Families: A Framework for Family Therapy.* New York: Norton.

McGoldrick, M., and R. Gerson. 1985. *Genograms in Family Assessment,* New York: Norton. Marcil-Gratton, N. 1998. "Growing up with Mom and Dad? The Intricate Family Life Courses of Canadian Children." Statistics Canada, Catalogue 89-566-XIE.

Martin, D., and M. Martin. 1992. *Stepfamilies in Therapy: Understanding Systems, Assessment and Intervention.* San Francisco: Jossey-Bass.

Mead, M. 1970. "Anomalies in American Postdivorce Relationships." In P. Bohannan, ed., *Divorce and After.* New York: Doubleday.

Miller, C. 1989. "Lesbian Stepfamilies and the Myth of Biological Motherhood." In N. Bauer Maglin and N. Schneidewind, eds, *Women and Stepfamilies: Voices of Anger and Love,* Philadelphia: Temple University Press.

Morrison, K., and A. Thompson-Guppy. 1985. "Cinderella's Stepmother Syndrome." *Canadian Journal of Psychiatry* 30: 521–29.

Papernow, P. 1993. *Becoming a Stepfamily.* San Francisco: Jossey-Bass.

Popenoe, D. 1993. "The Evolution of Marriage and the Problem of Stepfamilies." Paper presented at the National Symposium on Stepfamilies, Pennsylvania State University, University Park.

Ram, B. 1990. *New Trends in the Family: Demographic Facts and Features.* Ottawa: Statistics Canada.

Rapp, R. 1992. "Family and Class in Contemporary America: Notes toward an Understanding of Ideology." In B. Thorne and M. Yalom, eds, *Rethinking the Family: Some Feminist Questions,* rev. ed. Boston: Northeastern University Press.

Santrock, J., and K. Sitterle. 1987. "Parent-Child Relationships in Stepmother Families." In K. Pasley and M. Ihinger-Tallman, eds, *Remarriage and Stepparenting: Current Research and Theory.* New York: Guilford Press.

Schneider, D. 1980. *American Kinship: A Cultural Account,* 2nd edn. Chicago: University of Chicago Press.

Schneider, D., and R. Smith. 1973. *Class Differences and Sex Roles in American Kinship and Family Structure.* Englewood Cliffs, NJ: Prentice Hall.

Smith, D. 1990. *Stepmothering.* Hertfordshire, England: Harvester Wheatsheaf.

Stone, L. 1977. *The Family, Sex and Marriage in England 1500–1800.* London: Weidenfeld and Nicolson.

———. 1990. *Road to Divorce: England 1530–1987.* Oxford: Oxford University Press.

Vanier Institute of the Family. 1994. *Profiling Canada's Families.* Ottawa: Vanier Institute of the Family.

Visher, E.B., and J.S. Visher. 1988. *Old Loyalties, New Ties: Therapeutic Strategies with Stepfamilies.* New York: Brunner/Mazel.

White, L. 1993. Stepfamilies over the Life Course: Social Support. Paper presented at the National Symposium on Stepfamilies, Pennsylvania State University, University Park.

White, L., and A. Booth. 1985. "The Quality and Stability of Remarriages: The Role of Stepchildren." *American Sociological Review* 50: 689–98.

Whitehead, B.D. 1993. "Dan Quayle Was Right." *The Atlantic Monthly* (April): 47–84.

Part V

Problems, Policies, and the Law

Aside from the economy, laws governing marriage and divorce and social policies that provide varying levels of support to families establish much of the context in which people make and sustain families. Family law has changed to attempt to reflect the changing expectations about and reality of marriage and family life. Social policy, however, is dictated more directly than law by politics, and thus largely reflects the interests of powerful groups in society—at least it does so in the absence of mass grassroots mobilization putting pressure on governments to meet popular demands.

What follows are two articles, one on changes in Canadian family law governing the conditions of divorce settlements, and the other on Quebec's family policies that address the incompatibility of employment and family for dual-earner couples. First, however, an article on the causes of serious violence against women, by men, addresses a family problem not examined elsewhere in this anthology.

Chapter 27

Tragically, relationships presumably based on love sometimes feature violence. We need to understand why the home can be an unsafe place for some women, as well as for some children. This chapter is a review of the main findings of a large study of women who were killed in Ontario between 1974 and 1994. Rosemary Gartner and her colleagues review their findings, and draw on other researchers' findings, to conclude that gender is central to men's violence against women.

Confronting Violence in Women's Lives

Rosemary Gartner, Myrna Dawson, and Maria Crawford

Woman Killing: Intimate Femicide in Ontario, 1974–94

In March 1988, a young mother of two was killed by her estranged husband in a northern Ontario town. The killer had been visiting his wife who was staying in a shelter for abused women. Convinced that she was not going to return to him, he shot her twice at close range. Later that year, in a small-town outside of Edmonton, a woman was shot dead in her home by her estranged husband who then shot and killed himself. Miraculously, the woman's three-year-old girl, whom she was holding in her arms when she was shot, was not wounded. These women were two of the 202 female victims of homicide in Canada in 1988. They shared with 68 other female victims a marital relationship with their killers. These two women also shared the experience of having been clients and friends of women who worked in shelters for abused women in Ontario.

In response to these and other killings of women they had worked with, eight women met in January 1989 to share their experiences and provide each other emotional support. Within a few months the group had named itself the Women We Honour Action Committee, setting itself the task of learning more about the phenomenon of women killed by their intimate partners. With the support of a grant from the Ontario Women's Directorate, they conducted a literature review on women killed by their intimate partners, or intimate femicide.

That literature review led to a number of conclusions about the then-existing state of knowledge about intimate femicide (Women We Honour and R. Gartner 1990). First, obtaining an accurate estimate of the number of such killings in Canada or in Ontario from statistics in official publications was not possible because official publications restricted their classifications to "spouse killings," which excluded killings by estranged common-law partners and current or former boyfriends. Second, information on the nature of intimate femicide—its dynamics as well as its structural and cultural sources—was incomplete. In part this reflected researchers' reliance on small, highly select samples, on offenders' recollections of their crimes, and on traditional psychological and psychiatric concepts and classifications. Third, much of the research had been conducted in the United States which is atypical in both the quantity and quality of its homicides. That is, spousal homicides make up a much smaller proportion of total homicides in the United States compared to many other nations. Moreover, the ratio of female to male victims of spouse killings is more balanced in the United States than in other countries (about 1.3:1, compared to about 3:1 in Canada, Australia, Denmark, the UK, and other countries) (Wilson and Daly 1992b; Regoeczi and Silverman 1997).

It was to address these limitations that the Women We Honour Action Committee approached the Ontario Women's Directorate for funding to conduct their study of intimate femicide in Ontario. The study had three goals: to document for Ontario the incidence of killings of women by intimate partners, including legal spouses, common-law partners, and boyfriends, both current and estranged; to describe the characteristics of the people involved in and the circumstances surrounding these killings; and to present the stories of a small number of women who had been killed by their intimate partners. That study, completed in 1992, compiled and analyzed data on all intimate femicides known to authorities in Ontario from 1974 to 1990 (Crawford, Gartner, and the Women We Honour Action Committee 1992). A second study, designed to update the data through 1994, was completed in April 1997 (Crawford et al. 1997).

In this article, we describe the major findings of these two studies of intimate femicide. Our purpose is twofold: first, to provide an overview and statistical picture of intimate femicide in Ontario for the 21 years from 1974 to 1994; and, second, to locate this statistical picture in what is now a substantially larger and more sophisticated literature on violence against women by intimate partners. That literature encompasses studies similar in many ways to ours—that is, studies of the incidence and characteristics of relatively large numbers of femicides—as well as work designed to provide a theoretical and conceptual framework for understanding intimate femicide. We draw on that literature below in discussing our findings.

Framing the Issue of Intimate Femicide

After completing our literature review in 1989, we concluded that intimate femicide is a phenomenon distinct in important ways both from the killing of men by their intimate partners and from non-lethal violence against women; and, hence, that it requires analysis in its own right. This view was in contrast to much of the existing literature which treated "spousal violence" as a relatively undifferentiated phenomenon arising out of the intense emotions, stresses, and conflicts that often characterize marital relations (Goode 1969; Boudoris 1971; Chimbos 1978; Blinder 1985). These analyses tended to locate the sources of "spousal violence" in patterns of learning early in life, in the disinhibitory effects of alcohol consumption, and in dysfunctional patterns of communication between marital partners. Much of this early work also tended to devote limited attention and analysis to gender differences in spousal violence.

In response to this neglect of gender, a number of analysts have made gender a central feature of their accounts of spousal violence. Sex-role theorists highlight gender differences in socialization which teach males to view toughness, power, and control as masculine attributes. Evolutionary theorists argue that violence is an adaptive strategy for males facing the loss of status and control over their partners. Resource theorists view violence as the ultimate resource available to men when other means of exerting control over their partners are exhausted. General systems theorists argue that for men the rewards of violence against their wives are greater than the costs, because of society's failure to adequately sanction such violence. The arguments of these more gender-sensitive analyses resonated with the experiences of members of the Women We Honour Action Committee. Power, control, and domination were themes that they encountered daily in talking with abused women and that they detected in relationships ending in intimate femicide.

In recent work specifically focused on women killed by their intimate partners, these themes have been elaborated and, in the case of feminist analyses, placed in a historical and institutional context (Campbell 1992; Kelkar 1992; Marcus 1994; Maloney 1994). For example, Wilson and Daly (1992a) cite "male sexual proprietariness" as the predominant motive in the killing of wives across cultures and historical epochs. "Men exhibit a tendency to think of women as sexual and reproductive 'property' that they can own and exchange. . . . Proprietary entitlements in people have been conceived and institutionalized as identical to proprietary entitlements in land, chattels, and other economic resources." They go on to note, "That men take a proprietary view of female sexuality and reproductive capacity is manifested in various cultural practices," including claustration practices, asymmetrical adultery laws, and bride-prices. From this perspective, an extreme, if apparently incongruous, manifestation of male proprietariness is intimate femicide. If unable to control or coerce his partner through other means, a man may exert the ultimate control over her by killing her.

Thus, male proprietariness, or male sexual jealousy, has been placed at the centre of many empirical and theoretical analyses of intimate femicide. For example, research on intimate femicide and spousal homicide in Canada, Australia, Great Britain, and the United States (Dobash and Dobash 1984; Wallace 1986; Daly and Wilson 1988; Polk 1994) has identified a common core in these killings of "masculine control, where women become viewed as the possessions of men, and the violence reflects steps taken by males to assert their domination over 'their' women" (Polk 1994). This empirical work challenges many of the popular notions about the characteristics of such crimes, for example, the belief that they are explosive, unplanned, and unpredictable acts of passion. At the same time, it contests the validity and coherence of the concept "spousal homicide" with its connotations of sexual symmetry in violence by revealing distinct differences between intimate partner killings by men and those by women. As Dobash et al. (1992) note:

> Men often kill wives after lengthy periods of prolonged physical violence accompanied by other forms of abuse and coercion; the roles in such cases are seldom if ever reversed. Men perpetrate familicidal massacres, killing spouses and children together; women do not. Men commonly hunt down and kill wives who have left them; women hardly ever behave similarly. Men kill wives as part of planned murder–suicides; analogous acts by women are almost unheard of. Men kill in response to revelations of wifely infidelity; women almost never respond similarly.

In sum, there have been significant advances in both empirical and conceptual analyses of lethal violence against women by their partners since the literature review that served as the impetus for our research. Those advances have not, however, filled all of the gaps identified in our earlier review. In particular, empirical research in Canada has continued to rely largely on official statistics from police sources, which exclude from their classification of spousal homicides killings by men of their estranged common-law partners and girl-friends. Relying on these official statistics also restricts analyses to the information and coding schemes employed by police agencies and personnel. Because of our concerns about the potential for lost information and for the introduction of unknown biases, we relied on a wider range of information sources than typically used in previous research. In this way, our study is unusual in the comprehensiveness of its data. As we see below, it is not however unique in its findings about the nature of intimate femicide.

Data Sources

We began our data collection by searching death records kept by the Office of the Chief Coroner for Ontario. Coroners' records provide a centralized source of information on all deaths in Ontario, and a means of identifying and assessing records for deaths identified by the Coroner's Office as homicides. These files frequently contain copies of police reports as well as medical reports on the condition of the body, the way in which the woman was killed and the violence suffered—details often not available from other sources. However, coroners' records, like all official sources of information on homicide, are imperfect measures of the actual number of deaths due to homicide. For example, cases of homicide in which no body has been found will not typically appear in coroners' records. As a consequence, we expect our estimates of the incidence of intimate femicide to undercount the true incidence, an issue we discuss in more depth below.[1]

We were able to cross-check and supplement data from coroners' records by reviewing police homicide investigation files for many of

our cases.[2] In the second study, we were also able to review data from Crown Attorney files on many of the cases in which charges were laid between 1991 and 1994. In both studies, we supplemented our data from official sources with information from newspaper and magazine articles on some of the killings and on trials of some of the alleged offenders.

We compiled this information so that it could be used in both quantitative and qualitative analyses. Our final data collection instrument was designed to provide codes for approximately 52 variables, as well as space to record a narrative of the case where further information was available.[3]

The Incidence of Intimate Femicide in Ontario, 1974–94

Between 1974 and 1994, 1,206 women aged 15 and older were killed in Ontario, according to official records.[4] In 1,120 (93 per cent) of these cases, the crimes were solved and the killers were identified. In 705 (63 per cent) of the solved cases, the killers were the current or former legal spouses, common-law partners, or boyfriends of their victims. Thus, in Ontario over this 21-year period, intimate partners were responsible for the majority of all woman killings and an average of 34 women were victims of intimate femicide each year. These data indicate that the focus in official publications and some academic research on "spousal homicides" of women provides an incomplete picture of the more general phenomenon of intimate femicide: excluding killings of women by their estranged common-law partners and current and former boyfriends underestimates the total number of intimate femicides by about 25 per cent.

The actual number of intimate femicides in Ontario during these years is undoubtedly higher than this. Intimate partners were certainly responsible for some portion of the cases in which no offender was identified or in which we had too little information to determine the precise nature of the relationship between victim and offender.[5] Adjusting for excluded cases, we estimate that intimate femicides may have accounted for as many as 76 per cent of all femicides in Ontario between 1974 and 1994. However, since it is impossible to know the number and characteristics of excluded cases, the analyses that follow focus only on those 705 cases in which the offender was officially identified as the current or former intimate partner of the victim.

Trends in Intimate Femicide

Between 1974 and 1994, the rate of intimate femicide (i.e., the number of victims of intimate femicide per 100,000 women in the general population) ranged from a low of 0.55 in 1978 to a high of 1.26 in 1991, but appears to follow no particular trend over time (see Figure 27.1).[6] Dividing the 21-year period in half suggests otherwise, however: the average annual rate for the second half of the period (1.01 per 100,000) was slightly higher than the rate for the first half (0.92 per 100,000).

On its own, this difference is insignificant statistically and, it might appear, substantively. However, when compared to the statistically significant decreases in other types of lethal violence, the slightly higher rate of intimate femicide in the latter period takes on greater importance. The annual rate at which women were killed by strangers or unknown assailants declined significantly from an average of 0.27 during 1974–83 to 0.16 during 1984–94. Moreover, the annual rate at which men were killed by their spouses also declined significantly, from an average rate of 0.31 during

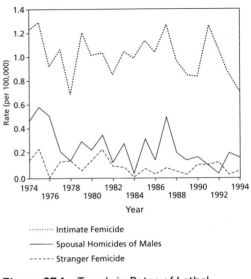

Figure 27.1 Trends in Rates of Lethal Violence, Ontario, 1974–94

1974–83 to 0.18 during 1984–94. In other words, during a period when women's risks from strangers and men's risks from spouses decreased, women's risks from their intimate partners increased slightly. Put another way, after 1984—a period of substantial expansion in services for abused women—men's risks of being killed by intimate partners decreased significantly whereas women's risks did not.

Without further analysis of these patterns—which is beyond the scope of this article—we can only speculate as to the reasons for this apparently counterintuitive finding. One possible explanation is that while the expansion of services for abused women may have resulted in the protection of abusive men from defensive violence by their intimate partners, these same services did not necessarily protect women from their male partners' violence. Research shows that women are most likely to kill their intimate partners after prolonged abuse and when they fear continued or more serious violence against themselves or their children (Browne 1987).

Where services for abused women are available, women in abusive relationships have an alternative to killing their partners. As Browne and Williams (1989) note, "By offering threatened women protection, escape and aid, [legal and extra-legal] resources can engender an awareness that there are alternatives to remaining at risk" and thus prevent "killings that occur in desperation." Their analysis of US data lends support to this interpretation: states with higher levels of services to abused women had lower rates of spouse killings of males, but not lower rates of spouse killings for females.

Characteristics of the Victims and Their Killers

In many respects, the women killed by their intimate partners and the men who killed them[7] are very similar to women and men in the general population of Ontario, as can be seen from the data in Table 27.1. For example, women killed by their intimate partners were, on average, about 37 years old; 51 per cent were employed; 80 per cent had children; and 76 per cent were born in Canada. These characteristics do not distinguish the victims from other women in Ontario.

In some other respect, however, victims of intimate femicide and their killers differed from women and men in the general population.[8] We can think of these differences as risk markers for intimate femicide because they tell us that some types of women and men face disproportionately high risks of intimate victimization or offending.[9] Each of the markers we discuss below has also been associated with increased risks of lethal violence against women in other research.

Relationship Status

Research based on data on spouse killings from Great Britain, Australia, the United States, and

Table 27.1 Characteristics of Victims of Intimate Femicide and Their Killers, Ontario, 1974–94

Characteristics	Victims	Offenders
Total Number	705	705
Average Age	37	41
% born in Canada	76	70
% with children	80	77
Employment Status		
% employed	51	64
% unemployed	17	21
% homemakers	18	0
% students	5	2
% retired or on disability pension	9	13
Relationship of Victim to Offender		
% legal spouse, cohabiting	–	39
% legal spouse, separated	–	16
% common-law partner, cohabiting	–	18
% common-law partner, separated	–	7
% divorced spouse	–	<1
% current girlfriend	–	12
% estranged girlfriend	–	8
% Aboriginal	6	6

Canada shows that two indicators of the status of the relationship—estrangement and common-law status—are associated with a higher risk of spouse killings of women (Wallace 1986; Campbell 1992; Wilson and Daly 1993; Johnson 1996). We find similar patterns in our intimate femicide data, although the limited availability of data on marital separation and common-law unions within the general population restricts our analysis somewhat.

Census Canada collects information on marital separations, but only for registered marriages. According to census figures, during the years of our study, 3 per cent of women in Ontario were separated from their legal spouses. According to our data, among the victims of intimate femicide, 16 per cent were separated from their legal spouses. Separation, then, appears to be a risk factor for intimate femicide, since women who were separated from their partners were greatly overrepresented among victims of intimate femicide. However, exactly how much greater the risks are for separated women cannot be determined from our data. This is because our measure of separation and the census measure of separation are not precisely compatible: the census measure captures largely long-term and relatively well-established separations, whereas our measure is more sensitive and captures short-term as well as long-term separations. Thus our measure will yield a higher estimate of separated couples. Nevertheless, we expect that even correcting for this difference, we would find separation to be associated with higher risks of intimate femicide.

Data on the prevalence of common-law unions in the general population have been collected only since 1991, so we can estimate the risks to women living in common-law relationships only for the most recent years of our research. According to census data, 4 per cent of women were living in common-law unions in 1991 in Ontario. According to our data, during 1991–94, 21 per cent of the victims of intimate femicide were killed by common-law partners with whom they were living. Based on our calculations, the rate of intimate femicide for women in common-law unions was approximately six times greater than the average rate of intimate femicide in Ontario in the early 1990s.[10] Clearly, then, women in common-law unions were greatly overrepresented among

victims of intimate femicide during the early 1990s, and perhaps in earlier years as well.

The higher risks associated with common-law status and estrangement have been interpreted in various ways. Compared to couples in registered marriages, common-law partners are more likely to be poor, young, unemployed, and childless—all factors associated with higher homicide rates. Compared to co-residing couples, estranged couples are more likely to have a history of domestic violence (Rodgers 1994; Johnson and Sacco 1995). This violence may be associated both with women's decisions to leave their relationships and with their greater risks of intimate femicide. In other words, "the fact that separated couples constitute a subset of marriages with a history of discord could explain their higher homicide rates" (Wilson and Daly 1994).

Male sexual proprietariness could also play a role in the higher risks for common-law and estranged relationships. If, as some have speculated, "husbands may be less secure in the proprietary claims over wives in common-law unions than in registered unions," they may be more likely to resort to serious violence to enforce those claims or to lethal violence when those claims are challenged (Wilson, Johnson, and Daly 1995: 343). Echoing a similar theme, several studies that have found elevated risks at separation have cited the male's inability to accept termination of the relationship and obsessional desires to maintain control over his sexual partner: "He would destroy his intimate 'possession' rather than let her fall into the hands of a competitor male" (Polk 1994: 29; see also Rasche 1989; Campbell 1992; Wilson and Daly 1993).

Ethnicity

Women in certain ethnic groups have risks of intimate femicide disproportionate to their representation in the population, according to several studies. For example, in the United States, African-American women face unusually high risks of intimate femicide. In Canada, such research is more difficult to do because of restrictions on the collection of crime statistics by race and ethnicity. However, Statistics Canada has collected data on Aboriginal victims of spousal homicides which indicate that Aboriginal women's rates of spousal homicide are between five and ten times higher than the rates for non-Aboriginal women (Kennedy, Forde, and Silverman 1989; Silverman and Kennedy 1993).

We had initially hoped to explore ethnic and cultural differences in the risk of intimate femicide in our research. Our community advisory group, which was composed of women from various ethnic backgrounds active in community organizations, encouraged us to do so.[11] However, our research agreement with the Ministry of the Solicitor General prevented us from compiling "statistics based upon social, cultural, regional, linguistic, racial, or ethnic group" from the coroners' records. Nevertheless, we were able to document the number of Aboriginal victims of intimate femicide during these years by relying on other sources of data.[12]

We estimate that at least 6 per cent of the victims of intimate femicide in Ontario between 1974 and 1994 were Aboriginal women. Census data for these years indicate that just under 1 per cent of all women living in Ontario classified themselves as Aboriginal. Thus, Aboriginal women in Ontario appear to be overrepresented among the victims of intimate femicide. Conversely, Aboriginal men are overrepresented as offenders, since all but four of the Aboriginal victims were killed by Aboriginal men.

A number of factors might explain the disproportionate risks of intimate femicide faced by Aboriginal women. Aboriginal Canadians, similar to African Americans, are an economically impoverished and politically disenfranchised ethnic minority. Considerable research has shown that economic, social, and political disadvantages are associated with higher homicide rates generally, as well as higher rates of serious spousal violence. In addition, Aboriginal-Canadian heterosexual couples also have disproportionate rates of other risk markers for intimate partner violence, such as common-law marital status, low income, bouts of male unemployment, exposure to violence in childhood, alcohol abuse, overcrowded housing conditions, and social isolation—all of which have been cited as reasons for the higher rates of family violence in Aboriginal communities (Health and Welfare Canada 1990; Long 1995). Some analysts situate these risk factors within a structural approach that views them as consequences of internal colonialism: "the conditions of colonialism [are] directly related to Aboriginal acts of political violence as well as rates of suicide, homicide, and family violence among the Aboriginal peoples" (Frank 1993; Bachmann 1993; Long 1995: 42).

Employment

Men's unemployment is commonly cited as a risk factor for wife assaults and is also associated with elevated risks of spousal homicide. Women's employment status, on the other hand, does not appear to be consistently associated with their risks of violence from their partners (Hotaling and Sugarman 1986; Brinkerhoff and Lupri 1988; Macmillan and Gartner 1996; Johnson 1996). The association between men's unemployment and violence against their female partners traditionally has been attributed to the stresses produced by unemployment and limited economic resources. But if this were the case, one would expect to find more evidence that women's unemployment is also associated with spousal violence, which is not the case. For those who see male violence against their partners as one resource for demonstrating power and control, the gender-specificity of the effects of unemployment is not surprising: men who lack more traditional resources (such as economic success) may "forge a particular type of masculinity that centres on ultimate control of the domestic setting through the use of violence" (Messerschmidt 1993: 149).

Our data on intimate femicide are consistent with this interpretation. For women, employment status is not associated with differential risks of intimate femicide: 51 per cent of women in both the victim population and the general population were employed during the period of our study. For men, however, employment status is associated with differential risks. Among intimate femicide offenders, 64 per cent were employed, whereas among males in the general population, 73 per cent were employed. In Ontario, then, male unemployment appears to be associated with higher risks of intimate femicide offending.

Offenders' Violent Histories

Several studies have shown that men who kill their spouses frequently have histories of violent behaviour, both in and outside their marital relationships (Johnson 1996: 183–6). As Johnson notes, "[a]lthough some wife killings are the result of sudden, unforeseeable attacks by depressed or mentally unstable husbands and are unrelated to a history of violence in the family, most do not seem to fit this description" (183). Because of this, risk assessment tools designed to assess battered women's risk of lethal violence typically include measures

of their partners' violence against their children and outside of the home, and threats of serious violence against their wives or others (Campbell 1995).

We also found evidence of unusual levels of violence in the backgrounds of the offenders in our sample. At least 31 per cent of them had an arrest record for a violent offence.[13] At least 53 per cent of them were known to have been violent in the past toward women they ultimately killed. This corresponds to data for Canada as a whole which indicates that in 52 per cent of spousal homicides of women between 1991 and 1993, police were aware of previous violent incidents between the spouses (Canadian Centre for Justice Statistics 1993). In addition, in at least 34 per cent of the cases of intimate femicide, the offenders were known to have previously threatened their victims with violence.[14] At least 10 per cent of the killings occurred while the offender was on probation or parole, or under a restraining order.

It is important to emphasize that these are *minimum* estimates of the number of offenders with violent and criminal histories. In over 200 of the 705 cases of intimate femicide we did not have enough information to determine if previous violence or police contact had occurred. Nevertheless, the information we were able to find clearly challenges the view that intimate femicides are typically momentary rages or heat-of-passion killings by otherwise nonviolent men driven to act out of character by extreme circumstances.

A Summary of Risk Markers for Intimate Femicide

Women killed by their intimate male partners and the men who kill them are drawn from all classes, all age groups, all cultural and ethnic backgrounds. However, the victims of intimate femicide and their killers in our study did differ from other women and men in Ontario in some important respects: they were more likely than women and men in the general population to be separated from their partners, to be in common-law relationships, and to be Aboriginal. In addition, men who killed their intimate partners were also likely to be unemployed and to have histories of criminal violence. These risk markers for intimate femicide have been noted in other research on spousal homicides, and have been interpreted from within various theoretical frameworks. We suggest that they are perhaps most consistent with a framework which views intimate femicide as the manifestation of extreme (if ultimately self-defeating) controlling and proprietary attitudes and behaviours by men toward their female partners.

Characteristics of the Killings

An adequate understanding of the sources of intimate femicide will need to take account of the particular characteristics of these killings. Prior research has devoted much less attention to these characteristics than to the characteristics of the individuals involved in the killings.[15] As a consequence, we are limited in both the comparisons we can draw between our findings and the findings from other research and in the interpretations we can offer of these findings.

Intimate femicides are typically very private acts: three-quarters of the victims were killed in their own homes and, in almost half of these cases, in their own bedrooms. Less than 20 per cent occurred in public places, such as streets, parks, workplaces, or public buildings. The most typical method was shooting: one-third of the victims were killed with firearms. Virtually all the other methods required direct and often prolonged physical contact between offenders and their victims: about two-thirds of

the offenders stabbed, bludgeoned, beat, strangled, or slashed the throats of their victims.

One of the distinguishing features of intimate femicide is the extent and nature of violence done to the victim. Unlike killings by women of their intimate partners, intimate femicides often involve multiple methods of far more violence than is necessary to kill the victim.[16] For example, in over half of the stabbings, offenders inflicted four or more stab wounds. Beatings and bludgeonings typically involved prolonged violence—leading some coroners to use the term "over-kill" to describe them. In about 20 per cent of the cases, offenders used multiple methods against their victims, such as stabbing and strangling or beating and slashing. In about 10 per cent of the cases, we also found evidence that the victim's body had been mutilated or dismembered.

The violence in these killings is much more likely to be sexualized than when women kill their intimate partners.[17] Records on approximately half of the cases in our study provided sufficient information for us to determine whether sexual violence was present. In 27 per cent of these cases we found evidence that the victims had been raped, sodomized, or sexually mutilated; in another 22 per cent of the cases the victim's body was found partially or completely unclothed.

Consumption of alcohol by offenders and/or victims was no more common in intimate femicides than in other killings: 39 per cent of the offenders and 32 per cent of the victims had been drinking immediately prior to the killing. In only 3 per cent of the cases was there evidence of drug use by offenders or victims immediately prior to the killing.

Establishing the motives in these killings is fraught with difficulties, as suggested earlier. We made our own determination of the motive after reviewing all the information available to us. In about one-fourth of the cases we felt we had insufficient information to make a judgment about the offender's motive. In the remaining cases, one motive clearly predominated: the offender's rage or despair over the actual or impending estrangement from his partner. This motive characterized 45 per cent of the killings in which we identified a motive. In contrast, women who kill their intimate partners only rarely kill out of anger over an estrangement (Browne 1987; Daly and Wilson 1988).

Suspected or actual infidelity of the victim was the motive in another 15 per cent of the intimate femicides. In 10 per cent of the cases the killing appears to have been the final act of violence in a relationship characterized by serial abuse.[18] In only 5 per cent of the cases did stressful life circumstances—such as bankruptcy, job loss, or serious illness—appear to motivate the killer;[19] and in only 3 per cent of the cases was there evidence that the killer was mentally ill.

Another feature that distinguishes intimate femicide from intimate partner killings by women is the number of people who die as a result of these crimes. The 705 cases of intimate femicide resulted in the deaths of 977 persons. Most of these additional deaths were suicides by the offenders: 31 per cent of the offenders killed themselves after killing their female partners.[20] But offenders killed an additional 75 persons, most of whom were children of the victims. In addition, over 100 children witnessed their mothers' deaths; thus, while they may have escaped physical harm, they obviously suffered inestimable psychological harm.

Our documentation of these characteristics of intimate femicide cannot sufficiently convey the complexity and context surrounding these crimes. Nevertheless, it serves important purposes. Comparing characteristics of intimate partner killings by males and females shows the distinctiveness of these two types of killings—a distinctiveness that is obscured in studies that treat intimate partner killings by men and women as instances of a single phenomenon. Compared to killings of men by intimate female partners, intimate femicides are much more likely to involve extreme and sexualized violence, to be motivated by anger over separation, to be followed by the suicide of the offender, and to be accompanied by the killing of additional victims. These features highlight the gender-specificity of intimate partner killings and are consistent with a perspective on intimate femicide which views it as based in a larger system of gender[ed] inequality and stratification which perpetuates male control over women's sexuality, labour, and, at times, lives and deaths.

The Criminal Justice Response to Intimate Femicide

In our initial study of intimate femicide, we had not intended to collect and analyze data on the criminal justice responses to men who killed their intimate partners—in part because our primary interest was in the victims of intimate femicide and in part because we did not expect information on criminal justice responses to be consistently reported in coroners' and police records. However, contrary to our expectations, we were able to obtain information on charges laid, convictions, and sentencing in a substantial number of the cases. In 90 per cent of the 490 cases in which we were able to establish that offenders did not commit suicide, we found at least some information on criminal justice processing.

In 94 per cent of these cases, the offenders were charged with either first- or second-degree murder.[21] The proportion charged with first-degree murder increased over time, from 34 per cent of the cases in the first half of the period to

52 per cent in the second half. Of the 346 cases for which we found information on dispositions, 10 per cent were convicted of first-degree murder, 35 per cent of second-degree murder, and 38 per cent of manslaughter. Murder convictions increased over time: from 32 per cent of the dispositions in the first half of the period to 56 per cent in the second half. Acquittals accounted for a total of 13 per cent of the cases: 11 per cent were verdicts of not guilty by reason of insanity and 2 per cent were straight acquittals.

Sentencing information, available for 302 of the men convicted of killing their partners, also indicates that criminal justice responses to intimate femicide increased in severity over time. Prior to 1984, 7 per cent of convicted offenders received no jail time, 14 per cent were sent to secure mental institutions for indefinite periods, 25 per cent were sentenced to less than five years in prison, 38 per cent were sentenced to between five and ten years, and 15 per cent received sentences of more than ten years. After 1983, 4 per cent of convicted offenders received no jail time, 7 per cent were sent to secure mental institutions, 10 per cent received sentences of less than five years, 37 per cent received sentences of between five and ten years, and 41 per cent were sentenced to prison for more than ten years.

This evidence clearly shows that criminal justice responses to intimate femicide became increasingly punitive over the 21 years of our study. How much of this trend reflects increasing punitiveness toward all violent criminals and how much reflects growing public awareness and intolerance of violence against women is an issue requiring further research.[22]

The Gender-specific Nature of Intimate Femicide

We have alluded to the gender-specific nature of intimate femicide at various points in our analysis. Here, we develop our ideas about this gender-specificity by considering what is known about gender differences in homicide more generally. We base this discussion on a large body of criminological research on homicide, as well as on data on over 7,000 homicides collected by Rosemary Gartner and Bill McCarthy as part of a separate research project.

Among those who study homicide, it is well known that women and men are killed in different numbers, by different types of people, and in different circumstances. Women are less likely to be victims of homicide than men in virtually all societies. Canada and Ontario are no different: men outnumbered women as victims of homicide by a ratio of approximately 2:1 in Canada and in Ontario between 1974 and 1994.

This may appear to indicate that women have a sort of protective advantage over men—that, at least in this sphere of social life, women are not disadvantaged relative to men. However, if we consider gender differences in offending, a different picture emerges. Men accounted for 87 per cent of all homicide offenders in Ontario during these years; and males outnumbered females as offenders by a ratio of almost 7:1. When women were involved in homicides, then, they were almost three times more likely to be victims than offenders; when men were involved in homicides they were more likely to be offenders than victims. In other words, women are overrepresented among victims and underrepresented among offenders; for men the opposite is true.

Women were also much more likely than men to be killed by someone of the opposite sex, as these figures imply. Fully 98 per cent of all women killed in Ontario between 1974 and 1994 were killed by men. Only 17 per cent of adult male victims were killed by women.

Thus, man killing appears to be primarily a reflection of relations within a gender, whereas woman killing appears to be primarily a matter of relations between the genders. Because women are the majority of victims in opposite-sex killings, such killings can be seen as one of the high costs to women of male dominance and desire for control in heterosexual relationships.

It is in intimate relationships between women and men that male dominance and control are most likely to erupt into physical violence. Women accounted for 75 per cent of all victims of spouse killings in Ontario during the last two decades.[23] So women outnumbered men among victims of spouse killings by a ratio of about 3:1. Moreover, spousal homicides accounted for over 50 per cent of all killings of women but less than 10 per cent of all killings of men.

If males, unlike females, are not killed primarily by their intimate partners, who are they killed by and under what circumstances? In Ontario, about 60 per cent of male victims are killed by acquaintances and strangers; another 20 per cent are killed by unknown assailants. Most male–male homicides are the result of arguments or disputes that escalate to killings. In many cases, both victim and offender have been drinking, and who becomes the victim and who the offender is a matter of happenstance.[24] One classic study of homicide (Wolfgang 1958) concluded that male–male homicides, as an instance of the more generally physically aggressive behaviour of males, converge with notions of masculine identity.

When males kill their intimate female partners, their methods of and motives for killing take on a character distinctive from male–male killings—a character that denotes the gender specificity of intimate femicide. As noted above, a substantial number of intimate femicides involved multiple methods, excessive force, and continued violence even after the women's deaths would have been apparent.[25] The violence in intimate femicides also frequently involves some form of sexual assault, a very rare occurrence in killings of men.

The motives in intimate femicide also point to its gender-specificity. The predominance of men's rage over separation as a motive in intimate femicides has no obvious counterpart in killings of men—even killings of men by their intimate female partners. We agree with others who see this motive as a reflection of the sexual proprietariness of males toward their intimate female partners.

In sum, our analysis of intimate femicide and our review of other research and data on gender differences in homicide suggest that women killing in general and intimate femicide in particular are uniquely gendered acts. By this we mean these killings reflect important dimensions of gender stratification, such as power differences in intimate relations and the construction of women as sexual objects generally, and as sexual property in particular contexts. Intimate femicide—indeed, probably most femicide—is not simply violence against a person who happens to be female. It is violence that occurs and takes particular forms because its target is a woman, a woman who has been intimately involved with her killer.

Conclusion

Our purpose in this article has been to document the incidence and provide a description of the phenomenon of intimate femicide. For some, our approach may be unsatisfying, because we have not proposed a systematic explanation of, nor outlined a detailed strategy for preventing, these killings. Obviously explaining and preventing intimate femicides are critical tasks, but both require comprehensive knowledge of the phenomenon. The statistical data we have gathered and analyzed are intended to contribute to this knowledge.

Nevertheless, we recognize that our overview of the extent and character of intimate femicide in Ontario between 1974 and 1994 has raised at least as many questions as it has answered. Why, for example, did women's risks of intimate femicide increase slightly when public concern over and resources available to abused women were also increasing; when other forms of lethal violence were decreasing; and when criminal justice responses to intimate femicide were becoming more punitive? Why did some women—such as those in common law relationships and Aboriginal women—face disproportionately high risks of intimate femicide? Were there other types of women with elevated risks of intimate femicide—for example, immigrant women or women with disabilities—whom we couldn't identify because of the limitations of our data? Why are intimate partner killings by men and women so distinctively different? All of these questions deserve answers, but the answers will require research that goes beyond the data and analysis we have been able to present in this paper.

There are other types of questions raised by our research that are more immediately pressing, questions about how to prevent intimate femicides. Our research has shown that intimate femicides are not the isolated and unpredictable acts of passion they are often believed to be. Most of the killers in our study had acted violently toward their partners or other persons in the past and many had prior contact with the police as a consequence. Many of the victims had sought help from a variety of sources. In a substantial portion of these intimate femicides, then, there were clear signs of danger preceding the killing, signs that were

available to people who might have been able to intervene to prevent the crime. We believe this information could be combined with what we know about the risk factors for intimate femicide—such as estrangement—to develop interventions that would save women's lives.

This is the question that has been at the core of our research and the recommendation that we tabled at the conclusion of both of our studies. We urged the establishment of a joint forces initiative that would include police, coroners, researchers, experts working in the field, as well as survivors of intimate violence, who would be charged with developing a system to respond more effectively to women when they are at greatest risk of intimate femicide. Such a response would need to be swift and focused on ensuring the victim's safety and deterring the offender from further violence or threats.

Of course, this kind of intervention must be coupled with efforts to address the underlying sources of intimate femicide. If, as we and others have argued, the sources lie at least in part in attitudes and behaviours that have been supported for centuries by patriarchal systems of power and privilege, those attitudes and behaviours, as well as the systems supporting them, must be confronted and contested. Some feminists argue that one means of doing this is through refining and reformulating law as a weapon against men's intimate violence against women. Isabel Marcus (1994), for example, argues for identifying domestic violence as terrorism and, as such, a violation of international human rights accords. Elizabeth Schneider (1994: 56) suggests redeploying the concept of privacy, not to keep the state out of intimate relationships as the concept has been used in the past but to emphasize individuals' autonomy and independence. She argues this affirmative aspect of privacy could frame a new feminist agenda against woman abuse.

As these and other analyses emphasize, preventing intimate femicides will require that the public as well as those working in fields relevant to the prevention of violence begin to see intimate femicide as a preventable crime. From our own and others' research on intimate violence, it should be apparent that these crimes are patterned and predictable. The danger lies in maintaining the view that violence is inevitable, unavoidable, and inherent in intimate relationships. Such fatalism must be challenged, so that women's safety in and outside their homes is seen as an achievable and pre-eminent goal.

● Notes

Major funding for the studies described in this paper was provided by the Ontario Women's Directorate. The Ministry of Community and Social Services and the School of Graduate Studies at the University of Toronto each provided additional funding for one of the studies. The analyses and opinions in the paper are those of the authors and do not necessarily represent the views of any of these funders.

1. Coroners' records are limited in another obvious and unavoidable way: they are observations removed in time and space from the actual killing. As a consequence, the description in the records will be shaped by the interests and perspectives of the observer. A coroner's perspective is that of an investigator after the fact, and his/her primary interest is in determining the cause and means of death. Thus, the information recorded by coroners is intended to serve these purposes, not the interests of researchers.

2. Different procedures were used in the two studies to obtain access to municipal police and OPP records. These records are not centrally compiled and it was impossible to contact and obtain co-operation from all of the forces around Ontario which investigate and keep records on cases of homicide.

3. Obviously, the coded data provide only a partial and, in some respects, an incomplete portrayal of intimate femicide. The lives and deaths of the women represented in these statistics cannot be sufficiently understood from counts and categorizations. For this reason, we devoted a considerable portion of our first study to reconstructing the stories of some of the women who died through interviews with their family and friends.

4. Our research has looked only at killings of females aged 15 and older because the killing of children differs in distinctive ways from the killing of adults.

5. The number of intimate femicides is undercounted in official records for other reasons as well. For example, in some cases of intimate femicide, the woman's death may be incorrectly classified as due to suicide, accident, or natural causes. Among the intimate femicides in our study, at least eight were not initially classified as homicides and only reclassified after further investigation. Another example of this occurred while this article was being written: the body of a southern Ontario woman who died by hanging was exhumed and an investigation revealed she had not killed herself, as originally determined, but had been killed by her boyfriend.

6. Although there are no statistics on the rate of intimate femicide for Canada as a whole, there are statistics on the rate of spousal killings of women. Since the mid-1970s, trends in Ontario's rate have paralleled those for Canada as a whole; and the mean rate for Ontario (0.77) is very close to the mean rate for Canada (0.83).

7. Of the cases of intimate femicide between 1974 and 1994, we found only three in which the offender was a woman.

8. Identifying differences between victims or offenders and women and men in the general population requires establishing the proportion of victims (or offenders) with the particular characteristic and comparing this to the proportion of women (or men) in the general population of Ontario during the years 1974–94 with the same characteristics. If the former proportion is larger than the latter proportion, this indicates that women with that particular characteristic are overrepresented among victims of intimate femicide. Tests for statistically significant differences are not appropriate

here because the data are based on populations, not samples. Because we used information from census reports to determine the characteristics of women in the general population of Ontario, we were limited in our search for risk markers of intimate femicide to characteristics which are measured in the census.

9. By highlighting these characteristics, we do not mean to obscure the fact that women from all types of backgrounds and in all types of relationships are victims of intimate femicide; nor do we mean to imply that certain characteristics of women make them likely targets for intimate violence. Rather, we would suggest that certain groups of women may be more vulnerable to intimate violence because they share characteristics that have isolated them, limited their access to resources for protection, or prevented them from obtaining a level of personal security that many Canadians take for granted.

10. The average annual rate of intimate femicide (per 100,000 women aged 15 and older) for the years 1991–94 was calculated by: (1) dividing the number of victims during those years (159) by the number of women aged 15 and older in the Ontario population in 1991 (4,130,450); (2) multiplying this figure by 100,000; and (3) dividing this figure by four (the number of years). This yields an average annual rate of 0.96 per 100,000 women aged 15 and older.

   The average annual rate of intimate femicides of women living in common-law unions was calculated by: (1) dividing the number of victims living common-law during those years (45) by the number of women aged 15 and older in Ontario living in common-law unions in 1991 (182,155); (2) multiplying this figure by 100,000; and (3) dividing this figure by four. This yields an annual average rate of 6.18 per 100,000 women aged 15 and older living in common-law unions.

11. This group was formed at the beginning of our first study and met with the principal researchers regularly to review the research for cultural sensitivity and validity. At the completion of the first study, its members also reviewed and made contributions to the final report.

12. The final report for our first study (pp. 67–76) documents the problems with collecting information on race and cultural backgrounds of crime victims and offenders, as well as the procedures we followed to gather the data on Aboriginal victims.

13. Another 30 per cent had been arrested and charged with non-violent criminal offences.

14. In contrast, in only 6 per cent of the cases were the victims known to have been violent toward their killers in the past; and in only 2 per cent of the cases were the victims known to have previously threatened their partners with violence.

15. What researchers can describe about homicide and femicide is largely determined by the types of information officials collect. This means that many details about the events leading up to the killing, the dynamics of the interaction immediately preceding the killing, or the states of mind of victim and offender are absent or at most only hinted at in official reports. Some characteristics of intimate femicide can be easily and reliably determined, such as where they occurred or whether weapons were involved. Other characteristics—such as the offender's motivation—are more susceptible to post hoc reconstructions that introduce the inevitable biases of observers and officials. When we collected and coded information, we reviewed all the information available to us and made our own best judgments about these characteristics. We recognize, however, that our judgments are necessarily based on limited information about extremely complex events. Our discussion of the characteristics of the killings therefore should be viewed with these limitations in mind.

16. We base this and other conclusions about the characteristics of intimate partner killings by women on data from an ongoing study by the first author of over 7,000 homicides in two Canadian cities and two US cities over the twentieth century.

17. Indeed, none of the data or research with which we are familiar indicates that women who kill their intimate partners exact sexual violence against their victims.

18. This does not mean that offenders who appeared to act for other motives had not engaged in systematic abuse of the women they killed. Rather, it indicates that in 10 per cent of the cases, the only motive we could identify was systematic, serial abuse that ultimately led to the woman's death.

19. Typically, offenders who kill under these circumstances are characterized as extremely depressed, and are more likely than other offenders to commit or attempt suicide after the killing. Nevertheless, some have argued that sexual proprietariness can

still be seen in killings apparently motivated by stressful life circumstances (e.g., Daly and Wilson 1988). According to this view, when men kill their wives (and often their children as well) because they feel they can no longer provide for them, their acts suggest that they see their wives as possessions to dispose of as they see fit and/or that they cannot conceive of their wives having an existence separate from their own.

20. Other research has noted the high rates at which offenders suicide after intimate femicides, and has contrasted this to the rarity of suicides by women who kill their intimate partners (see, e.g., Carolyn R. Block and A. Christakos, "Intimate Partner Homicide in Chicago over 29 Years," *Crime and Delinquency* 41 (1995): 496–526. Daly and Wilson (1988) have suggested that this pattern is grounded in males' feelings of possessiveness and ownership over their partners.

21. Murder is first-degree when the killing is planned and deliberate, when the victim is an officer of the law, or when a death is caused while committing or attempting to commit another offence, such as kidnapping. Any murder that does not fall within these categories is second-degree murder. According to the courts, the distinction between first- and second-degree murder is made solely for sentencing purposes. While anyone convicted of murder is sentenced to imprisonment for life, the parole ineligibility period varies between first- and second-degree murder.

22. Some analysts (e.g., Elizabeth Rapaport, "The Death Penalty and the Domestic Discount," in *The Public Nature of Private Violence: The Discovery of Domestic Abuse,* eds M. Fineman and R. Mykitiuk [New York: Routledge, 1994], 224–51) have speculated that the killing of a woman by her intimate male partner is treated more leniently by the criminal justice system than other types of homicides, such as killings of men by female intimate partners. However, empirical evidence in this area is sparse and not conclusive.

23. We use the category "spouse killings" here because we could find no statistics on the number of men killed by intimate partners, only statistics on men killed by spouses. To be comparable, we compare these figures to the number of women killed by spouses—a subset of all intimate femicides.

24. Marvin Wolfgang has noted in *Studies in Homicide* (New York: Harper & Row, 1967) that where males are victims of homicide, victim precipitation of the violence is fairly common.

25. Wolfgang (1967) found a similar pattern in his study of homicides in Philadelphia.

● References

Bachmann, R. 1993. *Death and Violence on the Reservation: Homicide, Family Violence, and Suicide in American Indian Populations* (New York: Auburn House).

Blinder, M. 1985. *Lovers, Killers, Husbands, and Wives* (New York: St Martin's Press).

Boudoris, J. 1971. "Homicide and the Family," *Journal of Marriage and the Family* 32: 667–76.

Brinkerhoff, M., and E. Lupri. 1988. "Interspousal Violence," *Canadian Journal of Sociology* 13: 407–34.

Browne, A. 1987. *When Battered Women Kill* (New York: The Free Press).

———, and K. Williams. 1989. "Exploring the Effect of Resource Availability on the Likelihood of Female-perpetrated Homicides," *Law and Society Review* 23: 75–94.

Campbell, J. 1995. "Prediction of Homicide of and by Battered Women," in *Assessing Dangerousness: Violence by Sexual Offenders, Batterers, and Child Abusers* (Thousand Oaks, CA: Sage), 96–113.

Campbell, J.C. 1992. "'If I Can't Have You No One Else Can':
Power and Control in Homicide of Female Partners," in *Femicide: The Politics of Woman Killing*, eds J. Radford and D.E.H. Russell (New York: Twayne), 99–113.

Canadian Centre for Justice Statistics. 1993. *Homicide Survey,* unpublished statistics.

Chimbos, P.D. 1978. *Marital Violence: A Study of Interspousal Homicide* (San Francisco: R & E Associates).

Crawford, M., R. Gartner, and M. Dawson, in collaboration with the Women We Honour Committee. 1997. *Women Killing: Intimate Femicide in Ontario, 1991–1994* (Toronto: Women We Honour Action Committee).

———, and the Women We Honour Action Committee. 1992. *Woman Killing: Intimate Femicide in Ontario, 1974–1990* (Toronto: Women We Honour Action Committee).

Daly, M., and M. Wilson. 1988. *Homicide* (New York: Aldine de Gruyter).

Dobash, R.E., and R.P. Dobash. 1984. "The Nature and Antecedents of Violent Events," *British Journal of Criminology* 24: 269–88.

Dobash, R.P., R.E. Dobash, M. Wilson, and M. Daly. 1992. "The Myth of Sexual Symmetry in Marital Violence," *Social Problems* 39: 81.

Frank, S. 1993. *Family Violence in Aboriginal Communities: A First Nations Report* (British Columbia: Report to the Government of British Columbia).

Goode, W. 1969. "Violence among Intimates," in *Crimes of Violence,* Vol. 13, eds D. Mulvihill and M. Tumin (Washington, DC: USGPO), 941–77.

Health and Welfare Canada. 1990. *Reaching for Solutions: Report of the Special Advisor to the Minister of National Health & Welfare on Child Sexual Abuse in Canada* (Ottawa: Supply and Services).

Hotaling, G., and D. Sugarman. 1986. "An Analysis of Risk Markers in Husband to Wife Violence: The Current State of Knowledge," *Violence and Victims* 1: 101–24.

Johnson, H. 1996. *Dangerous Domains: Violence Against Women in Canada* (Toronto: Nelson Canada).

———, and V. Sacco. 1995. "Researching Violence Against Women: Statistics Canada's National Survey," *Canadian Journal of Criminology* 3: 281–304.

Kelkar, G. 1992. "Women and Structural Violence in India," in *Femicide: The Politics of Women Killing,* eds J. Radford and D.E.H. Russell (New York: Twayne), 117–23.

Kennedy, L.W., D.R. Forde, and R.A. Silverman. 1989. "Understanding Homicide Trends: Issues in Disaggregating for National and Cross-national Comparisons," *Canadian Journal of Sociology* 14: 479–86.

Long, D.A. 1995. "On Violence and Healing: Aboriginal Experiences, 1960–1993," in *Violence in Canada: Sociopolitical Perspectives,* ed. J.I. Ross (Don Mills, ON: Oxford University Press), 40–77.

Macmillan, R., and R. Gartner. 1996. "Labour Force Participation and the Risk of Spousal Violence Against Women," paper presented at the 1996 Annual Meetings of the American Society of Criminology.

Maloney, M.A. 1994. "Victimization or Oppression? Women's Lives, Violence, and Agency," in *The Public Nature of Private Violence: The Discovery of Domestic Abuse,* eds M.A. Fineman and R. Mykitiuk (New York: Routledge), 59–92.

Marcus, I. 1994. "Reframing 'Domestic Violence': Terrorism in the Home," in *The Public Nature of Private Violence: The Discovery of Domestic Abuse,* eds M.A. Fineman and R. Mykitiuk (New York: Routledge), 11–35.

Messerschmidt, J.W. 1993. *Masculinities and Crime: Critique and Conceptualization of Theory* (Lanham, MD: Rowman & Littlefield).

Polk, K. 1994. *When Men Kill: Scenarios of Masculine Violence* (Cambridge: Cambridge University Press).

Rasche, C. 1989. "Stated and Attributed Motives for Lethal Violence in Intimate Relationships," paper presented at the 1989 Annual Meetings of the American Society of Criminology.

Regoeczi, W., and R. Silverman. 1997. "Spousal Homicide in Canada: Exploring the Issue of Racial Variations in Risk," paper presented at the 1997 Annual Meetings of the American Society of Criminology.

Rodgers, K. 1994. *Wife Assault: The Findings of a National Survey* (Ottawa: Canadian Centre for Justice Statistics).

Schneider, E. 1994. "The Violence of Privacy," in *The Public Nature of Private Violence: The Discovery of Domestic Abuse,* eds M. Fineman and R. Mykitiuk (New York: Routledge), 36–58.

Silverman, R., and L. Kennedy. 1993. *Deadly Deeds: Murder in Canada* (Toronto: Nelson Canada).

Wallace, A. 1986. *Homicide: The Social Reality* (New South Wales: NSW Bureau of Crime Statistics and Research).

Wilson, M., and M. Daly. 1992a. "Til Death Do Us Part," in *Femicide: The Politics of Woman Killing,* eds J. Radford and D.E.H. Russell (New York: Twayne), 85.

———. 1992b. "Who Kills Whom in Spouse Killings? On the Exceptional Sex Ratio of Spousal Homicides in the United States," *Criminology* 30: 189–215.

———. 1993. "Spousal Homicide Risk and Estrangement," *Violence and Victims* 8: 3–16.

———. 1994. "Spousal Homicide," *Juristat Service Bulletin* 14: 8.

———, H. Johnson, and M. Daly. 1995. "Lethal and Nonlethal Violence against Wives," *Canadian Journal of Criminology* 37: 343.

Wolfgang, M. 1958. *Patterns in Criminal Homicide* (Philadelphia: University of Pennsylvania Press).

Women We Honour Action Committee, and R. Gartner. 1990. *Annotated Bibliography of Works Reviewed for Project on Intimate Femicide* (Toronto: Women We Honour Action Committee).

Chapter 28

Family law shapes the lives of heterosexual couples most directly and powerfully when and if they divorce. For gay and lesbian couples, until 2005 it had a more profound effect. Many legal challenges were necessary before gay and lesbian couples acquired the same rights and benefits as heterosexual couples enjoy—including the right to marry. A series of legal decisions upholding equal rights were what pushed politicians to change family law in a way that expanded its definition of "family" to include same-sex partners.

This chapter is an article that legal scholar Mary Jane Mossman wrote just before same-sex marriage became legal in Canada. In it, she reviews important recent developments in Canadian family law. To understand her discussion, it is important to know something about the dramatic changes to family laws that occurred across Canadian provinces in the late 1970s. Old family laws had defined marriage as the union of a man and a woman in which the man owed the woman financial support and the woman owed the man domestic and sexual services. Getting rid of the gender differences in responsibility, the new laws defined marriage as a contract between two individuals in which each is responsible for their own support first, and then, given need and ability, for the support of their spouse—as well as their dependent children. With that change in law, the objective guiding the terms of divorce settlements revolved around the goal of enabling the two separating adults to make a "clean break" and become independent as soon as was possible. Toward that end, ongoing support (or alimony) following divorce was discouraged, and the emphasis was placed on an even division of "family property."

Unfortunately, these guidelines were problematic when put into practice: Many couples had very little property to divide between them, and women who had been home full-time, or employed only part-time, while married—because they and not their former husbands had cut back on paid work in order to prioritize child-care needs—were in such a weak position in the labour market that they were often unable to support themselves, much less their children. Evidence indicated that women's earnings significantly declined following divorce and men's did not. Mossman reports here that in response to this inequality in post-divorce outcomes Canadian courts in recent years have been expanding the responsibility of family members (that is, former spouses) to support dependent family members (former spouses and children) after divorce. She argues that this change recognizes both gender inequality in the labour force and the rise in neoliberal policies that have weakened the social-safety net. Mossman discusses the connection between the expanded definition of *family* (now including cohabitors and gay/lesbian couples) and the expansion in the responsibility held by families.

Conversations About Families in Canadian Courts and Legislatures: Are There "Lessons" for the United States?

Mary Jane Mossman

I. Trends in Canadian Family Law: Two Themes

I worry about governmental uses of relationships to serve governmental ends, like reducing governmental financial obligations. And I worry that by advocating expansive, functional definitions of family in some contexts, I may be fuelling this kind of governmental control in others.[1]

The field of family policy is not without controversy. . . . [But] there has been a new emphasis placed on strengthening families. Yet those who applaud new family forms are suspicious of the call for "a family policy" because they fear that it could represent a conservative agenda opposing greater equality for women, gays, and "families of choice." Creating social policies which bring together these two opposing viewpoints and deal adequately with the multidimensional aspects of family life is indeed a challenge.[2]

As these quotations demonstrate, issues about defining and supporting families create dilemmas for legal and social policies in both the United States and Canada. This article provides an overview of recent developments in Canadian family law, and some reflections on whether, or to what extent, Canadian developments offer "lessons" in relation to current American initiatives that challenge ideas about marriage, democracy, and families. For Americans seeking "lessons beyond borders," do recent experiences in Canada provide fruitful sources of inspiration and strategy?

In providing this brief assessment of Canadian developments, two interconnected themes are particularly significant. One is the new relationship between courts and legislatures in the recognition of "new families" in Canada. Like other western jurisdictions, Canadian legislatures have traditionally tended to enact guiding principles for family law, leaving Canadian courts to interpret and define how these principles should be applied in particular factual circumstances. However, the scope for expansive interpretation in Canadian courts has greatly increased in the past two decades, mainly as a result of constitutionally entrenched guarantees of equality in the *Canadian Charter of Rights and Freedoms* ("*Charter*").[3] As a result of the *Charter*, it is courts that have provided most of the impetus for legal recognition of "new families" in Canada, including recent decisions in three Canadian provinces which have declared that legal principles restricting marriage to only heterosexual couples violates the equality guarantee in the *Charter*.[4] In fact, many legislative reforms in Canada have been driven by these *Charter*-based judicial decisions, with legislatures often enacting reforms only after being compelled to do so by decisions of the courts. In relation to same-sex marriage, for example, the federal government has submitted a constitutional reference to the Supreme Court of Canada seeking the court's guidance with respect to proposed Parliamentary legislation.[5]

From an American perspective, however, this significant activism on the part of Canadian courts and judges may reflect a critical difference between our two countries at the present time. As a former member of the Supreme Court of Canada suggested a few years ago, constitutional interpretation in Canada, particularly in relation to human rights jurisprudence, has increasingly diverged from United States approaches because Canada's Constitution reflects the culture of international human rights in the late twentieth century:

> The United States Bill of Rights reads quite differently than most twentieth-century constitutions, which are drafted in language which has its sources in European and international human rights conventions, are more detailed, and frequently expressly permit limitations of the enumerated rights, either within the rights themselves or as a general limitation provision.[6]

Thus, Canadian family law currently reveals a pattern of activism on the part of courts and judges in interpreting the *Charter's* guarantees to recognize "new families" in law, with legislative reform frequently flowing out of this judicial decision making. Whether this pattern offers useful "lessons" for the United States, in the context of a different culture of constitutional rights, is an important question for those seeking family law reform.

A second and related theme in recent Canadian developments is the relationship between families and the state with respect to responsibility for dependent "family" members. In addition to active intervention in the legal recognition of "new families," Canadian courts have also been active in defining "new family obligations," including much expanded entitlement to ongoing spousal support, and obligations to pay child support for both biological and non-biological children, after separation or divorce.[7] Recent federal and provincial legislation has similarly confirmed that the primary obligation for support for children after separation or divorce rests with their parents, rather than the State.[8] In all of these contexts, primary responsibility for dependent individuals has been assigned to (former) family members and governmental support for dependency has declined.[9] In the context of social security, moreover, several Canadian legislatures have significantly reduced the level of payments to needy individuals and families in recent years, and the Ontario legislature (re)defined family relationships in 1995 so as to disentitle sole-support mothers who formed any kind of attachment to male persons.[10] Interestingly, the Ontario Court of Appeal recently declared that this legislative action contravened the *Charter,* striking down the relevant legislative provisions.[11] Thus, paradoxically, expansive judicial intervention that has recognized "new families" and "new family obligations" in the family law context has also been employed to strike down a legislative effort to create family relationships for sole-support mothers and thus disentitle them from continuing to receive financial assistance from the state. Although the *Charter* was once again significant in creating scope for this judicial activism, it is important to explore the underlying principles used by courts to define the obligations for *families* and for the *state* in these differing contexts of economic dependency. Moreover, since the Ontario Court of Appeal rejected the government's argument that its legislation was justified by the need to treat married and cohabiting couples in the same way,[12] these principles may offer useful "lessons" for the American context.

This article begins with an overview of Canadian developments in relation to the recognition of "new families." As explained above, this part of the article focuses primarily on judicial decisions, but it also includes references to some legislative reforms that have resulted from *Charter* claims. The article then provides an overview of recent developments concerning "new family obligations" and the relationship between family and state responsibilities for economic dependency. In this context, both judicial and legislative actions frequently intersect. In relation to these two themes, the article also focuses on some recent decisions of the Supreme Court of Canada which may signal a change in direction in relation to ideas about "new families," "new family obligations," or both, and on recent governmental policies concerning the definition and regulation of "families."[13] In this context, the article offers some reflections on the extent to which there may be Canadian "lessons" that are relevant to current concerns about marriage, democracy, and families in the United States.

II. Recent Legal Developments about Families in Canada

A. "New Families"; The Impact of *Charter* Jurisprudence

As in many western countries, Canada traditionally used marriage as the legal marker for "family."[14] However, by 1995, married couples with children at home constituted only 45 per cent of all families in Canada, a figure that had fallen from 64 per cent in 1961.[15] Demographically, opposite-sex cohabitees have represented an increasing proportion of all Canadian families; in the province of Quebec, for example, nearly 50 per cent of

babies were born in 1993 to mothers who were not legally married, and most of these births were to cohabitating couples.[16] Precise numbers about same-sex couples are more elusive, although questions were included, for the first time, about same-sex couples in the census in 2001.[17] The number of sole-parent families has also been rising; in 1995, for example, 22 per cent of Canadian families were headed by only one parent, and in 80 per cent of these families, the single parent was female.[18] And, the proportion of blended families or stepfamilies had also increased to about 10 per cent of all families in 1995.[19] Moreover, recent longitudinal studies have tracked the dynamic nature of family life; as one commentator suggested, "the modern Canadian family is like a giant amoeba, constantly joining, splitting, and rejoining in new configurations."[20] However, the statistics also suggest that there are significant differences in levels of household income in different kinds of families, with single-mother families most at risk of living below the poverty line.[21]

Traditionally, there has been some legal recognition of "family status" for opposite-sex couples who are not married, but such recognition for same-sex couples is relatively recent.[22] Thus, in the twentieth century, a patchwork of legislative provisions across Canada provided some legal recognition for "spouses" in opposite-sex couples in defined circumstances.[23] In addition, provincial family law statutes, which defined the entitlement of former spouses to ongoing financial support after separation, expanded the definition of "spouse" to include opposite-sex cohabitees.[24] Although these same provincial statutes also created principles for property sharing at separation or divorce, these principles were reserved for married couples only; they were not available to opposite-sex cohabitee.[25] Thus, although there was some legal recognition of opposite-sex couples as "families" in Canada, such families were nonetheless still excluded from some legal benefits provided to married couples.

However, same-sex cohabitees were not generally recognized at all in federal or provincial legislation, and there were a number of unsuccessful challenges to their exclusion from legal recognition as "families" even prior to the *Charter*.[26] After the enactment of the *Charter* in the 1980s, however, the number of litigation challenges to the exclusion of same-sex couples from the benefits of "family status" increased, although initially they were not often successful. The lack of success of the first litigation challenges resulted from two problems: first, sexual orientation was not included as a prohibited ground of discrimination in the *Charter*,[27] and second, early equality jurisprudence under the *Charter* strongly reflected the "similarly situated" test in American jurisprudence.[28] However, beginning with *Andrews v. Law Society of British Columbia*[29] in 1989, the Supreme Court of Canada began to articulate a new approach to equality jurisprudence that focused on the historic disadvantage experienced by persons such as a claimant in relation to immutable personal characteristics.[30] In addition, by the early 1990s, courts in Canada held that sexual orientation was an "analogous ground" to those listed in the *Charter* as prohibited grounds of discrimination.[31] In the context of these developments in *Charter* jurisprudence, challenges to the exclusion of same-sex couples began to attract judicial support. For example, a 1992 decision held that the policy of the Canadian Armed Forces excluding homosexuals contravened the *Charter*.[32] In relation to family status, moreover, a judge in Ontario wrote a compelling opinion in 1993, dissenting from the majority view that the exclusion of same-sex couples from marriage

did not infringe the *Charter*,[33] and a judge in British Columbia declared that a same-sex partner was entitled as a "spouse" to medical coverage under his partner's insurance plan.[34] Thus, although the issue of marriage for same-sex couples remained contested, same-sex partners were gradually being recognized by courts as entitled to equality of treatment and to some of the benefits of "family status."

In this context, the Supreme Court of Canada decided two cases in 1995 that required it to assess the fundamental nature of marriage, and to determine whether it was legally distinguishable from cohabiting relationships, including both opposite-sex and same-sex relationships. The court released decisions simultaneously in *Miron v. Trudel*,[35] concerning opposite-sex cohabitees, and in *Egan v. Canada*,[36] concerning same-sex cohabitees. In *Miron*, John Miron claimed accident benefits for injuries which he sustained in an automobile accident, on the basis that he was the "spouse" of the insured, his cohabitee Jocelyne Valliere.[37] The insurance company refused to pay the benefits, claiming that the word "spouse" in the insurance policy was limited to married couples only.[38] Although the insurance company succeeded in the lower courts, five of nine judges in the Supreme Court of Canada held that the policy discriminated on the basis of marital status, and that the discrimination could not be justified pursuant to section 1 of the *Charter*.[39] Among other reasons for their different conclusions, the dissenting judges expressed concern that "where individuals choose not to marry, it would undermine the choice they have made if the state were to impose upon them the very same burdens and benefits which it imposes on married persons."[40] In spite of such concerns, however, *Miron* clearly established that a majority of the court was determined to adopt a functional approach to married and cohabiting relationships, and the benefits flowing from such relationships.

In the related case, *Egan,* the claimant was a partner in a gay relationship which had existed since 1948.[41] When his partner became entitled to a pension pursuant to the Old Age Security Act, the claimant applied for an allowance that was payable to the "spouse" of a recipient within a married or cohabiting heterosexual relationship.[42] His claim was rejected by the government, and, with the exception of one dissenting opinion, the lower courts held that there was no discrimination in this case.[43] In the Supreme Court of Canada, however, all of the judges accepted that sexual orientation was an analogous ground of discrimination pursuant to the *Charter,* and five of nine judges held that the denial of the claim constituted discrimination on the basis of sexual orientation.[44] However, one of these five judges also held that the discriminatory treatment could be justified pursuant to section 1 of the *Charter.*[45] Thus, in the end, the claim was unsuccessful by a vote of five to four, with the majority asserting that marriage and opposite-sex cohabitation could be distinguished from all other societal units because of "the biological and social realities" of heterosexual relationships.[46]

Both of these cases have continuing significance for defining "families" in Canada, although most of the subsequent litigation has focused on *Egan,* at least until very recently.[47] Thus, in 1998, the Supreme Court of Canada redefined the "pressing and substantial" test for justifying discriminatory legislation pursuant to section 1,[48] and the federal government then announced that it would forego an appeal from Ontario that had decided that the exclusion of same-sex partners as "spouses" in relation to tax benefits in pension plans constituted

unjustifiable discrimination.[49] More significantly, the Supreme Court of Canada decided in May of 1999 that provincial legislation that excluded same-sex couples from entitlement to post-separation spousal support contravened the equality guarantee in the *Charter* and was not justified pursuant to section 1.[50] As a result, Ontario amended the definition of "spouse" to include same-sex couples, on the same basis as opposite-sex couples, in 67 provincial statutes in late 1999; significantly, the provincial government's reluctance was aptly reflected in the name of the amending legislation, *An Act to Amend Certain Statutes Because of the Supreme Court of Canada Decision in* M. v. H.[51] In early 2000, the federal government similarly enacted amendments to provide for the extension of benefits to same-sex couples in federal statutes.[52] Significantly, however, the federal legislation included an interpretation section, which was added during Parliamentary debate, stating that, "[f]or greater certainty, the amendments made by this Act do not affect the meaning of the word 'marriage,' that is, the lawful union of one man and one woman to the exclusion of all others."[53]

In this context, the Supreme Court's decision in *M. v. H.,* and the legislation that resulted from it, confirmed that same-sex couples were entitled to "family status." Yet marriage still remained the preserve of heterosexual couples. However, shortly after the decision in *M. v. H.,* same-sex marriage cases were initiated in the courts of three Canadian provinces: British Columbia, Ontario, and Quebec. In October of 2001, a single judge in a British Columbia court decided that the common law limitation of marriage to heterosexual couples did not constitute discrimination pursuant to the *Charter,* and that if there was discrimination, it was justified under section 1.[54] By contrast, in July 2002, a three member Ontario court unanimously held that the prohibition against same-sex marriage did constitute discrimination and was not justified pursuant to section 1 of the *Charter*. [55] The Quebec court followed the decision of the Ontario Court.[56] Although all of these decisions necessarily engaged with the nuances of *Charter* jurisprudence, one of the judgments in the Ontario court explicitly addressed the nature of marriage from a historical and societal perspective.[57] Identifying the procreation function as the basis for the exclusion of same-sex couples from the entitlement to marry, Justice Blair assessed the competing arguments and concluded that "[t]he underlying question, then, is whether the law in Canada today is sufficiently open and adaptable to recognize a broader rationale as the defining characteristic of marriage than heterosexual procreation and its surrounding religious paraphernalia. In my view, it is."[58]

In early 2003, the British Columbia Court of Appeal allowed the appeal in that province, but ordered that its decision would be suspended for two years to permit appropriate legislative action.[59] In early June of 2003, the Ontario Court of Appeal released its decision confirming the lower court decision in Ontario; however, the Ontario appellate court held that there was no reason to suspend its declaration of invalidity.[60] As a result, same-sex marriage became available in Ontario on June 10, 2003. A subsequent motion in the British Columbia court a few weeks later, requesting that the court's suspension be lifted, was unopposed by the federal and provincial governments.[61] Thus, same-sex marriage is currently available in the provinces of Ontario and British Columbia.

Even this brief overview demonstrates how significant the *Charter's* human rights protections have proved to be for advocates of same-sex family status, and even marriage:

the broad scope for judicial activism pursuant to the *Charter* has been critical to the legal recognition of same-sex families. By contrast, legislatures in Canada have tended to play "catch up" as and when judicial decisions have required them to act. As a result, it is courts that have primarily shaped and expanded legal definitions of "families" in Canada in recent years. Thus, although the federal government established a Parliamentary committee to examine the issue of same-sex marriage, and the federal Department of Justice issued a discussion paper in the fall of 2002;[62] they have been overtaken by these judicial decisions. As a result, the federal government has decided that legislation must be enacted to ensure uniformity of marriage law (a matter within federal constitutional jurisdiction) throughout Canada, and the government has now submitted a constitutional reference to the Supreme Court of Canada to determine how to shape such legislation to conform to *Charter* requirements.[63] In this context, it appears that Parliament is seeking direction from the court with respect to its constitutional obligation to extend marriage to same-sex couples in all provinces and territories.

Yet, the "success" of this human rights litigation for gay and lesbian families masks an important aspect of the litigation process: the fact that it has required advocates to argue that same-sex relationships are functionally *the same* as heterosexual relationships. As scholars in both Canada and the United States have argued,[64] this emphasis on functional similarity may necessitate the suppression of individual aspirations and undermine the efforts of same-sex couples (particularly lesbians) to (re)define their intimate relationships "outside" the law.[65] Yet, while their family relationships may not be fully recognized by law, the family lives of same-sex couples are nonetheless shaped by law, at least in some respects. As Shelley Gavigan argued, "[l]esbians do not live outside the law in a kind of legal limbo, nor do they exist in a legal vacuum."[66] In their engagement with the courts, both in human rights challenges and in other family law disputes, and in the law's definition of family rights and responsibilities, same-sex couples are both shaping and being shaped by legal and social relations in Canada. Thus, according to Gavigan, the "success" of a test case in Ontario, which permitted the lesbian partners of biological mothers to legally adopt their children, was flawed because it *required* the court to hold that the partners were "spouses."

> As profound as the challenge of the lesbian adoptions is, it is clear that striking down of the opposite sex requirement alone does not, cannot, address the constraints and assumptions that are embedded in the adoption legislation in Ontario. Under this legislation, it is not enough for the lesbian social parents to be "parents." In order to make a joint application, . . . they must also be spouses. . . . In order for the lesbian parents to be full parents, they had to be spouses, same-sex spouses to be sure, but spouses nonetheless.[67]

Thus, while it is clear that human rights challenges pursuant to the *Charter* have succeeded in expanding the legal definition of families to include same-sex couples, issues about precisely *how* to define families in law remain profoundly contested and challenging. In this context, a major report of the Law Commission of Canada attempted in 2001 to re-examine fundamental issues for defining families in Canada in the twenty-first century,[68] but its impact has been muted by the same-sex marriage debate. The report's significance for future developments in Canada is addressed later in this article.[69]

B. "New Family Obligations"; Responsibilities for Dependency for Families and the State

In spite of law's acceptance of the ideas of autonomy and independence for individuals within classical liberalism, it is evident that "dependence can be viewed as a necessary part of the human condition."[70] Although age, infirmity, and other conditions may render an individual adult dependent, children are inevitably dependent when they are born, even though the extent of their continuing dependence into adulthood varies according to economic and other circumstances within their families. Economic dependence may also occur for adult caregivers, whose ability to continue to engage in paid work is compromised by their caregiving responsibilities, a situation which commonly affects custodial parents (usually mothers) at separation or divorce. More systemically, governmental economic policies that assume a level of national unemployment contribute to the economic dependency of workers and their families, as do levels of minimum wages that do not result in family incomes above the poverty line.[71] Yet, recognizing that economic dependence is part of everyday life is much easier than determining who is responsible to support dependent individuals and families.

Although Canada has a history of support for publicly funded health care, education, and other social services, the division of legislative authority between the federal and provincial governments has often inhibited coordinated policy initiatives in relation to social security.[72] In the context of governmental concerns about deficit reduction in recent decades, moreover, there has been a trend to replace universal programs with benefits that target the poor and disadvantaged, an approach which has arguably reinforced the stigma of poverty.[73] In addition, some of these changes have been reflected in judicial decisions about responsibilities for economic support for dependent family members.[74] As sociologist Margrit Eichler argued, familial obligations to provide support may have both functional and normative aspects:

> As far as the support function of families is concerned, there is widespread consensus that families not only do support their own, but *should* do so. What is often overlooked is that there tends to be a direct opposition between the notion of the family as a support system and social security programs: to the degree that the proper locus of support for an individual is seen to lie within that individual's family, the individual becomes *disentitled* from public support.
>
> . . .
>
> [T]o the degree that we make social security programs available to individuals, we guarantee, as a society, some income security to individuals. Conversely, to the degree that we let eligibility for the social security programs be determined by family status, we disentitle individuals from access to social support on the basis of their family status. This disentitlement is usually justified by reference to the support function of "the family" . . . [75]

In my view, the trend of judicial decision making and legislative initiatives in the past two decades has reflected an expansion of the scope of family obligations for dependent individuals, with a corresponding reduction in the role of state support for dependency. Moreover, this trend has not simply occurred as a result of the functional vacuum created by the state's retreat from social security programs, but has also been characterized in normative terms. Thus, in spite of permanent separation or the finality of a divorce order, former spouses and their children have been categorized by the Supreme Court of Canada as a "post-divorce family unit" who *should* have continuing economic and other obligations to provide support for dependent family members.[76] This development was evident in relation to the issue of ongoing financial support after separation or divorce. For example, although the Supreme Court of Canada appeared to narrow the circumstances for enforcing responsibilities of ongoing *spousal* support in 1987 in the *Pelech* trilogy of cases,[77] even when former spouses had negotiated a binding separation agreement that limited their continuing economic relationship,[78] the principles of spousal support have increasingly been interpreted as recognizing ongoing obligations of the "post-divorce family unit." Significantly, the principles were initially expanded to recognize a need to provide effective compensation to former spouses (particularly wives) for their contributions to unpaid labour during the marriage.[79] Thus, in 1992, the Supreme Court of Canada expressly recognized "the feminization of poverty [as] an entrenched social phenomenon" in Canada,[80] and declared that the objectives of spousal support set out in the *Divorce Act* (which included compensation for the disadvantages of marriage or its breakdown) required Mr. Moge to continue to pay spousal support to his former wife almost 20 years after they had separated.[81] Judicial recognition of this "family obligation" was further expanded in 1999, when the Supreme Court of Canada determined in *Bracklow v. Bracklow*[82] that economic need on the part of a former spouse was all that was required to ground the obligation of a former family member to provide support.[83] As Chief Justice McLachlin stated, the "mutual obligation" view of marriage recognizes that spouses' lives become intermingled as a result of cohabitation over a period of time in a family relationship, and that it is unrealistic to assume that all separating couples will be able to move immediately from mutual support to absolute independence.[84] In addition, however, she suggested that this view of marriage "places the primary burden of support for a needy partner who cannot attain post-marital self-sufficiency on the partners to the relationship, *rather than on the state,* recognizing the potential injustice of foisting a helpless former partner onto the public assistance rolls."[85]

These cases revealed the court's commendable recognition of the precarious financial circumstances experienced by many women after separation and divorce, and they took into account both the need to compensate women for their unpaid contributions in intact families, as well as the post-divorce circumstances that often lead to economic need even in the absence of compensatory entitlement. This recognition is, of course, laudable in terms of ensuring that legal principles reflect the economic reality of women's lives. At the same time, however, both *Moge* and *Bracklow* conflated the clear economic need of former spouses (mostly women) with an assertion that the obligation to respond to this need belonged entirely to (former) family members, and not to the state. Of course, in a context in which the state was withdrawing support, any other decision would leave dependent family members in poverty. Yet, these judicial decisions may create difficulty in cases where former spouses, unlike those in *Moge* and *Bracklow,* do not have sufficient financial resources to support both current and former families.

Regardless of these issues, however, my point here is the narrower one of demonstrating how these decisions evidence a shift away from state-funded support programs for dependents and towards "new family obligations." More significantly, because of the expanded definition of "spouse" in family law legislation, these new family obligations extend to former cohabitees, both opposite-sex and (as a result of *M. v. H.)* same-sex partners. In this way, both the expansion of the category "spouse" and the shift to family, rather than state, obligations for economic support for dependency work together to make the family, including the "post-divorce family," the primary site for ensuring economic security for individuals.

These conclusions in relation to spousal support obligations were also reflected in the enactment of a system of national child support guidelines in 1997,[86] prescribing tables for defining the amount payable on the part of a non-custodial parent for their children after separation or divorce.[87] In this context, the state opted to use its resources to enforce support payments by parents, rather than to transfer benefits, economic and social, directly to children.[88] Moreover, both the federal and provincial statutes define "parent" so as to include non-biological children for whom an adult stands "in the place of a parent." Thus, in its 1999 decision in *Chartier v. Chartier*[89] the Supreme Court of Canada ordered a former husband to pay child support to his former wife, not only for their biological child but also for the wife's child from a previous relationship because he had stood "in the place of a parent" to this child.[90] In this case, the adults had been married for only a little over one year,[91] and although the court's decision was consistent with the authorities in Canada,[92] its policy implications were questioned by a commentator on the *Chartier* case:

528   Part V ● Problems, Policies, and the Law

The fact that adults live together does not amount to a commitment that they will remain together. Many relationships are of short duration. Many people are not inclined to make the accommodations necessary to ensure that their relationship will continue. In light of this, should the courts impose a long-term financial commitment on a person who was pleasant to a partner's child for a short time? The Supreme Court of Canada apparently believes that it should.

. . .

The task facing many lawyers will be to advise their clients on how to prevent that from happening to them. It appears that the only way to prevent a long-term child-support commitment is never to establish a parent–child relationship with a partner's child. Social scientists will have to decide whether that is a good way to force people to interact.[93]

Notwithstanding these concerns, Canadian courts have tended to enforce parental relationships with non-biological children, even when the relationship with a child's parent has terminated.[94] As a recent decision in Manitoba declared, "must as the status of a biological parent continues after the relationship between the adults has ceased, so one who stands *in loco parentis* continues to do so after cohabitation ceases. Neither bond can be unilaterally terminated by a parent."[95] Although there are important policy issues about law and family relationships in such cases, my point here is to demonstrate the shift in responsibility for dependency, once again, from the state to the "family," including the "post-divorce family."

In addition to this shift in family law principles, legislative changes concerning social security have also tended to limit state obligations

for dependency. For example, when the newly elected government in Ontario wished to implement its election promises about reducing the welfare rolls in 1995,[96] it adopted two strategies: reducing levels of welfare payments by over 20 per cent, and redefining "spousal" relationships.[97] Poverty activists challenged both of these actions, using the *Charter*. In relation to the government's right to set the levels of welfare payments, the challenge was unsuccessful, with the courts deferring to the legislature.[98] However, after protracted procedural challenges, the Ontario Court of Appeal held in 2002 that the new definition of "spouse" in the 1995 legislation violated the equality guarantee of the *Charter*.[99] The definition particularly affected single-mother families in receipt of welfare if the mother resided with a male with whom she shared any expenses. The claimants were all single mothers who were living with men who were not the fathers of their children, and they had arrangements for sharing rent, food costs, and other household expenses.[100] They argued that, pursuant to Ontario law, none of these male cohabitees had responsibility to provide financial support to the mothers or their children.[101] Significantly, some of the mothers had previously experienced abusive relationships and were hoping that these new relationships might become permanent, but they all wished to "test" the relationships for a time and to maintain their financial independence from these male partners while doing so.[102] In characterizing the regulations as violations of the *Charter*'s equality guarantee, the court stated:

> [T]he impact [of the Regulations] is severe, compromising, as it does, the respondents' ability to meet their own and their children's basic needs. Because of the definition, each [claimant] lost her entitlement to social assistance as a single person.

Beyond purely financial concerns, more fundamental dignity interests of the [claimants] have been affected. *Being reclassified as a spouse forces the [claimants] and other single mothers in similar circumstances to give up either their financial independence or their relationship. . . . Forcing them to become financially dependent on men with whom they have at best try-on relationships strikes at the core of their human dignity.*[103]

Thus, while the governmental regulation defining "spouse" in relation to welfare entitlement was consistent with family, rather than state, support for dependency, this judicial decision in the welfare context reassigned responsibility for the economic dependency of single-mother families to the state. Clearly, this judicial decision appears initially incongruous with cases that have expanded "family obligations" in the family law context. At the outset, it may be possible to find a distinction in the fact that "family obligations" were enforced, in cases like *Moge* and *Bracklow,* where the "spouses" had been married. By contrast, support obligations are not generally enforceable against cohabitees until their relationships meet the legislative threshold for liability, usually by the expiration of a three-year period or the birth or adoption of a child.[104] Thus, the claimants in *Falkiner* argued that they suffered discrimination because they were treated differently, and less advantageously, than single-mother families who were not in receipt of welfare payments.[105] Moreover, since their cohabiting partners acquired no legal responsibility to support them until the expiration of the three-year period, the claimants were particularly vulnerable in their economic dependency.[106]

These arguments may be important in relation to governmental assertions that welfare programs, and particularly these impugned regulations, were consciously designed to ensure equality in the treatment of married and cohabiting (opposite-sex) couples.[107] In rejecting this argument, the court held that the definition of "spouse" in the regulations did not "capture spousal relationships reasonably accurately [because] it embrace[d] many relationships that [were] not marriage-like in their economic component."[108] From this perspective, the court struck down legislation that was designed to reduce welfare expenditures by creating "new family" relationships. Thus, although the legislation did not function to encourage marriage *per se,* as does the recent proposal in the United States,[109] the overall purpose of the Ontario statute was to transform relationships into "families" and to replace state support for economic dependency with "new family obligations." In striking down the definition of "spouse" in welfare legislation, the court thus established one limit on the extent to which governments may transfer responsibility for dependency from the state to families. However, other than this limited situation, Canadian family law policy has tended to create expectations that families, expansively defined to include opposite-sex and same-sex cohabitees, will be the primary source of responsibility for economic dependency—rather than the state. Moreover, Canadian legal policy has achieved this goal without the need to enact legislation encouraging marriage.

C. Converging/Diverging Principles in Current Family Law and Policies

This overview of recent Canadian developments reveals how courts have significantly contributed to an expanded definition of "families." Using the constitutionally entrenched equality guarantee in the *Charter,* courts have responded positively to a number of claims presented by opposite-sex cohabitees and by gay and lesbian activists for legal recognition of their "families," including entitlement to marry. However, such claims for judicial recognition of same-sex families have generally been designed to attain equal access to the *benefits* of "family status," many of which were previously available only to families involving marriage and/or heterosexual cohabitation. Yet, as this overview has also demonstrated, courts have *at the same time* been redefining responsibility for economic dependency within families, including "post-divorce families," and in shifting primary responsibility away from the state by creating "new family obligations" for dependency. Unlike the same-sex family status cases, which have been driven by principles reflecting fundamental human rights and equality, the cases that have defined "family obligations" have reflected courts' increasing recognition of the reality of economic need, particularly for women and children post-divorce or separation, and they have been decided against a political backdrop of declining levels and categories of eligibility for social security. Although there has not been much political debate about roles and responsibilities for economic dependency in Canada, courts have responded to clear and demonstrable needs by creating "new family obligations." In this way, judicial decisions about "new families" and the evolving jurisprudence about "new family obligations" appear to have converged to expand not just the *rights*, but also the *obligations*, of Canadian families, including same-sex families.

Recent decisions of the Supreme Court of Canada, however, may signal changes in these judicial views about "new families" and "new family obligations." In *Gosselin v. Québec*,[110] for example, the court reviewed a legislative scheme in Quebec that significantly reduced the level of welfare benefits payable to recipients who were under 30 years of age, unless they participated in education or work experience programs.[111] A majority of five to four held that the age distinction, which determined different levels and qualifying criteria for persons over age 30, by contrast with the claimant and others who were under age 30, did not violate the equality guarantee of the *Charter*.[112] The majority concluded that the ameliorative purpose of creating incentives for young persons in receipt of social assistance to participate in education and work programming removed the possibility of discrimination:

> Even if one does not agree with the reasoning of the legislature or with its priorities, one cannot argue based on this record that the legislature's purpose lacked sufficient foundation in reality and common sense to fall within the bounds of permissible discretion in establishing and fine-tuning a complex social assistance scheme. Logic and common sense support the legislature's decision to structure its social assistance programs to give young people, who have a greater potential for long-term insertion into the workforce than older people, the incentive to participate in programs specifically designed to provide them with training and experience.[113]

In addition to this approach to *Charter* protection for equality, which seems to insulate from judicial scrutiny any program for which the government can identify beneficent objectives, the court also rejected the claimant's arguments that the government's failure to provide sufficient places for education and work opportunities for all social assistance recipients under 30 consigned her to living in poverty.[114] Interestingly, it was the views of a dissenting judge that revealed that the rationale for this treatment of recipients under the age of 30 was a governmental assumption that they would receive assistance, particularly in relation to housing, *from their parents*.[115] Yet, as Justice Bastarache concluded, "no effort was made to establish what living conditions were and a presumption was adopted that all persons under [30] received assistance from their family."[116] Unfortunately, this normative assumption about "family obligations" was untrue for Ms Gosselin, so that she was forced to live on an amount of social assistance that was less than the amount defined by Quebec legislation as the basic survival amount.[117] Thus, by contrast with the Ontario court's decision in *Falkiner,* the Supreme Court's recent decision in *Gosselin* appears to reinforce the scope for governments to shift responsibility for economic dependency to families, and to legislate on the basis of normative assumptions about "family obligations," whether they really exist in fact or not.

However, the outcome in *Gosselin* was achieved by a close vote,[118] with a number of dissenting opinions,[119] a feature that may suggest a significant divergence of opinion among judges on the court. By contrast, much greater unanimity was evident in another recent decision, *Nova Scotia v. Walsh,*[120] where eight of nine judges confirmed that Nova Scotia legislation did not violate the equality guarantee of the *Charter* when it restricted access to the statutory property-sharing regime to married couples who separated or divorced.[121] Walsh and her opposite-sex cohabitee had lived together for 10 years and they were the parents of two children, but her cohabiting partner held title to most of the accumulated property of the relationship. Thus, at separation, Walsh applied for a declaration that her exclusion from the statutory regime, which entitled each party to a marriage to an equal share of accumulated property, violated her *Charter* equality rights.[123] Although the appellate court in Nova Scotia had unanimously upheld her claim,[124] the Supreme Court concluded, with one dissenting opinion, that Walsh had not suffered discrimination on the basis of her status as a cohabitee.[125] Thus, the court held that there was no violation of Walsh's equality rights pursuant to the *Charter.*

Did *Nova Scotia v. Walsh* signal a new direction in the court's views about "new families" or "new family obligations"? In responding to this question, relationships between *Walsh* and some of the earlier cases must be assessed. For example, there were obvious similarities between the plaintiff's claim to be a "spouse" pursuant to an insurance policy in *Miron v. Trudel,*[126] and Walsh's claim to be a "spouse" for purposes of accessing property-sharing principles in the provincial statutory scheme at separation. In both cases, opposite-sex cohabitees were seeking legal recognition for their "spousal" relationships, even though they were not married.[127] Moreover, since opposite-sex cohabitees had long been recognized in legislative provisions across Canada,[128] it was widely expected that the court would decide that the exclusion of opposite-sex couples in *Walsh* violated the *Charter.*[129] In addition, since the Supreme Court of Canada had held in 1999 that the distinction between opposite-sex and same-sex cohabitees violated the equality guarantee in the *Charter,*[130] a decision that the exclusion of opposite-sex cohabitees from the statutory scheme for property-sharing at separation contravened the *Charter*'s equality guarantees appeared likely to apply to same-sex cohabitees as well. In this context, a decision confirming the decision of the Nova Scotia Court of

Appeal would have significantly enhanced the convergence of legal principles applicable to married couples, opposite-sex couples, and same-sex couples at the point of separation or family breakdown.

By contrast with this reasoning, however, the Supreme Court of Canada held that the exclusion of opposite-sex couples from access to the statutory scheme for property-sharing at separation did not violate the *Charter*'s equality guarantee, and distinguished *Miron*.[131] According to the court, *Miron* represented a claim against a third party in which the opposite-sex cohabitees were in agreement about the nature of their relationship, while *Walsh* involved a claim by one cohabiting partner against the other in circumstances where they had *chosen* to cohabit, rather than to marry.[132] For the majority of the court, the opportunity for individual choice in defining "families," whether by marriage or cohabitation, was critical:

> Where the legislation has the effect of dramatically altering the legal obligations of partners, as between themselves, choice must be paramount. The decision to marry or not is intensely personal and engages a complex interplay of social, political, religious, and financial considerations by the individual. While it remains true that unmarried spouses have suffered from historical disadvantage and stereotyping, it simultaneously cannot be ignored that many persons in circumstances similar to those of the parties, that is, opposite sex individuals in conjugal relationships of some permanence, have chosen to avoid the institution of marriage and the legal consequences that flow from it. . . . To ignore these differences among cohabiting couples presumes a commonality of

intention and understanding that simply does not exist. This effectively nullifies the individual's freedom to choose alternative family forms and to have that choice respected and legitimated by the state.[133]

By contrast with this majority view, Justice L'Heureux-Dubé's lone dissenting opinion focused on evidence of the rise in the numbers of cohabiting relationships in Canada,[134] arguing that "[t]he increased incidence of heterosexual unmarried cohabitation as a means by which children are raised and socialized and as a form of economic, emotional, and social interdependence dictates some form of recognition of the functional equality displayed by both heterosexual married and unmarried cohabitants."[135] Moreover, she expressly rejected the government's argument that the distinction in the legislation reflected different choices that were defined by the agreements between married couples by contrast with those of cohabitees about the nature of their relationships:

> [T]he fact that marriage gives rise to legal obligations does not, by itself, signal that the source of those obligations is some bargained-for exchange or the product of a consensus. While the price of a haircut is known in advance and can be contracted for (with a higher price for perms than for brushcuts), the same cannot be said about marriage. The marital relationship changes over time. Houses and other assets are bought and sold, one of the partners is promoted or loses their job, children are born, accidents occur, or a member of the family becomes ill. These and other events are rarely anticipated at the outset and appropriately bargained for. Further, neither spouse can anticipate who will contribute what to the marriage.

As a consequence, even the most intelligent of adults lacks the capacity to evaluate the commitments involved in any agreement dealing with the consequences of a dissolution that will only come after great change occurs in the relationship.[136]

Citing empirical research in the United Kingdom about the wide range of intentions among heterosexual cohabitees,[137] Justice L'Heureux-Dubé suggested a need to take account of the fact that:

[T]he choice not to marry is not a matter belonging to each individual alone. The ability to marry is inhibited whenever one of the two partners wishes to marry and the other does not. In this situation, it can hardly be said that the person who wishes to marry but must cohabit in order to obey the wishes of his or her partner chooses to cohabit. This results in a situation where one of the parties to the cohabitation relationship preserves his or her autonomy at the expense of the other. . . . Under these circumstances, stating that both members of the relationship chose to avoid the legal consequences of marriage is patently absurd.[138]

Interestingly, in 2003, the Supreme Court also allowed the appeal from the Ontario Court of Appeal in *Miglin,* with the majority concluding that choices reflected in private agreements between divorcing spouses should be respected, particularly where both spouses were represented by counsel in their negotiations.[139] By contrast, the two dissenting judges articulated the problems of vulnerability and economic need for such spouses, particularly women.[140] Thus, like the Supreme Court's decision in *Walsh,* the views in *Miglin* also

emphasized ideas of choice in the formation and dissolution of different kinds of family relationships, Moreover, while *Walsh* appears difficult to reconcile with the Supreme Court's earlier decision in *M. v. H.,* which recognized a violation of the *Charter*'s equality guarantee in the differential treatment accorded to opposite-sex and same-sex relationships for purposes of spousal support at the end of the relationship,[141] some of the views expressed by the majority in *Miglin* may signal a different approach to spousal support principles enunciated in *Bracklow*. As a result, these cases raise perplexing questions: is it significant that the claim in Walsh concerned property while the claim in *M. v. H.* concerned only spousal support? More fundamentally, what is the significance of "choice" for individuals who are involved in "family" relationships, and for governmental obligations to provide support for dependency? How should individual choices about family relationships and state regulation of the consequences of such choices be connected, if at all, in the twenty-first century?

III. Reconceptualizing "Families" and "Family Obligations"

Particularly as a result of the "same-sex marriage" cases, the federal government in Canada is now actively involved in reviewing the status of marriage. In the discussion paper issued by the federal Department of Justice in 2002, the government has suggested three alternatives, including the *status quo* (marriage only between a man and a woman), and secondly, the extension of marriage to same-sex couples,[142] The "third option" proposed would eliminate legal marriage, and replace it with "registered partnerships"; although the third option would not prohibit religious ceremonies of marriage, such ceremonies would have no legal impact in the absence of registration.[143] However, the discussion paper's proposals have been substantially overtaken as a result of the judicial decisions about same-sex marriage in Ontario and British Columbia, and federal legislation concerning marriage is expected to be introduced in Parliament in 2004, following release of the decision in the government's constitutional reference to the Supreme Court of Canada.[144] On the basis of the jurisprudence, it seems likely that Canada will enact same-sex marriage legislation applicable to all provinces and territories, although any such legislative proposals will also continue to attract political controversy.[145]

By contrast with recommendations focusing explicitly on marriage, a broader perspective about defining families in Canada was proposed by the Law Commission of Canada in 2001.[146] Although the Commission's report has not attracted much discussion in the context of the same-sex marriage decisions in the courts, it was considered carefully in the lower court decision in Ontario.[147] Indeed, the options proposed by the Commission persuaded Justice Blair that the issues should be addressed by legislatures so as to take into account the range of possible reforms to the law of marriage.[148] According to the Commission, "marriage" law should respect values of equality, autonomy, and choice in personal adult relationships, and its recognition of these relationships should ensure certainty, stability, and publicity.[149] Although conceding that marriage currently demonstrates some of these features, the Commission concluded that it was no longer sufficient because it does not "respond to the variety of relationships that exist in Canada today": older people living with adult children, adults with disabilities living with their caregivers, or cohabiting siblings, whose relationships may also be "characterized by emotional and economic interdependence, mutual care and concern and the expectation of some duration."[150]

In considering how to foster these differing relationships, the Law Commission's report reviewed four arrangements: private contracts (the only model available to conjugal and non-conjugal relationships outside marriage); ascription; registration; and marriage. Interestingly, in the context of recent decisions in the Supreme Court of Canada, the Law Commission's report identified serious disadvantages with private ordering in personal relationships: problems of inadequate knowledge and inaccessible legal advice, as well as issues of potential inequality between the parties. As the report noted, "[t]he contractual model may respect the value of autonomy but often falls short of fulfilling other values such as equality or efficiency since too few individuals are prepared to negotiate the terms of their close personal relationships."[151] In addition, it assessed the ascription model as less useful because it must treat all relationships as just the same; thus, it is "a blunt policy tool in that it treats all conjugal relationships alike, irrespective of the level of emotional or economic interdependency."[152] By contrast with these models; the report suggested that registration would permit greater personal autonomy, while providing models for achieving the partners' goals.

> A registration scheme provides a way in which a broad range of relationships, including non-conjugal relationships, can be recognized, while also promoting and respecting the value of autonomy. A registration scheme has a number of advantages specifically related to the value of autonomy and choice. In such a scheme, rights and responsibilities are based on

the mutual and voluntary decisions of the individuals in the relationship.[153]

In addition to individual autonomy with respect to such registered partnerships, however, the report also recognized a continuing state interest in restructuring financial relationships at the breakdown of such relationships: "[t]he state should ensure that the reasonable expectations of partners are not undermined on the breakdown of the relationship."[154]

The report also carefully addressed the fourth model: marriage.[155] At the outset, it assessed the continuing role for marriage in the context of proposed registered partnerships, suggesting that it was advantageous to remove the link between marriage and legal consequences: "[b]y establishing a civil registration scheme open to all persons in committed relationships, the state could focus more clearly and effectively on accomplishing the underlying objective currently accomplished incompletely by marriage, namely, recognizing and supporting committed personal adult relationships by facilitating an orderly regulation of their affairs."[156] Yet, as the report also noted, this recommendation may be inconsistent with established patterns of marriage in Canada, since civil marriage ceremonies now constitute a growing proportion of marriages solemnized in many parts of the country.[157] Partly for this reason, the report also considered the desirability of requiring a civil marriage for legal consequences (as is the custom in a number of European jurisdictions).[158] More significantly, however, the report reviewed the arguments about same-sex marriage and concluded that the reservation of marriage to heterosexual couples can no longer be justified.

There is no justification for maintaining the current distinctions between same-sex and heterosexual conjugal unions in light of current understandings of the state's interest in marriage. The secular purpose of marriage is to provide an orderly framework in which people can express their commitment to each other, receive public recognition and support, and voluntarily assume a range of legal rights and obligations. The current law does not reflect the social facts: as the Supreme Court of Canada has recognized, the capacity to form conjugal relationships characterized by emotional and economic interdependence has nothing to do with sexual orientation. . . . If governments are to continue to maintain an institution called marriage, they cannot do so in a discriminatory fashion.[159]

Such comments reveal both a functional analysis of the nature of family relationships as well as recognition of new normative principles for governing the state's relationships to families. Interestingly, moreover, the views of the Law Commission's report are similar to the results of opinion polls in Canada, conducted between June 1999 and June 2001, which revealed "that between [40] per cent and [65] per cent of Canadians [then] favour[ed] recognition of same-sex marriages."[160] In such a context, however, it is also clear that individuals' aspirations for recognition of their "new families" in accordance with the *Charter*'s human rights protections are increasingly congruent with the state's interest in transferring "new family obligations" for economic dependency to families. As a result, some Canadians may wish to embrace judicial decisions which grant the dignity of legal recognition to "new families," while lamenting at the same time the privatizing agenda of governments that are abandoning public responsibility for economic dependency by implementing "new family obligations." In the result, the level of financial support for dependency is entirely determined by the economic resources of former family members, and economic relationships must continue long after emotional ties may have shattered, or at least fluctuate as time and circumstances change. In this way, the concerns identified by the two scholars, one American and one Canadian, at the outset of this article clearly represent similar and significant challenges for family law and policy in both countries. At the same time, the current policy contexts in our two countries differ significantly: while the American government wishes to promote marriage as a panacea for welfare problems, and to exclude same-sex partners from entitlement to marry, recent trends in Canadian courts and legislatures appear to be in flux in relation to issues about family and state obligations for dependency, but recognition of same-sex marriage appears very likely. Moreover, the report of the Law Commission of Canada suggests that there are fundamental issues about families, and their relationships to law, which require serious consideration in both of our countries. In such a context, there may be a continuing need for all of us to examine "lessons beyond borders."

● Notes

1. Martha Minow, "Redefining Families; Who's In and Who's Out?," 62 *U. Colo. L. Rev.* 269, 283 (1991).

2. Maureen Baker, "Thinking about Families: Trends and Policies," in *Canada's Changing Families: Challenges to Public Policy* 4 (Maureen Baker ed., 1994) [hereinafter *Canada's Changing Families*].

3. See *Can. Const.* (Constitution Act, 1982) pt. 1 (Canadian Charter of Rights and Freedoms). § 15(1). In a recent assessment of the *Charter*'s impact, it was noted that the enactment of the *Charter* "was a turning point for the Canadian legal and political system and culture. prompting much speculation and a great deal of debate about what the effect of the *Charter* would, and should, be." "Reflections on the Twentieth Anniversary of the *Canadian Charter of Rights and Freedoms*: A Symposium." 40 *Osgoode Hall L.J.* 215, 215 (2002) (editors' introduction).

4. See generally *Egale Canada Inc. v. Canada (A.G.)*, [2001] 95 B.C.L.R.3d 122, 19 R.F.L.5111 59, 71 (B.C. S.C.), overruled by *Egale Canada Inc. v. Canada (A.G.)*, [2003] 13 B.C.L.R.A4th I; *Halpern v. Canada (A.G.)*, [2003] 215 D.L.R.4th 213, aff'd, [2003] 225 D.L.R.4th 529; *Hendricks v. Quebec (A.G.)* [2002] J.Q. 3816, varied by *Hendricks v. Quebec*, [2003] CarswellQue 93; see also Kathleen A. Lahey. "Legal 'Persons' and the Charter of Rights: Gender, Race, and Sexuality in Canada," 77 *Can. Bar Rev.* 402 (1998).

5. See Kim Lunman & Drew Fagan, "Marriage Divides the House," *Globe & Mail*, Sept. 17, 2003, at A1.

6. The Hon. Claire L'Heureux-Dubé. "The Importance of Dialogue: Globalization and the International Impact of the Rehnquist Court," 34 *Tulsa L.J.* 15, 32 (1998).

7. See, e.g., *Monkman v. Beaulieu*, [2000] 149 Man. R.2d 295 (extending child support requirements to stepchildren as well as biological children); *Bracklow v. Bracklow*, [1999] 1 S.C.R. 420 (grounding ongoing support on spouse's need).

8. See, e.g., Dep't of Justice, Canada, Parenting After Divorce, at http://canada.justice.gc.ca/en/ps/pad/about/ (last updated Apr. 14, 2003) (discussing current and proposed legislation).

9. See Sherri Torjman, "Crests and Crashes: The Changing Tides of Family Income Security," in *Canada's Changing Families: Challenges to Public Policy* 69 (Maureen Baker ed., 1994) (indicating a trend of shrinking reliance by Canadian families on government resources); see also Mary Jane Mossman, "Child Support or Support for Children? Re-Thinking 'Public' and 'Private' in Family Law," 46 *Univ. New Brunswick L.J.* 63, 81 (1997).

10. See, e.g., *Falkiner v. Ontario*, [2002] 59 O.R.3d 481, 484–85.

11. See *id* at 513–14; see also Andy Mitchell et al., *Five Years Later: Welfare Rate Cuts Anniversary Report* 2 (2000).

12. See Falkiner, 59 O.R.3d at 511.

13. See, e.g., Law Comm'n of Canada, *Beyond Conjugality: Recognizing and Supporting Close Personal Adult Relationships* (2001) [Hereinafter *LCC Report*]; Dep't of Justice Canada, *Marriage and Legal Recognition of Same-Sex Unions* (2002) [hereinafter *Legal Recognition*], available at http://canada.justice.gc.ca/en/dept/pub/mar/index.html.

14. See Winifred Holland, "Intimate Relationships in the New Millennium: The Assimilation of Marriage and Cohabitation?," 17 *Can. J. Fam. L.* 114, 117 (2000).

15. See Elaine Carey. "'Alternate' Families Outweigh Tradition," *Toronto Star* (Metro Edition), June 20, 1996, at A2 (quoting Statistics Canada, *Canadian Families: Diversity and Change* (1996)).

16. See "Younger Couples Choose Not Marry," *Toronto Star* (Metro Edition). June 14, 1995, at A11.

17. See Elaine Carey, "Are You Gay? How Next Year's Census Will Pop the Question," *Toronto Star* (Metro Edition), May 7, 2000, at A1.

18. See Carey, *supra* note 15.

19. See *id*.

20. "Figures Reflect Changing Family Scene," *Globe & Mail,* Apr. 12, 1996, at A10.

21. See *Vanier Institute of the Family, Profiling Canada's Families* 77 (1994) (stating that 95 per cent of single-mother families with no earners lived below the poverty line in 1991). See generally *Vanier Institute of the Family. Profiling Canada's Families* II (2000).

22. See Nicholas Bala, "Alternatives for Extending Spousal Status in Canada," 17 *Can. J. Fam. L.* 169, 192–93 (2000).

23. See *LCC Report, supra* note 13, at 116; Modernization of Benefits and Obligations Act, ch. 12, 2000 S.C. (Can.) (extending certain spousal benefits under Canadian federal law to "common-law partners").

24. See, e.g., Adult Interdependent Relationships Act, S.A., 2002, ch. A-4.5 (Alb.); Family Maintenance Act, R.S.M., 1987. ch. F20 (Man.).

25. See, e.g., Family Law Act, R.S.O., ch. F.3, § I (1990) (Ont.) (defining "spouse," which applies in relation to property-sharing in Parts I and II of the Family Law Act). The courts have developed a lively jurisprudence to award proprietary interests to cohabitees, including both same-sex and opposite sex cohabitees, pursuant to the equitable doctrines of unjust enrichment and constructive trust. See *Ontario Law Reform Comm'n, Report on Family Property* (1993); see also *Regnier v. O'Reilly,* [1997] 39 B.C.L.R.3d 178 (applying equitable principles to a will challenge brought by decedent's same-sex partner).

26. See generally Martha A. McCarthy & Joanna L. Radford, "Family Law for Same Sex Couples: Chart(er)ing the Course," 15 *Can. J. Fam. L.* 101 (1998).

27. Section 15 of the *Charter* includes a list of prohibited grounds of discrimination, but jurisprudence now recognizes "analogous" grounds, including sexual orientation. See e.g., *Egan v. Canada,* [1995] 2 S.C.R. 513, 528–29; *Haig v. Canada,* [1992] 9 O.R.3d 495, 500.

28. See, e.g., *Andrews v. Ontario,* [1988] 49 D.L.R.4th 584, 589 (finding that same-sex couples are not similarly situated as heterosexual couples and refusing to include same-sex partners as dependents under the Health Insurance Act).

29. [1989] I S.C.R. 143 (challenging the requirement of citizenship for application for admission as a lawyer in British Columbia).

30. See *id.* at 171 (McIntyre, J., dissenting in part) ("It is clear that the purpose of s. 15 is to ensure equality in the formulation and application of the law. The promotion of equality entails the promotion of a society in which all are secure in the knowledge that they are recognized at law as human beings equally deserving of concern, respect and consideration. *It has a large remedial component"* (emphasis added). For an overview of equality jurisprudence, see The Hon. Claire L'Heureux-Dubé, "What a Difference a Decade Makes: The Canadian Constitution and the Family Since 1991," 27 *Queen's L.J.* 361 (2001).

31. See *Haig,* 9 O.R.3d at 501.

32. See *Douglas v. Canada,* [1992] 98 D.L.R.4th 129, 134–40.

33. See *Layland v. Ontario,* [1993] 14 O.R.3d 658, 667–82 (Greer. J., dissenting).

34. See *Knodel v. British Columbia,* [1991] 58 B.C.L.R.2d 256, 1991 A.C.W.S.J. Lexis 33837, at*72–73.

35. [1995] 2 S.C.R. 418.

36. [1995] 2 S.C.R. 513.

37. See *Miron*, 2 S.C.R. at 430–32.

38. See *id.* at 431.

39. See *id.* at 465–511. Section 1 of the *Charter* is an express "limit" in relation to constitutional violations. Thus, a violation may be upheld if it is a "reasonable limit[] prescribed by law as can be demonstrably justified in a free and democratic society." *Can. Const.* (Constitution Act, 1982) pt. I (Canadian Charter of Rights and Freedoms), § I.

40. *Miron*, 2 S.C.R. at 450 (Gonthier, J., dissenting).

41. See *Egan*, 2 S.C.R. at 528.

42. See *id.*

43. See generally *Egan v. Canada*, [1993] 3 F.C. 401; *Egan v. Canada*, (1992) 1 F.C. 687.

44. See *Egan*, 2 S.C.R. at 572 (Sopinka, J., concurring).

45. See *id.* (Sopinka. J., concurring) (agreeing with four other justices that the distinction constituted discrimination contrary to section 15 of the *Charter*, but holding that the "infringement [was] saved" under section 1).

46. *Id.* at 536.

47. See, e.g., *Rosenberg v. Canada (A.G.)*, [1998] 38 O.R.3d 577, 582–84 (finding that the exclusion of tax benefits on the grounds of sexual orientation violates section 1 of the *Charter); M. v. H .* [1999] 2 S.C.R. 3, 25 (analyzing whether the definition of "spouse" in section 29 of Ontario's Family Law Act, R.S.O., ch. F.3 (1990) (Ont.), infringes section 15(1) of the *Charter*, and, if so, whether the legislation is saved by section 1 of the *Charter*).

48. See *Vriend v. Alberta*, [1998] 1 S.C.R. 493. 554–57; see also Brenda Cossman, "Lesbians, Gay Men, and the *Canadian Charter of Rights and Freedoms*," 40 *Osgoode Hall L.J.* 223, 231–32 (2002).

49. See *Rosenberg*, 38 O.R.3d 577 (applying the principles enunciated in *Vriend*).

50. See *M. v. H.,* 2 S.C.R. at 26–27.

51. Ch. 6, 1999 S.O. (Ont.) The amending legislation was enacted in October 1999, just barely within the timeframe permitted by the court in *M. v. H.* See *M. v. H.,* 2 S.C.R. at 87 (Iacobucci, J.) (suspending the severance of the offending section of the Family Law Act for six months to permit the legislature to assess the decision's impact on other statutes with similar definitions).

52. See Modernization of Benefits and Obligations Act, ch. 12, 2000 S.C. (Can.).

53. *Id.* § l.1.

54. See *Egale Canada Inc. v. Canada (A.G.)*, [2001] 95 S.C.L.R.3d 122, 19 R.F.L.5th 59, 71, overruled by *Egale Canada Inc. v. Canada (A.G.)*, [2003] 13 B.C.L.R.4th 1.

55. See generally *Halpern v. Canada (A.G.)*, [2002] 215 D.L.R.4th 223, aff'd, [2003] 225 D.L.R.4th 529.

56. See *Hendricks v. Quebec (A.G.)*, [2002] J.Q. 3816, varied by *Hendricks v. Quebec*, [2003] CarswellQue 93.

57. See *Halpern*, 60 O.R.3d at 345–55 (Blair, R.S.J., concurring).

58. *Id.* at 356 (Blair, R.S.J., concurring).

59. See *Egale Canada Inc.*, [2003] 13 B.C.L.R.4th at ¶161.

60. See *Halpern*, [2003] 225 D.L.R.4th at 456.

61. See *Egale Canada Inc. v. Canada*, [2003]15 B.C.L.R.4th 226.

62. See *Legal Recognition, supra* note 13.

63. See Lunman & Fagan, *supra* note 5.

64. See Katherine Arnup, "Lesbian Mothers. Lesbian Families: Legal Obstacles, Legal Challenges," 14 *N.Y.U. Rev. L. & Soc. Change* 907, 907–08 (1986); Nancy Polikoff, "'Mothers Just Like Others': Lesbians, Divorce, and Child Custody in Canada," 3 *Can. J. Women & L.*, 18, 30–31 (1989).

65. See, e.g., Susan B. Boyd, "Lesbian (and Gay) Custody Claims: What Difference Does Difference Make?," 15 *Can. J. Fam. L.* 131, 139–42 (1998); see also Susan B. Boyd, "Family, Law and Sexuality: Feminist Engagement," 8 *Soc. & Legal Stud.* 369, 381–82 (1999); Cossman. *supra* note 48, at 241–42.

66. Shelley A.M. Gavigan, "A Parent(ly) Knot: Can Heather Have Two Mammies?," in *Legal Inversions: Lesbians, Gay Men, and the Politics of Law* 103 (Didi Herman & Carl Stychin eds., 1995).

67. Sheltey A.M. Gavigan, "Legal Forms, Family Forms, Gendered Norms: What Is a Spouse?," 14 *Can. J. L. & Soc'y* 127, 156 (1999).

68. See generally *LCC Report, supra* note 13.

69. See *infra* text accompanying notes 147–61.

70. Pamela Symes, "Property, Power and Dependence: Critical Family Law," 14 *J.L. & Soc'y* 199, 202 (1987).

71. See generally Torjman, *supra* note 9; Linda Duxbury & Christopher Higgins, "Families in the Economy," in *Canada's Changing Families, supra* note 2, at 29.

72. See Maureen Baker, "The Effectiveness of Family and Social Policies," in *Canada's Changing Families, supra* note 2, at 129.

73. See Torjman, *supra* note 9, at 71.

74. See *Bracklow v. Bracklow,* [1999] 1 S.C.R. 420, 438 [1999] ("[A spousal support award] places the primary burden of support for a needy partner . . . on the partners to the relationship, rather than on the state, recognizing the potential injustice of foisting a helpless former partner onto the public assistance rolls").

75. Margrit Eichler, *Families in Canada Today* 110 (1983).

76. See *Thibaudeau v. Canada,* [1995] 2 S.C.R. 627, 702 (Meuchlin & L'Heureux-Dubé, J.J., dissenting).

77. See generally *Pelech v. Pelech,* [1987] 1 S.C.R. 801; *Richardson v. Richardson,* [1987] 1 S.C.R. 857; *Caron v. Caron,* [1987] 1 S.C.R. 892.

78. See *Richardson,* 1 S.C.R. at 866 (explaining that the *Pelech* line of cases suggests that it is within a court's discretion to alter a settlement agreement in the event there has been a "radical change in the circumstances of a former spouse," provided that the change is the product of "economic dependency generated by the marriage relationship").

79. See generally *Law Reform Comm'n of Canada, Maintenance on Divorce* (Working Paper No. 12, 1975), microformed on Canada Law Reform Commission (William S. Hein & Co., Inc.).

80. *Moge v. Moge,* [1992] 3 S.C.R. 813, 99 D.L.R. 4th 456, 482.

81. See *id.,* 99 D.L.R.4th at 479–85; see also Divorce Act, R.S.C., ch. 3, § 15(7)(a) (1985), amended by ch. 1, 1997 S.C. § 15.2(6)(a) (2d Supp. 1997) (Can.).

82. [1999] 1 S.C.R.420.

83. See *id.* at 448.

84. *Id.* at 437–38.

85. *Id.* at 438 (emphasis added).

86. Federal Child Support Guidelines, S.O.R./97-175, amended by S.O.R./01-292, available at http://canada.justice.gc.ca/en/ps/sup/grl/ligfed.html (last updated Apr. 24, 2003).

87. See Canada Department of Justice, "Federal Child Support Amounts: Simplified Tables," at http://Canada.justice.gc.ca/en/ps/sup/grl/Pdftab.htm (last updated Apr. 24, 2003).

88. See Julien D. Payne, "Spousal and Child Support after *Moge, Willick* and *Levesque*," 12 *Can. Fam. L. Q.,* 261, 298–99 (1995) (critiquing legislated child support guidelines as not likely "to resolve the economic crisis of separation and divorce for women and children").

89. [1999] 1 S.C.R. 242, 168 D.L.R.4th 540.

90. See *id.* 168 D.L.R.4th at 557.

91. See *id.* at 543.

92. See *id.* at 556–57.

93. J.G. McLeod, Annotation to *Chartier v. Chartier* (1999), 43 R.F.L.4th 1, 4.

94. See e.g., *Samson v. Samson,* [2003] 2003 N.LC. Lexis 140 at 24 (holding that when respondent took on role of father figure for eleven years to his wife's children from prior relationships, he stood in the place of a parent and was obligated for their support upon divorce from their mother); *Beaudry v. Gillcash,* [2001] 2001 Man. R.2d Lexis 272 at*5 (granting visitation to a non-biological parent who was "the only father [the child had] ever known").

95. *Monkman v. Beaulieu,* [2000] 149 Man. R.2d 295, 115.

96. See Betsy Powell, "Tory Squad to Retrace Path of NDP Probe," *The Record,* Aug. 21, 1995, at A3.

97. See *id.*

98. See *Masse v. Ontario,* [1996]134 D.L.R.4th 20, 42 (finding no right to social assistance benefits as the legislature was free to repeal or amend the statutes providing for it).

99. See *Falkiner v. Ontario,* [2002] 59 O.R.3d 481, 513.

100. See *id.* at 496.

101. See *id.*

102. See *id.* at 485, 495–96.

103. See *id.* at 512 (emphasis added).

104. See Family Law Act, R.S.O., ch. F.3, §§ 29–30 (1990) (Ont.).

105. See *Falkiner,* 59 O.R.3d at 503.

106. See *id.* at 513–14.

107. See *id* at 485, 514.

108. *Id.* at 498.

109. See Personal Responsibility, Work, and Family Promotion Act of 2002, H.R. 4737, 107th Cong. § 103 (2002) (authorizing grants to the states specifically to "promote and support healthy, married, 2-parent families").

110. [2002] 221 D.L.R.4th 257.

111. See *id.* at 276.

112. See *id.* at 275–309. The arguments focused not only on the section 15 equality protection, but also on the guarantee of "liberty" and "security of the person" in section 7. See *id.* at 301–04.

113. *Id.* at 290.

114. See *id.* at 291–92.

115. See *id.* at 360–61.

116. *Id.* at 361 (Bastarache, J., dissenting).

117. See *id.* at 361–62 (Bastarache, J., dissenting).

118. See *id.* at 275–309.

119. See *id.* at 309–24 (L'Heureux-Dubé, J., dissenting), 324–85 (Bastarache, J., dissenting); 386–424 (Arbour, J., dissenting), 424–37 (Lebel, J., dissenting).

120. [2002] 221 D.L.R.4th 1.

121. See *id.* at 36.

122. See *id.* at 14.

123. See *id.*

124. See generally *Walsh v. Bonn,* [2000] 183 N.S.R.2d 74.

125. See *Nova Scotia (A.G.) v. Walsh,* 221 D.L.R.4th 1 at 36; see *id.* at 37–89 (L'Heureux-Dubé, J., dissenting).

126. [1995] 2 S.C.R. 418.

127. In both *Miron* and *Walsh,* legal recognition of these claims did not result in courts creating new financial obligations for governments by extending such benefits to new categories of families, a concern that has often been used to distinguish the differing outcomes in *Miron,* and *Egan.* See text accompanying notes 34–45.

128. See *Miron v. Trudel,* [1995] 2 S.C.R. 418, 499.

129. See R. Thompson, Annotation to *Nova Scotia v. Walsh,* R.F.L.

130. See *M. v. H.,* [1999] 2 S.C.R. 3, 26–27.

131. See *Nova Scotia (A.G.) v. Walsh,* [2002] 221 D.L.R.4th 1, 32–33.

132. See *id.*

133. *Id.* at 28–29.

134. See *id.* at 56–58 (L'Heureux-Dubé, J., dissenting).

135. *Id.* at 58 (L'Heureux-Dubé, J., dissenting); see also *Law Reform Comm'n of Nova Scotia, Final Report: Reform of the Law Dealing with Matrimonial Property in Nova Scotia* 21 (1997) (discussing changes to the laws of property-sharing at separation as necessitated by the functional equivalent of heterosexual married and unmarried cohabitants).

136. *Walsh,* 221 D.L.R.4th at 65 (L'Heureux-Dubé, J., dissenting).

137. See *id.* at 67 (L'Heureux-Dubé, J., dissenting) (citing Carol Smart, "Stories of Family Life: Cohabitation, Marriage and Social Change," 17 *Can J. Fam. L.* 20, 50 (2000)).

138. *Walsh,* 221 D.L.R.4th at 68 (L'Heureux-Dubé J.,

dissenting).

139. See *Miglin v. Miglin,* [2003] 2003 Can. Sup. Ct. Lexis 23 at *84–106.

140. See *id.* at *182–93.

141. See *M. v. H.,* [1999] 2 S.C.R. 3, 26–27. Significantly, one partner in *M. v. H.* was seeking entitlement to spousal support at the breakdown of the relationship, while the other partner objected to being treated as functionally similar to opposite-sex cohabitees for this purpose. See *id.* at 30, 42. On its face, this claim appears substantially similar to the situation in *Walsh,* in which one partner was claiming access to property-sharing principles available to married couples, while the other partner resisted.

142. See generally *Legal Recognition, supra* note 13.

143. See *id.* at 26. This proposal would require agreement between the federal, provincial, and territorial governments, because of the division of legislative authority for "family law" in Canada. See *id.* All references to marriage would be eliminated and federal divorce law would apply only to existing marriages. Registered partnerships and their breakdown would be governed by provincial law. See *id.*

144. See *supra* note 5 and accompanying text.

145. See *id.*

146. See *LCC Report, supra* note 13; see also *Legal Recognition, supra* note 13, at 8 n.4. (stating that "further study would be needed before Parliament can decide whether it is appropriate to treat nonconjugal relationships in the same way as spouses or common-law partner in all federal laws").

147. See *Halpern v. Canada (A.G.),* [2002] 215 D.L.R.4th 223.

148. See *id.* at 375–76 (Blair, R.S.J., concurring).

149. See *LCC Report, supra* note 13, at xi, xv–xvi.

150. *Id.* at 113–14.

151. *Id.* at 115.

152. *Id.* at 116.

153. *Id.* at 117–18.

154. *Id.* at 120.

155. See *id.* at 123–31.

156. *Id.* at 123.

157. See *id.*

158. See *id.* at 126.

159. *Id.* at 130.

160. *Id.* at 136 n.58.

Chapter 29

Canada's approach to social policy has been what policy analysts label "liberal," which means that the government's role has been to enable corporate interests rather than monitor and intervene in the marketplace—except when the economy causes severe problems (e.g., unemployment, injury in the workplace) or is in trouble (e.g., during economic recessions or depressions). This approach contrasts with that of Scandinavian countries and some continental European countries, in which the role of the government is seen as ensuring the basic social security of every citizen, and even ensuring that all citizens have a decent standard of living. In the last two decades, an enhanced kind of liberal approach, known as neoliberalism, has governed social policy in Canada. As a result, an obvious solution to one of the most common problems facing a majority of Canadian parents of young children—the dearth of affordable, good-quality child care—has not been addressed in English-speaking Canada. Universal affordable, quality daycare is still an unmet need despite several decades of feminist lobbying for it.

In Quebec, the situation is different, as is the political culture. In the late 1990s, after systematic review of evidence and popular need, several family policies were implemented. One of them ensured a very affordable space in a daycare facility for every child in need of it. This chapter, by Diane-Gabrielle Tremblay, describes the policy approach that Quebec has taken and the resulting policies.

Quebec's Policies for Work–Family Balance: A Model for Canada?

Diane-Gabrielle Tremblay

Quebec's policies on child care, parental leave, and other measures to improve the work–family balance are often presented as a model for the rest of Canada. This chapter will compare and assess recent changes in both Quebec and at the federal level in Canada to ascertain the extent to which public policy addresses problems related to the balancing of work and family. In particular, it will examine the ways that current policies at the federal level and in Quebec affect gender equity in the labour market and the family.

The chapter will first set out a typology of family policies based on the classifications developed by Hantrais and Letablier (1996). Second, it will present a brief history of federal and Quebec policies regarding parental-leave and child care-services while attempting to situate them in relation to this typology. Recent federal policy orientations reflect a vision that differs greatly from Quebec's on family policy goals. I argue here that the rest of Canada and the federal Conservative Party are pursuing a conservative or laissez-faire doctrine, while the federal Liberal Party seems to favour a policy aimed at alternating between work and family, which is also a conservative position. Quebec generally favours a policy of work–family balance that involves a combination of work and family and parental responsibilities, although the Action démocratique du Québec (ADQ) had proposed a policy that would have moved Quebec in a conservative direction. In Quebec, a shift to the right may, however, be difficult for any government to accomplish because of the extent to which new programs have encouraged paternal leave.

In January 2006, the government of Quebec established a new parental-leave insurance plan (QPIP), thereby implementing a different policy from that of the rest of Canada. Parental leave is now more flexible (either a shorter leave with a higher earnings replacement benefits rate or a longer leave with a lower earnings replacement rate), with three to five weeks of the entire leave period (of almost one year) reserved exclusively for fathers. There seem to be political forces pulling in different directions at the moment, and since the present Quebec government is a minority government, family policy is high on the agenda.

The third objective of this chapter is to present available data on the use of parental-leave and child-care services as evidence of the impact of these policies on equity issues. This chapter will argue that Quebec's child-care and parental-leave policies would be good models for the rest of Canada. Data on parental leave show that the majority of users are still women, despite increasing participation in child care, as well as in play and educational activities, on the part of fathers. Although the extension of parental leave to one year throughout Canada, in 2001, was viewed by some as constituting considerable progress in terms of employment equity, this policy could further reinforce traditional mothering roles without having a strong influence on fathers' participation in parenting, and thus negatively affect the goal of labour force equality. Low-cost child care in Quebec ($5 a day per child at the beginning of this program, raised to $7 a day per child in 2003, versus approximately $30 a day per child before government funding was introduced) is a progressive measure that seems to have affected female labour force participation rates and child-care enrollment.

Since the new parental leave came into effect, Quebec has noted an increase in births, which were up to 82,500 in 2006 in comparison with 76,250 the previous year. This is the highest increase (8 per cent) since 1909. It is clearly too early to attribute this increase to the new regime, especially since some parents may have slightly delayed giving birth to be able to take advantage of the new regime. Nevertheless, the fertility rate in Quebec increased to 1.6, which is higher than the Canadian average, and up 0.1 point from the previous year. In the context of an aging population, fertility rates are of interest. The evidence in this chapter will demonstrate that it is mainly because of the more inclusive characteristics of the parental-leave program that this program should be envisaged for implementation elsewhere. The new parental-leave policy is more inclusive in that it provides more mothers with coverage (e.g., it includes the self-employed) and means a higher probability that fathers will participate in parenting because some weeks of leave are reserved for them. Parental-leave policy is not the only element necessary to facilitate work–family life balance, however: child care, flexibility of working time, and telework, among other measures at the firm level, are also important (Tremblay 2002; Tremblay et al. 2006a; 2006b; 2006c; 2007b). If well designed, though, parental leave can contribute significantly to fathers' involvement in the care of children, the sharing of family responsibilities, and thus work–family balance.

National Models

The forms that work–family relationships take vary according to country and geographical region, with northern and southern Europe holding clearly opposite positions, as do the United States and northern Europe. The work–family relationship takes on very different forms depending on social, demographic, and cultural contexts, as well as the public policies in place (and the latter is our main research interest in this chapter).[1] Most countries are linked to a model without perfectly fitting it, and this is also true of Quebec and Canada, as we will see.

Work–Family Balance or Cumulative Model

In the countries that draw on the work–family balance, or cumulative model, the aim of public intervention is to balance the demands of family life and work by allowing individuals, both women and men, to remain employed while also meeting their family responsibilities. In other words, the work–family balance, or cumulative, model makes it possible to combine family with employment without having to sacrifice one for the other. This model offers the best quality and the greatest variety of public measures for adjusting the work–family relationship, that is, accessible and highly developed public child-care services, excellent working-time arrangements, and paid and flexible parental leave.

In countries that draw on this model greater importance is given to the equal treatment of men and women than in countries that draw on other models. Laws and public policies related to work–family balance apply to both men and women, to encourage a more equal sharing of both work-related duties and family responsibilities. Measures related to parental leave, for example, provide for special incentives to encourage men's participation. This type of family policy is based more

on the notion of citizenship to the extent that it is first and foremost a policy of gender equality and a childhood policy, since children are considered to be future citizens. In a nutshell, the work–family balance model underpins a policy of social integration (Hantrais and Letablier 1995: 44). Countries such as Sweden, Norway, Finland, and Iceland fit into the work–family balance model (Tremblay 2004; 2005).

Work–Family Alternating Model

The main aim of the work–family alternating model is not to integrate family with work, as in the work–family balance model, but rather to encourage employed parents, generally women, to opt for a strategy of entering and exiting the labour market to balance work and family by giving priority to one sphere over the other at different times. The state encourages women to leave their jobs or reduce their work hours in order to take care of their children, and then to return to the labour market later, most often on a part-time basis when the children reach school age. This policy approach generally affects only mothers because, although it is desirable that work and family responsibilities be shared more equitably by both parents, it is rare that fathers leave their work or reduce their work hours to devote themselves to the family (Tremblay 2002; 2004).

Countries oriented to the work–family alternating model share a conception of the family that is based on the gendered division of work, relying mainly on the mother's role in linking work and family. They share a "privatist" assumption about the responsibility for raising children, in the sense that public intervention leaves families with this exclusive responsibility. The work–family alternating model covers countries such as Germany, the Netherlands and, in some aspects, France. Germany, for example, offers little support for child care and has fiscal incentives for mothers to stay at home. Programs described as "cash for care," which give financial incentives to mothers who take care of children or who do not use the public child-care system when available, are measures that fit into this model. They contribute to women staying at home, often for a few years, since the programs sometimes have higher incentives as the years go by or for a third or subsequent child.

Non-interventionist Model

Countries oriented to the non-interventionist model are characterized by the virtual absence of any state measures for adjusting the work–family relationship. Among these countries, a distinction should be made between those in which there is little or no state intervention due to insufficient resources, as has been the case, for example, in some southern European countries (Spain, Greece, and Portugal), and those in which state intervention is weak based on principle, as in the United Kingdom and the United States. Both cases result in a purely privatist conception of the work–family relationship, where any accommodation between the two spheres is left entirely up to the initiative of individuals and employers. In this latter case, it can be concluded that collective bargaining at the company level must compensate for the lack of public policy and state intervention. This third model is characterized by weak state measures for adjusting the work–family relationship. Canada is often associated with the United States as representative of a non-interventionist model, but there are significant differences between the two countries, in particular with regard to the provision of the one-year parental leave and, until the January

2006 election, a proposed national child-care program (which was, and remains, already in place in Quebec).

These different models have distinct effects on women's participation in the labour market (Cette et al. 2007). The work–family balance model yields the most positive results for women's participation in the labour market in terms of the rate of participation, stability of employment, and number of hours worked each week. The work–family alternating model also produces positive results for women's participation in the labour market, but causes more frequent interruptions in employment, in addition to reducing the number of weekly work hours—both factors having consequences for women's income, skills level, career opportunities, and so on. In contrast, the non-interventionist model yields more diversified results, depending on the context of the particular country—the nature of gender relations, specific historical conditions, and the national economic situation, among other factors. This non-interventionist model usually has a more negative impact on fertility and labour market participation, but situations vary.

The Situation in Quebec

Quebec is close to the work–family balance model. In practice, not all policy measures meet expectations, and much remains to be done to catch up with the situation in the Scandinavian countries, but Quebec nevertheless clearly stands apart from the rest of Canada, and especially from the United States, where the model of non-intervention predominates. Even so, there are some threats to the Quebec model: for example, the Liberal Party envisaged an increase in child care rates. It lost the election in 2012, however, and the Parti Quebecois (elected in Sept. 2012) proposes to increase the number of child-care spaces to ensure all children have a place. The majority of the population, including mothers in the labour force, strongly favour maintaining the public child-care system as well as developing more measures to strengthen the work–family balance model. The high labour force participation rate of women with children under six years of age seems to confirm the need and support for the cumulative, or work–family balance, model.

History of Policies

The Quebec government's interest in family policy can be explained by two main factors: (1) socio-demographic changes, especially involving a drop in fertility, a decline in marriage, and an increase in marital instability; and (2) an increase in mothers' participation in the labour force. Women's increased labour force participation makes it essential to think about family and work–family balance policy and explains the recent gains achieved by policies fostering this objective. Although the demographic changes are not unique to Quebec, their pace in Quebec represents a special case within Canada, and the measures adopted over recent decades also make Quebec a distinct case within Canada.

The 1960s were a socially determining period for Quebec. The government became increasingly interventionist, and the significant social changes that took place during this time are often referred to as the Quiet Revolution. Feminism became an important social movement, and women's participation in the labour market increased markedly. Over the years, public policies gradually began to take this fact into account. Laws and measures such as maternity leave and subsidized child care, came into being as a result of the struggles of the women's movement and other

popular movements. The first interventions regarding maternity leave came from the federal government. In 1971, the eligibility criteria for the Unemployment Insurance (UI, after 1996 Employment Insurance, or EI) program were broadened to include a 17-week maternity leave, whereby 15 weeks were paid at 60 per cent of insurable earnings (now reduced to 55 per cent, but with the length of parental leave increased to about one year). This EI program, which still constitutes the only income security for many Canadian women, nevertheless contains important limitations that the new Quebec Parental Insurance Plan of 2006 addresses, as will be seen below.

From the 1980s onwards, the Quebec government began to take a close look at the transformations in the family and women's participation in the labour market, publishing many policy statements over the years (see, e.g., Tremblay 2008, 2004). An important 1987 statement on family policy was behind the creation of the Conseil de la famille, which became the Conseil de la famille et de l'enfance (Council of Families and Children). Together with the Conseil du statut de la femme (Council on the Status of Women), this organization was among the most vocal on public policy issues concerning women, family, and child care. Over the years, these two organizations published many analyses and called for policy changes; they were largely supported by women's groups and activists on gender equality. All these endeavours were important over the 1980s and 1990s, but the concrete measures were slow in materializing, except for some support for child care.

Then, in 1997, a review process that took place in many government organizations led to the establishment of three goals: (1) to ensure equity through universal support provided to families and increased assistance to low-income families; (2) to facilitate a balance of parental and work-related responsibilities; and (3) to foster child development and promote equal opportunities (Québec 1997a: vii).

These goals were made top government priorities but, except for support to child-care services and the federal parental-leave program, a number of years went by before concrete measures were proposed. The Quebec government asserted that it had to obtain federal government funding to proceed with the new proposed parental-leave plan. An agreement was concluded in 2005 and, in January 2006, Quebec was able to implement its own Quebec Parental Insurance Plan. The work–family balance policy, however, which had been the object of consultation since 2003, and which did not require that funds be transferred, was nevertheless set aside by the Liberal government of Quebec, possibly because of opposition from employers, since a few employers' organizations were quite vocal in opposing any governmental intervention.

An explicit work–family balance policy, as envisaged in the 1997 review process, is to this day the main element missing that would situate Quebec clearly in the work–family balance, or cumulative, model. Indeed, while child-care support is important, and comes first in the demands of Canadian mothers for a work–family balance, Quebec parents are more and more requesting that employers actively facilitate a work–family balance, with measures such as working-time flexibility, telework, flexible career plans, and the like. The demand for a work–family policy and for incentives and pilot projects along these lines remains present in Quebec.

Maternity Leave

In Quebec, up until January 2006, the financial support provided to mothers who were expecting a child or had had a child came from three different income replacement programs. One fell under federal jurisdiction (Canada) and the other two fell under provincial jurisdiction (Quebec). The federal Employment Insurance program was the main parental leave benefits program administered by Human Resources and Social Development Canada (HRSDC). Benefits were paid to parents after a 14-day waiting period. The allowance corresponded to 55 per cent of insurable earnings. This leave, which used to last six months, was extended to one year in January 2001, and could be shared by both parents; however, unlike Sweden, incentive measures to encourage fathers' participation did not exist.

The Quebec Maternity Allowance Program (PRALMA) was under the responsibility of the Ministry of Employment and Social Solidarity (MES). Instituted to cover the 14-day waiting period imposed by the federal EI program, PRALMA offered a $360 maternity allowance to mothers who were eligible for employment insurance. Although not an immense amount, this program nevertheless supported low-income parents and would surely be welcomed by many Canadian mothers. The new Quebec regime covers the 14-day waiting period, and this program is thus no longer necessary, since it has been integrated into the new regime.

The Quebec Safe Maternity Program is administered by the Commission de la santé et de la sécurité du travail (CSST, or Occupational Health and Safety Board), and it allows a pregnant worker to stop working if her workstation or position poses risks for her own health or that of her fetus. During the first week of compensation, the employee receives her full salary from her employer. Subsequently, she receives compensation from the CSST through benefits that correspond to 90 per cent of her net income. This program is still in effect in Quebec.

The Labour Standards Act in Quebec stipulates that working women have the right to a maternity leave of 18 weeks. This leave is unpaid, however. This is the minimum to which women are entitled, in any case. But if eligible for the new program, women are entitled to benefits.

Paternity Leave

Paternity leave, in particular paid leave reserved for the father, is not very common worldwide, although it exists in Norway, Finland, and Sweden (2 months), as well as in Iceland (3 months). In general, where there is paternity leave, the tendency is to integrate it into general parental leave. In Canada, parental leave was extended in 2001 within the EI program, with the expectation that parents could share the leave between them. But there is still no financial incentive or time reserved specifically for fathers under the federal program. In Quebec, however, since January 2006, fathers have the right to take a three- to five-week paid paternity leave, based on the option chosen (longer leave with lower benefits or shorter leave with higher benefits). Combined with the parental leave, which has been extended to one year, this measure may favour a greater sharing of the leave between mothers and fathers—as has been observed in the Nordic countries—especially given the additional incentive offered by Quebec (better paid leave that is not transferable to the mother). Some analysis on the take-up of parental leave in Europe, however, indicates that fathers use what leave is reserved for them, but little more (Moss and O'Brien 2006). If the time reserved for them is long enough, as in Iceland—where three months are reserved for the father, three for the mother, and three can be shared—public policy can clearly lead to more sharing of parental responsibilities.

Parental Leave

Parental leave is in principle aimed at men as well as women, although in reality it is mainly used by women. In relation to the goal of furthering gender equality, parental leave is supposed to play a key role because it should help to distinguish between the physiological demands of pregnancy and childbirth on women—demands for which maternity leave was designed—and the care and raising of children.

Ultimately, the role of parental leave is to allow both parents to balance their work and family lives. It is essential that men participate in the same way as women; otherwise, parental leave translates into a kind of extended maternity leave and thus reproduces the traditional division of roles and related economic inequalities between men and women. Because the Canadian government has not introduced any measures to encourage fathers' participation, however, the latter has not increased greatly since extended parental leave was introduced. As women generally earn less than men, and the arrival of a child generally represents considerable expense, the lower earner usually takes care of the baby. Parental leave was extended in 2001, and in the years 2001–04 only about 10 per cent of fathers took some part of parental leave, and on average they took less than one month. The Quebec plan was designed to remedy this problem by introducing clear incentives, that is, a period reserved specifically for fathers.

The 2006 Quebec Parental Insurance Plan

Since 1997, Quebec had been trying to adopt a parental-leave plan that is distinct from that of the federal government, and it requested that the sums needed for this purpose be transferred to it from the federal scheme. Following an agreement reached in 2005, the new Quebec Parental Insurance Plan came into effect in January 2006. The new QPIP has a number of advantages in terms of the population that is covered, flexibility in taking the leave, and the earnings replacement benefits rate, as will be seen below (see also Table 29.1).

In Quebec the QPIP replaces parental-leave measures under the federal program. The new provisions do not change the provisions stipulated in Quebec's Labour Standards Act, which specify the duration of maternity leave (18 weeks) and parental leave (52 weeks) for a total of 70 weeks without salary, as well as the rights and obligations related to departure from and return to work. The new QPIP does, however, introduce four major changes.

The first change provides for weeks reserved for the father that cannot be transferred to the mother, which is an innovation in Canada and North America. Quebec fathers are now entitled to a three- to five-week paternity leave with higher benefits than under the federal program, since the income-replacement rates and maximum eligible earnings have also been increased. In contrast, the federal parental-leave program provides for a leave that can be shared by the father and the mother. Statistics Canada survey data indicate that this measure has not been enough to increase fathers' participation since mothers still took an average of 11 months off in 2004 and only about 11 per cent of fathers took part of the leave that year (Table 29.2 below). Data from 2005 indicate an increase in fathers' participation, to 14.5 per cent. In Quebec, the take-up of leave by fathers was 22 per cent in 2005, and with the new QPIP leave scheme, this has increased to 78 per cent in 2011 (Tremblay, 2012a, b).

The second change involves the increased income offered by the QPIP. In addition to abolition of the 14-day waiting period stipulated

under the federal parental leave program (two weeks without benefits, as is the case with EI, with which this program is associated), the new QPIP increases the maximum insurable income to $66,000, and not $45,900, as is the case with the federal parental leave. This has been shown to be important for fathers' participation, since countries where replacement earnings rates are higher have higher participation of fathers.

The third change relates to the introduction of more flexibility in the QPIP, since parents now have two options: a basic plan (longer leave with lower benefits) or a special plan (shorter leave with higher benefits). The latter might interest those who need a higher earnings-replacement rate (especially if their employment income is relatively low) or who cannot afford to miss work for very long because of various personal or work-related reasons. The federal program provides for benefits corresponding to 55 per cent of the maximum insurable income ($45,900) during the 15 weeks of maternity leave and 35 weeks of parental leave (accessible to both parents, but with a 14-day waiting period in each case). The new Quebec basic plan offers benefits of 70 per cent of the average weekly income for 18 weeks of maternity leave and 5 weeks of paternity leave. The QPIP offers two options for parental benefits, that is, either 70 per cent of earnings for 25 weeks and 55 per cent of earnings for 25 weeks for the basic regime or 75 per cent for 40 weeks in the special regime. Adoption leave can be shared by both parents, and provides for either 12 weeks of benefits at 70 per cent of earnings or 25 weeks at 55 per cent.

The QPIP special plan provides for higher earnings-replacement rates, but for a shorter period. Under this plan, maternity- and paternity-leave benefits are equivalent to 75 per cent of the weekly salary and are paid for 15 weeks and 3 weeks, respectively. Parental

Table 29.1 Parental Leave Benefit Plans, 2012

	Canada Employment Insurance	Québec basic plan	Québec special plan
Eligibility	600 hours	$2,000 earnings	
Self-employed workers[2]	Covered only since 2011 ($6,000 minimum earnings)	Covered since 2006	
Basic replacement rate	55% for 50 weeks	70% for 25 weeks 55% for 25 weeks	75% for 40 weeks
Low income replacement rate[3]	Up to 80%	Up to 80%	
Maximum insurable earnings	CAN$45,900	CAN$66,000	
Waiting period	2 weeks (per couple)	None	
Duration[4]	15 weeks maternity 35 weeks parental No paternity leave	18 weeks maternity 32 weeks parental 5 weeks paternity[3]	15 weeks maternity 25 weeks parental 3 weeks paternity

leave is also compensated at 75 per cent for 25 weeks and can be shared by the father and the mother. Under this special plan, the mother can receive benefits for a maximum of 40 weeks (versus 50 in the basic plan), and adoption leave can be shared by both parents, for 28 weeks at 75 per cent of earnings.

Lastly, it must be underlined that the new QPIP is more accessible and will allow more parents, including self-employed workers and students, to receive benefits since it no longer requires individuals to have worked 600 hours over the previous 52 weeks, but simply to have earned an insurable income of $2,000. The funding of this program is based on additional contributions that employers, employees, and self-employed workers must pay into the QPIP. Employers and employees, of course, continue to contribute to the federal EI program for unemployment coverage.

It is still too early to assess the full impact of this new QPIP on fathers' participation in parental responsibilities, since the experience of Nordic European countries has shown that it takes a few years for fathers' participation

to increase. However, based on what has been observed in other countries that have introduced a paternity-leave period not transferable to mothers (Moss and O'Brien 2006), it is clear that there should be an increase in the participation of Quebec fathers, at least for these reserved weeks, and recent data show that 78 per cent of fathers participate and, on average, they take seven weeks of leave. Because the earnings-replacement rate has been increased, it is now easier to take the leave at a time when financial needs are considerable. In the rest of Canada, the rate of uptake was increased to 23 per cent by 2006, in part because of Quebec fathers taking leave with the new regime there. In Quebec, 32 per cent of eligible fathers took leave under EI in 2005. This rate increased to 78 per cent in 2011 with the new Quebec Parental Insurance Plan.

We have so far discussed only paid leave, but it should be underlined that the Quebec Labour Standards Act was also revised in 2003 to take families' needs into account and to protect the part of the workforce not eligible for paid parental leave. In Canada, 75 per cent of mothers who have a child under 12 months of age have insurable employment, entitling them to maternity-leave and parental-leave benefits (under the federal plan; Statistics Canada data for 2003, 2004, and 2005 present the same percentage). In Quebec, workers who do not have access to this plan, nevertheless have rights under the Labour Standards Act, which provides for a number of rights related to departure from and return to work. Due to limited space, it is impossible for us to report on all aspects of this issue; however, it should be pointed out that since 1 May 2003, employees in Quebec have the right to miss 10 days of work (instead of 5 days, as was previously the case) in order to assume family responsibilities.

Use of Parental Leave by Canadian Women

We will now examine the effect of the 2001 extension of parental leave to one year, under the federal program (Pérusse 2003; Marshall 2003). Table 29.2 presents some interesting data (despite the fact that Statistics Canada's Employment Insurance Coverage Survey focuses mainly on mothers, and considers fathers only as spouses who might take up part of the leave; it is hoped that with the incentives offered to fathers in Quebec, more interest will be shown in their leave patterns). Table 29.2 shows that, in 2004, about three-quarters of mothers who had a child aged 12 months or less had insurable employment, entitling them to parental benefits; almost 66 per cent of these mothers received benefits, while about 35 per cent did not. Among those who did not have insurable employment, 9 per cent were self-employed—a situation remedied by the QPIP since it makes self-employed or independent female workers eligible for the plan in Quebec. It should be pointed out that under the new

QPIP, individuals—including self-employed female workers—are required to have worked 200 hours during the previous year. It is also interesting to note that, whereas the average duration of leave was five months before the federal government extended the period of parental leave in the EI program to one year, it is now 11 months: In 2004, over 62 per cent of women took a 9- to 12-month leave, and almost 17 per cent took more than 12 months, while fewer than 12 per cent took between five and eight months and fewer than 9 per cent took from zero to four months.

Thus, even though the parental leave under the federal plan can theoretically be equally shared between the two spouses, women have extended their duration of parental leave while men have not made a lot of effort to take this leave. The higher rate of taking up parental leave by Quebec fathers, even before the new regime, suggests that Quebec fathers are more interested in participating in child care. (Tremblay 2003, 2012a,b,c). Indeed, it may be that the important coverage given to work–family issues in the media over the years and in recent elections in Quebec, but also the very strong commitment of women's groups, unions, and government bodies (e.g., Conseil du statut de la femme, Conseil de la famille et de l'enfance), explain the fact that Quebec fathers feel more comfortable in taking time off for their children, despite potential impacts on their careers (Tremblay and Genin, 2011, 2010). Some of our research highlights that fathers are not fully comfortable in taking time off or with flexible working-time arrangements in some firms or sectors (Tremblay 2003, 2012b), but nevertheless it seems easier, or more legitimate, to take paternity leave in Quebec than in the rest of Canada.

Since our aim is to classify Quebec in relation to the main models of work–family balance described at the beginning of this chapter, some elements of child care services will now be presented.

Child Care

Child-care services constitute a fundamental measure for balancing work and family. The number of daycare spaces, the operating hours of child-care centres, their geographical locations, and their costs are constant concerns for employed parents. These factors have a direct effect on the time-management problems faced by parents. An effective child-care system allows parents to better plan their schedules and it can reduce tensions between family and professional responsibilities. Thus, we will briefly describe the situation in Quebec in this regard.

Since the 1990s, a network of child-care centres has been created in Quebec to provide educational child-care services to children four years of age and under. Child-care centres and daycare in family homes provide reduced contribution services (currently $7 a day per child) for children and babies. The number of child-care spaces is far too low to meet the demand and needs, however. The number of spaces is insufficient, and the operating hours too restrictive, for many parents who work on non-standard schedules especially. A survey by the Institut de la statistique du Quebec (Québec 1997b) revealed that 28 per cent of parents would like services to be more easily accessible in the evenings, nights, and on weekends. This proportion corresponds to the proportion of parents who work on a casual basis or on non-standard schedules. Moreover, school holidays and after-school hours represent care issues for a great number of parents. Despite these criticisms, Quebec parents are strongly attached to their network of child-care services, and years ago they reacted negatively when the federal

Conservative government proposed to cancel the contributions paid to Quebec for these services and offer instead $1,200 per year for each child under the age of six to women who stay at home to care for their children—a plan it implemented. The Quebec child-care services network took action to defend its gains, and the Quebec government has recognized that public support for child-care is such that it needs to be maintained, and even the number of places for children increased, over the coming years. Researchers at the Université de Sherbrooke (Audet et al. 2006) conducted a preliminary analysis of the Conservative federal government's policy reform (replacing child-care services funding with an annual subsidy of $1,200 for each child under age six, paid directly to parents). Audet and colleagues (2006) assessed the impact that this policy would have on poverty and inequality should the Quebec government decide to reduce current public funding of child-care services, something that had effectively been envisaged by Quebec. According to the authors, although the effects on poverty and inequality in the general population are not highly significant, the effects increase in scale when the population targeted by these policies is considered: couples with children and lone mothers are obviously most affected. In the case of the latter, Audet and colleagues predict that observed poverty, based on an index that captures all the dimensions of poverty, may increase by 60 per cent. This may, of course, have consequences for women's labour-force participation and fertility: it could lead to an increase in labour-force participation, to the extent possible, but also to a decline in fertility.

Conclusion

The effectiveness of the Quebec and the federal Canadian models in terms of the work–family

Table 29.2 Eligibility of Mothers for Maternity and Parental Benefits and Duration of Leave, 2004

Mothers with child aged 12 months or less (*n*)	350,000
With insurable employment (%)	74.3
Received maternity or parental benefits (%)	65.9
Did not claim or receive maternity or parental benefits (%)	8.4
Without insurable employment (%)	25.8
Had not worked in two years or more (%)	16.6
Other (includes self employed) (%)	9.1
Mothers who received maternity or parental benefits as a proportion of mothers with insurable employment (%)	88.7
Mothers with known return plans or already returned to work, paid employees only (*n*)[a]	211,000
Average duration of planned leave (months)	11
Median duration of planned leave (months)	11
0 to 4 months (%)	8.9
5 to 8 months (%)	11.6
9 to 12 months (%)	62.7
More than 12 months (%)	16.9
Spouse or partner claiming or intending to claim parental benefits	30,000
Mothers with spouse claiming or intending to claim benefits (%)	9.5

[a] Excludes mothers who have not worked in two years and self-employed mothers, since the survey does not provide information on their intentions to return to work.

Source: Statistics obtained by the author from Statistics Canada division responsible for employment insurance survey data.

relationship can be assessed by comparing their results with those obtained in other countries that implement other models, in particular in terms of women's labour-market participation rates. An analysis of women's rates of participation in the labour market in Quebec and across Canada shows that these rates are increasingly high, in particular for women of childbearing age and for women who have children. Currently, two-thirds of Quebec adult women are in the labour market, and the rate is higher than that in some Canadian provinces (e.g., Ontario). Consequently, the number of dual-earner families, that is, the number of families in which both parents work, has increased considerably. The proportion of employed women who had children between the ages of three and five years was 41 per cent in 1976; by 1991 this proportion had increased to 68 per cent, and it has remained steady ever since.

In the 1990s, public policies, both federally and in Quebec, tended to evolve towards the work–family balance model. The federal government's extension of parental leave, under its Employment Insurance program, to around one year brings it closer to the work–family alternating model—or the conservative model—however. Similarly, the newer federal program that pays a lump sum of $1,200 per year per child to all mothers of children under six years of age, including those who do not enter the labour force, places Canada firmly in the conservative model, which favours alternating work with family and, in particular, the withdrawal of women with young children from the labour market.

With its child-care service network and its new Parental Insurance Plan, Quebec more closely resembles the work–family balance model, especially since it provides more flexibility in the duration of the various kinds of leave. In addition, if the incentive to fathers' participation leads them to exceed the three to five weeks of leave specifically reserved for them, Quebec could be considered to be resolutely in line with the work–family balance model in which family responsibilities are shared by both parents. Finally, it must be said that, while a good model for the rest of Canada, Quebec is still far from the Scandinavian standard, since its parental-leave time (including the time reserved for fathers) is shorter. Furthermore, some political parties in Quebec (namely, the ADQ, which came second in the 2007 election but has now disappeared as a party) have proposed policies

that are quite conservative, such as "cash for care"—$100 a month for parents of children who are not in the daycare system—or a "baby bonus" of $5,000 for the third (or subsequent) child. While this kind of approach may be attractive to stay-at-home moms, it is very risky for those less educated to stay out of the labour market for many years, because they lose their marketable skills and often are at greater risk of poverty, especially if they end up as lone mothers. In any case, Quebec's family policy appears to be somewhere close to the Nordic model at the moment, although the ADQ's propositions would bring it closer to a conservative alternating model, were they ever implemented.

Finally, the absence of working-time policy measures is a weakness of both Quebec and Canadian policy regarding work–family issues. A national child-care system and measures such as the new parental leave of Quebec would certainly be an improvement for women and men with children in other provinces of Canada.

● Notes

1. Elements of the typology presented in Tremblay (2004) will be used here; these, as well as those of Hantrais and Letablier (1995; 1996), can be consulted for more information on the various countries found in each of the models.

2. As we wrote in Doucet, Lero, and Tremblay (2011): "On 3 November 2009 the Government of Canada introduced Bill C-56, which proposed to extend EI special benefits to the self-employed on a voluntary, 'opt- in' basis. The legislation, which was passed in January 2010, allows the self-employed to claim, starting January 2011, federal EI special benefits: Maternity (up to 15 weeks of benefits), Parental (35 weeks), Sickness (15 weeks), and Compassionate care (6 weeks). Unlike the Canada Pension Plan, where the self-employed pay both employee and employer contributions, under this system the self-employed are only expected to contribute the employee portion of the cost, which would be around CAN$750 (€566) for 2010. A further

requirement is that the self-employed person will have earned at least CAN$6,000 (€4,526) in net income in the previous year. Self-employed individuals who wish to be eligible for EI special benefits must register at least one year before claiming benefits. Once the self-employed person opts into the program and receives an EI benefit, he or she cannot opt out again. Coverage of the self-employed in Québec has been in place since the adoption of the new regime in 2006." Adapted and updated from "Child Care Spaces Recommendations" Report from the Ministerial Advisory Committee on the Government of Canada's Child Care Spaces Initiative, Government of Canada, January 2007.

3. Under both plans, a net family annual income of less than $25,291 is required to be eligible.

4. Maternity and paternity leave are non-transferable individual entitlements. Parental leave is a shared entitlement.

● References

Audet, Mathieu, Dorothée Boccanfuso, and Paul Makdissi. (2006). L'impact de la politique conservatrice de réforme du financement des services de garde sur la pauvreté et l'inégalité au Québec. *Interventions économiques* 34: ch. 9. Electronic version retrieved from http://www.teluq.uquebec.ca/pls/inteco/rie. entree?vno_revue=1&vno_numero=4.

Cette, Gilbert, Dominique Méda, Arnaud Sylvain, and Diane-Gabrielle Tremblay. (2007). Activité d'emploi et difficultés de conciliation emploi-famille: Une comparaison fine des taux d'activité en France et au Canada. *Loisir et société (Leisure and Society)* 29(1): 117–54.

Doucet, A., D.-G. Tremblay, and D. Lero (2011). "Canada." In Moss, P. (2011) (dir.). *International Review of Leave Policies and Related Research 2011*. Employment Relations Research Series. Retrieved at http://www.leavenetwork.org/lp_and_r_reports/country_notes/?type=98.

Hantrais, Linda, and Marie Thérèse Letablier. (1995). *La Relation Famille-Emploi: Une comparison des modes d'ajustement en Europe.* Paris: Centre d'études de l'emploi.

———. (1996). *Families, Travail et Politiques Familiales en Europe.* Paris: Presses universitaires de France.

Marshall, Katherine. (2003). L'avantage du Congé Parental Prolongé. *Perspectives on Labour and Income.* Ottawa: Statistics Canada, Cat. 75-001: 5–13.

Moss, Peter, and Margaret O'Brien (eds). (2006). *International Review of Leave Policies and Related Research 2006.* Employment Relations Research Series No. 57. London: Department of Trade and Technology.

Pérusse, D. (2003). New Maternity and Parental Benefits. *Perspectives on Labour and Income.* Statistics Canada Cat. 75-001: 12–16.

Québec. (1997a). *Nouvelles Dispositions de la Politique Familiale: Les enfants au coeur de nos choix.* Quebec: Secrétariat du comité des priorités du ministère du Conseil exécutif.

———. (1997b). Survey. Quebec: Institut de la statistique du Québec.

Tremblay, Diane-Gabrielle. (2002). Balancing Work and Family with Telework? Organizational Issues and Challenges for Women and Managers, 157–70. *Women in Management 17(3/4).* Manchester: MCB Press.

———. (2003). Articulation Emploi-Famille: Comment les pères voient-ils les choses? *Les politiques socials* 63(3–4): 70–86.

———. (2004). *Conciliation Emploi-Famille et Temps Sociaux.* Quebec: Presses de l'Université du Québec et Octares.

———. (ed.) (2005). *De la Conciliation Emploi-Famille à une Politique des Temps Sociaux.* Quebec: Presses de l'Université et Octares.

———. (2008). *Conciliation Emploi-Famille et Temps Sociaux,* 2nd edn. Quebec: Presses de l'Université du Québec et Octares.

———. (2012a). *Articuler emploi et famille: Le rôle du soutien organisationnel au coeur de trois professions* (infirmières, travailleuses sociales et policiers). Québec: Presses de l'université du Québec.

———. (2012b). *Conciliation emploi-famille et temps sociaux,* 3rd edn.Québec: Presses de l'Université du Québec. 406 p.

———. (2012c). Work-family balance; is the social economy sector more supportive and if so, is this because of a more democratic management? *Review of Social Economy* (http://www.socialeconomics.org/).

Tremblay, Diane-Gabrielle, and Émilie Genin. (2010). Parental Leave: When First Hand Experience Does Not Measure up to Perception. *International Journal of Sociology and Social Policy,* 30(9/10).

———. (2011). Parental Leave: An Important Employee Right, but an Organizational Challenge. *Employee Responsibilities and Rights Journal.* DOI: 10.1007/s10672-011-9176-0. Online first: http://www.springerlink.com/openurl.asp?genre=article&id=doi:10.1007/s10672-011-9176-0.

Tremblay, Diane-Gabrielle, Renaud Paquet, and Elmustapha Najem. (2006a). Telework: A Way to Balance Work and Family or an Increase in Work-Family Conflict? *Canadian Journal of Communication* 31(3): 715–31.

Tremblay, Diane-Gabrielle, Elmustapha Najem, and Renaud Paquet. (2006b). Articulation Emploi-Famille et Temps de Travail: De quelles measures disposent les travailleurs canadiens et à quoi aspirent-ils? *Enfances, Famille, Génération* 4. Electronic version retrieved from http://www.erudit.org/revue/efg/2006/v/n4/index.html.

Tremblay, Diane-Gabrielle, Catherine Chevrier, and Martine Di Loreto. (2006c). Le Télétravail à Domicile: Meilleure conciliation emploi-famille ou source d'envahissement de la vie privée? *Interventions économiques* 34 (June). Electronic version retrieved from http://www.teluq.uquam,ca/interventionseconomiques.

Tremblay, Diane-Gabrielle, Renaud Paquet, and Elmustapha Najem. (2007a). Work-Family Balancing and Working Time: Is Gender Determinant? *Global Journal of Business Research* 1(1): 97–113.

Tremblay, Diane-Gabrielle, Catherine Chevrier, and Martine Di Loreto. (2007b). Le Travail Autonome: Une meilleure conciliation entre vie personnelle et vie professionnelle . . . ou une plus grande interpénétration des temps sociaux? *Loisir et Société (Leisure and Society)* 29(1): 191–214.

Glossary

Affines   relatives by marriage

Apprentice   a teen or young adult who lived and worked in the household of a master (or mistress) craftsperson and thus learned the skills necessary to practise a trade; in pre-industrial Europe, guild membership was given upon completion of an apprenticeship

Autonomy   freedom, liberty

Binuclear family   a family that lives in two residences following separation or divorce

Capitalism   a type of economy in which one class that owns the resources essential to production (for use as well as for the market) pays a wage to people who do not otherwise have access to resources essential to producing their own livelihood

Charivary   a loud, unruly mock serenade by the community demonstrating disapproval of marriages or remarriages that were deemed to violate local customs or norms (e.g., the marriage of a widow too soon after the death of her spouse)

Colonialization   foreign conquest or settlement establishing power over an indigenous group of people, which involves that group's loss of control over vital resources as well as the weakening of their customs, identity, and laws

Conjugal   marriage-like

Cottage industry   production occurring in the household in which household members were supplied (by a merchant) with raw materials that they manufactured into goods for that merchant; they were paid a wage (and usually by the piece)

Dowry   property that women must bring into a marriage

Egalitarian   a characteristic of a type of society or set of relationships in which no group is in a material position that provides them the basis of power over another group, or in which no group

can impose its will on another group (e.g., men vis-à-vis women)

Enclosure   a legal process that transformed public land into private property

Endogamy   customs that require that marriage occurs between people who are members of a clearly defined group

Ethnographic research   qualitative research that explores social organization, culture, and behaviour common in a society, community, institution, etc.

Evolutionary psychology   an approach that assumes that certain human behaviour related to biological reproduction is innate, and is the product of a process of natural selection of behaviour that, over the course of human evolution, enabled individuals to adapt to their environment and maximize the number of offspring they left behind

Exchange theory   related to rational-choice theory, this approach focuses on the exchanges of work, help, and support that occur between and among people, and assumes that there is some rational calculation in the exchange (e.g., the expectation of reciprocity when help or resources are given)

Exogamy   customs that prohibit marriage between people who live in a clearly defined group

Extended family   a type of family that is more complex than a nuclear family, one involving more than just parent–child and spousal relationships

Family economy   a type of economy in which the household is the unit of productive work, and in which the relations of the household and those of work are entangled; 'family economy' can also refer more generally to the economic arrangements (i.e., the allocation of work and responsibility) in any household or family

Family wage   a wage that is large enough to support a family; an ideal the union movement struggled to achieve beginning in the nineteenth century, and one that assumes that men should be income earners and women and children are dependants

Feudalism   a type of society that existed in medieval Europe (between the ninth and fifteenth centuries) in which a warrior nobility was tied to the king by vows of loyalty and obligation, and the peasantry were legally obligated to provide labour and surplus crops to the nobility

Guest worker   someone who has a temporary work permit to work in a country where she or he is not a citizen

Hegemonic masculinity   a concept proposed by R.W. Connell decades ago that refers to the patterned practices that have allowed men as a group to dominate women as a group; behaviour associated with men who are in powerful positions in society

Heteronormativity   the assumption that heterosexuality, heterosexual relations, and institutions based on heterosexual relations (like conventional nuclear families) are natural and not socially produced

Incest   a sexual relationship, usually between two people who are kin, that is socially taboo

Indenture   a legal contract binding a person to work for another person for a designated period of time, which usually involves payment, often payment in kind—the provision of housing, clothing, etc.—and/or payment of the worker's travel costs if the worker came from another country

Journeyman   a person who finished an apprenticeship, had guild membership but not money sufficient to open his own shop; an itinerant worker

Kin keeper   a lifelong role that usually went to a daughter, which involved retaining information on family members, helping family members in need, and arbitrating disputes among family members;

kin keepers cared for elder parents and generally were the centre of family communication

Labour power   the ability to work

Lineage   a kinship group defined by members' descent from a common ancestor

Matrilineal   the practice of defining social identity and kinship ties by descent through the mother and her female ancestors

Matrilocal residence   a tradition that involves a married couple and their children living with or near the wife's kin

Modernization theory   a theoretical approach that developed in the 1950s that explained the development of industrial capitalist societies as a series of stages, each more complex (and assumed to produce a better outcome) than the one before

Neoliberalism   a political philosophy that assumes that individuals are responsible for their own welfare and that they can support themselves doing waged work; the approach assumes that the state should not intervene in the marketplace other than to address significant problems created by the workings of the economy

Neolocal residence   a tradition that involves a married couple and their children living independently of either the wife's or husband's kin

Nuclear family   a type of family composed of two adults in a conjugal relationship and their children

Patriarchy   a type of society in which male household heads (or fathers) have power over all other household members, and sometimes over the members of their lineage. Some feminist writers use the term to mean a type of society that systematically works to enable men (collectively) to control and dominate women.

Patrilineal   the practice of defining social identity and kinship ties by descent through the father and his male ancestors

Political economy   an approach that is interdisciplinary and that focuses on social relations and social organization, especially as they are related to the economy; it is an approach that assumes that the political, economic, social, and cultural dimensions of any society can only be understood in relation to each other

Polyandry   a marriage system in which a woman is married to more than one man

Polygamy   a marriage system in which there are either multiple husbands or wives

Polygyny   a marriage system in which a man is married to more than one woman

Poststructuralism   A postmodern approach, poststructuralism rejects any assumption that material reality in the social world is distinct from the theoretical approaches and concepts that social scientists use to interpret that social world. More specifically, poststructuralism rejects structural arguments, like many made by Talcott Parsons and Emile Durkheim, that social institutions determine the behaviour of the people in them. Poststructuralism instead emphasizes human agency, which it assumes is only influenced (and not determined) by social-organizational and cultural forces. Assuming that there is no essential or innate human nature, poststructuralists shift the focus of analysis to culture and the ways in which individuals engage with the ideas, or discourses, associated with different social contexts. They assume that people's subjectivity is created as they engage with ideas that are specific to their social contexts.

Primogeniture   a type of inheritance system in which property is inherited by the eldest child, usually the son

Privatize   [as opposed to socialized] when work or responsibility is done in, or borne by, households, families, or individuals, and not (at least in part) by the larger society

Proletarianization   a social process in which people who have access to land, and produce their subsistence from growing food on it and/or grazing animals on it, lose access to that land and must work for wages as a result

'Putting out' system   production done in households for factory owners, usually paid by the piece

Rational-choice theory   an approach to understanding behaviour that assumes that people act in ways they think will maximize their well-being; it assumes that people weigh costs and benefits when they make decisions

Social reproduction   the physical, mental, and emotional work of feeding, clothing, and otherwise caring for loved ones, which reproduces the next generation and sustains adults

Socialized   the opposite of privatized; when responsibility is held by, or work is carried out in, a social setting

Stem family   a family system in which the son who is intended to inherit the family land lives with his parents as well as his wife and children

Structural functionalism   a theoretical approach developed in the post–World War II period that is especially concerned with social organization and largely explains it in terms of the functions served by a society's institutions (like families) and the social roles that are common in them

Symbolic interactionism   an approach that examines the meanings that individuals construct in interaction and about their experiences

Tabula rasa   Latin for 'blank slate'

Vivilocal residence   a tradition that involves a married couple and their children living with or near the husband's kin

Wet nurse   a woman, usually a peasant, who was paid to breastfeed and care for a baby for several years

Index